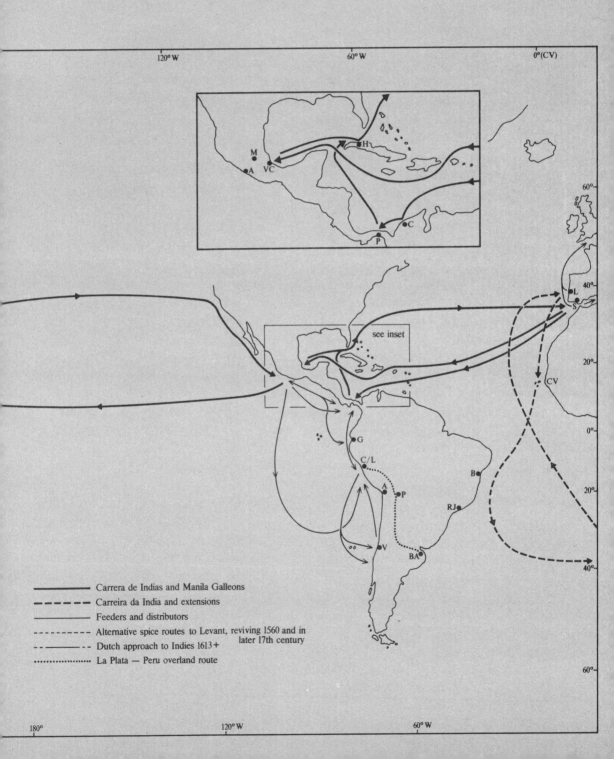

120° W   60° W   0°(CV)

• M
• A • VC   • H
                                              • C
                                          • P

see inset

• G
• C/L
• A • P   • B
                                            • RJ
• V   CV
• BA

────────── Carrera de Indias and Manila Galleons
– – – – – – Carreira da India and extensions
───────── Feeders and distributors
- - - - - - Alternative spice routes to Levant, reviving 1560 and in
                 later 17th century
– ·· – ·· – Dutch approach to Indies 1613+
············· La Plata — Peru overland route

60°
40°
20°
0°
20°
40°
60°

180°   120° W   60° W

The Spanish Lake

The Spanish Lake

O. H. K. Spate

'Let Observation with extensive View,
Survey Mankind, from China to Peru . . .'

UNIVERSITY OF MINNESOTA PRESS

MINNEAPOLIS

First published in Australia 1979.

Published in the United States of America by the University of Minnesota Press.

Printed in Australia

© O. H. K. Spate 1979

Library of Congress Cataloging in Publication Data

Spate, Oskar Hermann Khristian.
The Spanish lake.

(His The Pacific since Magellan; v. 1)
Includes bibliographical references and index.
1. Discoveries (in geography)—Spanish.   2. Pacific
Ocean.   3. Oceanica—History.   I. Title.   II. Series.
G288.S68   910'.09'164   78-23614
ISBN 0-8166-0882-2

In memoriam

ARMANDO CORTESÃO

homem da Renascença renascido

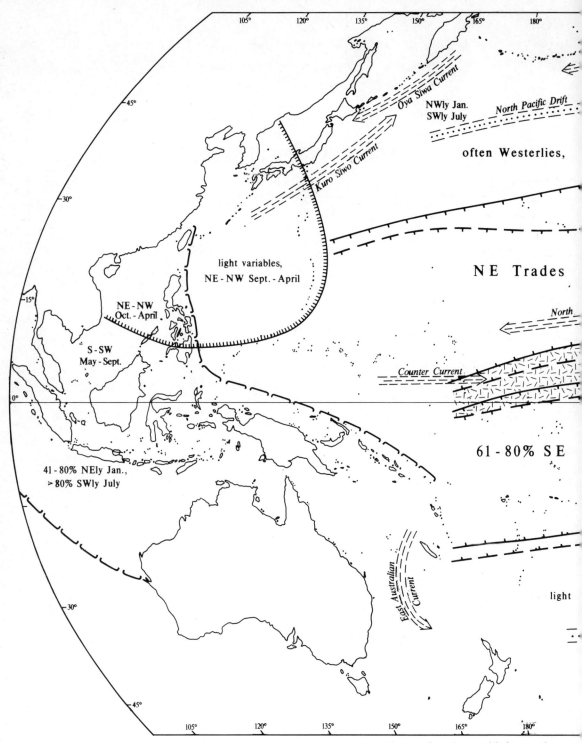

Figure 1. PACIFIC WINDS AND CURRENTS.   1, approx. limits of Trade Wind belts, April-September; 2, same in October-March; 3, approx. trend of main currents; 4, of main drifts; 5, encloses area dominated by Southeast Asian monsoons; 6, areas of high typhoon risk, especially July-October; 7, belt of calms and light airs (Doldrums). Figures indicate frequency of prevalent wind in total observations, excluding calms. Central meridian 165°W.

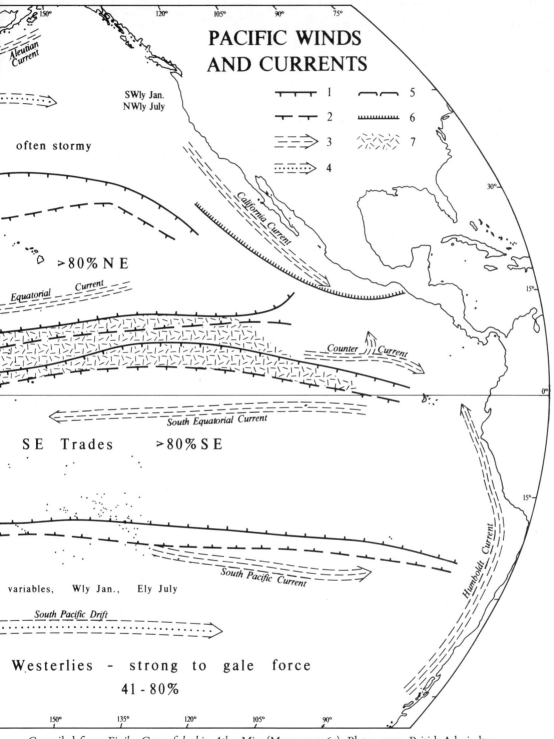

PACIFIC WINDS
AND CURRENTS

⊢⊤⊣⊤⊢ 1		⌒⌐ 5	
⊢−⊤⊣ 2		⋯⋯⋯ 6	
⇢⇢⇢⇢⟶ 3		⤫⤫⤫ 7	
⋯⋯⋯⟶ 4			

Aleutian Current

SWly Jan.
NWly July

often stormy

>80% N E

Equatorial   Current

California Current

Counter   Current

South Equatorial Current

S E   Trades   >80% S E

South Pacific Current

Humboldt Current

variables,   Wly Jan.,   Ely July

South Pacific Drift

Westerlies - strong to gale force
41 - 80%

Compiled from *Fiziko-Geograficheskiy Atlas Mira* (Moscow 1964), Plates 40–1; British Admiralty
Charts 5215, 5216. Base map by courtesy of American Geographical Society, New York.

Preface

This book is written in the spirit of Lucien Febvre's words introducing the Chaunus' great work *Séville et l'Atlantique*: 'these studies of maritime relations, these reconstructions of the histories of the Oceans considered as real entities, historical personalities, primary factors in the collective efforts of men. . . .' I have no illusions that in this to some extent impressionistic outline I can measure up to that monumental work; but then I may perhaps claim the indulgence due to the pioneer *por mares nunca dantes navigados*, through never-navigated seas. Many sectors of my theme have been illuminated by scholars of the first order; little attempt has been made to see the Pacific as a real entity, as a whole over space and through time.

The aim of my work, of which this is a first instalment, is to seek to explicate the process by which the greatest blank on the map became a nexus of global commercial and strategic relations. From the very beginning, the implications of Magellan's voyage made the Ocean a theatre of power conflict. For this reason, some attention must be given to the political background in Europe, and more to the economic background of Spanish America, an extrusion of European polity which was naturally in far closer contact with the Ocean than was the metropolis; or rather perhaps the fulcrum by which, in this first or Iberian phase, Europe extended its power in the opposite half of the globe.

This is a history of the Pacific, not of the Pacific peoples, a difference which I have sought elsewhere to explain; as such it may seem, in this age, somewhat Eurocentric. But then there was not, and could not be, any concept 'Pacific' until the limits and lineaments of the Ocean were set: and this was undeniably the work of Europeans. To say this is in no way to disparage the achievements not only of Aztecs and Incas, Chinese and Japanese, but of the peoples whose skill and daring found and peopled the remote and scattered islands of Oceania. Of this great diaspora, more will be said in a later volume; even in this one, in an Asian context the Iberians must appear less than the unchallenged Conquistadores that they were depicted in the historiography of imperialism; but no less human and heroic for that. The fact remains that until our own day the Pacific was basically a Euro-American creation, though built on an indigenous substructure. This is changing, and not before time, and in that change I may say *pars minima fui*. The change will demand a new historiography, which is indeed in hand; for this, despite inclination, I have not the skills, and my work will perhaps appear a requiem for an era of historiography, which yet must serve as a basis for that which is to come.

If it would take a lifetime to visit all the shores and islands of the Pacific, one sometimes feels that it would take nine lives to master fully the vasty literature of the deep. All that the explorer can do is to mark some positions and take some soundings; and if mine are not a close net like that of Chaunus' Atlantic charting, I may at least hope that I have run my lines with enough intelligence to bring out the main lineaments of the Ocean. The work is inevitably based on secondary sources and on printed collections of primary and sub-primary sources; with all respect for archival historians, whose work is often fundamental, not all that is found outside archives is insignificant, and not all that is found in MSS. really matters. I can only say that I have tried to arrive at a synthesis drawn from reputable authorities. I have no doubt at all that specialists will find superficialities and errors in my treatment of some of the multitudinous topics which a study of this scope and scale involves. But this is the occupational hazard of playing the generalist game, and I have also no doubt that it is a game well worth playing, as an effort to see the theme as a whole and not as cut up into discrete sectors; and it is great fun to play—nor is a feeling for fun, that neglected factor in human affairs, incompatible with serious intent.

As for the skill and success with which I have played the game, that is of course altogether another matter. I have written elsewhere at more length on the methodological and even ethical problems involved in such work; and on these papers I would rest my case.* In the last resort, one can always console oneself with the noble apologia for unavoidable error, and the canons of criticism there implied, with which Samuel Johnson closed the Preface to his *English Dictionary*.

How much the execution of such a work falls short of his ideal, only its author can truly know; he alone also knows both its drudgeries and its delights. The drudgeries have been lightened, the delights immeasurably enhanced, by the constant loving kindness of my wife.

O.H.K.S.

Canberra
18 March 1977

---

* 'The Pacific as an Artefact', in N. Gunson (ed.), *The Changing Pacific: Essays in honour of H. E. Maude* (Melbourne 1978), 32–45; 'Prolegomena to a History of the Pacific', *Geographia Polonica* (Warsaw) 36, 1977, 217–23.

Acknowledgements

It is impossible to name all who have helped me, especially amongst my colleagues in The Australian National University. To begin with a debt of piety, my much-loved friend Jim Davidson was an inspiration to my first steps in Pacific history. I owe much to Gavan Daws, his successor as head of the Department of Pacific and Southeast Asian History, to Harry Maude, doyen in Australia of Islands historians, and to Pat Croft of the ANU Press, for their constant interest and encouragement; and to Professors Anthony Low, the Vice-Chancellor, and Wang Gungwu, Director of the Research School of Pacific Studies, for their blessings and support to an ambitious project. In the Department itself, Bob Langdon and Tony Reid let me borrow at will from their private libraries, Norah Forster fed me with references, and Robyn Walker enlivened her meticulous typescript with pencilled marginalia, always to the point and always welcome. The maps owe everything except their conception to the care and skill of Keith Mitchell of the Map Room, Department of Human Geography. But indeed the whole ambience of the ANU is in itself a magnificent support for scholarship.

I must thank staff members of the following libraries for their always courteous assistance: in Australia, the ANU and National Libraries, Canberra, and the New South Wales Public Library and the Mitchell, Sydney; in Chile, the Biblioteca Nacional, Santiago; in Peru, the Biblioteca Nacional, Lima; in the United Kingdom, the Bodleian at Oxford, and in London the British Library and those of the Institute of Historical Research, the Institute of Latin American Studies, the Royal Geographical Society, and the University of London; in the United States, the University of California and the Bancroft Libraries, Berkeley.

In South America, I received most generous hospitality from Messrs Noel Deschamps and W. R. Carney, respectively the Australian Ambassador to Chile and Chargé in Peru; but most of all my thanks are due to Claudio Véliz, who made my visit possible by inviting me to the memorable Conferencia del Pacífico held in 1970 at Viña del Mar. Far to the North, in Nova Albion, Professors D. W. Hooson and J. J. Parsons very kindly gave me office facilities in the Department of Geography, University of California at Berkeley; and I received valuable assistance from Professors Woodrow Borah and Robert F. Heizer of the University and Mr Robert H. Power of Nut Tree. Fr Michael Cooper of Sophia University, Tokyo, was most kind in helping me to secure photographs for the plates, as was Miss Elizabeth Ellis of the Map Room in the National Library of Australia.

Scholars who have kindly answered specific queries are acknowledged individually in the notes, but I must mention in particular Dr Helen Wallis, in charge of the Map Room of the British Library, and Captain Brett Hilder of Queensland.

Finally, the dedication of this book reflects my gratitude to a great scholar, whose generosity was unfailing for twenty years from my first approach to him as a diffident novice to a Master *nos feitos que os portugueses fizeram*. It is a great sorrow that my tribute must be posthumous.

Contents

Maps

Plates

Preliminary Data

I. BIBLIOGRAPHICAL

References

For a work cited more than once, the full title with place and date of publication is given at its first appearance, with a short title in brackets, thus: E. C. Chapman, *A History of California: The Spanish Phase* (New York 1921) [*California*]. This full reference is repeated for every chapter in which the work recurs. Where several places of publication appear on the title page, only the first so listed is given. Where citations are from a paperback edition, the name of the series is given: A. L. Rowse, *The Expansion of Elizabethan England* (Cardinal ed. London 1973). Where it appears significant, the original date of reprinted works is indicated. It is worth noting that when the place of publication is Berkeley, this normally implies the University of California Press; Amsterdam, Israel; Harmondsworth, Pelicans or Penguins and their brood.

Sub-titles of articles in journals are sometimes omitted, when they add nothing to the point.

Abbreviations

A few works are so often cited that they are referred to by author's or editor's name only:

Blair & Robertson E. H. Blair and J. A. Robertson, *The Philippine Islands 1493–1803[–1898]*, 55 volumes, Cleveland 1903–9; reprinted in Manila, *c.* 1962.

Chaunu Huguette and Pierre Chaunu, *Séville et l'Atlantique (1504–1650)*, 8 volumes in 12 tomes, SEVPEN, Paris 1955–60—a mighty work based on the analysis of 17,761 trans-Atlantic voyages. The first seven tomes, by both authors, are the 'Partie statistique', including a volume of graphics; the last four form the 'Partie interpretative' by Pierre alone. The most important for this book is Tome VIII.1 (cxxv+1212 pages), *Les structures géographiques*, and unless otherwise stated all references are to this one.

Hakluyt R. Hakluyt (ed.), *The Principall Navigations, Voiages and Discoveries of the English nation* . . . , London 1589. All references are to the Everyman edition in eight volumes, London 1907.

Abbreviations for periodicals are self-explanatory, except for:

HAHR	*Hispanic American Historical Review*, 1918+.
MM	*Mariner's Mirror*, 1911+.

and also:

HS 1st	Publications of the Hakluyt Society, First Series 1847–1899,
(2nd) Ser.	Second Series, 1899+ (serial number also given).

General

Translations are by myself, except when quoted from previously Englished works as indicated in the notes.

A formal bibliography of works consulted would be inordinately long, and unless made longer by being turned into a *catalogue raisonnée* would add little of value to the documentation in the notes. 'To end a book with a display of the machinery by which it has been assembled is to stress the toil which has gone into its making, not the pleasure'—C. M. Rourke, quoted in G. Seldes, *The Stammering Century* (Colophon ed., New York 1965), 412. The machinery and the toil of the making of this book are adequately illustrated in its notes; and some of them will reflect, and I hope give, the pleasure.

This seems the appropriate place to mention two works not directly drawn upon but covering some of the same ground as my own. O. Hardy and G. S. Dumke, *A History of the Pacific in Modern Times* (Boston 1949), is a soberly researched college text; its Pacific includes a lengthy treatment of China, surely continental rather than oceanic, but *per contra* nothing on Pacific Spanish America after Independence: a stout effort, but routine in its approach and at times naïve in interpretation. C. Hartley Grattan, *The Southwest Pacific to 1800* (Ann Arbor 1963), combines a clear narrative with lively and intelligent comment, though its sequel—*Since 1800*—seems written rather more *con amore*. Finally, the encyclopaedic four volumes of the (British) Naval Intelligence Division's Geographical Handbook on the *Pacific Islands* (1943–5) form an indispensable *vade mecum* for factual information on Oceania.

2. GENERAL

Dates

There is no difficulty about dates until 1582–3, when the Catholic states of Europe accepted Pope Gregory XIII's correction of the Julian calendar, by which 5 October 1582 became 15 October; most Protestant states followed suit in 1700, but Great Britain not until 1752. In this book, dates for *English* voyages after 1582 (Cavendish, Richard Hawkins) are in Old Style (ten days behind New), but the year is taken as beginning on 1 January, not 25 March as was contemporary English practice.

Leagues

Although the metric system is used in this book, distances are often given in leagues, since these were the most common unit used at sea for distance run. The 'sea league', Portuguese in origin, was 4 Roman miles (3·2 nautical or approximately 3·7 statute miles, 5·9km). However, following the erroneous Ptolemaic estimate of the circumference of the globe, the Spanish reckoned 16⅔ leagues to a degree instead of the better Portuguese value of 17½: a factor of great importance in the Luso-Castilian debates over the partition of the globe. Moreover, 'English sailors, however, at least in the last half of the [16th] century, used the value of 20 leagues or 60 miles' to the degree, for convenience (a mile a minute!), neglecting the difference between Roman and English miles (Taylor). It is worth remembering that the mean length of a degree of latitude (or of a degree of longitude on the Equator) is roughly 69 statute miles or 111km.

See C. Jack-Hinton, *The Search for the Islands of Solomon 1567–1838* (Oxford 1969), 1–2, 99–101; E. G. R. Taylor (ed.), [Roger Barlow's] *A Briefe Summe of Geographie*, HS 2nd Ser. 69 (London 1932), 186–7; D. W. Waters, *The Art of Navigation in England in Elizabethan and Early Stuart Times* (London 1958), 65–6.

Money

Sums of Spanish money in our period are given in *maravedis*, *ducats*, or *pesos*, of which the first two after 1497 became merely moneys of account, the ducat being 375 maravedis, while salaries and so on were usually expressed in maravedis. Actual coinage was in *reales* or subdivisions or multiples of them. Much the commonest unit in our sources is the peso, but unfortunately it is often not clear which of several pesos is meant; and scholars as authoritative as Chaunu (I.269–71) and H. R. Wagner (*Sir Francis Drake's Voyage around the World*, Amsterdam 1966, 506–8) give different values in maravedis for the *peso de oro*.

Pesos de oro of 16 reales (544 maravedis) are sometimes stipulated, but the 'heavy' *peso ensayado* or *de minas* (13¼ reales, 450 maravedis) was more usual as a money of account in the Indies. It must be remembered that much 'monetary circulation' was in uncoined silver bullion. Much the most important actual coins seem to have been the Mexican *pesos de a ocho reales* or *pesos corrientes* (8 reales, 272 maravedis); these, the famous 'pieces of eight' or 'Mexican dollars' were destined to a great future as an international medium (see Ch. 7). According to Wagner, the piece of eight was worth between four and five English shillings of the time, but others make it nearly twice as much. Very roughly, 30,000 gold pesos could be taken as rather over £13,500—J. A. Williamson, *Hawkins of Plymouth* (2nd London ed., 1969), 148. The wild debasements of the seventeenth century (see Ch. 7) introduce further confusion.

With these uncertainties, and given the inflations of the sixteenth and twentieth centuries, not to mention the vastly changed conditions of economic life, any attempt to translate these currencies into modern equivalents seems a nonsense.

The figures in pesos cited in this book are, then, given for what they are worth, and that is simply as indices or orders of magnitude.

Non–English names and terms

Accents were not used in sixteenth century Spanish, and are omitted here except in one or two given names (Andrés, Bartolomé); they are of course retained for quotations, personal names, and book titles in modern Spanish. They have also been omitted from place-names: Perú, Panamá seem pedantic. As a rule Spanish or English forms of place-names are used according to context: Magellan's 'Puerto San Julian' becomes 'Port St Julian' when visited by Drake or Cavendish. Occasionally there may be a bastard form in quotations, e.g. Hakluyt has 'cape of S. Lucar' when either 'Cape St Lucas' or 'Cabo (de) San Lucar' would be correct. Normally the form used today in the respective country is used, e.g. 'Cape Mendocino' (California) but 'Cabo Deseado' (Chile). Some inconsistencies may doubtless be found.

Titles of rank are given as in the original language, e.g. 'Marques de Montesclaros', with some exception for world-famous figures whose titles have taken on an English style, such as 'Duke of Alba' (not 'Duque de Alba') and 'Prince Henry', not 'Infante Dom Henrique' (still less 'Henry the Navigator'!). Names of foreign sovereigns are also as in the original, e.g. 'João III' (of Portugal), not John. But for the Emperor Charles V and the Philips of Spain, this would be mere pedantry, since they are so well-known in English historiography. But sometimes there is a departure from this rule for the sake of emphasis; e.g. in the context of the Treaty of Zaragoza, 'D. Carlos I' makes the point better than 'Charles V'; similarly at times with 'Nueva España' and 'New Spain'.

Spanish terms such as *encomienda*, *almiranta/almirante*, *obraje*, Japanese such as *daimyo*, and so on, are italicised at their first appearance, thereafter in Roman. Their meaning is given (sometimes by context) at first appearance or main treatment, and these can be found from the index.

Shipping tonnages

Like the currency, the question of shipping tonnages is almost intolerably complex. The basic English 'ton' in our period derived from the tun (French *tonneau*) of the Bordeaux wine trade, which when full and including the weight of the cask itself was reckoned as 2240 lbs (1016 kg) in England and 2000 *livres* (979 kg) in France. Allowing for the space wastage resulting from the shape of casks, the cubic equivalent was reckoned at about 60 cu. ft ($1·7 m^3$). Payment by weight at this equivalence for lighter cargoes than wine was obviously not in the carrier's interest, since his ship's space would be full before she had taken on as much weight as she could carry, and hence 'In England the space obtained by paying for a ton [weight] of freight became standardised fairly early at 40 cu. ft [$1·13 m^3$]' (Lane, 354). In Spain the corresponding unit was the *tonelada*, and early in the sixteenth century the equivalents are straightforward: 1 deadweight ton = 1 *tonneau de mer* = 1 Seville *tonelada*, all of which luckily approximate to 1 metric tonne burden. Conveniently also, 1 tonne in weight terms is very close to 1 ton avoirdupois. So a ship of 100 tons could carry 100 tuns of wine, or translated into volume, she had a cargo capacity of 56–60 × 100 cu.ft (1·58–1·70m³) (Lane, 364, 366). Deadweight tonnage was the difference between the displacement of the ship empty and laden, i.e. the maximum weight of cargo which could be safely carried, and this was used for heavy cargoes, which would bring the ship to its maximum draft long before it was 'full'. (Venice had the equivalent of 'Plimsoll lines' in the thirteenth century.)

So far all is more or less straightforward, but now conveniency ceases and complications set in. The units varied from time to time, from place to place, from function to function; there was a continual interplay between a desire to keep the nominal tonnage down, so as to minimise port dues and so on, and one to keep it up so as to charge more when the ship was chartered or (as was very common) hired by the government for war; hence the development of various 'registered tonnages', complicated by various formulae for equating the dimensions of a ship with the reckoning of its tonnage, while the methods of measurement varied in English, Spanish, and French practice.

For our purpose, the most important points are the differences between English and Spanish reckoning. In 1520 the ton and the *tonelada* were virtually the same, but during the century the Spanish reckoning changed, and by 1620 the Spanish registered *tonelada* was only about 0·6 of a ton. The date generally given for this change is 1590, but Chaunu (I.132–6) argues plausibly that so great a change could hardly be made at a stroke of the official pen, but was in effect a codification of a practice which had been going on since mid-century: that of reckoning in a sort of registered ton, based on the ship's dimensions rather than on *toneladas*. The upshot was that a ship of 500 *toneladas* at the end of Charles V's reign would be only, say, 350 tons at the end of Philip II's; and hence an English ship of 100 tons would be the equivalent of a Spanish of about 145 tons, more or less. There was a further difference between Spanish 'Merchant' and 'War' tonnage, a merchantman taken into the Armada Real having 20 per cent added to her nominal tonnage. (This practice seems to have come much later in the Royal Navy—Lane, 364–5.) By the time comparisons are significant for this book (say 1570 +), the differential between Spanish and English reckonings was substantial, and the necessary adjustments are damaging to the patriotic English view of the odds in 1588: thus the *San Salvador* was registered in Spain as 953 tons, but when measured by her English captors came out as only 600 (M. Lewis, *The Spanish Armada* (Pan ed., London 1966), 75).

The tonnages given in this book are those in the immediate source, Spanish or English; and all such figures should be regarded, like sums of money, as orders of magnitude rather than as absolutes: according to Naish, Drake's *Golden Hinde* could be 100, 120, or 150 tons, according to where and how she was measured. The important point to remember is that by the time of Drake's activity in the

Pacific, one must add 30 to 45 per cent to an English figure to get the Spanish equivalent.

It is not necessary at this stage to go into the more modern refinements of registration, such as: is a deckhouse an enclosed space?—a matter of financial importance when it comes to tolls (see G. Mack, *The Land Divided* (New York 1944), 522–8). Given the differences not only in laws but in ship construction, comparisons with modern figures are pointless. One must agree with Joseph Needham (*Science and Civilisation in China*, Vol. 4, Part 3 (Cambridge 1971) at 628), that 'Perhaps the most urgent need of naval archaeology to-day is a systematic, sober and definitive study of estimated tonnage in all historical periods and cultures. Obviously this work cannot be done here.'

This note is based mainly on F. C. Lane, 'Tonnages, Medieval and Modern', in *Venice and History* (Baltimore 1966), 345–70 (also in *Econ. Hist. Rev.* 2nd Ser. 17, 1964, 213–33), and Chaunu, I.130–41. See also C. R. Boxer, *The Great Ship from Amacon* (Lisbon 1959), 13; F. C. P. Naish, 'The Mystery of the Tonnage and Dimensions of the *Pelican-Golden Hind*', MM 34, 1948, 42–5; L. G. C. Laughton, 'English and Spanish Tonnages in 1588', MM 44, 1958, 151–4; A. P. Usher, 'Spanish Ships and Shipping in the Sixteenth and Seventeenth Centuries', in A. H. Cole *et al.* (eds), *Facts and Factors in Economic History* (Cambridge (Mass.) 1932), 189–213 at 208; J. H. Parry, 'Transport and Trade Routes', in *The Cambridge Economic History of Europe*, III (1967) 155–219 at 218–19. The only other measure which needs mention is the *quintal*, which was 46kg or 100lb avoirdupois.

Plates

Every effort has been made to trace the owners of the copyright in the plates; any omission is inadvertent and will be willingly rectified.

The abbreviations 'ANU' and 'NLA'—respectively The Australian National University and the National Library of Australia—indicate the sources of some of the plates.

Special usages

'Straits' unless otherwise stated or clearly implied by context means the Straits of Magellan; 'Cape', the Cape of Good Hope; 'Islands' (except for named groups such as Falkland Islands), those of Oceania; 'Galleon' or 'Galleons' when capitalised refers to those used on the Manila-Acapulco run, as distinct from galleons in general. A distinction is made between the shores of oceans or seas and the coasts of landmasses. 'Conquista' with initial capitalisation is used for the historical process, on the analogy of the 'Reconquista' in Spain itself, or the 'Reformation'; 'conquista', with lower case 'c', for specific episodes.

Chapter 1

THE WORLD WITHOUT THE PACIFIC

I will confute those blind Geographers
That make a triple region in the world,
Excluding Regions which I meane to trace . . .

. . . the trade of Asia is the foundation of commerce . . .

Before Magellan

Strictly speaking, there was no such thing as 'the Pacific' until in 1520–1 Fernao de Magalhãis, better known as Magellan, traversed the huge expanse of waters, which then received its name.[1] Eight years earlier, in a moment which in the saga of the New World ranks only second to the landfall of Columbus, Balboa had seen—not the Pacific. He had seen the Mar del Sur, the South Sea—and so it remained, in common speech and very generally in maps and academic discourse, for over two centuries—until in fact the fur-traders following Cook, and after them the whalers, brought European shipping north of the Equator, into seas until then scarcely traversed except by the annual Galleons between Manila and Acapulco. What sea it was Balboa did not really know, though presumably beyond it lay the true Indies and Cathay, and just to be sure he claimed, with vast panache and formality,

> real and corporeal and actual possession of these seas and lands and coasts and ports and islands of the south, and all their annexures and kingdoms and provinces to them pertaining . . . in the name of the Kings of Castile present or to come, whose is that empire and lordship over those Indies, islands and Tierra Firme northern and austral . . . whether within or without the tropics of Cancer and Capricorn . . . both now and in all times, as long as the world endures until the final day of judgement of mortal man.[2]

A comprehensive assertion, leaving no gaps: but still the South Sea, the claims of Their Catholic Majesties notwithstanding, was the greatest blank on the European map of the world; and by 1513 no other people had a world-map remotely comparable in scope and accuracy with that already acquired by Europe in the mere century since Prince Henry had sent the first of the Portuguese caravels creeping out to the Azores and down the desert coast of Africa. It had not always, nor long, been so; before 1421, the probable date of the first Henrician voyage, there can be no question but that Chinese and Arabs taken together, or even separately, had a far wider knowledge of the world than had Europeans.[3] The far side of the globe was only a vast void—though, significantly, it *could* be thought of as merely a narrow gap—across which Magellan carried a thin line marked with three island-dots, establishing also its vastness; a track almost lost in a waste of mystery and darkness. The major theme of this book will be the essentially European and American achievement of turning this emptiness into a nexus of economic and military power.

And yet, and of course, Europeans were not in truth the first discoverers. It is in one sense loose thinking to use 'discovery' as meaning simply the first sighting or exploration, whether by Europeans or others, that we know of: since few even of the remotest islands of the Pacific (the Atlantic is different) were un-inhabited when Europeans came upon them, there were discoveries of which we know nothing, except that they happened. However, in a more limited context it is not rationalising too much to take 'discovery' in another sense, requiring the placing on written or graphical record, available (at least potentially) to seamen, merchants, and scholars all round the world, of the existence and position of the newly found lands and seas; and for the Pacific this placing of facts on enduring record was basically a European achievement.[4] Yet the drama of exploration and exploitation was played out upon an already peopled stage; and the priorities of Pacific exploration are intra-European relativities, not absolutes.

To Europeans in the brief interval between Columbus and Magellan (and setting aside Columbus's own confusion between his own 'Indies' and Cathay), where is now the Pacific was only a nameless naked space between the known to the west and the known to the east; simply the convexity of the globe, of greater or less extent according as one followed more modern (really more ancient!) or Ptolemaic estimates of the figure of the earth. But for those who lived on its continental shores there was an objective entity: here, a mysterious and limitless expanse of strangely salt water, a barrier; there, an avenue for active but littoral or thalassic, not oceanic, trade. And for those who lived on the islands 'lost over its blue expanse like a handful of confetti floating on a lake',[5] the ocean was, if not a highway, then at least a net of local ways with a few widely-known nodes within an extensive but closed system. Clearly, it cannot always have been closed on all sides, at least not to one-way and perhaps one-time passage: the Islanders must have come from somewhere, though the whence and the how are still matters of sometimes hot dispute.

From the Equator to middle latitudes the Asian margins of the Ocean were the seats of great and ancient civilisations, with continuous polities long antedating the European polity painfully built up from the ruins of the Roman imperium. Tens of thousands of years before the Vikings and Columbus, men had filtered round the eastern shores, from Alaska to Tierra del Fuego, and there too, on the plateaus of Mexico and Peru, they had built up great cities and highly organised empires; those of Peru had some maritime capacity. From either side forays into the unknown Ocean may well have been made. Because of the set of winds and currents, these are more likely to have been from the eastern shores except in the north, where in the belt of the west-east Kuro Siwo current and the Westerly winds there are many historic records of involuntary crossings by castaways from Japan.[6] It is becoming clear that it is not so much a matter of whether men made some sort of Pacific crossing, but rather we must ask to what extent they did so, and whether contacts were on a scale sufficient to leave significant and lasting cultural effects. Some metallurgical techniques in the New World, for example, seem specific enough to suggest direct Chinese or Southeast Asian origins.[7] But it is very difficult to envisage return voyages, and whatever such links as may once have existed, by the time of European contact their memory had been lost 'in the dark backward and abysm of time.'

Farther south, the peopling of the Oceanic Islands was the last major migration of mankind into a previously unpeopled realm: so far our earliest radiocarbon date is only some 3000 years ago. Even so, it is salutary to reflect that, by whatever combination of purpose and accident it took place, 'this incredible maritime venture was under way when sailors in Europe and Asia were barely ever leaving sight of land.'[8] The achievement of those who so early ventured on the oceanic, as distinct from the marginal, Pacific—'over those never-navigated seas'[9]—is indisputable; not so the highly controversial problems involved in its understanding.

South again, the great island of New Guinea paradoxically enough was visited, not merely sighted, by Jorge de Menezes within thirty years of Vasco da Gama's landfall at Calicut, and yet deserves the name given it by its historian Gavan Souter in the title of his book: *The Last Unknown*. Not until 1933, and after preliminary aerial reconnaissance, did white men cross the jungle-clad and savagely eroded flanks of its central mountain core to find on its savannah plateaus vigorous and still entirely Stone Age peoples,[10] though we now know of the existence of man in New Guinea 25,000 years ago, and of an advanced horticultural economy three millennia before our time.

And finally Australia, 'the last of lands', geomorphologically the oldest of the continents (taken as a whole, and perhaps barring Antarctica), yet to many of its earlier European settlers a mere afterthought of the Creator.[11] Here again the work of the last few years has revolutionised our concepts of the antiquity of man in the Pacific region. It is now beyond doubt that man was firmly established in Australia between 25,000 and 30,000 years ago; in Tasmania, isolated by the rising postglacial sea, 'a tiny universe of 4,000 hunters survived as direct inheritors' of Palaeolithic culture 'until they were destroyed in one generation by civilised man early last century.'[12] Both antiquity and failure to survive are in marked contrast to the position in the Islands.

Such, in baldest outline, is a sketch of the Pacific side of our globe as it was before

Magellan. When he sailed, the best-informed European would have known the outlines of most of the Atlantic shores, and have had some knowledge—incomplete and inaccurate—of the East Indies, together with a tiny glimpse across the Isthmus of Panama and some distorted pictures, vague yet highly coloured, of China. The first reports of Yucatan had reached Spain, but there was as yet little firm knowledge of what was to become Nueva España. All the rest was beyond European ken, and the North Pacific and the east coast of Australia remained so for another two, or two and a half, centuries; and these centuries added little to knowledge of the Islands except some exceedingly spotty reports.

In the remoter phases of the long story of human endeavour in the countries around the Pacific there are still many gaps, many mysteries; and to some of these problems, in Oceania, we may return. But the scope of this book as a whole is temporally more limited, essentially to the Euro-American phase, which, be it remembered, even for the Pacific Islands, the most recently peopled division of the globe, is little if any more than a tenth of their total time-span. For a fair proportion of its sectors, this phase of the Euro-American expansion suffers rather from an embarrassment than a paucity of documentation. The ostensible starting point looks clear cut: Magellan's voyage of 1520–1. Even so, for its antecedents we must go back as far as classical antiquity, and specifically to Ptolemy the Geographer, writing about A.D. 150–60, and to Eratosthenes in the third century B.C.

The shrunken Globe and the opened Sea

Neither the intent nor the achievement of Magellan's voyage was to demonstrate that the earth was a globe; that had been common knowledge, to the educated, for centuries. The picturesque names of Cosmas Indicopleusthes, 'the Indian Traveller', and of his book *Christian Topography* (*c.* 540), are all too easily adaptable as light relief in elementary textbooks; so is his extraordinary model of the world, just like an old-fashioned trunk with rounded lid and inner tray corresponding to the Firmament. This engaging irrelevancy is perhaps in part responsible for the vulgar error that, until Columbus and Magellan, only a very few unorthodox persons did not believe in a flat earth; an error persisting to our own day.[13] While Cosmas himself had very little influence, and 'the passionate declamations of a Lactantius or a Cosmas are only individual opinions' and did not commit the Church,[14] it is also true that most of the early Fathers repudiated sphericity, with more or less conviction; but some, and those of the greatest, seem doubtful—Clement, Origen, Augustine—or, like St Ambrose and St Basil, simply regard the question as irrelevant to a Christian's beliefs.

But obscurantism was perhaps never total, and did not endure. Already the Venerable Bede (673–735) seems to have inclined to believe in a globe. While one cannot always be sure that a medieval writer who refers to a 'round' earth is thinking of a disc or a sphere, yet in general 'By the eighth century the Church appears to have largely forgotten its early doubts about the shape of the earth

and to have accepted the saner opinions of [most of] the Ancients',[15] and seventy
years ago Beazley wrote

> It is almost unnecessary to repeat that the roundness of the earth,
> so clearly stated by Bacon and so finely illustrated by Dante, is
> everywhere assumed by the greater schoolmen (writing as
> geographers), from the thirteenth, and even from the twelfth, century.[16]

Unfortunately, although in the twelfth century William of Conches could return
Cosmas's hysterical attacks on believers in the sphere by asserting that flat-
earthers were 'bestial',[17] it still seems necessary to repeat it.

In the Middle, as distinct from the 'Dark', Ages the real debate was on the
question, theologically much more serious, of the Antipodes: whether there were
lands on the other side of the globe, whether they were accessible, whether
anyone could live there. Although, as is usual with the Holy Writ of any belief,
texts could be taken in differing ways, there was nothing in Scripture incompatible
with a spherical earth. 'The world also is stablished, that it cannot be moved',
God 'hangeth the earth upon nothing'—both texts would fit neatly into the
Ptolemaic scheme of spheres; and God 'sitteth upon the circle of the earth.'
But—Adam was the father of all men, the Apostles were commanded 'Go ye
into the world, and preach the gospel to every creature';[18] and how could that
be if, as had been generally held from antiquity,[19] the Antipodean lands, if indeed
they existed, were barred from the Oecumene, the known habitable world, by
a zone so torrid that in it human life was impossible? And hence the Antichthones
or Antipodeans themselves, if *they* existed, how could they be sons of Adam?

The struggle over the Antipodes was longer and sterner than that over the
Globe; nevertheless by the twelfth century the concept of antipodal lands seems
to have been very generally accepted; one powerful line of argument saw an
Austral land-mass as necessary to preserve the balance of the globe. Some thought
that such lands were habitable, a few that they were inhabited—perhaps (but
this was indeed dangerous thinking) by an entirely different race of men, not of
the seed of Adam. For one thing, the reports of Marco Polo and of the Arabs
who had travelled far to the south in Africa seriously eroded the northern
frontiers of the supposedly uninhabitable zone; for another, men of the weight
and standing of Albertus Magnus and Roger Bacon argued the question acutely
and came down firmly in favour of habitable lands beyond that zone.[20]

No doubt for centuries the mass of the illiterate populace, if they thought at
all about such things, were content to live out their laborious lives under the
dome of heaven and on an undefined middle-earth; but global thinking was not
confined to academic speculation and treatises in Latin. The travels of that genial
impostor 'Sir John Mandeville', written about the 1350s, became the most popular
science fiction of the Middle Ages, the top best-seller; but, like modern writers
in the genre, Sir John had provided himself with an extensive if uncritical scientific
background. Mandeville, whoever he was, gathered his materials from any and
every available source, but these included solid works such as the *De Sphaera*

(*c.* 1220) of John of Holywood or Sacrobosco, a standard manual for at least 300 years. The chapter of the *Travels* on the evil customs of the Isle of Lamory (Sumatra) deals concisely with nudity, community of women, and cannibalism, and then plunges into a demonstration not only that 'the earth and the sea be of round form and shape' but also that there existed habitable, and inhabited, Antipodes:

> And therefore I say sickerly [with certainty] that a man might go
> all the world about, both above and beneath, and come again to
> his own country . . . For ye wot well that those men who dwell
> even under the Pole Antarctic are foot against foot to those that
> dwell even under the Pole Arctic . . . For ilk a part of the earth and
> of the sea has his contrary of things that are even against him . . . .

And this was written in a book which became 'a household word in eleven languages and for five centuries', surviving in some 300 MSS.[21]

Nevertheless, dread, especially popular dread, of the torrid zone long persisted, and had to be reckoned with. To antiquity, the obstacles were searing heat, deserts, vast mountains, though on some versions of the world there was an equatorial sea. In the Middle Ages the seas themselves, beyond known limits, came to be considered evil, the home of unspeakable horror—

> The very deep did rot: Oh Christ!
> That ever this should be!
> Yea, slimy things did crawl with legs
> Upon the slimy sea.[22]

Such terrors applied especially to the seas which were most relevant to any hope of a waterway to the Indies around Africa. The prime source for these tales of mystery and terrified imagination seems to be Arabic: from the tenth to the fourteenth centuries writers of the stature of Masudi, Idrisi, and Ibn Khaldun had spoken of the Western Ocean as a 'Green Sea of Darkness', viscous and yet storm-swept, shrouded in thick and perpetual gloom; and ships might be dragged down to the hideous deep by some many-tentacled monster, or even (perhaps) by the giant hand of Satan himself.[23] Practice rather than theory dispelled this myth; nevertheless for fifteen years, 1419–34, the bastion of Cape Bojador, the 'bulger', girt by treacherous shoals, reefs, and currents, marked a *ne plus ultra* to the Portuguese thrusts to the South.[24]

Ptolemy is conventionally known as the Geographer, but this was not his role until very late in the Middle Ages: for most of these centuries he is the great cosmologist of the *Almagest*, with its complex system of epicycles to account for the movements of the heavenly bodies. His geographical work was known to the Arabs, but had singularly little impact in the Christian world.[25] But a Latin version of his *Geographia*, direct from the Greek, was made in Italy about 1406, and there are over forty MSS. still extant in one or the other language; the work was printed in 1475.[26] The special feature of Ptolemy's work, excellent in theory, was his introduction of a system of co-ordinates for some 8000 places throughout the then-known world; given the lack of instrumental techniques, the longitudes in particular could not be anything but exceedingly rough approximations, often grossly incorrect even in the Mediterranean. But they gave a spurious air of precision, and from them maps could be constructed, or reconstructed (Plate I).[27] These maps had a strong influence on geographical thinking in the fifteenth century, and, for the Spanish under Columban influence, even later.[28]

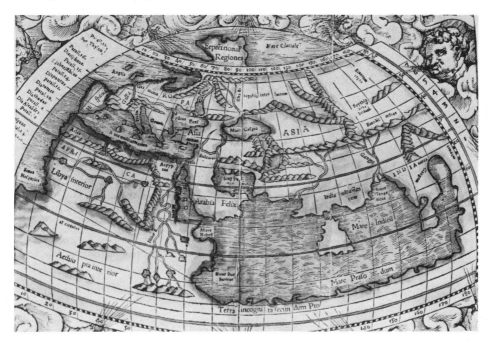

Plate I. THE PTOLEMAIC WORLD MAP. For comment, see text, pp. 7–9. From the Nürnberg Chronicle, *c.* 1480. NLA.

By a most happy scientific error, perhaps the most fruitful in all history, Ptolemy rejected the remarkably good estimate for the circumference of the globe made by Eratosthenes nearly 400 years before him, and accepted a value about one-sixth too small.[29] He compounded this error by inflating the longitudinal extent of the Oecumene, from the Fortunate Isles (the Canaries) to the land of the Seres or China, making it no less than 180°, half the world's round, instead of a true distance of about 140°—and moreover he set no eastern limit to China, so that the land of Eurasia might stretch out eastwards indefinitely. He thus reduced the globe by about one-sixth and then stretched Eurasia, in the relevant latitudes, over one-half (or more) of this reduced extent, instead of two-fifths. Columbus, as we shall see, improved even upon this; he had other authorities, but without that of Ptolemy—as it were his minimal case—it is unlikely that he would have got the backing for his voyage.

The idea that Asia might be reached by sailing westwards from Europe has a long and respectable pedigree; indeed, the very first hint is in Eratosthenes himself.[30] But his work survived only in fragments quoted by other writers, and he had no influence in the Middle Ages, except that through Macrobius (c. 395–423) his value for the size of the globe was widely accepted; but Roger Bacon, for instance, followed Ptolemy in thinking that the distance between Spain and 'the beginning of India' was quite small.[31] More important was the virtual rediscovery of the *Geographia* after 1406, in fact one of the most important episodes in intellectual history.

Pierre d'Ailly, Cardinal of Cambrai, had produced about 1410 the *Imago Mundi*, a careful conspectus of the academic geography of his time. By 1414 he had seen a Latin version of Ptolemy's *Geographia* and hastened to exploit this new source in further geographical works, which formed an important part of Columbus's documentation. Ptolemy had cited, though he did not accept, the view of his predecessor, Marinus of Tyre, that the extent of the habitable world was at least 225° of longitude; and again Marinus set no limit to the eastwards extension of Eurasia.[32] Columbus seized upon this extension—nearly two-thirds instead of one-half—and by adjusting every variable or uncertainty to his own desires he managed to reckon the distance from the Canaries to Cipangu (Japan) as a trifle of 4445 km, well under a quarter of the true distance. Marinus brought China as far east as Hawaii; Columbus brought Japan to the Virgin Islands![33]

The total effect of the geographical speculations of the fifteenth century was, then, to envisage a globe much more manageable, in dimensions at least, than it was in reality.

Another aspect of the Ptolemaic scheme, however, was much less convenient. This was the view that the southern coasts of Asia curved round in a vast arc to join Africa, making of the Indian Ocean an enclosed sea. To accept this was indeed to make a retrograde step, but fortunately its significance was much greater in academic circles than in the world of affairs.

The geographical compilers of the later Middle Ages by and large ignored the first-hand travel reports which could have been available to them. Mandeville, a 'popular writer', of course raided everybody, but although there were exceptions (such as Bacon's mention of William of Rubruck's mission to the Great Khan), scholars usually preferred the endless rehashing of classical authority, mixed with material from the vast and confused compilations of the Dark Ages. By critical examination of conflicting classical views the greater writers did indeed attain to some originality, but this was more in the direction of cosmographical speculation—the Antipodes, the Oecumene—than in topographical geography. Marco Polo was not as universally derided or ignored as tradition suggests—the number of manuscripts, no fewer than 119, attests this. By the fifteenth century, however, he was being taken more seriously, especially perhaps his exaggerated view of the wealth of Cipangu, which he had not seen. His book was studied not only by

Columbus but by Prince Henry; a manuscript of it was presented to the latter's brother Dom Pedro by the Doge of Venice.[34] Nevertheless the general cast of academic geography was excessively bookish.

But alongside the clerisy, though outside business dealings not much in touch with it, was the merchantry. Ptolemy, as J. H. Parry remarks, was both stimulating and enslaving—

> The exploring activity of the late fifteenth and early sixteenth
> centuries was dominated by a small group of men, regularly
> employed in difficult and dangerous tasks. They were not for the
> most part learned men. The fifteenth-century revival of ancient
> learning affected them only at second hand; that, no doubt, was
> one reason why they were not intimidated by Ptolemy.[35]

But much earlier such men, perhaps less regularly commissioned, had pioneered new trade routes or reopened old ones: Polo himself is witness, and his successor Pegolotti, who advises the overland trader into central Asia to pick up a Crimean woman as cook and concubine: there is no obligation, but life will be easier that way.[36] 'Now it is this more humble kind of people whom we must consider as the principal mediators and teachers' between Islam and Christendom;[37] as well as concubines, such hard-headed and professionally observant characters undoubtedly picked up also a vast amount of firm geographical knowledge from their peers, of all races and creeds, in the ports and caravanserais from the Crimea to the Nile. This would have included the knowledge that the African coast ran south far beyond the remotest Ptolemaic cape.

The Arab cartographic tradition seems always to have shown Africa as encircled by sea on the south, and this tradition is carried on by the Sanuto world-map, between 1306 and 1321; but these are 'disc-maps', reminiscent of the 'T–O' type common in the earliest Middle Age, and of limited value as evidence of real knowledge. Really extraordinary is the Laurentian Portolano of 1351–70, as Beazley says 'among the confounding things of history'—*if* we could accept it as all of a piece, which is impossible. This shows an outline for the whole African continent which is astonishingly real, and yet no known or even legendary voyage—at any rate since the Phoenician one from east to west, reported by Herodotus—could have accounted for it; but most likely everything south of Cape Non, or at best Sierra Leone, is a later addition under Portuguese influence.[38] We may also recall the Vivaldi brothers, who sailed from Genoa in 1291 to seek the trade of the Indies by sea. They were probably not the first to venture down the Mauretanian coast, never to return.

By 1457–9 the Genoese World-Map and Fra Mauro show Africa as a peninsula, and the Indian Ocean as an open not an enclosed sea; and half a century before the Ptolemaic map was in print, Prince Henry's men were disregarding the Ptolemaic view of Africa as curving round to join India.[39] The complex claims to priority of Castilians, French, Genoese, Portuguese, and even (and perhaps) one English couple,[40] in the eastern Atlantic islands and on the opposite African coasts do not concern us here. What is significant is the Portuguese drive down the west coast, beginning soon after the capture of Ceuta from the Moors in 1415 and, though occasionally interrupted by other political concerns, maintained with remarkable steadiness until complete success was achieved at the end of the century. This involved the acquisition of accurate knowledge of winds, currents, and sailing courses, especially the *voltas* or return routes, which were well off-shore: Vasco da Gama's great westwards sweep on his way to the Cape was perhaps less daring but better-prepared than is generally allowed. This drive of course was the great enterprise of the Infante Dom Henrique—the title of 'the Navigator' is a spurious piece of British romanticism. It is an exaggeration to institutionalise the group that Henry gathered round him into a formal 'Academy of Sagres'; but it was remarkable in that it included some of the best informed cosmographers and most practical seamen of the age; some of its scholars were Jews in close touch with the Arab tradition. Motives were doubtless highly mixed—the Crusade against the Moors, the geostrategic advantage of holding Moroccan fortresses, the propagation of the Faith, gold, slaves, adventure, fame, intellectual curiosity. 'Guinea gold', slaves, ivory, and the inferior 'malagueta' pepper of West Africa had long been available in Mediterranean ports from Muslim traders—at a price; and the desire to cut out these middlemen was certainly a factor. It would be difficult to say just when the trade, especially the spice trade, of the Indies became a dominant, but the Papal Bull *Pontifex Romanus* of January 1454 definitely speaks of Henry's intention to circumnavigate Africa, though in a context of struggle with the infidel rather than of trade. Nevertheless, while D. Henrique 'certainly was always imbued with religious fervour . . . after the earlier years of his career he was, above all, the administrator of an economic enterprise of national importance and international consequence.'[41]

Alfonso X, the Wise, King of Castile from 1252 to 1284, a notable patron and indeed practitioner of learning, sponsored the revision of the Ptolemaic astro-nomical tables, and is reputed to have exclaimed that if he had been consulted at the Creation, he would have planned a simpler and tidier Universe.[42] It is perhaps fitting that the definite breach of Ptolemy's barrier between Europe and the Indies should have been made by Castile's rival Portugal just over a century after Aljubarrota, the 'Bannockburn' which broke the Castilian hold over the smaller kingdom. In 1488 Bartolomeu Dias sailed far beyond Cabo Tormentoso, his Cape of Storms, renamed by the King Dom João II the Cabo da Boa Esperança.[43] The way to the Indies lay open.

The European background

Europe was still under the shadow of the Black Death when Prince Henry launched the first modest voyages which were to lead, in almost exactly a hundred years, to the first girdling of the earth by men. That plague had carried off one-quarter, or more, of the population of western Europe;[44] and recovery from the wrath of God, or the bite of the flea, was inhibited by the wars of men. Whatever factors lay behind the sudden, if thin-spread, European expansion far beyond the ends of their then-known earth, population pressure was not one of them.

The political *leit-motiv* of most of the fifteenth century in Europe, and of most of its individual countries, was disunity and internecine war; and this in face of the continuing advance of the Ottoman Turks, who even before the century opened held much of the Balkan peninsula, and during it took not only Constantinople but also the rest of the Balkans (up to and including Bosnia), Greece and the Ionian Islands, and even—briefly (1480-1)—Otranto in Italy itself. Not even this manifest menace could impose any but the most local and temporary alliances within Christendom; the years from 1402 until 1454, when 'a concerted Italian effort' might have saved Europe from the Turks, 'were consumed by three of the wealthiest and most advanced communities in the world [Florence, Milan, Venice] in a contest which had no significance for civilization.'[45] Pius II died at Ancona waiting vainly for Venetian galleys to take him on his crusade, and the quick recovery of Otranto owed more to the unexpected death of Mohammad II than to the modest local league formed to regain it.[46]

In the Holy Roman Empire, the burning of Jan Huss in 1415 was followed by twenty years of Hussite Wars; and the long reign of Frederick III (1440-93) was a time of internal weakness and constant encroachment by border powers—Burgundy, Poland, Bohemia, Hungary—only relieved, towards the end, by the marriage which brought most of the Burgundian territories to his son Maximilian, and paved the way to the unwieldy but giant domain of Charles V. In 1415, again, England, flushed with the delusive spirit of the Agincourt song, was fatally embarked on the losing game of the conquest of France; and when that dream was wrecked she plunged into her own thirty years' war, which by a bitter irony has received the chivalric, almost idyllic, title of the Wars of the Roses. Long after the end of the Hundred Years' War some of the finest provinces of France—Normandy, Gascony, the Ile de France itself—were still devastated, and some tracts had almost reverted to wilderness.[47] The recovery under Louis XI was slow and painful, impeded at first by the ambitions and arrogance of Charles the Bold of Burgundy; and the strength so carefully and unscrupulously built up by Louis was soon perverted by Charles VIII to the adventurism of the Italian wars. In Iberia, both Aragon and Castile were more than normally wracked by endemic dynastic and feudal conflicts until the Union of their Crowns in 1474. Only Portugal seems to have escaped internal war, but for a brief and slight affair in 1448-9. It is perhaps only as a chance result of dynastic accidents that the Crown of Castile was united with that of Aragon rather than of Portugal.

Nevertheless, beneath this surface agitated by the showy or bloody futilities of princes and dukes and bishops, there ran the continuities of commerce, expanding into new factors potent to shape a new world. The fall of Constantinople was very far from closing down trade with Asia—there was another Islamic power, that of the Mameluke Sultans, in Egypt until 1517—but despite some 'shrinkage of the Mediterranean trade system',[48] Venice and Genoa still sent their great ships to northern ports, and these fleets had a multiplier effect:

> . . . a sudden rush of vital forces to the periphery of the European
> continent facing the Atlantic Ocean. An all-water route [between
> the Mediterranean and the North Sea] presupposed concentrations
> of manpower, investment capital, and sizable monetary exchanges;
> it presupposed also organization, the training of sailors, the
> establishment of ports of call on the very long route (at Seville
> and especially Lisbon) . . . A division of responsibilities was
> necessary if such exchanges were to run smoothly and grow. A young
> and alert [merchant] capitalism favored these commercial relations.[49]

The capitalism of the age may have been young, but it was already far from primitive, nor was it confined to commodity trading. While most manufacture was literally done by hand, the great textile industries of Flanders and Italy had long been in the hands of moneyed entrepreneurs who put out piece-work to artisans working in their homes, a form of organisation which, on the scale of the times, might be considered mass production. But a few industries demanded a more centralised plant: a great Venetian ship, for example, could be over 1000 tons and was a most complicated machine, and the state shipyards of Venice called for a large specialised labour force. New trades such as printing and gun-founding, the extension of mining to deeper levels, called for organisational as well as technological innovation.[50] The Fuggers began as simple cloth merchants and graduated to finance; the second Jacob Fugger (1459–1525) managed an economically virtuous circle of lending to the Habsburgs on the security of mining royalties, by which he secured the mines themselves and more money for more lending. . . .[51] Monopolies, corners and cartels were already incipient. As the bankers for Charles V's wars, the Fuggers were the power behind the Imperial throne; almost, the first multinationals.

'Of all the economies, [Europe's] was the most imbued with monetary techniques utilizing both hard cash and other media of exchange', and hence already in the fifteenth century Europe had 'established herself at the center of a vast but weak world economy.'[52] This early lead in money power certainly contributed not only to the organisation of the Discoveries in the specific sense of financial backing, but to the whole climate which impelled to them. All actions had their reflex; gold made more wars possible, more wars bred the need for more gold. The great work of the latter part of the century in England, France, and Spain was the reduction to order of a turbulent nobility. The cost of guns was a factor limiting the attractive prospects of war for private ends; the bigger the ruler, the better the credit for guns and men. Bankers and monarchs were natural allies.

From about 1435, then, we have in the west four relatively well-knit and increasingly 'national' states; and if England was as yet relatively weak and isolated, and France seduced into the Italian adventure, Portugal and Spain, poised on the very edge of the Westerly-Trade Wind circulation, of vital importance to the development of ocean routes, were well placed to initiate the expansion.[53]

We must however distinguish: Castile rather than Spain, for Aragon was still deeply involved in the western Mediterranean, and the Kingdom of the Two Sicilies was still under her Crown. Indeed, the American Conquista was almost exclusively a Castilian prerogative, and until 1596 this restriction had the force of (often breached) law.[54] Portugal, as we have seen, had enjoyed a full century of domestic peace after the national rising (1383–5) which had brought the bastard but able House of Aviz to the throne, a rising of the gentry and of the towns and the *arraia-miuda* or *menu peuple* rather than of the nobles, who feared to 'affront so great a Lord as the King of Castile.'[55] Crown and people were thus well in accord, and the resulting dynamism—'Bliss was it in that dawn . . .'—which still thrills through the pages of Fernão Lopes's *Crónica de D. João I*, coupled with the very unusual team spirit of Prince Henry and his brothers, the grandsons of John of Gaunt, provided a very encouraging milieu for the grand design. And one reason for Portuguese priority on the real road to the Indies may be that suggested by Livermore: the discovery had to wait until the maritime technology was ready, but this once given,

> Perhaps an even stronger obstacle was the simple habit of journeying east to get to the East. Only a nation which had not its gaze fixed on the conventional trade-routes of the Mediterranean could foresee that the nearest seaway to the East lay due south.[56]

As the sequel will show, the Portuguese had taken the measure of Ptolemy to a much greater degree than had the Spaniards.

The lure of Asia

Always, since the Crusades, Europe had been conscious of Asia as a land of marvels and of wealth. Commercial relations between the Mediterranean world and the Orient were of very long standing, though subject to many vicissitudes and at times to almost complete breakdown. Roman publicists, notably the elder Pliny, deplored the drain of precious metals to the East in exchange for effete luxuries—silks, spices, perfumes—and in Graeco-Roman times there was an active maritime trade via the Red Sea to the littorals of the Arabian Sea. This is attested not only by the 'manual for navigators and traders'[57] known as the *Periplus of the Erythrean Sea* but also by the discovery near Pondicherry of a depot for the return trade from the Mediterranean—to judge from the large numbers of amphorae, largely in wine.[58] Alexandria was the main entrepôt for sea trade, Antioch for the overland traffic, mainly in silks from China. Later, Byzantium monopolised a smaller trade, but while the smuggling of silkworm eggs in Justinian's time reduced Europe's dependence on Chinese silk, spices remained an Asian monopoly.

While the early expansion of Islam from Antioch to the Maghreb (Morocco) may not have had the catastrophic and catalytic results ascribed to it by Henri

Pirenne in *Mediaeval Cities*, there was undoubtedly a very marked decline in commercial contacts, more especially in the western Mediterranean. The consolidation of Muslim power had an ambivalent effect: on the one hand the Crusades brought the Franks of the West into direct contact with the Levant and increased the demand for oriental luxury goods; on the other, it effectively debarred the West from direct communication with lands eastwards from the narrow littoral of the Crusader kingdoms. Until the thirteenth century, European ideas of Asia beyond Euphrates were vague and distorted in the extreme, far below the level of knowledge in the Graeco-Roman world.

A new opening to the East came in the aftermath of the Mongol invasions; after their great reflux from the borders of the Holy Roman Empire to their ancestral steppes, the image of the Mongols in European eyes changed, in remarkably short order, from that of devilish blood-drinking monsters to one of civilised potential allies against the nearer threat of the Seljuk Turks. Between 1245 and 1253 four missions, diplomatic and evangelical, were sent to the Court of the Great Khan.[59] Not much success accrued to their primary aims: the heretical Nestorian Christians were well established in the East, and that mighty Christian potentate Prester John proved singularly elusive. But these emissaries, highly literate and conscientious reporters, brought back a good deal of useful information as well as agreeable fantasy, and Trade soon followed the Cross. After the Polos a whole new world was opened to the traders of Venice and Genoa, the latter working from their advanced bases in the Crimea. For about a century from 1250, the 'Mongol peace' of Kublai Khan and his successors maintained firm order over the vast area from the Volga to Cathay, and when Pegolotti wrote his handbook, about 1340, the long caravan routes were still safe 'by day or night', and probably a good deal safer than many a King's Highway in Europe. Later in the fourteenth century, however, the huge but insubstantial empire broke up, and Asia entered upon a period of turbulence symbolised by the daemonic figure of Timur Lenk, Tamburlaine the Great. But at their height Italy's trade relations stretched from Norway to China, though her role was essentially a middleman's; very little of the traffic east of the Levant was directly in Italian hands, despite the presence of Genoese merchants in India and China.

Silk and spices were the great staples of the trade, though of course there were other high-value low-bulk lines—luxuries such as gems, dyes, drugs, fine brocaded fabrics. Chinese and Persian silks had a higher reputation than those produced in Europe; the trade in these seems to have been mostly overland and largely in Genoese hands. Given the monotony of foodstuffs available in Europe, the necessity of preserving the flesh of animals slaughtered for want of winter feed, and the badness of the wine (which often needed doctoring to be drinkable), spices might well be considered a necessity of life for people above the bare subsistence level of the peasantry; pepper especially was needed in large quantities for the winter 'salting' of meat. Venice was the great mart for spices, bought mostly in Alexandria from Muslim merchants. But in the fifteenth century these great trades were increasingly shackled by political obstacles; not only disruptions of stability on the overland routes, but obstruction at the Levantine and Byzantine outlets into the Mediterranean.

Instability in Asia; the rise of a new Turkish power under the Osmanlis, tougher and more efficient than their Seljuk predecessors; the devastating incursions of Tamburlaine—all these imposed severe economic strains on the older states of southwest Asia such as Persia and Egypt. Twenty-five years before the fall of Constantinople, the Soldan of Egypt 'nationalised' pepper exports, raising the Alexandria price by over 60 per cent; a Venetian attempt at a boycott in 1480 failed before threats of violence.[60] Byzantium had been for so long islanded by Ottoman power that its fall in 1453 merely set the seal on a virtually accomplished fact; despite the long warning, the psychological shock to Christendom was great, but not great enough to impose a decent unity. Economically, it meant the end of the special commercial privileges held at Byzantium by Venetians and Genoese, and for the latter (compromised by their gallant part in the last days of the Christian city) the loss of their Black Sea colonies: Caffa, the modern Feodosiya, fell to the Turks in 1475. Moreover, before the marked rise in European silver production which began about 1450, output of precious metals in Europe was declining,[61] while clearly both Egypt and Turkey were screwing up the terms of trade. Venice was thus in the paradoxical position of holding a monopoly squeezed at both ends, by ruthless price maximising by the suppliers and by an inelastic purchasing power of the customers. Yet by this time Asian luxuries were necessaries to Europe—necessary at least to the expected standard of living of her ruling classes.

The room for manoeuvre within the established trading system was thus narrow, and to all appearance narrowing; the room for manoeuvre by outflanking the established routes was limitless, or at least limited only by ignorance and fear of the unknown. For by now western Europe had the technological and organisational capacities to break out of the circle, and an increasing need to do so. The tools were to hand, and it needed only courage and imagination to accomplish this truly revolutionary task.

Renaissance ships and navigation

Shipbuilding underwent a virtual revolution in the fifteenth century, although the vital adoption of the stern rudder was at least two centuries earlier. This revolution sprang from a very fruitful interaction between the traditions of the Mediterranean and the northern seas. Iberian builders, particularly those of Biscay, played an important role in this development, without which the Discoveries would not have been possible.[62]

Mediterranean oared craft ranged from light fighting galleys to the great Venetians which sailed to Southampton and Bruges: three-masted and lateen-rigged, using their banks of oars in calms and for entering and leaving port, they were not only the largest but also the most dependable ships of their day—

at any rate outside the China Seas!—and hence favoured for passengers and valuable cargoes. Minor cargo in the coastal trade was largely carried by small or medium-sized lateen-rigged craft, fast and readily manoeuvrable, especially in light airs. Keels were curved, and hence a vessel could not be simply beached or allowed to settle aground on the ebb, but had to be shored up; this was not so serious a handicap in the almost tideless Mediterranean as in the Atlantic, though it made careening difficult. A major limitation to the usefulness of both oared and lateen-rigged craft, on long voyages, was their demand for large crews, with consequent reduction in pay-load. On the other hand, the Mediterranean carvel-built construction, with planking edge to edge and bolted or pegged to stout ribs, was superior to the over-lapping clinker-built sides of the northern ships, and in the sixteenth century clinker building was abandoned except for small coastal craft and sometimes for upper works.

The standard northern merchantman was the cog, roomier than equivalent Mediterranean vessels, better fitted to rough seas, and, with its straight keel, able to ground on the ebb without damage. In the fourteenth century the cog had usually only one mast carrying a single large square sail, but improvements in rigging and the handling of sails were continuous. Square-rig called for fewer seamen on large ships—for a vessel of 250 tons, say twenty men, as against fifty for lateen. Hence for bulk traffic where speed was not a primary factor, such as the very important alum trade, square-rig became generally adopted in the Mediterranean except for small coasting and fishing craft, and its advantages over lateen in the heavier weather of the open Atlantic were soon recognised: square sails were much easier to handle and to furl in strong winds than lateen on their very long yards. But the North in turn soon realised the advantage of having more than one mast: either a foremast or a lateen mizzen greatly increased manoeuvrability. Thus from about 1430 a bewildering variety of hybrids were developed, initially it seems largely by the Basques; the technical differences are of intense interest to the *cognoscenti*.[63] The end result, the standard big ship for most of the sixteenth century, was the carrack: three masts, with a lateen mizzen, high castles (especially aft), and a large central cargo hatch. This was the *nao* of the Spanish *Carrera* and the *nau* of the Portuguese *Carreira* to the West and East Indies respectively. By the 1590s such ships sometimes exceeded 1500 tons, though 700 to 1000 would be more usual; these figures had been exceeded by Chinese vessels two centuries earlier, and it is salutary to reflect that three of the essentials for oceanic navigation by *large* ships—the mariner's compass, multiple masting, the axial rudder—existed in China long before their adoption in Europe. Although their European initiation and development are probably independent, the remarkably rapid flowering of European ship design from about 1450 may owe something to borrowings from China via the Arabs of the Indian Ocean.[64]

Early in the sixteenth century there was a rash of competitive prestige building of 'Ships Royal' such as the *Henry Grace à Dieu*, which might have four masts with three fighting tops on the main, and fantastic sail plans. More to the point

Plate II. AN ELIZABETHAN GALLEON. Reconstruction of a late sixteenth century warship of about 700 tons. From D. Macintyre and B. W. Bathe, *Man-of-War* (New York 1969), by courtesy of the publishers.

was the invention about 1501–2 of the gun-port, which meant that much heavier armament could be carried, guns to damage masts and hulls instead of light essentially anti-personnel weapons mounted on high 'castles' at bows and stern.[65] The future was not with the huge parade ships but with the galleon, developed as a specialised fighting ship, with lower castles (especially the forecastle) and finer lines than the carrack. Usually between 250 and 500 tons and carrying up to forty guns, some reached 800 or 1000 tons by the end of the century (Plate II).[66] Galleons formed the escorts of the Spanish trading fleets to America, carrying no licit cargo themselves except royal bullion, although the enormously important Manila-Acapulco run was worked by '*the* Galleon'. Another major evolution of the later sixteenth century was the development of more effective sail plans, including topsails on all masts except the mizzen, which long retained its lateen, and even topgallants.

THE LOST CARAVEL

Although caravels are frequently mentioned in sixteenth century writings, there are remarkably few extant pictures of them. These five, based on contemporary drawings, demonstrate the variety of rigs employed. They have been redrawn from illustrations accompanying an article on caravels by R. Morton Nance in the 'Mariner's Mirror' 1913, vol. 3, p. 265-71.

CARAVELS

Plate III. CARAVELS. From R. Langdon, *The Lost Caravel* (Sydney 1975), by courtesy of the author and Pacific Publications Pty Ltd. ANU.

Alongside these greater ships there was of course a host of smaller types, of which the most important was the caravel (Plate III), the main instrument of Portuguese exploration until the Cape had been rounded. The Portuguese caravel—the Spanish version differed—was apparently a home-grown product, developed from small coastal *barcas*. At first they were very small, under 50 *tonéis*, only partly decked, with two or three lateen masts; later they reached 150 to 250 tonéis or more, with three or four masts, the *caravela redonda* having one or two square sails on the foremast. Light and very handy, good at sailing near the wind, they were regarded as very versatile, as indeed they were; but, except for the largest, they had only a very modest superstructure on the poop and provided very little accommodation. Admirable for inshore work, they were not really tough enough for long-distance exploration in the open ocean; but as auxiliaries in war and trade, especially in littoral seas, they lasted until near the end of the seventeenth century.[67] In the north, the Dutch *fluyt* or flyboat became prominent as a medium-sized cargo vessel before 1600, and as the *felibote* played an important part in the colonial trade of Spanish America (Plate IV).

Finally there was a large assortment of small craft: pinnaces, *pataches*, *barcos*, *bergantins*. This last type must be distinguished from the later brigantines, as is sufficiently shown by the fact that Cortes built thirteen of them in seven weeks

Plate IV. DUTCH FLUYTS. Roomy and cheap to build and work, the *fluyt* (English 'flyboat', French 'flûte', Spanish 'felibote') was much used as a general service cargo vessel from the later sixteenth century onwards. From R. Davis, *English Merchant Shipping and Anglo-Dutch Rivalry in the Seventeenth Century* (London 1975), by permission of the National Maritime Museum, London. ANU.

for his final attack across the Lake of Mexico.[68] The original bergantin seems to have been essentially a light galley with an auxiliary lateen (later square) sail, suitable for river or inshore coastal work, the oars making it possible to work against wind or current. Later the term recurs constantly in the records of the Spanish American coastal trade, along with the patache, which was like a small brigantine in the modern sense. In this context also the Spanish *fregata*, until quite late in the eighteenth century, often meant not a fairly large warship but a small or medium-sized coastal trader or felibote, often built in American yards, for coasting in the first place but capable in emergency of making trans-Atlantic passages.[69] The maid-of-all-work on English voyages was the pinnace, the counterpart of the bergantin.

It is a far cry from the galley and the cog to the great and complex ships of the seventeenth and eighteenth centuries, with broadside armaments which, unless in extraordinary circumstances, rendered them virtually impregnable to any opponents to be met with in extra-European waters. The continual increase in the size of long-distance ships had a sound economic basis, once coastal or littoral exploration had yielded to exploitation. For initial voyages over long distances out of sight of land, with no known ports of supply and little possibility of estimating the length of the voyage with much accuracy, safety demanded ample provisioning, with consequent loss of cargo space, though economy might dictate the use of smaller vessels, in twos or threes to spread the risk of loss.

To equip a ship of 65 tons for two years' exploring practically ruled out any pay-load, at least on the outward journey, though commodities as valuable for their bulk as bullion or spices could be brought back. But once commerce was established, a ship of 700 tons was much more economic than one of 300; the larger ship, with a crew of eighty or ninety, would demand a 'poids moteur'— food, stores, wine, water—of only 10 per cent of its transport capacity; the fifty or sixty men on the smaller would need 13 to 15 per cent. Hence the tendency to ever-increasing size in the Carreira da India (and to a lesser degree on the Carrera) and in the great Indiamen of the seventeenth and eighteenth centuries.[70] One possible limitation on this growth, the need to make up full cargoes, could be met by feeders to a few great ports, the 'country trade' of South and Southeast Asia in East India Company days, the *cabotaje* of the Caribbean and the Pacific in the days of the Puerto Bello fairs. For such miscellaneous carriage, as distinct from the great main lines, fluyts, later on brigs and barques, were essential. The real limitation in size was simply the cost and time of building the giants.

Navigation at the end of the fourteenth century, at least outside the Mediterranean, was still almost entirely a matter of empirical experience, with the simplest instrumentation: little beyond the compass and the lead, greased to bring up samples of the sea-bottom; pilotage rather than true navigation. The range of expertise of the ordinary skipper was still that of Chaucer's Shipman, relying on an intensely detailed memory of tides and currents, ports and landmarks, essentially rule of thumb; although could he read, written pilot-books or rutters were probably already available. But the next century saw the gradual, and very uneven, introduction of theory. In the long run this was to change a craft 'mystery' into an applied science; already in the early sixteenth century the Casa de Contratacion in Seville had charge of a formal system of examinations for certificating Spanish pilots, who by this time had to acquire some mathematical skills.[71]

The date at which astronomical navigation was introduced is uncertain, although there can be no doubt that the necessities of their Atlantic voyaging made the Portuguese the pioneers: mere dead reckoning, even assisted by the traverse table, was no longer adequate, as it was in the Mediterranean. The first references to the observation of the altitude of the Pole Star are those by Cadamosto, who was on two voyages with the Portuguese in the 1450s; his terms—'the height of a lance' or of a man—do not imply instrumental navigation, but Portuguese students find it difficult to envisage regular two-way voyages between Lisbon and the Azores (officially colonised in 1439) without some techniques for taking heights of the Pole Star.[72] Be that as it may, before 1480 the astrolabe and the quadrant had been adapted for use at sea (possibly by Prince Henry's Jewish expert, Master Jacome of Majorca), and tables of latitude had been drawn up for points as far south as the Equator—using the sun, for the Pole Star was too low to be easily observed as far south as Guinea. These tables are found in 'the oldest surviving navigational manual', the *Regimento do Astrolabio e do Quadrante*, of which an edition, probably not the first, was printed in Lisbon in 1509.[73] Later the Jacob's Staff and the back-staff (which avoided direct sights at the sun) superseded the cumbersome astrolabe, until the introduction of improved quadrants by Davis in the seventeenth century and James Hadley in 1731.

So much for latitudes: those of the *Regimento* are often correct to within ten minutes, so this was no longer a serious problem. The accurate determination of longitude at sea, however, remained in practice impossible for two and a half centuries after Pope Alexander VI had made it 'a live issue' by decreeing a meridian as the demarcation line between Portuguese and Spanish hemispheres. The theory was there—Vespucci and the Dieppois Jean Rotz had attempted to use lunar distances before 1540, Columbus tried the timing of a lunar eclipse, and Rotz and others thought that magnetic variation was or might be sufficiently regular in its distribution to give an indication of longitude.[74] But neither the observational nor the timekeeping instruments available were adequate to attain the precise readings which were needed. In effect, the mariner had to fall back on course steered and distance made. Distance was checked, all too roughly, by various log devices, all crude—though once again theory, with the concept of a geared instrument, was ahead of practicability. As for course steered, the traverse board, on which the time run on each bearing during a given period could be recorded, was an ingenious, if rough and ready, graphical solution. With all these devices, latitude sailing—going north or south until one reached the latitude of the destination, then easting or westing—became a practicable and much-used procedure; to be safe from piling up on shore, one usually adopted the biggest possible estimate of longitudinal distance made.[75] But longitudes still remained a matter of dead reckoning, and the results can be seen in the vagabond habit of Mendaña's Islas de Salomon, discovered in 1568 and in the next two centuries placed anywhere between the longitudes of Cooktown in Queensland, 145°E, and the Marquesas, 140°W—a difference of 75 degrees! Those seen by Mendaña actually lie around 160°E.[76]

Mediterranean sailors had long had the assistance of the portulan chart, which, especially in its fully developed Catalan form, gave an accurate delineation of the shores of the Mediterranean, and of the Atlantic as far north as the Narrow Seas; it had a linear scale and a system of wind-roses from which a pilot could work out his bearing from port to port.[77] It had no grid of latitude and longitude, and hence no projection; the earth was treated as a plane surface. For the Mediterranean, with its short north-south span, this did not greatly matter, since the convergence of the meridians over some 15 degrees of middle latitudes was too slight to induce really serious distortion. It was otherwise when the range of latitude involved stretched to the Equator and beyond, still more when the globe itself had to be plotted on a flat sheet.

This problem was not, of course, anything new, but it had hitherto been an academic one; the theory was well within the grasp of Renaissance mathematicians. It was once more the necessities of Portuguese navigation in the Atlantic which led to the first steps, again seemingly at the hands of the learned Master Jacome. Initially, these steps were modest enough, merely the addition to portulan-type charts of a north-south line marked off in degrees of latitude, originally just a line on magnetic north, later allowing for the variation by a similarly divided true meridian at the appropriate acute angle. Tables of the length of a degree of longitude according to latitude were produced, and early in the sixteenth century the Portuguese Jew Pedro Nuñes devised a quadrant by which these values could be read off directly. He also worked out the true spiral form of rhumb-lines— lines to intersect all meridians at a constant angle—but this was well above the heads of practical seamen, who needed a simple chart on which such a course of constant bearing could be plotted as a straight line. He was unable to provide this, but he led the way to Mercator—or perhaps more correctly Edward Wright —who did.[78] Nuñes anticipated Jonathan Swift in a fine, but more scientific, scorn for cartographers who used plenty of gold paint and planted all over the place flags, camels, and 'elephants for want of towns.'

The European moment

Western Europe in the year of Agincourt and Ceuta, 1415, was as yet only reaching out to Madeira and the Azores, though the Canaries, closer to the African

coast, had been known for over half a century. By 1485 the second great Portuguese thrust under João II was under way, and Columbus had just proffered to
that king his alternative westwards course to the Orient. In seventy years Iberia,
building on the experience of voyagings from the Azores to the Bight of Benin,
had become technologically equipped for the vaster achievement of girdling the
globe. But the use of this technology for so unprecedented an enterprise not only
called for organisational capacity, but depended also on a particular ideological
or moral climate.

An adequate technology, and powers of organisation, were indeed available to
other peoples: to the Arabs, whose shipping and navigation were certainly not
inferior to those of Europeans and whose commerce extended from Sofala in
Mozambique to Canton and beyond; to the Chinese themselves. Indeed, in the
very month of the taking of Ceuta, the fourth expedition of Cheng Ho returned
to China from the east coast of Africa. This was through seas long navigated,
from known port to known port; but his fleets were numbered in tens or even
scores of ships and thousands of men; some of the ships themselves, and their
numbers, were certainly much larger than those of any armada of the King of
Portugal, then or for three centuries thereafter. The objectives were part commercial and part diplomatic, showing the flag on a giant scale, demanding tribute.
But there was no follow-up; after the seventh expedition in 1431–3 such activity
abruptly stopped, perhaps because of Mongol pressures on the northern frontiers
of the Ming Empire.[79]

But Europe needed Asia far more than Asia needed Europe. Islam was 'the
unavoidable intermediary', seemingly securely entrenched with no compelling
motive to attempt improving on a most profitable middleman's position; and
China, despite the dramatic excursions under the Ming dynasty, returned into
her basically self-sufficing self. Myron Gilmore suggests that one factor, and a
main factor, in the European seizure of the initiative was that 'the attitude of the
European world' to those beyond its horizons was never 'completely closed and
assured'; and the openness of European society allowed for a fruitful co-operation
of individual and state enterprise. It seems at all events that the great intellectual—
and emotional—opening of the Renaissance coincided in time with a phase of
relative stasis, if not of decline, in the Arab world, which had lost some of the
outgoing energy of its earlier centuries, and with one of retreat to the home base
in the Chinese.[80]

The mental ardours of the age of Humanism, its desires 'Still climing after
knowledge infinite, And alwaies mooving as the restles Spheares',[81] must surely
have played their part. But neither intellectual curiosity nor fervour to spread
the Faith would have been likely to secure the necessary backing without the
auri sacra fames, the cursed lust for gold which could compel the hearts of men not
only to infamy but also to deeds of high courage. In an age when 'the amassing
of a hoard of bullion' was among 'the prime objects of statecraft', any state able
to do so was bound to further the discovery and exploitation of new sources of

wealth, whether in the precious metals themselves or in commodities which commanded high prices, such as pepper and the other spices.[82] This demanded capital and organisation on a scale not available in Portugal and Castile, except for the preliminary exploring voyages, and then often with difficulty. For major exploitation, outside sources of capital increasingly became necessary: Genoese, Florentines, the great German houses such as the Fuggers and the Welsers, took their shares:

> the first great moves in oceanic discovery were the work, for the
> most part, of adventurous Portuguese and Spaniards; but the
> development of discovery, the foundations of settlement, trade and
> empire, were paid for by capitalists whose bases were in the older
> commercial centres of the Mediterranean and south Germany.
> To those centres, the profits mostly returned. International finance
> made the Reconnaissance the concern of all Europe.[83]

Nor would it be realistic to think that non-material factors, except sometimes a desire for adventure or escape, had much weight for the rank and file who manned the ships. For the officer class, duty to one's Prince was initially probably as important a motive as any; later, fame and El Dorado were always around the next peninsula. A few young gentlemen joined up to see the world and share the glory—Pigafetta, sailing with Magellan, is an outstanding exemplar. But the ordinary seaman, who shipped glory with every wave, would doubtless 'have preferred a coat For keeping off the spray'.[84] For the most part, unless compelled, they seem simply to have signed on for the job, accepting risks philosophically: it was just an extension of an already tough, hard, life. These, the unknown crews, faced dirt, rough living, poor food, disease, danger, in conditions to which the only modern parallel would be life in a concentration camp.[85]

Seventy years after Ceuta, the two options had been delineated: Columbus's way, west across the Atlantic; da Gama's, south around Africa. A century after Ceuta, both these great avenues of traffic and endeavour were well entered into a vigorous life, though it was already sure that Columbus had found not Cipangu and Cathay but a New World. Between the Old World and the New, between the furthest thin-drawn tentacles of European penetration east and west, lay the last and greatest unknown quantity, the as yet unchristened Pacific.

Chapter 2

BALBOA, MAGELLAN,
AND THE MOLUCCAS

Mas he tambem razão, que no Ponente
Dhum Lusitano hum feito inda vejais,
Que de seu Rey mostrando se agrauado
Caminho ha de fazer nunca cuidado . . .
O Magelhães, no feito com verdade
Portugues, porem não na lealdade.

Columbus and Portugal

The background to European entry into the Pacific must include the ancient and never-healed rivalry between Portugal and Castile. In 1479 the Treaty of Alcaçovas liquidated the unfortunate Portuguese intervention in the Castilian succession; Portugal recognised the Spanish possession of the Canaries, but secured the other eastern Atlantic islands and an exclusive free hand along the African coast—not that this stopped interloping by other merchant adventurers, including Spaniards, though this became more hazardous after the building of the massive Portuguese fortress at El Mina (in Ghana) in 1481–2. Conflict, or at least hostility, between the two powers never quite ceased, despite dynastic marriages and the ground-rules established by the Treaties of Tordesillas in 1494 and Zaragoza in 1529, which set the geopolitical pattern in the earlier Iberian phase of Pacific history.

Whether the plans presented by Christopher Columbus in 1483–4 to the new and energetic King of Portugal, D. João II, pointed directly to Cathay and the Indies, or merely to Atlantic islands, has been, like every other aspect of his life and achievements, the occasion of intense controversy, much of it pointless in a broad view.[1] On the one hand, the trifling trade goods such as beads, mirrors, needles, and the like which, according to las Casas, Columbus demanded were hardly appropriate to commerce with the immensely rich empires of the East; on the other hand, when he did sail he carried a letter from Ferdinand and Isabella addressed to the Great Khan of Cathay.[2] In any case, the expert committee which D. João appointed to examine the proposal would have had no difficulty in demolishing Columbus's wild cosmography, while the would-be discoverer,

---

Luis de Camões, *Os Lusiadas*, X.138, 140—'Yet it is just to look westwards on the achievement of a Lusitanian who, feeling himself affronted by his King, took a way never before imagined . . . Magellan, truly a Portuguese in deed though not in loyalty.'

never one to undervalue the claims of a divinely-appointed pioneer, demanded exorbitant terms. Talk of islands to be found beyond the Azores had been in the air for generations, and in Portugal the immediate result of Columbus's initiative seems to have been merely a mild flurry of interest and official support— all aid short of financial—for voyages which would have the advantage, from D. João's point of view, of being by Portuguese subjects at their own expense. Nothing came of these, but the scale of the 1486 project of Fernão Dulmo— a voyage of six months—and the phrase 'ilhas ou terra firme per costa' ('islands or a continental coast') in the royal warrant, are significant as suggesting know-ledge or presumption of a trans-Atlantic mainland, and this in turn was a possible or even probable factor in the Portuguese stance on shifting the 'Line of Demarca-tion' at Tordesillas.[3] Meanwhile, the royal resources were devoted to the more serious purpose of opening the African route to the Indies, made a certainty by Dias in 1488.

On 4 March 1483, however, the man whom D. João had written off as 'a man talkative and vainglorious . . . more fantastic with his imaginings of his Ilha Cipango than certain of what he said'[4] (an accurate description, as far as it went) came across Lisbon bar, bringing gold and natives from 'Antilha and Cipango.' This time the result for Portugal was a diplomatic crisis. Fears that Columbus had been poaching in Guinean waters were soon dispelled, and despite some anxiety at the sight of natives who clearly were not from Africa, the Portuguese were not slow in discounting his claims to have discovered Japan or the real Indies. But obviously Castile was likely to follow up this striking success, and from the Portuguese point of view the whole balance of the globe might be upset.

The initial reaction was bellicose, the fitting out of a squadron with the implied threat of falling on any further Spanish expedition. But the Spain of 1493, flushed with the conquest of Granada, was much stronger than that of 1479, when Ferdinand and Isabella were only beginning to consolidate their grip on the joint kingdoms of Aragon and Castile, and for the moment D. João's bluff was called: he had at least served notice that his claims could not be ignored. However, the Spanish monarchs were in the happy position of being able to call the spiritual arm to their aid. By immemorial prescription, only the Papacy could authorise missions to heathen lands, and naturally such authority was normally accorded to specific rulers or religious Orders: the Bull *Pontifex Romanus* of 1455 was accorded to Prince Henry in his capacity as Governor of the Order of Christ, itself a survival from the *Reconquista* of the Peninsula. The salvation of unbelievers, obviously, might depend on secular strength, and that in turn on economic resources; mission rights, at least in the view of their recipients, carried with them as a necessary corollary rights of exploitation, and these could be best secured, perhaps only secured, by a monopoly in favour of the power behind the mission. This was the thinking behind *Pontifex Romanus*, 'the charter of Portuguese imperialism', which confirmed in the clearest terms the exclusive rights of the Crown of Portugal, and Henry as its agent, to discovery, conquest and commerce south of Cape Bojador and as far as the Indies. The labourer in the vineyard was worthy of his hire.[5]

The Alexandrine Bulls and the Treaty of Tordesillas

Most conveniently for the Spanish cause, the spiritual arm was represented by the less than spiritual Rodrigo Borgia, who became Pope Alexander VI in August 1492. The Borgias were a Valencian family, and Alexander, already much beholden to Ferdinand and Isabella, needed their support in his efforts to create an Italian principality for his son Cesare: hence he was 'like wax' in their hands, to the extent that they could write to Columbus saying that if he thought it necessary one of the bulls would be modified.[6] The Spanish sovereigns at this time were at Barcelona, in close touch with Rome; requirements could be sent from Spain and a bull received there in six or seven weeks. Hence the *camera apostolica* became almost an extension of the Spanish Court, which secured a rapid succession of bulls virtually liquidating Portuguese claims. The first of these, *Inter caetera*, is dated 3 May 1493 but was prepared in April, and being based on preliminary information is vague in its terms, merely granting to Spain all discoveries in the West. Much more serious for Portugal was the second *Inter caetera*, nominally dated 4 May but actually issued in June—after the Spanish sovereigns had been thoroughly briefed by Columbus. This drew the famous 'Papal Line' running from Pole to Pole 'to the west and south to be distant one hundred leagues' from any of the Azores or Cape Verdes, a definition which at first glance reflects no credit on the papal chancelry's drafting, since there is a difference of nearly eight degrees of longitude between the extreme points of these groups. Beyond this line no person of whatever rank, 'even imperial and royal', was to trespass without the express permission of the 'Catholic Kings' Ferdinand and Isabella, under pain of excommunication; but the rights of any Christian prince in possession beyond the line were preserved. But Alexander VI and his legists were not so 'sloppy' (Mattingly's word) as to define an area as lying west and south of a meridian only; a latitude must also have been assumed. Vast confusion has arisen from the indiscriminate use of the phrase 'No Peace beyond the Line'; Mattingly wittily shows that this 'proverbial' saying 'suddenly bursts into full bloom' in the twentieth century! The 'Line' was latitudinal, originally perhaps that of Cape Bojador (26°N) but finally becoming fixed as the Tropic of Cancer.[7]

The last of the series, *Dudum siquidem* (26 September) was extreme: it simply swept away all rights previously granted by the Papacy and not yet taken up by actual occupation,

> so as to secure to you [the Catholic Kings] all islands and mainlands
> whatsoever that are . . . discovered and to be discovered, are
> or were or seem to be . . . now recognised as being in the waters of
> the west or south and east and India.[8]

Moreover, without Spanish permission no person whatsoever was to enter these comprehensive regions, even for fishing. Portugal was not mentioned by name, but, though her rights had been confirmed by Sixtus IV as recently as 1481, *Dudum siquidem* most explicitly set aside all previous papal awards. Nowell may be rather too picturesque in asserting that 'a small reconnoitering expedition' was held to have given Spain the entire non-Christian world, while after a century of effort Portugal was left with her Atlantic islands and the African forts at Arguin and El Mina; she still had the African route, if she could exploit it quickly enough—and she was already far on the road. But even though the Portuguese may have been reasonably sure that Columbus had discovered not Asia but a New World, the line in the Atlantic was itself restrictive, and the New World might not be a barrier to Spanish westwards penetration of the Orient. Indeed, thirty years later Columbus's son Fernando relied on *Dudum siquidem* to assert Spanish rights over everything east of the Cape of Good Hope; but by then that was no longer practical politics even for a Columbus.[9]

João II very sensibly declined to enter into a hopeless competition at Rome; he seems simply to have ignored the bulls, thus neither admitting their authority nor defying the Church. If Rome was in Ferdinand's pocket, highly placed personages at the Spanish Court were in his, and kept him well informed of its moves. He chose a direct approach: the hasty reaction of early 1493 was succeeded by skilful negotiation, from the position of strength afforded by Portugal's strategic situation, herself athwart the seaways from Spain to the Antilles and in possession of bases in the Azores and Madeira. The assertion *à l'outrance* of Spanish claims might well be too costly, and the second expedition of Columbus, a much larger royal investment than the first, at risk either going or returning. A proposal to delimit spheres along the latitude of the Canaries, Portugal taking all to the south, was rejected by Castile; for one thing, Columbus's new islands lay south of this line, though the Portuguese were as yet unaware of this.[10] The suggestion may however have led to the proposed longitudinal line of the second *Inter caetera*, and—with Columbus away on his second voyage— it became apparent to reasonable Spaniards that *Dudum siquidem* was not so much a trump card as a too obvious fifth ace. The compromise reached was not quite so advantageous to Portugal as the rejected latitudinal delimitation, but it gave her all she needed—at least until East and West should meet.

This extreme Spanish position once cleared out of the way, agreement was reached with surprising speed and smoothness; neither side paid any attention to Alexander's bulls, which indeed had not even been appealed to in Spanish protests to Henry VII about the Cabot voyages. Nothing could alter the Portuguese geostrategic position, D. João had laid his ground at the Spanish Court with cunning and skill, and his diplomats were abler and better briefed than their counterparts. The main provision of the treaty signed in 1494 at Tordesillas, an obscure little town in Valladolid, was the placing of the demarcation line at a position 370 leagues west of the Cape Verdes; and Alexander's jurisdiction was specifically set aside.[11]

Neither the Pope's line nor the new one 'divided the world like an orange', as is so often stated;[12] it divided Atlantic zones only. After all, nobody had been to the other side of the world since the Polos and the fourteenth century missionaries—certainly nobody by sea and in an official capacity—and there was little point and less possibility of making a precise demarcation of the utterly unknown.[13] Had there been a definite idea of extending the line in the full meridian great circle round the globe, it would not have been to Portuguese advantage to shift it too far to the west, since this might jeopardise their claims in the Orient, when they should reach it. This strengthens the presumption that they had some fore-knowledge of Brazilian lands—officially discovered by Cabral only in 1500— and were prepared to risk the East (they might well feel ahead in the race thither) in order to make certain of securing their western flank in the Atlantic. The Spanish also were content, since if Columbus were right, they were not too distant from their goal.

However, since the whole Luso-Castilian concept of zones of exploitation was predicated on eastwards and westwards voyaging to the Indies and Cathay, and obviously these voyagings could converge, the presumption grew up that the division must apply on the other side of the globe. This, as we shall see, lay at the core of Magellan's position, and when both Spaniards and Portuguese should reach the Moluccas the twain would have met and the question become acute. For the time, however, it was in abeyance.

The Treaty contained a provision for determining the line within ten months, by a joint expedition—Portuguese pilots in Spanish ships and vice versa—which should sail due west from the Cape Verdes for 370 leagues 'measured as the said parties shall agree'. This would surely have been a most interestingly acrimonious enterprise, but quite impracticable even with the best of good will on both sides, and it quietly lapsed. Nowell draws attention to a probably more significant point; Tordesillas confirmed Alcaçovas, but to make assurance doubly sure D. João secured a supplementary agreement binding Spain not to send or allow any ship to Africa south of Cape Bojador for three years. The inwardness of this is made patent by two dates: the Catholic Kings ratified Tordesillas on 2 July 1494; Vasco da Gama cleared the Tagus on 8 July 1497.

'a peak in Darien'

For the time being, then, the rivals were busily engaged in staking out claims in opposite directions. Westwards, the twenty years after Columbus's first landfall saw the small beginnings of empire in the Caribbean, based on Española, where after a number of false starts Bartolomé Columbus founded Santo Domingo, now Ciudad Trujillo: this first European city in the New World dates from 1496. The economy of these first colonies had a very narrow basis: range cattle and swine for local subsistence and for provisioning further voyages, cane-sugar and

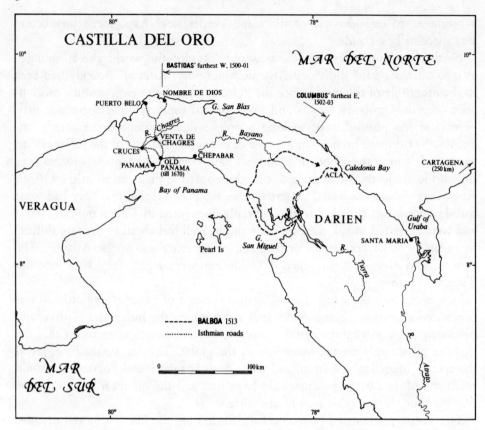

Figure 2. CASTILLA DEL ORO. Adapted from maps in G. Mack, *The Land Divided* (New York 1944) and C. O. Sauer, *The Early Spanish Main* (Berkeley 1966).

gold for export, the latter procured by ruthlessly forcing the helpless natives to work scattered deposits. Depopulation set in with frightful rapidity; the resources, human or mineral, of any one small area were soon used up, and the only answer was slave-raiding and the extension of this literally robber exploitation.[14]

Apart from this spur to expansion, there were of course the lure of riches just over the horizon, the lure of fame, the continuing lure of a way to the Orient. The outlines of Middle America, on its Atlantic flank, were taking shape: the great embayments of the Caribbean and the Gulf of Mexico could be discerned. There was as yet no real reason to suppose that a continuous land barrier existed, and to Columbus and many others these waters must lead on to not-too-distant Cathay and Cipangu: 'The problem at this time [*c.* 1497] was to find the passage to the south of [Ptolemy's Golden] Chersonese—that used by Marco Polo—which led from the Atlantic to the *Indian* Ocean'[15]; there was as yet no idea that a third ocean was inset between these two.

We need not linger over the details of the voyages by which these shores were revealed, replete as they are with adventure and intrigue, false hopes and golden rewards, suffering and daring. In 1498, on his third voyage, Columbus realised that the coast over against Trinidad was continental, though he assumed as a matter of course that it was Asia, if not indeed the Terrestrial Paradise. By the very first years of the new century the South American coast, Tierra Firme, was known from the eastern angle of Brazil to the Gulf of Darien, and valued for its wealth in pearls; Vicente Yañez Pinzon, brother of Columbus's captain, had been at the mouth of the Amazon, or perhaps more probably the Orinoco, and thought it was the Ganges.[16] The fourth and last voyage of Columbus in 1502–4 is particularly significant, though a sad last act in a life so strangely compounded of obsession and of heroic resolution. By this time not only da Gama but also Cabral had reached India and returned to Lisbon, so that

> As for Spain, unless some drastic and decisive operation were
> mounted, she had no choice but to recognise that in the race for . . .
> the Indies she had been defeated by her rival. A possible solution
> was to accede to the importunities of the Admiral and allow him to
> stake all on one more venture . . . the arrival of the Portuguese
> in India proper . . . must be countered at all cost.

Hence Columbus should take Arabic interpreters, were they available (they were not), and in case he should actually meet the Portuguese in the Orient he 'was . . . provided with a passport addressed not to that shadowy potentate, the Great Khan, but to Vasco da Gama himself.'[17]

Columbus made the coast of Honduras near the modern Trujillo, meeting with a large canoe carrying a varied cargo of fine textiles and metal goods— the first hint, not understood, of the rich mainland cultures. The coast turned south at the significantly named Cabo Gracias a Dios, and by Christmas Day 1502 Columbus was off the site of the present town of Colon,[18] at the northern entrance to the Panama Canal. In this region, Veragua, soon known as Castilla del Oro, 'Golden Castile', he spent some months; and here he would seem to have heard of a great sea on the other side of the mountains; but the strait or passage which must be there eluded him. . . . Somehow he managed to convince himself that the unlettered Indians knew they were but ten or twenty days' sail from the Ganges. . . .

Before and after this voyage, other explorers, coming from the west, reached the Isthmian region; fever-ridden harbours were receiving names destined to figure in the geostrategic projects of the Maritime Powers when Panama should become a great node of Spanish inter-oceanic traffic. So Bastidas and la Cosa in 1500 had named Cartagena and reached the site of Nombre de Dios, itself so named nine years later by Nicuesa, who also built a small fort at Puerto Bello; in 1504 La Cosa and Vespucci had explored the Gulf of Uraba, the southwards continuation of that of Darien, and had found the Atrato River. There was no way through, but there was gold enough to confirm Columbus's thrilling reports of Castilla del Oro.

Formal settlement of Tierra Firme began in 1509, when Alonso de Ojeda and Diego de Nicuesa were granted rights to colonise from the Gulf of Venezuela to the Atrato and from that river to Cabo Gracias a Dios respectively. The history of these first settlements is one of unmitigated violence and rapine, fear and petty intrigue; poor, nasty, and brutish. The first and only effective joint action of Ojeda and Nicuesa was the burning of an Indian village (and its inhabitants) near Cartagena, where la Cosa was killed by a poisoned arrow. In a few months only some sixty of Ojeda's 300 men, and a similar number of Nicuesa's 785, survived.

The first settlement, San Sebastian, was held for a time by Francisco Pizarro, later of Peruvian fame, Ojeda having returned to Española to bring succours with his partner Fernandez de Enciso, a judge of that island; but food was short and here too arrows were poisoned. In 1510 the survivors founded Santa Maria de la Antigua del Darien, west of the Gulf of Uraba, now lost in the jungle but until its supersession by Panama City in 1519 a sufficient base:[19] a fort and some tens of hutments, but at least located where food could be found and where the local Indians, unfortunately for them, did not know the use of poisoned arrows. Meanwhile Nicuesa had mismanaged everything; he and his wretched survivors were brought to Darien, where he was ill-advised enough to try to assert an authority already damned by his own incompetence.[20]

And here Vasco Nuñez de Balboa steps on to the stage of history, traditionally out of a provision barrel and accompanied by his dog Leoncico. It may indeed have been by his advice (he had been with Bastidas in 1500) that the new site was chosen. Balboa had failed to make good in Española, and had stowed away on one of Enciso's ships; probably assisted by the local knowledge gained with Bastidas, he soon came to the fore in the despondent community, riddled with feuds and fevers, of Darien. Resolution, decision, daring were common form among the *conquistadores*, though lacking in Nicuesa and Enciso; but Balboa had other assets, among them a fundamental fair-mindedness which was not so common among them. He had also the intelligence to see that the utterly indiscriminate terrorism hitherto exercised on the Indians was worse than useless. He was probably not the 'verray parfit, gentil knight' of his more romantic admirers—he was not very likely to have long survived had he been such; the case arising, he could be as ruthless as any. But he supplemented acts of ferocity with acts of generosity and even camaraderie. Enciso was too pettily legalistic, Nicuesa too pettily arrogant, to hold sway over the toughened survivors who made up the Darien town's meeting; the former was soon stripped of all authority, the latter sent off 'home' in a leaky brigantine, to meet an unknown but doubtless horrible end. Balboa remained in command, by the suffrage of his peers.

A compound of battle, terrorism, gifts, marriage with a chief's daughter, and (reasonably) honest alliances enabled Balboa not only to retain but to expand a tiny empire in the swamps and jungles of Darien. To the new bureaucrats of

Española, to the Court in Spain (and despite a provisional legitimation by Columbus's son, Diego Colon, as Viceroy of Española) his was a usurped power. Its real base was his hold over the colonists, and in face of royal censure, and sapped by local personal discontents, that might well prove but a sandy foundation. As early as possible—in April 1511—Balboa had taken the essential precaution of sending to the Spanish Court as much gold as he could; but Enciso went with it, and was soon busy in intrigue. In January 1513 Balboa received two letters: one was his royal appointment as temporary captain and governor of Darien; the other, later in date, was news from his own agent that Enciso had so poisoned the royal counsels that his fall was prepared. More gold, and yet more, was the only possible answer; and that meant more forays into the interior.

Already in 1511 there had been the picturesque incident when the son of an Indian chief had scattered, as mere trifles, the golden artefacts the Spaniards had collected and in return for alliance had promised to lead them against his father's enemies across the mountains, where there was much more gold—and a great sea. Early in September 1513 Balboa sailed with some 200 men to the narrowest part of the Isthmus, and set out on the arduous journey from Acla, another of the little lost towns (recently rediscovered) of Darien. On 25 or 27 September, alone, he looked down on the great waters of the ocean. The solemnity of the occasion was recognised—the conquistadores were always self-conscious of their Place in History. So a cairn was built, and the names of all Spaniards present— now, through sickness, no more than 67—were recorded. On the 29th Balboa himself waded into the salt water of the Gulf of San Miguel—he had to wait hours for the tide to come up—banner in hand, and formally took possession of the Mar del Sur, and all its lands.[21]

The rest is anticlimax. Balboa returned to Darien, laden with gold and pearls— as he himself said, 'with more gold than health', but with little or no loss of life— in January 1514; at the end of June arrived his replacement, Pedro Arias de Avila (Pedrarias), one of the few historical figures who has found no historical defender. Balboa remained in the administration, in the subordinate role of Adelantado del Mar del Sur—a title surely of honour to posterity, but of rankling jealousy to Pedrarias. Balboa's vision had immediately envisaged navigation on the South Sea; his energy compelled him to a tremendous effort of organisation which (at great cost in Indian life) transported marine stores, anchors, tackle, even timber, from Acla across the jungles, swampy where not mountainous, of what by his efforts was known and forever known as *the* Isthmus. He occupied the Pearl Islands in the Bay of Panama, and sailed for a hundred miles or so to the south—already there were rumours, derived from the Indians of San Miguel, of the richer kingdoms which Pizarro was to seize. The four little ships were his undoing: his plans—to golden lands in the south? to the Spice Islands? to Cathay? —were enough to inflame the never-sleeping jealousy, disguised in smooth cordiality, of Pedrarias. Arrested by Francisco Pizarro, a fit instrument for such work, Balboa was tried on trumped-up charges, and beheaded at Acla. His achievement, but for the immortal priority of the South Sea,[22] died with him; under Pedrarias his even-handed good order amongst Spaniards was replaced by legalistic tyranny, his relative humanity amongst Indians by the most savage exploitation and devastation. The humanist Peter Martyr, reporting from Spain to the Pope, summed it up: 'no other thing was acted saue to kill, and be killed, to slaughter, and be slaughtered.'[23]

Meanwhile, far away on the other side of the South Sea, these very years of Balboa's agonies and endurances saw the Lusian rival make good his bid. In 1511 the great Afonso de Albuquerque took Malacca; a gallant part in the action was played by a young officer, Fernão de Magalhãis. From his new base Albuquerque sent Antonio de Abreu and Francisco Serrão on the great voyage which first put the true Indies firmly—if as yet somewhat erratically—on the map of the world. The fleet coasted right along the northern coasts of Sumatra, Java, and the lesser islands further east, reaching Ceram and Amboyna. Serrão was wrecked near Banda, but made his way in native craft to Ternate in the Moluccas, the Spice Islands themselves, where he remained to attain a very influential position in local politics. His position was ambiguous: was he a loyal Portuguese subject, or a freelance playing his own hand, the first precursor of the Rajah Brookes of the Orient? Indubitably he was a close friend of Magellan, who had saved his life in a Malay ambuscade at Malacca; and this friendship played some part in the conception of Castile's real countermove to the Portuguese advance, a move which became, probably by accident rather than design, the first circumnavigation of the globe.

Magellan: the man and his motives

Magellan was born of the minor Portuguese nobility, probably about 1480 and probably at Oporto.[24] After service as a page in the household of Queen Leonor, he went East with the great fleet of Francisco de Almeida, first Viceroy of India, in 1505, and saw much action. He took part in the decisive naval battle off Diu in 1509, when the Egypto-Gujerati counter-offensive was shattered;[25] he was probably with Albuquerque in the first assault on Goa in 1510, and certainly at Malacca both in 1509, when he rescued Francisco Serrão, and for the successful siege of 1511. He is now thought not to have been on de Abreu's Indies voyage, but would have heard all about its results. From the scattered notices of his life before 1517, we have the impression of a man short in stature but impressive, gallant and resourceful in action, at once realistically calculating and daring, capable both of generosity and violence, independent in temper, secretive and over-taciturn, and very dogged as to his rights. His whole life shows him as a tough leader, driving men hard because driven by his own daemon. Even as a junior officer, he was capable of dissenting in open council from the terrible Albuquerque.

Magellan was back in Portugal in time to take part in the capture of Azamor in Morocco in 1513; here he was wounded in the leg, so that he limped ever after, and was promoted to *quadrilheiro mor*, an officer in charge of the disposition of booty. The post was an invidious one, and Magellan was soon involved in unfounded charges of misappropriation. He did not help his case by returning to Portugal without leave, and demanding a token increase in stipend. The King, D. Manuel, sent him back to face the charges; these were dropped and his name cleared, but Magellan's demands for further recognition of his services both in the Indies and Morocco were very brusquely refused: there is no doubt that D. Manuel, never noted for generosity towards his servants, was prejudiced against Magellan, who in turn was clearly not a man to swallow insult, even from his sovereign, with any patience. This petty squabble, endlesssly paralleled in Renaissance courts, had global consequences, for Magellan determined to transfer his services to Castile—'What mighty contests rise from trivial things'!

It is of course possible that there were deeper reasons, and some authors have thought that Magellan must have broached to D. Manuel plans for a westwards voyage to the Indies:[26] few proposals could have been less welcome, and Magellan would surely have realised this in advance. Quite apart from any prudential reluctance to trespass across the Tordesillas line, this would have been a ridiculous waste of effort for Portugal, already in firm possession of the African route, and indeed completely contrary to her interests: why open new and less controllable doors? The eventual discovery of the Southwest Passage was highly unwelcome to the Portuguese, who must have read with no displeasure of the hardships and horrors of the Straits and the Ocean passage. Lagôa sums up: although the elements for Magellan's enterprise were collected while he was in the East, the idea of executing it was formed after his quarrel with D. Manuel. By this time 'to go to the Moluccas for the Portuguese Crown, after de Abreu's voyage, would be an inglorious feat', and a man of Magellan's temper could hardly reconcile himself to a life of inaction, the normal result of a prince's displeasure. Lagôa goes on to say that 'the failure of Juan de Solis, coinciding with the affront inflicted on Magellan, called his attention to the momentous problem whose solution besides honour and riches, would provide him with the only way to revenge the royal insult.'[27] This seems the fairest summing-up of the question of motive.

From about 1514, then, the grand design must have been forming in Magellan's mind. How far he was influenced by the reports of his friend Serrão's position of influence, almost independence, in the Moluccas, and the letters exchanged between them, must be doubtful. According to Barros, Serrão wrote to Magellan that he had found a new world, greatly exaggerating the distance between Malacca and the Moluccas in order to inflate his own achievement (this of course would tend to place the Moluccas in the Spanish zone), and his papers, examined after his death by the Portuguese commander in the Moluccas, included a letter from Magellan saying that 'if it were God's pleasure, he would soon be with him; and if it were not by way of Portugal, it would be by way of Castile, for his affairs were tending that way.'[28] Lagôa inclines to discount the importance of Serrão's influence: a factor but not as important as the tradition suggests. In any case, by 1516 Magellan knew what he wanted to do; and it could be done only by renouncing his natural allegiance.

In judging this transfer of loyalty, it must be remembered that there was a constant interchange of personnel, especially perhaps of those engaged in maritime affairs, between Spain, Portugal, and other countries; Juan de Solis, for example, was probably also a Portuguese, and served Castile and France as well as his own country.[29] There was already a group of Lusian exiles in Spain; Magellan married into the family of one of them, Diogo Barbosa. For many men of position loyalty was as much personal to their prince as national, and repudiation of an ungrateful sovereign may well have been deemed (except by that sovereign) merely somewhat censurable rather than really disreputable; more in doubtful taste than actually treasonable. So great was the interchange of services in the Peninsula that it seems safe to assume that Magellan's real offence was his titanic success, without which not so much would have been made of his defection; although paradoxically, this contributes to the modern tendency to condonation.[30]

In October 1517 Magellan went to Seville and formally naturalised himself as a subject of Carlos I (the Emperor Charles V); he was joined in December by Ruy Faleiro, a man of repute as a cosmographer but of somewhat unbalanced mind. Magellan and Faleiro had sincerely convinced themselves that the Moluccas lay within the Spanish sphere, assuming the Tordesillas line to be carried on round the globe; and indeed a number of Portuguese who remained loyal to their Crown were either doubtful of Lusian rights or of the same belief, whence some embarrassment for D. João III's envoys at the Badajoz conference which met to consider the new situation created by Magellan's voyage.[31] By way of insurance D. Manuel obtained a new Bull, *Praecelsae devotionis* (1514), from Pope Leo IX, who had been gratified by the gift of a performing elephant sent back by Albuquerque; this confirmed *Romanus Pontifex* and in very sweeping terms gave Portugal rights to any heathen lands wheresoever which were reached by sailing eastwards, in effect restricting the Tordesillas line to the Atlantic.[32]

The officials of the Casa de Contratacion, the royal agency busily organising the Antillean Indies from Seville, were mostly unimpressed by Magellan's promise that he could lead them to the Spice Islands without trespassing on Portuguese preserves; but one of them, Juan de Aranda, took Magellan and Faleiro more seriously. Aranda had the ear of the immensely powerful Juan de Fonseca, Bishop of Burgos and the head of the Casa; but, to Faleiro's fury, he drove a hard bargain for his good offices, insisting on an eighth of any profits that might accrue to the pair. Support was also received from Cristobal de Haro, a member of a Burgos merchant family who had worked with the Fuggers in financing the pepper trade, but had broken with D. Manuel over the latter's insistence on a crown monopoly and general tough dealing with the German investors, and more personal grievances. Haro was apparently behind a small Portuguese expedition under João de Lisboa and Estevão Frois which between 1511 and 1514 reached the La Plata estuary or even perhaps the Gulf of San Matias in 42°S, and according to the manuscript *Newen Zeytung auss Pressilandt* in the Fugger archives, thought itself to have been only 600 leagues from Malacca; this is probably the source of the strait in 45°S shown on Schöner's map of 1515.[33] Haro came to Spain in 1516 and immediately allied himself with Fonseca. The joint efforts of the group secured the royal *Capitulacion* issued on 22 March 1518: the design, foreshadowed by Vespucci and the Solis voyage of 1515–16, was not for a circumnavigation but for a Southwest Passage to the Moluccas; and another possible objective in Magellan's mind was the gold of Tarshish and Ophir, identified with the Lequeos—the Ryukyu Islands—already known to the Portuguese, having been visited by Jorge de Mascarenhas in 1517.[34] Whether it *originally* included a circumnavigation may be left open, but on the whole is very doubtful, although, according to Pigafetta, Magellan had decided on this route before his death. *Pace* Morison, it would not make sense for a Portuguese defector to Castile to return through the Portuguese zone, against the tenor of his instructions; but, as Magellan's rashness on the day of his death suggests, hubris may already have set in.[35]

The voyage: background and preparations

Amerigo Vespucci, who on his three or four voyages was never in command, indirectly gained (though many would say he had not earned) the honour of having his name bestowed on the New World, since it was through the publication of his letters, most notably by Waldseemüller in 1507, that

> all Europe recognised America for what it was, a new continent
> and a barrier between Europe and Asia. To everyone except
> the Portuguese it was an unwelcome barrier.[36]

The recognition of course was not automatic and universal; it is fair to say that in 1504 Columbus's conviction that he was only a couple of weeks from the Ganges might be scouted, but also that it had some respectable authority behind it and was quite widely accepted by disinterested parties, such as Italian geographers; and a similar concept retained acceptance by a much interested party— the Castilians—at least as late as the Badajoz conference in 1524. Nevertheless the concept of a continental barrier increasingly took hold.

The contrast is strikingly shown by the maps of Contarini and Ruysch (1506 and 1508) and Stobnicza-Waldseemüller (1507). In Ruysch's map (Plate V) from the 1508 edition of Ptolemy, Greenland and 'Terra Nova' (Newfoundland) form part of an eastwards peninsula of Asia, separated from 'Terra sancte crvcis sive Mvndvs novvs' (Venezuela-Brazil) by a wide sea with only a few islands, the most notable being '[E]spagnola' and a misshapen Cuba, with an inscription attached to the latter indicating that Spanish ships had reached it; on this map Polo's Zaiton (in Fukien) is only eighteen degrees of longitude beyond the latter,

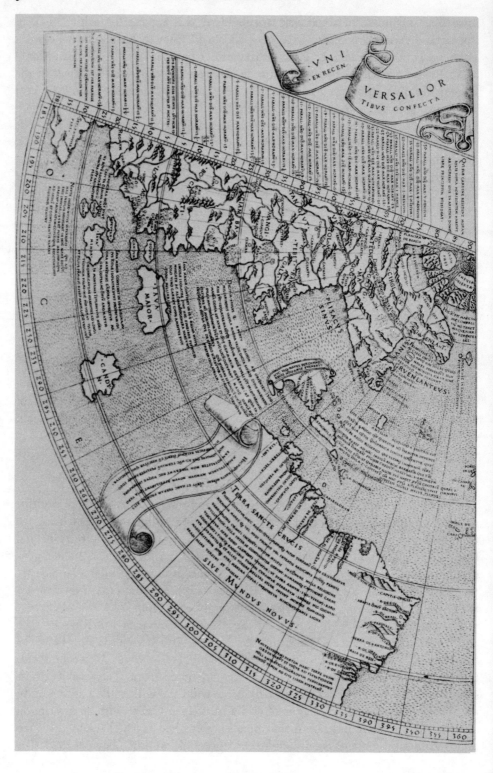

and between them is another inscription suggesting, rather doubtfully, that 'spagnola' may be Cipangu. Beside this elegant map, Stobnicza's inset on Wald-seemüller's world map is crude (Plate VI); but it shows an (American) continent continuous from 50°N to the bottom edge of the map in 40°S; the western 'coasts' of this land-mass are shown diagrammatically, as not known but intelligently inferred; Cipangu lies nearer to this land than to Asia. Yet the older concept lingered on: in the planisphere of Franciscus Monachus (1529) we have the Spanish version: America is a vast projection from southeast Asia (with a guessed-at strait somewhere in central America) and the Indian and Pacific Oceans are one.[37]

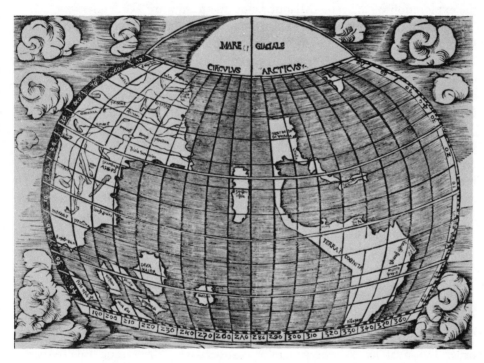

Plate VI. THE AMERICAN INDIES: STOBNICZA 1512. Copied from an inset on Waldseemüller's world map of 1507, from J. Fischer and F. von Wieser (eds.), *Die Älteste Karte mit den Namen Amerika* (Innsbruck 1903). NLA.

◄*Plate V.* THE COLUMBAN INDIES: RUYSCH 1508. The inscription to the left of the island corresponding to Cuba is obscure, owing to a superfluity of abbreviations, but says in effect that as Marco Polo states that 'Sipangu' is '1500 miliaribus' east of Zaiton (Ch'uan-chou in Fukien), Ruysch dare not insert it on the map under that name, since the position so indicated is occupied by islands found by the Spaniards; very oddly, it is then suggested that 'Sipangu' and 'Spagnola' may be the same since the letters forming the two words are the same. (I am indebted to Mr R. W. Barnes of the Department of Classics, Australian National University, for help with this difficult text; but the responsibility for the interpretation is in the last resort mine.) From *Universalior Cogniti Orbis Tabula*, reproduced in A. E. Nordenskiold, *Facsimile Atlas* (Stockholm 1889). NLA.

How far the barrier extended north and south was unknown, nor whether any through passages existed; by 1518 there had been several probes in both directions. Unless Vicente Yañez Pinzon's cruise of 1499 along the coast of Venezuela, and possibly of northern Brazil, be counted, the first of these probes to go in a southerly direction was that of the Portuguese Nuño Manuel, with Vespucci, in 1501–2. How far south this expedition reached is a matter of dispute; Vespucci claimed 52°S, though somewhere between 20 and 32° is more favoured.[38] But at any rate it found no passage, and Vespucci's last voyage, in 1503–4, did not get so far. Indeed, however much Vespucci and Haro might be interested in a South-west Passage, their then master D. Manuel can have been concerned only with the exploration of the trans-Atlantic lands due to him by Tordesillas.

Proposed expeditions under Pinzon—with Vespucci, now again in Spanish service—in 1506 and by Vespucci in 1508 lapsed or were diverted as a result of Portuguese protests, and Vespucci became head of the Casa de Contratacion's school for pilots. It was becoming clear, however, that the coast of the new continent trended far beyond the Tordesillas limit. The last voyages of significance before Magellan's were those of Frois and of Juan de Solis in 1515–16; this had definite instructions to find a way to the Mar del Sur and thence to Castilla del Oro. Near the modern Montevideo, which he calculated to be (as it was) well on the Spanish side of the Tordesillas line, Solis took possession of the country for Castile, and sailed up the La Plata estuary, the freshwater 'Mar Dulce', far enough to be assured that it was a great river and no passage. Here he was eaten by cannibals, and the expedition returned to Spain in disarray. But the idea of a strait was 'in the air' and Magellan's proposal well timed.[39]

When he sailed, then, Magellan knew that he would have to go beyond 30°S to avoid Portuguese waters, and that any passage lay far beyond that—perhaps about 50°S, possibly even twenty or more degrees further still.

Magellan's troubles were but beginning: at first the Casa de Contratacion took hardly the issue of the capitulacion over its head, but when briskly called to order by royal letters was generally co-operative. The erratic Faleiro was a constant source of troubles, and there was a marked reluctance all round—not least amongst the putative crews—to engage in the enterprise. And all the time the Portuguese were doing their best to sabotage a venture which was against their country's material interests and also—Magellan's breach with D. Manuel being notorious—damaging to their amour propre as Portuguese, and to that of their Prince—factors which weighed greatly in the Renaissance world.

Five ships were allotted to the voyage: San Antonio, 120 tons, 31 metres long, 9·8 in the beam; Trinidad, 110; Concepcion, 90; Victoria, 85; Santiago, 75.[40] They were old and the worse for wear—the Portuguese factor or consul at Seville, Sebastião Alvares, said that he would not risk sailing to the Canaries in them,[41] but Magellan threw himself with tremendous energy into the task of refitting at royal expense through the Casa; but by 1519 funds were running short, and

Cristobal de Haro had to put up one-fifth of the cost—which he was repaid, with no profit or interest, eighteen years later.[42]

Recruitment was the worst problem: there were plenty of Portuguese agents to spread alarmist stories. D. Carlos had wished for all-Spanish crews, with Portuguese limited to at most the five pilots and a few boys; he had to accept twenty-four, and in the event perhaps forty sailed, some enlisted as Spaniards. This amounted to one out of six in the total complement of 237 men, and even so Magellan, almost on the eve of sailing, had to fill up with aliens: about thirty Italians, a score of Frenchmen, Flemings, Germans, Levantines, nondescript mixed-bloods, and one Englishman, the master-gunner Andrew of Bristol, who died in the Pacific.[43] With Portuguese pilots, and staff officers unavoidably but dangerously mixed between Portuguese and Spaniards, there was material enough for the seditions and dissensions of the voyage, though both nations contributed both to Magellan's supporters and to his deserters and mutineers.

Repeated efforts were made by the Portuguese, especially Sebastião Alvares, to re-seduce Magellan from his new allegiance; Alvares pointed out the dangers, 'as many as the Wheel of St Catharine', stressed Castilian suspicions of Magellan (which he had done much to manufacture), and held out rewards, at one point flattering himself that he was very close to success. But quite apart from Magellan's position as a man of honour pledged to his new and more generous Lord, on which Lagôa lays much stress, it is not very likely that an intelligent man of the Renaissance would put so much trust in princes. Alvares had more success in stirring up discord in general, and in particular a waterfront riot over the false allegation that Magellan had displayed Portuguese ensigns on the *Trinidad*. This was in October 1518; Magellan's firm appeal to the King greatly strengthened his hand with unco-operative local officials; and the too-obvious Portuguese anxiety to disrupt the expedition was counter-productive, indicating that a Spanish presence in or control of the Spice Islands would indeed be profitable.

Although Ruy Faleiro's vanity and bad temper must have been most detrimental to the project, his prestige as a scientific expert had played a large part in its acceptance, and in mid-1519 Magellan still considered him, in Lagôa's phrase, as his 'colleague in the high command', whereas had he been really mad, as is so often stated, the Captain-General would have been anxious to get rid of him. Faleiro's supersession in July 1519, however, seems not to have been due to his mental instability, much exaggerated by Sebastião Alvares after failing to lure him back into the Lusian fold. Some were sceptical of Faleiro's boasted cosmography, which others attributed to the promptings of a familiar daemon, and altogether he must have seemed less stable and safe than the impressive Magellan. Above all, it must have seemed much wiser to have a Castilian next to or alongside Magellan, rather than two Portuguese at the top; the machinations of Alvares had stimulated not unnatural doubts and apprehensions among the royal advisers.

Faleiro, then, was excluded by the Casa, being soothed by the promise of taking charge of a follow-up expedition; perhaps also he feared to put to the test his unorthodox methods—to determine longitude by isogonal lines—in utterly unknown regions, although Magellan himself insisted that he should be given Faleiro's book of pilotage before acquiescing in his replacement as chief pilot by Andrés de San Martin. It was only after Magellan's departure that Ruy Faleiro became really insane.[44]

The critical appointment of Juan de Cartagena, Fonseca's man—his nephew or perhaps bastard—as *Veedor-general* and captain of the third ship was definitely a reinsurance against Portuguese predominance in the command. The office of *Veedor-general* might best be described as a super-supercargo, charged to look after the royal financial interests, and such an appointment was a perfectly normal procedure; but a royal *cédula* of 10 May 1518 is explicit:

it is convenient that there should be a third with the said
Portuguese, in case of death or in case the said Portuguese should
not follow the route which they should to complete the voyage
which is to be made and perchance the affairs of our service
should not come to a good end.

This has been held to indicate that Cartagena was in effect a commissar, or at least a spy, with secret powers, or a second in command—that is the whole point of the cedula—and his actions suggest that in his own view he was joint commander. In addition to the ordinary functions of a veedor, he was to advise on colonisation and to be *alcalde*, or governor, of the first fort to be constructed. But his own instructions of 6 April 1519, in Lagôa's words, 'were not of a type to allow any intervention in the functions of the Captain-General, being limited to giving him powers to control the commercial side of the enterprise.'[45]

On the other hand, *any* officer was given the right to report in writing, uncensored, on the conduct of the expedition, so that the chief might be called to account on return; such a *residencia*, or post-mortem, on a governor's actions was normal in Spanish colonial practice, though in this case somewhat pointed towards Magellan. But had Cartagena been given any powers beyond this, he could hardly have failed to appeal to them at his trial at Puerto San Julian, at least for the record, even if the immediate verdict might be a foregone conclusion. In Lagôa's view, the King may have considered giving Cartagena such powers, but desisted lest Magellan should be impelled to accept Portuguese offers by such a mark of no-confidence. Obviously the likelihood of a serious rift in the command was great, in fact the worst weakness of the expedition.

Final instructions were based on standard Iberian practice for long voyages. Magellan was not to take any risks by going ashore himself, but to send officers and take hostages. No arms, axes, or iron were to be sold to natives. No native women were to be touched, and cards and dice were banned—a counsel of perfection going beyond the Portuguese model, which allowed play for low stakes. All these, except the provision already noted for independent reporting, were fairly normal for contemporary expeditions, if not normally followed with exactitude. One other directive was most important: on no account should Magellan infringe on the Portuguese zone. According to las Casas, directly reporting (but forty years later) his own talk with Magellan, if he failed to find the Southwest Passage the Captain-General would take the African route—or perhaps a more daring plan, predicated on the quasi-Ptolemaic map of Lopo Homem (1519), which prolongs the coast south of Brazil in a great Antarctic sweep to join up with Cathay, thus reconciling Ptolemy's closed Indian Ocean with da Gama's discovery: the ocean is still closed but it takes in both the Atlantic and the Indian.[46] Such an immense navigation along the coasts of an unknown Terra Australis would certainly have given Magellan good reason to conceal his plans from his officers; but this reticence was a major provocation to the mutiny which could have wrecked his whole project.

After two postponements, all obstacles being at last overcome, the fleet dropped down the Guadalquivir from Seville in early August, and after final victualling at San Lucar de Barrameda cleared the estuary on 20 September 1519, Magellan flying his flag on the *Trinidad*.

The voyage south

Friction began early, after the Cape Verdes had been passed; probably following Portuguese *roteiros*, Magellan kept on a southerly course instead of striking across the Atlantic, and this may well have alarmed the Spanish officers: was the Captain-General luring them into Portuguese waters? Juan de Cartagena was plainly insolent and insubordinate, garbling and then omitting the regulation evening greetings to the commander, and at a suitable opportunity Magellan deprived him of his captaincy of the *San Antonio* and put him under arrest. So matters stood as the fleet passed across to Brazil and, in January 1520, explored the La Plata estuary. Hopes were raised by this great opening, but there was no passage either here or in the Gulf of San Matias further south, and on 31 March Magellan reached Puerto San Julian, in 49°20'S, where he decided to winter. Here, faced with a long wait on reduced rations in a cold climate, discontent broke into open mutiny, and an officers' mutiny at that.

Representations, more or less mutinous, demanding a return were very common from crews wintering in high latitudes. Magellan succeeded in talking down the desire of the seamen to turn back, partly by pointing out that things would be much easier in the spring and that wood, water, fish and birds were plentiful, so that rations could be supplemented; partly by an appeal to pride; most of all, perhaps, by driving leadership: he himself was determined to find a passage, as far south as 75° if need be, or to die. The sedition of the officers was far more serious.

At Easter,[47] only one of the captains—Magellan's cousin Alvaro de Mesquita, now in command of the *San Antonio*—accepted his invitation to Mass and a feast on the flagship. During the night the conspirators, led by Juan de Cartagena and

Gaspar de Quesada, took over the *San Antonio*, *Victoria*, and *Concepcion*. Next morning there were negotiations, probably of doubtful sincerity on either part; Magellan sent a small party with concealed arms to the *Victoria*, ostensibly to arrange a conference; her captain Luis de Mendoza was stabbed without warning, and the ship seized, to join with the loyal *Trinidad* and *Santiago* in blocking the harbour mouth. At night the *San Antonio* made a feeble attempt to break out, but the swift retaking of the *Victoria* had taken the heart out of the mutineers. After their surrender Alvaro de Mesquita presided over a court, which sentenced forty men to death, including Juan Sebastian del Cano, whom the rebels had put in command of the *San Antonio*. Obviously this sentence on well over a sixth of the complement was a formality; in the event only Quesada was beheaded and quartered, as was the body of Mendoza. Juan de Cartagena was not executed, probably because of his royal commission, but sentenced (perhaps after a second attempt to stir up revolt) to be marooned.

There can be no doubt at all that Magellan had contributed very greatly to the outbreak by his overbearing manner, secretiveness, and partiality for Portuguese officers. That said, and considering the stakes, he can hardly be blamed for meeting rebellion with ruthlessness and little scruple. Mutiny was a constant nightmare of exploring captains until well into the eighteenth century; and unless the commander struck at once and hard, the voyage was doomed; a century later Richard Hawkins was to write

> By this and the like experience, remembring and knowing, that, if
> once I consented to turne but one foote backe, I should overthrow
> my Voyage, and loose my reputation, I resolved rather to loose
> my life, than to guie eare to prejudiciall Counsell . . . for I haue
> not seene, that any man haue yeelded therevnto, but presently
> [immediately] they haue returned home.[48]

It was in effect on suspicion of projected mutiny that Drake executed Thomas Doughty in this very Puerto San Julian; and here his people found the remains of what they took to be a gibbet 'with men's bones underneath it', a grim memento of the bloody Eastertide nearly sixty years earlier.[49]

During the winter the little *Santiago* was lost on a reconnaissance to the south, but the crew was able to make its way back to San Julian; contact was made with the inhabitants, to the delight of Pigafetta (who had the instincts of an anthropologist) and the tale of the Patagonian ('big feet') giants was launched on its long history. Perhaps fearing the results of long inaction in this port of evil memories, Magellan took the four remaining ships to sea in late August, leaving behind Juan de Cartagena and an accomplice, with wine and some bags of biscuit.

Ten degrees farther south the fleet spent two months at the Rio Santa Cruz, taking on wood, water, and fish. With spring, they put to sea again, and four days later, in about 52° 30′S, they saw on 21 October, St Ursula's Day, a cape which they named for her Eleven Thousand Virgins, and beyond it 'certain inlets of the sea . . . which had the appearance of a strait.'

The voyage: the Straits and the Ocean—Mactan

Mooring inside the new cape, possibly on the southern shores of the embayment, Magellan sent on the *San Antonio* and *Concepcion* to reconnoitre; a great storm came on the night of their departure, and it was feared that they had been lost, until they were seen approaching, guns firing and crews cheering as they drew near. They had passed the First Narrows—well named Angostura de la Esperanza —and found a great opening, narrowing at the further end but then widening out again, and obviously running far into the land. This was no La Plata or Mar Dulce; the indications were for a true passage, and the fleet pressed on.

The chronology of the passage is confused. At one point Magellan sought counsel in writing of his officers, professing (from one's general impression of his character, most disingenuously) that he was always open to advice; so far as is known, only Andrés de San Martin replied, though on this or another occasion Estevão Gomes (or Esteban Gomez), a Portuguese disgruntled at not receiving command of a ship, objected to continuing the voyage: now that a passage had been discovered, it would be better to return to Spain and come out again with a better-found expedition. As Zweig says,

> From the logical, the objective outlook, Gomez's proposal to return
> forthwith to enjoy the honours they had won was eminently
> sound. Had it been accepted, the commander and nearly two
> hundred other members of the expedition who were foredoomed
> to perish, would have got home safely.[50]

Once again Zweig invokes the prerogative of a genius: 'who wishes to act heroically, must act unreasonably.' But even discounting his intense egoism, Magellan was not unreasonable in finding the proposal utterly unacceptable: anything would be better than returning with his task half-done, his promises half-fulfilled, to face all over again the frustrations, intrigues, and hazards of resurrecting the project. It is likely that Magellan's conciliatory gesture was only *pro forma*; it is now that he is said to have declared 'in a most composed manner' that he would go on even if they had to eat the leather from the yards. According to Pigafetta, the Captain-General knew of a hidden strait from a map by Martin Behaim which he had seen in Portuguese archives; and it is largely on this that Nunn and Nowell base their view that Magellan thought of South America not as a new continent but as a southerly extension from Asia, and the Mar del Sur as Ptolemy's Sinus Magnus. Whatever the truth on this point, it seems impossible that a passage shown by Behaim along the Tropic of Capricorn should be 'The strait which Magellan sought for and thought he found': an error of nearly 30° in *latitude* is too much by far. Even if he had seen a map by or based on Behaim, it would have represented the knowledge of the 1490s, and by 1520 Vespucci and Solis had exploded it. It is true that the conviction that Columbus had found not Asia but Mundus Novus was not as yet universal, but it was already general, and apart from this reference by Pigafetta, there is little or no evidence that Magellan was much influenced by Behaim. It seems more likely that, as Lagôa argues, he was confusing Behaim with that other Nurnberg cosmographer Schöner, whose globes and maps were far more in accord with the general knowledge and opinion of the time.[51]

At the head of Broad Reach there is a fork: Magellan went up the southwestern channel (between Brunswick Peninsula and Dawson Island) with the *Trinidad* and *Victoria*, sending the other two ships to explore the branch to the southeast. Many smokes were seen on the land to the left, hence named Tierra del Fuego, and the broad sounds and open desolate country of the eastern shores of the passage were replaced by narrow fiords walled in by densely forested and snow-capped mountains; but despite the notorious difficulties of navigation in narrow waters liable to sudden squalls from the side-valleys, the passage—some 600km, the length of the English Channel—seems to have been a fairly smooth one. At the 'River of Sardines', rather more than halfway through, Magellan stopped to take in wood and water; but the other two ships had not rejoined, and he turned

Plate VII. MAGELLAN IN THE STRAITS: THE HEROIC IMAGE. The hero is shown steering (apparently backwards, since Tierra del Fuego is to starboard of the ship) between the Land of Giants and the Land of Fire; the Patagonian giant using an arrow as an emetic is mentioned by Pigafetta and became a standard item in Magellanic iconography (cf. Plate XX); the roc is obviously a stray from Madagascar. From Theodore de Bry, *America*, Part IV (1594), by permission of the Trustees of The British Library.

back to look for them. He found only the *Concepcion*; the *San Antonio* was missing; in fact, Estevão Gomes had seized her and deserted.[52] Giving her up for lost, the fleet returned to what Magellan now knew to be the main channel, since while at the River of Sardines he had

> sent a boat well provided with men and victuals to find the cape of
> the other sea. They took three days going and returning, and told
> us that they had found the cape and the great open sea; at which
> the Captain-General, for the joy he had, began to weep, and
> named that cape Cape of Desire [Cabo Deseado, close to the modern
> Cape Pilar], as a thing much desired and long-time sought.

The channel was narrow but deep, the flood stronger than the ebb: there could no longer be any doubt that the Passage was found.

On 28 November they passed the Cape of Desire, and now other tears, not of joy, were to be shed:

> we entered into the pacific sea where we stayed three months and
> twenty days without taking on victuals or other refreshments, and
> we ate only old biscuit turned to powder all full of worms and
> stinking with the odour of the urine the Rats had made on it, after
> eating the good part. And we drank putrid yellow water. We also
> ate the hides of cattle which were very hard because of the sun,
> rain, and wind. And we left them four or five days in the sea,
> then put them for a little while over the coals. And so we ate them.
> Also rats which cost half a crown each one. And even so we
> could not find enough of them.[53]

And Pigafetta goes on to describe the worst horror of all, the scurvy. But the sea was well named the Pacific, for they met with no storms.

During the whole traverse to Guam, they saw only two small uninhabited islands. The generally accepted version of Magellan's route takes him up the Chilean coast to about 32 or 34°S (so as to reach warmer climes as quickly as possible) and thence across the Ocean in a generally west-northwesterly direction, borne on by the Southeast Trades. The two islands seen, San Pablo and Los Tiburones ('The Sharks') are generally identified respectively with Pukapuka, Fangahina, or Angatau, outliers of the Tuamotus, and Caroline, Vostock, or Flint in the Line Islands. G. E. Nunn, however, puts forward a closely argued but unconvincing case for a track right up the South American coast to about 10°S, thence northwest to the area of Cipangu (which he holds to be a main objective of Magellan's) as shown on Waldseemüller's map of 1507—that is, a large rectangular island extending from Baja California to about 8°N. Not finding this island, Magellan gave up the search and meeting with favourable winds—the southern limb of the Northeast Trades—he struck west, in accordance with the principles of latitude sailing. On this view the two islands would be Clipperton and Clarion (in the Revillagigedos), about 10 and 19°N respectively—

surely much too large a difference from the 16–19°S for San Pablo and the 9–14°S for Tiburones given by Pigafetta, Francisco Albo, and the 'Genoese pilot', the three recorders who were actually on the voyage. The main basis of Nunn's argument is that the pilot Albo, who alone gives a coherent sequence of positions, consistently falsified his results after Magellan's death (but what is the force of this?) so as to make sure that the Spice Islands would be shown in the Spanish half of the world. Much of Nunn's argument seems circular.[54]

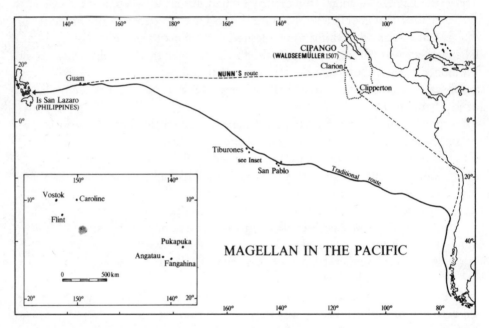

Figure 3. MAGELLAN IN THE PACIFIC. Adapted from map by G. E. Nunn, *Geographical Review* 24, 1934, 616.

The 'incidental remark' by Pigafetta about Cipangu on which Nunn relies is so extremely vague and confused that nothing can be safely built upon it. The fact that Magellan saw only two islands before Guam is certainly rather surprising, but by no means so extraordinary a phenomenon as Nunn asserts: in the relevant longitudes (that is as far west as 160°W, where the traditional track enters an island-free zone), the island screens are arranged *en echelon*, and Magellan was passing along them, not athwart. Schouten and Le Maire in 1616 saw only four islands east of 160°W, all in the Tuamotus and all within four days; Byron in 1765, in a course close to the traditional track of Magellan in these longitudes, saw five, again all in the Tuamotus and again all so close together as hardly to count as more than two; the ship of Magellan's immediate successor Loaysa met with one island only. Nunn arrives at his course largely, if not mainly, by correcting for compass declination; but it appears from Pigafetta—in a less dubious reference than that to Cipangu—that Magellan did insist on his pilots

adjusting for declination, and a further correction would be gratuitous and mis-
leading. The Nunn route is materially longer—by nearly 2800 km—than the
traditional one, and it seems highly unlikely that Magellan, already very short
of provisions and with one mutiny and one probably presumed desertion behind
him, would have risked setting his pilots such a course, especially when he had
found favourable winds in the Southeast Trades—that would have been an open
invitation to further discontents. It seems also gratuitous to labour the suspicious
precision of Albo's latitudes and the discrepancies between his and other accounts
for San Pablo and Los Tiburones (only three to five degrees) while at the same
time insisting that all the early authorities were either deceivers or deceived to
the tune of 25 to 30 degrees. Why should Pigafetta, an Italian and a Knight of
Rhodes, join in the deception? and while he was by no means a professional, he
could surely tell the difference between 10 or 20° *south* and 10 or 20° *north*—in
January! Nunn's paper is an elegant essay in deduction, but there seem to be too
many interdependent variables for it to carry conviction. Nor, given the Spanish
clinging to a Ptolemaic view of the world, the complete and natural uncertainty
as to the width of the gap between Asia and Castilla del Oro, and the genuine
doubt as to the position of the Spice Islands relative to an extension of the
Tordesillas line around the globe, can one see any very compelling reason for the
falsification.

Plunged into the wastes of the Ocean, and however desperate the physical and
moral condition of the company, obviously 'returning were as tedious as go
o'er.' The long agony drew near an end, or at least an intermission, when on
6 March 1521 they sighted three islands, inhabited and promising: Guam, Rota,
and perhaps Saipan. But this first contact between Europeans and Oceanians was
far from happy. Magellan wished to obtain fresh supplies, but the natives came
aboard and stole everything they could carry away, dexterously making off
with a small boat from the *Trinidad*'s stern. Going ashore with forty armed men,
Magellan burned houses and boats in reprisal, killing seven men. Leaving these
Islands of the Ladrones, or Robbers, on 9 March, they came a week later to a
high island of considerable size: Samar.

Magellan had taken a course which brought him well north of the Moluccas,
allegedly giving as a reason that food would be in short supply there, but perhaps
rather on the scent of Tarshish and Ophir, thought of as in the Lequeos (Ryukyus),
or with a more realistic idea than Columbus's of the location of Cipangu. On
any view, he must have thought himself near Asia, and perhaps his motive was
the simple and sensible desire to replenish his supplies and recuperate his crews
before a possible encounter with the Portuguese in the Moluccas. The islands
he had reached were obviously large and desirable; not yet christened the
Philippines, they were named for the day of their discovery, the Islas de San
Lazaro. The barrier that Vespucci had divined, the great sea that Balboa had
glimpsed—both had been overcome.

Landing on a small uninhabited island, they set up tents for the sick, and two days later a canoe with nine men arrived.[55] Magellan commanded his people to wait in silence; but these men were welcoming. Trade trifles were exchanged for fruit, coconuts, and arrack, and more provisions were promised. With rest and fresh food, all took new heart; the Captain-General gave coconut-milk to the sick with his own hand. Relations with the local people remained cordial, and on 28 March, when they had moved on to another little island, they met a man who could converse with Magellan's Malayan slave Enrique: it was now certain that they had reached the confines of Asia.

The first Easter after the mutiny at Puerto San Julian was marked by an impressively solemn Mass, at which two local 'kings' kissed the Cross. They were among a people of civility, even elegance, who had justice, weights and measures, intriguing customs; Pigafetta was fascinated by such strange new things as betel-chewing and flying foxes. There was also gold. . . . Accompanied by their new friends, they moved on to the large island of Cebu, where these first favourable impressions were enhanced.

The Rajah of the island, Humabon, startled and impressed by gunnery salutes, yet wished for 'tribute', pointing out a merchant from Siam who had paid his dues. The Captain-General replied that he was servant to a great King, one greater than the King of Portugal, who paid no man tribute; war or peace was at the Rajah's choice. The Moor merchant interposed: be careful, these are the men who have conquered Calicut, Malacca, India. Doubtless reflecting on the artillery, the Rajah chose peace, accepting Spanish protection and desiring to be received into the Church of these powerful strangers. On 14 April he and his wife were baptised under the names of Don Carlos and Dona Juana, in honour of the King-Emperor and his mother; five hundred of their subjects followed them into the Faith. All this was done with great ceremony and solemnity; one wonders if Pigafetta remembered the party a few days earlier, where he had enjoyed the dancing of three girls, quite naked.

Cuius regio, eius religio—as the King, so the religion—seems to have applied as it did in contemporary Europe; once the Rajah led the way, mass conversion followed perforce. But some of the neighbouring vassal chiefs were recalcitrant, and—against his instructions—the Captain-General decided to intervene personally; if 'Don Carlos' was to be of use as a puppet king to maintain Spanish influence in the islands, he must be supported to the full. Doubtless Magellan saw the affair as a test of credibility; this was to be by no means the last time in these regions that a client was to drag a 'great and powerful friend' into disaster. Had he succeeded, Magellan might have been called many things, but we would not have heard of his lack of judgment; and the Portuguese in the East were wont to take on very heavy numerical odds against much stronger foes: as at Cannanor, as at Diu, as at Malacca, in all of which actions Magellan had served.

At midnight of 26 April 1521 the Captain-General and Humabon-Don Carlos set out with sixty Europeans and several hundred Cebuans to bring into their joint allegiance the Rajah of Mactan, Lapulapu, now honoured as the first hero of Filipino resistance to colonialism. Next morning forty-nine men waded ashore, for Magellan, here truly and arrogantly injudicious, had asked the Rajah and his men to stay in their boats and see how Spaniards could fight. The 1500 defenders opposed them with unexpected resolution and tactical skill; musket and crossbow fire was opened at too great a range to be effective, and finally Magellan ordered a retreat. All but six or eight of his men fled; the mortars in the boats were too far away to give adequate covering fire. In the end the Captain-General, bravely covering the flight, was overborne by numbers and hacked to death. The disheartened survivors tried to ransom the body, to be told that they of Mactan would never give up such a man, such a trophy, for the wealth of the world. The last words must always be Pigafetta's simple tribute: 'so great a captain'.

The ends of the voyage: Victoria and Trinidad

Whatever discontents remained after the recuperation in the Islas de San Lazaro—and it is not likely that all shared Pigafetta's devotion to 'our mirror, our light, our comfort, and our true guide'—all must have been daunted by the loss of the Captain-General's iron leadership. They chose Juan Serrano (or Serrão) and the Portuguese Duarte Barbosa, two of Magellan's most loyal officers, as leaders, and sadly prepared to go on. Their position had been more seriously undermined than they knew, for the Rajah of Cebu (possibly incited by the interpreter Enrique, threatened with a lifetime of slavery in Spain—despite his manumission by Magellan's will) had resolved to rid himself of these dangerous but unsuccessful allies. He invited them to a feast on 1 May, at which the jewels promised for the King of Spain were to be presented. Fortunately for posterity as well as for himself, Pigafetta had been too badly wounded at Mactan to walk into the trap. Two of the twenty-nine who went ashore suspected foul play and returned; the rest, including Barbosa, were slain. At the water's edge Serrão implored with tears his bosom friend João Carvalho to save him, but the company was too shaken to act.

They sailed on, still in quest of the Spice Islands, under Carvalho. There were now only 115 men left, too few to man three ships, and the Concepcion was burned at Bohol. They passed across from Mindanao to Palawan, where they were well received, and found pilots who took them down the Borneo coast to the rich town of Brunei. Relations, at first friendly but suspicious on both sides, soon degenerated; men were detained ashore, including a son of Carvalho's by a Brazilian girl; there was a successful skirmish with the Rajah's praus, and semi-piratical seizures of junks for hostages; it was soon time to move on. In August they careened at an island off the north point of Borneo, and here Carvalho, a most ineffective leader, was deposed: Gonzalo Gomez de Espinosa took general command, and Juan Sebastian del Cano took over the Victoria. They sailed again on 27 September, and after wandering through the Sulu archipelago and skirting the southern coast of Mindanao, at last reached the Spice Islands, anchoring on 8 November 1521 at Tidore.

Politics in the Spice Islands were highly confused by the rivalries of the Rajahs of Ternate and Tidore. Francisco Serrão had died some months earlier in mysterious circumstances,[56] but Portuguese influence was strong on Ternate, and Tidore was open to a countervailing alliance. Luckily for the newcomers the Portuguese had at the moment no ships in the islands. But they were already moving to control the clove trade, from Malacca, and had promised to build a factory: whichever nation and whichever island first secured such a base would gain commercial hegemony in the Moluccas. Hence 'the ancient feud between Ternate and Tidore was intensified in a new rivalry to secure this European support',[57] which yet had obvious dangers: the factory would also be a fort. So there were cross-currents; a week after the Spaniards arrived they were visited by a Portuguese, Afonso de Lorosa, like Serrão a freelance, who came over from Ternate. From him they learnt that, despite ostensible cordiality on both sides, the Rajah of that island mistrusted the Portuguese (as well he might) and would also be glad of Spanish friendship; but they also learnt that Lopes de Sequeira, Magellan's commander in the Malacca days and now Viceroy, had been ordered to seek out and destroy Magellan's fleet should it reach the Moluccas. Two months were spent in negotiating trade and protection agreements and in buying cloves, obtaining so many that sixty quintals had to be left behind for fear of overlading. When they were putting to sea, the *Trinidad* leaked so much that she was clearly unseaworthy. It was decided that she should be repaired and then make east for Darien—there was as yet no New Spain, and it was still thought that the Spice Islands were not far distant from the Isthmus. The *Victoria* would continue westwards for Spain. Pigafetta records the decision almost casually, but there must have been much anxious debate, and some remained behind for fear of foundering or of hunger.

Del Cano left Tidore on the last great lap of the first circumnavigation on 21 December 1521. In February the *Victoria* sailed from Timor and into the Indian Ocean, and strictly speaking out of our history. The voyage home was as agonising as the Pacific crossing had been, but Del Cano proved a worthy successor to his Captain-General,[58] rejecting pleas that they should seek succour from the Portuguese in Mozambique. As Morales Padrón remarks, Del Cano had a shipload of spices but nothing to eat, and was compelled by manifold distresses to put in to the Cape Verdes, pretending to come from America; but the secret leaked out and the Portuguese seized some of his diminished crew. Forty-seven Europeans and thirteen Malays had left Tidore; eighteen and four reached Spain, in wretched plight but with spirit enough to fire a salute as they came alongside Seville quays on 8 September 1522. Pigafetta went to Valladolid and presented to D. Carlos 'neither gold nor silver' but, amongst other things, a holograph copy of his narrative, the precious record of the greatest single voyage in all history.

The *Trinidad* was long in the repairing, and did not leave Tidore until 6 April 1522. Lorosa, unfortunately for him, had thrown in his lot with the Spaniards and sailed with them; a few men were left behind in a tiny factory, the first formal European base in Indonesia, to look after the remaining trade goods and the surplus spices. They touched at some islands, including probably Agrigan in the northern Marianas, and battled on northeastwards, dead into the Trades, apparently reaching 42 or 43°N.[59] Here, cold, famished, and sick, they ran into a prolonged storm. Probably not even Magellan could or would have pushed on; there was no recourse but to return to the Spice Islands, which they reached early in November.

They returned to find that in May seven Portuguese ships under Antonio de Brito had arrived at Ternate; the little factory on Tidore had of course at once been seized. Thirty-five of the fifty-four men with whom Espinosa had left Tidore were dead, and he had no option but to throw himself upon the mercies of the Lusian rival. These were not tender; the Portuguese seem at first to have been moved to compassion by the miserable state of Espinosa's people; but they seized ship, cargo, instruments, papers and charts, refusing receipts. Lorosa was promptly executed and the Spaniards made prisoners, according to some accounts being put to work on building the Portuguese fort at Ternate. De Brito wrote to the new King of Portugal, D. João III, that his best service would have been to cut their heads off. He did not venture to go so far, but obviously regretted having to send them to Malacca, instead of keeping them in Ternate where the climate might kill them off. Eventually four (including Espinosa) of the forty-four reached Spain, to be denied pay for the time they were captives and hence not serving the Crown. . . . With Del Cano's eighteen, and thirteen of his company sent on from the Cape Verdes, thirty-five men in all had completed the circuit of the globe. As for the *Trinidad*, she broke up in a squall at Ternate, and her timbers were used for the fort. For the time being, the Portuguese were in undisputed possession.

Stalemate at Badajoz

Deducting all costs and losses, the spices brought back in the *Victoria*, the first shipment direct from the Spice Islands to Europe, showed a moderate profit on the outlay for the whole expedition. Del Cano came home to fame and honours, including a coat of arms charged properly with cinnamon, nutmegs and cloves, and for crest a globe with the motto *Primus circumdedisti me*; Magellan's memory had to bear the angry reproach of his countrymen, and in Spain was not enhanced by the partial evidence of Del Cano and others at the enquiry into the voyage. Nevertheless, the great achievement was not to be denied: the circling of the globe was made possible only by the forcing of the Southwest Passage.

The most immediate result of the voyage was a new Luso-Castilian diplomatic crisis. João III demanded that the *Victoria*'s spices should be handed over to him, and the circumnavigators punished, since they had clearly trespassed within his

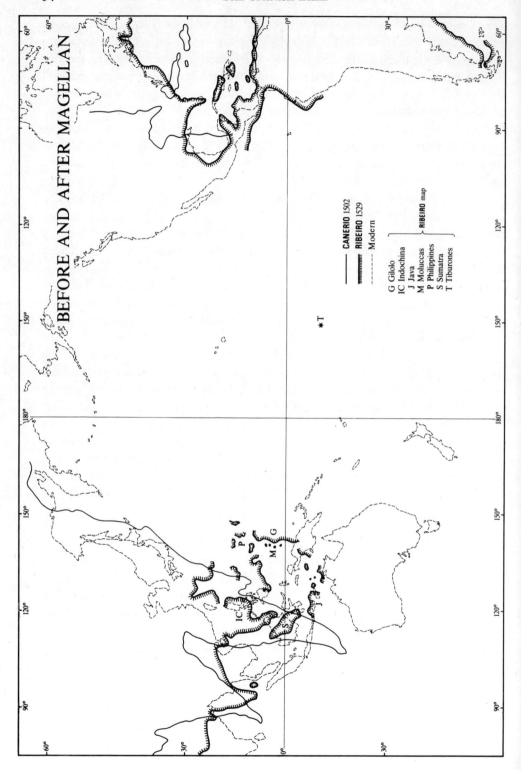

BEFORE AND AFTER MAGELLAN

CANERIO 1502
RIBEIRO 1529
Modern

G Gilolo
IC Indochina
J Java
M Moluccas
P Philippines
S Sumatra
T Tiburones

RIBEIRO map

dominion; each monarch should send out a ship with competent experts to agree on the true position of the Spice Islands. D. Carlos took up this singularly impracticable suggestion, which stemmed from a neglected clause of the Treaty of Tordesillas, adding that the Pope might send a third ship as referee. All this was probably time-spinning, as was the Portuguese proposal that, pending such a procedure, neither side should send a fleet to the disputed area, which would in effect freeze a *status quo* to Portugal's advantage. In fact, both parties were secretly preparing Moluccan voyages. In the circumstances, the Junta of experts from

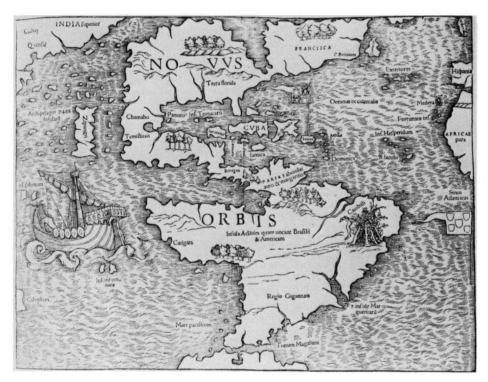

Plate VIII. THE AMERICAS, 1540. Note Magellan's 'Unfortunate Islands' and the archaic position and rendering of 'Zipangri' (Cipangu, i.e. Japan); but the Americas are firmly seen as what they are, a 'Novvs Orbis' between the two Oceans. From the Basel edition of Ptolemy, reproduced in Nordenskiold, *Facsimile Atlas* (Stockholm 1889). NLA.

both sides which met in April-May 1524 on the bridge over the Caya, the boundary between the two kingdoms, with sessions in the town halls of Badajoz and Elvas, can hardly have been regarded by either side as anything but a face-saving and time-winning device.[60]

◄*Figure 4.* BEFORE AND AFTER MAGELLAN.   Adapted from maps by E. A. Heawood, *Geographical Journal* 57, 1921, 431–46, and in A. Cortesão and A. Teixeira da Mota, *Portugaliæ Monumenta Cartographica* (Lisbon 1960), I. Plates 39–40 (for Ribeiro, see ibid., 82–106).

In one sense, as Nowell stresses, the Portuguese were on the defensive: there was sufficient leakage of obsolete but damaging maps, originally prepared to exaggerate the distance and hence the difficulty of the way to the Indies, and sufficient general doubt amongst the well-informed, to make Spanish claims seem plausible, though in fact the Portuguese positions were much nearer the truth than the Spanish, and the antimeridian of the Tordesillas line (134°40′E) is in fact some 7° east of the Moluccas, though this could not then be known.[61] The Spaniards made much play with minor discrepancies in the Portuguese calcula-

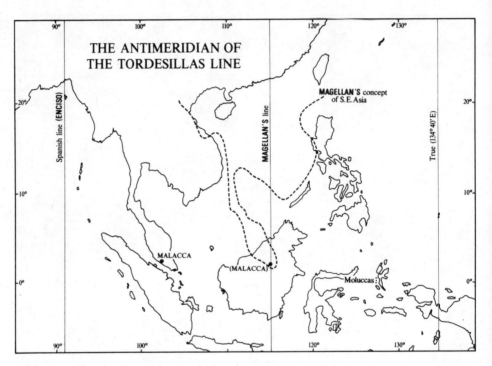

Figure 5. THE ANTIMERIDAN OF THE TORDESILLAS LINE. Note that on various reckonings the antimeridian can be placed at 129, 131.18, or 133.21 degrees east of Greenwich. In part adapted from maps by R. A. Laguarda Trías in A. Teixeira da Mota (ed.), *A Viagem de Fernão de Magalhães e a Questão das Molucas* (Lisbon 1975), 146–9.

tions and with the methods they proposed to fix the longitudes, which they alleged would take much too long (this would have been true had they been feasible) and to be against the spirit of the agreement for the conference. Scorn was heaped on the official Portuguese map which, very naturally, showed only a few key points between Lisbon and the Moluccas, leaving out the useful detail.

To all this, the Portuguese delegates could only stonewall and refuse to sign anything. They were strengthened in this attitude by the wild inaccuracy of the Spanish arguments, still sticking to Ptolemy and his inadequate length of an equatorial degree. Pliny, Marinus, Ptolemy, Polo, even Mandeville and King

Solomon were cited; and Fernando Colon, Columbus's illegitimate son, claimed for Castile 'all of Persia, Arabia, and India.' As Denucé says, these 'oratorical demonstrations . . . contrast singularly with the calm and knowledge of the Portuguese delegates to whom history has done justice . . .'.[62]

Argument on such divergent bases was clearly pointless; only occupation would suffice: the race was on again, and the logistic odds were strongly in favour of Portugal. She had firm bases much nearer Ternate and Tidore than were Seville or even Panama and the petty ports just being born in New Spain;[63] and the way from Malacca to the Moluccas was through well-travelled seas with many points of supply. The Spanish riposte to Antonio de Brito, when it did come (below, Ch. 4), was heroic but pathetic.

Magellan's voyage, whatever his own initial beliefs, ensured the final destruction of the lingering remnants of the Ptolemaic world: the achievement is writ large on contemporary maps. Even the hapless last voyage of the *Trinidad* at least showed that the great new ocean extended indefinitely, with a vast breadth, into northern latitudes; no rehashing of Cipangu or Ptolemy's Sinus Magnus could possibly fit the new facts. There were limitations: the Passage was too difficult to be of reliable use so long as it was confined to the actual Straits of Magellan. Although while in the Straits Magellan's people had thought that they could hear the surge on a distant coast to the south, and had correctly deduced that the land to their left was insular, yet, as J. H. Parry points out, Tierra del Fuego gained 'a new lease of cartographical life' for Terra Australis,[64] the temptation to carry it on across the Mar del Sur proving irresistible to generations of cosmographers. Yet even this was a spur to new exploration. No other single voyage has ever added so much to the dimension of the world.

Chapter 3

SPAIN: ENTRY AND DOMINION

Comme un vol de gerfauts hors du charnier natal,
Fatigués de porter leurs misères hautaines,
De Palos de Moguer routiers et capitaines
Partaient ivres d'un rêve héroïque et brutal . . .
Chaque soir, espérant des lendemains épiques
L'azur phosphorescent de la mer des Tropiques
Enchantait leur sommeil d'un mirage doré . . .

To castrate the Sun, for that the strangers came.

Beginnings on the Isthmus

The year 1519 was indeed a year of destiny for the Pacific. A month before Magellan sailed from San Lucar, the city of Panama had been founded; three weeks before he sighted Brazil, Cortes and his men were gazing at the Aztec palaces 'rising from the water . . . like an enchanted vision from the tale of Amadis. . . .'[1] Although there were still hankerings after *el estrecho duvidoso*, 'the doubtful strait', by the time the *Victoria* returned to Seville (September 1522) probes north from Panama and south from Mexico were narrowing the gap within which it might yet be hoped for; and puny little shipyards were beginning to secure the Spanish grip on the eastern shores of the Pacific, a hold which in a territorial sense was not seriously challenged (despite Drake's Nova Albion and the Russians in the far north) until the Nootka crisis of 1790.

The Mar del Sur, however, was still only an exciting potentiality, not yet an exploitable maritime space, even though it would without doubt contain 'many islands rich in gold, pearls, precious stones, spices, and other unknown and admirable things.'[2] Balboa had revealed that the barrier, even were it to prove continuous, was in at least one area very narrow, and the first step was to tie in the new Sea with the already dominated Caribbean. In effect, this was secured by the founding of Panama City; 'In its origins, Panama belongs to the West Indies; in its later role, historically, to Peru and New Granada. . . .'[3] This at

---

José-Maria de Heredia, *Les Conquérants*, 1893: 'Like a flight of falcons from their charnel-house nest, the reivers and captains set out from Palos and Moguer, weary of the burden of their proud poverty, drunk with an heroic and brutal dream. Each night, hoping for an epic morrow, the phosphorescent blue of the tropic sea bewitched their slumber with a gilded mirage.'
The Mayan Chilam Balam de Chumayel, cited in N. Wachtel, *La Vision des Vaincus*, Paris 1971, 59.

least was the achievement of Pedrarias, who was as tough—he died at ninety—
and realistic as he was unscrupulous.

He had arrived at Darien in June 1514 with some 1500 men, mostly gentlemen
adventurers, carpet knights and their hangers-on, eager for easy pickings in
Castilla del Oro, a name by now little better than a promoter's trick. The little
settlement was in no case to cope with this influx; tension with Balboa's toughened
veterans was inevitable and immediate, and something like half of the newcomers
were soon dead of disease or hunger. Pedrarias's instructions stressed the importance of securing the Pacific slopes; his first action was to send a lieutenant on a
savage foray against Balboa's Indian allies on the Atlantic side. It seems likely
that Balboa's enterprise of 1517, the hauling of needless timber across the divide
to build bergantins, was wished on him by Pedrarias to get him out of the way.
The Governor was expecting a successor from Spain, and this meant a residencia,
an official enquiry into his acts, at which Balboa would surely have stressed the
ruin of his careful pattern of alliances by the new régime's atrocious mistreatment
of the Indians. Despite sickening setbacks, Balboa did build ships, occupy the
Pearl Islands, and carry out some coastal exploration before being trapped and
judicially murdered by Pedrarias, who had the greatly undeserved good luck that
the new governor arrived and died forthwith. A residencia was formally held and
informally rigged; in such things Pedrarias was a master.[4]

Despite the penetration of 1512 of some 250km up the Rio Atrato south of
Darien—the first foray *into* South America—interest shifted from this promising
but extremely difficult and hostile region to the west, where in 1511 Balboa had
gathered the first news of the South Sea.[5] His trans-isthmian journey had begun
from Careta, renamed Acla by Pedrarias when he built a fort there; for some
years this became the main base for penetration, superseding Santa Maria del
Darien. A direct route from Santa Maria to the Gulf of San Miguel was indeed
pioneered as early as 1514, but its name—Trepadera, 'the clambering'—indicates
its limitations. The easiest way across, only some 65km through fairly open
country with a summit under 300 metres, was from the Gulf of San Blas to the
mouth of the Rio Bayano or Chepo, where the estuary afforded a fairly good
harbour. Balboa had intended to settle this place, Chepabar; but his recom-
mendation of course ensured rejection by Pedrarias, and no more rational
explanation of the latter's choice of a tiny Indian fishing village as the site of
Old Panama can be found.

The site was indeed very central on the shores of the Gulf of Panama, but that
is about all that could be said in its favour. The harbour was very poor, and much
use had to be made of the tiny outport of Perico some 10 or 12km to the west,
to which neighbourhood the city was moved after Morgan's sack of 1671. The
hinterland, although suitable for stockrearing, was of very little use for agriculture; flour had always to be imported, and was difficult to keep in the near-
equatorial humidity.[6] Chaunu stresses not only the pearls of the Pearl Islands
(still, by exception, a source of wealth), but that the islands 'guard' the Bay; but

this cut both ways, as they became on occasion a handy temporary base for buccaneers.[7] Nevertheless, given the geostrategical pattern, somewhere on this short stretch of coast there had to be a great base; and just as in the case of Madras on the Coromandel coast, a chance initial selection pre-empted the options.[8] To begin with, Panama was a gateway leading nowhere very much, and in the next phase only to Nicaragua; but that was soon to change dramatically as the Conquista moved southwards to the riches of Peru and Potosi.

It is not very likely that so early as 1519 security was, as Chaunu implies, an important factor in the choice of the Pacific side of the Isthmus for the main base: rather that the unknown but surely great opportunities of the Mar del Sur could not be so readily exploited from across the land-barrier. But a northern port of entry was obviously essential, and pre-emption on the south carried with it pre-emption on the north. The Gulf of San Blas was thus set aside in favour of the nearer ports of Nombre de Dios and Puerto Bello, though these, and especially the former, were most miserable places, except during the seasonal fairs when the *galeones* came in from Seville; then they became miserably over-crowded. Communication across the Isthmus was by a land route for passengers and high-value goods, or more slowly and with more risk to health (it took a week in the best conditions but often two) by canoe up the Rio Chagres to Cruces, thence by mule-train to Panama.

Only the vaguest rumours of great wealth to the south were afloat when Panama was founded; there was still hope that the doubtful strait might be found to the north. Already in 1517 Gaspar de Espinosa had explored the Azuero Peninsula beyond Nata, west of Panama, devastating a rich maize-producing country; by 1522 Gil Gonzalez Davila had reached the Gulf of Nicoya and his colleague Andrés Niño that of Fonseca, in modern Costa Rica and Honduras respectively. From the former Gonzalez crossed the neck of land to Lake Nicaragua: there might not be a strait, but he was told that there was a navigable outlet to the Atlantic, the Desaguadero or Rio San Juan. He reported that from the Mar del Sur to the Lake was only three leagues, two of which could be crossed by waggons: 'It is narrow enough to permit the transport of spices . . .'—so early, as Mack says, began the Isthmian rivalry between Panamanian and Nicaraguan sponsors.[9] But when the Desaguadero was explored, in 1529, it proved an outlet indeed, but disappointingly full of rapids and shoals and without even a proper anchorage at its mouth.

Forewarned again that a new governor of Castilla del Oro was on his way, Pedrarias determined to ensconce himself in this new land. In 1524 two of his lieutenants founded Granada and Leon on Lakes Nicaragua and Managua; but by this time there were competitors from the north. Gonzalez, eluding Pedrarias and obtaining from the authorities of Española a commission to discover the outlet of his lake, entered from the north coast of Honduras; Cortes's lieutenant Pedro de Alvarado, a notable swashbuckler even by conquistador standards, was in control of Guatemala; another of Cortes's men, Cristobal de Olid, had been sent to find the by now more than doubtful strait, but was playing his own hand; and there were others. The struggle was confused and treacherous even beyond the normal annals of the Conquista; when it was over, Alvarado was in control of his own Captain-Generalcy of Guatemala, Pedrarias had in effect managed to exchange Castilla del Oro for Nicaragua. But, although not without resources, these were only marchlands.[10] The weight of Spanish power had shifted north, to the 'New Spain of the Ocean Sea' so swiftly built up by Hernan Cortes who, almost alone of the conquistadores, had a genius for polity as well as for conquest.

Cortes on the Mar del Sur

Montezuma's lake-girt capital Tenochtitlan, the heart of an empire or con-federation whose nominal subjects (many of them however far from submissive) may be counted as somewhere between fifteen and twenty-five millions,[11] fell in mid-August 1521. It was only forty months since Cortes had reached the already known northwest tip of Yucatan, with about 600 men, including the crews of his ships; of these only thirty-two were crossbowmen and thirteen musketeers, and they had seven small guns. He had quelled two near-mutinies, destroyed his ships, and set up a municipality at Vera Cruz before setting out with some 400 men and fifteen horses on the march of about 625 km to the central valley of Mexico. There by inducements and menaces Cortes brought Montezuma to accept Spanish suzerainty, and there he learnt that he himself had been proclaimed a traitor by Panfilo Narvaez, sent from Cuba to supersede him. He had to divide his little force and dash back to the coast, where he won over nearly all of Narvaez' army of over 800 infantry and 80 cavalry, twice his own numbers. But meanwhile a massacre of Aztec nobles by Pedro de Alvarado, left in command at Tenochtit-lan, had provoked a rising. The useful puppet Montezuma was killed by his own people, disgusted by his capitulation;[12] and all was to do again.

At the end of June 1520 the enlarged but still very small force had to cut its way out of Tenochtitlan over the lake causeways, losing over 400 men (some two-thirds of its Spanish strength) in the confused fighting of *la noche triste*. The remnant retreated to independent and friendly Tlaxcala, which after a stout initial resistance had joined the invaders to break the Aztec stranglehold on the little 'Republic'. Here Cortes reorganised, bringing his numbers up to 600 again by the seduction of reinforcements meant for Narvaez and from chance arrivals at Vera Cruz. Then came the building of the thirteen bergantins at Tlaxcala and their portage to the Lake of Mexico, the reduction of the lakeside towns, and the final assault, nearly three months of filling-in the constantly renewed breaches in the causeways and destroying the city block by block, against a most gallant and desperate resistance.[13]

Many factors contributed to this amazing triumph. Armour, horses, crossbows, firearms, disciplined tactics and valour, all important, would not by themselves have sufficed against the numerical odds. But the harsh, and often recent, Aztec domination was bitterly resented by many of the tributary states, some of which were in chronic rebellion, and Cortes marshalled these discontents with surpassing diplomatic skill: this was perhaps the most important factor. Tlaxcala had never submitted to Aztec power, but was walled in by it and under constant attack, never pressed home since the wars provided a perennial source of prisoners for sacrifice on the altars of Tenochtitlan; it formed a loyal and secure forward base, and the Tlaxcalans were not alone in preferring the new yoke to the old. Gomara's estimate that Cortes had 200,000 men under his command at the siege may be a large exaggeration, but the indigenous allies certainly greatly outnumbered the Spaniards.[14]

Cortes was a master in the manipulation of men, and ably seconded by his Indian mistress Marina; Montezuma was cut off from reality by his almost sacerdotal position, which yet was more that of the head of a tribal confederacy than one of autocratic power, and both he and his people were unnerved by portents of disaster. Indeed, the 'Aztec Empire' was scarcely a consolidated state structure, but rather a very frangible one, and its chiefs were naturally unable to react decisively—until the bitter final struggle—to a crisis so novel as to be incomprehensible. Their wars had been bloody but not total: more important than the destruction of the enemy was the capture of victims for the human sacrifices which in their cosmogony were the only means of preserving the fabric of the universe. Their ruthlessness and that of the Spaniards were of different orders. They seem to have been gripped by a general premonition of doom; in Chaunu's words, an inner cosmic anguish, sapping resistance.[15]

Be this as it may, the Conquest of New Spain was now an achieved fact, and Cortes could turn his great administrative gifts to the task of building the new dominion. High on his priorities was the extension of that dominion to, and over, the South Sea.

Already in Montezuma's time Cortes had heard that this other sea was only about twelve or fourteen days' march from Mexico; and soon after the fall of the city he received an offer of vassalage from Michoacan, an independent territory lying to the west. He lost no time in sending out two pairs of Spaniards—such was their self-confidence—who were to take 'Royal and entire possession' of the South Sea; both assignments were carried out by the first weeks of 1522. Alvarado was despatched with some 400 men, a large force for the times, to the conquest or pacification of Tutupec, on the Pacific coast in Oaxaca, and before March 1522 possession had again been taken. During the next two years Alvarado pressed on, close to the coast, into southern Guatemala, and by October 1524 Cortes was able to claim that over 500 leagues along the South Sea were under Spanish subjection.[16]

'Possession' by rhetoric was one thing; exploitation another. Cortes's Third Letter to the King (15 May 1522) states that he had already, 'with much diligence', provided for the building on the South Sea of two caravels for exploration and two bergantins for coastal work; in the Fourth Letter (15 October 1524) he speaks of sending expeditions south to explore the land discovered by Magellan and north to the supposed strait, precursor of 'Anian' (below, Ch. 9), linking the Mar del Sur with Los Bacallaos in the Mar del Norte—that is, with the cod fisheries of the Newfoundland region, known since around the turn of the century from the voyages of the Cabots and the Corte Reals, if not indeed to men of the Azores and Bristol a generation earlier. Such a discovery would shorten the distance between Spain and the Spice Islands by two-thirds.[17]

The beginnings of maritime history on this coast are known in fascinating but sometimes confused detail. There seems to have been pre-Spanish trade in sailing canoes between Tehuantepec and Panama, and there are vague and unsubstantiated references to a Portuguese ship blown from the Moluccas to the Mexican coast in 1520,[18] but the first European craft actually to sail in Mexican Pacific waters was probably the pinnace *Santiago*, not locally built but direct from Spain. The *Santiago* had become separated from Loaysa's fleet (a follow-up to Magellan; below, Ch. 4) after passing the Straits and, being short of food, made for New Spain, ending up in July 1526 near Tehuantepec—it is said after fifty days on a daily ration of 2½ ounces of biscuit dust per man.[19]

Although shipbuilding had begun four years earlier at Zacatula, northwest of Acapulco, Cortes's reports to the King somewhat anticipated results. He brought in forty artisans, but two of his ships were burnt in the yards, and of the four completed in 1526 two sank and two went with Alvaro de Saavedra for the Moluccas in October 1527, sailing from Zihuatanejo. By 1526 Cortes's estate at Tehuantepec was an active building centre: the harbour was only a poor roadstead but there were fine stands of large 'pines', and gear could be brought from Spain via Vera Cruz and the Rio Coatzacoalcos, which was navigable to 120 km from the Pacific (or for small canoes 30 km), whence the portage to Tehuantepec was at only 200 or 230 metres above sea-level. It was soon rivalled by Guatulco or Huatulco, about 60 km to the southwest, which had a far better harbour, and became the principal Pacific port of New Spain from about 1537 until the rise of Acapulco in the 1570s. Guatulco had much better connections with central Mexico than that town, though even so the 'roads' were mostly unpaved trails, for the most part suitable only for pack-mules, though ox-carts could be used in the broader valleys. By the mid-1540s Guatulco was building substantial ships, and later in the century it had a church and a customs-house, 'very faire and large', some hundred brush and wattle huts, and a number of resident traders. Such as it was, it may stand as a type of the bush ports on this hot (in summer broiling) coast, ports for the most part even less developed. By 1538 Cortes had nine ships based in this region, employed in exploration to the north and in victualling other conquistadores from the produce of his estates; but he suffered from a shortage of pilots.[20]

Thus within two decades of the first penetration to the South Sea in New

Spain, its shores were dotted with a great number of tiny ports and shipyards (Fig. 6),[21] including from 1528 Acapulco, a fine harbour but set in a poor and unhealthy hinterland, and linked in 1531 with Cortes's seat at Cuernavaca by a difficult trail. The great days of the 'City of the Oriental Galleons and the Modern Sirens' were not to come for another four decades, when the return route from the Philippines was discovered.[22]

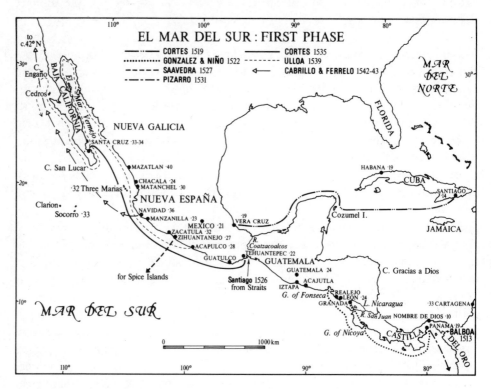

Figure 6.   EL MAR DEL SUR: FIRST PHASE.   Dates shown thus, '.33', are those of foundation or first mention, a preceding '15' being understood.

Compiled from various sources, but especially D. D. Brand (see Ch. 3, note 18).

Although suitable shipbuilding timber was available in several places, the ports of New Spain were not so well off for local raw materials as those beyond Tehuantepec: Nicaragua had pitch and excellent fibres for sails and cordage, while New Spain often fell back on second-hand gear from Europe. After mid-century Tehuantepec decayed and Guatulco was used mainly for repairs, but the yards at La Posesion, the fine port of Realejo in Nicaragua, were capable of bigger things, up to the 700-ton *Santa Ana* captured by Cavendish off Baja California in 1587. But this was very exceptional; the general run, even in the 1580s, would have been 12–15 tons for cabotage, 60–120 for inter-colonial trade. But the port was lively enough: discovered in 1523 by Davila and Niño, ten years later it had between fifteen and twenty slaving caravels. This trade had been organised by Pedrarias, and was fostered by the impracticability of moving Indian slaves overland.[23] Much basic equipment for shipping, especially metal work, still had to cross the Atlantic and then the Mexican plateaus, although Cortes had begun the exploitation of the abundant copper and less rich tin and iron deposits of central Mexico, and the sulphur of the volcanoes for gunpowder.[24] Spanish building on the eastern shores of the Pacific never reached the high standard of the Manila yards, which could marry European technology with the traditional skill of Chinese shipwrights; in Borah's words, most American vessels were 'poor, nasty, brutish, and crank', and there is abundant evidence of this even in the eighteenth century.[25] Moreover, shipping in American waters was always highly vulnerable to the *broma*, the boring ship-worm which could make timbers 'like a honeycomb or a sponge', and although lead sheathing was tried on the ships with which Pedrarias came to Darien in 1514, a very early use, it was too expensive, too unreliable, and too cumbersome for general application.[26] Later, worm-resistant timbers were found, and contributed greatly to the rise of Guayaquil as the great shipbuilding centre of the American South Sea; but these of course were not available at all times and places. Crews were also a source of difficulty; they might have a core of real seamen, but were for the most part drawn from the scrapings of a badly mixed society.

Probes to the north

Conquistadores from the north and the south had met in central America by 1524-5, and there was no longer room for a doubtful strait in that region: if one existed, it must be well to the north. From 1528 to 1530 Cortes was in Spain, trying to mend his political fences; he had after all slipped away from Cuba in 1519 in disregard of authority, and his later legitimisation—first by his own obviously managed creature, the Vera Cruz town meeting, and then by royal favour after his triumph—had left him with many foes at Court. He returned to New Spain with the title of Marques del Valle de Oaxaca and vast estates in that valley and elsewhere, which he exploited with imaginative capacity; but he was cut off from real power. At the age of forty-five, a man of his temper could hardly be content with the life of an improving landlord, on however grand a scale (the original grant had perhaps a million souls)[27] and however much he excelled at it. He turned his attention to the exploration of the northern shores of the Mar del Sur; it was not yet realised that winds and currents would greatly hamper coastwise sailing to the north.

Cortes's first effort, two ships sent from Acapulco in 1532, was a fiasco, ending in mutiny, shipwreck, and the disappearance of the commander, though it did discover the Tres Marias, islands beautifully located to become a handy point of repair for pirates.[28] In the next year he sent out two more ships from Tehuantepec: one found Socorro in the Revillagigedos; the pilot of the other killed his captain and was himself killed by Indians at La Paz in Baja California, now first seen by

Europeans. Not surprisingly, Cortes decided to take personal command of the next voyage, devoted to gathering up the remnants of the earlier misadventures, searching for reported pearl-banks, and colonising the new country. He sailed from Tehuantepec with three ships and reached La Paz (also called Santa Cruz) in May 1535. Some exploration was done, but two ships were lost; the country was sterile, and it was impossible to support the little colony, which was abandoned about the end of 1536.

Cortes made one more effort before returning to Spain permanently in 1540; in July 1539 he sent out two or three small ships from Acapulco under Francisco de Ulloa. This voyage had notable results: both shores of the Mar Vermejo (the Gulf of California) were explored to its head, demolishing the hope that this long inlet might be the much-desired strait, and establishing the peninsular nature of Baja California—the idea of California as an island comes much later, and reaches its full flowering only in the seventeenth century. The ocean coast of the peninsula was also followed as far as 29°N, beyond Cedros Island, and perhaps indeed as far as the modern San Diego. But Ulloa himself was probably lost on the voyage, and it is more likely that Cabo Engano—'Cape Deception' or 'Disappointment'—marks the end of the voyage. This was the last of the deeds of Cortes, and to some extent an anticlimax.

Nor did more success attend the expeditions sponsored by Cortes's rival, the Viceroy Antonio de Mendoza. One of these, under Francisco de Bolanos (1541), may be responsible for the name 'California', the origin of which is literally romantic, stemming ultimately perhaps from the Chanson de Roland and more immediately from Queen Calafia in the romance *Las Sergas de Esplandidian* (*c.* 1498): this lady ruled the Island of California, which lay quite near the Earthly Paradise but was inhabited solely by black Amazons. A concept worthy of Hollywood; but it is possible that the name was bestowed by Cortes's enemies in irony, on a land that certainly did not flow with milk and honey. The only other voyage of note was that by Hernando de Alarcon in 1542, which entered the Colorado River but otherwise added little.[29]

This first phase on the Mar del Sur, however, saw one more important voyage, that of Juan Rodriguez Cabrillo, a Portuguese, and Bartolomé Ferrelo in 1542-3.[30] These men sailed from La Navidad, which was established about 1536 and for a time was a notable base: Villalobos and Legaspi sailed thence for the Philippines.[31] Leaving at the end of June 1542, Cabrillo reached on 28 September a port 'closed, and very good, which they named San Miguel'; this was the site of modern San Diego, and they were the first Europeans to land on the Pacific coast of what is now the United States. Here, and at other points, Cabrillo heard tell of white men to the east, presumably rumours of distant encounters with parties from Coronado's great sweep in search of golden Quivira and the Seven Cities of Cibola, which began in 1540 and went past the Grand Canyon of Colorado and into central Kansas. Some of these encounters had been violent, and Cabrillo was careful to conciliate the Indians by generous gifts.

In October he discovered the Santa Barbara Islands off the present Los Angeles. The two little ships pressed on, despite adverse gales, and in mid-November made a landfall some 50km north of San Francisco, close to the site where two and a half centuries later the Russians were to build Fort Ross. Driven south, they came to Drake's Bay, and were then forced back to the Santa Barbara Islands. Here on 3 January 1543 Cabrillo died from an accidental injury he had received at the same place in October, but in dying he charged his men to carry on. Ferrelo took over, and in late February reached his farthest north, probably off southern Oregon; at this point they met furious storms from the north and northwest and had to turn back, still exploring the coast; they returned to La Navidad on 14 April 1543.

This was a well and resolutely managed expedition, finding some 1300km of new coast and pushing the doubtful strait to that extent northwards; in one voyage, they had paralleled the entire coast of the modern State of California. Cabrillo seems to have been an admirable leader; but his achievement was to be half or quite forgotten, and duplicated sixty years later by Vizcaino. His names were not retained on the map; his sorrowing crew renamed his 'Posesion', where he died, Isla de Juan Rodriguez; it is now San Miguel. It is strange that modern American piety has not revived so deserved a tribute to the true discoverer of Alta California; the more so as it seems likely that the original stone set up on his grave still exists.[32]

The drive to the south

Nueva España by the early 1530s was settling down. The areas of high Indian civilisation and dense population were under control, and Aztec Tenochtitlan was being transformed into the great city of Mexico. But Indian stocks of gold had been ransacked, placer gold was falling off, and there was no Spanish market for cotton cloth, cacao (as yet), or maize. Many rank and file conquistadores had not done well in the scramble for grants of Indian lands or Indian labourers; the authorities, fearing a drain of manpower, forbade emigration and the export of arms or horses. But to many a veteran the sanction of losing his *encomienda*, if he had one, meant little, and it was impossible to police the ban. Some went north, still in search of gold and Indians, into New Galicia and its arid marches, beyond which might lie the golden cities of Cibola and Quivira; but probably more filtered south towards Realejo in Nicaragua, whence the first 'export trade' of New Spain was in soldiers and their gear, her first 'market' the new conquista beyond the Equator.[33] Later, as in the Californian and Australian gold rushes, those with some capital might find provisioning the rush a less arduous and much safer road to fortune.

In 1522, when Davila and Niño set out west and north from Panama, Pedrarias sent Pascual de Andagoya in the opposite direction. He did not get very far, but far enough to bring back fairly definite news of 'Biru', a strange and wealthy realm to the south. If, as some state, he reached the Rio San Juan in the south of

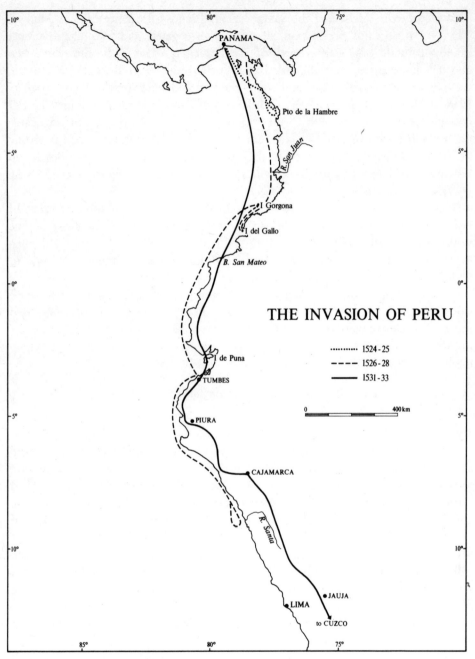

Figure 7. THE INVASION OF PERU. Adapted mainly from maps in J. Hemming, *The Conquest of the Incas* (London 1970).

modern Colombia, he would be at about the northern limit of a lively balsa-raft traffic from Tumbes, which had been for some forty or fifty years a part of the Inca Empire. The trade was a luxury one: gold, pearls, conch-shells, emeralds, cacao.[34]

Exploitation fell into the hands of Francisco Pizarro and Diego de Almagro, both of them illegitimate and illiterate, with the financial backing of the priest Fernando de Luque, an associate of Pedrarias, who gave permission but no more— naturally against a share of the profits. The two ships which sailed under Pizarro in November 1524 and Almagro a little later included 'one of Balboa's brigantines which had miraculously escaped destruction by rot or shipwreck', and the crews included 'the vagabonds of Panama'; Pizarro lost a quarter of his men and ended at Puerto de la Hambre, 'Port Famine'.[35] Somehow Luque scraped together funds for a second venture, two ships and 160 men, in early 1526. On this expedition the pilot Bartolomé Ruiz became the first European to sail southwards across the Equator in the Pacific; he met a large balsa-raft sailing north from Tumbes and into the speculations of a modern Viking over four centuries later.[36] Of more immediate importance was its revelation of luxury and civilisation: a cargo of finely worked silver and gold, emeralds and chalcedony, richly coloured and embroidered fabrics. Almagro returned to Panama for new and better recruits, and then with combined forces they went on to modern Ecuador: a country well worth the conquest, but needing more men for the task, since the Indians were numerous and hostile. Once more Almagro went back, after a quarrel with Pizarro, who naturally resented being left on the outposts while Almagro shuttled back and forth to the comforts, and the useful contacts, of Panama.

Pizarro waited it out on the desolate but secure Isla del Gallo, about 2°N; discontents naturally arose, and he sent back his remaining ship, perhaps in emulation of Cortes, more likely to get rid of dissidents. Shocked by the appearance of Almagro's men and the smuggled accounts from some who had stayed, the new Governor of Panama, Pedro de los Rios, sent two ships to bring back the foolhardy adventurers; but they also carried counsels of persistence from Almagro and Luque. At this point took place the famous incident of the thirteen who dared accept Pizarro's challenge to cross a line on the sand and stand by his fortunes; an episode much inflated, perhaps all but invented, by the chroniclers.[37] The fourteen moved to the larger and less depressing island of Gorgona, further north. Here, after seven months, they were rejoined by Almagro, bringing no reinforcements beyond his crew: de los Rios would not allow any more wastage of men, had any been willing to volunteer. With new heart, they set out again, through the Gulf of Guayaquil to Tumbes; and here at last they were actually within the Inca realm: a sizeable town, an active coasting trade, paved roads, admirable irrigation, a civil people—and gold in the temples. Relations were friendly—this was only a reconnaissance, and not in force, and Acts of Possession were not understood. After reaching the Rio Santa, in 9°S, the expedition returned

to Panama eighteen months after its departure. The contrast between the horrors
of the beginning and the amenity and promise of the ending was doubtless well
displayed in official relations and in tavern tales.

So much was prologue to the great enterprise. Pizarro went to Spain, reaching
the Court at Toledo in mid-1528; he returned in 1530 with full powers as
Governor and Captain-General and with three half-brothers; volunteers came
especially from the tough and poor minor gentry of backward Extremadura,
Pizarro's own country and that of Cortes, who was helpfully in Spain at the
time. Almagro was allotted only the commandancy of Tumbes—perhaps because
the Court foresaw friction if both men were promoted too high. But he was
naturally furious, and only pacified by the promise of an independent conquista
beyond Peru; whence the conquest of Chile, but also the first of the civil wars
which within ten years were to provide a dreary preview of the history of Peru
and Bolivia in the nineteenth century, a rehearsal for the plague of *caudillismo*,
the turbulence and tyranny of local magnates and war-lords.

Pizarro sailed from Panama at the end of 1530, with three ships and about
180 men. After two weeks he landed in the north of Ecuador, which had taken
nearly two years to reach in the preliminary reconnaissances; thence he advanced
slowly, partly by land and partly by sea, exploring the country, receiving reinforcements, fighting local resistance, pillaging towns and villages. Tumbes was
in ruins, the first evidence of the civil war which perhaps made the conquest
possible. Over a year was spent on this approach: Pizarro was building a base
before risking an entry into the great wall of mountains always visible to the east.
In mid-1532 he founded San Miguel de Piura, the first Spanish town on the Pacific
coast of South America. After leaving sixty men there, he had sixty-two horses
and 106 infantry for his field force. The stage was set for the assault on the Inca
realm, which was much more of an Empire than that of the Aztecs. It was fortunate for the Spaniards that it had recently been ravaged by a great epidemic
spreading from the north, and was riven by a wide and bitter civil war.

The conquest of Peru

The Inca power, unlike that of Montezuma, was absolutist, based on control by
a hierarchy of officials over the forced labour of the core area of Cuzco and of
tribes subjugated in about a century and a half of expansion. Most aspects of life
were meticulously regulated from above, and the net effect was that the resources
of the Empire, apart from the necessary subsistence of the masses, were channelled
into providing the power, the glory, and the luxury of 'the Incas', the ruling
family and its associates, and above all of 'the Inca', the autocrator at the head of
the pyramid; but this was a cosmic structure, as much sacred as secular, and the
Inca, the son of the Sun, was the source from which all blessings flowed—light,
life itself.[38] Elaborate records were kept by the *quipus* or knotted cords; two paved
roads, along the coast and along the plateau, with transverse links through the

mountains (altogether some 15,000 km), ensured communications from Ecuador to northern Chile; they were well provided with *tambos* or post-inns and an elaborate system of relay runners, so that it took only five days to send a message from Quito to Cuzco, 2000 km.[39] The roads and runners were important factors in the rapidity of the Spanish conquest of the country, the tradition of massive forced labour in its exploitation when conquered. As in Mexico, local discontents and revolts and political rivalries greatly facilitated the conquista.[40] There was no lack of Indian agents, puppets, and allies; nor of terrorised porters to provide the transport services of the armies. If the weakness of the Aztecs was that they were not yet consolidated into a firm state structure, but caught at the 'moment of crystallization' from a tribal to an urban-centred society, the weakness of the Incas was the converse—a state structure too rigid and centralised to take the shock of a blow directly to its head—the Inca Atahualpa.[41]

At the time of Pizarro's arrival, Atahualpa had recently defeated his half-brother Huascar in a bitter succession war, and was endeavouring to exterminate any possible rivals in the imperial family. He waited for Pizarro at Cajamarca, high up on the plateau, apparently thinking that there this strange but tiny invasion could be crushed or absorbed; and it is fair to say that the fate he envisaged for them was probably a ghastly one: it was slay or be slain.[42] Within an hour or two of the meeting of the two men, on 16 November 1532, the Spaniards had seized Atahualpa's person—which was sacrosanct—and slaughtered thousands of his followers, too bewildered to resist. Some months later, having collected a huge ransom, they charged Atahualpa with 'treason': he accepted baptism to purchase death by strangling rather than by burning alive. Some of the conquistadores were horrified by this foul play, although probably more were in favour, and may indeed have enforced it on Pizarro. There yet remains a beautiful but heart-rending native elegy for Atahualpa: all things, all people, are engulfed into suffering. . . .[43] For now the Empire seemed no more than a headless trunk, utterly at the disposal of the victors.

This was at the end of July 1533; a year less a day from the meeting at Cajarmarca, Pizarro entered Cuzco. By the middle of 1534 the Quitan provinces had been secured; Pedro de Alvarado of Guatemala, who had diverted a projected South Seas voyage to the nearer and surer riches of Quito, was bought off, leaving his ships and many of his men as reinforcements to the more authorised conquistadores. The seal was set on the conquista by the formal establishment of Spanish municipalities at Jauja, Cuzco, and Quito.

More significant than these was the foundation, on 6 January 1535, of the Ciudad de los Reyes (the Three Kings of the East), better known as Lima. The contrast with Cortes's rebuilding of Mexico is striking: although its fabled and its real wealth lay on the high Andean plateaus, Spanish Peru, much more than Nueva España, was oriented to the Pacific. Simple climatic factors played a part, for one can hardly envisage a metropolis in the unhealthy *tierra caliente* of Mexico, while Lima is not only more hospitable than the plateaus, with their extreme

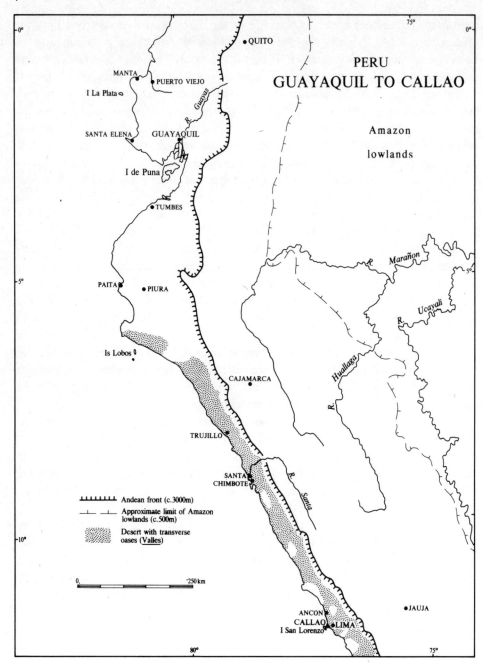

Figure 8. PERU: GUAYAQUIL TO CALLAO.   Blanks within desert areas are not oases but *lomas*, dew-fed grazing land—see P. James, *Latin America* (London 1942), 173.

temperatures and rarefied air, but owing to the Humboldt or Peru Current is remarkably cool for its latitude.[44] The Conquista at this stage was looking to landed settlement rather than mining—there was still much Indian gold to be collected, and the silver of Potosi was unknown—and the irrigated coastal valleys were again much more favourable than the plateaus for Iberian agriculture and horticulture. But the *raison d'être* of Lima and its adjacent port Callao was to be a secure base by the sea; the more so as, after the first shock, Inca resistance was rallying.

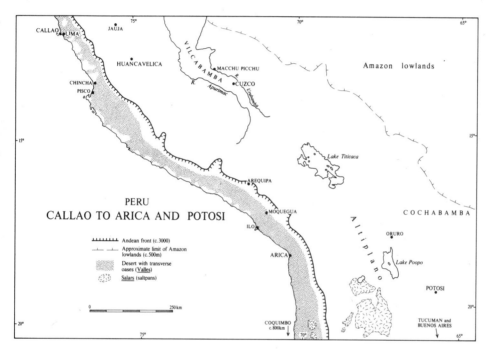

Figure 9. PERU: CALLAO TO ARICA AND POTOSI

Resistance culminated in 1536, after Almagro's departure with a large proportion of the Spanish force on the first *entrada* into Chile—the 'New Toledo' promised him beyond Pizarro's 'New Castile'; this was clearly Pizarro's diversion of an over-strong rival. But during Amalgro's absence a great rising was led by the Inca Manco Capac, whose brother Paullu, however, had gone with Almagro and on his return was to prove the most committed of Spanish associates. Manco himself had been recognised as puppet Inca, but suspicion was mutual; he was subjected to (literally) obscene outrage and escaped to seek revenge. There was very desperate fighting at Cuzco, and Lima itself was threatened. Appeals for aid brought responses from Cortes—probably with ulterior motives—in New Spain and Espinosa in Panama, and Alvarado came from Guatemala, though he merely added another element to the internecine factions of the conquerors.

Once the first major effort at Cuzco had failed, Manco was unable to maintain his immense but ill-organised forces. By the end of 1539 resistance was broken; Manco retreated to the tangled mountains of the Amazonian slope, between the Apurimac and the Urubamba. Here, only some 125 km from Cuzco, he reigned in sadly diminished state until in 1544 he was murdered by Spanish refugees from the civil wars, to whom he had given hospitality. This pathetic relic of Inca power around Vilcabamba survived, a thorn in the flesh of Spanish authority, until 1572, when the last of the Incas to rule, Tupac Amaru, was captured and 'executed'—after the customary 'conversion' to the Faith; a judicial murder by the Viceroy Toledo which shocked the more settled colonial society of the time. The name Inca lived on as an honorific for those Indian grandees of the royal line who had come to terms, which might be very comfortable terms: Manco Capac's great grand-daughter, whose father was a great-nephew of St Ignatius Loyola, was created Marquesa de Oropesa, the only hereditary fief in Peru. But in the last great nativist rising, in 1780–1, a direct descendant of Tupac Amaru, Jose Gabriel Condorcanqui, proclaimed himself Tupac Amaru II: with his failure and barbarous execution, even the name of Incas was blotted out, being proscribed as a formal signature.[45]

Aftermath: the first naval campaign

Almagro's return to Cuzco in 1537 initiated the civil wars—seven between that year and 1554—which at one time threatened to tear the New Castile from any allegiance to the Old, and which saw the death in battle of the first Viceroy from Spain, the execution of Almagro by Pizarro, and his own assassination by Almagro's *mestizo* son. By 1550 the shrewd and resolute little lawyer Pedro de la Gasca had restored royal power, in the form of an Audiencia which was able to cope with the last two risings, in the interim (1552–6) between the death of the second and the arrival of the third, the first effective, Viceroy. But the victory of law in the abstract was secured only by discarding the particular 'New Laws' intended to protect the Indians against their brutal exploitation by the *encomenderos* to whom Pizarro had parcelled out land and serfs.

The bloody details of these coups and counter-coups do not concern us, except for one 'campaign' in which hardly any blood was shed: the competition for command of the sea between the royalist leaders and Gonzalo Pizarro, brother and successor of Francisco and at least strongly tempted to set up as an independent, and undeniably wealthy, monarch. Just as the civil wars in general are a preview of post-Independence internal strife, so this episode is a preview of the paramount importance of seapower in the Wars of Independence and the 1879–81 War of the Pacific. All three emphasise the fact that the littoral communities, till at least the end of last century, were really to all intent islands, 'oases', or 'compartments' freely accessible only by sea.[46]

Gonzalo was able to secure the King's ships off Peru, and to build others, and correctly decided to seize Tierra Firme, or at least the Isthmus, to forestall a counter-attack. His captains twice occupied Panama; they did not take over the administration, but men were sent across the Isthmus to Nombre de Dios, and there was some seizing and burning of ships on the Nicaraguan coast. But when la Gasca arrived at Panama, with offers of amnesty and annulment of the hated New Laws, Gonzalo's fleet went over. He made the mistake of burning five ships at Callao, to prevent desertions; and with nothing to stop it, the now royalist fleet proceeded methodically down the coast. Whatever local successes the Pizzarists might achieve, they had no possibility of reinforcements. Panama was the key—the only blood spilt was in a skirmish at Nombre de Dios—and the events there the turning-point. But as Garcilaso sums up, 'it was the revocation [of the New Laws] and the general pardon that fought the war and gave the empire to La Gasca.'

The Peruvian conquistadores have traditionally been regarded as a rough, not to say ruffianly, lot; and certainly Pizarro was well below the moral and intellectual stature of Cortes. But Lockhart has shown that they were much more a fair cross-section of Spanish society than has been generally believed, and beneath the savage tumults the solid work of colonisation was going on. This was based, it is true, on extremely brutal exploitation of the Indians; against the greed of the men-on-the-spot and the need of the Treasury, the numerous and sincere royal ordinances to remedy abuses were simply unenforceable. 'Though the King's allies always won in the civil wars, the King's legislation was soundly defeated' and the 500 encomenderos became virtually absolute lords of the land, and of Indian lives, while 'Conversion of the Indians seems to have become a major casualty'[47]—and this last, in the eyes of respectable Spain, was the justification of the Conquista.

Between 1532 and 1548 fourteen towns were founded, most of which remain important. Perhaps about a quarter of Spanish males were really rootless adventurers; but of something over 4000 Spaniards in Peru in 1555, about 500 were artisans (though the backbone of the artisan labour force was Negro), and there were probably over 750 women; there were respectable Spanish matrons—one or two—at Piura and Jauja as early as 1533 and 1534. By 1537 Lima had already 2000 Spanish *vecinos* (burgesses), while Callao, in 1537 merely 'a tavern by the sea', was developing into a flourishing port, striving to secure autonomy from the Lima town council.[48] But the beginnings were nasty and brutish: in 1535 it was forbidden to throw dead Indians into the Lima streets: penalty, twenty pesos.[49] Nevertheless, twenty years after Cajamarca there was an articulated and ordered society in Lima and the major towns.

The farthest frontier: Chile

Farthest, not last; there were still entradas to be made in the jungles of the Andean/ Amazonian borderland, and Spain's northern frontier in the Americas had a last expansive phase which reached Nootka in 1790, while in the south her heirs, the Argentine and Chilean Republics, did not overcome the last Indian resistance in

Patagonia until the late 1870s and 1880s. But Chile was the last phase of the
Conquista proper, and its farthest reach.

Almagro set out from Cuzco in July 1535, in detachments totalling at least
500 Spaniards.[50] He went past Lake Titicaca and down the Atlantic slope into the
northwest corner of Argentina, thence across the desolate Puna de Atacama, at
some 4000 metres; gruelling journeys in which thousands of his Indian supply-
train died of cold, hunger, and mountain sickness. He recuperated near Copiapo;
only one of the supply ships for which he had arranged made contact, and
probably reached the bay of Valparaiso. His main body advanced as far as the
Aconcagua valley, a little to the north of modern Santiago, and patrols to the
Rio Maule. This was in the depths of a probably unusually severe winter, for
the reports of this beautiful and now productive country were gloomy. But here,

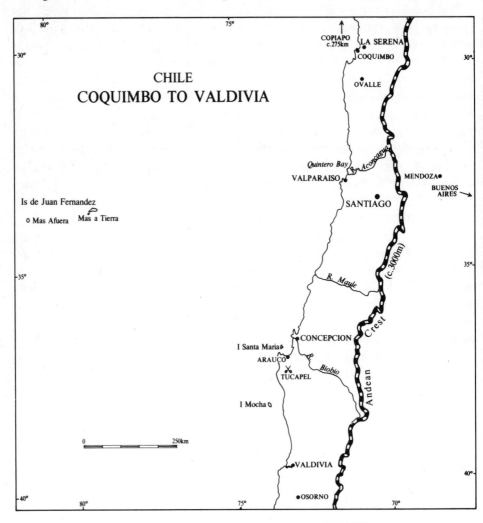

Figure 10. CHILE: COQUIMBO TO VALDIVIA

on the very verge of Inca influence, they met only a few rude and tough tribes; there were no roads, no cities, no possibility of a coup as at Tenochtitlan or Cajamarca; above all no gold. The return was made along the coast; the first entrada was a failure.

The Conquistador of Chile, Pedro de Valdivia, was a man of better stamp than the average of his fellows; nearer to Balboa or Cortes than to Pizarro or Almagro. His first force consisted of only about 150 Spaniards; in effect the defeated in the first civil war, and with each upheaval in Peru there were new recruits from the losing side. Indeed, it is clear that on the local level, and sometimes on the viceregal one, the entrada was practically an instrument of policy to rid the community of the failures and the more intolerable swashbucklers of the Conquista.[51]

Valdivia left Cuzco in January 1540; avoiding Almagro's dreadful Andean route, he pushed slowly down the coast, taking a year to reach central Chile, now—it was summer—a smiling country. Here, on 14 February 1541, he founded the city of Santiago. Indian resistance, slight at first, now stiffened with this evidence of a permanent intrusion; in September the Indians sacked and burnt the primitive townlet. They were repelled, but for two years the 'captives of their conquest', isolated from Peru, could achieve no more than modest consolidation, and at times they even faced extinction. In 1544 what is now the delightful little town of La Serena was founded, with thirteen citizens, to be destroyed by the Indians and rebuilt in 1549, by which year the total Spanish population was about 500. Political events in Peru now gave Valdivia a freer hand and reinforcements, which could enter through the new port of Valparaiso. Some placer gold was found, but the colony was already becoming, as it was long to remain, one of agricultural and pastoral settlement. There were more city foundations: Concepcion in 1550, Valdivia in 1553.

However, as the expansion sought to pass the Rio Biobio, it became apparent that there was a new dimension in the Indian resistance. The Spaniards were now face to face with the Araucanians, a numerous loose confederacy of determined warriors who proved able to marry Spanish fighting methods with their own. Valdivia himself was killed at Tucapel in December 1553, and his tiny force annihilated. It seemed that the limits of the Conquista had been passed. But the Indian leader Lautaro could not induce his people to undertake what might well, at that stage, have been a decisive counter-offensive across the Biobio. He in turn was slain in battle in 1557, and thenceforward the Araucanians were on the defensive. But most of the country south of Concepcion, except for Valdivia, remained a debatable ground for generations. In this 'Flanders of the Indies', with no organised state to overthrow and take over, the conquest had to be piecemeal and 'There was no possibility of applying the "Cortes plan".'[52] Some advanced positions lost in the sixteenth century were not regained until the nineteenth; Osorno, sacked by the Indians in 1600, was rebuilt in 1796, following the original plan of 1558. The final settlement was not reached until

1883, after the War of the Pacific. In Chaunu's words, 'Chile was saved by amputation', and 'Araucania remained, for three centuries and to its misfortune, in the hands of the Araucanians'[53]—though it might be thought that if one must be conquered, it is better to wait, if one can, till the conquerors have themselves gained something in conscience and in civilising capacity.

The frontier struggles left their mark on Chilean colonial society; with so much of it a marchland, and its economy based on the land, colonial Chile never became so diversified a society as Mexico and Peru, never attained their wealth and sophistication. An outlier, cut off from the flowering of Peru by the Atacama deserts, walled in by the Andes (some spillover on to the Argentine glacis was a source of weakness rather than strength), fronted by 'the greatest desert of all', the South Pacific, Chile could not really break out of its shell until the opening of that Ocean as a locus of world trade: then Valparaiso could become one of the great relay-ports. Till then, the mark of Chile was a modest but tough provincialism, in fact rusticity: the first university dates from 1756, the first printing press was almost unbelievably late, perhaps not until 1812. The corresponding dates for Mexico and Peru are (at latest) 1553 and 1539, 1571 and 1584.[54]

The nature of the Conquista

The Conquista from the beginning was with rare exceptions not so much directed by the Crown of Castile as authorised by it. The bands of at most a few hundred men that in a scant half-century had fanned out first from Española, then from Mexico, Panama and Peru, were private enterprises, working as it were under licence and to guidelines laid down from Spain, but themselves normally setting the immediate targets: 'profit-making enterprises financed by contracts stipulating how the profits were to be shared. These enterprises resembled government in some respects, business in others.'[55] This flexibility enabled the expansion to be extraordinarily rapid—with each new focus of Indian wealth taken over, new options appeared, until by the end of the 'exponential phase' about 1536, before the first check in Chile, it covered some 2·5 to 3 million square kilometres, from the 500mm isohyet bounding humid Mexico to the southern frontiers of the Inca Empire; basically the great plateaus and the littoral strips essential for access to them. The Spanish hold was of course by no means even: the Conquista was most solid where it seized upon and supplanted solid economic and political structures; there was a net of towns, the nuclei of control, surrounded by zones more or less completely farmed out in encomiendas but with interstices and a vast penumbra where Indian life went on much as before. Chaunu stresses that the Conquista acted much more on men than on their land, basically seeking to control the Indian labour force and to take over its surplus product.[56] Hence the leap-frogging over non-productive pockets and the much slower extension of control—hardly completed even in this century, with its new forms of mobility—over the marginal areas of the Amazonian slopes.

The executants came for the most part from the gentry, younger sons of the minor nobility, and semi-professional soldiery. One cannot escape the impression that for such people the enterprises of the Indies provided a vast liberating hope; not only of material wealth, though that was a most material factor, but also of adventure, honour, fame, self-expression, and for those so inclined, ample sexual opportunity. Attaining these, however, entailed not only a commitment to months or years of most desperate hardships and hazards, but first of all getting the royal warrant, often in the face of cut-throat competitors, and arranging finance, usually on hard terms: 'The small and informal armies . . . were bound together by personal loyalty, by joint hope of gain and by debt.'[57] There was a constant tension between a fantastic individualism and an equally fantastic legalism; and between the lure of another Eldorado in the next valley but two and the desire to settle down as a man of property. Those who lost out in the scramble for encomiendas, habituated as they were to the hand-to-mouth but exciting existence and the rough mateship of the entrada, provided the raw material for new ventures, and indeed were often eased on their way by the more provident (or lucky) and respectable. The clearest case, but it is only one of many, is the quest for Eldorado by Pedro de Ursua in 1560, which was taken over by Lope de Aguirre, of whom Peru was obviously better rid: Aguirre, a vicious psychopath, left a trail of rape and murder all along the Rio Negro and the Orinoco to the sea.[58]

Gold and God, in that order, were at bottom the main motivations of the average conquistador; the official vindication of the Conquista put God first, and the Crown from time to time made efforts, usually unavailing, to live up to this priority. In effect, the Indians were to mediate the gold to the Spaniards, the Spaniards to mediate the true God to the Indians. This was at the root of the greatest tension of Spain in the Indies: that between the Crown's struggle for social justice, and the tempering, or rather blunting, of its efforts by the sheer brute facts of colonial life.

Once the immediate loot, the tangible gold, silver and jewels had been shared out (the Crown taking its *quinta* or fifth), the aim of the more sober conquistador was to obtain an encomienda. This was not exactly a feudal fief, though it became something like it; it was not a grant of land, but rather a grant of the labour service of the Indians of a given tract of land; a concept stemming from the Reconquista from the Moors in Old Spain. The encomendero was supposed in turn to 'instruct the Indians in the Christian religion and the elements of civilized life, and to defend them in their persons and property'.[59] But, since any economic life beyond sheer robbery depended on the exploitation of Indian labour, the possibilities of abuse were obvious and enormous. The question of tenure was important: it could be argued that a mere life tenure meant more racking exploitation for a quick fortune; but, apart from humanitarian considerations (which however bulked large), the Crown was naturally fearful of allowing a hereditary feudality in these distant scarce-controllable realms. The first royal attempts to protect the Indians were in 1502; encomiendas were accepted by the Laws of Burgos in 1512, with careful (but unenforceable) regulation in Indian interests; there was an attempt at abolition of encomiendas in 1530, with such disastrous economic results in New Spain that in 1535 life grants were extended to the life of a widow or one child. The New Laws of 1542 forbade new encomiendas and the inheritance of old ones; we have seen their fate. But in New Spain, at least, they did to some extent 'tame the encomienda', and the continuing decline in Indian numbers enforced attention by encomenderos to their more positive functions; in the seventeenth century the system faded away as a really significant economic factor, being succeeded by debt peonage. The exploitation went on, and indeed the public sector took an increasing share with the Viceroy Toledo's codification of the Peruvian *mita* in the 1570s; this massive corvée swept the Indians by thousands into Potosi and the yet more hellish mercury mining of Huancavelica.

Yet it is difficult to see that, given the premise of spreading the Faith by Empire and the agents available for the task, any other system could have worked; and in the conditions of colonisation, no government could have controlled it effectively. The Crown's efforts were sincere, its discussions anguished, caught between economic and political necessity, and the claims of human—or divine—justice. The reiteration of protective ordinances attests their failure; nothing could bridge the inevitable gap between the impeccable humanity and morality of the *cédula real* and the inhumane immorality of the very peccant frontier; a problem of empires in all ages.

This is perhaps best illustrated by the procedure of the *Requerimiento*, which might sardonically be described as a strange form of Justification of Empire, or murder, by Faith. Since the moral justification of conquest was to mediate the Gospel to those sunk in blind idolatry, they had to be given the opportunity to freely embrace the new Faith:

> Bar this pretence, and into air is hurl'd
> The claim of Europe to the *Western World*.[60]

This was to be secured by insisting that a formal and sonorous proclamation should be read to the Indians for their acceptance or rejection; if they persisted in their blindness, their blood would be upon their own heads. The results were of course a bloody farce: the *Requerimiento* was read out of arrow-range, in deserted villages, in camp before moving out, even from shipboard. . . .[61] It should be recalled also that if many royal laws were entirely humane in intent, others were exceedingly discriminatory and exploitative; and these there was no difficulty in enforcing. The royal interventions 'proposed to commit iniquities humanely, and to consummate injustices equitably'.[62]

The human suffering of the Conquista cannot be estimated but was certainly immense, probably more terrible even than that of the greater wars and revolutions of our times. In its own day the burning protests of Dominican Bartolomé de las Casas—himself a one-time encomendero—provoked much heart-searching and some real, though mostly ineffective, action by the royal authorities. It is undeniable that the unscrupulous use of his work, illustrated by the gruesome and perennially reprinted engravings of de Bry, fixed on the Spanish name the disgrace of the *leyenda negra*. Perhaps the best attitude to this 'black legend' should be Dryden's to another black legend, the Popish Plot: complete acceptance, complete rejection, are alike mere foolishness.[63]

Certainly some of the modern 'revisionist' defences seem naïve or disingenuous in the extreme; it is difficult to find in the Third World the 'universal plebiscite' in favour of 'that genial colonising Europe which has radiated its high culture and its well being over all the earth's round' of which Menéndez Pidal speaks; truly, Don Quixote rides again![64]

Concentration of the debate on the highly emotional las Casas obscures the evidence of the conquistadores themselves; their matter-of-fact recording of their own atrocities is as terrible as any of his searing protests.[65] It also obscures the fact that las Casas was far from alone in his stance: many a missionary friar and some courageous officials made full use of the right, positively encouraged by the Crown, to comment freely to the authorities in Spain on any aspect of Spanish activities in the Indies: the testimony and the protest are not from partisan outsiders but from Spaniards themselves. (Nor should we overlook the fact that many aspects of Aztec and Inca society were very far from idyllic, in fact extremely brutal.) This internal criticism contributed to the very high intellectual and moral standard of the debate on the very fundamentals of Faith and Empire initiated by Francisco de Vitoria, the virtual founder of International Law, at the University of Salamanca in 1539. For another example of a great empire permitting such profound questioning of its very right to be an empire, one might have to go back to Buddhist India, to Asoka's reaction to the horrors of his Kalinga war. This is highly to the honour of Spain; the dishonour of the Conquista is black, but in the last resort we are all the children not only of Adam, but of Cain who slew his brother. . . .[66]

The vast destruction of Indian life, and lives, cannot of course be ascribed mostly to direct assault; the disruption of the norms of social life, hunger and over-work in the mines and perhaps above all as human beasts of burden, accounted for very much; but most was due to epidemics of new diseases—Chaunu makes the point that, unlike such devastating invasions as those of the Mongols in Eurasia, the Conquista 'came by sea, not by land; this implies fewer invaders, but an incomparably greater microbiotic shock'.[67]

On these ruins, from these remnants, the Spaniards built a unique and fascinating culture; but this was not the work of the conquistadores themselves—though they laid the foundations of power—but of the officials, clerics, lawyers, merchants and artisans who followed them. The Crown very soon took in hand the taming of its too individualistic and too turbulent advance agents:

Private commanders like Cortés, Pizarro, Belalcázar, and Nuño de
Guzmán, if they escaped the knives of their rivals, were for the
most part soon displaced by royal nominees . . . Some succeeded
in settling down as *encomenderos*, ranchers or miners; . . . some, like
Bernal Díaz, lived on in obscure poverty in America; some, like
Cortés, returned to Spain with their winnings and spent their last
years in bored and litigious retirement. Very few were trusted by
the Crown with any real administrative power. They were not
the stuff of which bureaucrats are made.[68]

The organisation of the Indies

All great empires depend on their bureaucracies; but few can have been so totally
bureaucratic, from top to bottom, so given to the recording of everything, as
that of Spain. Over all hung the shadows of the notary and the priest, more
immediate figures than the King; no entrada was without its notary, few if any
without its priest. 'One day in 1544 two shoemakers . . . had an impressive
document drawn up devoted to nothing more than their arrival in Lima'; for
a brief, a very brief, spell the Crown sought to ban lawyers from Peru, but
'Reality soon repealed the law'.[69] And it was not the first Viceroy but the lawyer
la Gasca who reduced Gonzalo Pizarro's recalcitrant satrapy to its allegiance.
In the seventeenth century the famous *Recopilacion de leyes de las Indias* managed
to reduce over 11,000 laws, drawn from about 400,000 cédulas, to around 6400.[70]

The Crown of Castile, under God (a limitation taken seriously), was absolute
in the Indies, and in theory very little indeed could happen without the specific
approval of the Crown through its Council of the Indies, a body which naturally
soon became notorious for procrastination. A classic, if extreme, case of bureaucratic delay is afforded by the University of Chile, as we have seen a late starter.
The first letter to Spain on this subject was in 1602, but that century was not
propitious. With better, Bourbon, times, a proposal was made to the Cabildo
of Santiago in December 1713 and referred to the Council of the Indies for twenty
years of correspondence. The Council approved in 1736 and in 1738 issued a
decree which arrived in Santiago in 1740, but owing to lack of funds the University was not formally inaugurated until 1747, and courses started in July
1756:[71] 154 years betwixt the first motion and the acting; truly, if no empire
has been vaster, none has been more slow.

At the apex of the hierarchy in the Indies were the Viceroys. The Viceroy was
also Captain-General over his immediate province; the subordinate Captains-
General of the outer provinces, however, became 'more and more regarded as
little Viceroys.' These were the executive heads; but the most important other
officers were directly appointed by the Crown and could correspond directly with
it: whence divided counsels. Even the routine activities of the Viceroys were
subject to the minute detail of the all but uncountable royal ordinances, many of
them *ad hoc*. This over-centralisation was of course mitigated by local circum-

stance, 'the unconscious influences of the widely varying nature in the different provinces . . . events and forces [which] rarely rose above the Madrid horizon'.[72] It was also mitigated by the time it took to communicate with Spain; an able and enterprising man could get away with a good deal 'in anticipation of sanction', to borrow a phrase from another great imperial bureaucracy, that of the British Raj. If the royal commands were too hopelessly unsuited to the situation, they could be accepted with the respectful formula *obedezco pero no cumplo*—'I obey, but do not comply' (or rather 'fulfil'), in effect a referral back, an informal decentral-ising device.[73] In the sixteenth century and after the Bourbon reforms in the eighteenth, many of the Viceroys were remarkably able men; but in the interim, probably most were mediocrities, taking away with them when they went home a good deal, and 'leaving little behind but their portraits' in the museums. Where so much depended on the interpretation of a mass of often conflicting and half-forgotten regulations, there was room for much assistance to favourites or for financial consideration; the main check was the residencia or open post-mortem on an incumbency, but that could often be swamped in contradictory detail or otherwise fixed.

The main territorial sub-divisions were styled the *Audiencias*, each of which generally corresponded to a Captain-Generalcy. The Audiencia itself was in effect the provincial supreme court and an advisory council to the Viceroy or Captain-General; it had also the important task of carrying on government during accidental vacancies of the chief executive post. The Viceroyalty of New Spain, established in 1535, included the Audiencias or Captain-Generalcies of New Galicia, Mexico, Guatemala, the West Indies, Venezuela, and Panama, until in 1567 the last was definitively attached to Peru, for which it was of course the vital link with Seville. After some administrative vicissitudes New Granada, based on Bogota, became an independent Captain-Generalcy in 1563 and under the Bourbons (1739) a Viceroyalty, taking over Panama. Although the Vice-royalty of Peru was founded nine years after that of New Spain (1544), it became the superior office, the apex of a colonial career; under the Viceroy at Lima were Peru itself, Quito, Charcas (the nucleus of Bolivia), and the outlying and definitely inferior Audiencias or Presidencies of Chile and Buenos Aires. In 1776, however, the last of the Viceroyalties, Buenos Aires, was set up, and included Charcas: a belated recognition of the significance of the La Plata-Potosi routeway.[74] There were of course changes in the administrative layout from time to time, but these are the general lineaments, which alone concern us.

Municipal traditions in Spain had always been strong and—as we have seen with Balboa, Cortes, Pedrarias, Pizarro, Valdivia—the formal establishment of a municipality was among the first priorities of the successful conquistador: it gave him a quasi-legitimacy and a power base. At first these little towns were virtually self-governing, but this did not last for long: the patronage was too useful, and the Crown too suspicious of local privilege. From 1528 royal life nominees constituted the *cabildo* or town council of Mexico, and only in a few cases, mostly on the frontiers, did an elective element survive—Quito, Santiago de Chile, turbulent Potosi, isolated Buenos Aires. In common with most offices, membership of the cabildo was open to purchase, and with commissions (also purchasable) in the later militias, this provided the principal opportunity for Creoles, the locally-born Spaniards, to hold office, since many posts, and practically all of importance, were reserved for *Peninsulares*. Moreover, in times of emergency a *cabildo abierto* or 'open council' might be convened; this was not open to all, only to invitees, but was obviously subject to local pressure. As a centre for mobilising Creole opinion and action, the cabildo abierto was one of the most effective agencies in the opening struggles for Independence.

By 1574 there were said to be something over 150,000 Spaniards in the Indies, probably an overestimate; of these only some 6000 were encomenderos.[75] Basically life was oriented around two or three hundred 'towns', from great cities like Mexico, Lima, and Potosi, with total populations numbered in scores of thousands and with thousands of Spaniards, to wretched little ports and bush hamlets, where a few poverty-stricken vecinos held sway over a few score Indians. The real towns were nearly all built to a rectangular grid—laid down in royal ordinances—with central plazas and *alamedas* or main boulevards;[76] and the more substantial had splendid baroque buildings, especially churches and monasteries. The Church itself was the most active builder, as well as practically the only purveyor of educational and hospital services, which ranged from the miserable to institutions of high standard.

The Church was in important respects an arm of the State; it was obviously at once the protector, to the extent possible, of the Indians, and the main instrument by which they were subsumed into the new hybrid culture and kept safe for the Establishment. The Inquisition was less rigorous than in Spain; it was most active in Lima, where Portuguese New Christians and crypto-Jews infiltrated from La Plata and were important in commercial life.[77] Spanish culture in the Indies was more lively and diversified than might be expected; books were not only freely imported, in very large numbers, but exempt from all but one of the taxes levied on other imports. It is true that in 1531, 1543, 1575, and 1680 'books of romance, vain and profane stories such as that of Amadis' were prohibited imports; but it is believed that most of the first edition of *Don Quixote* in 1605 was—not inappropriately!—shipped direct to the Indies. Even books on the papal *Index Librorum Prohibitorum* found their way thither in the eighteenth century.[78]

Economically, all this activity was organised on the strictest mercantilist lines: the *raison d'être* of the Indies was to provide a continual stream of bullion to Spain, and to receive Spanish manufactures. With few exceptions (such as Huancavelica mercury, an essential factor in silver production), the State left economic activity in private hands, but subjected it to minute and often self-stultifying regulation. The system has been called, picturesquely, a gigantic

Common Market, in which 'The defence of the consumer was the sole law'.[79] This view seems difficult to defend in view of the activity of the *Consulado* or chamber of commerce of Seville, whose powerful influence was persistently exerted for the material interests of a small ring of merchants; it was responsible, for example, for the legal suppression in 1631–4 of the very lively and valuable trade between New Spain and Peru.[80]

The driving-belt of the whole immense system was the corporate activity of the Casa de Contratacion in Seville, which will be a significant theme in Chapters 7 and 8. The Casa was originally intended to be a royal monopoly trading in spices, on the Portuguese model; but 'ni llegan especias ni hay contratación'— it received no spices and it had no trade.[81] It became a government agency which organised the *flotas* and *galeones* of the Carrera de Indias; collected duties and taxes and the revenues remitted by colonial treasurers; trained and licensed pilots; kept up-to-date the official master-chart or *padron real*; ensured (or tried to) that ships were adequately manned and provisioned, and seaworthy; acted as a court for commercial cases and shipboard crimes; ran the postal services and the *avisos* or despatch boats for the Indies.[82] A unique institution, it was not only remarkably comprehensive but in many ways remarkably competent; and yet it was the main component in a top-heavy structure of over-regulation which ended up crushing itself by its own weight; a standing invitation to corruption and the contraband trade which sapped not only the wealth but the actual power of the Empire.

It was certainly an extraordinary achievement to cover, so swiftly, such enormous and enormously diversified realms with a net of law and common administrative practice. Clumsy, inordinately time-consuming, a fine culture for the bacteria of corruption, crammed with tensions and frictions, this extraordinary bureaucracy was for three centuries the stout skeleton of one of the most astonishing empires the world has ever seen. In the seventeenth century, with Spain itself, it was grievously afflicted with a Parkinsonian creeping paralysis; yet it was largely revitalised by the Bourbon reforms of the eighteenth century. One must agree with Ramos that the mere maintenance of this gigantic edifice, some of whose components were founded merely on their own 'functional apparatus', was almost a miracle, considering the distances, the terrain and climate, and the diverse environments, linked with Seville by shipping routes which in times of war were often worse than tenuous.[83]

The Pacific littorals of Nueva España and Peru were the bases by which, in the half-century succeeding the half-century of the Conquista, the Ocean was turned into virtually a Spanish lake. Mexico was the middle term of a highly organised commerce which spanned both Oceans, from Macao and Manila via Acapulco and Vera Cruz to Seville; Peru not only the financial heart of the system, but the base for the probes in depth by Mendaña and Quiros, the essential first steps through which

The Pacific no longer appeared as it had done to Magellan, a
desert waste; it was now animated by islands, which, however, for
want of exact astronomical observations, appeared to have no fixed
position, but floated from place to place over the charts.[84]
To this oceanic endeavour we now turn.

Chapter 4

MAGELLAN'S SUCCESSORS: LOAYSA TO URDANETA

... aqueles ilhas ... são um viveiro de todo mal, e não teem
outro bem senão cravo; e por ser cousa que Deus criou, lhe podemos
chamar boa; mas quanto a ser matéria do que os nossos por êle
teem passado, é um pomo de tôda a discordia. E por êle se podem
dizer mais pragas que sobre o ouro ....

Malacca and the Moluccas

Between Antonio de Abreu's return from Amboyna to the newly acquired
Portuguese base at Malacca, in December 1512, and Del Cano's to Seville in
September 1522, the Portuguese had acquired a knowledge of the Indonesian
seas more extensive and far firmer than Polo's, even if for the most part coastal.[1]
The world in which Lusitanians and Castilians were here involved was far
different from that of the Americas: a congeries of petty but civil kingdoms, in
the shadow of huge and mysterious empires, and linked by an active and diversified thalassic commerce, which was run by men with little to learn in the arts of
trade. Violence by sea and land was not lacking, but the entrada was to be replaced
by the embassy; despite forays in Cambodia and pipe-dreams of over-running
China, there was to be only one conquista, that of the Philippines.

Dominating the entire region, commercially, was Malacca, a good harbour in
either monsoon, and in the hands of its Muslim rulers controlling both sides of
the strait through which the traffic between the Indian and the Chinese seas was
funnelled.[2] Born of piracy, like many another Indies Sultanate, Malacca's rise was
fostered by its use as a forward base for Cheng Ho's voyages to and across the
Indian Ocean[3]—the name first appears in a Chinese record of 1403. By the early
sixteenth century its harbour saw the arrival of about a hundred big ships a year,
and of course a multitude of small craft. Its direct contacts extended from Gujarat
to Japan, or at any rate to the 'Gores' of the Lequeos or Ryukyu Islands.[4] The
Gujaratis were intermediaries for the Venetian trade via the Red Sea—arms,
cloth, quicksilver, glassware—while from the farther East the main commodities

---

João de Barros, *Asia*, III.5.v (Lisbon ed. 1945–6, III.261–2): 'these
islands ... are a warren of all evil, and have no one good thing
but the clove; and since it is a thing that God has made, we can
call it good; but in so far as it is the material cause of our people
going there, it is an apple of all discord. And one could curse it
more than gold itself. ...'

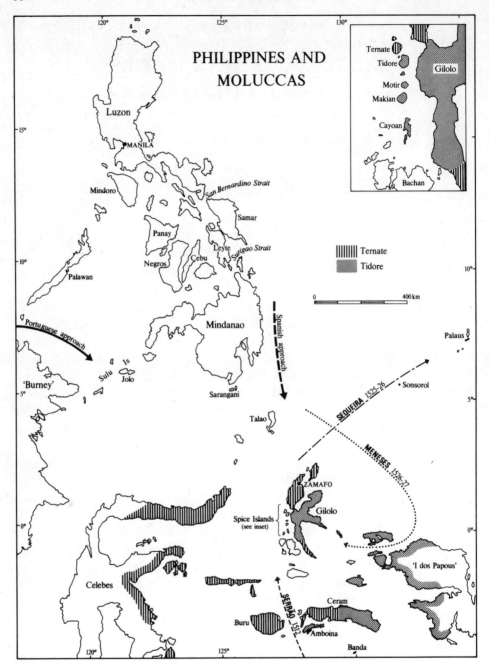

Figure 11. PHILIPPINES AND MOLUCCAS. Inset: The Spice Islands. The Portuguese approach shown was used mainly after 1545.

were of course spices, sandalwood, 'birds from Banda for plumes for the *Rumes*'—Camoes' 'aureas aves', the Birds of Paradise—from the islands; from China, silks, porcelain, and the more mundane salt and saltpetre. The great return trade to China was pepper, up to ten large junk-loads a year.[5]

The seizure of this great emporium by Afonso de Albuquerque in 1511 dislocated but was far from demolishing the commerce of the local trading powers, such as Atjeh (Achin) and Patani in Siam, both between themselves and with the farther East, and even to some extent with the Red Sea and Venice. Although, as Tomé Pires said, 'Whoever is lord of Malacca has his hand on the throat of Venice', the grasp was not always effective—there was a marked revival of European spice imports through Alexandria about 1560, and full control had to wait on the bureaucratically much more efficient Dutch monopoly, when the grip of Malacca was replaced by that of Batavia.[6] Nevertheless, though the new base would have to be supplemented by points farther east, its possession gave the Portuguese a position of strength, and of opportunity, and they lost no time in exploiting it. Albuquerque took Malacca in August; in November he sent de Abreu on his voyage along the north coasts of Java and the islands eastwards as far as Ceram.

By 1517 Tomé Pires could claim that the navigation from Malacca to the Moluccas, by-passing Java, was safe and easy, though the Portuguese authorities took good care that an opposite view was widely circulated.[7] Pires himself was sent in that year as ambassador to China, with which the first contacts had been made in 1513–15; he was imprisoned and died there, and for some thirty years from 1521 Portuguese trade with China was illicit and hazardous. The Moluccas were first reached by an official Portuguese fleet (as distinct from Francisco Serrão's free-lancing venture) in 1515; they were more tractable in themselves—five small islands; more obviously rewarding as the Spiceries *par excellence*; and, in view of Magellan's thrust in the service of Castile, a much more urgent objective. On 24 June 1522, between the *Trinidad*'s departure for Darien and her dejected return, Antonio de Brito set the foundation stone of the fort of São João at Ternate, on the best harbour of the group.

The Spice Islands proper—those of the clove—were Ternate, Tidore, Motir, Makian, and Bachan (Fig. 11), all volcanic with deep but thirsty lava soils; sago was an important article of diet, but their people depended for much of their food on the nearby large island of Gilolo (now Halmahera, then often Batachina), so that Magellan's stated reason for not making directly for them may have been genuine. Although all the Moluccan rulers were Muslims, there was precious little Islamic brotherhood: political life revolved around the rivalries of the Rajahs of Ternate and Tidore, with interventions from Gilolo; and since the rulers depended 'entirely on the revenues derived from trade, imports, and middleman profits',[8] the arrival of Portuguese and Spaniards presented fine openings for quadripartite manipulations in both war and trade. The first round, the seizure of the tiny factory on Tidore and of the *Trinidad*'s crew, went to the Portuguese.

The Spanish riposte: Loaysa

Charles V was elected Holy Roman Emperor just before Magellan sailed, and for much of the duration of the voyage he was engaged in a successful struggle to assert his challenged authority in Spain itself. Del Cano's return was thus psychologically most timely; new horizons of empire were opened, and in the last four months of 1522 thirty-three 'privileges' were issued for Spanish subjects willing to equip a Moluccan voyage.[9] But matters hung fire pending the procrastinatory Badajoz discussions, and it was not until the end of July 1525 that seven ships, under the command of Garcia Jofre de Loaysa, with del Cano as the obvious choice for Chief Pilot, sailed from Corunna, where a (short-lived) Casa de Contratacion, specifically for the Spiceries, was set up.[10] Amongst the company, as an accountant, was Andrés de Urdaneta, destined to make a great name in the annals of the Pacific. Three of the four Malays brought to Spain by del Cano were aboard for repatriation, though they seem not to have survived the voyage out; the fourth was kept in Spain, having shown himself all too inquisitive about the spice trade, and all too shrewd in appreciating the price differential between Europe and the Indies.[11]

Materially, the voyage was a succession of disasters. The *Sancti Spiritus*, with del Cano, was wrecked at the Cape of the Eleven Thousand Virgins, though all but nine men were saved; two ships deserted; the caravel *San Lesmes* was driven to 55°S and saw what 'appeared to be the end of the land', presumably the first sighting of Staten Land, so named by Schouten and Le Maire in 1616. The *San Lesmes* rejoined, and four ships entered the Pacific, to be scattered within a few days by a great tempest. The pinnace *Santiago* made its way to New Spain; the *San Lesmes* disappeared, and its wreck on Amanu in the Tuomotus may be taken as proven by the discovery there of four cannon.[12] Another caravel, *Santa Maria del Parrel*, reached Mindanao on its own; the few survivors of wreck and mutiny became captives of the islanders, and of the three picked up by Saavedra one was hanged for mutiny and one went bush.

The flagship *Santa Maria de la Victoria* sailed on alone; although by leaving in July rather than September Loaysa avoided wintering before passing the Straits, the Pacific crossing took almost as long as Magellan's, and only one island was seen, Taongi, the northmost outlier of the Marshalls; this, named San Bartolomé, came to bulk large in Urdaneta's thinking. The same ills as had afflicted Magellan's crews prevailed; Loaysa died on 30 July 1526 and del Cano took command, to die himself only five days later, a victim to his own courage in daring that terrible crossing for a second time. His successor Alonso de Salazar tried to make for Cipangu (Japan) before changing course directly for the Moluccas; eight days after their arrival at Guam (4 September), Salazar died in his turn, to be succeeded by Martin Iniguez de Carquisano. At Guam they were hailed in good Spanish by a naked 'Indian'; he was a surviving cabin boy from Magellan's *Trinidad*. It was now the Southwest Monsoon season, the wrong time for sailing from the Ladrones to the Moluccas, and progress was slow; but after touching at Mindanao and Talao to the south of it, at the end of October they reached Zamafo on the east of Gilolo: of the total 450 men who left Corunna, 145 had been on the *Victoria* when they passed the Straits, only 105 reached Zamafo. The people here were vassals of Tidore, and the Rajah of that island retained Spanish sympathies from the time of del Cano and Espinosa, so that the Spaniards were among friends. Contact with Tidore was soon made; but after outfacing the terrors and horrors of the Ocean Sea, they had now to meet the intense hostility of their fellow-Christians.

Tidore town had just been taken and sacked by the Portuguese; its Rajah was in the mountains, and eager for assistance in his revenge. The expedition's instructions were ambivalent: Article I, in the standard form, forbade touching at any land 'within the limits of the king of Portugal'; XVIII recommended avoiding contact, but a Portuguese presence should not inhibit a Moluccan landing; XXII directed that if the Portuguese had arrived, if they had ill-treated Magellan's survivors, and if they could be overcome without risking the fleet, then overcome they should be—but if they were too strong, the fleet should go elsewhere.[13] The Portuguese were not ambivalent: their commander, Garcia Henriques, sent to say that if the Spaniards came in to him at Ternate, they would be honourably received; if not they would be compelled by force of arms, or sunk with all hands. The Spaniards did come, but to Tidore, where they anchored on 1 January 1527.

The Portuguese attacked twelve days later, but were beaten off, though the *Victoria* was so badly strained by the firing of her own guns that she had to be burnt.[14] Rather desultory petty warfare followed, full of treasons and stratagems —Urdaneta accuses a new Portuguese commander, Jorge de Meneses, of a whole-sale poison plot,[15] and, on a lighter note (though it was very serious to good Catholics facing death unshriven), the Spanish chaplain, visiting Ternate to be confessed by his Lusian counterpart, was unsportingly kidnapped and had to be exchanged (unequally) since there was no other confessor available, but plenty of sins to confess. For the time being the local rulers found their account in these hostilities: with Spanish competition, the price of cloves rocketed. Ternate stood stoutly by the Portuguese, Tidore by the Spaniards, who also had a base and powerful support on Gilolo. For some fifteen months, with lulls due to Portuguese dissensions, these handfuls of men, Lusians and Castilians, raided and slew each other at the end of the earth from their homelands. The Spaniards clung desperately to the hope of succours from Spain; when help came at last, it was from an unexpected quarter: not Spain but New Spain.

America to the rescue: Saavedra

Cortes's original plans for discovery in the Mar del Sur, coasting north, were modified by a royal missive of June 1526: the Emperor-King was anxious to know of the success of Loaysa as soon as possible, but his recent marriage to a Princess of Portugal had made an expedition direct from Old Spain less than

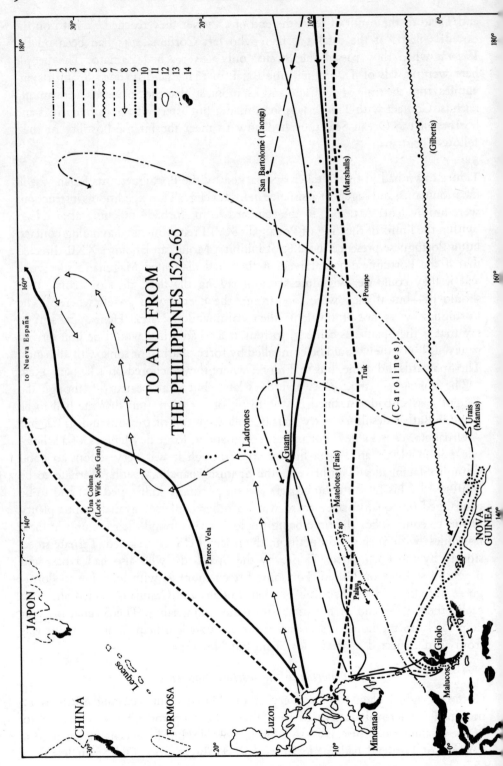

TO AND FROM
THE PHILIPPINES 1525-65

tactful. New Spain was the answer: Cortes had boasted of his ships, and details could be left to him. He therefore instructed his kinsman Alvaro de Saavedra Ceron to sail for the Moluccas, via Cebu where he was to look for any Magellanic survivors. 'Cortes hoped to make the Moluccas an outpost of New Spain'—as the Philippines were to become—and Saavedra was told to bring back, surreptitiously, various spice plants, with directions for their cultivation.[16]

After a three weeks' shake-down cruise north from Zacatula, two caravels and a bergantin left Zihuatanejo on 31 October 1527; the total tonnage was at most 120, with 110 men, fifty of them in the flagship *Florida*. The pilot was a Portuguese from the *Santiago*, Loaysa's pinnace which had reached Tehuantepec; but he died before the Ladrones were reached. After a week the *Florida* was leaking badly, and his officers urged Saavedra to transfer to another ship; but he replied in the spirit of Sir Humphrey Gilbert that he would be lost or saved on his own ship: ironically, the other two ships disappeared for ever in high winds in mid-December. Around the New Year Saavedra found four small islands in the Marshalls;[17] repeating Loaysa's mistake of trying the eastern or weather coast, he failed to find an anchorage at Guam, and on 1 February 1528 reached the east coast of Mindanao. He had sailed at the right time to catch the *brisas* or Trade Winds—by accident, as very little was yet known about the wind systems[18]— and made fairly good time to Guam. His course (Fig. 12) had several advantages: it was in the right latitudes (10 to 13°N) to pick up the Trades (if the timing was right) but avoided the dangerous concentration of atolls in the main Marshalls, so easily unseen until a ship was almost upon them; and it had a virtually assured landfall in the high island of Guam, stretching for nearly 50km athwart the track and rising to 390 metres.[19]

At the end of March 1528 they reached the Moluccas, five months out from New Spain. The Portuguese whom they met pretended that there were no Spaniards in the islands, but by mere chance Saavedra had already made contact with his countrymen on Gilolo: 'From that time the war proceeded with much greater heat.' Once the first almost incredulous joy was over, counsel had to be taken. The obvious course was to send the spices already collected—seventy quintals—to New Spain, and to draw new succours thence.

While Saavedra's outward course was to prove the correct one, 'it was a route of no return. Few who ventured on it between 1527 and 1564 saw New Spain

◄*Figure 12.* TO AND FROM THE PHILIPPINES, 1525–65. 1, Sequeira (Portuguese), 1525–6; 2, Loaysa, 1526; 3, Saavedra, 1527; 4, Saavedra's first return, 1528; 5, Saavedra's second return, 1529; 6, Grijalva's mutineers, 1536–7; 7, Villalobos, 1542–3; 8, de la Torre, 1543; 9, de Retes, 1545; 10, Legazpi, 1564, and Urdaneta's return, 1565; 11, Arellano's return, 1564–5; 12, reasonably known coasts, *c.* 1550 (*c.* 1575 in Philippines); 13, vaguely known coasts; 14, Portuguese contacts by *c.* 1545.

Compiled from maps and texts in H. Friis (ed.), *The Pacific Basin* (New York 1967); A. Sharp, *The Discovery of the Pacific Islands* (Oxford 1960); G. Souter, *The Last Unknown* (Sydney 1963); H. Wallis, The Exploration of the South Sea, 1519 to 1644 (unpublished Oxford D.Phil. thesis 1953–4).

again'.[20] Early in June the *Florida* left Tidore and rounded Gilolo northabout, then taking a southeasterly course which brought her to Manus north of New Guinea (the first European visit to the Admiralty Islands) and thence into the Carolines; adverse winds compelled a return through the Ladrones, reaching Tidore late in the year. Hernando de la Torre, in command since Carquisano's death, suggested going to Spain by the Cape of Good Hope: at least del Cano had succeeded. But Saavedra insisted on trying again his earlier route; he sailed on 3 May 1529, was becalmed round the Admiralties, and then made his way northeast through the Carolines and skirting west of the Marshalls, probably discovering Ponape, Ujelang, and Eniwetok. Whatever the exact course, the *Florida* reached 31°N before being again forced back; Saavedra died before the turn was made. Twenty-two men reached Zamafu on 8 December 1529—to find that the gallant game was over.

Portuguese pressure had increased, especially in October 1529 when de la Torre injudiciously committed about half his scanty force to eastern Gilolo. It was now the Spaniards' turn to suffer dissension: there seemed little chance of a new fleet arriving, and it was apparent that the enemy could draw on Malacca. Perhaps more decisive was the discovery that both rivals had outstayed their welcome, and that there was a serious risk of a general rising against both sets of intruders; a *rapprochement* was clearly indicated. The little fort on Tidore capitulated five weeks before the *Florida*'s return; the Spanish had still considerable strength in the Gilolo alliance, and a truce was patched up. The Spaniards raised provisions from Gilolo for the Portuguese, now besieged by a revolt on Ternate, and Urdaneta claims that they mediated peace on that island. But once the Portuguese were again secure on Ternate, they pressed on for Gilolo, the Spanish maintaining a dangerous neutrality, despite pleas from the allies who had served them so well. It is hard to blame them: when Gilolo fell, there were only seventeen Spaniards surviving.

After the truce, an embassy to Goa confirmed that the Moluccan question had been settled not by force of arms in the Indies but by a cash transaction in Spain. There was now no point in staying, and in February 1534 the little remnant took Portuguese shipping for India. Urdaneta and another stayed on as factors for cloves already under contract; the Portuguese naturally soon put a stop to this. A tiny handful of survivors reached Lisbon in mid-1536; they included Urdaneta and Vicente de Napoles, who petitioned 'for help in his work, and they ordered him to receive 14 ducats. These were the mercies of the Council'.[21]

Zaragoza 1529: the Moluccas and the Straits

The Treaty of Zaragoza (5 April 1529) confirmed D. João III of Portugal in the gains of D. João II at Tordesillas: the interests of Charles V, Holy Roman Emperor of the German Nation, outweighed those of D. Carlos I, Rey de Castilla.

Charles, deeply involved in European wars and politics and, as ever, deeply in need of hard cash, was wise to cut his losses; and in view of French piracies and menaces against Brazil and Guinea, D. João also was ready to come to terms. The major provision of the Treaty was that a line of demarcation should be adopted from Pole to Pole, defined by laying off 19° on a bearing NE by E from the Moluccas; beyond this line (which in real terms, then of course not known, gave Portugal about 187° of longitude against Spain's 173°) the King of Castile should not claim, trade, or sail. There was an escape clause, which can hardly have been meant as anything but a face-saving *pro forma*: should future investigation establish accurately that the Moluccas lay east of the true antimeridian of the Tordesillas line, the agreement would be void. In return, João III would immediately pay over 350,000 ducats: an advance on his starting offer of 200,000, but a substantial shortfall from the original Castilian demand of 1,000,000. Technically this was not, as it is sometimes called, a sale of rights, rather a mortgaging. Probably nobody was deceived by this aspect; in Spain the transaction was seen as an almost shameful surrender.[22] Incidentally, this was the first European treaty on claims in the Pacific.

Spanish sell-out or no, it was commonsense: as Nowell points out, in ten years fifteen ships had sailed for the Spice Islands from the Spains, Old and New; one only, del Cano's *Victoria*, had come home—and that only by illicitly and perilously running the Portuguese gauntlet round the Cape.[23] The costs in blood and treasure of maintaining a foothold were too great. Although, Tomé Pires notwithstanding, the voyage from Malacca (and *a fortiori* from Goa) could be long and hazardous, the logistic advantages were on Portugal's side, and were enhanced by a much more detailed and comprehensive knowledge of the lands and seas surrounding the Moluccas, and (not less important) of the pre-existing network of trade and political relations. That the Spaniards were able to put up so bold a front for so long, despite the extreme fragility of their lines of communication, was due as much as anything else to the extraordinary indiscipline and self-seeking of the Portuguese leaders, who except for Antonio Galvão paid scant heed to the general interest of their king and country, being more intent on personal booty.[24]

Yet in the end, despite the daring and endurance of so many men, 'For all practical purposes, the status of the two countries in the Moluccas was again what it had been before Magellan appeared at the Spanish court. . . .'[25] Spain was indeed to trespass successfully over the new line, in the Philippines; but that had to wait for over thirty years, when the base in New Spain had become stronger. Even then, the Spanish presence was tenuous until the problem of the return route had been solved, and that in turn was only after two disastrous failures, those of Grijalva and Villalobos.

The real significance of the voyages of Loaysa and Saavedra lies in their dearly-bought experience. On the positive side, Saavedra did find the correct outward course from New Spain; on the negative, his ill-starred attempts to return should have shown the folly of trying to beat back in low latitudes, where currents and winds (when there were winds) were adverse. The lesson was not immediately learnt, but even these failures doubtless contributed to the deductions of Urdaneta and others, by which the true return route, north into the Westerlies, was found.

Loaysa's was the second Spanish trans-Pacific voyage to use the Straits of Magellan—and the last for over two centuries. The navigation was too long and difficult, compared with that from New Spain, to be worthwhile. Only two more Spanish attempts at a westwards traverse of the Straits were made in the sixteenth century, and both had more limited objectives than the Moluccas. In 1535 Simon de Alcazaba penetrated the Straits with a commission for an entrada into Patagonia: of the forty-one named members of his company, nineteen (including himself) were drowned, murdered, hanged or headed, starved or marooned. Four years later the Bishop of Plasencia sent out Alonso de Camargo to open a route to Peru, judging that the longer navigation would be offset by avoiding the double break-of-bulk at the Isthmus. Of Camargo's three ships, only his own reached Valparaiso (the first ship to anchor there) and Callao, possibly sighting Juan Fernandez; one was wrecked, one returned to Spain, though it seems to have penetrated the Strait of Le Maire and wintered in the south of Tierra del Fuego.[26] But this promising if limited success was not followed up, doubtless because it would have interfered with the system of Seville and the vested interests built up at Panama. Into such disrepute did Magellan's great discovery fall that it was rumoured that his Straits had been blocked by some natural disaster.[27]

With the settlement of Zaragoza, the Moluccas, hitherto so significant as a magnet for trans-Pacific voyaging, begin to fade out of Pacific history proper, to revert as it were to a Southeast Asian allegiance. The Portuguese remained deeply suspicious of anything suggesting a new Spanish approach; but until the Union of the Crowns in 1580, such Spaniards as reached the Moluccas were strays, as were Grijalva's mutineers, or enforced by real distress, like Villalobos. With the advent of the Dutch in 1599, the Spice Islands were drawn more and more into the ambit of the Indian Ocean rather than that of the Pacific. With few exceptions, of which Drake's visit was most notable, not the Moluccas but the Philippines and the Marianas (especially Guam) became the main objective of trans-Pacific voyaging, until in the eighteenth century the role was taken over by Batavia, but with a differing function: refitting, not plunderage. Nevertheless, until 1662 the Moluccas remained indirectly involved in Pacific affairs, largely as an outreach of the Spanish presence in the Philippines.

Two failures: Grijalva and Villalobos

The first crossing from Peru to the East Indies was unofficial in its origin, inconsequential and mutinous in its progress, and miserable in its ending. It was in fact a by-blow of the great Inca revolt of 1536: Hernando de Grijalva, sent by Cortes with succours to Pizarro, decided to try his luck in searching for rich islands rumoured to lie west from Peru—perhaps seduced by the legends of Tupac Inca which were later to inspire Sarmiento and Heyerdahl, perhaps under secret instructions. Antonio Galvão thought that Cortes, anxious to forestall the first Viceroy of New Spain, Antonio de Mendoza, had instructed Grijalva to sail 'to Maluco to discouer that way a long vnder the equinoctial line';[28] but then as Governor of the Moluccas Galvão was properly suspicious of stray Spanish ships.

Grijalva left Paita in April 1537, and after sailing apparently a long way to the southwest attempted to make New Spain or California, but was defeated by winds from east and northeast, the Trades being still strong as far west as Hawaii in this season. According to the Portuguese historian Diogo do Couto (with Galvão one of the two main sources), the crew then demanded that they should make for the Moluccas, the winds seeming favourable, and on Grijalva's prudent refusal to trespass into Portuguese waters they killed him. They sailed on west-wards close to the Equator—the first crossing in so low a latitude—sighting two islands over a thousand leagues from Peru.[29] Most of the mutineers died in the dragging traverse along the belt of equatorial calms; the ship simply broke up somewhere on the north coast of New Guinea, and three survivors were rescued from the 'Papuans' by Galvão. The voyage was a failure from first to last.

Much more serious, though in its end almost as disastrous, was the voyage of Ruy Lopez de Villalobos in 1542. Charles V and his subjects were still convinced that the Moluccas were properly theirs, and though their claim had been hypothe-cated at Zaragoza, there were other islands where the Portuguese were not yet active—the Islas de Poniente, 'Islands towards the West', Magellan's San Lazaro. Pedro de Alvarado, the conquistador of Guatemala, was in Spain when the remnants of Loaysa's and Saavedra's people arrived from Lisbon, including Urdaneta, who presented a full and euphoric report on the possibilities not only of the Moluccas but of these islands to the north. Alvarado seized his chance, obtained a commission, and built eleven ships at Iztapa and Acajutla. His first cruise—to the north, lured by tales of the golden cities of Cibola—alarmed the Viceroy Mendoza, who succeeded in claiming first a third and then a half of the putative profits. Alvarado's death in a minor Indian war gave the Viceroy a free hand to appoint Villalobos, a relative by marriage, to seek for a base in the Islas de Poniente, presumptively on Cebu, for trade with China and the Lequeos; to spread the Faith; and not least to ascertain a return route to New Spain.[30]

Villalobos sailed with six ships from Navidad on 1 November 1542, passing through the Revillagigedo Islands and the Marshalls. On 23 January 1543 they passed an island which they called Los Matelotes, since natives from canoes hailed them with 'Buenos dias, matelotes'; this was Fais in the Carolines, and João de Barros and do Couto were convinced that the greeting was in Portuguese, not Castilian, an echo from the furthest reach of Galvão's missionary efforts—as he himself claimed, and as indeed seems most likely.[31] Villalobos now committed an error by declining his pilot's advice to make for the north point of Mindanao, which would have brought him to Cebu by the Surigao Strait; instead he found himself stuck on the weather side of Mindanao, with no trading prospects—although porcelain was found in a hut on the little island of Sarangani, Chinese and Malays did not come to the east of Mindanao. The Portuguese had been there already, and the people were generally hostile. A base was made on Sarangani, which had been visited by both Magellan's and Loaysa's *Victoria*; here they were brought to eat 'horrid grubs and unknown plants', land crabs which sent people mad for a day, and a 'grey lizard, which emits a considerable glow; very few who ate them are living'.[32]

In August 1543 Villalobos sent the *San Juan de Letran* under Bernardo de la Torre to take news to Mendoza. This fourth attempt to find a return route reached 30°N but then, like its predecessors, was forced back by storms; however, de la Torre touched at Samar and Leyte, and in all probability discovered some islands in the northern Marianas as well as the volcanoes of the Bonins, and possibly Marcus Island. He was also the first European to circumnavigate Mindanao.[33] Before he got back to Sarangani, hunger had forced Villalobos to leave, after an unsuccessful attempt to reach Cebu; he was in the Portuguese zone (though he may well not have thought so) and the people around Sarangani refused supplies, whether through loyalty to Portugal (according to Galvão) or through Portuguese intrigues (according to the Spaniards).

Villalobos sought refuge on Gilolo, where there was still some support for Spain, though an appeal to the old alliance with Tidore failed. The Portuguese warned them off, but did not press too hard, and for the sake of peace the Castilians abandoned their old Gilolo friends. It was agreed to refer their position to the Viceroys of Portuguese India and of New Spain, and in the meantime the *San Juan* was to be refitted for yet another return attempt, under Ortiz de Retes. He sailed from Tidore on 16 May 1545 and coasted along New Guinea (which he so named) until 12 August, reaching somewhere near the mouth of the Sepik; but once more Saavedra's southern route proved an impasse. In October de Retes reached Tidore again, but so did a fresh Portuguese fleet, and Villalobos accepted repatriation. He himself died a few weeks after they set out (January 1546) in Amboyna, on Good Friday, receiving the last rites from St Francis Xavier: a good end for a man of his time and country. But this was also the end of any Spanish activity in the Spice Islands; henceforth such adventures were forbidden to the Viceroys.

Failure, but not the completely sterile failure of Grijalva's men. A great deal had been added, mostly by de la Torre, to knowledge of the Islas de Poniente; Villalobos, who had a taste for toponymy, named Mindanao 'Caesarea Karoli' for the Emperor, because of its greatness; the smaller islands to the north he called the 'Felipinas', for the prince who became Philip II.[34] These northern islands were free of Portuguese influences—they had no spices, except some poor cinnamon; but they had ample supplies of food and good timber, so a base was possible;

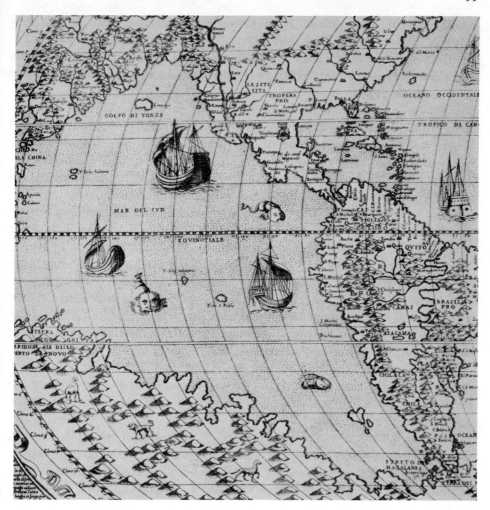

Plate IX. THE PACIFIC BY MID-CENTURY: FORLANI 1565. This is from Forlani's *Universale Descritiione* (Venice 1565) and its representation of the Mar del Sur is as in Gastaldi's map of 1546, on which the sea is too messily hatched to allow of a good reproduction. The map shows increasing recognition of the true outlines of the Pacific, though the width of the Ocean is still much too small and there is no Strait of Anian, and Cipangu is erratic in a new way. Reproduced in F. Muller, *Remarkable Maps* (Amsterdam 1595). NLA.

and this was vital, since

> Villalobos's disastrous voyage had shown more clearly than any the
> reason for the Spaniards' difficulty in finding the return route; it was
> that their ships started from the Archipelago in a condition unfit
> for a long and perilous voyage of exploration. The Spaniards could
> not discover the return route until they had a good base at which
> to equip their ships; they could not establish a base until they
> had discovered a return route; here was their dilemma.[35]

Small wonder, then, that St Francis Xavier thought it lamentable that new voyages should be projected, and asked a correspondent in Lisbon to beseech the King of Portugal to tell his fellow-monarch of Castile to send no more ships to be cast away in the Mar del Sur;[36] not that D. João would need much urging to send such a message.

Villalobos's underestimate of 1500 leagues for the distance from Navidad to the Philippines made the potential base seem easier of access than it was; and despite Legazpi's careful logging of 1900 leagues in 1564–5, the earlier figure had a strong influence on Spanish thinking; the much improved outlines of Gastaldi and Forlani (1546–65; Plate IX) still grossly understate the distance, and as late as 1574–80 Juan Lopez de Velasco could show this distance as 63° of longitude instead of over 130°.[37] On the more tangible and immediate point of managing the trans-Pacific crossing, the results were negative. It was borne in upon navigators and projectors—not Urdaneta alone—that the return must be looked for to the north, not by Saavedra's well-worn but dead-end track. But while Villalobos's outward course passed more hospitable islands than did his predecessors', those so far known were mostly dangerous low-lying atoll reefs, difficult to recover and identify, and his route missed the surer landfall of Guam. It also came to the Philippines on a lee shore, well south of the (later all-important) Surigao and San Bernardino passages leading to what was to be the centre of Spanish power, on Luzon. Outwards, Saavedra's track was better.[38] Moreover, it was not on the relatively quick and easy westbound passage that places of rest and refreshment were most needed, but on the long return in colder latitudes; and here they were absent.

But at least the boundaries of the problem were now far more firmly set; and, line or no line, the very name 'las Felipinas' asserted a claim.[39] The next attempt was to gain a new province for Christendom, and a giant extension for the Spanish mercantile system, which would span a continent and two oceans.

Finding and founding a base: Legazpi and Urdaneta

Felipe II, the Prudent (and slow), succeeded to the Spanish Crowns on the abdication of his father the Emperor Charles V, in January 1556. The death of his unhappy wife Mary Tudor in November 1558 and the Treaty of Cateau-Cambrésis with France in the following April freed him, for the time, from his more burdensome European preoccupations. Spice prices were rising sharply. It is, then, perhaps significant that less than six months after Cateau-Cambrésis the King wrote to Luis de Velasco, Viceroy of New Spain, definitely ordering 'the discovery of the western islands towards the Malucos';[40] and this was to be a directly royal expedition, not just an authorised entrada.

There had been previous correspondence, and Philip enclosed 'the letter that you think I should write to Fray Andrés de Urdaneta', the companion of Loaysa, now an Augustinian monk. There are modern doubts as to Urdaneta's real standing as a navigator, and he sailed simply as a missionary; but by contemporaries he was highly regarded as an expert on Pacific affairs, and was much deferred to by Legazpi, a personal friend, and by Velasco. The Viceroy replied to his master in May 1560, saying that he was preparing ships—ostensibly for Peru and coast defence—but raising the question of the demarcation: Urdaneta and others believed that the Philippines lay west of the Moluccas (as they do) and hence in the pawned and prohibited region. But Urdaneta himself hit upon the solution: 'some legitimate or pious reason is needed', and this can be the redemption of Spanish captives from earlier voyages, or their children, whose souls would be in obvious danger. Once the position and value of the Philippines were ascertained, the pawn might be redeemed. The academic geographers and lawyers in Spain, however, still clung to the belief that the Philippines were a legitimate target.[41]

At this point the objectives of the expedition were not at all clear. In a long memorandum (early 1561) Urdaneta lays stress on occupying 'San Bartolomé' (Taongi, discovered by Salazar in 1526) as an intermediate base; if a start could not be made before December 1561, New Guinea should be sought; if not before January 1562, then they should wait until March and sail northwest, along the coast which Cabrillo had found, and then strike west, perhaps from about 40°N, to somewhere near Japan. These alternatives depended of course on the seasonal winds, and the last was obviously a bad shot. The return track seems to have been left studiously vague, though the Ladrones were mentioned; but it is possible that Urdaneta was keeping a northern route in reserve. There were other experts in the field; Juan Pablo de Carrion, who had been with Villalobos and de Retes, attacked the idea of going to New Guinea (and especially of settling there) from personal knowledge of the island, and urged a direct course for the Philippines, where the Spaniards had contacts and whence the return should be easier to find; eight years later he claimed to have planned both the out and home tracks. Although an obvious choice for *almirante* or second-in-command,[42] and in fact so chosen, he did not go with Legazpi, being unwilling to work with Urdaneta.

Although Velasco had hoped that the expedition might leave early in 1562, there were as always delays; it was not until 21 November 1564 that four ships under Miguel Lopez de Legazpi sailed from Acapulco; the choice of that port was due to Urdaneta, who argued at some length its superiority over Navidad, and his insistence on by-passing Navidad on the return voyage may be said to have fixed Acapulco as the Mexican terminal of the Galleon route.[43]

Velasco had died four months earlier, and the final orders were issued by the Audiencia of Mexico. They were sealed; security was much to the fore, and Velasco may have spread the idea that the destination was China, both as cover story and to aid recruiting.[44] When the orders were opened, 100 leagues out, they proved to opt firmly for the Philippines: Carrion's plan, and on Villalobos's course. Urdaneta (apparently still hankering after New Guinea) and his friars protested, but acquiesced. The orders stressed trade (there was still some hope of spices), settlement if practicable, and conversion to the Faith; exploration could extend to the Japanese islands, believed to be in the Spanish zone but contacted by the Portuguese. Above all, the return route was to be found as quickly as possible, and Urdaneta was to come back with the first ship. While there was the usual licence for all to write to the King and the Audiencia, letters would not be forwarded until the Audiencia had received a full report, and precautions were to be taken against leakage. From all this it is clear that the prime objective was a serious attempt at colonisation, and probably also that Spanish officialdom, at least in New Spain, was by no means as sure of the international legal standing of the venture as it would have liked.

The four ships carried a total complement of 380, of whom 200 were soldiers for the settlement. The ships were soon reduced to three: on the morning of 30 November the patache *San Lucas*, which should have been ahead, was missing; a serious loss, as she was intended for close coastal work in the islands.[45] Between 9 and 12 January 1565, in about 10°N, they sighted five small islands in the Marshalls; on the 17th the pilots thought that they were already west of Villa-lobos's Los Matelotes (Fais) and hence might soon find themselves up against Mindanao on their lee. Urdaneta differed, and they agreed to go up to 13°N so as 'to avoid entering [the Philippines] at the hunger-point of Villalobos'.[46] Five days later Urdaneta was proved right, when what the pilots thought the Philip-pines turned out to be Guam: he had a clearer idea of the width of the Ocean than his fellows. On 26 January Legazpi made a formal Act of Possession of the Ladrones, and their arrival in the Philippines on 13 February was followed by a flurry of similar acts: six in all, on Samar, Bohol, and Cebu.

A Moro (Muslim) trading prau from Borneo was taken after a sharp fight; Legazpi returned its cargo and received the useful information that the indigenous avoidance of the newcomers was due to devastating raids by Portuguese posing as Castilians. Reconnaissance showed that Cebu was populous and well provi-sioned; and in Spanish eyes the Cebuans were already vassals since Magellan's day. On 27 April 1565 the fleet anchored off Cebu; an attempt to negotiate peacefully failed. Women and children were fleeing to the hills, fighting men and praus were assembling: the Cebuans were obviously in apostasy and rebellion. A brief bombardment left most of the little town in smouldering ruins; but in a hut they found 'a marvellous thing, a child Jesus like those of Flanders, in its little pine cradle and its little loose shirt. . . .' Truly, a marvellous thing: forty-four years before Pigafetta, or possibly Magellan himself, had given it to the Queen of Cebu, and there could be no more moving omen, a holy joy, for Catholic men. On 8 May Legazpi broke ground for the fort and town of San Miguel, and proclaimed a possession that was to last for 333 years; the Niño Jesus was to endure longer yet, and still looks down on the faithful of Cebu in the Church of the Holy Child.[47]

Legazpi, more of a Cortes than a Pizarro, soon came to reasonable terms with the Cebuans; as ever, long-standing local rivalries provided the Spaniards with auxiliaries, and gradually Spanish lordship was extended over, or at least among, the islands between Mindanao and Luzon. Mindanao itself was to prove a tougher nut to crack, and the Moros of Jolo, in the Sulu archipelago to the south, tougher still: it would be wearisome to count, let alone to recount, the raids and counter-raids, the piracies and punitions, the pacifications and the treaties of short-lived eternal amity; and indeed as these words are written (1977) 'pacification' still pursues its weary and bloody way. To the north, however, 'The Hispanization of the Philippines'[48] was powerfully influenced by the Augustinians, later by Franciscans and other Orders; and if the friars too often became themselves exploiters, the excesses of the entrada and the encomienda were at least attenuated in the Philippines.

There was an ever-present danger, and sometimes the actuality, of famine; the local subsistence agriculture could hardly cope with the injection of so many new and unproductive mouths, and the general disruption and hunger led to dissensions and plots. Apart from this, there was also a threat not from pagans or Muslims but from fellow Christians. The first contacts with the Portuguese were made in November 1566, wary and shiftily evasive on both sides. Two ships arrived from New Spain in August 1567 with 200 men and badly needed supplies, though not on the scale asked for in urgent messages to Mexico.[49] The *San Juan* was sent off in July 1568 with over 400 quintals of cinnamon; she was wrecked off Guam, and although her company was saved, the loss of the spice cargo, relied upon to attract more support, was a serious blow. It was followed by a solid Portuguese threat: on 2 October 1568 four galleons, two galliots, and two smaller vessels under Gonçalo Pereira arrived from the Moluccas. There followed four months of sporadic skirmishing and lengthy diplomatic exchanges; at his last summons Pereira announced that he was 'weary of so many papers containing so many irrelevancies' (he had himself supplied the longest and most irrelevant of them). Velvety insults were traded; Legazpi protested that he would like nothing better than to depart, had he the ships to do so; perhaps Pereira might lend him some . . . ? In the end the Portuguese departed first, on 1 January 1569; and soon after Legazpi left, not for New Spain but for Panay, better-found than Cebu (whose resources were now badly strained) and farther from the Portuguese, who also were about at the end of their tether.

In June 1569 Juan de la Isla brought reinforcements (including fifty married couples), permission to grant encomiendas, and Legazpi's promotion to Governor and Captain-General; the couples were sent to a new town on Cebu. Reconnaissance brought information of the region around Manila Bay, central to the largest island, densely populated and with a good harbour; there was plenty of food, and reportedly gold; the people were civil enough to have artillery of a sort and even a foundry. Trade with the Moluccas and their spices was obviously barred, but the situation of Luzon gave promise of trade with China, always a background element in the project and soon to come to the fore. In May 1571 Legazpi landed at Manila and enforced a treaty of vassalage; in June he set up a cabildo for the new Spanish city. Within a year the populous areas of coastal

Luzon had been visited and some inland excursions made, and—a most significant development—a small colony of Chinese traders was establishing itself at Manila.[50]

When Legazpi died on 20 August 1572, he had laid foundations for one of the strangest of colonies. Itself a colony of colonial Nueva España,[51] it existed, apart from an intense missionary effort, by and for its one great emporium, Manila. The islands themselves produced little (wax, ginger, poor cinnamon, a little gold), and the military and administrative establishment had to be permanently subsidised by Mexico. Manila was an arsenal for the military and the Church Militant, but its supreme function was to be the pumping-station in a channel through which the silver of New Spain drew the luxuries of the Orient, above all Chinese silks, to America and to Seville. Well might Legazpi report 'We are at the gate and in the vicinity of the most fortunate countries of the world, and the most remote . . . great China, Burnei . . . Siam, Lequois, Japan, and other rich and large provinces'.[52] But Spain was not alone at the gate: after so much valour and suffering, Portugal still held the Spiceries, and since 1557 had been established at another emporium, Macao.

The return achieved: Arellano and Urdaneta

No time had been lost in seeking the return route; Urdaneta indeed had been anxious to settle at Guam and find the way back thence.[53] Only three weeks after the founding of San Miguel, he sailed (1 June 1565) on the fastest ship, the *San Pedro*, initially on much the same course as de la Torre's in the *San Juan*; the latter's 'Abreojos' is probably the island still called by Urdaneta's name for it, Parece Vela.[54] By 3 August the *San Pedro* was in 39–40°N, then dropping to 30° northwest of Hawaii; early in September they were again in 39° 30′N, and then sailed east and by south until, on 18 September, they sighted La Deseada, 'the desired', probably San Miguel where Cabrillo had died. Although short-handed (sixteen of forty-four men had died) they pressed on past Navidad for the better port of Acapulco, arriving on 8 October: nearly 20,000km in 130 days. But the triumph was dulled: the lost *San Lucas* had reached Navidad just two months earlier, on 9 August.

There had been no stress of weather to account for Alonso de Arellano and Lope Martin, captain and pilot of the *San Lucas*, parting company: it seems simple desertion. Arellano had pressed on for the Philippines—this was after all a known route—picking up eight islands in the Marshalls and Carolines, his most notable discovery being Truk. By his own account he was in Philippine waters for nearly three months, wandering around the inland seas from 29 January to 22 April 1565. This overlaps with Legazpi's stay by nearly nine weeks, and if as Arellano claimed he was really looking for the fleet, it seems strange that no news filtered through either way; on the other hand, his account of his wanderings among the islands is detailed and verifiable. On the return he claimed to have reached 43°N, and this part of his account is filled with strange stories, which have cast doubt on his general veracity: porpoises as big as cows present no difficulty, but it is unlikely that cooking oil would freeze in mid-summer.

After enquiry by the Audiencia, Arellano was neither punished for desertion nor rewarded for success, and there is little doubt that Lope Martin was the villain of the piece: a most shady character, who played a leading part in a maze of mutiny on the *San Geronimo*, sent to aid Legazpi in 1566, and who ended his days marooned in the Marshalls.[55] As Chaunu says, Arellano's exploit is anecdotal, a 'first' less significant in itself than as showing that the solution was in the air; but intrinsically the voyage, in a 40-ton pinnace with twenty men, was a great one.[56]

With these two voyages, the problem of the return was solved (Fig. 12)—on the lines tried forty-four years earlier by Espinosa's *Trinidad*. Quite apart from Arellano's narrow priority in time, it is a mistake to attach a single name to the achievement; as Wallis, a supporter of Urdaneta's claims, remarks, 'Every pilot of Legaspi's fleet probably thought that he knew the route', and Carrion had stated firmly that the Philippines 'have the best situation for the return voyage, because they are in north latitude'—Saavedra's lesson had at last been taken to heart.[57] There is no doubt that Urdaneta had the right contacts—Legazpi, the Viceroy, the Augustinian publicists—and, whatever his formal training, he clearly had a good seaman's intuition, as shown by his justified disagreement with the pilots. He stressed the importance of timing in relation to seasonal winds, though one may suspect that others who had been with, or in touch with, the series from Loaysa to Villalobos had begun to grasp the general trends of the wind circulation; perhaps by a subconscious analogy with the Atlantic. Urdaneta left Cebu at the right time—nearly June, with a westerly monsoon—and took the shortest track through the Trades to pick up the Westerlies. On the whole, despite his penchant for New Guinea and his vacillations, Urdaneta does seem to have had a clearer, or at least more clearly formulated, idea of the problem than did the others, and he alone seems to have appreciated fully the immense width of the Ocean: 'On all accounts, the intellectual discoverer is Urdaneta'.[58]

In a remarkably short time 'Urdaneta's route' became almost sacrosanct for the Manila–Acapulco run, and his chart was still considered standard, by the Spanish, into the eighteenth century. Late in the seventeenth, however, there was an unfortunate modification—a supposedly safer route, between 32 and 37°N, avoiding the colder and stormier higher latitudes. But here the Westerlies are less reliable, so that the passage was often prolonged, and no small part of the privations and disease of the voyage may be attributed to this change. At either end of the route, however, adherence to tradition had deleterious effects. The excessive risk of wreck in the maze of islands between Manila and the Embocadero, or debouchment of San Bernardino Strait into the Ocean, did not suffice to have this hazardous navigation replaced by the simpler and quicker, and on the whole safer, course up the west coast of Luzon, despite serious efforts, especially in the eighteenth century, to have this route adopted. On the opposite shores, even after the colonisation of Alta California from 1770 on, its ports were not used to refresh the weary and scurvy-ridden crews before they went on to Acapulco; this could also have stimulated Californian development, but mercantile interests in New Spain would not brook the short delay. Spanish bureaucracy and dockyards being what they were, it was more difficult to adhere to sailing-dates than to courses: sailings from Manila should have been between mid-June and mid-July, and usually were; but in practice they might be at any time between early May and late September. In any case, the voyage east usually took five to six months, that from New Spain only three.[59]

Establishment of the Galleon route meant enhanced importance and self-esteem for New Spain, now an essential link in a maritime system extending from Seville to China. The back-parts of Mexico no longer led nowhere in particular, though the increased value of the Pacific coast was narrowly concentrated in the single port of Acapulco. A contemporary letter from Seville says that 'those of Mexico are mighty proud of their discovery, which gives them to believe that they will be the heart of the world'; and it is notable that this letter, printed in 1566, contains the first use of 'Mexican' to mean non-Indian inhabitants of New Spain.[60]

Rica de Oro y de Plata; Hawaii?

The Galleon route had two by-products of interest: first the search for mysterious (and of course rich) islands in the Northwest Pacific; second—at a far remove— claims of a European discovery of Hawaii, long before Cook's visit in 1778.

Of all mythical isles of gold and silver, perhaps none has had a longer paper existence than Rica de Oro and Rica de Plata, supposedly lying between 25° and 40°N and at an indefinite distance east of Japan. Pedro de Unamuno searched for them in 1587 and, so early, expressed disbelief in their existence; but the Dutch looked for them in the 1640s, the Spaniards did not officially write them off until 1741—and one or the other of them appeared in atlases of repute as late as 1927.[61] Findlay in 1870 listed at least eleven highly dubious reports of islands in this general area, and his irritated comments recall those of the more level-headed Spanish officials.[62]

The origin of the fiction is in the report of a Portuguese ship—no name, no date—blown east from Japan to rich islands, with white and civil people; they were known, from a merchant on board, as the Armenian's Islands, later as Rica de Oro and de Plata. What core of experience there may be in the fable is not of vast import, but the story seems to stem from Francisco Gali's voyage of 1584, more important as really bringing home the vast width of the North Pacific. He took over a Manila Galleon which had put into Macao, obviously to take on cargo for New Spain—illicitly, for though the Crowns were now united, their colonies and commerce were by law as exclusive as ever. Gali probably heard the tale in Macao; at all events, he looked unsuccessfully for 'Armenicão'.

His report inspired Fray Andrés de Aguirre, who had been with Urdaneta in the *San Pedro*, to recall an old but seductive document he had seen long ago.

Dahlgren suggests that this account of Aguirre's is a recollection of a Portuguese letter of 1548 read by him with Urdaneta in 1565—two decades earlier!—and that the islands were in the Ryukyus (Lequeos), which in the earlier decades of European penetration in these regions were important and wealthy intermediaries between China and Japan, while both Chinese and Japanese were certainly civil people and commonly described by the Portuguese as white. Mere lapse of memory, with the lapse of time, would account for Aguirre's placing of them east and not south of Japan. Chassigneux finds this reasoning 'very ingenious . . . [but] very difficult to accept', and invokes a double typhoon, which could give the impression that a ship was blown far to the east when in fact it was brought south. His own reasoning is even more intricately ingenious than Dahlgren's: he opts for Okinawa, pointing out that its raised coral soil supports a temperate-looking vegetation, so that it might seem to be more northerly than it is, and that the trade of the Ryukyus had been so cut out by the Iberians that by 1573 they were virtually unknown. However, as Okinawa is the main island of the Ryukyus, all these distinctions end up in no difference at all.[63]

There were other factors in the quest for these islands than the sufficient one of gold and silver. The Bonin and Volcano groups, which lay athwart of the track of Galleons making their northing, offered no satisfactory way-station; they were rather hazards. Yet it was in this section that ships were most liable to hurricane damage and, as we shall see in Chapter 6, refuge in Japan carried other perils. It would, then, be most valuable to have a place for refitment *before* entering 'the great gulf of Nueva España', that is the vast North Pacific embayment. This was the main motivation in the early seventeenth century, and again in the 1730s, when efforts were made to re-awaken official Spanish interest in the search.[64] Another, though officially very minor, element was the desire to see whether the 'Straits of Anian' (below, Ch. 9), joining the Mar del Sur and the Mar del Norte or Atlantic, really existed, and if so to forestall other nations in their control.[65] Legendary and elusive, indeed totally fictitious, as Rica de Oro and its sister-isle were, they thus played a considerable role in the exploration of North Pacific waters.

Gali was commissioned to make a further search, but died before he could start, to be replaced by the obscure and possibly shady Pedro de Unamuno. He sailed from Manila in a small ship in July 1587; he found two small islands 'of no value for any purpose', but as for Rica de Oro, Rica de Plata, and the Armenian's Island or Islands—they did not exist. Despite this simple and negative report, the quest was not abandoned; instead of following up Sebastian Vizcaino's strong advocacy of a way-station at Monterey (below, Ch. 5), it was decided to resume the search for these western islands, and in 1611 Vizcaino was sent from Acapulco to Japan to look for them once again.[66] Schurz declares roundly that this diversion of energy 'was responsible for delaying the Spanish settlement of

California for a century and a half', but this is going much too far: the Spaniards had good reason to be wary of spreading small and isolated settlements, and despite Vizcaino and his advocate Fray Antonio de la Ascension, that country had really very little to offer. The renewed interest in it after 1770 took place in greatly altered geostrategic conditions, and was a response to fears of encroachment by other powers, especially the Russians in the north. Nevertheless, the two issues were clearly linked, and the choice was conscious. Vizcaino spent some time cruising east of Japan, and in his turn concluded firmly that 'there were no such islands in the whole world', though as late as 1620 Hernando de los Rios Coronel thought that in these seas 'God has placed an island . . . that serves us as an inn'.[67]

Another element was imported into these unknowns by João da Gama, who in 1589 or 1590 sailed direct from Macao to Acapulco, to the natural anger of the Governor of the Philippines. In the mid-seventeenth century his name was attached, originally on Portuguese maps, to a vague land he sighted northeast of Japan. By 1753, despite a vain search for it by Vitus Bering in 1741, 'Gamaland' was on some charts an archipelago stretching over some 13° of longitude.[68] Possibly it was Yezo itself, or one of the Kuriles, seen and named 'Compagnies Land' by de Vries in 1643.

This Dutch effort by de Vries was the last serious attempt at finding the shadowy Armenian's evasive islands. The first Dutch search was by Mathijs Quast and Abel Tasman in 1639, sailing far into the Pacific between 37° 30' and 40°N and as far as 175°E; naturally they found nothing, but on the way out they examined the Volcano and Bonin Islands more systematically than had the Spaniards. Four years later Maarten de Vries again failed to find Rica de Oro and its fellow, but he penetrated the Kuriles, finding Iturup and Urup; the latter he mistook for a mainland, taking possession and naming it for the Oost-Indische Compagnie.[69]

From time to time Galleon captains saw, or thought they saw, land or signs of land on the northern passage: Gemelli Careri, for instance, in his famous account of 1696–7, tells of a little wind-blown bird, like a canary, which the captain tried to keep alive, 'but being quite spent, with hunger and weariness, it dy'd the same day, and there was sand found in its belly.' All agreed that it could only have come from Rica de Plata, some thirty leagues to the south.[70] We may leave these isles of gold and silver to the oblivion to which they were consigned by Philip V of Spain in his reply (1741) to the demand of the Governor of the Philippines for a new search: the Galleons have got along without them since 1606; nobody has any idea of their position, size, resources, or the nature of their people if any: 'From all the information received, there appears no reasonable encouragement to attempt the aforesaid discovery . . .'.[71] An understatement.

On the maps of today the Hawaiian Islands lie so blatantly between the east- and west-bound tracks of the Galleons that it seems almost mandatory that some stray must have found them. The inference was first drawn by La Pérouse, who deduced from Spanish charts that islands named 'la Mesa', 'los Majos', and 'la Disgraciada', in the right latitude but much too far to the east, were in fact the Hawaiian group, la Mesa ('the Table') in particular being the main island with the great table-massif of Mauna Loa; the error in longitude was put down to Spanish failure to allow for currents. On one such chart is a note saying that Juan Gaetan, who was with Villalobos in 1542, discovered the group, and named it Islas de Mesa, in 1555; unluckily this chart also gives Cook's name, the Sandwich Islands. One must admit that if a non-Polynesian name were to be used, la Mesa would be much preferable to Sandwich.[72]

The argument from maps and documents has been fairly demolished by Dahlgren; it is yet another case of what the great geographer Elisée Reclus called 'the disorderly fluctuation of oceanic isles'.[73] One may, however, enter a caveat against Sharp's objection that to describe Mauna Loa 'as a table is fanciful, since it is a typical rugged volcanic mountain. La Pérouse himself did not see Maunaloa.' Rugged in detail, yes; but it is a shield-type volcano, and seen from the sea, with cloud hanging on the plateau, it would certainly look table-like.

There are also other than written or cartographical evidences: oral traditions, artefacts. Inferences from these have been severely criticised in a competent demolition job by J. F. G. Stokes, but new material has come to light since he wrote. R. A. Langdon makes out a convincing case for regarding the question of one-way Spanish contacts as much more open than it was left by Dahlgren and Stokes, who have received almost complete academic acceptance. Some elements adduced to indicate contact may be discarded, for instance the alleged Spanish style of helmets noted by Cook's officer James King: they are much more like Graeco-Roman or even Etruscan types than the standard Spanish morion or steel-cap, and one may reasonably suppose that King got his notion of armour from romanticised engravings or the stage costuming of his day. But the suggestive oral traditions may well deserve more respectful treatment than they have usually received from academics in reaction against nineteenth century romanticism; there are some intriguing linguistic clues.[74] While iron drifted in pieces of timber has certainly been a factor in the Pacific, the amount and nature of iron in Hawaiian possession in Cook's day may not be so facilely explained; but nor can the possibility of drifted junks from Japan be ruled out.[75] There is also a piece of woven fabric, very like sail-cloth, in an indubitably pre-Cook burial.[76]

It has been suggested that the oral tradition of seven castaways arriving at Kealakekua Bay long before Cook might be not Spaniards but Dutchmen, deserters from Mahu's ship Liefde in 1600; a nice ironic twist, but the decor of the tale and the latitude of the desertion rule this out.[77] But it would seem that Dahlgren's concession that 'It is not incredible' that Spanish castaways reached Hawaii and survived should be amended to 'It is very likely' that they did so. However, this is not 'discovery' in the reasonable sense that the event is put on record and the knowledge made available to others. The one clear thing is that there was no 'discovery' by Juan Gaetan in 1542 or 1555.

Chapter 5

EASTERN SHORES AND SOUTHERN LANDS

... the Spaniard from the east,
His flickering canvas breaking the horizon
That shuts the dead off in a wall of mist.

'Three hundred years since I set out from Lima
And off Espíritu Santo lay down and wept
Because no faith in men, no truth in islands
And still unfound the shining continent slept;

'And swore upon the Cross to come again
Though fever, thirst and mutiny stalked the seas
And poison spiders spun their webs in Spain. . . .'

The Californias: Cermeño and Vizcaino

Unamuno's voyage of 1587 in search of Rica de Oro was no more productive on the eastern shores of the Pacific than in its western waters. He did find a new port, San Lucas, near the present San Luis Obispo, but this seems to have made no impression on the authorities: the current Viceroy of New Spain, Manrique, was simply not interested, although the projected voyage of Juan de la Isla in 1572 and Gali's actual one of 1584 had certainly envisaged exploring the American coast north of 35–40°N.[1] The younger Luis de Velasco, Viceroy in 1590, was however much concerned with the sickness and privations normal in the latter stages of the Galleon passage, and secured authority to investigate this coast to see if there might not be some fit port of succour. To this end the Portuguese Sebastian Rodriguez Cermeño sailed from Manila in the 200-ton *San Agustin* on 5 July 1595.

Cermeño's first objective was Cape Mendocino, which seems to have been known from a disastrous Galleon crossing in 1584.[2] On 6 November, two days after his landfall somewhat north of the Cape, he was at Drake's Bay, which he named Bahia de San Francisco—one may be sure with no intention of a compliment to his predecessor, who was in these waters sixteen years earlier. Here he lost the *San Agustin* in a squall, but assembled a prefabricated launch, and on 8 December sailed south, crossing Monterey Bay (his Bahia de San Pedro) and near Point Concepcion meeting Indians who knew the words 'Mexico' and 'Christiano', probably from Unamuno's party. Food was very short—largely

Douglas Stewart, 'Terra Australis', in *Collected Poems*, Angus & Robertson, Sydney 1967; used (with a trifling emendation) by courtesy of author and publishers.

acorns bartered from the Indians—but despite strong pressure from his crew Cermeño insisted on examining the coast. At Isla San Martin, off Baja California, they were saved by finding a stranded fish said to have been big enough to support seventy men for eight days. Finally he reached Chacala on 7 January 1596.[3]

Cermeño had done his best, but the wrecking of the *San Agustin* robbed him of any reward. She carried (legally) private merchandise, and the ensuing enquiries into its loss concluded that he had crossed promising inlets instead of examining them properly, though it was allowed that he was driven to do so by hunger. The new Viceroy, the Conde de Monterey, drew the sensible inference that further investigation should be made not by trading vessels from Manila but by a special expedition from New Spain.

Sebastian Vizcaino is not an attractive figure, though it may be harsh to say with Wagner that 'there was hardly any Spaniard of his day . . . who wrote more and accomplished less'—in view of the Spanish mania for paper and the many fiascos, this is no small claim. A merchant, Vizcaino had like Cermeño been on the Galleon *Santa Ana* when Cavendish took her, and his letter to his father mentioning this misfortune gives a strong impression that his main interest in life was to make money; as a message from a distant son to an anxious parent, it lacks appeal.[4] Yet he completely supplanted the much finer Cabrillo, most of whose work seems to have been forgotten; only his harbour of San Miguel remained on the maps, until Vizcaino typically renamed it San Diego.[5]

Vizcaino's first voyage, June to December 1596, was financed by a partnership, on a quite substantial scale: three ships, one of 500 tons, and 230 men, with twelve cannon. The aims were colonisation in Baja California, and pearling; a town was founded at La Paz, Cortes's Santa Cruz, but half of it was burnt down, and the infant settlement was abandoned after two months. Vizcaino, clearly a smart operator, bluffed himself out of this fiasco: all that was wrong was the timing of the start, and there were numberless Indians crying out to be saved. . . .

The second expedition, in 1602, was much more tightly controlled by officialdom. The objective was definitely the exploration of the coast up to Cape Mendocino, and if possible beyond it; the Gulf of California and its pearls were strictly barred, unless on the return Vizcaino should find that he had time, good winds, and enough food to explore it—and on past form this last condition surely amounted to a veto.[6] The chronicler of the voyage, Fray Antonio de la Ascension, alleges ulterior aims, notably Quivira and the Straits of Anian. The Father, however, was obviously more romantic than well informed: he was responsible for reviving the idea that Baja California was an island, an idea which had been abandoned as long ago as 1539–40 but now persisted for most of the century—and indeed, despite new evidence that should have been conclusive against it, well into the eighteenth.[7] To Fray Antonio, the channel insulating California communicated with Anian. But he makes good reading: a gruesomely detailed description of scurvy is followed, without transition, by rhapsodies on

Monterey and its 'affable Indians of good disposition and well built [too significant words!] . . . [who] would have much pleasure in seeing us make a settlement in their country. Those who come from China in need of relief could very well resort to this port.' The good Father was also very much taken by the loving kindness of the pelicans in feeding their sick and maimed, and from compassion released one that the Indians were using as a decoy.[8]

Vizcaino sailed from Acapulco on 5 May 1602, with three good ships, 200 selected men, and provisions for a year. Progress against head winds was slow, and it was not until 10 November that he entered San Diego, which he described in nearly the same words as Cabrillo's party; and here, as with Cermeño's nomenclature, he breached his clear instructions to retain already given names; since he had with him one of Cermeño's pilots, he must have known at least the latter's names.[9] On 15 December, seven years after Cermeño, he came to Monterey Bay, which he and Ascension greatly over-rated as a port for the Galleons. At the end of the year Vizcaino sent back the worst of the sick in the almiranta (twenty-five of the thirty-four died) and himself went on with the *San Diego* and the launch *Tres Reyes*; he called in at Cermeño's Bahia de San Francisco (renamed 'Don Gaspar') and reached Cape Mendocino on 12 January 1603. The *Tres Reyes* was driven north to Cape Blanco, reporting a great 'Rio de Martin Aguilar' (named for her dead commander) which was probably either the Mad or the Rogue River of today. Despite their striking names, neither of these is of special note, but in the eighteenth century Aguilar's river became inflated into a mighty estuary, the entrance into the Strait of Anian.[10] Vizcaino was back in Acapulco by 21 March.

Considering his resources, and the aid of the pilot Bolaños who had been with Cermeño, Vizcaino's achievement compares unfavourably with that of Cabrillo sixty years earlier; but the work of his forerunners was for the time effectively blanketed by his new toponymy. However, in October 1603 the Marques de Montesclaros succeeded the Conde de Monterey, and the new Viceroy was not impressed by the glowing reports on the Bay named in honour of his predecessor. Although in 1606 a royal decree was issued naming Vizcaino to command a Galleon returning from Manila to 'ascertain in what manner the said port of Monterrey can be colonised and made permanent', it arrived after he had left for Spain, and the project lapsed in favour of another search for our old friends Rica de Oro and de Plata.[11]

Interest in the Californias, till near the end of the seventeenth century, relapsed into concentration on pearling ventures in the Gulf.[12] Vizcaino made large claims for Monterey; he also claimed to have been near China and Japan, an old illusion stemming from a supposedly marked northwestward trend of the coast of Alta California. The later riches of the modern State of California, except perhaps for timber, were not apparent from the coast; as Brebner says, the neglect of Alta California was not accidental, and even with the greater resources of the eighteenth century, there was very little economic development, extensive stock-rearing apart, in the three-quarters of a century of Spanish and Mexican rule.[13] Simply for rest and refreshment of the Galleon crews, a port on this coast would

Plate X. THE NORTH PACIFIC: DE JODE 1578. Islands in the Philippines are confused but recognisable; there is some notion of Japan, which is separated from the Lequeos; Anian and Quivira are established; but the Ocean is still far too narrow. From G. de Jode, *Speculum Orbis Terrarum* (Amsterdam 1578), facsimile published by Theatrum Orbis Terrarum BV (Amsterdam 1965). By courtesy of Mr N. Israel, Amsterdam. ANU.

have been helpful; but it would have meant delays unacceptable to the mercantile interests of New Spain. In any case, Cabrillo's San Miguel (San Diego) would have been more to the point than Monterey, which is within the area of fog risk and, as a colony, would have been much more isolated and vulnerable.

Three hundred leagues from New Spain the east-bound Galleons saw the first

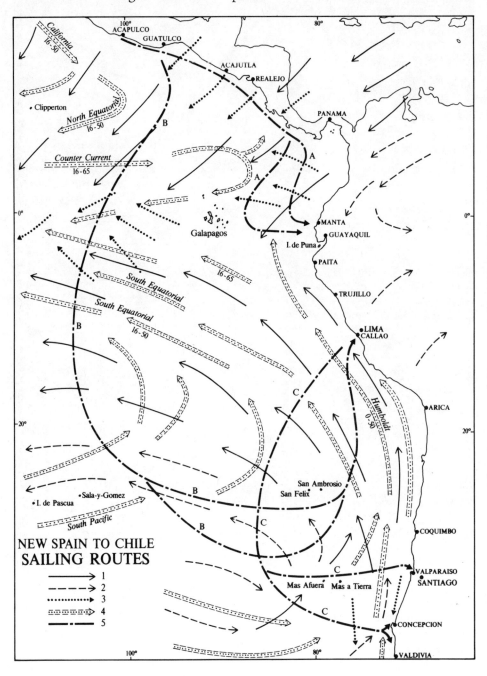

of the *senas* or signs of land—various seaweeds which appeared in a regular order, seals and dogfish—and then

> *Te Deum* was sung, and all persons congratulated one another with the sound of drums and trumpets . . . This unseasonable rejoicing was caus'd by that long and dreadful voyage of above 3,000 leagues; which makes them think themselves in the port, when they have 700 leagues to it . . . It now appear'd that the pilots had mistaken above 200 leagues in their accounts. . . .[14]

There were handsome tips for the first sailor to sight the *senas*, and a boisterous court was held, as for 'crossing the Line'. Careri brings the scene before us vividly, the release from tension when at last they knew where they were; life on the passage was poor, nasty, brutish—and *long*, so long!

The *senas* were indeed regarded as a reliable indicator of longitude. From this point the Galleons trended southeast until making a landfall; the coast was usually in sight, but it was regarded as dangerous and the people as hostile, so no landing was made: 'The prospect . . . of Acapulco, "the safest and finest port in all the North parts", was too strong an inducement'.[15] The very few landings which were made, under stress of weather, in sterile Baja California provided no inducement for sojourn.

As for the argument for a defensive base north of New Spain, Montesclaros disposed of it in a letter of 4 August 1607 from Acapulco, and in almost the same terms as Manrique had used twenty years before: the security of these parts lay simply in their inaccessibility. An isolated settlement would be but an added target for intruders, a bait rather than a bulwark; Dutch or English 'would find Spaniards with whom to treat and trade . . . as they do in the north of Santo Domingo'—that is, on the island which was the first base of Spanish power in the Indies: a give-away sentence indeed! Hence each Manila ship would need two armed escorts. . . . In short, as Wagner puts it, a Spanish settlement 'would have been of more service to the English than one of their own even if they could have maintained it'.[16]

The eastern thresholds; Juan Fernandez (Fig. 13)

Quite as important as these northern coastal reconnaissances, indeed a good deal more important until well after the middle of the eighteenth century, was the discovery of the open-sea routes between the Spanish centres on the eastern

◀*Figure 13.* NEW SPAIN TO CHILE: SAILING ROUTES. 1, dominant winds in January, over 80 per cent observations excluding calms; 2, in January, 25-80 per cent; 3, variations in July, all 41-60 per cent; 4, currents with speeds in km per day; 5, sailing routes: A, 'on the meridian'; B, 'on the latitude'; C, Juan Fernandez' route.

Compiled from *Fiziko-Geograficheskiy Atlas Mira* (Moscow 1964), Plates 40–1 (winds); V. I. Voitov and D. D. Tomarkin, map in W. G. Solheim (ed.), *Archaeology at the 11th Pacific Science Congress* (Honolulu 1967) at 89 (currents); British Admiralty Charts 5215, 5216. Routes from literary sources, approximate only.

shores of the Pacific. The Doldrums, the belt of equatorial light variable winds and calms, and the remarkably strong and persistent Humboldt or Peru Current running northwards from about 45°S to the Equator, closely parallel to the coast, are major obstacles to easy communication by sail. For most of the year, but especially in the northern summer, the westerly bulge of South America has prevailing south or southeasterly winds; and these conditions persist far south of Arica, where the coast takes a straight north-south trend. From the Isthmus to southern Mexico winds are weak and uncertain, with spells (often lengthy) of calms. In the northern winter, conditions are marginally better: Mexican and Nicaraguan waters have light winds from northeast to northwest, with occasional storms, 'Tehuantepeckers' or 'Papagallos', from north; while as far south as Ecuador there is a better chance of picking up a northerly wind, and from January to March there actually may be a southwards current (*el Niño*) for a short distance on either side of the Gulf of Guayaquil. 'El Niño' (so called from its advent about the feast of the Christ-child) is irregular in occurrence (though this is disputed) and is of less significance for navigation than as bringing heavy rains to the coast, leading to floods on land, and at sea, owing to an influx of warm water from the north, to catastrophic if temporary disruption of Peruvian fisheries.[17]

It follows that at least as far north as the Isthmus, sailing north is at all times easier than sailing south; indeed, while from April to September the passage Callao-Guatulco could often be made in four to six weeks, the reverse voyage could take seven or eight months. The normal time in the favourable (northern winter) season was two or three months, keeping fairly close to the coast (to keep the light northerlies) as far as the Gulf of Panama, then sailing (or trying to) south, perhaps as far as a sight of the Galapagos Islands. Landfall was made near Manta, a wretched little town (only seventeen *vecinos* in 1570) about 1°S, or at Santa Elena or Isla de Puna: these were better placed for shelter, water, food, and timber (with asphalt for caulking at Santa Elena), and served as outports for Guayaquil, whose deltaic approaches were difficult for ocean-going ships. The Galapagos themselves were accidentally discovered in 1535 by Bishop Tomas de Berlanga, on his way to Peru; perhaps the only prelate to make such a discovery, if we discount St Brandan. . . . This route 'on the meridian' was at any rate better than following the coast: near Manta the Bishop met people who had been on a galleon from Nicaragua for eight months. Little wonder that the run from New Spain to the Philippines was considered much easier than that to Peru.

In the unfavourable season, the voyage to Peru could be made 'on the parallel', striking south across the Trades to 30°S (or, later, even as far as Juan Fernandez, 30° 42′ S) and then northeast to pick up the southerly winds or currents of the Peruvian coast. This route was probably discovered about 1540-4, by a pilot with Cortes's man Diego de Ocampo; but as it still took three or four months, it seems to have been all but forgotten later in the century. In the good season, there was not a great gain in time over the meridian route, but in later colonial days the 'parallel' track, was used when ships could not wait for the open-

ing of the normal sailing season. Its analogue farther south, Juan Fernandez'
course from Callao to Chile, was more significant.

Between the discoveries of these two open-sea routes, notable work was done
in the maze of channels and islands along the stormy fiord coast of Chile south of
Chiloé: a most intricate and hazardous navigation, on shores still imperfectly
known in the first half of this century, and indeed not giving up all their secrets
until the advent of aerial survey.[18] The first southern voyage, under Francisco
de Ulloa and Cortes Ojea, in 1553–4, penetrated thirty leagues into the Straits of
Magellan, but was surpassed as a feat of seamanship four years later by that of
Juan Ladrillero and Ojea, which left Valdivia or Concepcion on 17 November
1557, with three very small ships and sixty men—commissioned, amongst other
things, to look for spices! (This may not be as absurd as it looks, since there may
well have been reports of the cinnamon-like 'Winter's bark', so named for
Drake's captain, and so useful to Sarmiento's wretched colonists.) Ojea, the
almirante, became separated, and reached nearly to the Straits; but he missed the
entrance, and jumped to the conclusion that some island torn from its moorings
by tempest had grounded and jammed the channel—presumably the origin of
the idea that the Straits had been blocked by an earthquake. Unfortunately, the
poet Ercilla gave currency to the myth in the opening canto of his very popular
epic La Araucana (1569); it at least reflects the fact that a major hindrance to the
west-east passage was the difficulty of identifying the right entrance in this maze
of inlets. On the return journey from his farthest fiord, still called 'Ultima
Esperanza', Ojea wintered in extremely harsh conditions, living largely on seaweeds, the staple of the local Indians; these were thievish, but friendly, presenting
the Spaniards with packets of coloured earth so that they could paint themselves
decently. After rebuilding his bergantin, Ojea reached Valdivia on 1 October
1558. Meanwhile, Ladrillero went down the wild western coast of the Fuegian
archipelago to the Canal Santa Barbara in 54°S, and then penetrated the Straits
to the Atlantic end. He wintered in more comfort than Ojea and was back in
Concepcion by mid-1559, bringing 'a detailed account of the hydrography of
the Chilean archipelagoes and the Strait of Magellan which was not improved
on until the nineteenth century',[19] except perhaps by parts of Sarmiento's survey.
Obscure voyages, all but forgotten, but resolute and daring.

Fray Reginaldo de Lizarraga tells of a Santiagueño 'conceived and born at sea' on
the Callao-Chile run, 'and his mother became pregnant again, and still they had
not reached the port of Coquimbo.'[20] A good story, which at least emphasises
the contrast between the northwards passage, running with winds and current,
taking only three or four weeks, and the southwards, at best as many months,
and sometimes the greater part of a twelvemonth. The discoverer of the open-sea
route which circumvented these inordinate delays was one of the twenty-six
people, several of them sailors, living in Santiago de Chile in the 1570s, and all
named Juan Fernandez; the meticulous researches of José Toribio Medina have

narrowed the field to one.[21] He also discovered the island long named after him, but since 1966, by official decree of the Republic of Chile, styled Robinson Crusoe's Island.

Juan Fernandez seems to have come to Chile about 1550-1, and in the next twelve years had much experience, as boatswain and later master, in navigation between Peru and Chile. In February 1574 he was in command of the *Nuestra Señora dos Remedios* from Valparaiso to Callao; and when, on 27 October 1574, he took her out on the return, there can be scarcely any doubt that his southwestwards track—into the open Pacific—was deliberate. The wind regime on the coast is such that he could hardly have been blown off-shore; on the other hand, he was a close friend of Gallego, Mendaña's pilot on the 1567 voyage to the Solomons, and from him he must have learnt that once out of the mainstream of the Humboldt Current, and well into the Southeast Trades, winds and currents made a good southing much easier than it was close to the coast.

On 6 November Fernandez sighted the barren rocky islands he named San Felix and San Ambor (a Saint so obscure, even to Spaniards, that he was soon replaced by San Ambrosio), and on the 22nd two islands which he named for the day, Santa Cecilia's. These were certainly the group known by his name, but it is not clear whether the two were Mas-a-Tierra and Mas Afuera ('Nearer Land' and 'Further Away') or the former and the nearby little island of Santa Clara. Thirty days from Callao he reached a Chilean port, either Valparaiso or Concepcion; and there was no further need for embarrassing confinements on board. Although his island did not appear on the maps until early in the next century, his 'new navigation' was soon adopted as the standard track.

One of the founders of Santiago, Juan Jufre (who introduced goats to Chile, and hence, at a remove, to Crusoe's Island), backed a reconnaissance in 1575, perhaps under Fernandez, though it is not certain the latter ever set foot on his islands. Nothing came of this, but in 1576 Fernandez was sent by Jufre (who had wanted Sarmiento for command, but that redoubtable figure was in trouble with the Inquisition) to discover 'the islands which are frontier to this kingdom.' Knowledge of this expedition rests on one of the memorials with which the highly uncritical Dr Luis Arias sought to revive, in the totally unfavourable climate of Philip III's reign, the grand designs of Mendaña and Quiros for a vast religious imperialism in the South Sea. Fernandez is said to have sailed, from about 40°S, on a westsouthwest course for one month—and to have discovered a land with well-clad white people and many fine rivers. In the eighteenth century this was taken up enthusiastically by Alexander Dalrymple—to whom it must of course have been Terra Australis—and considered more cautiously by James Burney; it has been variously identified as Easter Island, New Zealand, Australia, the Solomons, Tahiti, and (by the Chilean Vicuña Mackenna) as fantasy; which last seems most probable.[22] Arias himself is most confused, and his evidence is—at best—third-hand; Medina makes a gallant attempt to show that Fernandez found somewhere, say Tahiti, but carries no conviction. At all events, what with the Araucanian Wars and Drake's raid nothing could be done—the heretics might hear of it—and any follow-up was put off from day to day until Juan Fernandez died in 1599. The mantle fell on Quiros.

At this point it is convenient to sketch the history of Juan Fernandez Island, and its strategic significance, into the eighteenth century. An ineffectual attempt at colonisation was made in 1591–6, and again in 1599, by Sebastian Garcia, who became a Jesuit and deeded his grant to his Society; in 1642 Tasman proposed that it should be made a Dutch base, and there was a feeble Jesuit attempt at exploiting their claim in the early 1660s.[23] The earlier Dutch incursions missed the island, but Schouten and Le Maire found it in 1616, and 'it became thereafter a sought-after haven for navigators of all flags . . . but most particularly for those who would not find a welcome in the ports of Spanish America'[24]—which meant any flag but Spain's. Early and late in the period it was a place of refreshment for the Nassau Fleet (1624) and Roggeveen (1722), but above all it was a base for the English (and odd French) buccaneers—Sharp, Wafer, Dampier, Cowley, Cook, Davis, Rogers, Stradling, Shelvocke, Clipperton; only Morgan is missing from the roll-call. For the southeast Pacific it was as potent a magnet as Guam in the west; the South Sea Company had vague plans for 'the Gibraltar of the Pacific', and Roggeveen and de Brosses suggested settlement by the Netherlands and France respectively.

Spanish warships visited the islands in occasional defensive flurries, and from time to time left ferocious dogs to kill the goats so valuable to the buccaneers, or at least to drive them to inaccessible heights—a strange defence measure for an empire. But not until 1750, after the visit of the most illustrious corsair of all (after Drake)—Anson—did Bourbon Spain take the logical step of settling and fortifying an island which after all should have been easy to supply, only a few days' sail from Valparaiso. Soon after Anson's stay, Juan and Ulloa, as part of their famous inspection of the Pacific colonies, examined both Mas Afuera and Mas-a-Tierra, and made positive and specific recommendations for the fortification of the latter.[25] When it was at last done, it was done secretly and effectively: great was the surprise of Philip Carteret, in 1767, to find 'a great number of men all about the beach' and Spanish colours flying over a stone fort with a score of embrasures—a far cry from Alexander Selkirk's hut and his ballet of goats and cats.[26]

The Southland I: Mendaña and the Bay of the Star (Figs. 14 and 15)

King Solomon's servants had brought much gold from Ophir, bringing it to 'Eziongeber, which is beside Eloth, on the shore of the Red Sea': somewhere east of Suez, then—Scripture said it—lay a land of incalculable wealth. Ptolemy's Golden Khersonese was an obvious candidate; so were the mysterious islands of Veach and Locach and Maletur, 'the misbegotten progeny of Polo'; some Portuguese thought that Ophir would be found in East Africa, in the hinterland

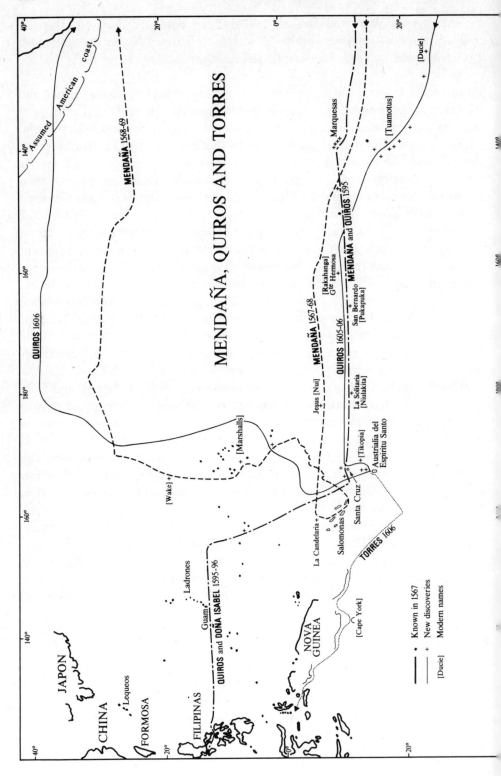

MENDAÑA, QUIROS AND TORRES

MENDAÑA 1568-69

QUIROS 1606

Assumed American coast

[Ducie]

[Tuamotus]

Marquesas

MENDAÑA and QUIROS 1595

MENDAÑA 1567-68

QUIROS 1605-06

[Rakahanga]
Gte Hermosa

San Bernardo
[Pukapuka]

Jesus [Nui]

La Solitaria
[Niulakita]

[Marshalls]

[Wake]

Austrialia del
Espíritu Santo

[Tikopia]

Santa Cruz

La Candelaria

Salomonas

TORRES 1606

Ladrones

Guam

QUIROS and DOÑA ISABEL 1595-96

NOVA
GUINEA

[Cape York]

JAPON

CHINA

Lequeos

FORMOSA

FILIPINAS

·   Known in 1567
+   New discoveries
[Ducie]   Modern names

of Sofala, where later romance would place 'King Solomon's Mines'; Magellan opted for the Lequeos, Columbus thought he had found it in Española: 'as geographical knowledge extended eastwards and westwards without Ophir being recognised, its supposed position moved with that knowledge, always a little ahead of the latest discovery.'[27] And in Peru a new element was added, particularly in the active mind of Pedro Sarmiento de Gamboa: tales of Tupac Yupanqui's Inca fleet with 20,000 men, which had found black people—and gold—in islands to the west; while across the Pacific in the Moluccas, Galvão had heard that in Chile Valdivia had news of an island king, beyond whom 'were the Amazones, whose queene was called Guanomilla, that is to say, the golden heauen', so that there must be great riches there, 'and also at an Island called Solomon'.[28] The resulting voyages—by Mendaña in 1567-9, Mendaña and Quiros in 1595-6, Quiros and Torres in 1605-6—are among the most remarkable in the whole history of maritime discovery, alike in their geographical results (long misunderstood as these were) and as a story of high ideals, bitter disillusions and sufferings, baseness and grandeur.

By the mid-1560s the Spice Islands were officially barred, the Philippines were becoming an annexure of New Spain; and quite apart from the restraints of policy, the developing knowledge of the wind-systems and the precedent of Grijalva's disaster were hardly encouraging for any Peruvian enterprise in these directions. The southwest was open, and already in the 1550s voyages thither were being mooted; and in 1565 there was a definite project for finding 'some islands, called Solomon, which lie over opposite Chile'—the first quasi-official use of the name.[29] This came to nothing—the scratch company recruited was suspected of planning to turn pirate, and hastily disbanded—but in 1567 the interim Governor Garcia de Castro appointed his young and inexperienced nephew Alvaro de Mendaña y Neyra to command two ships to find rich islands 'between New Guinea and this coast'. In Mendaña's mind the prime motive of settlement was the conversion of the heathen; this probably had only the most intermittent appeal for the rank-and-file or for Sarmiento, who later claimed to have initiated the project (he was at any rate active in its organisation) and to have declined the offered command, on condition of retaining overall control. This is unlikely; his position was captain of the flagship, not Chief Pilot, but in his own view he was at least on a par with that officer; as in so many Spanish voyages, the command was far from harmonious. Objectives were also unclear, as was doubtless inevitable, but seem to have been first of all Sarmiento's Western Isles, anywhere between 14 and 23°S and not far from Peru, and then Terra Australis itself, the great land-mass thought to run from New Guinea to Magellanica.

The hastily prepared *Los Reyes* and *Todos Santos*, with about 100 men, left Callao on 19 November 1567, the day of Santa Ysabel, who became patroness of the voyage. The *Los Reyes* was capitana, and carried Mendaña, Sarmiento,

◄*Figure 14*. MENDAÑA, QUIROS, AND TORRES

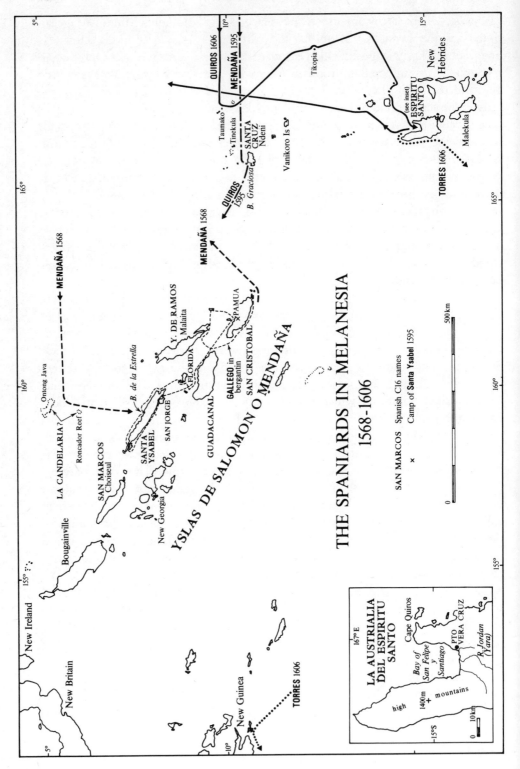

THE SPANIARDS IN MELANESIA
1568-1606

SAN MARCOS   Spanish C16 names
          ×   Camp of **Santa Ysabel** 1595

0   500 km

YSLAS DE SALOMON O MENDAÑA

LA AUSTRIALIA
DEL ESPIRITU
SANTO

Cape Quiros

Bay of
San Felipe
y
Santiago

PTO
VERA CRUZ

R. Jordan
(Yara)

high   mountains

1400m +

0   10 km

167° E

15° S

and the Chief Pilot Hernan Gallego, who had been with Ulloa and Ladrillero in Magellanic waters. They sailed westsouthwest to about 15° 45'S, then west by north and finally west. This change of course was strongly criticised by Sarmiento, who held that they were instructed to press on, and was also angry at Mendaña's refusal to investigate a cloudbank which Sarmiento thought might have been land. This insistence, and Gallego's promise on the last day of the year—already six weeks out—that they would find land by the end of January make it difficult to credit Mendaña's statement that they were provisioned 'for at least a month'. As Wallis says, that would mean not much over a month; but though the water was bad, it was not exhausted, and there seems no hint as yet of a real food crisis.[30] It is possible that in changing course Gallego had his own plan, to discover New Guinea from the east, basing himself on Bernardo de la Torre's Cabo de la Cruz (or Cruzes) on that coast, which was thought to be only 600 leagues from Peru.[31]

On 15 or 16 January 1568 they came to an 'Ysla de Jesus', most likely Nui or some near-by island in the Ellices. Here again Sarmiento made trouble, criticising the failure to land and take possession (Gallego being unwilling to risk the ships, or to delay), and later hinting to the soldiers that they had left behind a kingdom.[32] Continuing generally westwards, on 1 February, Candlemas Day, they reached some shoals they named 'Bajos de la Candelaria', either Ontong Java or Roncador Reef.[33] Then at dawn on Saturday the 7th they saw a large high land, no little atoll: Santa Ysabel, the largest truly Pacific Island yet seen by Europeans. It was fifteen leagues away, and they did not come close-to until late on Sunday: people came out in canoes, shy until a sailor swam to them, eager for caps and bells, thievish once they had nerved themselves to come aboard, but very friendly and soon imitating the sign of the cross and the Lord's Prayer. The ships could not find a harbour that night, but on Monday made port, being guided by a bright star, resplendent in full day-light—surely the Star of the East. Here in the Bahia de la Estrella (still so named), they landed and took possession, the Franciscans singing *Vexilla Regis prodeunt*—'the banners of the King press on'.[34]

The bright omen was deceptive, though for a time all went well. By early April they had built a bergantin, and in the next month it visited the north coast of Guadalcanal and circumnavigated Ysabel. By the time it returned to Estrella Bay, relations with the 'Indians' had deteriorated, and the whole expedition shifted to Guadalcanal, settling on 12 May at Puerto de la Cruz, the site of the present agreeable little capital, Honiara. A week later the bergantin went out again, following the north coast of Guadalcanal, then across to Malaita and down to San Cristobal, returning to Puerto de la Cruz on 6 June. The ships then moved to an anchorage on San Cristobal, where they careened while the bergantin explored the south coast of the island. The work done in six months by Gallego and his co-pilot Ortega was notable (Fig. 15): very much of the coasts of Santa

◄*Figure 15*. THE SPANIARDS IN MELANESIA, 1568–1606

Ysabel, Malaita (Ysla de Ramos), Guadalcanal, San Cristobal, and Florida had been examined, as well as many smaller islands, and Choiseul (their San Marcos) and New Georgia (Arrecifes) had been sighted. Although Gallego greatly over-estimated the sizes of his islands, many of his sites can still be identified with precision, and many of the Spanish names for the islands actually visited remain on the maps. This side of the work was done well. But the bright star had dimmed; the hopes of settlement and of converting the heathen had foundered utterly.

The first friendly reception, when after their visitors had come ashore the Indians had danced to Spanish fifes and guitars and their own Pan-pipes, when their leader Bileban-Arra and Mendaña had exchanged names—they were both *tauriquis* or chiefs—had gone sour. The islanders, faced with the intrusion of scores of non-producers demanding food, had gone into sullen retreat; the Spaniards naturally enough did not understand that their consumer demand meant the disruption of a nicely, even precariously, balanced economy. Mendaña, a genuinely honest and high-minded man, asked the friars what could be done; they—understanding something, but not enough—replied that parties should go out foraging for essentials: if nothing was offered, food and food alone could be taken, but the villages should not be stripped, and proper and adequate gifts should be left in exchange. It is clear that sincere efforts were made to live up to this semi-self-denying ordinance; but in time they inevitably broke down. Sarmiento, almost a throw-back to the earlier and tougher conquistadores, was not the best man to be put in charge of foraging. He was sent inland, and scaled the central range of Ysabel, a feat not repeated until this century. On the whole he held himself in hand for the time being, but it could not last: the gulf of misunderstanding was too great.

The Indians resorted to guerrilla harassment, interspersed with gestures, which in their own culture would show friendly intent. On at least one occasion these took the form of presenting human flesh for Spanish delectation, which was counter-productive. The dreary syndrome was repeated when the Spaniards moved to Guadalcanal; and we may be sure that news of the strange invaders had travelled ahead. The prizes of war were pigs, desperately needed by the Spaniards, central treasures in the local culture. Here, with a real food crisis, Sarmiento devastated a village (to Mendaña's anger) and took hostages by treachery. Nine Spaniards were killed in retaliation, and it became clear that cannibalism would not be kept within the family: the purser Catoira convinced himself that one Indian felt the legs of a soldier, his destined share of the feast, to see if they were tender. . . .[35] So a possibly friendly native group was counter-massacred, the quartered bodies being left where the Spaniards had been slain, and Sarmiento burned all accessible villages. The process began anew on San Cristobal.

It was time to go. A council was held on 7 August: Mendaña, assuming that the islands were outliers of a great landmass, wished to press south for another ten or twelve degrees; Gallego argued that, while they had enough provisions for a return voyage, little more food could be gathered by scouting round the islands—and the ships were in very poor shape. In view of the distance from Peru, much greater than had been anticipated, the food shortage, and native hostility, it was generally agreed that settlement was impossible; Mendaña, Sarmiento, and a couple of gold-hungry soldiers dissented, but Gallego won the day. Any course but a return would probably have meant disaster. Mendaña accepted the decision, but so reluctantly that he persistently tried to make the pilots head southeast, into the Trades, alleging that the winds would change with the Equinox and that they would thus make Chile, though it is clear that he was still hankering for a Southland. The pilots replied, unanswerably, 'the landsman reasons and the seaman navigates', and after a month formally protested against further vacillations: the only way of salvation was by New Spain. Only then did Mendaña give way completely.[36]

North of the Equator they came across an island which Gallego identified as Salazar's San Bartolomé (Taongi) but which was actually Namu in the Marshalls; some rope and a nail fitted to a stick were probably relics of Villalobos or the *San Geronimo* in 1566. Further on, in 19–20° N, they sailed round the very isolated atoll of Wake Island (not seen again until 1796), and in mid-October the almiranta, now under Sarmiento's command, parted company. The *Los Reyes* lost its main-mast in a great storm—in forty-five years Gallego had not seen its like—but they patched up a jury-rig, at first with no more sail than a blanket, and came through, although the ship 'being built only for the coast of Peru, for which work she was good enough . . . was only fit to drown us all'.[37] The soldiers, racked with scurvy and reduced (like Mendaña himself) to a daily ration of 'half a pint of water, and half of that was crushed cockroaches', clamoured that 'they no longer had any faith in charts and papers' and demanded to turn back, which presumably meant a course for the Philippines, where Legazpi was still on Cebu. Faced with this lunacy, Mendaña asserted himself, for once in accord with his pilots: land must surely be near. Murmuring continued until, next day, a log 'clean and quite free from barnacles' was picked up; but it was still eight more days until, on 19 December, they sighted Baja California. Near the tip of the peninsula they rested and watered, and the sick were fed on pelicans; a great white cockatoo brought from the Solomons, 'a very rare bird, the like of which has never been seen', had been sacrificed to the same end. They could not make Navidad, and it was not till 23 January 1569 that they entered a Christian port, Colima, where three days later Sarmiento rejoined in the *Todos Santos*.[38]

The voyage was not yet over, nor were their troubles. Sarmiento was the first problem: he was obviously insubordinate, and Mendaña had him arrested, prob-ably to obviate false charges against himself. The transaction is obscure; Sarmiento was soon released, but either he or Mendaña, or both, thought it imprudent for him to come on to Peru. The battered voyagers were well received at Colima, but it was not much of a port and they could not refit there, while all down the coast, from Acapulco to Realejo, they were met at first with alarmed suspicion, only allayed when Gallego was recognised by fellow-pilots: John Hawkins had been on the Atlantic coast two years earlier, and since 'it had not been certified that we were not Lutherans' they were taken for 'strange Scottish people', up to no good. At Realejo they were at last able to repair the ships, but only by Mendaña and Gallego pledging their personal credit. They did not reach Callao until 11 September 1569; they had been gone over twenty-two months.[39]

The Southland had not been found, and the position of the islands actually discovered was far from certain. Unable to make adequate allowance for the favourable South Equatorial Current, Gallego had greatly underestimated the distance run from Callao to the Bajos de la Candelaria, making it 1638 leagues against an actual 2284, about 9700 and 13,525 km—a shortfall of over 28 per cent. It is true that he was able to deduce, correctly, that the islands lay not far southeast of New Guinea; but this depended on a grossly reduced figure for the width of the Pacific. With the techniques at Gallego's command, the error is excusable; but it set the Solomons on a wildly errant career.[40]

Yet the existence of large high islands might well point to a mother-continent not far away, and indeed might not the islands seen to the west—Choiseul and New Georgia—be promontories from the main? If no *tierra firme* had been discovered, neither had any significant wealth been revealed; there were hints of gold, fallacious, but enough to spark off wild rumours along the waterfronts of the New World. Lopez Vaz, a Portuguese captured off La Plata by the Earl of Cumberland's men in 1587, spoke with great confidence of 40,000 pesos of gold, 'besides great store of cloves and ginger', brought back by Mendaña—this although the Spaniards 'were not seeking or being desirous of gold'! He added the intriguing suggestion that the Solomons had been so named 'to the ende that the Spaniards supposing them to bee those Isles from whence Salomon fetched gold to adorne the Temple at Jerusalem, might bee the more desirous to goe and inhabite the same'.[41] The Ophirian Conjecture was far from dead; only Ophir was as elusive as ever.

To Mendaña, the isles, and their souls crying for salvation, became an obsession. He went to Spain with his uncle the Governor in 1569, and presented a too-glowing prospectus of his discovery and the opportunities it offered. Doubtless by the influence of de Castro, now on the Council of the Indies, he obtained in 1574 authority for a substantial expedition to found a colony of which he would become marquis: it seemed as if the old days of the Conquista had come again. But when he arrived in Peru, in 1577, he found the climate changed. His uncle was far away, and the new Viceroy, the great Francisco de Toledo, saw no point in such expensive ventures, even as a way of getting rid of turbulent soldiers of fortune—after all, they came back just the same, and claimed rewards for their services. Sarmiento was high in Toledo's favour, and corsairs more real than the phantasmal *gente estrangera escoseses* were soon to rock the Spanish Pacific world: while Drake and Cavendish were at large, not a ship or man or peso could be spared for adventures however pious.[42] But with the capture of Richard Hawkins off modern Ecuador in 1594 the immediate threat was eased; and Sarmiento, after his abortive fortification of the Straits of Magellan against a second Drake, and a polite captivity in England and a harsher one by Huguenot Frenchmen, was safely off the scene. A new Viceroy, the Marques de Cañete, was more favourably disposed than the ferociously realist Toledo. But it was a quarter of a century after Mendaña's return to Callao before he could set out once more on his quest.

The Southland II: Mendaña and the Holy Cross, Quiros and Doña Isabel

In all 'the tragical history of the Sea' there can scarcely be a more moving and terrible story than that of Mendaña's second, and last, voyage, unless it be Sarmiento's lingering disaster in the Straits. Mendaña's story is recorded by a poet, Luis de Belmonte Bermudez, the secretary to the Chief Pilot, Pedro Fernandez de Quiros, or, to give him his Portuguese name, Queiroz. The substance of the account is definitely from Quiros; the words are often those of the poet; it is an astonishingly vivid narrative, with much use of direct speech, which has been an inspiration to poets in our own day. The story, with its sequel in Quiros's own voyage ten years later, is one of almost unrelieved tragedy, and tragedy in the true and highest sense, that of the collapse of an ideal which its holders believed to be divinely inspired, in the hands of the pitiable human instruments.[43]

Mendaña's aim was to found a God-fearing colony whence the light of the Gospel should spread. His instruments were four ships and 378 men and women, who included six religious; and also his wife Doña Isabel Barreto and her three brothers. On these, and on the Camp-Master Manrique, a quarrelsome old soldier, the divine light did not shine. The only leading figure, apart from the friars, who fully shared Mendaña's enthusiasm (the word is used in its older theological sense) was probably Quiros, though some humbler men and women had at least the gift of charity. There were others, such as the soldier rebuked by Quiros for wantonly shooting and slaying an islander with a child in his arms, who replied that he was very sorry the Devil had to take those destined for him, but then he had a reputation to maintain as a good shot.

From the start, the expedition was confused and disorderly. The moment he came aboard Manrique interfered in seamen's matters and quarrelled with Doña Isabel and Quiros. The two galleons and two smaller ships left Callao on 9 April 1595, and went north to Paita, provisioning, or rather requisitioning, at small ports en route: at one the almiranta was exchanged, by mixed force and fraud, for what they thought would be a better ship. At Paita there were more quarrels with Manrique, and only Mendaña's urgent pleadings persuaded Quiros to continue on board. After they sailed from Paita on 16 June, things improved for a while; winds and weather were favourable, and the ships made good progress southwestwards, and then in a generally westerly direction. Spirits were high, and there were fifteen marriages in the first month at sea. But if Mendaña's weakness as a leader was displayed at Paita, his limitations as a navigator were no less clearly shown at their first landfall.

He had instructed Quiros to prepare a chart showing only the Peruvian coast and two points in 7 and 12°S, 1500 leagues from Lima: these showed where the Isles of Solomon would be found; all else was omitted lest one of the captains should be tempted to go discovering on his own account. The course was easy: once in 7–12°S, all that was needed was latitude sailing westwards, with both winds and currents helping them on. Yet after 1000 leagues Mendaña was sure that the first islands he came to, on 21 July, were the Solomons: they were in the right latitude, but in reality nearly 50° of longitude distant from San Cristobal. It was soon obvious, however, that their fair-skinned smooth-haired people could not be the fuzzy blacks of the Solomons, and Mendaña gave his discovery the name, still in part retained, of Las Marquesas de Mendoza, for Cañete's family name.

Four hundred of their people came out in canoes, people 'almost white, and of very graceful shape', one youth so clear and fresh and beautiful that Quiros 'never in my life felt such pain as when I thought that so fair a creature [the word was more literal then] should be left to go to perdition'.[44] For a time there was merrymaking in a spirit of mutual curiosity, until the freedom with which the islanders helped themselves to odd gear about the ships became annoying. A gun was fired, which scared most of them off; but one man who would not leave the flagship *San Geronimo* was wounded in the arm with a sword, and his fellows brandished spears, threw stones, and tried to tow the ship ashore. Then the shooting began. It was repeated, with less provocation, on other islands; there were intermittent friendly passages, but when the Spaniards left, only two weeks later, Quiros estimated that 200 Marquesans had been killed, for the most part in mere wantonness. And this was the first substantial contact between Europeans and Polynesians.

Mendaña accepted that these were not the islands which he sought, but three or four days after leaving the Marquesas (that is on 8 or 9 August) he announced that they would find the land they were seeking before nightfall on that very day. Supplies were running out, but at this news people ate and drank more freely; and then they saw no land for days, until 20 August, 400 leagues from the Marquesas: and then the land was only an atoll, which they called 'San Bernardo'. Nine days later they came upon another island, 'La Solitaria', but the surrounding sea was studded with reefs, too dangerous to attempt a landing. The authorities, in unwonted agreement, identify these as Pukapuka (Danger Island; not to be confused with Magellan's 'San Pablo' in the Tuamotus) and Niulakita, in the Cooks and Ellices respectively. With these meagre sightings, murmuring grew among the soldiers, abetted by some of the pilots, jealous of Quiros: they had sailed over the hypothetical islands, erased from the chart he had produced at Mendaña's behest, and they could sail on forever, or at least to Great Tartary.

For the sake of his promised Marquisate, Mendaña was prepared to send them fishing for his boasted pearls, on the bottom of the sea . . . But the end of the outward voyage was at hand, though it was not the sought-for end. Thirty days after Mendaña had announced land for that very day, they saw ahead a great bank of dark smoke: a less auspicious but more appropriate omen than the bright star of his first voyage.

The morning, 8 September, showed them clearly a large and beautiful island, which they had seen when the rain lifted the night before: this was Ndeni, 'which Mendaña called Santa Cruz.[45] To the northwest was the source of the smoke-bank, the volcano of Tinakula rising steeply from the sea like a sugar-loaf, and in active eruption. But they could not see the almiranta, and a search by the smaller ships found no traces of her. This mystery of the sea was not cleared up until 1970-1, when excavations at Pamua, on the north coast of San Cristobal, turned up Spanish colonial pottery in quantities indicating a longer stay, by more people, than could be accounted for by Gallego's exploration in the bergantin in 1568, which did not camp on the coast: there can be no reasonable doubt that this represents settlement by the company of the *Santa Isabel*. Despite the fact that Mendaña had recently refused an appeal by her captain for more water, the parting was probably not deliberate: the almirante's wife was left behind on the flagship, San Cristobal could have been recognised from Gallego's description, and whether or not the ship, which was in poor condition, was wrecked, it would have made good sense for it to wait for the rest of the fleet at its presumed destination.[46]

At Santa Cruz, Mendaña again professed to recognise the island: the people were of the right colour, though their language differed from those of Santa Ysabel and Guadalcanal. The first reception was hostile, arrows being shot (harmlessly) from canoes; the arquebusiers soon drove off this feeble attack, with loss. After several tentative anchorings, the expedition finally came to rest at the head of a deep bay on the northwest coast of Santa Cruz, where the people were friendly, especially their chief Malope, who exchanged names with Mendaña. Here the settlement was commenced, at a point which can be precisely located from Quiros's relation, confirmed by pottery finds: Graciosa Bay still retains its singularly ill-fitting name.

The sickening cycle of friendly welcome, misunderstandings, sullen retreats, occasional reconciliations, robberies and killings began all over again, and was compounded by violent dissension within the thoroughly demoralised company. Mendaña stayed aboard ship—the Governor's house was not ready—and although the soldiers worked willingly at first, 'The Devil was able to work so well with some of them, that they kept in mind the delights of Lima'. Quiros was convinced that when matters had been put on a friendly footing with the inhabitants, some soldiers deliberately murdered villagers in order to provoke hostilities and so force the abandonment of the colony. Seditious petitions were signed, shots were fired over the ships—'I know not at what birds they were aiming'. When

Mendaña at last took action, it was, in Jack-Hinton's words, 'as little more than the vassal of Doña Isabel and her brothers.' The Camp-Master was cut down at Mendaña's behest and in his presence, and another malcontent killed; and on the same day the Spaniards' best friend, Malope, was murdered by some of Manrique's gang while actually feasting them. In a futile attempt at reparation, the head of the ensign mainly responsible was left at the door of Malope's house in his deserted village; the other murderer was reprieved—nearly 200 people had been lost with the almiranta, and not another man could be wasted—but died of shame and the scorn in which he was held. Manriques' head and that of the man killed with him should have been buried, but nobody bothered, and they were found on the beach, gnawed by dogs.

In all this, Quiros appears as an ineffectual peace-maker; such control as existed was in the arbitrary hands of the Barretos. Mendaña was ill and broken, sunk in a religious stupor; he died in mid-October, nominating his wife as Governess and his brother-in-law Lorenzo Barreto as Captain-General; but he in turn soon died of a wound received from the islanders. Naturally their hostility was now more persistent, and there were only fifteen healthy soldiers left. When most of the company moved to the ships, on 7 November, the first European colony in the South Seas ended its dismal and bloody existence of two months.

The agony, however, was far from ended. Morale was further depressed by the death of their conscientious Vicar, who had risen from his dying bed to confess Lorenzo Barreto. Two incursions were made for provisions, to a small off-lying island; the usual syndrome was acted out again. Mendaña's body was disinterred, that it might not be desecrated by the savages, but those on the capitana refused to take it aboard; it was placed on the frigate. They abandoned their dogs, which ran along the beach barking distractedly, all but the smallest one, which swam for the ships and 'for such fidelity was taken on board; and of him it may be said that fortune favours the brave.' At last, on 18 November, all three ships sailed, though Quiros had very sensibly proposed abandoning the two small vessels and using their men and gear on the capitana.

The plan was to sail westsouthwest as far as 11°S, in the hope of finding San Cristobal and the almiranta; failing that, to turn for Manila. Probably the *Santa Isabel*'s people were still camped at Pamua, a hill-top on a headland with excellent visibility to sea, and had the *San Geronimo* pressed on when 11° was reached, the two might well have rejoined; in which case, in all probability, all would have shared the same unknown fate, for the ships were rotten and supplies were short. But seeing no land at 11°S, Quiros bore northwest, to avoid New Guinea, which he thought was close at hand; had his ships been well-found, he would have preferred to explore the lands of which, a few days later, he saw signs—a tree trunk and masses of reeds. But in his desperate position he felt under the necessity of avoiding the hazards of unknown coasts and islands.[47]

The voyage to Manila was terrible in the extreme, and not relieved by human solidarity in distress. Unremitting labour, by weakened men, was needed to keep sails and rigging workable. Quiros did his best to see that the workers and the sick were looked after; the Governess refused to share her ample stores, and raided the scanty water supply to wash her clothes. She suggested hanging murmurers, but at last released two jars of oil for the sick, which did not last long. Probably the people were too weary and broken to mutiny; if ever an officer were justified in heading a mutiny, this was the time, but Quiros devoted himself to the desperate and thankless task of acting as peace-maker between the generality and the hard-core gang around the Barretos. The galleot parted company early in December, after being specifically warned not to do so, for Quiros feared that the capitana might sink at any moment. A few days later the frigate disappeared; in this case Quiros had wished to bring her worn-out crew aboard the *San Geronimo*, but was over-ruled. For lack of gear to hoist in the boat, he was unable to land at Ponape or at Guam, which he reached on 1 January 1596; but here they were at least able to exchange scrap-iron for provisions brought out in canoes, though two Guanamese 'were killed by an arquebus, owing to a matter of a piece of cask hoop'.

In mid-January they reached the Philippines, but Quiros had no charts of the archipelago, and without them it was difficult and dangerous to find safe anchorage; there can be little doubt that only his insistence on his own expertise saved the capitana from disaster almost in sight of relief. They met a man who had guided Cavendish through the islands, and he told them that the land which they saw was indeed Cape Espiritu Santo, the northwest point of Samar, for which Quiros had been making. Here they found a good port and above all food; some of the sick died from over-eating. Recalcitrant to the last, Doña Isabel ordered the flogging of a married soldier who had gone ashore for food, allegedly against her orders; but the tough old boatswain protested so strongly that she had to yield. She continued to threaten condign justice in Manila, and sent her two surviving brothers ahead to report. Before the ship reached Luzon, provisions were short again, and when Quiros approached the Governess she upbraided him for his ill-service to Mendaña, who had spent so much on the expedition, before she grudgingly gave up a calf. At the entrance to Manila Bay the Spanish coastguard came aboard, and was horrified at the sight of the sick and starving men and women—and babies—below, when there were two pigs—but Doña Isabel's pigs—on the deck above. At his angry 'What the Devil! Is this a time for courtesy with pigs?' she reluctantly ordered them to be killed. It was difficult, with a weak and sullen crew, to work into the Bay, but soon food and supplies were sent from Manila. Fifty people had died on the twelve weeks' voyage, and of the nearly 400 who had sailed from Paita, about 100 survived when, on 11 February 1596, they anchored at Cavite, and the long horror at last was over.

The galleot reached Mindanao, in such distress that it was said that her crew landed to kill and eat a dog they saw on the beach. Of the frigate bearing Mendaña's body, there was only a vague report that she had been seen aground on some unnamed coast, with sails set and all her crew dead. As for Mendaña's wife, on the voyage that evil woman had gone into retreat and prepared to meet her God; in Manila she met and married the Governor's young cousin.[48] Re-equipped and revictualled, the *San Geronimo* sailed for Acapulco, arriving there on 11 December 1597. There Quiros left her and sailed for Peru, but not out of this history.

Quiros, caught between the devil of Doña Isabel and the potentially turbulent sea of the sailors and soldiers, appears in all this as a man of stature approaching moral heroism; and it may plausibly be objected that the flattering portrait is drawn by himself or by his secretary, a poet who loved him. However, the account is not only psychologically and internally consistent, it is also consistent with what we know of him from other and not always friendly sources. His loyalty is unimpeachable, to Mendaña but also to Doña Isabel, whom he cannot have respected in herself, only in her office; indeed, this loyalty overrode his earnest desire to secure fair and decent treatment for his company. Those qualities of humanity and forbearance so apparent in the Quiros/Belmonte relation, and which so much appeal to us, are vouched for by a hostile witness, Prado, and indeed are precisely those qualities which earned Prado's scorn, and to a lesser extent that of a better man, Torres. And even in the relation, there are clear indications of the points where his very virtues became, in the context within which he had to act, failings and weaknesses.

As for his competence as a cosmographer, that was attested by such contemporary authorities as the notable Jesuit mathematician Clavius, the reformer of the calendar, and, given his technical resources, it stands up to modern criticism. It is notable that when he does assert himself, it is nearly always in matters of navigation, and he alone brought the *San Geronimo* through her dreadful voyage. The nobility of his dream, the intensity of his spiritual vision, will appear in the sequel; the passion with which he held them may seem to us, in an age psychologically conditioned to scepticism in such matters, extravagant to absurdity; but it must be seen in the context of his time, his country, and his Faith: he and Mendaña were men not of the Conquista but of the Counter-Reformation. His weaknesses are too marked to allow him true greatness; but he was a remarkable personality, and if not a great, then surely a good man: in no satiric sense, a 'Spiritual Quixote'.

The Southland III: Quiros and the New Jerusalem

Even while in Manila, Quiros seems to have determined on a return to the Islands; he begged de Morga to keep the existence of the Marquesas secret 'until his Majesty be informed and order what is most convenient for his service', since their central position in that South Sea would enable the English to do much harm should they hear of them and settle.[49] Back in Peru by June 1597, he tried to get a ship from the Viceroy Velasco, who (naturally, given the record) set a precedent for future dealings with Quiros by hedging. At his suggestion Quiros went to Spain to put his plans to the Court; he visited Rome as a pilgrim in Holy Year, 1600, and secured the support of the Pope (in a personal audience), of the Spanish Ambassador to the Holy See, and of leading mathematicians and cosmographers, who were impressed by his navigational skills. His holy design may have been implanted in his mind by the unforgettable sight of the young Marquesan, so beautiful and yet damned; but if he arrived in Rome as a man with a mission, it was here that he became a man possessed, and his possession held him through humiliating failure, grinding poverty, and the sickness of hope ever deferred, until death 'saved him from further frustration and humiliation and the Spanish authorities from further inconvenience'.[50]

In 1603 Quiros obtained the royal authorisation, the instructions to the Viceroy of Peru being couched in usually strong terms.[51] There was some opposition from Doña Isabel's new husband, who considered himself Governor of the Solomons in succession to Mendaña, but this was smoothed over on Quiros's assurance that they were not in his program. He was given two ships, the *San Pedro y San Pablo* as flag and another *San Pedro* as almiranta, with a *zabra* or launch for inshore work; the complement of 250 to 300 people, including six Franciscans, was provisioned for a year, with seeds and animals for a colony. But, as so often, the staff structure seems almost calculated to ensure conflict in the command. There was certainly prejudice against Quiros as a Portuguese. The almirante, Luis Vaez de Torres, was stout-hearted, competent, and loyal, though without great respect for his leader; but the reluctant Chief Pilot, Juan Ochoa de Bilboa, may have been a trouble-maker, though Brett Hilder implies that the trouble he made was merely his correct stand against Quiros in the dispute over the distance sailed. As for Don Diego de Prado y Tovar, as his style implies the most exalted personage aboard, he was a gentleman-volunteer with some hopes of succession to the command—perhaps even the Viceroy's nomination as such—and it is difficult to find in his own doctored account the virtues that H. N. Stevens ascribes to this 'much-maligned man': he convicts himself of malice, disloyalty, and an unscrupulous determination to exploit his ambiguous status. He forgot that, in the long run at least, 'Malice to be effective should be concealed'.[52]

There were very reasonable doubts in Lima as to the advisability of launching new colonies which would be difficult to support; the fleet's accountant, Iturbe, later alleged that Quiros shouted in the streets that the new Viceroy, the Conde de Monterey, was obstructing the intentions of the Council of State and the Pope, and it is possible that Ochoa and Prado were to some extent the Viceroy's watch-dogs; on the other hand Monterey wrote a month before sailing to ask Quiros, in most friendly terms, for a progress report, and it was not until after his failure that Quiros blamed it on the delay of ten weeks in starting, and that in turn on the Viceroy.[53] Vagueness and secrecy as to objectives probably contributed to the unease; but the real aim was to find a great Terra Australis beyond but fairly near the discoveries of 1568 and 1595: the Marquesas were well populated by a more or less civil people who could not have come from New Spain or Peru, still less from the western shores of the South Sea. Terra Australis failing, they would make for Santa Cruz and explore New Guinea, apparently facing the risk of unknown lee shores and, should New Guinea not be an island, of embayment. If the Southland were not found, the return would be by the East Indies and so round the world, which was politically practicable since the union with Portugal in 1580.[54]

The course was to be westsouthwest to 30°S, then in zigzags between 10 and 20°S, with Santa Cruz as the destination if no land were found, and the rendezvous in case of separation. The fleet left Callao on 21 December 1605, and by 22 January 1606 was in 26°S, when Quiros abruptly changed course; but Torres, Prado, Ochoa, and another pilot were for pressing on, alleging the usual promising cloud-banks. They sailed in a generally northwesterly direction until 19 February, when they were in 10° 20′S, sighting on the way the isolated Ducie and Henderson Islands and several of the Tuamotus;[55] at the most promising of these, 'La Convercion de San Pablo' (Hao, a large atoll, 50 km long) the people were friendly and landings were made. Quiros wished for a longer stay, though these were hardly the millions of whose salvation he dreamt; but he was ill and Ochoa disregarded his instructions. They now turned west for Santa Cruz, coming to an island which Quiros identified with Mendaña's San Bernardo (Pukapuka) but which was in fact Caroline. On 2 March they found a small well-populated island, covered with coconut palms, generally identified as Rakahanga in the Northern Cooks. The people were defiant, and there were martial passages, but also some amorous ones. Once more Quiros was dazzled by the physical beauty of the Islanders, and from his description Fray Juan da Torquemada in 1615 gave the island the most generally used Spanish name, 'Gente Hermosa', the beautiful people; but Quiros himself characteristically called it 'La Peregrina', the pilgrim, and Torres more realistically 'La Matanza', the killing.[56]

Long before this the inevitable murmurings had begun, abetted by Ochoa, and were not mollified by Quiros's well-meant lectures to the people on the evils of gaming, even if winnings were devoted to the souls in Purgatory, and the advantages of using the time on their hands to learn the three Rs, martial arts, and the use of the spheres. His temper was failing, and he hoisted a block to the yard-arm, *in terrorem*. But he had to admit, even to himself, that the voyage was dragging. Although, as Wallis says, nobody had yet had more experience of the South Pacific, the wind régime was not known. Even had they sailed in early October, not late December, they would still have been too late to take advantage of the winter extension of the Southeast Trades to the north, and they were now entering, in March, an area where monsoonal winds from the northwest prevail from December to April—they were running only ten leagues a day, instead of the twenty-seven of August-September 1595.[57]

On 25 March, Easter Eve, Quiros called a council, and discontent came to a head. Ochoa pointed out that they had been sailing for ninety-four days, against sixty-nine from Lima to Santa Cruz in 1595, and there was no sign of land; by this reckoning they had come 2300 leagues. Quiros applied various corrections, making much play with the fact that Ochoa's experience was merely coastal, and said that he had overestimated by 600 leagues: this would put them 1600–1700 leagues from Peru and well east of Santa Cruz. Actually Quiros had himself underestimated by about 600 leagues. Torres and the Portuguese pilot de Leza were also much closer to the truth than Quiros—about 2000 leagues to Taumako— but allowed themselves to be overborne. As far as Gente Hermosa the general estimates were not wildly out; the errors piled up as they passed out of the region where the Trades are steady even in winter. Quiros had his way: Ochoa was deposed and transferred to the almiranta, but the snake was scotched, not killed.

Water was short, despite the use of a condenser which Quiros rated too highly, and it was with great relief that, on 7 April, they sighted an island higher and more promising than the atolls so far visited. This was Taumako, under 150km northeast of Santa Cruz; Quiros was apparently running about half a degree north of the correct course for that island. The people here were friendly, with fine canoes, apparently knowing but disapproving of cannibalism; wood, water, and provisions were plentiful, and harmony was scarcely marred by the kid- napping of four young men for the salvation of their souls and their potential value as interpreters—factors barely distinguishable in the Spanish scheme of things. The chief, Tumai, was especially cordial; he told them of over sixty islands (some of them possibly as far away as Fiji or Tonga) and, 'by signs with fire', that the volcano seen in 1595 was five days to the west, and Santa Cruz could be seen from it. Obviously he had heard about arquebuses, and Quiros tried to explain away Malope's murder.

Santa Cruz was now in reach, but it was not the mainland of Terra Australis, it might be considered as Doña Isabel's territory, and to Quiros its memories were doubtless hateful; so on 18 April they headed southeast, with the tail of the monsoon, for the great land of 'Manicolo' of which they had heard at Taumako.[58] On 24 April the ships rounded Tikopia, where three of the men taken at Taumako escaped by swimming. Passing through the Banks Islands, the northmost New Hebridean group, they came on 1 May 1606, the day of SS Philip and James, to a great mountainous land, to Quiros the end of the quest: La Austrialia del Espíritu Santo. Or perhaps indeed 'La Australia . . . .'[59]

Espíritu Santo retains the name that Quiros gave it, the largest (3885km²) and most diversified of the New Hebrides, where a bizarre Anglo-French Condo- minium, an old-style land-grabbing colonialism, and nativistic movements such as Nagriamel are trying to come to grips with the twentieth century. To Quiros, the problem of bringing the islands into the seventeenth century was sublimely simple: the New Jerusalem (such and no less was his name for the colony) would be devoted to the propaganda of the Faith and the welfare, material but first of all moral, of the natives.

The history of the New Jerusalem was a phantasmagoria: Quiros was now in the grip of a religious mania. It began realistically enough with the exploration by Torres of the great bay, still called St Philip and St James, in which they found themselves: a fine fertile land, well-timbered and well-watered, with a river, the Jordan, which in Quiros's eyes was as great as the Guadalquivir at Seville and hence proof of a land of continental size, though others were sceptical of this. There was a good port, named Vera Cruz; but nowhere suitable to build bergantins for coastal exploration. The land was well peopled by jealously separate tribes; but the people were not the golden youth of the Marquesas and Gente Hermosa.

They came out in canoes, with bows ready, and Torres's idea of an embassy was a whiff of arquebus-shot. This was meant to terrify, and it did. In the next few days there were occasional very wary meetings and exchanges; but when, a week after their arrival, Torres led a reconnaissance in some force, a great crowd blocked their way. Its leaders drew a line on the ground and indicated that both sides should lay down their arms—to their cost, says the pilot Leza, this tribe knew nothing of the arquebus—but to Torres this was an insolence, and he advanced across the line. The first death may have been by impatience or accident —Quiros tries to put a good face on it—and then a hard combat began. It could have only one ending; but that meant also the end of any hope of saving souls for Christ, and he admitted sadly that his great intention was now 'but a sound'.[60]

Quiros was saddened but not deterred. A church was built of boughs and plantains, and on Pentecost Day, 14 May, he took possession of the land, as far as the Pole, in the names of the Trinity, Jesus, St Francis, John of God, and King Philip III. He hardly deserves the scorn poured on him for the creation of 'Ministries' when he was in fact setting up the standard Spanish municipality with the appropriate officers and magistrates, though thirty-four of one sort and another seems an excessive number. As Fray Martin de Munilla, the leader of the Franciscans, puts it, 'all the offices, which a well organised city should have' were distributed; and on normal Spanish form the early appointment of a Registrar of Mines was a very reasonable precaution. But this relative common sense was overlain by the trappings of the Order of the Holy Ghost which Quiros instituted, a bizarre medley of baroque chivalry and religiosity, dedicated, in Prado's words, 'to defend the Indians from their enemies and from the others who might wish to injure them, and other absurdities [*inpertinencias*] . . .'. Fray Martin (an old experienced man, in general very reserved about these enthusiasms) demurred at wearing the blue cross which was the badge of the Order—this would be against the Franciscan Rule—and overheard Quiros complaining of this to himself in words 'which could not be set down with ink on paper'. But the taffeta crosses were distributed to all—

> even two negro cooks were rewarded by such largesse . . . for their
> gallantry and courage. Besides, on that day he granted them their

liberty, though they did not belong to him, and what is more they afterwards continued in the self-same state of slavery.

Even the aged Fray Martin was satirical about the marvellous 'diversity of knights . . . negro-knights and Indian-knights and knights who were knight-knights'.[61] It is clear that Quiros's sense of reality, and his command over himself, were breaking down.

Prado claims to have attacked Quiros directly in the most insolent terms:

> . . . . you would give us so much gold and silver that we could not carry it, and the pearls should be measured by hatfuls . . . We have found only the black devils with poisoned arrows; what has become of the riches? . . . all your affairs are imaginary and have gone off in the wind.

Quiros should consider that he was dealing not with Indians but with Spaniards, some of whom had begged in the Ronda hills gun in hand, and 'those from the mud of Lisbon were just the same; look out for yourself . . .'. That this mutinous speech was made to Quiros before his friends may very well be doubted; but the feelings expressed must have been widespread.[62] In 1595 Quiros had carried such things off by his recognised superiority as a pilot (which now, with better competition, was not so evident) and a patient evasiveness; but he was now in sole command, there was no arbitrary Doña Isabel to provide the cover of higher authority, and he seems to have taken refuge in a nervous breakdown. On 25 May, Corpus Christi was celebrated with much festivity, though some thought it an artificial and precarious pomp, since the Spaniards were so few and the Indians so many; but Quiros and Fray Martin considered it a strikingly auspicious asseveration of the Faith. That same evening Quiros walked a league inland, past the already sprouting gardens he had planted, and on his return casually announced that since they stood little chance against native hostility, they would leave next day and visit the islands to windward. . . .[63]

Astonishing as this sudden decision must have been, there seems to have been no discussion. Obviously Quiros was overwrought, but probably by now hardly anyone had confidence either in the settlement or in the commander, and Prado's point was well taken—no gold or pearls had been found, only hostile Indians. So the second European colony in the South Seas endured a month, half the span of its predecessor. What followed for Quiros was anticlimax, both immediately and over the years; for Torres, an outstanding achievement.

The departure was delayed to allow the people to catch fish, and when they started on 28–9 May they were forced back by a resultant epidemic of fish-poisoning, though nobody died. Finally they sailed again on 8 June, but met strong southeasterly winds. Quiros decided to return and build a fort and a bergantin, waiting until the seasonal wind régime could be determined. The almiranta and the launch made the port of Vera Cruz, but the capitana apparently could not work up the bay, or at least the pilots so claimed. It was a confusing situation, and the accounts are confused; the true reasons for the ensuing separation on the night of 11 June are not likely ever to be ascertained.[64] Prado said confidently that there was a mutiny on Quiros's ship; but he was on the almiranta, having transferred probably at Taumako, and the wish is rather too obviously father to the thought for much credence to be given to his statement, even if he were in general a more reliable witness. But even if there were no mutiny, there was a breakdown in command: clearly Quiros had lost his grip and was ill mentally if not physically; the pilots must have been in effective control, and they decided that the ship could not safely beat back to windward. Quiros was left to revolve distractedly the causes of his failure—untrustworthy subordinates, the ten weeks' delay in sailing at Callao, the 'half hour of time' in the Bay which robbed him of so great an enterprise.

On the capitana, the first thought seems to have been to make for Santa Cruz, forgetting that it was presumably dropped as a rendezvous by the decision to turn southwest from Taumako; but there was a strong feeling that they should make for Guam or New Spain, though Iturbe made a formal protest against giving over the search for new lands. Quiros was doubtful about making for Santa Cruz: they might easily miss the island and then, unable to beat back east, be faced with the old spectre of embayment on some unknown lee shore of New Guinea. They bore generally north, seeing a sail, undoubtedly native; Iturbe was bitterly critical of the failure to follow it, which indeed would probably have brought them to Santa Cruz within hours. On 21 June they were in the latitude of Santa Cruz, but there was no sign of land, and they might be either east or west of it. Quiros, now somewhat recovered, had reasoned objections to making for either Guam and the Philippines or for New Spain: at this season the westerly *vendavales* would render it hazardous, if not impossible, to make Manila, and the way to Acapulco was very long, water and food were short, and it might not be the right season to cross the Equator. In council, some still argued for the Philippines—they could recoup expenses with the silk and porcelain of China—but at last all agreed for Acapulco, Iturbe apparently under duress. Like Mendaña, Quiros wearily acquiesced, with the face-saving proviso that if they found promising islands, they should build a launch and explore; if not, they should reconsider when they struck the Acapulco-Manila Galleon track in the latitude of Guam. He consoled himself, rather lamely: other expeditions had been totally lost, he had laid a good foundation, Torres might make further discoveries, and it was all in the Lord's will. . . .[65] He made his own testament, a rambling pathetic plaint against the greed and cruelty of men.

They did find one island, but it was only an atoll, Butaritari or the adjacent Little Makin in the northern Gilberts, and after reaching 38°N and suffering the accustomed privations (but only Fray Martin died, at 80) reached Navidad and four weeks later, on 23 November 1606, Acapulco. Thence Quiros went to Mexico and eventually to Spain, to wear his life out in the sad effort to rekindle the dead flame of his mission.

The Southland IV: Torres and New Guinea

At Vera Cruz, Torres thought that the departure of the capitana was plain desertion, 'for they did not sail on the proper course, nor with good intention'.[66] He spent two weeks looking and waiting for the lost ship and then determined to carry on with the voyage, against the majority opinion—'for my temper was different from that of Captain Pedro Fernandez de Quiros'. They sailed round a good deal of Espíritu Santo, enough to establish that it was a large island and not a main, and then southwest as far as 21°S. Seeing no land, Torres bore northwest and made what he correctly assumed to be the southeastern extremity of New Guinea. North of that land, as he knew, was a route which would take him to the Moluccas, but he could not weather the peninsula.[67] Unless he were to give up his purpose, he had no option but to sail west into the Strait which now bears his name; but it was a bold decision, since he must already have seen enough to realise that the surrounding seas were very dangerous. In fact, the 150km between Cape York, the northern tip of Queensland, and the nearest Papuan coast are crowded with reefs and shoals, many shifting, and in places masked by the muddy discharge of the Papuan rivers, especially off the great delta of the Fly.

The passage of the Strait was not repeated until Cook's 1770 voyage, and well might Torres write to the King 'these are not voyages performed every day . . . .'. He sailed along 'Magna Margarita' for some 600 leagues, taking possession at various points, until he met people with iron and 'China bells' and crockery, and Mohammedans who had guns and were converting Papuans to Islam; then he knew they were not so far from the Moluccas. After some adventures in those islands, he reached Manila on 22 May 1607. Torres sent an account of the voyage to Quiros before he wrote to the King—an index of his essential though not uncritical loyalty.[68]

In itself, the voyage after the entry to the Strait scarcely belongs to the history of the Pacific proper, and whether or not Torres saw Australia, while naturally interesting to Australians, is a trifle on a world view. His track is very difficult to determine, but the general consensus has been that he could not have sighted Cape York, The most recent examination however, by Brett Hilder, a seaman with nearly half a century of experience in the waters between New Guinea and Australia, seems definitive, and leaves scarcely a doubt that Torres did in fact see Cape York. Hilder's analysis on this point hinges largely on his recognition of the great bank or 'Placel' that Torres skirted; his discussion, both documentary and navigational, especially of Prado's maps, is meticulous, and in my view his case may be taken as proven.[69] Yet Torres naturally could not know that what he had seen was a mainland, and the continent had already been sighted by Willem Janszoon in the Duyfken from Bantam. He had coasted along the eastern shores of the Gulf of Carpentaria from 14°S to Mulgrave Island half-way between Cape York and Papua, some five or six months before Torres, in September 1606, was in the Strait; the Dutch priority is assured. But what matters is not a possible sighting of an unrecognised bit of land but the extent to which knowledge of the general lie of the land filtered through to Europe. The significance of the voyage was the determination of the insularity of New Guinea and the consequent northern delimiting of any possible Terra Australis, and the opening (though its use was long delayed) of an alternative western passage to and from the Pacific.

It is true that this significance was not widely recognised; with Spain's power in decline, it was more than ever to her interest to conceal such dangerous discoveries; but the concealment was not total. It is still sometimes stated, or implied, that the insularity of New Guinea remained unknown until Alexander Dalrymple, from a memorial by Arias found at the British capture of Manila in 1762, realised that there was a strait and named it after Torres.[70] But even though Torres's *name* may have 'passed out of history', some concept of his discovery can be traced in the cartography of the seventeenth and early eighteenth centuries.[71] Quiros was reckless enough to print and circulate some of his memorials; these may not have contained much specific reference to Torres's discovery, but they treated of many things 'well let alone', and the Council of the Indies, justly alarmed, got a royal order that Quiros should call them in. Too late: one memorial printed at Pamplona in 1610 had been published in German, Latin, and Dutch, and incorporated in de Bry's widely-read collections of voyages, by 1613.

As for Torres's results, an insular New Guinea appears in the Duchess of Berry Atlas (1615–23), in maps by the remarkable Luso-Macassarese cosmographer Manuel Godinho de Eredia (who had contact with Prado), and in Antonio Sanches's world-map of 1623; but these may be discounted as both manuscript and Iberian. The Van Langren globe of *c.* 1625 shows not only an insular New Guinea but—south of the Insulae Salomonis!—the Baia de S. Philippo y S. Jago and Porte Vera Cruz on the north coast of a continental *Terra Australis*; four of Prado's names in the Orangerie Bay area (Papua) are used by Van Langren and Vaugondy. Gerritz' Dutch chart of the South Seas (1622) is highly confused, but does draw on these or similar Iberian predecessors. Towards the end of the century du Val's 'La Mer du Sud' (1679) is a wonderful conflation of Gallego, Mendaña, Quiros, Torres, Janszoon, Schouten, and Tasman; but almost the only things shown on it with some approximation to accuracy are a firmly insular New Guinea and the shores of the Gulf of Carpentaria. In 1700 the Dutch version of d'Albancourt's *Neptune françois* shows a south coast of New Guinea with many Torres-Prado place-names, though its relations with Carpentaria are left vague. This map, or the tradition it represents, probably influenced Robert Vaugondy's 'Carte General' for Charles de Brosses' very well-known *Histoire des Navigations aux Terres Australes* of 1756: the map shows an island New Guinea and a wide strait separating it from the west coast of the Cape York peninsula; though once more Espíritu Santo (and 'Jerusalem la Neuve') are impacted into a hypothetical northeast coast of New Holland.[72] And de Brosses probably counted as much as, or more than, Dalrymple in Cook's thinking: certainly it is the former, not the latter, whom he cites when tackling the question of New Guinea's insularity.[73]

The knowledge, then, was there, 'would men observingly distil it out': why was it so long neglected? One may suspect that the reason was simply that the course of Empire was not yet setting that way. Spain felt herself over-extended, and was in no condition to follow up such an opening; and for her rivals there were the known and assured trans-Pacific tracks—Magellan's great diagonal before the Trades, and the Manila Galleon run—and known places of refuge, notably Guam and the Ladrones, and Juan Fernandez. Using these, there were plenty of pickings to be had without venturing so far into the unknown—booty on the South American coasts, the trade of the Indies, or the treasure of the Galleon itself.

The end of the Spanish saga

'With Quiros died the heroic age of Spain.'[74] When he reached New Spain, the Viceroy Montesclaros was cordial at first, but relations were soon soured by a disagreement over the disposition of the capitana, the complaints of members of the crew, and Quiros's liberal interpretation of his original cédula requiring royal officers to assist him; this took the form of a demand for 2000 pesos to take him to Spain. The Viceroy warned the Court that they might expect very wordy complaints from Quiros, who in turn resolved not to be satisfied in future with anything but the most precise commitments to him. He reached Spain in October 1607, in utter penury, by his own account (according to Markham) unable to buy even paper, and reduced to pawning the royal standard he had unfurled at the New Jerusalem. And he needed much paper for the bombardment of memorials which he now let loose. They had worked before, but he was now more discredited than he realised. One of Iturbe's letters, a more reasoned attack than Prado's (which seems to have been merely docketed), had preceded Quiros to Spain, and other unfavourable reports came in.

The bureaucracy's treatment of Quiros was, however, much more reasonable and considerate than is generally allowed. Procrastination and expedient evasion were of course inevitable; but on the main count nothing could be done: Quiros's demands were fantastic—1000 men and half a million ducats. The Council of the Indies thought that there were better uses for a treasury surplus, should there ever be one. Between his persistence and the increasing evidence of his unfitness as a leader, though his knowledge and talents were appreciated, the Council wearily noted that 'he is not a reliable man, although he has got it into his head that he is a second Columbus, and that is his affliction'—and indeed Quiros himself was not backward in making the same comparison, not to mention an implied bracketing of himself with Caesar, Hannibal, Alexander and Pyrrhus.[75] In 1609 his affairs came before the council at least twenty times; one must sympathise with the senior clerks who had to read those endless memorials, and soothe down this intolerably monomaniac old bore.

But he retained some influential supporters, and it was felt that he must be handled gently lest he—of all people!—should defect to the heretics. Something should be done: perhaps a post as cosmographer, perhaps send him to Peru to pacify him? At one point he was given 3000 ducats for his debts and a monthly retainer of 100 ducats—on condition that he ceased for a time to press his demands. As Kelly says, he 'memorialized' himself out of favourable consideration. The famous, or infamous, story that he was betrayed by being sent to Peru with two despatches—an open one entirely favourable, a secret one countermanding it— is not strictly true, for whenever Quiros received a favourable response, he demanded something much more specific, and once more no action was taken.[76] There were also theological objections to the component of conquest which, despite his experiences at Santa Cruz and Espíritu Santo and his protests at the cruelty of the Conquista, Quiros still included in his plans.

At last a decision of a sort was reached: Quiros was to go out to Peru with the new Viceroy, who was to do his best to send him on his way to the Southland. . . . It was not much, and probably it was indeed meant as a fobbing-off: one can almost hear the great sigh of relief as the Council minuted 'and with this it can be taken that we have settled with this man'. But it was obviously the best that he would get and, perhaps with confidence, perhaps with misgivings, he acquiesced. He sailed with the Viceroy in April 1615, but he was never again to see Peru, let alone the Southland: he died on the voyage, probably at Panama.

His dream did not quite die with him: the Franciscans and the Chilean lawyer Juan Luis Arias continued to plan and petition for a great missionary effort in the Austral Regions. The last Franciscan appeals to the Crown were made in 1630-3, but it was then far too late: the springs of the national energy were running down. Abroad the Empire was increasingly hard put to defend itself, at home economic decline was well advanced.[77]

The last voyage of Quiros was virtually the end of new Spanish enterprise in the Pacific for a century and a half, until the Bourbon revival brought the great northwards thrust in California and the Tahitian voyages, both in the 1770s. Even in the sixteenth century, security in the South Sea had been rudely shaken by Drake and Cavendish; in the seventeenth, the Dutch made the running in Pacific activity. But their efforts were rather of geostrategic than of strictly geographical significance. The Mar de Sur was still a Spanish lake, its axis between the poles of Manila and Acapulco, and the English and Dutch forays are best considered as threats to the Spanish system; with the notable exception of the voyage of Schouten and Le Maire, and of Tasman in 1642-3, their geographical results were secondary, the result of accident rather than design.

Those memorials of whose diffusion the Council of the Indies was so nervous did indeed play some part in this new phase of Pacific navigation: Celsus Kelly relates

> the scene on board the *Eendracht* on 25 October 1615, the very
> morrow of Quirós' death, when in mid-Atlantic Jacob Le Maire
> summoned his ship's company, depressed by scurvy and adverse

weather, to announce the purpose and commission of the voyage:
the *Terra Australis* of Quirós. 'I read to them in the cabin', he says,
'the memorial of Quirós in order to encourage them;' and Le
Maire goes on to say that all were encouraged and rejoiced.[78]
The work had fallen into other hands; but it had been initiated by the religious
enthusiasm of Alvaro de Mendaña and Pedro Fernandez de Quiros, which
brought them only an ambiguous Quixotic fame, some few moments of ecstasy,
then disillusion and heartbreak.

Chapter 6

ASIAN EMPIRES, CHRISTIAN TRADES

Aqui o soberbo imperio, que se afama
Com terras, e riqueza não cuidada,
Da China corre, e ocupa o senhorio
Desdo Tropico ardente ao Cinto frio . . .
Esta mea escondido que responde
De longe aa China donde vem buscarse,
He Iapão, onde nace a prata fina,
Que illustrada sera coa Ley diuina.

'The Background of Eastern Seapower'[1]

The timing of the European arrival in the China Sea was fortunate, for Europeans: in effect they entered a power vacuum, occupied only by small trading city-states and by pirates. Central to the international relations of the region was the Chinese tributary system; but this was no longer backed, as it had been, by a very considerable, highly organised and effective naval power. Nor was it translated effectively into Chinese commercial power; there were of course many Chinese merchants in the ports of the 'Southern Seas', some of them long settled there, but their activities were unofficial, as it were extra-legal, and often, from the Imperial point of view, actually illicit. However, a concept analogous to the 'factory', the alien merchant community extra-territorial as regards its own administration and (within limits) its law, though not so in sovereignty, was as indigenous in Asia as it was in the Europe of the Hansa and of the Genoese and Venetian colonies of the Levant.[2] This greatly eased initial commercial penetration; but in dealings with major powers—Mughal India, China, Japan—it meant that European activity was not so much imposed on them, as it often appears in Eurocentric histories, as infiltrated into them, on Asian terms and sometimes under severe restrictions. It was often otherwise with the pettier states of Southeast Asia, a geopolitical fracture-zone.[3]

This setting largely conditioned the mechanisms of European trade, and some account of it (perforce too brief and hence over-simple) is needed for the 'placing' of a drama which in the West is still too often seen as simply the forceful and

Luis de Camões, *Os Lusiadas*, X.129, 131: 'Here stretches the proud empire which boasts of lands and riches yet unknown, China, holding dominion from the burning Tropic to the frigid zone . . . This [isle] half-hidden, lying far off against China, whence it must be sought, is Japan, where the fine silver is born, soon to be illuminated by the divine Law'.

picturesque activity of the European protagonists. Forceful and picturesque it indeed was, but the action was moulded by the setting of the stage and the reactions, often themselves very forceful, of other actors in the play.

Centuries before Portuguese keels first furrowed the Indian Ocean, or even the Atlantic, Chinese ship-building and maritime activities, especially in the south-eastern provinces of Fukien and Kuangtung, had reached a much higher pitch than European technology and organisation were to attain until well into the sixteenth century. Chinese ships sailed to Java in the fifth century of our era; in the thirteenth the prolonged resistance of the Southern Sung dynasty to the Mongol invasions was largely a naval affair, with some remarkable technological developments; and the anti-Mongol revolt of 1348 in sea-oriented Fukien was essentially a naval campaign, intercepting the convoys of rice and tribute to northern China. The Mongol Emperor Kublai Khan mounted full-scale overseas expeditions against Japan (a disastrous failure), Champa or Annam, and Java (another failure). Already in Sung times ocean-going ships could exceed 500 tons burthen and may have reached twice that size; Marco Polo and Ibn Battutah were mightily impressed by, amongst other things, the individual cabins, sixty or more in the larger ships, with some private baths—which would have been difficult indeed to find on European vessels before the passenger liners of the later nineteenth century. Archaeological evidence, including an 11-metre long rudder post, indicates that by Cheng Ho's time (1405–31) the greatest Treasure Ships were at least 100–150 metres long and of 2500 tons burthen, 3100 displacement, approaching the practicable limit of wooden-hulled sailing ships in the nineteenth century.[4]

The Chinese were very probably in contact with East Africa by the tenth century (as suggested by finds of 'Chinese porcelain by the shovelful' and by an intriguing reference in Idrisi (c. 1154)); there is a near-certainty that Cheng Ho's ships sailed into the Mozambique Channel, and even a possibility that they rounded the Cape of Good Hope from the east. Obviously these voyages, made by thousands of men in scores of ships, did not come out of the blue; they seem to have been essentially a reassertion and an extension by the new Ming dynasty of the Chinese suzerainty into which their predecessors the Mongols had brought all the organised kingdoms of Southeast Asia; it was obviously desirable for a new and native dynasty to demonstrate that its prestige was no less than that of the old. As an organiser of voyages Cheng Ho would seem *sans pareil*, as a navigator he must have ranked with Vasco da Gama and Magellan, with the single allowance (a large one) that north of Kilwa his voyages were by long-navigated seas to known ports. But surely he more than Columbus might claim the title 'Admiral of the Ocean Sea'.[5]

Unlike the Mongols, the Ming did not seek military expansion; the two or three warlike incidents which took place on Cheng Ho's voyages were just that, mere incidents. There may well have been an element of serious scientific enquiry into resources; but the voyages were also a form of disguised state trading: the 'tribute' brought back included not only exotic rarities such as ostriches and 'the auspicious giraffe' but also fine timbers, copper, sulphur, spices, and (perhaps especially important) drugs. The counter-presentations were largely luxury or ceremonial *objets d'art*, easily spared by China but very flattering to the local rulers, who welcomed both the recognition and the display. This tributary relation, while bulking large in the minds of the rulers on both sides, seems to have had little practical effect except in kingdoms actually contiguous to China, such as Annam and Korea. After the Portuguese took Malacca, its refugee Sultan did indeed appeal to his overlord in Peking, but received at first a dusty answer, and no practical help; by this time the Ming court was preoccupied with the northern frontier.[6] Sometimes the effects were negative: misunderstandings of the relationship—innocent, wilful, or generated by interested intermediaries— bedevilled Sino-Japanese negotiations during Hideyoshi's Korean wars.[7]

But this was after the decline of Ming sea-power, a decline more sudden than its rise and seemingly more difficult to explain. One factor was certainly the increasing involvement with revived Mongol power in the north—already in 1421 the capital was moved from Nanking to Peking; another the drying-up of special fiscal resources devoted to such expeditions. Cheng Ho himself was a Muslim eunuch; the voyages were sponsored by the Emperor personally and carried out by his eunuch-dominated household staff, and hence met with the bitter and effective hostility of the Confucian officials, who saw in this venturing overseas at once a departure from the agrarian polity rooted in ancient tradition,[8] a drain of funds, and more power to the eunuchs, their hated rivals in Imperial counsels. The navy's prestige must have been weakened by several defeats in the successful revolt of the northern Vietnamese against the Chinese occupation of 1406–27. Needham points out also that the remodelling in 1411 of the centuries-old Grand Canal (1705 km from Hangchow to Peking, and still active today) fitted it for transport at all seasons, so that grain convoys by sea could now be dispensed with. The great ship-building capacity of littoral China was diverted to inland water transport; in 1431 the naval crews were set to transporting rice on the Canal, 'thus reducing them from fighting men to stevedores'.[9]

As a result of all these factors, even the record of Cheng Ho's achievement was so far as possible buried: when a later Ming Emperor showed some interest in reviving overseas enterprises, the files were officially 'lost'. The Ming navy, which in 1420 comprised some 3800 units, some very large—a force which would have made any contemporary European mind boggle—'simply fell to pieces by the end of the century', and in the next even private trading overseas was legally banned, though this was far from completely enforceable. Decidedly the Portuguese were lucky in their timing![10]

Chinese maritime commerce did not cease with the end of official voyages; the eunuchs switched their capital into private ventures, and in the later fifteenth century there was some revival of trading enterprise. But it was increasingly subject to official hostility; by 1500 it was (theoretically) death to build a three-masted sea-going junk; in 1551 it was decreed that those who went down to the sea in ships 'committed a crime analogous to espionage by communicating with foreigners'. As in Japan in the next century, this 'agoraphobic mentality' was basically motivated by a desire to maintain a pure polity, uncontaminated by dangerous alien thoughts and *mores*; the Great Wall played an analogous role *vis-à-vis* the nomads of the north. In both cases there was some rationale in exclusion.[11] For the Ming, it was a desperate attempt to cope with the virulent problem of piracy, a merely negative reaction once the positive solution of naval power had been scrapped; but as Spain was to find in her Spanish American empire, the result was erosion of control by smuggling: 'The Minister at Madrid' or Peking 'may give what orders he pleases . . . but still a people who want goods will find out wayes for a supply. . . .'[12] In the fifteenth century legitimate maritime trade came to be dominated by two great entrepôts: Malacca in the Southern Seas and in the north the Ryukyu Islands, known to Europeans as the Lequeos or Loochoos or variants of that name.

Although Malaccan ships went as far as India and China, the Sultanate lacked capacity for building large vessels, as distinct from light war-craft, and seems on the whole to have been less a great trading-state in its own right than an emporium, for which its location was unrivalled: a good defensible harbour on a strait only 65 km wide, strategically situated in relation to the alternating monsoons of the Indian Ocean and the China Seas. This was 'the only point throughout the 8,000 miles [13,000 km] of the trade-route [between the Moluccas and the Mediterranean] at which a monopoly of spice distribution could be established'; for Tomé Pires, 'there is no doubt that Malacca is of such importance and profit that it seems to me it has no equal in the world'.[13] By 1460 its Sultan held both shores of the Straits for some 700 km; such a position was not likely to escape the fine geopolitical eye of Afonso de Albuquerque, who duly took the town in 1511 and, as we have seen made of it the forward base whereby Spanish intrusions in the Spice Islands were thwarted.

As for the Ryukyuans, from the 1370s until the mid-sixteenth century they were 'self-made agents of entrepot trade'. They profited greatly when the expansionist atmosphere of Cheng Ho's day was succeeded by the Ming policy of inhibiting foreign trade; many Chinese merchants and seamen transferred themselves to the 'southern lands', and in fact most of the executive officers on Ryukyuan ships were of Chinese origin. Later, the Ryukyuans picked up the threads of Malayan trade, after the fall of Malacca to the Portuguese: Patani on the Gulf of Siam became an alternative entrepôt, and Siam was Ryukyu's most important trading partner in Southeast Asia. Chinese trade continued under the guise of tribute missions. The islands themselves produced sulphur and horses; their traders distributed to the 'Southern Seas' Chinese porcelain, silks, and other fine textiles, metal goods and drugs, and Japanese weaponry, lacquer, and gold. Returns included exotic beasts and birds, camphor, rhinoceros horn and other *materia medica*, but especially dyewoods and spices, above all pepper, which sold in China at several hundred times the buying price.[14]

The Ryukyuans seem to have provided an element of stability and respectability in an often fluid and tricky half-diplomatic half-adventuring context. The trade was a royal monopoly, and it was for example to the advantage of Japanese traders, whether agents of the local lords of Kyushu or private merchants, first to carry Ryukyuan official envoys (trading in tributary guise) and later to act themselves as such, since both Chinese and Korean authorities were very ready, and not without reason, to see Japanese commerce as being compounded with piracy. But the increasing instability of the later sixteenth century, the decline in the effectiveness of Ming power with the resulting rise of smuggling and piracy, and finally the extension of Portuguese competition and even control, confined Ryukyuan trade to the more limited, though still profitable, role of carrier between China and Japan. Early in the seventeenth century the little kingdom became a vassal to the Shimazu, lords of Satsuma in Kyushu: but both sides played the dependency relation down so that Ryukyu could continue to act as a channel for Sino-Japanese trade, otherwise illegal from the expulsion of the Portuguese from Nagasaki in 1638 until a relaxation of the Chinese ban in 1684. There was even a secret manual for Ryukyuans going to China, who were instructed to fob off awkward questions by saying that their money and merchandise came from 'Treasure Island'. Probably nobody was much deceived, but appearances were preserved.

Japan's Wars of the Roses were also a Hundred Years' War: 'The Emperor in Kyoto sat powerless upon his throne, his shogun or generalissimo could exercise no authority over the regional lords'.[15] This time of troubles, the 'Warring States', lasted from 1467 until 1568, when Oda Nobunaga, the first of the three unifiers of early modern Japan, occupied Kyoto and was able to dominate his rivals. As a State, therefore, and despite its population of 15–20,000,000, Japan hardly comes into the reckoning before Nobunaga; for example, St Francis Xavier made an arduous journey to Kyoto in 1550, seeking imperial favour for his mission, but soon realised that he must fall back on the local lords or *daimyo*.[16] But if Japan did not count, Japanese did: they showed such interest in Western ways that they almost at once took rank, in European eyes, as the most 'civilisable' Asians—an elegant and intelligent people, 'the best who have yet been discovered', said Xavier. But they were also the tough cruel men who formed the core of the 'Wako', the pirates who scourged the coasts of eastern Asia before and after the periods of Mongol and Ming naval strength, and as such were 'not suffered to land in any port in India with weapons; being accounted a people so desperate and daring, that they are feared in all places where they come'.[17] So early was the love-hate relationship born on both sides.

The century of turbulence which began in 1467 saw a slide into a completely decentralised feudalism, as a result of which 'The daimyo domain became in essence a petty principality' where the lord ruled with 'only the haziest reference to . . . sanction from the Shogun and emperor.'[18] At the same time, however, the wars themselves demanded supplies and servicing, and merchant communities were growing up in the interstices of feudal power; in a few cases they were approaching, rather distantly, the position of European free cities. The most notable were Hakata and especially Sakai, near Osaka, which for long was the main port for trade with Korea, Fukien, and the Ryukyus. Although obviously not so well placed for Korean trade as Hakata and Hirado on the Tshushima Straits, Sakai was closer to the heart of consuming Japan—the core area between Kyoto and Edo (now Tokyo)—and by going south of Shikoku and Kyushu its ships could avoid the petty pirates (protected by local daimyo) of the Inland Sea. The city could hold its own against the local lords; it was a centre of arms supply and had its own defences and its own oligarchic government by thirty-six senior merchants, and even after being forced to accept a governor from Nobunaga, it retained much significance under his successors Hideyoshi and Ieyasu—all three had a keen sense of trade values.[19] Exports to China were copper, sulphur, craft work, and great numbers of swords; imports raw silk, porcelain, strings of cash, drugs, books. The trade was from a Chinese point of view a tributary one: the ships were despatched by the Japanese Emperor, the Shogun, great lords and monasteries, but their fitting-out and the business arrangements were in the hands (and much to the profit) of the Sakai and Hakata merchants. But this commerce was of course vulnerable to the increasing restrictiveness of Chinese policy, and by the 1540s it was collapsing, to be replaced by piracy on a grand scale.

The China Seas, with their multitude of coves and off-shore islands, were a highly favourable milieu for sea-bandits, and piracy was of great antiquity and endemic in times of turbulence. The decline of shogunal power allowed the daimyo of the west—especially of strategically located Kyushu—to take over the missions to China, officially tribute missions but *de facto* trading convoys. The Ming authorities naturally endeavoured to recognise only one mission at a time; rejected groups turned to smuggling, with the active connivance of Chinese merchants, increasingly inhibited in legal trade by official policy, and sometimes of the mandarins themselves. Thence it was but a short step to piracy.

In 1523 the quarrels of rival Japanese 'embassies' led to serious disorders, with the loss of Chinese lives and property, in Ningpo, the official port for trade with Japan; all trade with that country was forthwith prohibited. This absolute ban was relaxed, but the continually changing restrictions made the formerly licensed trade impracticable, smuggling and piracy increased, and eventually the Ming reacted by banning *all* sea-borne commerce, presumably on the principle of no trade, no pirates. Of course trade went on, but with no Chinese sea-power and no central control in Japan, it ceased to be merely illicit and became utterly lawless. Some daimyo found their account in co-operating with the pirates; the feudal wars provided plenty of daring leaders, whose crews were swelled by the forcibly unemployed Chinese seamen, who in fact were numerically the great majority in the Wako gangs. By the 1540s Fukien and the region of the Yangtse delta (where the Chusan Islands were a handy base) were subject to pillage, rape and murder by the almost continuous incursions of bands sometimes numbered

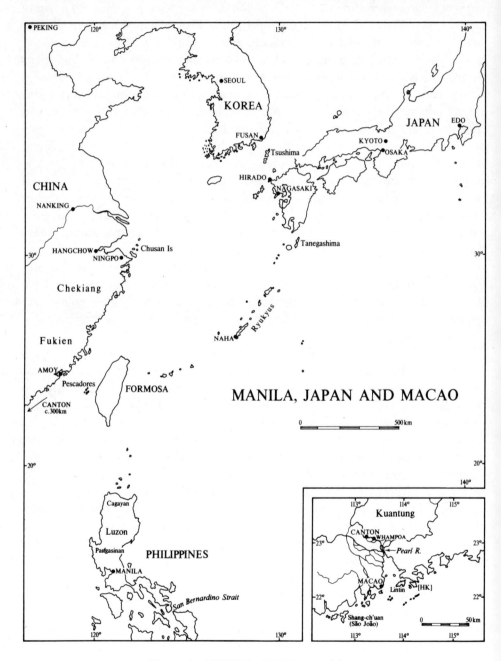

Figure 16.   MANILA, JAPAN, MACAO

in thousands; to such a pitch that some littoral areas were evacuated and a scorched earth policy adopted.[20] This was the milieu in which the Portuguese attempted the commercial penetration of China and Japan, and the evangelisation of the latter.

Macao and the 'Great Ship to Japon'

The monopoly of eastern trade by the Portuguese was not absolute even in theory; apart from the fact that illicit dealings by officials and others soon crept in, Asian as well as Portuguese merchants were licensed to trade, except in spices and a few other commodities, in the areas under Lusian dominance. Except for de Abreu's voyage of 1511–12 into the Indies and a mission to Siam in 1518, initial penetration beyond Malacca was by individual pioneers carried in Asian ships. In 1513 or 1514, soon after Francisco Serrão had thus reached the Moluccas, Jorge Alvares came in a junk to Lintin Island, about 100 km southwest of Canton and in the main embouchure of the great delta south of that city (Fig. 16), which was the official port for trading with southeast Asia as Ningpo was for Japan and Foochow for the Philippines. Once it was reported that 'there is as great a profit in taking spices to China as in taking them to Portugal', the Portuguese authorities in Malacca planned to open official relations; at the taking of that town, local Chinese merchants, at odds with the Sultan, had offered their help, and so the prospects of friendly trade were thought to be good.[21]

Accordingly a fleet was sent to Canton under Fernão Peres de Andrade, carrying Tomé Pires as ambassador to the Emperor; but a promising start was ruined by Fernão's brother Simão, who came out in 1519 and forthwith started building a fort, interfering with Asian shipping, and carrying off (or 'buying') young people. Initially the local officials seem to have covered up this outrage, against bribes, and Pires was allowed to proceed to Peking. But when more reliable news came through from Canton, the embassy collapsed: its staff was to be imprisoned until justice was done to the Sultan of Malacca, and trade was forbidden. Pires and his people died in captivity.

Nevertheless, the pepper and sandalwood brought by the Portuguese was highly desirable to the Cantonese, and two Malacca fleets arrived in 1521. The first did good business, but after orders came from Peking to expel the 'Fo-lang-chi' (Feringhis or Franks) the second had to fight its way out. There was further fighting, in which the Portuguese were unsuccessful, in 1522, in which year Canton was officially closed to all foreign commerce. Ming naval forces were after all not entirely negligible, and the Portuguese feared an attack on Malacca itself. They gave over any more official visits, and the Chinese fitted out more ships. But these had more than enough to do in coping with local pirates; with closure of the port, customs duties ceased and local salaries fell into arrear; and there were no spices for the Court.[22]

Vested interests—merchants, local gentry, some mandarins—favoured commerce with foreigners, and the Portuguese continued to trade, illicitly, around the

Bay of Amoy and at Ningpo, hovering off-shore, camping on islands, and using
Malay or Siamese front men. Law enforcement varied from province to province
and from time to time; a forceful counter-attack in 1547–8 by Chu Wan, Viceroy
of Fukien and Chekiang, on the smugglers, banditti, and pirates (who included
some Fo-lang-chi) was successful initially, until local resentments and intrigue
led to his fall and suicide: his hard line had completely alienated 'a large group
of disciplined, tough men', used to the sea, and their friends—local officials,
gentry, and consumers—who found their account in a live-and-let-live policy.
Chu Wan 'rais[ed] the level of antagonism from that of smuggling to that of
piracy',[23] and the next decade saw the devastating razzias at their height: in 1555
the Wako penetrated well beyond Nanking, over 300km inland. Piracy shaded
off into trade and *vice versa*: one Wako chief, the Chinese salt merchant Wang
Chih, driven from the Chusan Islands by Chu Wan, based himself at Hirado
and supplemented piracy with a large more or less licit business with the Southern
Seas, especially in sulphur, important for textile industries as well as explosives.
He was taken by a trick and executed in 1559, and in the 1560s major piracy
subsided, though it long continued on a smaller scale. Against this background
of ferocious anarchy, the Portuguese reputation as the violent disruptors of peaceful Asian trade, perhaps true enough for the Indian seas, must surely look a little
different in those of China.

Three factors were important in the decline of piracy: in China, sensible
relaxation of the prohibitions, which led to some revival of Chinese shipping;
in Japan, the renewal of central control under Nobunaga—the first of these took
away much of the *raison d'être* of illicit commerce, and both cut down recruitment
to the Wako; finally the legitimation, within limits, of Portuguese trade, since
the light Wako craft could not cope so easily with their solid well-armed ships.
Indeed, one element in the eventual allowance to the Portuguese of a settlement
near Canton may well have been their usefulness in putting down local pirates.

Since direct Sino-Japanese trade had never recovered from the Chinese embargo
of 1523—the Japanese reputation for violence was such that they were banned
again in 1579, 1599 and 1624, after which they shut themselves out—there was a
place for the middleman, as the Ryukyuans had seen; and should the Portuguese
secure the necessary base beyond Malacca, instead of having to make do with
off-shore trading and precarious island camps, there would then be nothing to
prevent them from entering and eventually dominating the carrying trade.
Even so, indigenous Asian trading continued and even thrived, but often by
avoiding Portuguese ports—in the long run, a weakening of Lusian economic
strength through the fall-off in customs and port revenues.[24]

In the face of Chu Wan's offensive, the Portuguese in the 1550s began to shift
their attention back to Kuangtung, where in 1530, as a result of local pressure,
Canton had been reopened to foreign trade. The Fo-lang-chi were still excluded,
though, as previously in Fukien and Chekiang, the connivance of local officials
and merchants enabled them to conduct trade from the islands of Shang-ch'uan

(São João, where St Francis Xavier died in 1552) and Lang-pai-kau (Lanpacau), really on an annual fair basis, the temporary hutments being burnt at the end of the August-November trading season. In 1554 Leonel de Sousa secured permission for regular trade, paying customs dues, and by 1557 a town was growing up on the Bay of A-ma (most appropriately the goddess of seafarers), officially 'the City of the Name of God in China', in history Amacon, Macao, Macau (Plate XI).[25]

Plate XI. MACAO, 1598. Obviously a stylised view, with a few concessions to local colour; note the absence of fortifications, very often the most conspicuous features in this type of illustration. From Theodore de Bry, *Indiæ orientalis* (Frankfort 1607). NLA.

The transaction was a verbal one, and indeed while the Portuguese ceased paying a rent in 1849, their sovereign rights were not fully admitted by China until 1887; but from the beginning Macao enjoyed a practical extra-territoriality. As Boxer says, 'the agreement suited both parties, and consequently had a much longer lease of life than one would expect from an oral arrangement made after much junketing on board the Portuguese flagship.' The reason for this is well put by Chang, in words nearly as applicable to the Hong Kong of 1957 as to the Macao of 1557:

> [the Chinese authorities] saw their aim attained: they could now reap
> the benefits of foreign trade without either permitting foreigners
> to visit Canton or Chinese to leave their country. Here, right at
> the doorway of Canton, was a settlement of foreigners who eagerly
> took what China could offer to other countries, and brought to
> her what she needed from abroad on such terms as were favourable
> to her. On the other hand, however, the Chinese watched the
> mushroom growth [of Macao] with a certain amount of apprehension
> . . . At times the foreigners were treated with singular generosity
> and showered with rare favours, while at other times, they were
> suspected, closely watched and subjected to grotesque restrictions.[26]

Meanwhile, between the first arrival off Canton and the founding of Macao, a
new sphere of enterprise had been opened: in 1542 or 1543 three Portuguese
adventurers had arrived, in a junk and by chance, at the island of Tanegashima,
south of Kyushu.[27]

The advantages of Portuguese trade with Japan were mutual; the daimyo of
Kyushu were immediately responsive, and especially did they appreciate the
virtues of the arquebus, long known simply as the 'Tanegashima weapon'.[28]
There was also an eager demand for European novelties such as time-keepers,
whether clocks, dials or hour-glasses, some fine textiles, and leather goods, as
well as Chinese porcelain and other Asian luxury items. But commercially these
were marginal: the great staple import was Chinese raw silk, superior to the
home-grown and in great demand; later on were added fine silk stuffs and, in
the 1590s, gold for Hideyoshi's wars. Exports included swords and other traditional Japanese lines such as lacquer work and, in the next century, copper for
the gun-foundries of Goa and Macao; but the staple was silver to pay not only
for the silk of China but also for the spices of the Southern Seas: the value of
silver in relation to gold in Japan was a little below that in Europe but about
twice that at Canton, and the Chinese demand for silver was apparently insatiable.
After the initial curiosity had been met, there was little market for most European
wares, and the Portuguese trade in the China Seas was essentially a carrying
trade in Asian products; but with direct Sino-Japanese trade usually banned, and
the silver:gold ratios what they were, this was a middleman's dream.[29]

For the first few years of contact, trade was in the hands of private venturers
coming to various ports of Kyushu, notably Hirado and Kagoshima. The daimyo
were in active competition for Portuguese visits, which brought some prestige
as well as material benefits; and along with the merchants came the missionaries.
As a result of Xavier's brief mission and the work of such devoted and able
successors as Luis Frois, a remarkable number of Japanese—as many as 150,000
by the early 1580s—became Christians, and very many of them far from merely
nominal ones, as their steadfastness in fearful tortures and martyrdoms was to

show.[30] This notable success had political implications, and following Gibbon's example we may glance at some of its 'secondary causes'.

Initially, some Japanese seem to have thought that as Christianity was brought from India, it was only a new sect of Buddhism, and hence acceptable in a land of many such sects; conversely, and at a different level, Nobunaga, rising to power in the 1560s, was a bitter enemy of the great Buddhist monasteries, as recalcitrant and over-mighty subjects as any daimyo; one sect at least, the True Land (Jodo) had dangerously radical social tendencies.[31] As a natural consequence Nobunaga showed some favour to the new faith. Christianity had a certain appeal to the poor and oppressed, who were offered new consolations and kindly attention by the Fathers, especially perhaps in the later Franciscan phase of mission activity; conversely again, there was an element of *cuius regio eius religio*, leading to mass conversions at the lord's behest. The 1584–6 'embassy' of young Japanese nobles, hand-picked by the Jesuits and carefully shepherded through their splendid receptions in Iberian and Italian courts and cities, was of course designed to such an end: the manipulation of an élite.[32] While some daimyo, including for example Hideyoshi's very able and loyal general Konishi Yukinaga, became truly sincere Christians, others thought adherence to the foreign belief a small price to pay if Jesuit influence brought Portuguese shipping to their ports: 'In short, it was the Great Ship' from Macao 'which was the temporal mainstay of the Japan mission'.[33] It may well be, as Hall says, that to speak of 'The Christian Century in Japan' is really 'something of a Western conceit';[34] but, as we shall see, at several points Christianity impinged very significantly on Japanese external affairs, political and economic.

At both ends of the trade, the free-for-all did not long endure: 'after the Viceroy at Goa got wind of this new Eldorado, the voyage was placed on the usual monopoly footing under the control of a captain-major' of the China voyage from Goa and Malacca; until 1623 he was also captain-general of Macao while actually at the port, which in the interim was ruled by its own *Senado* or Council.[35] This Crown appointment was by way of reward for services, royal favour, or purchase, and in addition to the captain-major's own investment there were also sundry charges and commissions on consignments financed by various parties—Macao merchants, both Portuguese and Asian; the Jesuits, who would not have been able to finance their mission otherwise; Kyushu daimyo, and even Hideyoshi and Ieyasu. Naturally so lucrative a post or job was surrounded by much corruption, faction, and intrigue, and there were also of course occasional interlopers, licensed or illicit. After 1550 the China voyage was usually made by only one or two ships a year, presumably in the interests of the royal fisc; but these were great Indian-built teak carracks of 600 to 1600 tons, known to the Japanese as the *Kurofune* or 'Black Ships', a favourite and lively theme of Namban or 'Southern Barbarian' art.

At the other end, in Japan itself, the trade was not completely regularised until 1571; before that various ports were visited, sometimes on a political basis—

Plate XII. THE GREAT SHIP AT NAGASAKI. Japanese screen painting, reproduced in M. Cooper SJ (ed.), *The Southern Barbarians* (Tokyo 1971). By courtesy of Kobe Municipal Museum of Nanban Art.

the Jesuits naturally tried to favour those daimyo who favoured them—but this was not conducive to stable trade relations. But the Christian daimyo Omura Sumitada offered an uninhabited peninsula on the first-class harbour of Nagasaki as a secure base, and by 1579 a Christian town of about 400 houses had grown up (Plate XII). Although authorities disagree as to whether there was an actual cession of land, in practice the Jesuit Superior nominated the daimyo's Governor from about 1580 until Hideyoshi took over the town some ten years later, and even then, after a decent spell, the Church regained an effective if discreet control.[36] The year 1571 saw, then, the founding of the port which for over two centuries from 1641 was to be the only licit point of contact between Japan and the outer world; it saw also the founding of Manila, the spearhead of attempted penetration of China and Japan by Portugal's rival Spain, and again for over two centuries the only licit point of contact between Pacific America and Asia.

The Philippines: dreams and realities

The reduction of the Philippines to Spanish rule was the work of men of the sword; the retention of rule was largely due to men of the Cross. Although King Philip's treasury paid heavily to establish and maintain the network of mission stations, their close supervision and moral domination of the country people helped a mere handful of Spaniards—never more than 5000 until the very last years of the régime—to maintain a hold over the scores of jungly and mountainous inhabited islands (Plate XIII).[37] Even so, that hold was at times precarious, and in the Muslim south never really complete and assured: although, after the occupation of a 'royal' village in 1578, Governor Sande officially annexed the whole of Borneo, even the treaty made three hundred years later (1876) with the Sultan of much smaller Jolo was 'written on water',[38] and Cross and Crescent remain in armed conflict to this day. The hispanisation of the Philippines by the Gospel was a continual drain on the royal treasury—only in 1701–31 was there a surplus, for the rest the administration was carried on by heavy subsidies from New Spain;[39] but the Galleon trade put much treasure into private pockets—not least into those of Philippine ecclesiastics.

Here indeed, in a vulnerable wedge between the farthest eastward penetration of an expanding Islam and the expansionist Japan of Hideyoshi, was the end of the world for Iberian expansion westwards. The Philippines were 'Spanish by the grace of New Spain, of Legazpi and Urdaneta, the true testamentary executors of the abortive dream of Columbus'.[40] It follows that the islands were the colony of a colony, and all through the voluminous reports to Spain run complaints of the alternate indifference and interference of the Viceroy in Mexico. These documents in the earlier volumes of Blair and Robertson give a wonderful view of the agitated intrigue, the tinsel grandeurs and real miseries of life in this small frontier pond, which was yet too close to mighty and mysterious Asian empires to be merely a backwater.

Each new Governor reports proudly that he has built or is building an efficient

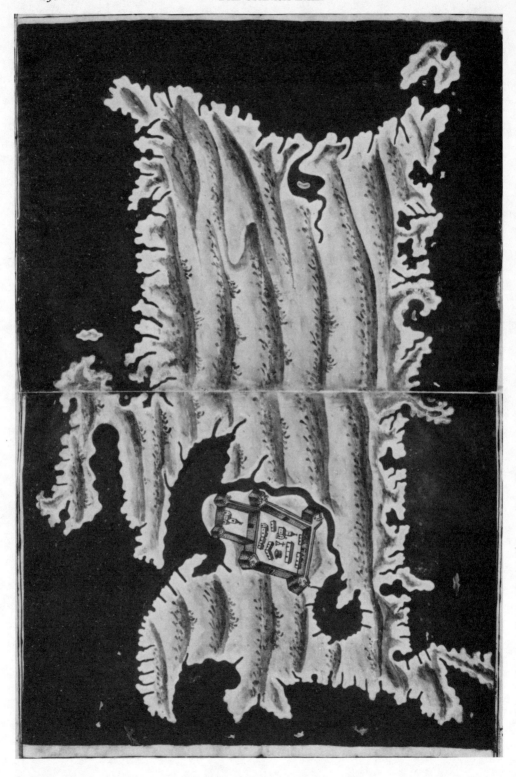

galley fleet to cope with the Moros; each successor finds only a few rotting boats, or none. The Chinese traders and artisans—the 'Sangleys'—are a constant problem: they bring poor shoddy silk and will take only gold and silver, making profits of 100 or 200 per cent; their cheap cottons ruin local crafts and drive the 'Indians' into laziness and vice; they force up prices. Yet we need them for the commodities they bring (including, after two decades of settlement, even food) and to carry on the artisan and retail trades that Spanish gentlemen cannot be expected to handle; and then there are doubtless vast possibilities in China, both for commerce and conversion. We ought to put down the infamous crime of sodomy that the Sangleys are said to perform on their ships, corrupting the simple Indians—'but, since the punishment may hinder commerce, it will be necessary to observe moderation' until your hard-pressed Majesty advises us. Between the Chinese and the Mexicans, the Manila merchants are squeezed out, and so much money is drained away. The widows of noble conquistadores marry beneath them to keep the encomienda in the family, which is a disgrace to civil society, bad for morale and morals. Church and State are often at loggerheads: Bishop Salazar, playing the las Casas, vehemently attacks the atrocious ill-usage of the Indians, but *per contra* officialdom alleges that 'the friars make use of them by the hundreds . . . whipping them as if they were highwaymen', and have 'no grief or pity'. Manila has 'not even a prison, and that under an Audiencia'. To get money for the urgently needed fortification of the city, Governor Dasmariñas monopolises the sale of playing-cards and imposes a 2 per cent property tax, but applying this to the clergy he incurs 'the censure of the bull of the Lord's supper' and is excommunicated. He retorts that the clergy are 'all better merchants than students of Latin', and this is backed up by a list of consignors to Acapulco by the Galleon—all ecclesiastics or Audiencia officials. With under 600 Spanish citizens in 1599, the colony doesn't really need an Archbishop and three Bishops and all their underlings—'one is sufficient'. We may let an Archbishop have the last pungent word: Majesty in Madrid

> should not enquire into the particular vices of Don Francisco Tello,
> but should picture to yourself a universal idea of all vices, brought
> to the utmost degree and placed in a lawyer: this would be Tello,
> who is your Majesty's governor in the Philippines . . .
> he has not even an indication of a virtue.[41]

With all this, there was a great deal of vigour and panache. Legazpi died in August 1572, and his followers took far too seriously, given their scant resources, his boast that 'we are at the gate' of the great realm of China. Within eighteen months of his death, his notary Fernando Riquel was writing (January 1574)

◄ *Plate XIII.* MANILA AND LUZON, 1635. The distorted lineaments of Luzon are recognisable, but in contrast to Macao (Plate XI) the emphasis is on Manila as a fortress in the bush: unrealistic cartography, but a symbolism appropriate to the realities. From P. Barretto de Resende, Livro do Estado da India Oriental, Sloane MS 197, by permission of the Trustees of The British Library.

that the many very populous cities on the year's journey between Canton and Peking 'could be subdued and conquered with less than sixty good Spanish soldiers'—*con menos de 60 españoles buena gente*.[42] Even assuming that a cipher has been dropped out, Tomé Pires, dying in a Chinese jail half a century earlier, could have told him better. It is a neat comment on these delusions of grandeur that before the year was out Manila itself nearly fell to the assault of a mere pirate.

This Cantonese sea-rover, Lin Ah Feng, or to the Spaniards Limahon, commanded some three score well-armed junks and was seeking a new base, having made the China coast too hot to hold him: his most prominent lieutenant was a Japanese. He landed near Manila on 29–30 November 1574, and his two assaults were beaten off only by very desperate fighting, and some luck. He retired to Pangasinan, some 175 km north of Manila, and set up a little kingdom, which in March 1575 was blockaded by land and sea by Juan de Salcedo, Legazpi's youthful grandson and the most notable conquistador of Luzon. During the blockade Salcedo met a Chinese warship under Wang-kao ('Omoncon'), sent to track Limahon down. This was of course an excellent opportunity to open relations with China, and Wang agreed to take an embassy, led by Fray Martin de Rada, back to Fukien. Unluckily, Salcedo thought that Limahon was safely boxed up, and conducted a leisurely investment: the pirate was an abler man than the Spaniards accounted him and was able to build up a fleet of small craft from the remains of his fleet, burnt by Salcedo. At the beginning of August he slipped away, to meet an obscure end.

The result for the Fukienese embassy was disastrous: the Chinese suspected collusion. After an initially good reception, Rada and his companions were brought back to Manila by a Chinese mission, and there were further misunderstandings with the foolishly arrogant new Governor, Francisco de Sande. The Chinese wanted Limahon's head, or at least presents suitable to their rank; Sande could not produce the first and on a point of pique would not provide the second. The envoys agreed to carry Rada and another friar back to Fukien, but beached them in northern Luzon; and there was no further talk of the virtually promised Spanish base on the Bay of Amoy, the very site for which had been pointed out to Rada. Sande's reaction was an absurd antipathy and scorn for all Chinese, so that this very promising opening for friendly relations was replaced by crazy schemes of conquest—schemes which in their wild disregard of common-sense, let along logistics, recall King Picrochole even more than Don Quixote.[43]

There were tremors also in the south: Drake was at Mindanao and the Moluccas in 1579, and eight years later Thomas Cavendish sailed into San Bernardino Strait and right through the southern islands, as though the Spaniards were in the Philippines to no purpose.[44] These were mere premonitions; more immediate was the threat from the north. In 1580-1 a Japanese freebooter set up a base in Cagayan, in the north of Luzon, and was expelled in 1582 only after very hard fighting. Japan had been included, rather vaguely, among those neighbour kingdoms whose conquest would be both pious and glorious, and perhaps easy, but more sober thoughts began to creep in: 'These occasions are not so much a matter of jest as they have been hitherto; for the Chinese and Japanese are not Indians' but as valiant as many Berbers 'and even more so'. Matters were to become even more serious from 1582, for in that year Nobunaga was assassinated, to be speedily avenged by his even abler general Hideyoshi. Hideyoshi's advent to power heralded an intensified drive towards consolidation in Japan, if not an end then at least a very marked limitation to the freedom of action of the Kyushu daimyo, and in due course a menacing expansionism. By 1593 any merriment was on the other side: 'The Xaponese laughed [and] said that the defence of these islands was merely a matter for jest. . . .'[45]

In 1582 also news reached Manila and Macao of the forcible union in 1580 of the Portuguese and Spanish Crowns. A completely separate Portuguese administration in the Indies as well as in Europe was guaranteed by the Cortes of Thomar (1581), which accepted the Spanish takeover, and until late in the 'Sixty Years Captivity' the promise was honoured; nevertheless the change could not but lead to complications—commercial, political, religious, military. The ancient rivalry survived in the forced marriage, and was often very sharp indeed. Loyalty to a single Crown could not wish away the competition for the trading, and mission, rights in Japan.

Manila and Macao

The Galleon was more to Manila than even the Great Ship to Macao; the Portuguese had their carrying trade, and it would seem a more enterprising free-lance element, and it was these that enabled Macao to adapt and survive even after the Dutch had blockaded the Malacca Straits and the Japanese had expelled them from Nagasaki.[46] Trans-Pacific crossings were almost annual from the foundation of Manila,[47] and in 1593 the Galleon trade was regulated at a normal two ships a year, practically in the form in which it was to persist until the end of Spanish rule in Mexico, except for a great increase in unit-tonnage—originally the ships were to be limited to 300 tons, but this, like so much else in Spanish regulations, was a dead letter almost from the start, and already by 1614 there were 1000-tonners.

The hope of tapping the spice trade from the Philippines soon dwindled away (although as late as 1579 Sande was still yearning after the Moluccas);[48] it became clear that economically only the China trade could justify the Spanish presence in the islands. The profits from Chinese silk could be enormous; it had to be paid for with silver, but here Mexico was a providence: 'The extraordinary luck of the Spanish Philippines was to be at the point of contact between two monetary systems, a world of dear silver and a world of cheap silver.'[49] But the silk, and the minor wares—porcelain, drugs, luxury craft-work—came to Manila in Chinese junks, and after 1604 also in Portuguese ships from Macao, and on this side the Spanish 'part in the trade was a stationary one', simply sitting on a fine harbour splendidly situated to be a focus of shipping in the Southern Seas. But for two or three months of the year Manila was a chaos of shipping and forwarding.[50]

The organisation of the Galleon trade was extraordinary: reading Schurz's chapter 'City and Commerce' one has almost the strange impression that the entire colony acted as both individual shareholders and managers of a joint-stock company; whence, naturally, some confusion.[51] There was a *permiso*, or global quota of cargo, which throughout the seventeenth century was set at a value of 250,000 pesos; within this total all citizens had in theory the right to consign, in proportion to their wealth, on the King's ships, each person's entitlement being apportioned by a committee, the *junta de repartimiento*. In practice, the trade fell increasingly into the hands of a few active entrepreneurs, who bought up the *boletas*, or permits, of the small fry, a highly speculative affair. A large share was taken by groups such as the cathedral chapter and the *obras pias*, or charitable foundations, which ran orphanages, hospitals, and the like services. These, by their continuity of experience and policy, amassed large capitals and were able to act as bankers for the shippers, lending at anything from 20 to 50 per cent.

As well as securing his boleta from the junta de repartimiento, the consignor had to secure his goods from the commissioner of the *pancada*, the bulk-buying scheme which in theory handled all Chinese merchandise for export on the Galleon. When we add to this the normal complications of Spanish shipping and customs regulation, and the fact that the 250,000 pesos in Manila would (even officially) be worth 500,000 in Mexico, it will be seen that the system, like so much in the Spanish combination of bureaucratic control with private financing, was guaranteed to produce delays and corruption on every hand. The real value of the cargoes was always grossly in excess of the permiso, often several times greater. Everybody was in the racket: each seaman even was allowed to carry one chest, 'which had a most expansive capacity'; and the Chinese packers were artists in the compaction of the small-bulk high-value staples of the trade. The resulting overlading between and even on decks, often at the expense of space for necessary stores and gear, interfered with the working of the ships and was responsible for several wrecks; and the loss of a Galleon, by storm or capture, meant a ruinous year for the city. But the profits were enormous: officially set at a permissible 83 per cent, represented as a miserable 5 to 10 in Manileño petitions, inflated up to 1000 in jealous Dutch or English eyes, they ranged in actuality between 100 and 300 per cent.

The Union of the Crowns was only reluctantly accepted at Macao;[52] although now officially brethren, Lusians and Castilians often behaved in less than fraternal fashion. It is an ironic comment on the Union that the Cabildo of Manila wrote to the King that the Audiencia should be suppressed since not only was it superfluous for seventy Spanish households in Manila and seventy in the rest of the islands (plus a few troops), but, as they alleged, 'our Portuguese neighbours cannot believe that it has been established for so few people' but 'imagine that it is . . . to overpower and govern them' and so 'have shut the door to the commerce, friendship, and intercourse which was commencing. . . .'[53]

Naturally Manila (and Mexico) wanted to get into the direct China trade; equally naturally the Portuguese saw in this the complete ruin of their 'Eastern Yndias', and argued that Castille itself would suffer, since China would drain 'all the money and coin' from New Spain 'and none will go to Hespaña' (it must be remembered that Macao's silver came from Japan). This consideration carried weight in Madrid itself, so much so that in 1586 the King signed a decree prohibiting Mexican imports from China altogether, partly in the interest of cloth exports from the home country. The Viceroy of New Spain, Manrique, put up an able counter-argument and, more to the point, simply saw 'fit to disregard your Majesty's orders, until you direct me further'.[54] There was a Cabildo in Mexico City as well as in Manila, and trade with the Sangleys went on.

Rigid separation between the two Iberian spheres was more easily applied to the large and bureaucratically organised long-distance trades: the voyages of Francisco Gali in 1584 and João da Gama in 1589-90, direct from Macao to Acapulco, were exceptional and caused scandal. But the Macao-Manila silk trade was sufficiently profitable to both sides to survive repeated official bans, and it remained in Portuguese hands (so far as it was not in Chinese) despite the demand in 1586 by a junta of the leading officials and citizens of Manila that they should be allowed to 'make voyages to Japon, Macan, and all other kingdoms and posts, whether Portuguese or pagan'. The memorial of this junta is indeed a most remarkable document. Much of it deals with internal problems and is a level-headed and liberal reform program; all that is wrong is that for it to work successfully the Castilian leopards—officials, ecclesiastics, merchants, encomenderos—would have had to change their spots. The rest is a plan for the conquest of China, at least more realistic than Riquel's sixty stout soldiers: the forces needed would be 10-12,000 Spaniards and Portuguese, 5-6000 'Indians' from Visaya ('a spirited and sturdy people'), and 5-6000 Japanese, who might prefer to go in with the Portuguese, whom they knew already, and could be guided by the fathers of the Society of Jesus. Such large forces would be needed to overawe any thought of resistance; otherwise the Spaniards would win but, as they did in once-populated but now desert countries like Cuba, at the price of wrecking everything, including the 'so wonderful' Chinese government. In that case we shall lose 'our reputation and the bright hopes we now have of getting the port of Macan and a passage into Japon'.[55]

This went into the discard; the one project of conquest that these forward-policy men-on-the-spot got away with was a confused and abortive adventure in Cambodia, an absurd dispersal of scanty forces when more than all available strength might well have been needed for defence against Japan.[56] The Manileños persisted in attempts to secure a base on the China coast, the Macaonese as persistently blocked them. The 'bright hopes' received their quietus in 1598-9, when Cantonese officialdom had at last been persuaded to let the Spaniards settle 'in perpetuity' at 'El Pinal', somewhere between Canton and Macao. Far from co-operating in the conquest and conversion of China, the Portuguese informed the mandarins that the Spaniards were 'robbers and insurrectionaries, and people who raised revolts in the kingdoms they entered'; finding words not enough, they tried to expel their fellow-subjects and fellow-Christians by force of arms. They were staved off, but El Pinal was abandoned.[57]

Already, however, the focus of rivalry had shifted to Japan, where nationalist, mercantile, and missionary motives were nicely compounded in a paradigm: Portingall: Castilian, Macaonese: Manileño, Jesuit: Franciscan.

Japan united

Oda Nobunaga began his career as a very minor baron, held in scant respect by his peers. He was lord of Owari at the head of Ise Bay, around the modern Nagoya, a small fief but strategically located between the ancient capital Kyoto and the largest lowland of Japan, the Kanto (Kwanto) Plain where Tokyo stands. The country was racked by the endless confused struggles of the warlords, for whom however Kyoto retained its mystique: ambitions could be legitimated by securing from the shadowy Emperor, through his little less shadowy Ashikaga Shogun, a commission doubtless disguised as for the defence of the realm against (other) over-mighty subjects, in practice to subjugate or destroy these rivals— a procedure far from unknown in medieval Europe. In 1560 Imagawa of Suruga, a much more potent magnate than Nobunaga, the lord of three provinces between Owari and Kanto, was moving on Kyoto to this end, across Nobunaga's territory. He had 25,000 men, Owari could muster a bare 3000: Imagawa saw no problem. Nobunaga surprised, routed, and slew him. By an adroit combination of political intrigue and war he then built up a power which enabled him to enter Kyoto itself in 1568, nominally in support of a claimant to the Shogunate, whom he formally installed in that dignity, only to depose him five years later.[58]

Nobunaga's hegemony was far from undisputed, and his period of dominance was filled with much hard fighting, not least with the great Buddhist monasteries which sided with his enemies: these he crushed with great slaughter. By the time of his murder in 1582 he controlled, directly or through vassals, thirty-two of the sixty-odd provinces, and these centrally located in a belt from the borders of Kanto to the northern shores of the Inland Sea, the very heartland of Japan.[59] He had a rough military approach to civil affairs, but this was needed, and he had grasped the importance of sound administration. Under his rule the many tax barriers which compartmented the country were abolished, and the hold of the merchant guilds on internal trade was weakened by the favouring of free markets as service centres to the castles of himself and his vassals; Nobunaga asserted his authority over Sakai, but fostered the city in its role as a major source of armaments.[60] An innovator in tactics, making much use of arquebusiers, and in fortification, he also initiated policies later extended by Hideyoshi, notably a new land survey and the disarming of the peasantry, far too much given, in these times of troubles, to agrarian risings. He also anticipated Hideyoshi in dreaming of the conquest of China. Basically an iron-hearted soldier, he had yet an enquiring mind which, perhaps as much as his hatred of the Buddhist monks and his taste for overseas luxuries, led him to listen courteously to the learned and tactful Jesuits.[61]

Remarkable as Nobunaga was, he was outclassed by his successors Toyotomi Hideyoshi and Matsudaira Motoyasu, the latter better known as Ieyasu, the first Tokugawa Shogun. They could be no less ruthlessly cruel on occasion, but were more prepared to use conciliation and finesse. The three are well summed up in their traditionary reactions to the caged bird that would not sing: Nobunaga—wring its neck; Hideyoshi—force it to sing; Ieyasu—wait till it sings.[62]

Hideyoshi, Nobunaga's leading general, was unique amongst Japanese rulers in being of humble birth: in a rough European approximation, if Nobunaga began but little above the gentry, Hideyoshi's birth was little if at all above the yeomanry.[63] But, until in his latter years he overreached himself, he was a soldier and a politician of genius, who like Cromwell

> Could by industrious Valour climbe . . .
> And cast the Kingdome old
> Into another Mold.[64]

It is ironic that by his ruthless 'Sword Hunt', completing the disarming of the peasantry, and by his census, land survey, and other legislation, he froze the social structure of Japan into a hierarchy of closed classes, which lasted into Meiji days: warriors, peasants, artisans, merchants, conceptually and nominally in that order, though in the nature of things the peasantry soon sank to the bottom.

When one of his generals assassinated Nobunaga at Kyoto, Hideyoshi was away in the west of Honshu, engaged in the reduction of the Mori who dominated that area. He lost no time in patching up a truce and dashing back to the capital: within twelve days he had defeated and slain the murderer. Other leading generals were absent, Nobunaga's sons ruined their chances by fratricidal quarrelling, and Hideyoshi was able to control events. He called a meeting of notables and literally carried into them Nobunaga's baby grandson, who was proclaimed heir, with a council of four army leaders to run the country. Such an arrangement could hardly last, and it was not long before Hideyoshi as Regent began to concentrate power in his own hands. This of course meant more fighting, but by mid-1583 he controlled thirty provinces, and could operate on interior lines against Kyushu or Kanto at his choice. The most dangerous rival, Ieyasu, had kept aloof from events, but now took up arms with some success; but the two were realist enough to come to an honourable arrangement, and Hideyoshi was now free to complete Nobunaga's work of unification.

He had already a footing in Shikoku, which he subdued in 1585; in 1587 he took advantage of internal strife in Kyushu to compel the dominant lord of the

island, Shimazu of Satsuma, to come to terms. The Mori, who had helped in
the tough Kyushu campaign, did not finally submit until 1591. By that time
Hideyoshi and Ieyasu had together overrun the Kanto Plain, which was given
to Ieyasu, who seated himself in Edo (today's Tokyo), in exchange for his three
provinces of Mikasa, Totomi, and Suruga—the very three whence Imagawa
had launched the entry into Nobunaga's lands in 1560, the beginning of the whole
coalescence. In the still backward and peripheral north there was only one really
powerful lord, Date Masamune, who submitted in 1590; Hokkaido was as yet,
and long remained, a barbarous no-man's land, This apart, a common soldier's
son was now master of all Japan.

The building of the great castle at Osaka, which was to overshadow Sakai as
a commercial centre, set the seal on Hideyoshi's dominance; with the reduction
of Kyushu and the taking over of Nagasaki, he was brought into more direct

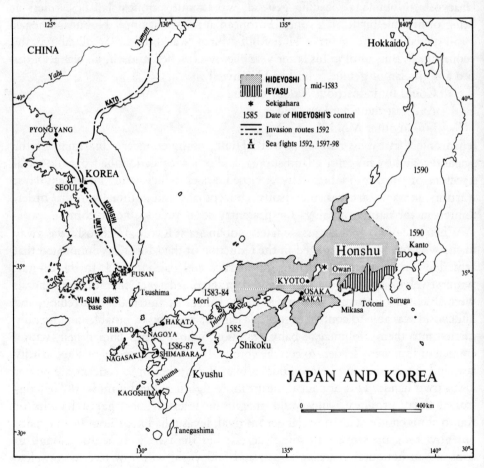

Figure 17. JAPAN AND KOREA. In the later sixteenth century. Based on maps in J. Murdoch,
A History of Japan (London 1949), Vol. II, and A. L. Sadler, in *Trans. Asiatic Soc. of Japan* 2nd Ser.
14, 1937, 177–208.

touch with the Europeans. He could now think of asserting himself on a wider stage than the Japanese islands, and Macao and Manila were face to face not with a congeries of rival lordships but with a state which, however strange and composite its organisation—paradoxically, a sort of centralised feudalism—was yet comparable in real power with any European monarchy.[65] The resulting involvement of those European outposts with Japanese politics was to be fateful both for the expansion of Iberian Christendom and for the polity of Japan itself.

Hideyoshi and the Jesuits

Immediately, Hideyoshi's accession to power made little difference to Macao and the Jesuits; to them, probably, the warm welcome given to a storm-driven Spanish ship in 1584 by the daimyo of Hirado (losing trade to Nagasaki) may have seemed more ominous. Indeed, as the daimyo suggested that missionaries other than Jesuits would be well received, it was the first hint of a crack in their mercantile and religious monopoly. Only two or three years later the innocent maladroitness of the Jesuit Vice-Provincial, Gaspar Coelho, precipitated a crisis which, however, was bound to come fairly soon, given the rate of conversion among the western lords and their retainers, and the obvious danger of divided loyalties that this implied. *Cuius regio, eius religio* could after all go into reverse, and on a bigger scale.

In 1586 Coelho paid a courtesy visit to Hideyoshi at Osaka; the interview was cordial—as it turned out, too cordial. The Regent confided his plans for the invasion of Korea and China, asking for the aid of two Portuguese carracks. Anxious to please, and showing much less than the traditional subtlety of his Order, Coelho rashly agreed, and even proffered further Portuguese aid for the Korean war, though obviously he had no way of making good such promises. Worse, he went on to pledge—unasked—his influence to rally the Christian daimyo of Kyushu against Shimazu; just the interference in local politics that wiser Jesuit heads had always warned against. To Hideyoshi, here was clearly another over-mighty subject in the making, the more dangerous for his foreign backing. The Christian lords were horrified at Coelho's presumption, but Hideyoshi kept his own counsel, even granting the Jesuits privileges superior to those of the Buddhist priests, and Coelho nestled happily in his fool's paradise.[66]

In July 1587 Hideyoshi was at Hakata after the Kyushuan victory, and here Coelho entertained him on shipboard.[67] To all appearance the party was a great success, and Hideyoshi went ashore with some of Coelho's Portuguese wine—which ironically may have incited rather than mollified him. In the middle of the night a shaken Coelho was roused by the Regent's couriers and presented with four extremely pointed questions about Jesuit and Portuguese activities, ranging from alleged forcible conversions, destruction of temples, and slaving, to the eating of useful animals like horses and cows. He made what reply he could, but during the day—25 July 1587—an edict was issued giving all Jesuit Fathers twenty days to leave Japan; but 'As the Great Ship comes to trade, and this is quite different, the Portuguese can carry on their commerce unmolested'. A leading and actively Christian daimyo, Takayama Ukon, had already been stripped of his fief for refusing to recant.

Coelho temporised, pointing out that they could leave only by the Great Ship, not due to sail for some months, and this excuse was accepted; but the ban was strengthened and extended: all symbols of the Faith were prohibited, and all Japanese Christians were ordered to recant, or to suffer exile or death. Coelho now tried to incite armed resistance by the Christian lords and wrote to Goa, Macao, and Manila for armed succours; all of those he approached had much more sense than to comply, and his ecclesiastical superiors were furious at his ineptitude. Their cooler stance was justified: Hideyoshi took no serious steps to enforce expulsion, and only a handful of Jesuits actually left; the rest carried on, if less publicly than of old, though a quarter of their establishments were actually destroyed. Takayama had obviously been disciplined *pour encourager les autres*; but other leading converts, such as Konishi Yukinaga, soon to make a great name for himself in Korea, were even moved to the danger-spot of western Kyushu.

In fact, the Jesuits were considered (fallaciously, in their own opinion) as indispensable interpreters and intermediaries with the Macaonese traders, a factor of special importance when Hideyoshi was amassing supplies and wealth for the Korean project; as Father Alessandro Valignano put it, with gentle cynicism,

> with this Great Ship, and with our doing them all these little
> favours, they deceive themselves, and they are nearly all of them
> convinced that if the padres were not here, the Japanese could not
> deal with the Portuguese, which opinion is of no small help to us
> at this juncture.[68]

Valignano, who had taken the Japanese youths to Rome in 1582, was officially permitted to bring them back in 1590.[69] His earlier experience in Japan (when he had supported a policy of acculturation by the Fathers to Japanese ways), his tact, the splendour of his embassy and the presents it brought, put things back on the old footing, and Hideyoshi even defied 'his own prohibition by strolling through the gilded halls of the Juraku palace wearing a rosary and Portuguese dress'.[70]

Nevertheless, a clear warning had been given. Coelho's good wine, missionary interference with the supply of girls for Hideyoshi's court pleasures, were trivial secondary factors, if factors at all; more important perhaps was the Regent's increasing tendency to arbitrary action on impulse, a resultant of success and power. But while it is true that 'The dictator who changed three and twenty daimyo from their fiefs in a single day' had no need to dissimulate in his earlier effusive display of friendship to the Jesuits, or 'to truckle to [the] petty lordlings' of Kyushu,[71] it was just as certainly not at all irrational for him to see in the rapid advances of the new Faith the beginnings of a subversive fifth column.

This, the simple view of his volte-face, is surely the right one, and it explains amongst other things the singling out of one Christian daimyo only, Takayama Udon, as an example and a warning.

The real threat to the Jesuits, when it did come, came doubtless not by the intent but without doubt by the actions of their co-religionists and fellow-subjects, the Franciscans of Manila: the storm had blown over for the time, but a cloud was rising in the south. Before it reached Japan, however, Hideyoshi had plunged into his Korean campaign, the greatest Japanese overseas operation before the wars, in the same waters, of 1894–5 and 1904–5.

The Korean adventure

Narrowly considered, Hideyoshi's Korean war may seem to have but a tenuous connection with the Pacific at large; but its significance, if negative, was real enough. Immediately, it diverted Japanese attention from a known option to the south; longer-term, its failure seems to have implanted a distaste for expansion and outside contact, a factor in the eventual self-internment of the country. Simply as a strategic study, the war is of great interest, a preview of the Korean campaigns of 1894–5 and even 1950–3. The naval historian must lament the absence of Coelho's promised carracks, which could have tested their technical capacities against the Korean 'tortoise-boats', while a European eye-witness account would have been of inestimable interest.

Hideyoshi's main motive seems to have been a megalomaniac lust for glory: Korea in fact was to be but the bridge-head for the conquest of China, a belated *revanche* for Kublai Khan's attack on Japan through the peninsula, three centuries earlier. Secondary motives probably included the need to divert discontents stirred up by his tough land policies; to find employment for the masterless or landless warriors left over from the wars—the *ronin*, obviously a potentially dangerous group; and to secure trade without tribute, or even with tribute coming to Japan. The decision was not a sudden impulse; the project had been long in Hideyoshi's mind and may have been taken over from Nobunaga.[72] Pretext was found in the Chinese refusal to extend facilities for trade by ships licensed under Hideyoshi's 'Red Seal', and in that of the Korean king to pay homage and tribute (he was of course already tributary to Peking); he warned Hideyoshi that to attack China would be like 'a bee stinging a tortoise', which was more true than tactful.[73] There were many minor irritations which could be blown up by either side into quarrels—the overlordship of the Ryukyus, piracy—and the diplomatic exchanges were complicated by local vested interests such as those of the daimyo of Tsushima (lying between Japan and Korea), the reasoned policy calculations of competent generals in the field such as Konishi and the unreasoned reactions of other warriors, and the inveterate if very natural tendency of the intermediaries to tamper with their instructions when these would obviously offend the recipient: one Chinese envoy, for example, when reporting to Peking habitually represented a Japanese desire for 'peace' as one for 'submission'.[74]

A total of some 225,000 men were mobilised, with Nagoya (in Shikoku, not the modern city on Ise Bay) as the main and Tsushima as the advanced base; organisation was meticulous, and hundreds of craft, small and large, were assembled for transport—the one-time pirates of the Inland Sea found a new opening for their talents. The first three divisions, under Konishi Yukinaga, Kato Kiyomasa, and Kuroda Nagasama, numbered some 52,000. On 24 May 1592, aided by mist, Konishi made an unopposed crossing of the 75–80 km between Tsushima and Fusan (or Pusan, the chief southern port of Korea), which he took the next day. He was joined almost at once by Kato and Kuroda; the government of the country was in a miserable state, and the Japanese 'swept through Korea like a swift wind blowing away dead leaves'; they were much aided by their possession of firearms, which the Koreans lacked.[75] By 12 June Konishi was in Seoul, having covered 440 km in under twenty days.

In the meantime, however, and almost simultaneously with Konishi's occupation of the capital, the fatal errors in Japanese planning were revealed: the lack of an effective supreme command in the field, Hideyoshi remaining at home, and above all the neglect of sea power. The Korean Court seems not to have taken the threat seriously at first, but even had orders to oppose the crossing been issued, the naval commander at Fusan, Won Kiun, was so worthless that they might not have made much difference. Strategically poised in a group of islands near the southwest corner of the peninsula, however, was his colleague Yi-sun Sin, a man of a very different mettle, and this soon became apparent. The Japanese fleet contained a number of large ships built for war, but on the whole these seem to have been inferior to Korean and Chinese vessels. Probably the Japanese crews and some individual captains were as skilled seamen and sea-fighters as their opponents, and many of them must have had naval experience in Nobunaga's blockade of Osaka (1578) and the Kyushu campaign; but there was no unified command. The squadron commanders were soldiers, and as in the land fighting they were inspired by intense rivalries; but the spirit of 'marching to the sound of the guns' was more hazardous at sea, faced as they were with an opponent with superior armament and very clear ideas on how to use it.

By contrast to the Japanese commanders, Yi-sun appears a professional—his achievement in fleet-building alone shows that—and he was an admiral of such resolution, intelligence, and power of leadership that in the second naval campaign (1597–8) the chief of the Chinese contingent served under him, which in view of the normal Chinese stance towards lesser powers would seem almost against nature. He had also the advantage of the 'tortoise-boats', which were novel to the Japanese although they did not, as is often implied, spring new-born from Yi-sun's brain—they had a long prehistory in Chinese war-junks. Nor were they, as Ballard styles them, the Dreadnoughts of the time, though perhaps weightier than Sadler's alternative of torpedo-boats.[76] They probably had some form of armour-plating, certainly a carapace-like deck studded with spikes to cripple the boarders on whom the Japanese relied too much—like another Armada only four years earlier, their ships were crammed with troops. The offensive capacity of Yi-sun's ships depended on fire-power—guns (in cannon, as against small arms, they were ahead of the Japanese), fire-arrows, something like Greek fire— and their use of the ram has been generally much exaggerated; by and large, any ramming seems to have been largely incidental.

By 7 June, with Konishi well on the road to Seoul, the main Japanese naval forces were scattered among the numerous off-shore islands west of Fusan, where Yi-sun fell upon them: by 10 July, in seven tactically beautiful actions, he had shattered their flotillas in detail, destroying at least 160 substantial vessels. But by the beginning of September the remaining Japanese ships, still a formidable fleet, were concentrated under the fortifications of Fusan, now turned into a powerful base, and Yi-sun's attack was beaten off. Nevertheless, steady reinforcement and supply of the armies in Korea was made very difficult, and these armies had now to meet counterattack from across the Yalu River.

On 15 July Konishi had taken Pyongyang, and the Korean king had fled to the banks of the Yalu, appealing for aid to his overlord in Peking. In October a small Chinese force was trapped and nearly destroyed in Pyongyang itself, while on Konishi's right Kato had advanced into northeastern Korea, at one point crossing the Tumen into what is now Manchuria. But the Koreans were recovering from their initial collapse; not all their provincial governors were incompetents, some rallied forces and achieved local successes, aided (despite Japanese efforts at conciliatory administration) by a strong guerrilla movement. Resistance throughout the country was hardening, while the alarming naval news from the south weakened the morale of the more thoughtful Japanese leaders. Despite his successes, Konishi accepted a truce. The Chinese were now taking the invasion more seriously, and when they struck again, in February 1593, it was in such force that Konishi had to withdraw to Seoul. Kato fought his way down from the northeast to join him, and together they defeated the Chinese in fierce fighting. But the pressure continued, and in May they felt forced to abandon Seoul pending negotiations, and retreated, unhampered by the Chinese, to a fortified zone covering Fusan.

Hideyoshi was far from disheartened. By this time he seems to have lost touch with reality, and apart from a peace party led by Konishi (and it had to be very cautious) his courtiers did little to help him regain it. He had still a bridge-head in Korea (Konishi realistically saw little point in the half-way policy of hanging on to it), and although the Chinese had virtually left the Koreans out of the war and the negotiations, they themselves had left only a small garrison in Seoul. The Chinese terms for peace included a demand (doubtless much softened in the presentation) that Hideyoshi should be invested by the Chinese Emperor as King of Japan; he countered with demands for the southern provinces of Korea, resumption and extension of the 'Red Seal' trade, and the hand of the Emperor's daughter. Negotiations dragged on in an atmosphere of intrigue and arrogance on both sides, with the diplomats tempering their principals' demands to the point of deceit. The moment of truth came at the end of 1596, when a Chinese embassy actually brought over the robes for Hideyoshi's investiture as a vassal. A milder man might have exploded as he did.

The war began again in March 1597, but in a different atmosphere from that of 1592. At least the naval lesson had been learnt on one side, lost on the other; Yi-sun had been dismissed through palace intrigue, and his fleet allowed to decay. Won Kiun was in command again and Konishi, now a general at sea, had no difficulty in soundly beating the drunkard who had fled from the first encounter five years before. On land the Japanese advanced with less speed and drive than previously, until in January 1598 they were forced back by new Chinese armies. There were very bitter battles north of Fusan, the Japanese more than holding their own: Konishi bore much of the brunt, surely one of the great subordinate commanders of history. The impasse was resolved in October, when news arrived of Hideyoshi's death on 15 September: there was now no point in staying. But Yi-sun had been recalled and with a reorganised navy he fell upon the retreating squadrons: the Japanese got away with very heavy losses, perhaps half their ships and men. Yi-sun himself was killed in the thick of his last battle.

The Korean war was as futile as any in the long grim competition of futile dynastic wars. It had however some useful economic effects in Japan itself. Korean captives contributed notably to the excellence of Japanese ceramics, one group brought over by Shimazu developing the famous Satsuma ware; more important was the great expansion in ship-building and allied industries.[77] Politically, the absence from the story of Ieyasu's name is significant: that wary prince sent a small force to Nagoya, but himself sat out the war safely in Kanto, biding his time, which was very near: as in 1582, he could wait for the bird to sing.

The relevance of the war to Pacific history is that it helped to settle the geostrategic position of Japan for over two and a half centuries, estopping a very likely development of incalculable effect. Without the war, it seems all but certain that Hideyoshi would have struck south, to the Philippines. It is inconceivable that the small Spanish forces there, barely beating off Limahon, incapable of definitively subjugating Mindanao and Jolo, with little effective naval power, could have withstood the assault of even a third of the highly organised forces committed to Korea. With the metropolitan base so close and so populous, the manpower would have been available for an easier and more complete subjugation of the local peoples than that achieved by the Spaniards. By the time the Dutch and English arrived in any strength—like the Iberians, at the extreme range of their effective action—the Japanese would have been perfectly capable of meeting them on more than equal terms, and borrowing from them what they needed to adapt to a more open polity. It is easy to envisage, with Ballard, 'a fleet of Japanese 74's dominating the whole Western Pacific'.[78] The statesmen of mercantilist Europe would have had ample cause to thank God for Hideyoshi's folly, had they known of it. Setting aside any might-have-beens, the Franciscans who came from Manila to Japan in the 1590s were playing with fire; some of them all too literally.

Hideyoshi and the Philippines

The Jesuits had pulled in their horns after Coelho's disastrous gaffe; guided by Valignano they had recovered lost ground, but its retention depended on continued discretion. Valignano argued cogently for one single control in the Japanese mission field—naturally, that of the Society of Jesus—and in 1585 he procured a papal bull confirming the Jesuit monopoly. The ardent Franciscans of Manila were not to be deterred by this embargo, and they were backed by more mercenary interests in the Philippines.[79]

Soon, however, the Jesuits were hoist with their own petard, in the shape of one of their converts, Harada (Farada in Spanish documents). This man was a Sakai merchant who had traded in the Philippines; in 1591 he and others proposed to Hideyoshi an invasion of the islands, but the eve of the Korean war was hardly a propitious time, and instead a relative of Harada was entrusted with a message for the Governor, Gomez Perez Dasmariñas. This document, most beautifully and elaborately packaged, was less pleasing in content: it contained a demand for an embassy, on pain of such a conquest that 'that country shall repent'. Dasmariñas, startled as he was, and understandably suspicious of an 'ambassador' of such lowly status (who was also the only available translator), replied tactfully, making these points but promising to refer the matter to Spain. In the meantime, to 'show willing', he sent a Dominican, Father Juan Cobo (presumably chosen as being a Chinese expert) to make and to receive further explanations.[80]

Nothing positive came of Cobo's mission: he did not even report, being lost on Formosa on his return voyage. It had however some awkward negative results: an increase of Spanish-Portuguese tension, and probably the strengthening of latent suspicions in Hideyoshi's mind. Cobo did not contact the Jesuits, who if not anxious to help could at least have interpreted more reliably than Harada, but instead joined with a couple of disreputable Spanish merchants with grievances against the Portuguese. Their complaints led to some renewed action against the Jesuits in Nagasaki, but this soon blew over. Cobo is also said to have shown Hideyoshi a globe, pointing out the wide spread of Philip II's realms.[81]

Harada now took the game into his own hands, himself carrying to Manila a second letter from Hideyoshi. This was more than explicit:

> Formerly I was an insignificant man . . . but I set out to conquer
> this round expanse under the sky, and those who live beneath the
> sky upon the earth are all my vassals . . . [Korea refused homage
> and is conquered] The kings of other nations are not as I . . .
> Thou shalt write the following at once to the king of Castilla:
> 'Those who insult me cannot escape. . . .'

Dasmariñas stalled for time—if the Japanese could be amused for four years, Manila might then be ready for them, though as the required force was estimated at 1517 men, this may reasonably be doubted. In May 1593 the Governor sent a second embassy of Fray Pedro Bautista and three other Franciscans: this was in breach both of Japanese decrees and of the bull of 1585 (as the Jesuits did not fail to mention), but was supposedly justified by the claim that the Fathers were going as government envoys rather than as missionaries. The real mischief was that the shady Harada had fraudulently represented that Hideyoshi, and indeed the whole country, positively desired the Franciscans, and with this encouragement a steady trickle of friars went to Japan. Hideyoshi had, it is true, warmly welcomed the embassy; but in religious matters he was a *politique* to the marrow, and his real desire for it was as 'a bait for the Manila traders in the same way as the Jesuits were considered to be part and parcel' of the Macao trade.[82] With the fiscal strain of the Korean war, any competition between traders was welcome.

The Franciscan embassy also gave Hideyoshi an opportunity to exercise what was for him diplomacy: his next letter (1594) reads like Marlowe's Tamburlaine—at his birth the sun had shone on his breast, portending his destiny, which was nothing less than that all kingdoms must bow down at his door or be destroyed. Gomez Perez Dasmariñas had been killed by his Chinese rowers on an expedition to the Moluccas, and the task of replying fell to his son Luis, assisted by a full council of war: with the omission of a lesson on cosmogony in the first draft, the letter as sent was a masterpiece of polite hedging.[83] There was a lull in the exchanges, but it was the proverbial lull.

The storm broke in 1596. The four friars had stayed on in Japan and had been allowed to preach in Kyoto; at least in his relations with Hideyoshi, Bautista was tactful. It is however clear, even if we assume some Jesuit exaggeration, that the friars were far from content with Valignano's cautious (and temperamentally sincere) policy of adapting so far as possible to Japanese ways; after all, they had been used to dealing with submissive 'Indians', not proud and sophisticated daimyo. They also appealed more directly to the poor and oppressed than did the Jesuits, and in general the sons of St Francis behaved in a far more forthright and uncompromising way than those of Loyola. Their flouting of Hideyoshi's bans became more and more flagrant; but for the time being he had other pre-occupations, and in July 1596 Antonio de Morga could write to Philip II, in all innocence, that 'Xapon is kept quiet by the presence of the Franciscan religious whom we have there.'[84] But the situation was highly unstable, and in October it was brought to a head by a chance happening, the wreck of the Acapulco-bound Galleon *San Felipe* on Shikoku.[85]

The cargo was very rich, and the local daimyo and his samurai seized most of it—as Boxer remarks, 'the coastal inhabitants of any European country would have done the same.' The Spaniards naturally appealed to Kyoto, using the good offices of Fray Juan Bautista rather than those proffered by the Jesuits, who were after all mostly Portuguese. The Japanese intermediaries double-crossed the claimants; between the demands of the war and the losses caused by severe earthquakes, Hideyoshi was in financial straits, and accepted the suggestion that he should confiscate this gift from the sea. (He might after all have cited, had he known of it, a tactless precedent—Elizabeth's legal but scarcely moral seizure of the Spanish treasure forced into her ports in 1568.) It is possible also that his suspicions were roused by the Spanish pilot who, in a natural desire to assert the powerful backing he might expect, is said to have displayed on a map the world-wide empire of his own sovereign, and have added that the religious were used as an advance-guard to soften up the King of Spain's prospective vassals. The similarity to the story told of Cobo is suspicious.

Be this as it may, it is certain that Hideyoshi's suspicions were aroused, and inflamed by the go-betweens and others around him; after all, he had given a clear warning to Coelho and Takayama Ukon, but had then held his hand; and now his reward was a reckless defiance of his commands. No ruler of his time could have been expected to accept such a situation. Even so, his wrath was discriminating. Presumably because after the *San Felipe* affair trade prospects with Manila were dim, and hence Macao's must be nursed, the Jesuits were still exempt from extreme measures, save for three Japanese lay-brothers mistakenly included in the mass crucifixion at Nagasaki on 5 February 1597. On that day six Franciscans and seventeen of their converts suffered; Morga prints a moving letter from the friars, warning that Hideyoshi, 'his appetite whetted by what he has stolen from the *San Felipe*' plans to take the Ryukyus, Formosa, then Manila: the letter is subscribed 'On the road to the gallows'.[86]

Further and greater persecutions were to face the Christians of Japan, but not at Hideyoshi's hands, although he did finally order the expulsion of all but a handful of Jesuits, an order again generally evaded. In August 1597, feeling his death near, he appointed a Regency council of five on behalf of his four-year-old bastard Hideyori; Ieyasu was not one of the five, but was asked to be guardian of the child: an arrangement not likely to be any more viable than the council Hideyoshi had himself subverted after Nobunaga's murder. In September 1598 Hideyoshi—and Philip II—died. Factional intrigues soon began; by 1599 Ieyasu had pledges of support from so many daimyo that he was able to occupy Osaka castle. A 'western alliance' was formed against him, but was itself riddled with faction, and in the great battle of Sekigahara it was utterly defeated: among those executed after the fighting was the gallant Konishi Yukinaga. A few days later Ieyasu was again in Osaka, nominally acting for Hideyori, in practice master of Japan.

Sekigahara was fought on 20 October 1600. Exactly seven months earlier a small, battered ship, with only a quarter of her hundred-odd crew still alive, was towed by the local boatmen into a small harbour of Kyushu. She had come by the Straits of Magellan, her pilot was an Englishman, but she herself was Dutch: the *Liefde* ('Love' or 'Charity'!). Only seven weeks after Sekigahara, Oliver van Noort and Antonio de Morga were locked in a bitter sea-fight in the approaches to Manila Bay. More than the spectacular forays of Drake and Cavendish, the arrival of the Dutch heralded the end of the Iberian monopoly of the world, as distinct from the local, trade of the Spice Islands and the China Seas.

Chapter 7

THE SILVER TIDE

Reina del grand' Océano dichosa,
sin quien a España falta la grandeza . . .
¿Cual diré que tú seas, luz hermosa
da Europa? . . .
No ciudad, eres orbe; en ti admira
junto cuanto en las otras se derrama,
parte de España más mejor que el todo.

(Herrera)

Derramado y sonoro el Océano
era divorcio de las rubias minas
que usurparon la paz del pecho humano . . .

Y España, con legítimos dineros,
no mendigando el crédito a Liguria,
más quiso los turbantes que los ceros.

Menos fuera la pérdida y la injuria
si se volvieran Muzas los asientos;
que esta usura es peor que aquella furia.

(Quevedo)

Herrera, who died in 1597 (a year before Philip II), rejoices in Seville, the lovely light of Europe, not a city but a world: a part of Spain greater than the whole. Quevedo, born eight years before the Armada and writing long afterwards to Olivares, minister and favourite of the Prudent King's less prudent grandson Philip IV, speaks the sombre truth: once Spain was separated by the Ocean from the mines which have ravished peace from the human heart; once she had a valid

---

F. de Herrera (1534–97), *A Sevilla*: 'Fortunate Queen of the great Ocean, without whom greatness would be wanting to Spain . . . what shall I say you are, lovely light of Europe? . . . You are no city but a world; in you can be admired all that is dispersed through other cities, oh part of Spain much greater than the whole.'
F. de Quevedo y Villegas (1580–1645), *Epistola satírica y censoria . . . a Don Gaspar de Guzmán, Conde de Olivares*: 'The wide-spread and loud Ocean severed them [earlier Castilians] from the ruddy mines which have ravished peace from the human heart . . . And Spain, with a valid coinage, not begging to the Genoese for credit, cared more about [Moorish] turbans than about ciphers. Less would be the loss and damage if the loans were turned to Moorish chiefs, for this usury is worse than that fury.' The Muzas, father and son, were ninth century Muslim rulers in Aragon. Both in J. M. Cohen (ed.), *The Penguin Book of Spanish Verse* (Harmondsworth 1956), 171–2, 274–5.

currency and did not go a-begging to the Genoese; now the usury of their loans—the *asientos*—is more devastating than that ancient fury of the Moors. The genius of the poet and victim expresses the burden of the plaints of many contemporary *arbitristas*,[1] and of many modern economic historians, with greater concision, clarity, and poignancy. But not for the first time or the last, the pen of the accountant, not the poet, outmatched the sword.

For the tragedy of Spain was that, dominating and exploiting the New World and the (then-known) Pacific by zealous valour, whether missionary or soldierly, she was in turn dominated and exploited by good business practices, zealous ciphering, and the force of coin—coin struck from her own wealth, a wealth itself basically ill-gotten, wrenched as it was from the agony of millions of Indians. The vast outpouring of American treasure was mediated to the rest of Europe (and much of it ultimately to Asia) by Spanish dynastic wars and follies,[2] by capitalist chicanery, by piracy (or, politely, privateering), by contraband trade carried on (not least by Spaniards themselves) through corruption or 'at point of pike'; yet without this inflation, without the productive or predatory enterprises which it stimulated, the transition from the late medieval to the modern world would at the least have been much slower, though not necessarily less painful. In 1977, this transition itself may seem a much less assured good than it seemed to the generality of Western observers in 1877 or 1777; and yet, human nature being what it is, it is not very likely that modern times would have been much, or any, more peaceful without American silver. It was in the last resort that *auri sacra fames*, the accursed lust for gold, which assured that Latin America should quickly become something more than a mere littoral fringe.[3] Alongside the devastation was construction, the *mise-en-valeur*, as part of the world economy, of great continents.

The Indies: people, land, and labour

Spanish domination in the last quarter of the seventeenth century extended from the Tropic of Cancer in New Galicia to 40°S in Chile. As with other intruding empires, its rule was most easily and firmly based in areas such as Mexico and Peru where existing well-organised political structures could be taken over; and it frayed out into the merest 'presence' on the more arid or jungly margins. Both the northern and the southern frontiers were far from being well settled in any sense. On the arid marches of New Galicia, the Chichimecas around the silver town of Zacatecas were not fully pacified, after several decades of ferocious guerrilla war, until 1600, and then 'not by the sword [our 'military solution'] but by a combination of diplomacy, purchase, and religious conversion', including the settlement on the frontier of Tlaxcalans, stout peasant types with a 'special relation' who could be exemplars to the Chichimecas of a more civil existence.[4] It was just at this time that in the far south the Araucanians compelled a local but long-enduring retreat. Spanish control was exercised from no more than three large cities—Mexico, Lima, Potosi—with a handful of second-rank towns, and thence through scores of small district centres, tiny ports, missions and mining camps, many of them wretchedly rough places. There were many gaps where climate and terrain were more effective defences than armed force: so near the heart of the Indies as the Isthmus of Panama, Spanish power was so feeble, or so ill co-ordinated, that in 1698 the Scots could insinuate their Darien colony, un-molested by the Spaniards for over a year—though by the same tokens of climate and terrain, it was quite debarred from any growth or useful activity of its own.

Within these limits and limitations a small (though constantly increasing) Spanish minority was able not only to control a large (but constantly decreasing) Indian majority, but also to maximise the latter's productive capacity by a most ruthless exploitation. It is true that exploitation had its indigenous precedents; as Lynch says, 'Whereas before the Peruvian Indians had toiled to build temples of the Sun, now they laboured to satisfy the bullion demands of the world economy',[5] and both the old masters and the new were powerfully aided by the bonds of religion. But the old system had more reciprocity—at least in the under-standing of the people—and the Spanish exploitation was often so intense and uninhibited (except by laws promulgated far away in Spain, and disregarded) as to become counter-productive. Its workings were at first sustained but in the long run undermined by Indian fatalism in face of the break-up of their world, a fatalism at once a cause and an effect of appalling population decline.

Despite the apologetics of writers like Salvador de Madariaga, using selective data and faulty method, this demographic disaster, probably the most catastrophic in all human history, cannot be gainsaid.[6] The pre-conquest population cannot of course be known with certainty. The most serious recent proponent of a low figure is Angel Rosenblat, who in 1935 estimated that of Mexico and Central America as 5,300,000 in 1492; but the very careful work of Simpson, Borah, and Cook, using Aztec tribute lists as well as Spanish data, indicates a 1523 population of 16,800,000 in central Mexico, roughly the Aztec domain; since initial de-population is known to have been very rapid, a 1519 population of 20–25,000,000 is possible. By mid-century it was about 6,000,000 and in 1605 only 1,075,000; two or three decades later a slow recovery was in train. The earlier figures have been challenged by Rosenblat on grounds of 'manipulation'; but, as Borah says, he simply repeats himself in 1967 'without change in the estimated figures, although with enormous additions at the foot of the page'. Such exact adherence over thirty years—and years of remarkable progress in the techniques of historical demography—is the more strange in that Rosenblat's figures were originally put forward as tentative. There seems a certain rigidity of mind, and Rosenblat's arguments are as a whole unconvincing.[7]

It seems likely that there was already pressure on resources in the fifteenth century, and the Spanish shock may have simply tipped over an already precarious Malthusian balance; but discount the earlier figures even to Rosenblat's, and the story is still terrible. First place among the responsible factors must undoubtedly go to epidemic disease—'bacteria and viruses recognised the unity of the planet long before man', and areas that were so to speak kept out of this unity by oceanic barriers—America, Australia, Oceania—owed to this spatial quarantine a total lack of immunity to new infections. The rest of the world had knocked together for millennia; now for the Americas the barriers to epidemic invasion were destroyed in decades, with results of course the most devastating precisely where population was densest.[8] But there was also a great toll of life in the wars, by actual slaughter, economic disruption, and famine; Spanish labour demands did the rest, together with that most universal solace of the dispossessed and oppressed, alcohol; and probably a weariness of living in the confused regimen of a disordered world, where 'To castrate the Sun, for that the strangers came'.[9]

For Andean America, Venezuela through Chile, Rosenblat gave a 1492 total of 5,100,000, of whom only 2,000,000 were in the present Peru, and this last figure, falling to 1,500,000 in 1570, is often quoted.[10] *A priori*, it seems too small, especially in comparison with Mexico; Chaunu speaks of the richness of Peru lying in its mass of 4–5,000,000 Indians. A recent review by Nathan Wachtel, using Spanish local enquiries as well as overall estimates, suggests tentatively but quite reasonably a pre-Pizarro population for the Inca Empire of 7–8,000,000, possibly 10,000,000; whatever the starting point, there was a steep decline to 2,500,000 in 1560, then a slower fall to 1,500,000 in 1590. The causes were as in New Spain: 'Abus, guerres, epidemies' and, except for a few favoured Inca grandees, a trauma perhaps more acute than in less centralised and absolutist Mexico, for with the violent death of *the* Inca the arch of the world's fabric had collapsed.[11]

One may reckon, then, on an initial mass of ten million souls at the very least, more probably forty million, dwindling with fearful rapidity and hence supplemented, especially in hot coastal lowlands, by slaves imported from Africa, though for a century these were numerically but a small element barely on a par with the all-controlling whites. In 1570 Europeans may have numbered 63,000 in New Spain (18,000 in Mexico City), 25,000 in Lower Peru and 7000 in Upper (roughly Bolivia). By 1630 these figures had risen respectively to 125,000 (48,000 in the capital, say half the population of Madrid or Vienna), 20,000 and 50,000, this last great increase reflecting the rise of Potosi, whose wealth became proverbial in other languages than Spanish, and whose total numbers, including Indians, rivalled all but a handful of European cities.[12]

The *raison d'être* of Spanish settlement (the glory of God apart) was essentially the extraction of treasure from the earth, and both then and now the world's gaze has been caught by the dazzling mining economy of Spanish America. But the miners had to be fed and clothed, and to this end, often in disregard of metropolitan interests, there was a remarkable development of agriculture and stockraising, with some consumption manufactures, and these were oriented to the market—even if in some places a very local market with the mine, corn-supplying arable farm, and ranch for meat, leather and tallow, in one close-knit complex. Farms and plantations and ranches of course depended on the acquisition of land, and of the labour to work it.

Whether by right of conquest or of Papal donation, the Crown of Castile considered itself the owner of the land of the occupied Indies, and it was in its own interests quite as much as those of the Indians that it strove to prevent the encomienda becoming effectively an hereditary landed fief. Direct land grants were initially carefully restricted, but laxity soon set in, and there were many opportunities for expansion: taking over land left vacant by the dying Indians, forced purchase or legal chicanery at Indian (or 'poor White') expense, simple squatting in a country where some delineations of title long remained 'by eye'— that is, as far as could be seen from a given point.[13] In New Spain at least the difficulty was not so much in acquiring an estate as in manning it, and as the encomienda declined the repartimiento and its Peruvian equivalent the mita (for which there was Inca precedent) grew in importance. This was a forced levy of a proportion of the working population of each Indian community, drafted for several short periods in each year to work at low wages either on public corvée or for private applicants.[14]

The system was obviously cumbrous, with great wastage—especially in travel time—and disruption of Indian subsistence farming, and liable to vicious abuse. Early in the seventeenth century the norms were changed in New Spain: the labourer could now choose his employer, and with falling population there may have been some reality in the choice; but offsetting this, the proportion in the village so compelled to choose was raised from one-seventh to one-quarter. Finally, in 1632, the Mexican repartimiento was abolished, except for mines and public works; not so much a concession to the Indians as an effort to retain labour for these essentials. By this time the encomiendas were being replaced by great landed estates or *haciendas*, and the repartimiento was simply unable to meet their labour needs, which were supplied by the wage-labour, at least nominally 'free labour', of the old occupants. Much of this new-old labour force was naturally soon gripped by debt peonage into an almost serf-like status. In the more northerly mining areas of New Galicia the locals were far too well armed and mobile, and far too little tamed, to be shared out by repartimiento, and here the mines attracted labour from older centres, in marked contrast to the ever-attempted flight from mining in Peru. On this isolated frontier it was easy to get the workers so attracted into debt-bondage and to hold them there; nevertheless the new conditions did mean some betterment for many Indians, and it may well be significant that it is around the 1630s that the Indian population begins, however slowly, to increase in numbers.[15]

But the solution reached by so much trial and error was essentially the creation of latifundia: Iberian America was basically a 'big man's frontier', with little place for the simple squire or the intensive small farmer, except around a few city markets such as Lima or Panama or in such favoured areas as Antioquia. For well over three centuries, until the Mexican revolution of the 1920s, the latifundist solution gave social, though not political, stability of a sort; it articulated 'property into a system which, though it was neither feudal nor seignorial, established a rigid social hierarchy'.[16] But after the Mexican *ejido* and Cuba, the price of this stability is still being paid today, in blood; even in Chile, so long the model of *orden, progreso, libertad*, those three words which sum up so much of the slogans of Latin America, so little of the realities.

Agriculture, livestock, workshops

'It was the unforeseen discovery of America which changed the agricultural map of the world . . . the only crops common to both the Old and New Worlds were cotton, coconuts and some gourds', with the dog as the only shared domestic animal.[17] The list of borrowings from the Indies is formidable—maize, potatoes 'Irish' and sweet, tobacco, rubber, cassava, groundnuts, capsicums, tomatoes, pineapples, cacao, coca, and cinchona (whence quinine); but these are offset by wheat and other cereals, rice, sugar, the silk mulberry, the olive and the vine; later, eucalypts. The Americas were rich in dyestuffs, but their cochineal is matched by indigo (añil), and while Eurasia sent to America horses, cows, sheep, goats, pigs, poultry, it received in return only the turkey and, for what it is worth, the guinea-pig. This great work of intercontinental cross-fertilisation was carried out mainly by Spaniards and Portuguese, and largely in the first century of Ibero-America.[18]

In New Spain the economy of the humid south was largely agricultural: little of its output entered Pacific trade, despite Cortes's efforts to supply the Panamanian victuallers of Peruvian entradas with the wheat, biscuit, pork, sugar and cheese piling up on his Oaxaca estates. Initially indeed there was a brisk one-way traffic south in livestock and planting materials, but once Peru was stocked Mexican imports were soon cut out, last of all sugar.[19] There is, however, an important if negative Pacific connection in that a flourishing silk industry, half a century old, was nearly ruined when the Union with Portugal carried with it the final abandonment of the idea that Manila was to be a great spice mart, while the opening of the return route enabled her to become the channel for Chinese silks. Between 1579 and 1593 the Mexican price of raw silk fell by 80 per cent, flat against the general inflation of the time; the Chinese product was exactly competitive with the Mexican, being either of very high quality, which could stand round-world transport costs, or very cheap lines 'with which they clothe the galley-slaves at Manila'. The fall of the Mexican industry was a decline, not a sudden collapse, and the causes were complex. Rearing and reeling were confined to Indians, weaving to Spanish artisans, and for some uses Mexican yarn was preferable to Chinese. Falling numbers in the work force for a labour-intensive industry (especially in the great epidemic of 1576–7) and forced production quotas, with minimal returns to the Indian producers, led them to abandon or sabotage the rearing side. But, initially at least, the finishing side actually benefited from cheaper yarn and enforced specialisation in finer lines. However, the falling-off in local raw silk and continuing Chinese competition undermined the Mexican industry, and the suppression (1634) of all legal trade to Peru was simply the *coup de grâce* to a moribund craft. There was still a trifling Indian production, for home use or the most local markets; but attempts at revival in the last decades of Bourbon rule were futile.[20] The main item in overseas trade on the Pacific side of New Spain became cochineal from Michoacan.

The more arid north, New Galicia, was the main provider of the motor force for New Spain's macroeconomic activity: silver mining. The mines provided a market for tropical foodstuffs such as sugar and, where grain farming was not possible near at hand, for wheat, maize, and flour. The north was also the great stock-rearing zone: 'cattle more than men' competed with the Chichimecas for the land. It is difficult for us today to realise, and impossible to overstress, the importance then of cattle, sheep, and goats, not only for food (including jerked and cured meats for camps and ships), saddlery, and footgear, but also for a multitude of uses now served by metal, glass, or plastics. Leather goods included cordage and lassos; shields or targes, caps and helmets, cuirasses or buff coats, breeches for the soldiery; bookbindings; boxes and containers of all sorts—skins for brandy, pouches for cacao, flasks to transport the all-important mercury of Huancavelica. Eventually American hides were to displace those from Mediterranean sources in Spain itself. Lard was essential for cooking in the many places where olive oil was not easily procurable; tallow for soap-making, but above all for the mines, where there was an insatiable appetite for it for lighting and lubrication. In sum, it may not be much of an exaggeration to say with Perez: 'Beyond all doubt, the greatest triumph of economic colonisation consisted in the acclimatisation and astonishing proliferation of European livestock'.[21]

More important than Mexican export through the South Sea ports was the import of cacao from Soconusco and Sonsonate (in Guatemala and Salvador), usually shipped from Acajutla to Guatulco; this trade was very flourishing until monoculture led to utter exhaustion of the soil—and of the Indian work force. The onset of this crisis coincided with Cavendish's ravages off the coast (1587: he burned some 300 tons of cacao), and the major centre of production shifted far south to Guayaquil, which was exporting by 1610. Guatemala turned to indigo (añil), exported to both New Spain and Peru for the textile *obrajes*. Beyond Sonsonate, the connections of Nicaragua and Costa Rica were essentially with Panama rather than New Spain, and did not amount to much, except for the shipbuilding of Realejo; though Costa Rica, with few people and a considerable food output (including European fruits from the hills) supplied provisions and, most importantly, mules to the Isthmus.[22]

The Isthmus itself was much more important as consumer than as producer: cattle and pearls, fish, a little rice, about sum it up; but of course its activity as a transport node was transcendent, to the great envy of Realejo and other wishfully potential isthmian nodes to the north. The littoral from Panama to the

Equator was all but valueless, as it still is—mountainous to Buenaventura, plain beyond that, but both tropical jungle. Chaunu devotes three very solid pages to demonstrating the insignificance of Buenaventura, and even the small would-be outlets for the intermont basins around Quito—places like Ancon, Puerto Viejo and Manta, Santa Elena—were little more than places of occasional and often probably reluctant call. Santiago de Guayaquil, however, some 120km up a big complex estuary, had access to great stores of excellent worm-resistant timbers, easily floated down streams which converged on the Rio Guayas itself: with local fibres and with asphalt from Santa Elena for caulking, it became the greatest shipbuilding centre on the whole Pacific littoral. It also became the chief exporter of cacao, some even reaching Spain; and this despite disadvantages—a shoal-crowded river, and a notoriously unpleasant and unhealthy climate.[23]

Beyond Paita began the desert, stretching from 5° to 30°S, broken only where crossed by widely-spaced wedges of irrigable floodplain. It was in 'forty or so oases created by the descent of Andean waters to the coasts of Peru',[24] and far away to the south in the central valley of Chile, that the most solid, diversified, and enduring agriculture of the Spanish Pacific littoral took root, and for Peru this was as early as the mid-1530s—the planting of the first wheat was 'an honour claimed by practically every Spanish woman who reached Peru before 1537'.[25] By the early 1540s Lima, Arequipa, and probably Trujillo were surrounded by what would now be called truck-farming zones, and since they depended on irrigation, many holdings were small enough for intensive cultivation. Pigs were first slaughtered in 1536; wheat-flour mills date from 1539, by 1549 there were four cane-crushing mills, and the import of sugar from Mexico was beginning to be squeezed out; in 1551 came the first vintage.[26] Many of the larger enterprises, especially for sugar (which was capital-intensive, with big demands also for labour and land), were run by the Jesuits, who provided continuity of management and economic integration of diverse agro-pastoral activities; like other ecclesiastical entrepreneurs, they were greatly strengthened by mortmain.[27]

Trujillo, the most populous place between Panama and Lima (it had about 300 householders in 1570), was the most important of the northern *Valles* or oases, and the only one to adopt from the Indians the use of guano as fertiliser. These Valles were basic to the provisioning of Lima and Callao and the latter's shipping; they had a wide range of production: wheat, maize, barley, sugar, tobacco, cotton; pork, pig and goat hams; fruits, vegetables, olives (not introduced until about 1560), wine. The Valles south of Lima were the more important for vine-yards; a flourishing export sprang up, especially in wine—so flourishing, in fact, that the home authorities, initially encouraging, tried to restrict or to prohibit altogether new plantings of both olives and vines, fearing, in Thomas Gage's words, that in 'those parts . . . certainly had they but wine, [they] needed not any commerce with Spain.'[28] In 1600 the doctors of Panama denounced Peruvian wine as a source of fevers, and an obliging Cabildo banned its import; but it could be brought in for personal use or as 'unsolicited gifts', a large loophole, and a royal veto of 1614 had to be repeated several times in the next twenty years. There was also judicial blending of local wine with that of Spain. Then again the Church needed oil and wine for the Sacraments, and surely Divine needs should prevail. . . . By such shifts colonial enterprise, often severely restricted, was never completely defeated, until at last the Bourbons wisely abandoned any pretence of prohibition.[29]

This littoral zone of European-style agriculture extended as far south as the piedmont oases of Arequipa and Moquegua; there was then a great gap, over 1000km of desert and high Andes, until the outliers of Spanish culture were reached: the beautiful central valley of Chile from La Serena through Santiago to Concepcion, and beyond that the outpost of Valdivia. Chile, where not a wild frontier, was provincial in the extreme, but it had a very virile population: it is reported that in one week of the year 1580, sixty mestizo children were born in a garrison of 160 men.[30] As if to compensate for poverty in minerals (except placer gold, soon exhausted, and copper), the climate and terrain in the central valley were like those of the milder and more agreeable parts of the homeland: Chile was dominated by the hacienda, not the mine. The main crops were maize and the vine, with hemp for cordage; wheat was grown from the first, but its export did not become really important until after 1687, when earthquakes and blight had disrupted much Peruvian agriculture. There was also a large export of hides, *charqui* or jerked meat for mining rations, and tallow for mining candles.[31] Finally, fishing had been of great importance in pre-conquest Peru; it was menial, and economically trivial enough to be left largely in Indian hands. But there was of course a large market for smoked and dried fish, some of which was exploited by small Spanish 'companies', and the Chilean *róbalo* and dried eels were famous. The enthusiastic Fr Alonso de Ovalle SJ, to whom all prospects in his native land were pleasing, also draws attention to the value of kelp as food and of powdered starfish as a cure for alcoholism.[32]

Alongside these agro-pastoral developments, and based on the raw materials they provided, was the manufacturing of minor consumption goods, carried on mainly in small workshops or *obrajes*. The original Spanish entrants of course included a complement of artisans and, as always on frontiers, these had to be able to turn their hands to anything at all resembling their specialism, especially in munitions of war: 'even a builder of musical instruments could make wooden powder flasks.'[33] Initially the home government, and Castilian public opinion, favoured American self-sufficiency, to offset the sharp rise in prices of consumption goods, which was ascribed to the American demand backed by the high purchasing power of successful conquistadores. In 1552 the Cortes of Valladolid demanded the import of foreign textiles and a complete ban on exports, and the last major expression of this consumers' concern was the sending to Peru, in 1559, of Maestro Francisco of Segovia (the leading textile centre of Spain) with a team of weavers, shearers, combers, carders, and dyers. But under Philip II there was a trend towards a stricter mercantilism; stricter at any rate in intent, for the many regulations to protect both Indian workers and Spanish suppliers were rarely effective.[34]

The obrajes were manned, or womanned, mostly by Indians, who after the more or less nominal abolition of repartimiento were held by debt peonage, or simply illegal coercion, this most often at the hands of the *corregidores de indios*, or local 'justices', in alliance with Indian *caciques*, or chiefs: both parties were supposed to be protectors of the Indians, and both earned an ill name for eager use of their ample opportunities to impose forced labour as a penalty for alleged crimes. An attempt in 1601 to prohibit the employment of Indians, replacing them by Negroes or others, lasted eight years; perhaps some 10,000 Asians (mostly Chinese) may have come to New Spain, over a longer period, and some of these ended as virtual slaves in the obrajes.[35] Despite efforts at amelioration, conditions in the shops remained abominable throughout colonial times; they survived as an evil necessity.

Obrajes had a wide range geographically—from Guadalajara to Tucuman— and in products, though textiles, woven mostly by Indian women, bulked as the largest single line on almost any index: so soon was set the standard pattern for infant colonial industry in the imperialist world. For the most part the obrajes were devoted to cheap products for the masses—coarse cottons and woollens, blankets, ponchos, with silks in Mexico and some vicuña stuffs in Peru; there were also specialisms such as lamp-wicks for mines, slow-match for arquebuses, and so on. Leather goods probably ranked next to textiles, in output, variety, and geographical spread. Furniture, unless in the form of chests, was obviously too heavy and space-consuming to be generally imported: at first somewhat clumsy and 'frontier', colonial woodworking, in all its forms, was to reach very high levels of craftsmanship; but here we are entering the realm of the artisan. Of luxury trades, silversmithing—again hardly likely to be left to the obrajes!— was probably the most important. Nor should printing be overlooked: the first press was opened in Mexico City in 1539.

These various enterprises, but more particularly the agricultural ones, were the basis of a lively coastal and intercolonial trade (below, Ch. 8)—perhaps not the first long-distance trade in the Pacific,[36] but the first to be linked to world exchanges. It also involved substantial shipbuilding, especially at Realejo and Guayaquil. There was also of course much building, including great cathedrals and palaces, and major public works such as the drainage of the Valley of Mexico undertaken in the 1630s.[37] Major road-building, however, lagged badly; most routes were merely pack-trails, even the all-important Isthmus crossing. Carreri about 1700 thought it a miracle that he got safely from Acapulco to Mexico by the grandly named *Camino de China*, while Gage's account of his journey over the windy mountains between Tehuantepec and Chiapas is hair-raising; but there was a cart-road from Mexico City to Zacatecas, some 700km, constructed between 1542 and 1570. In Peru, the Inca 'roads' were meant for human porters or llamas, and they ran longitudinally to the mountain grain: invaluable pathways for the penetration of the Conquista, they were of much less use in the later *mise-en-valeur* of the Andean region, and the mining centres had to develop transverse pack-trails to the sea. It was not until the eighteenth century that much was done in the way of up-to-date road-building.[38]

All these economic activities, important as they were and essential to the working life of the Indies, were overshadowed by the giant: mining.

Mining: Zacatecas to Potosi

The first phase of mineral exploitation hardly concerns us: it consisted of *orpaillage*—gold-washing—and the rapid pillage of long-accumulated Indian ornaments in the Caribbean, New Spain, and Central America; in this phase gold was dominant and, with the massive loot of the Incas, gold consignments to Spain did not reach their peak until the 1550s. But in 1527–30 the first silver from New Spain reached Seville, by mid-century it was closing up to gold, if not ahead, and after 1571–80 was never less than 98 per cent by weight and 90 by value of officially recorded consignments. The great take-off of silver came with the discovery (1546) and working (1548) of the deposits at Zacatecas (still today a producing area) and the introduction from 1554 onwards of the *patio* or mercury amalgam process of extraction from the ore (Plate XIV). Peru enters the scene with the accidental discovery of Potosi (1545) and draws ahead of New Spain from 1575, after her Viceroy, the extremely able Francisco de Toledo, had been convinced by demonstration that the amalgam process would work, and had cut through legal and illegal tangle to arrange what he called 'the most important marriage in the world, between the mountain of Potosi and the mountain of Huancavelica'.[39] The latter produced more mercury than the combined output of the only European mines, at Almaden in Spain and Idria just north of the Adriatic. Shipments of bullion, overwhelmingly silver, remained high up till about 1630, peaking in the 1590s according to Hamilton or in the next decade according to Chaunu; there was then a decline, quite slow at first but precipitous after 1650.[40]

This is the standard account, based on Earl Hamilton; his figures were clearly minima but acceptable at least as indices, with some modification by Chaunu, who took volume of shipping at Seville as an index. Recently, however, a new approach, using the annual amounts of mercury made available for amalgamation, suggests a rather different scale and tempo. Mercury figures are relatively reliable, since there were only three sources of the metal, all under Habsburg control, while other indices (registered bullion imports, the Royal Fifth or *quinto*) were liable to understatement. There are still of course unknowns and unreliables—the exact ratio between mercury used and silver reduced; the amount of silver produced by smelting, which continued when and where mercury was in short supply—but this approach suggests a summit in the 1620s, perhaps as late as 1625–40, for the Indies as a whole, New Spain peaking before Peru. The really catastrophic drop would be not in the 1650s but some thirty years later—when

planche. XXII.   page. 138.

A *Llamas ou moutons du Perou* : E *Plan de la desazogadera*
B *Trapiche ou moulin a minerai* : F *Profil de la desazogadera*
C *Buiteron ou cour ou lon petri le minerai* G *La pigne*
D *Bassins a lauer* : H *Fourneau atirer le vifargent*

Plate XIV. LLAMAS AND MINING. Note the crushing-mill (B), the patio (C), and the distillation of mercury from the ore (H). From A. F. Frezier, *A Voyage to the South Sea* (London 1717). ANU.

indeed all accounts agree that the Spanish state and Spanish society were at their nadir.[41]

Although Hamilton's work was meticulous, it was based on the official records of imported bullion, as registered at Seville. But obviously the books could have no entries covering precious metal smuggled into Spain to avoid the royal charges (and the risk of seizure in times of fiscal stress), or seized by the King's enemies, or used for contraband trade with foreign interlopers, or diverted licitly or illicitly to the Philippines, or expended in the Indies on public or private account: a formidable list of omissions. However, Hamilton's figures do have the merit of representing the amount the Spanish government and private agencies had to work with in Europe; and even without any upward adjustment his totals are impressive: from 1503 to 1660, Seville registered 185,000kg of gold and 16,886,000 of silver—67 per cent of this last amount between 1581 and 1630. And this is absolutely the minimum influx. To strike a modern equivalent, in our own inflationary age, is impossible, nor is it easy to see it in terms of its own time. Earlier estimates were that the input added one-fifth to the gold stock of Europe in 1500, but tripled that of silver;[42] more recent ones tend to scale up European holdings of precious metals in 1500 (admittedly much of them locked up in the treasuries and Chapter Houses of the Church) and suggest an increase of something like 50 per cent. But this took place in only a century and a half; the old stock had been built up over nearly twenty centuries, the new input came in at unprecedented speed, and into an economy already equipped with credit and fiduciary devices, so that there was a great increase in the velocity of circulation.[43]

Serious mineral development had indeed a less lustrous side: before Cortes sent Charles V his parade cannon cast in silver, he had mined and smelted tin and copper to make more realistic guns of bronze. By and large, however, non-precious metals were not much mined in the Indies, except for Chilean copper or when European supplies were cut off by war.[44] Between 1525 and 1530 a number of silver lodes were worked in the present States of Mexico, Jalisco, Nayarit, and Guerrero, but these were not of much significance. The main advance began between 1546 and 1555, along the axis of the Sierra Madre Occidental through Guanajuato, Zacatecas, and Durango, this last about 800km from Mexico City (Fig. 18), 'The mine needs men but fears water',[45] and these places lie near the 500mm isohyet, in a zone dry enough to obviate drainage problems (at least in the earlier, shallower, mining phases) but still not in really desert country. Pachuca and Real de Monte, quite near the capital, date from 1551; but Parral, some 350km north of Durango, and San Luis Potosi, nearer Mexico City but in more arid country, were not developed until the last decade of the century; the latter is surely an early example of the Norte Americano booster name!

In contrast to the wide spread of silver mining in New Spain, that of Peru was dominated, almost from the beginning (1545) until well into the next century, by Potosi; but Potosi was dependent in turn on the mercury of Huancavelica; as another Viceroy Toledo said in 1648, these were like 'two poles which support this kingdom, and that of Spain'.[46]

Huancavelica was indeed the key to the vicissitudes of silver mining at all times in Peru, and at some times in New Spain. The mine was under 300 km from Lima and 200 from the sea, in a well-peopled area; these were essential factors in its success. At first the mercury was sent to Potosi via Cuzco and Oruro, but by the end of the century it went to the nearest harbour, Chincha, and thence by sea to the main port of Upper Peru, Arica (Fig. 9).[47]

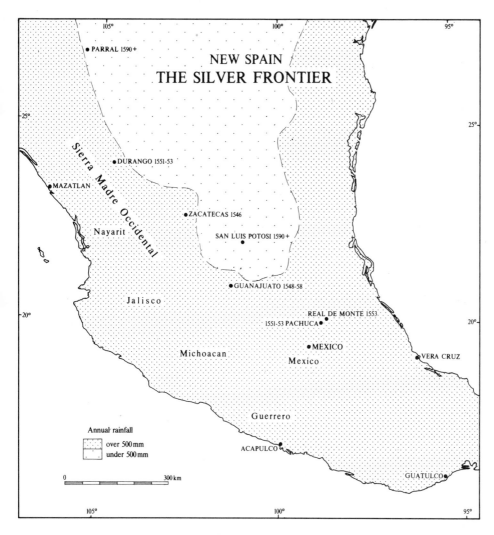

Figure 18. NEW SPAIN: THE SILVER FRONTIER

In both Viceroyalties, fuel for smelting was scarce; the mines of New Spain nearly all lay in steppe or at best scrub country; Potosi is in the desolate wind-swept *puna*, and the Indians who originally refined its ore had to use dry grass or llama dung.[48] Whether the patio method had long been known in central Europe, or whether, as Hispanic authors naturally assert 'with an almost undue alacrity', its onlie begetter was the Sevillean merchant Bartolomé de Medina (who himself said that he got the general idea from a German in Spain), is not a matter of the first moment.[49] The important facts are that amalgamation meant that lower-grade ores could be used, and with a great saving in fuel—indeed, some variants were cold and needed little or no fire. On the other hand, it did need more capital equipment and more power for ore-crushing, the power being generally animal in New Spain and water in Peru; and it tied processing to a commodity at once 'heavy and liquid, the traditional terror of seaman and muleteers',[50] a commodity moreover at first produced in only two places, both across the Atlantic.

This however was soon changed: the quicksilver of the New World was tracked down by a Portuguese merchant and poet, Enrique Garcés. This son of Mercury noticed that the Indian women used its ore cinnabar as ornament or cosmetic, and proceeded to search for a source. His first finds were disappointing, but in 1563–4 one Amador de Cabrera found the Huancavelica deposits: his troublesome claims for special privileges as the discoverer were not extinguished until 1591, and indeed his heirs were demanding a Marquisate and much else as late as 1680. . . . Garcés, however, had a prior licence for exploitation. In 1568 (or 1572) a shipload was sent to New Spain, and later Garcés and Fernando de Velasco much improved the mercury process, which in Peru was carried out in containers, not in an open patio or courtyard as in New Spain. As a result of these endeavours Garcés prospered, returned to the Peninsula, published a Castilian version of *Os Lusiadas*, and won the approbation of Cervantes: an attractive ending to a career, but he left a hell behind him.[51]

The politics of quicksilver were peculiar. There was an element of rape in Toledo's 'marriage', since it involved the virtual expropriation of the mine as a Crown monopoly; though the working itself was leased out to contractors, whose *gremio*, or guild, was for two centuries a resolute and usually successful opponent of any serious innovation. Since the costs of shipment were so high as to inhibit private tenderers, by the 1590s the Crown found itself compelled to take over trading in mercury, buying (in theory) the entire output at rates negotiated in an asiento, and this trading monopoly enabled it to manipulate, albeit often clumsily, a delicate mercantilist balance. Almaden and Huancavelica, despite the disparity in map distance, were at much the same effective distance from Mexican mines, and although Huancavelica could normally have supplied both Viceroyalties, as a rule its surplus over Peruvian needs was used as a stop-gap only when Almaden supplies to New Spain were interrupted by war or accident; otherwise it was stockpiled as a reserve despite the risk of leakage by rotting of the leather containers: how serious a risk is shown by the loss of four-sevenths of the Almaden mercury shipped to Callao between 1623 and 1650, though we may be sure that by no means all of this loss was accidental. One factor in this policy was the fear, surely justified, that licit mercury shipments would facilitate illicit general trade between Peru and New Spain. For some years after 1623 Almaden mercury was largely diverted to Peru to make up for shortfalls from Huancavelica; the Crown had a greater interest in retaining Peruvian rather than Mexican output at a high level, since in Peru the royal share was still the *quinto*, 20 per cent, while in New Spain most producers had gained the concession of paying only the *diezmo*, 10 per cent.[52] When this emergency had passed Almaden itself was declining, and in the later seventeenth century the situation became chaotic: there were serious shortfalls in supplies from Almaden, while appeals from Mexico to Huancavelica produced only irregular and inadequate shipments, so that by the 1690s New Spain was looking to Idria and even, with scant success, to China. Indeed, as early as 1600 the Viceroy of Peru itself, Luis de Velasco, wished for supplies from China, but this was in connection with his desire to get rid of underground work by the Huancavelica mitayos.[53]

In the next century Huancavelica's performance was extremely irregular, and towards its end Potosi (from 1776 in the new Viceroyalty of La Plata) and other Peruvian mines at times depended quite heavily on Almaden or even Idria. There was also a chronic shortage of cash for working expenses—'no silver without mercury, no mercury without silver [coin]'—and payments to mine operators by the Crown, the only legal buyer, were often in arrear; hence much selling on the side and smuggling. The fluctuations in output were due not only, perhaps not as much, to mine accidents and the exhaustion of richer or easier-worked deposits, though both these played their parts, as to the erratic changes of official policy in its efforts to cope with the inefficiency (for everything but corruption and obstruction) of the gremio, and the latter's dreadful exploitation of the labour force.

If Toledo's marriage had an element of fiscal rape, the gremio brought an element of sheer murder into the operation. There can be no rational doubt that the mita of Huancavelica was exceptionally frightful. To the merely normal hardships and dangers of gas, cave-ins, fire, pneumonia, over-work and under-feeding, was added the horror of mercurial poisoning: '" the disease of the mine" . . . *in less serious cases* rotted and ulcerated the gums, destroyed the dental system through excessive salivation [*ptialismo*], and led to paralytic symptoms or a "sleeping sickness" [*modorra*].'[54] As the shafts and galleries had to go deeper, unit returns fell, mortality increased, and the region lost people by death or flight. Lohmann Villena discounts the more sinister legends of mitayos receiving funeral honours when drafted from their villages and of long chain-gangs; such stories were spread not only by zealous priests but by interested parties wishing to keep Indian labour for themselves. He points out that there were numbers of volunteer labourers; but these strongly preferred to work above ground and were able to

stand out for higher wages. Luis de Velasco wished to obviate the evils of the
mine by turning the whole hill into an open-cut; even if technically practicable,
in Huancavelica's climate this might have been as bad for the mitayos as work
below the surface. In 1604 restrictions were placed on underground work; Fugger
interests, jealous for their Almaden monopoly, may have had some influence
in this, but there can be little doubt that the Crown's main motive was a conscientious and honourable one, to mitigate suffering. But output fell by nearly 50 per
cent, and a few years later economic reasoning and the needs of the Treasury once
more prevailed, as they did in 1716–19 when the complete closure of the mine,
for humanitarian reasons, was seriously considered.[55]

As might be expected, as a general rule (there were exceptions) reliance on the
mita went hand-in-hand with technological stagnation; New Spain was much
more innovative, and under the Bourbons outstripped Peru. But in the great
days, twenty-five or forty years from 1575, something like half the world's
silver came from one mountain, the Cerro de Potosi (Plate XV).

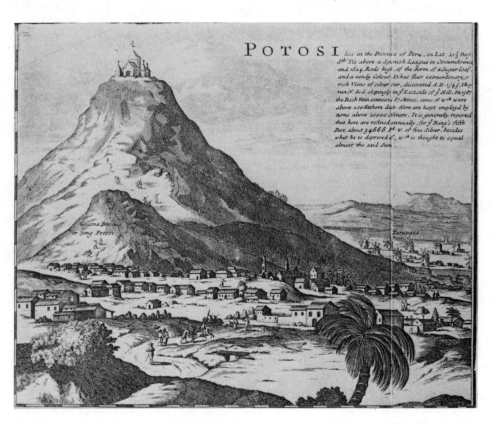

Plate XV. POTOSI AND THE CERRO.   Somewhat stylised, but giving the essentials. The
legend ends, realistically, 'refined annually, for y^e King's fifth part, about 34,666 p^d w. of fine
Silver, besides what he is deprived of, wch is thought to equal almost the said Sum.' From H. Moll,
South America (London *c.* 1719). NLA.

Potosí, over 4100 metres above sea-level (c. 660 higher than Lhasa!), was a sport, a freak; by far the highest city in the world, it was itself dominated by the Cerro.[56] This immense ruddy cone rose nearly 650 metres higher still, and was riddled by the veins of one of the world's richest ore-bodies; the surface exposure found in 1545 was ninety by four metres and 50 per cent silver. Altitude and terrain were themselves advantages from a technical point of view, since there was no fear of flooding and much of the ore was accessible, to begin with at least, by adits and relatively short shafts. But these factors added a new dimension of suffering for the mitayo: an average winter day may range from -16 to +7°C; some mine entrances were at 4500 metres, nearly 15,000 feet. In the shafts, up which men and women carried heavy burdens on dizzying ladders, the air was hot and humid, poor in oxygen but rich in carbonic gas; at the exits, sweating and under-nourished bodies were plunged immediately into icy and rarefied air, well above the altitudinal optimum even for Andean Indians. Well might it be said that only the heat of human greed could temper such a climate.[57] Yet on this highly unfavourable site, too dry and cold for cultivation, rose one of the greatest cities, numerically, of the early modern world. It had some 120,000 souls of all colours in the late sixteenth century, and by 1650 claimed 160,000—as large as Amsterdam or any Italian city, probably twice as large as Madrid itself.[58] The European population was numbered in thousands or even tens of thousands, and a very mixed lot it was.

The basis however remained, as it had to, the Indians, whether conscripted mitayos or more or less free 'fringe dwellers'. Until the introduction of the amalgam process, the refining itself was in Indian hands, and primitive enough, carried on in over 6000 little clay furnaces: some Indians could attain a modest competence, or rather more. With the new capital-demanding technique, the Spaniards took over: between 1574 and 1621 over a score of reservoirs were formed to supply water and power to the crushers and stamping-mills. By 1585 the Cerro was honeycombed by 600-odd adits and shafts, with about 1500 registered mine-owners; but a much smaller number of azogueros—'mercury-men'— controlled the refining, and they in turn depended for capital on a dozen or so big silver merchants. By an odd twist, however, a custom grew up by which anybody—and that meant mostly Indians—had the right to dig for themselves in any mine, from Saturday night till Monday morning. 'Remember the Sabbath day, and keep it holy'?[59]

The creation of this freak market in a mountain wilderness had a strong multiplier effect on the Peruvian economy, and not only on the export of silver or merely local trade.[60] The mitayos lived mostly on chuño,[61] frozen and dried potatoes, and kept themselves going by chewing coca leaves (the source of cocaine) from the eastern Andean slopes and Cochabamba, whence also mine timbers had to be brought. Amalgamation needed great quantities of salt—1500 quintals a day in the 1630s—but this was available from the great salt-pans of the Altiplano 200 km or so to the west (Fig. 9).[62] Staple European foodstuffs came from Arequipa or from Salta, Jujuy, or Tucuman, which was also a great provider of mules; further south the inland plains of La Plata supplied leather and tallow. While the official port of entry and outlet was Arica, this reaching down into the northern marches of modern Chile and Argentina was to become a major, though officially improper, trade route. Silver exports to Europe by La Plata were forbidden (a ban not so irrational as it looks (below, Ch. 8)); but since silver could be sent for normal trade as far as the customs station at Cordoba, and this was more than half-way to Buenos Aires, there was a standing invitation to *contrabandistas*. In time this was to prove a major lesion in the system of Seville.

Alongside this mundane trade in subsistence and production goods was that in sinfully costly frivolities for the conspicuous consumption of the newly rich élite. Bartolomé Arzáns de Orsúa y Vela, the gloriously inconsequential eighteenth-century chronicler of the city, gives a glittering and much-quoted list of the luxuries which flowed in from all quarters of the world for the pleasures of opulent Potosinos;[63] many of these came through the back door, brought from La Plata by Portuguese merchants, the notorious *Peruleiros*—another leak from the official channels of exchange.[64] Between these *Peruleiros* and the *Peruleros*, the merchant capitalists of Lima or their factors at Seville, the profits of Potosi were largely drained away; enough were left, however, to support a society raffish on the grand scale, out-Westerning the Hollywood West. Solid piety and good works did exist, but were overlaid by an atmosphere of fiesta and brawl: along-side the eighty churches were fourteen dance-halls and thirty-six gaming-houses, staffed by 700 or 800 professional gamblers. Civil commotion was violent and endemic. Respectable Spanish women were relatively few, partly because child-birth at the high altitude was thought dangerous; but apart from many Indian women living by *exercicios amorosos*, there were 120 professional ladies, at their head one Doña Clara, who lived in a style ranking her with the *grandes horizontales* of the French Second Empire or Third Republic.[65] And all around, gasping in the mine or shivering in the thin sharp air, the drafted relays of mitayos choked their lungs and lives out.

New Spain and Peru

Publishing in 1552, Lopez de Gomara, Cortes's secretary, struck a comparison which for two or three centuries did not need much qualification, and is indeed not altogether invalid today:

> Although the mines [of New Spain] have not been so rich, nor the
> remittances as heavy, as those of Peru, yet they have been
> continuous and great . . . Few ships come which do not return laden,
> which is not the case in Peru, which is not so fully supplied with
> such profitable husbandry. So New Spain has been as great a source
> of wealth for Castile as Peru, although Peru has the reputation . . .
> In Christianity and the preservation of the natives, New Spain has a

great advantage over Peru, and is more settled and full of people.
The same holds true for cattle-raising and agriculture . . .
It may happen that Peru will grow and become enriched with
our things like New Spain. . . .[66]

Over four centuries later, Lynch and Chaunu say much the same thing of the two
Viceroyalties in Habsburg times: New Spain is less hostile to European life, with
more diverse economic activities (including more manufacturing), and with more
and more diverse involvement of Indians in European modes of production.

If in the seventeenth century recession in silver output set in earlier in New
Spain than in Peru and was initially more severe, the Mexican recovery under the
Bourbons was the more striking: by 1798 New Spain was producing 67 per cent
of the American total, an almost exact reversal of the position a century earlier.
The single site of Guanajuato, though one of the earliest exploited, was now
producing more than Peru or La Plata, which included Potosí. 'This outstanding
achievement rested upon the long-term in-built tendencies of the period prior
to 1630', assisted by a resurgence at Almadén and a Bourbon policy of throwing
Habsburg restrictions almost into reverse—for instance, by halving the price of
mercury. There were other factors—territorial expansion of mining; a higher
level of enterprise and expertise in New Spain, with a greater readiness to accept
innovation; official measures such as the cut in mercury prices and replacing the
quinto by the diezmo did not produce equivalent results in Peru. Of the longer-
term factors in this reversal, one of the most fundamental was the renewed
increase of the Mexican Indian population, accompanied by the rise of a class of
free mine-workers—mestizos, mulattoes, Indians—whose wages were low but
supplemented by a modest share in the product. In Peru the Potosí mita at its
height took roughly one-seventh of the adult males of the region between
Cuzco and Potosí, perhaps 13,500 men, to work at the mines for one week in
three—for the other two they could hire themselves out. Demographic recovery
must have been retarded by this disruption of normal life (some 'journeys to
work' took two months!), and while this 'massive input of cheap labour' had
enabled Potosí to reach its heights, it was cumbrous and not conducive to enterprise. By the eighteenth century the Toledan mita, though much attenuated, was
merely 'a wearisome anachronism' subsidising inefficient management.[67]

We have taken the story of silver forward into the eighteenth century since it
brings out the differing roles of New Spain and Peru in 'Le Pacifique des Ibériques'.
It is in keeping with the generally more sophisticated and modernising aspect of
the Mexican economy that it acted as a sub-metropolis not only to the Philippines
(the Pacific wind circulation would account for that) but to the nominally
richer Peru. The latter, much less diversified, had a much higher price level, and
when Peru did 'become enriched with our things', its exports were primary
products—silver first of course, sometimes mercury, then (but a long way after)
wine. New Spain exported consumption goods, not just metals and foodstuffs,
of her own making, as well as European re-exports; and Acapulco was the great

entrepôt for Asian trade, though the initiative, the control, and the lion's share of the profits remained with merchants of Mexico City.[68]

Geopolitically, the maritime relationships of the two Viceroyalties were paradoxical. Physically, much of the Pacific littoral of New Spain is a rather narrow coastal plain, either semi-desert or tropical rainforest, backed (often not very far back) by rugged mountains: the Pacific States of modern Mexico have roughly 30 per cent of its area and only 19 of its people. The country as a whole looked to the Atlantic (despite the difficult and unhealthy Gulf coast) and was of course in far readier touch with the metropolis than was Peru. Acapulco itself was isolated, a town more than half deserted except when the Galleon was in, and the rest of the seaboard was (as much still is) economically backward.[69] By contrast, the coastal departments of Peru have 20·5 per cent of its area, 55·5 of its population; the desert coastal plain is traversed by the fertile irrigated Valles. Doubtless the Andean plateau weighed more heavily in the economy in colonial times; but the littoral was 'enriched by our things' and had half a dozen busy ports, even excluding Guayaquil and Valparaiso, in contrast to the narrow concentration on Acapulco. And it held Pizarro's capital, by far the nearest rival to Mexico City as a centre of government and culture; although the younger in creation, Peru was recognised as the superior Viceroyalty in status. Beside Lima and Callao, Acapulco was nothing. This active Pacific seaboard was separated from the Atlantic by the immensities of the Andes and the Amazonian *selvas*.

Yet the *oceanic* Pacific played a greater part in the life of New Spain than of Peru; conversely, what was essentially *thalassic* navigation, in the nearer Pacific waters, played a much larger role in Peru, whose external relations (when not with Pacific New Spain—a trade carried on even when officially barred) were with the Atlantic, whether legally by Panama or illicitly by Buenos Aires. Apart from the voyages of Mendaña and Quiros, which in effect came to nothing, Peru's share in truly oceanic enterprise was limited to one or two attempts to get into the Asian trade:[70] these, and the thalassic shipping to Panama and Acapulco or Realejo. The rest was no more than an active cabotage, from Guayaquil or Manta to Valparaiso and Concepcion. In contrast, New Spain played the key role in establishing the trans-Pacific link with Manila, taking over where Old Spain had failed with Loaysa; and through the Galleon and Macao trade on one hand, Vera Cruz and the *flota* on the other, she spanned two oceans, linked three continents. Once again, the motor force in all this, and much else, was silver.

American silver and the world

If Gomara had little doubt as to the superiority of New Spain, 'although Peru has the reputation', Garcilaso de la Vega was firm on the other side:

> For as the trade and commerce of mankind spreads from one
> province to another and one kingdom to another, and everything
> depends on the hope of gain, and the empire of Peru is an ocean

of gold and silver, its rising tides bathe all the nations of the
world, filling them with wealth and contentment. . . .[71]

It is true that El Inca himself bewails the rise in the price of everything since he arrived in Spain fifty years earlier, and has to concede that some think that this flood of wealth has done more harm than good, making the rich richer and the poor poorer; in fact, he hardly knows what to think about inflation, in which he has not been alone, then or since. On the main point he was wildly wrong: the treasure of Peru was a debilitating gift to Spain. Yet the silver tides did 'bathe all the nations of the world', even as far as China, bringing to some much wealth, if not contentment. But tides ebb.

The present writer is perhaps not much better equipped to deal with monetary theory than was the innocent Garcilaso, and though he is generally not averse to extra-mural forays beyond the bounds of his own discipline, a foray into a maze is daunting. Nonetheless, any discussion of the Spanish imperium, even or perhaps especially of its activities on Pacific shores and waters, cannot avoid reference to the intricate and shifting background for the 'conjuncture' of the 'long' sixteenth century in Europe: a general inflation, in Spain amounting to some 400 per cent by 1600, followed by recession.[72] Averaged over a hundred years, 400 per cent seems ludicrously mild in our own day; but of course it was not an even rise, and it came as an inexplicable phenomenon to societies lacking not only the expertise to control inflation (who has yet gained it?) but even that needed to recognise the mechanisms of the problem—and that at least has been painfully learnt over the centuries.

Earl Hamilton's straightforward approach, a direct relation between treasure flowing in and prices rising, is to some extent *démodé*: Braudel for instance 'turn[s] the hour-glass' and reverses the explanation: 'the economic surge created the rise in prices and provoked and stimulated the import of metals from the New World'.[73] Even so, if the already initiated expansion of European capitalism called forth silver, this expansion itself could hardly have proceeded so far and so fast without the reasonable expectation of yet more; its advance would have been more halting. The capitalists of Europe would have had to cut their coats according to their cloth, as in fact they had to do in the next century, until after about 1690 Brazilian gold came to the rescue. Even before the definite down-turn began—say in the 1590s for Spain and the Mediterranean, by 1640 for the Netherlands and England—there had been difficult periods, when for one reason or another the inflow of treasure fell short of expectations. One such was in the later 1550s, when the patio process was just being introduced in New Spain and before Potosi had really boomed. This precipitated the bankruptcy of 1557— the year after Philip II's accession, a gloomy augury—and brought on, for sheer lack of resources, peace with France at Cateau-Cambrésis.

Although the inflationary syndrome was more complex in its causes than Hamilton seems to allow, it is still agreed that the injection of treasure, especially when silver imports became really massive, could not fail to have had a marked effect on the volume of monetary circulation and its velocity. There were some offsetting factors—for instance, the much lesser handiness of silver as against gold for transport and storage—but this was itself to some extent offset by the development of credit devices. As might be expected, the relationships between treasure imports, prices, and economic activity were neither smooth in time nor regularly distributed in space.

In view of the use of bullion to adjust international trading balances, 'a ridge of high monetary pressure' developed over Spain,[74] and although 'In theory at least nothing entered Spain, nothing left, without the consent of a suspicious government, relentlessly watching over all outgoings of precious metals',[75] an outflow from this anticyclone was inevitable. One way was by commodity supply. In 1594 treasure formed 95·62 per cent of cargo from the Indies (the balance was in cochineal, hides, and indigo); about a quarter of this was on public account.[76] Of the rest, some would be accounted for by remittances, including those of returning officials or fortune-hunters (very often the same persons) who had made their piles, and of this much would be invested in land or spent on conspicuous consumption or building; little would be invested industrially. But much also of the total would be on trading account, to pay for a variety of consumer goods, from books to wine, and some raw materials, such as iron. This new demand certainly played a part in forcing up Spanish prices, an old complaint; but except in some lines such as textiles (still in good form in the 1590s) Spain had difficulty in meeting her own needs, let alone in finding a surplus for the Indies. Hence increasingly her exports across the Atlantic were really re-exports which had to be paid for, and preferably in silver—whether the transfer was licit, by government licence, or by smuggling; and by the end of the seventeenth century the genuinely Spanish share in legal exports from Seville was almost derisory—sometimes only about 5 per cent.[77]

The Royal share of American treasure, which included the net proceeds of taxation and of the sale of mercury as well as the quinto or diezmo, was a much smaller proportion of total revenue than was and is generally supposed—perhaps 10–12 per cent in the mid-sixteenth century, 20–25 in the 1590s, 10 per cent or less under Philip III—but it was a critically important fraction: negotiable bullion 'with no strings', it was unconditionally the King's, to do with as he would.[78] It was therefore, or it seemed, ideal security, and the international financiers of the day were normally willing enough to lend on it: first the Fuggers and the Antwerp bankers, then as the troubles of the Netherlands mounted in the 1570s the Genoese (always a strong element in Seville) became dominant. Since there was naturally a feeling that 'there is always plenty more where it came from', financiers and Crown alike were tempted and fell, until the Prudent King imprudently slid into a costly imperialism. The first major event after the marriage of Huancavelica and Potosi was the rape of Portugal in 1580. This was an immediate gain in strength, and in the Pacific meant an end to possible complications;

even though attempts had soon to be made to bail out the Portuguese who were
in trouble in the Moluccas, it was not until the surge of Dutch aggression some
thirty or forty years later that the Portuguese holdings began to be liabilities. But
the Armada of 1588 was a most costly disaster, and as for the Low Countries
themselves—to yield them was unthinkable, to attempt to keep them ruinous. It
meant a double drain—money spent on fighting the rebels, money to pay those
cheerful Dutch traders with the enemy who alone could supply such essentials
as Baltic grain, and who turned their profits to more insurgency by land and sea.[79]

In principle, to be sure, this Spanish imperialism was defensive, the maintenance
of inherited legal rights—even in Portugal, where Philip's claim was more than
plausible, the other pretendants being a bastard Prior and a woman, albeit a
Duchess. But from 1567 there had been religious riots, finally risings, in the
Netherlands; by 1572, despite or because of the Duke of Alba's ruthlessness, the
rebels had a firm territorial base in Holland and Zeeland (though Amsterdam
and some other towns still held for the King). They also had a leader of political
genius in William the Silent. Spain was now committed to a war of conquest
over difficult terrain and at the end of long and fragile lines of communication.
The standard route for men, money, and supplies was by the Atlantic to Antwerp,
but this was ceasing to be safe; apart from the Dutch Sea-Beggars, there were
Huguenot privateers—it was some of these who in 1568 forced Alba's pay-ships
into Plymouth and Southampton. Here the treasure was seized by Elizabeth's
authority, under cover of a simple transfer of a loan, the money technically
belonging to Genoese bankers until delivered at Antwerp.[80]

Except for occasional shipments by fast zabras or 'frigates', the Atlantic route
was abandoned in favour of shipping silver from Barcelona to Genoa, whence it
was forwarded by various routes under Spanish control or influence. This naturally
strengthened the Genoese hold; her bankers had the resources to make advances,
even monthly, against the annual (and sometimes less frequent) arrivals of treasure
at Seville. It goes without saying that the Genoese charges were very high: in
crises over 50 per cent interest might be exacted. The inevitable result was the
hypothecation of treasure long before its actual arrival (four years ahead in 1607),
sequestration of private bullion against copper or bonds, finally bankruptcies or
suspensions, forced conversions accepted by the bankers as salving something.
Such operations took place in 1557, 1575, 1596, 1607, 1627, 1647; that of 1607
shook out those old and faithful backers the Fuggers, who 'settled on their
Swabian estates as Imperial counts'; the Genoese hung on.[81]

The decline in bullion registered at Seville, after 1620, comes close together
with the end of the Twelve Years' Truce (1609–21) with the Netherlands and the
initiation by Olivares of a 'forward policy' which by 1640 led to revolt in Catalonia and successful revolution in Portugal. Waning resources, waxing expenditures; the silver, coming more slowly, ran out of Spain as fast as ever. The
official response (and many nations have seen much the same in our time) 'was
neither policy nor logic but only a kind of fiscal desperation that contradicted

every kind of sense and ignored all advice'.[82] Spain's own currency needs were met in a fashion by the reckless coinage of copper money or *vellón*; and this base currency was itself devalued more than once. By mid-century entire fleets and armies were financed to over 95 per cent in vellón; one wonders how the pay-chests left room for the ammunition-boxes. The acme, or nadir, of price-fixing was surely reached in 1627, when copies of a price-fixing ordinance fetched 36 per cent over the legal maximum it set for itself. Finally, a crushing comment, the Indies guard-ships of 1643 brought to Seville a cargo of copper for the mint. This went on until in 1680 drastic deflation brought prices down by nearly 50 per cent: Spain was left dazed, shaken, purged, but set for recovery, however agonisingly slow.[83]

For the Pacific, this melancholy story had a peculiar significance. The virtual paralysis of the metropolis forced the Indies more and more on to their own resources. There was another side to this chronicle of coinage. While these extraordinary debasements were going on in the mints of Old Spain, those of New Spain were turning out 'piezas de plata de a ocho reales'—the 'pieces of eight' of pirate lore—in which the silver content fell by only 5·9 per cent from 1535 to the turn of this present century. This coin became a standard medium of exchange, if not *the* medium,'along the coasts of Asia, from Siberia to Bombay'; it was only rivalled in geographical range (though not in longevity) by the Maria Theresa or 'Levant' dollar and became father, or at least godfather, to the United States dollar itself. Not until the 1890s was it displaced in the western Pacific, partly by gold and partly by the British Indian 'Straits dollar'.[84] Long before Canning, a New World had been called upon to redress the balance of the Old; the domination of Atlantic Seville over the Pacific was weakening.

The Pacific gains on Seville

The Asientos which paid for Spanish fleets and armies in the Mediterranean, Italy, Germany, France, above all Flanders, were not the only drain on American silver: much of it never set out for Seville at all. Not even the Casa de Contratacion would expect Indies silver for the payment of Indies officials to be checked in first at Seville, and this was an increasing charge as administration extended beyond the littorals and the core mining areas, and became more diversified. Colonial defence costs were constantly rising, and the Indies took an increasing direct share of them—indeed, while the *Armada de Barlovento* or Windward Fleet was paid for by the Indies and nominally stationed in the Caribbean, it often took over trans-Atlantic export duties and some of its ships served in European waters.[85] From the days of Drake and John Hawkins onwards, the Caribbean was obviously vulnerable, and its fortification a major charge. In the Pacific there were of course flurries of anxiety after the raids of Oxenham, Drake, and Cavendish; counter-measures included Sarmiento's attempt, costly in lives as well as money, to seal the Straits. There was a lull after Richard Hawkins's defeat

(1594), and Dutch attacks did not become serious on this side of the Pacific until after 1615; the heavy costs of the five-galleon *Armada de la Mar del Sur*, based on Callao, were then supplemented by expensive fortification at Acapulco, Panama, Callao, and Valdivia. Acapulco of course was a charge on New Spain, the others on Peru, where 'by 1650 defence costs alone absorbed about 20 per cent of total viceregal revenue'; and as Lynch points out, this expenditure amounted to reinvestment in local industries and ancillary services. There were also *situados*, subsidies to less-developed provinces such as Chile. Over the period 1651–1739, under 21 per cent of the Lima Treasury's receipts were remitted to Spain; the rest went on local defence and administration. The regular annual silver shipment to Panama was dropped, until in the 1680s–90s two or three sailings in a decade became the rule. 'In general Spain's loss was Peru's gain . . . The colony had become in some degree its own metropolis.'[86]

As for New Spain, that colony also was a metropolis—for the Philippines, which except for thirty years (1701–30) were heavily dependent on situados of over 500,000 pesos a year; exceptionally, in 1639–40, over 1,000,000.[87] Military costs came to 40 or 50 per cent of total expenses, and in some years a third of the receipts of the Manila Treasury went on the upkeep of the clergy. Conversely, 90 per cent of customs duties at Acapulco were paid on the Galleon's cargo. To the situados must of course be added the private silver sent from Acapulco to pay for imports, mostly from China, which as we have seen greatly exceeded the permitted 500,000 pesos a year. The drain was real, but vastly exaggerated by Sevillean enemies of the Galleon and the New Spain-Peru trade. One critic said picturesquely that 'The King of China could build a palace with the silver bars from Peru which have been carried to his country';[88] Chaunu comments no less picturesquely that if by some miracle the alleged total of silver had been loaded on to the Galleon, there would have been no room for crews, stores, or arms, and even so she would have sunk at her Acapulco moorings under the sheer weight. 'The Philippines cost Spain, in the palmy days [*à la belle époque*], some 10 to 15 per cent of what she might have received from the Indies'—this in public finance; but altogether the Orient took two-thirds or perhaps three-quarters as much as New Spain sent to Europe.[89]

This would include of course the silver sent or brought to Acapulco by Peruvian merchants buying into the Manila trade, in which they were denied direct participation. Having more silver at command, they could outbid the Mexicans, and to a large extent Acapulco became an entrepôt for re-export to Peru: in 1602 the Cabildo of Mexico City claimed, tendentiously, that Peruvian money accounted for three-fifths of an estimated flow to Manila, and ultimately China, of 5,000,000 pesos a year.[90] We shall discuss this trade in the next chapter; it was an index of increasing colonial autonomy, so striking an index in fact that it called forth the extreme counter-measure of complete official suppression. Finally we must add the silver, in its origin Spanish but passing through other than Spanish hands, which went to Asia by way of the Cape: Chaunu's final estimate is that perhaps a little over one-third of American production eventually reached the Orient.

All this indicates by no means a break-up of the Spanish Empire, but at least a weakening of the bonds of Seville. It must be seen against a background of increasing diversification of the Spanish American economy (despite 'New Spain's century of depression') and of increased internal investment, at least in part due to merchants leaving their returns in America to avoid the risk of seques-tration at Seville. Lynch puts it forcibly: 'The crisis in the *carrera de Indias* occurred not because the American economies were collapsing but because they were developing and disengaging themselves from their primitive dependence on the mother country. This was the first emancipation of Spanish America.'[91] Or perhaps more accurately a first stage in a transfer of dependency from an enfeebled Spain to new and aggressive commercial imperialisms, in the eighteenth and much of the nineteenth centuries, in our own day most notably North American. Initially by smuggling on a vast scale, after the gaining of political independence by more normal forms of economic infiltration and domination, external suppliers, investors, and monopsony customers continued to call the tune, as indeed they often still do. 'The New World returned to dependence on the Old with indecent haste.'[92] The truth probably lies between these two extreme statements by Lynch and MacLeod.

The system of Seville

Attempting as it did to bring commercial exchanges, literally from China to Peru, under one vast bureaucratic structure, to funnel the undreamt-of wealth of two continents through the narrow estuary of the Guadalquivir, the system must appear as a first gallant but hopeless effort to construct a planned and con-trolled world economy: a gigantic Common Market, but scarcely as Ramos describes it, one in which 'the defence of the consumer was the supreme law'; rather that law was the need of the Spanish Treasury and dynastic wars, overriding the sincere but pathetically ineffective desire to mitigate the exploitation of the Indians, and it was vulnerable to the conflicting interests of pressure groups both in Spain and the Indies. But we must agree with Ramos that, considering the distances and the diverse environments, it seems almost a miracle that some sort of equilibrium was achieved and maintained for three centuries, without more contact with Spain than a few 'fragile vessels which from time to time . . . reached a few specified shores.'[93] Indeed, in the last resort the warranty for what seems crazy over-regimentation by the Crown may be that without such legalistic promulgation of an ideally overriding Law, ever ill-enforced but ever asserted, the Indies might have split up into independent dominions and lordships, intern-ally autocratic and probably in a state of anarchy between themselves.

In this day and age, littered with the débris of such attempts and yet convinced of the inadequacy of *laissez-faire*, we must have much sympathy with the ideal of a wide-spreading and yet more or less flexibly integrated Commonwealth.

As with our view of the *étatisme* of the Byzantine Empire, our changing times mean that we no longer look on such strivings with the pitying contempt of Manchester School economists; rather with a feeling of common cause in the perhaps hopeless endeavour to control economic destinies. Even had the bureaucracies of the Crown and the Casa possessed well-trained development economists from LSE or Harvard or Sussex, in itself an absurd thought, the task would have been too great: as it was, the mass of statistical data they did record, without benefit of computer, compels respect. But the technical means to overcome the giant barriers of distance were just not there: it took five years for the round transit Seville-Manila-Seville, or Lisbon-Macao-Lisbon, and hazardous years at that. 'One does not construct a firm, or an Empire, on a lucky combination of circumstances. What counts is not getting to America or the Moon, but getting back'; from some hundreds of cases, it can be reckoned that the merchants, officials, and missionaries who went from Europe to these ends of the earth had about one chance in three of making the round trip and returning to live out the rest of their days among their own kin.[94]

No Crown on earth had the world-wide contacts of that of Spain in 1600; but the strain was too great, too much energy was poured out for too little return, and the returns, vast as they seemed in their day—witness Garcilaso's naïve raptures—were dissipated in the maelstrom of European politics. In that same year 1600, two years after the death of Philip the Prudent, the arbitrista Martin Gonsalez de Cellorigo wrote, with a sombre magnificence perfectly in keeping with his nation and his age, the terrible words: 'Truly, it seems that this Republic has become a republic of men bewitched, living outside the natural order of things.'[95] Yet with Don Quixote rode Sancho Panza, and this perishing Republic survived for another two centuries, a monument to ill-directed fortitude.

Chapter 8

SEVILLE AND THE PACIFIC

él hace del tiempo una nave y dirige este siglo al océano,
al ancho y sonoro Pacífico, sembrado por los archipiélagos . . .
Lord del mar, la cadena española nos cierra los ojos!
Lord del mar, nos amarra los sueños la noche española!

Seville: bases and fleets

Seville's ships were confined to the North Atlantic; not so her mercantile empire, which was powerful enough to secure the absolute suppression (at least in official theory) of the flourishing and economically rational commerce between New Spain and Peru. It is true that the happy coincidence of China's thirst for silver and New Spain's argentiferous profusion, with the profits so made, enabled Mexico and Manila to stand up against Seville's pressures, despite their own conflict of interests as buyer and seller; but they were always on an uneasy defensive, compelled to justify their tampering with the sacred principles of Sevillean monopoly. Lima had no autonomous outreach on the scale of the Acapulco Galleon trade—its tentative efforts at direct Peruvian-Philippine contact were quashed, since here the interests of New and Old Spain were in alliance; Callao was, however, the focus of a thalassic commerce whose extreme reaches were at Acapulco and Concepcion. Again, Seville restricted almost to nothingness any legal outlet from Peru to the Atlantic by La Plata, logical as such an alternative outlet might seem on the map. All routes—that is, all *legal* routes—led sooner or later to Seville and its outports, whose domination was based initially on solid advantages of location and tradition, backed by international capital (especially Genoese) and the interests of local magnates such as the Dukes of Medina Sidonia.[1] The Andalusian control was exercised through the elaborate machinery of the Casa de Contratacion and the Consulado or Merchants' Guild. Except at the very beginning, it would be wrong to describe the relation as umbilical: quite soon the mother country was giving less nutriment than she received, though this in turn was being passed on to other and insatiable offspring in Europe, most notably the French and Netherlands wars, while the Genoese midwife took her toll. But clearly there was a maternal bond which became irksome to the lustier children who had adventured overseas.

Pablo Neruda, *Lord Cochrane de Chile*—'[the mariner] makes Time into a ship and drives this century to the ocean, to the broad and sonorous Pacific strewn with its islands . . . Lord of the sea, the Spanish bonds shut on our eyes! Lord of the sea, the Spanish night binds down our dreams!'

The monopoly, at least the attempted control, of Seville thus affects all but the most local economics of the Indies; one might say that its Atlantic fleets were the keys, its Caribbean bases the locks, to Spanish trade in the Pacific. This was by fiat of the Crown—not, however, an entirely arbitrary fiat of an economically irrational Crown. It was logical that somewhere in Andalusia should be the main base for the Indies trade, and within Andalusia Seville was by far the most important centre.[2] Concentration on the massive intake of bullion has tended to mask the fact that trade across the Atlantic was two-way, with diversified exports to supply many of the consumption and construction needs of the New World settlements; and not only was Andalusia the province with the nearest ocean frontage to the vital Trade Winds belt, she was also one of the most productive regions of Spain. The other Atlantic littoral provinces, Galicia, Asturias, Vizcaya, had a more active maritime tradition than Andalusia; indeed, they had an overwhelming dominance in ship-building, and Biscayan seamen were disproportionately to the forefront in maritime enterprise. But these mainly mountainous provinces could not compare with Andalusia either in location or general productivity. The Casa de Contratacion formed at Corunna immediately after the *Victoria*'s return, especially to handle trade with the Spiceries and backed by Cristobal de Haro, never got off the ground: it foundered before Lusian and Sevillean opposition, and its resources were diverted to 'the silver dream of the Indies', specifically to Sebastian Cabot's 1526 expedition to La Plata—which sailed from Seville.[3]

Indeed, when in 1529 Charles V gave permission for outward sailings to the Indies, from nine ports, mostly northern, little advantage was taken of it; perhaps the point of the concession was frustrated by the limitation that the return must be to Seville, to register cargo, but in any case there seems to have been little interest. By mid-century the need to form convoys against freebooters enforced concentration, and even had Seville not had a head-start, it would probably have been the obvious choice, together with its outports of San Lucar de Barrameda, at the mouth of the Guadalquivir, and Cadiz; in 1573, by which time the privateering menace was much greater, it was ordered that all departures, as well as returns, must be via Seville. But the city lies about 100 km up a winding river, and large ships had often to carry out some of their lading or unlading outside the San Lucar bar. Cadiz gradually began to creep up on Seville, and in 1547 received a subordinate branch of the Casa and the assignment of a third of the Indies tonnage. In the seventeenth century the increasing size of ships took Cadiz ahead, until in 1717 the Bourbon government precisely reversed the roles and statuses of the rivals: Cadiz had now the Casa and two-thirds of the tonnage, Seville the branch and one-third.[4]

The functions of the Casa have been outlined above (Ch. 3). The Consulado, founded in 1543, was a tight oligarchic pressure group, which came to have executive functions: in 1562 it took over from the Casa the collection of the *averia* or tax to pay for escort ships, and from 1573 had a direct say in organising the convoys. As Vicens Vives says, Casa and Consulado 'were bound together by a common cause: protectionism at any price'; also by discreet family and financial ties. The price included attempts at regulating not only the direct Atlantic trade to the Indies, but its offshoots in the Pacific; we have seen one small but typical example, the ban on Peruvian wine at Panama. Apart from such meticulous official regulation, the method of control was basically the chronic undersupply of a captive bullion-rich market—although given the distance-times involved, it would have been difficult in any case to ensure smooth supply to American markets, which were usually either in glut or dearth. It is perhaps illustrative of Sevillean ways that when in 1582 it founded a Stock Exchange, the building (now, pleasingly, occupied by the Archives of the Indies) was partly financed by a small octroi-type tax: the building was finished in 1598, the tax was collected until 1826.[5]

Initially the system was in reasonable accord with the economic views of the age: a not irrational attempt at 'maximization of the limited possibilities of a backward metropolitan economy' by protective monopoly.[6] It had a strong element of the Just Price, and a perhaps stronger one of unjust price-fixers. In the not very long run, Spanish resources proved simply not equal to the integration of a complex economy over such a vast and diversified space, or even to its basic supply. To begin with, the economy, especially in Castile which had the sole responsibility for the Indies, was badly distorted by a bias in favour of wool production, often in great latifundia, over industry and crop farming.[7] As a consequence, the productive capacity of the metropolis was not enough to keep the colonies supplied, and there were plenty of outsiders eager to break in. The system was exceedingly vulnerable to cracks and leaks at both ends and in the middle: at the American end, by smuggling, illicit trading (on the Galleon or by La Plata), disregard of inconvenient regulations; in between, by the direct pillage of French, English, and Dutch sea-reivers, commissioned or freebooting; at the European end, by more smuggling, the infiltration of foreign merchandise and interests wearing a Spanish mask,[8] and above all by the drain of the Habsburg wars. Martial glory and the defence of the Faith had to be paid for at rates which led to that succession of six defaults in ninety years.[9] As with the armoured dinosaurs, the defence mechanism, until the Bourbon reforms, was usually more of the same, a hypertrophy of the protective structures.

And yet this astonishing contraption worked, however creakingly and cumbersomely, for three centuries. At the time of its foundation, probably no other European country with the power to do so would have failed to set up such an organisation; it was well adapted to the thinking of its times. Perhaps also no other country would have kept it so long scarcely modified; but the innovating spirit departed from Spain with the century. The shadow of Seville was thrown on to Pacific waters, since the rhythm of economic life from Mexico to Peru was closely bound in to the rhythm of her fleets, even if that rhythm was often more regular in theory than in practice.

As early as the 1520s merchant ships were forbidden to sail for the Indies singly, and the first royal armada was sent out in 1537. In 1543—the year of the establishment of the Consulado—more formal convoy regulations were promulgated, and in 1564-6 Pedro Menendez de Aviles, an able naval administrator who had been appointed Captain-General of the *Armada de la Carrera de Indias*, set up the organisation of scheduled and escorted fleets which lasted through the Habsburg era, and indeed in an attenuated and irregular form long after that.[10] Menendez' policy had three parts: fortified bases in the Indies; compulsory convoys; Indies-based fighting squadrons. The last of these, obviously an essential for any really serious defence scheme, was initiated by 1598 but not effectively developed until the Dutch admiral Piet Hein had taken an entire silver fleet at Matanzas in Cuba in 1628, and even then, as we have seen, this *Armada de Barlovento* was liable to be diverted to general convoy duties. But after the shock of Drake's 1585-6 raid, when Santo Domingo and Cartagena were sacked, the fortifications were taken in hand, if with much procrastination, after a survey by a trained military engineer, Juan Bautista Antonelli—one of whose reports fell into Richard Hakluyt's hands.[11] Meanwhile with all its inefficiencies the convoy system, plus the occasional fast zabra, did good service for over a century: at Cadiz in 1656 and Santa Cruz in 1657 the English gains, though substantial, did not equal the Spanish loss. At Vigo Bay in 1702 all the silver could have been saved had not the Casa delayed the unloading by objecting to the payment of customs at Vigo instead of Cadiz, but even so (and allowing for a considerable diversion of silver to Spain's ally France), 'the 4,587,493 dollars retained by the King of Spain was a greater sum' than in any year before or after—in part because the transfer to Vigo had disrupted the normal arrangements for smuggling.[12] As a rule, the King's enemies did less damage than Acts of God; hurricane disasters were quite frequent, though better management would have avoided the hurricane season, as the regulations provided.

Outwards, there were two convoys: the New Spain *flota* for Vera Cruz, the *galeones* for Tierra Firme[13] and the Isthmus (Fig. 25). The former normally sailed from San Lucar in May, and was usually a smaller affair than the Isthmus fleet, sometimes being escorted by only two warships. The latter usually left in August, on a rather more southerly course, with an escort of as many as six or eight large galleons; after a stop at Cartagena, whence a notice was sent to Panama and Peru, it went on to Nombre de Dios or Puerto Bello, normally reached in ten or twelve weeks from Spain. Here took place the central feature of the whole operation, the great fair where the merchandise of, or at least from, Seville met the silver of Peru. Both fleets rendezvoused at Habana in March, to victual and refit before the summer hurricane season, and then made north to pick up the Westerlies. As with the Manila Galleon, it was easier to adhere to courses than to times, and the failure of the Peruvian silver ships, despite an early warning system, to synchronise with the galeones (or vice versa) was a constant complaint of the merchants; as even a modern Spanish revisionist must admit, the timings were precise, but not for long: 'Poco duro esta prática.'[14] Although of course the Camino de China and the Camino de Castilla met in Mexico City, it was through the galeones rather than the flota that Seville impinged upon the Pacific, with the Isthmus as the great interchange.

The Isthmus as portal to the Pacific

Panama has the distinction of being the first Spanish city on the Pacific, founded the day before Cortes set out from the Atlantic coast for Mexico (15 and 16 August 1519); but in the beginning its range of action was limited. As the gold and the Indians of Castilla del Oro were rapidly worked out, and Darien showed itself to be (as it still is) highly intractable,[15] entradas probed north in 1522, the year in which Cortes first made contact with the South Sea; but in two or three years they came up against prior claimants to conquest on the marches of Guatemala. Thus shut in on the north, the Panama base had a far greater sphere for expansion to the south, but one much more difficult to take up, since it was guarded by a great expanse of unknown sea flanked by extremely inhospitable shores. Southern exploration also started in 1522, but it was ten years before the seizure of Atahualpa at Cajamarca put Castile in possession of another empire as fabulously wealthy as that of New Spain, and completely changed the geographical values of central America.

But this new empire lay on the Pacific, and the Portuguese held the entry by the Indian Ocean and, in Brazil, lay athwart or flanked any possible routes across South America, while the Magellanic passage was useless for continuous traffic. Thus to link Spain and Peru 'America had to be crossed, involving a certainty of illegal trade. The solution finally settled upon simply crossed America at the least objectionable place and restricted trade as much as possible.'[16]

'Glance-at-the-map geography', hindsight, and Panama's eventual success have focused attention on that isthmus as the pass through the barrier between Atlantic and Pacific; but there are of course several constrictions of the land between Tehuantepec and the Atrato. As we have seen, rivalry between a Nicaraguan and a Panamanian route goes back to 1522, and the precise choice of a Pacific terminal on the Isthmus itself seems to have been largely due to chance.[17] Tehuantepec had its prospects; the summit level is not much over 200 metres. But the portage between rivers (Tehuantepec and Coatzacoalcos) is long and would have needed much labour, ports at either end were dangerous in the season of 'Nortes' winds (October-May) and too small for the bigger ships of the later sixteenth century, while if Vera Cruz and Guatulco were used as main terminals there would have been prohibitive breaks of bulk. The *coup de grâce* to Tehuantepec's chances came with the opening of the Philippines trade: not only was its port too small for the Galleons, but it was not so well placed as Acapulco for a direct Mexico-Manila link, or as Panama for a link between the Atlantic convoys and Peru. There was also agitation in the 1550s for Juan Garcia de

Hermosilla's projected route between Trujillo (Honduras) and Realejo, its long portages being supposedly compensated for by better going in a much more healthy and productive country than Panama. In 1560 such efforts seemed successful, since the Crown agreed to make Trujillo to the Gulf of Fonseca the isthmian crossing for trade with Peru; but 'Habit was already too strong' and the project lapsed. It was revived again in 1590, with the usual high-flown propaganda, to receive a cold douche from that objective surveyor Juan Bautista Antonelli. There were still proponents of Nicaraguan routes in the 1620s, using the only really solid argument, that sailing to Peru was much easier from Realejo than by beating out of the Bay of Panama.[18] But the tangible and intangible investment in Panama was much too great to be shifted.

The great arguments against Panama were its climate, with high mortality from disease and much damage to goods and foodstuffs from the very humid heat, and, later on, the virtual impossibility, in such jungly terrain, of suppressing the *cimarrones*, the runaway black slaves who plundered—and recruited—from the *requas* or mule-trains of the portage. In the 1570s the cimarrones formed, in Chaunu's words, a 'counter-colony' of 3000 or more people, with subsistence agriculture, laws, and a mud-walled town which Drake's men found 'kept so clean and sweet . . . very pleasant to behold'; in these respects at least it may have improved on Panama City. These stout recalcitrants had also, of course, a high capacity for collusion internally with the Negro muleteers of the requas, externally with any *corsarios luteranos* who might appear.[19] But in the event, once Nicaragua's Desaguadero had been tried and found wanting, nothing prevailed over the shortness and low altitude of the Panama crossing; the risk of disease and plunder-age was balanced against a speedy transit, which meant fewer halts and hence fewer opportunities for illicit trade.

Pioneers from Mexico and Panama had met by 1524–5, and so disposed of the 'doubtful strait': there was no natural channel through the barrier; yet before the end of the decade there must have been talk of making an artificial waterway. Galvão's statement that Saavedra 'if he had liued, meant to haue opened the land of Castillia de Oro and New Spaine from sea to sea'[20] may be hardly solid evidence: Saavedra's name would naturally come to the mind of a Portuguese Governor of the Moluccas, and he may have merely attached it to Gomara's list, which he gives, of four possible locations for a canal to shorten Spain's route to the Spiceries. It is a good list, concentrating on Panama and the Nicara-guan lakes, but adding Uraba-San Miguel and Tehuantepec as possible but more difficult, which is objective in Cortes's secretary and biographer; Gomara indeed set the priorities for nearly three centuries of debate. Both Galvão and Gomara published in the 1550s, but the former's reference suggests at least that somebody had the idea of a canal in Saavedra's day, and this is surely demonstrated by the fact that in 1534, after three surveys of the Rio Chagres in 1527–33, Charles V directed not only the clearance of obstructions as far upstream as possible, but also a feasibility study (with analysis of benefit-costs for neighbouring provinces) of a cut joining the Chagres and the South Sea. Pascual de Andagoya reported that this was not possible, but that a road would need only fifty Negroes to make and maintain.[21]

Canal schemes now went into the discard, though in the mid-fifties and again in the mid-sixties interest in the Nicaraguan route was revived, and Gomara made the spirited claim that, despite the mountains, 'For the spice trade, for the riches of the Indies, for a King of Castile, little is impossible.' There were indeed counter-arguments, amongst others the presumed difference in sea-level between the two coasts, with unpredictable hydrodynamic implications. Fr José de Acosta SJ thought this but vain discourse, stressing rather the 'strong and impenetrable mountaines' placed by God himself as a rampart 'to withstand the furie of two seas': even were men able to pierce them, they should surely fear His vengeance for impious meddling with the divine 'framing of this vniversall world'.[22] This remark was passed into legend: although a tradition grew up that Philip II took a similarly devout view and forbade, on pain of death, even discussion of a canal project, this seems a caricature of his undoubtedly intense piety, and to be con-flated with an actual but very local prohibition by Philip V, in 1719, of attempts to by-pass the Cartagena customs by using the Rio Atrato! The more genuine reasons for the long lapse in serious discussion of the idea are the cost of a canal and the fact that it would provide a target for attack and hence would need special defences; in 1535, Charles V actually refers to opening a door for Portu-guese or Frenchmen. The mule track dignified with the name of *el camino real* did not obviate the need for defence, but despite the fact that until well into the eighteenth century it was notoriously bad by the low standards of its time and region, '18 leagues of misery and curses',[23] the track did after all work; while a waterway, even if technologically and economically feasible, would not have avoided the breaks of bulk at each end, and the transit would probably have taken longer than by road or road-and-river, with consequently greater hazard to life, property, and the Royal Customs.

Chaunu puts it very strikingly: *before* the creation of Peru, Castilla del Oro had been functionally much the same as any other local base for Indian exploitation and further forays, and so much isolated in a disjointed and sparsely-peopled land mass as to seem insular rather than Tierra Firme; *after*, human activity is solely devoted to the passage function. After 1530, then, it became truly an isthmus, *The* Isthmus.[24] Before it could properly take up this role, it had to be repopulated, for the Peruvian rush had all but emptied it. This took six or seven years, until in 1538 Veragua and Panama were formed into the smallest Audiencia,[25] which could muster in 1570 only some 800 Spaniards, half of them in Panama City. This administration was simply to control the passage: an index of the intense concentration of traffic, wealth, and imperial interests on a few leagues of poor river and worse road. How intense can be judged from Chaunu's reckoning: from 1538–40 to the mid-seventeenth century, the Atlantic side of this 'complexe portuaire', Nombre de Dios and Puerto Bello, accounted for 55–60 per cent of the exchanges between Spanish America and the Old World; or—even including the trade of the Manila Galleon, of Brazil, and that carried on by foreign interlopers—35–40 per cent of all the external commerce of the New World. On the Pacific side, Panama ranked next to Callao in volume of trade, far ahead of any third port, and controlled 95 per cent by value of all trade between South America and Spain, though only 40 per cent by volume. These remarkable figures were of course overwhelmingly due to Peruvian silver.[26]

The Isthmian node really began at Cartagena:[27] a solid city, from 1570 on largely stone-built, with an excellent and easily fortified harbour: a port which was important in its own right as a commercial centre for Tierra Firme, despite water shortage and mediocre inland communications. So important was it in fact, and after 1580 so attractive to Portuguese merchants (always suspect as rivals to Seville, and as crypto-Jews), that in 1610 it was awarded its own Inquisition, which put it in the rank of Mexico City and Lima, since, as Chaunu remarks, only cosmopolitan places warranted this luxury. But its major functions were as a barbican, an outer guard to the Isthmus, and as the first stop of the galeones: significantly, its real foundation was in 1533, the year after Cajamarca. The fleet usually spent only a few days at Cartagena on the outward run before going on to Nombre de Dios or Puerto Bello, but it might spend weeks, depending on whether or not the silver fleet from Callao was on time at Panama: if it was not, the galeones waited at Cartagena, since health conditions were very bad at the Isthmus ports, and Nombre de Dios was practically defenceless and undefended. After the fair at the Isthmus, the fleet returned to Cartagena for refitting, which led to a ship-repairing industry that by the mid-seventeenth century had gone on to the building of galleons of 600 toneladas or more. Most of the legal South American trade not handled at the Isthmus itself was carried out during these stopovers, and without doubt covered a great deal of illegal trade.

Compared to Cartagena, a real city, Nombre de Dios was a dreadful place: the nearest thing to a good word that anyone ever said for it was Antonelli's remark that it would have been very well had the harbour been any good; but it was a bad and shallow haven, dangerously exposed and without good water.[28] Although at times handling about half the exchange values between the Old and the New Worlds, the 'town' had only about thirty permanent residents. Defences were derisory—the place was 'a shanty town on an open beach', not worth spending on. There were no stone buildings: since for most of the year the town was almost deserted except for a few caretakers, and then for a couple of months a mere camp for Lima merchants or their Panama factors, there was no point in building. Above all, Nombre de Dios had the notoriety of being the most disease- and death-ridden place in a region with many contenders for this bad eminence. Antonelli strongly recommended that 'this citie should be plucked downe and newly builded againe in Puerto Bello.' It took the shock of Drake's 1596 raid,

when the 'citie', such as it was, was destroyed, to compel action; Puerto Bello
was the obvious resort.

Here there was an excellent harbour, nearer the entrance to the Rio Chagres;
Puerto Bello became an altogether more impressive place than its discarded rival,
well fortified and with good stone buildings. As regards mortality, it was not so
deadly as Nombre de Dios, but bad enough, and like that wretched settlement
it really only came alive when the fleet was in. In 1637 Thomas Gage was offered
lodging for nothing—until the galeones came in, when he was charged six score
crowns a fortnight—perhaps about $US200, in 1946!—for a room 'but as a
mouse hole'. Food became 'so excessive dear' that fish and tortoises 'though
somewhat dear were the cheapest meat that I could eat'; cloths were sold not
by length but by weight and paid for not in coin but in weighed silver wedges.
In one day Gage counted 200 mules laden with nothing but silver ingots, which
'lay like heaps of stone in the street, without fear or suspicion of being lost.' A
century later the town 'en tiempo muerto' was 'solitary, poor, full of a perpetual
silence, and infusing total melancholy'; but then at the fair-time, 'this most
abhorrent shore' becomes 'the Theatre and magazine of the riches of the two
trades of Spain and Peru.'[29]

Panama Viejo itself—there has always been a certain mystery about that city.
To some it has been a sort of 'Golden Goa', a merchant princes' city of magnificent
palaces—timber it is true, but mahogany and cedar, richly carved; to others, a
mediocre town of some 500 to 700 huddled wooden houses. Nearly seventy
years after it was founded, Antonelli officially reported that the royal buildings
'are all of timber and bourdes, as the other houses are'—and this included treasury
and prison!—while fifty years later still Thomas Gage adds that even the churches
were of wood.[30] The idea of Panama's splendour seems to derive from
Exquemelin's glowing account of the city at Henry Morgan's sack of 1671, at
which he 'himself, of necessity, was present'. The genre—really on-the-spot
'I was there' journalism—is not unknown today; a priori, one might expect
some exaggeration, and without doubt there was some inflation in the contemporary Englishing of his tale.[31] On the other hand, timber building is quite
consistent with elegance and even luxury, and when the town was rebuilt after
the disastrous fire of 1644, some at least was in stone: the ruined Cathedral tower
still stands. But considering that this rebirth was in a period of deep economic
depression, one must agree that 'It is tolerably clear that the city never gave the
appearance of a great commercial metropolis';[32] a modest Phoenix.

For all that, and despite disadvantages already mentioned, on the economic
plane Panama was no mean city: well over half of the silver of the Indies must
have passed through its godowns. For 1607, by which time there were two
official and two private houses of stone, we can even construct a sociological
'profile' from the Audiencia's complaint of economic decline. There were 495
Spanish householders, plus 31 Portuguese, 18 Italians, 4 others, a total of 548;

of these, 29 were wholesale merchants, 21 retailers, 35 owners of the 850 mules of the requas. The rest would be clerics, royal and municipal officials, notaries, small planters and ranchers in the food-producing *umland*, artisans, sailors, soldiers. Of the 548 no fewer than 333 were single or widowers; but as it is implied that in addition to 2558 male slaves (about 1000 of them muleteers or other transport workers) there were 1138 females, one must presume that these 333 unattached white males could make do with *negras escravas*; or as Gage more picturesquely puts it (perhaps with a tang of sour grapes?), 'The Spaniards are in this city much given to sin, looseness and venery especially, who make the blackamoors (who are many, rich, and gallant) the chief objects of their lust.'[33] Indians are not counted—there were 300 or 400 families surviving in 1570— nor of course were the cimarrones within the pale of the census.

Trade relations with New Spain were practically non-existent, but Nicaragua was a main supplier of mules and provisions, and of pitch and cordage for a small ship- or boat-building or repairing industry. But essentially Panama looked to the south: to Guayaquil for cacao and fibres for ships' rigging, to Paita and northern Peru for sugar, and above all to Callao. There was some minor exchange of produce—rice from the Isthmus, maize and especially wine in return—but dominantly this was the great exchange of silver for Sevillean merchandise. In effect, Panama acted as factor between Seville and Lima, in so far as her own merchants were not simply individual factors or commission agents for the Limeños. More than any other American centre, Panama was completely locked into the Sevillean monopoly. The Audiencia in 1607 attributed the city's hard times to two things: the Manila trade, and that between Mexican ports and Callao, by which silks and luxuries from China and general merchandise from Europe (and some from New Spain itself) reached Peru.[34] The former certainly, the latter probably, cut into Sevillean exports or re-exports; but both undoubtedly by- passed the Panamanian intermediary.

The East Pacific trading zone

The beginning of intercolonial trade in the Pacific was, as we have seen (above, Ch. 3), the export of armed men on entrada, and their supplies. The first recorded direct voyage from New Spain to Peru was Grijalva's in 1536, ostensibly sent by Cortes to help Pizarro cope with the Inca revolt of that year, but actually planned as a trading venture (the contract was signed in Acapulco two months before the Indian attack on Lima), and possibly with the ulterior motive of intra- or trans-Pacific discovery. In fact most early ships on the Mar del Sur were owned by encomenderos or officials and intended in the first place for exploration and conquest, with trading ventures merely as side-lines to keep this capital-intensive equipment at work; they tended to be too large for profitable working in cabotage, which had to rely on snapping up small opportunities. Except for cacao, which was handled by smaller ships on narrow margins, there was no such solid coasting trade as developed in Peru, and it was not until the 1550s that merchants and masters or pilots took over as owners: according to Chaunu, as late as 1547 the Pacific trade was basically a support for emigration to Peru. But after the mid-seventies the opening of the Manila trade (with its big entrepôt potential) and the burst in Peruvian silver output transformed trading conditions, and the wealthy merchants of Mexico City joined in.[35]

Although it is said that in exceedingly exceptional circumstances a ship might reach Paita from Panama in under a fortnight,[36] as a rule the set of currents and winds made the southbound journey at least two or three months, and this if started in the most favourable season, January-February (above, Ch. 5 and Fig. 13); generally speaking a ship made only one round voyage a year, if that, and passengers for Peru often disembarked in the far north and went on overland from Piura. Getting out of the Bay of Panama was particularly difficult. Nevertheless, after the 1550s sailings on the routes north of Callao were reasonably regular, and on occasion news passed between Spain and Peru more rapidly via New Spain than via Panama.[37]

Callao, which had contacts with some two dozen ports from Acapulco to Concepcion, was the unrivalled focus for the shipping of the whole Pacific seaboard. Lying on an open bay, only 10 or 12 km from Lima, its harbour was not first class, but the long Isla San Lorenzo gave it shelter and the advantage of a double entry, from both south and north, the latter of especial value given the winds and currents; it was in Frezier's view 'the greatest, the finest, and the safest in all the South Seas', far better than the open roadsteads which were the rule along the Peruvian coast.[38] It lay halfway between Panama and Chile, and was an almost compulsory stop on the southwards run; until Juan Fernandez cut the Callao-Chile time to three or four weeks, a typical voyage might be three months Panama-Callao, three at Callao (careening, making up cargo, or waiting on a wind), and three more to Chile. There were usually long delays at Panama also. Hence a single round trip a year was normally the best that could be done, and probably even that needed some luck; the official silver convoys set up after Drake's raid maintained an annual service, but their individual ships had a two-year rotation. There were usually not more than three to five treasure ships a year to Panama: a modest tonnage sufficed for this high-value low-bulk cargo, while other Peruvian commodities were not valuable enough to warrant export across the Isthmus; they were handled almost exclusively by the small vessels of the local cabotage.[39] For the treasure, in effect a double fleet was needed to maintain yearly service, and with the recession of the seventeenth century it deteriorated: say three to five silver ships would sail one year, only one or two the next. However, the convoy system was never so rigid as in the Atlantic, since the risks were more sporadic, and much traffic was carried on by unescorted *navios sueltos* or 'free ships'. A stop at Callao was not so indispensable on the much quicker northbound run, but on the other hand there was probably no call for direct traffic Chile-Panama, even had it been officially favoured, while there were always good commercial reasons for putting in to Callao. There was indeed only one, and that a partial, exception to the hegemony of Callao: there was some direct shipping from Panama to Arica, but this was a duty-dodging device, since Arica had customs exemptions to serve the Andean mining.[40]

As for the scale of the traffic, there seem to have been between fifty and sixty ships on the Mar del Sur in 1562, of which perhaps only half a dozen were regularly engaged on the full New Spain-Peru voyage; this figure was probably doubled by the end of the century, when Callao had always about forty vessels at anchor, with a total of 250 or 300 entrances and clearances. In 1615–18, seventy-five units used the ports, fifty-two of them *navios*, the rest *barcos*, generally smaller craft which were officially supposed to keep within sixty leagues north or south of Callao. The biggest vessels were the King's galleons of the silver convoy, 200 to 400 or 500 tons; most private ships were from 60 to 135 tons, and the little coastal *fregatas* and *lanchas* ranged down to twelve or fifteen. Ships' companies, numbering anything from seven to thirty-odd all told, became far more professionalised than in the early days on the Mar del Sur of Cortes's time; but except for masters, pilots, and the notary carried on every ship, they were a rough mixed lot, with many Basques and Portuguese, not to mention Greeks, Flemings, mestizos, and Negroes. They were correspondingly despised by good Castilians, of whom exactly one is recorded amongst hundreds of known seamen. Already in 1572 it was necessary to use foreign masters and pilots for lack of Spaniards; they were heavily bonded and had to have a special licence to return to Europe, lest they should sell their knowledge and themselves to northern corsairs.[41] One difficulty confronting the maritime historian is that of nomenclature: about half the ships of 1562 were either *Santiago* or *La Concepcion*. To overcome this, resort was had to nicknames: the officially styled *Nuestra Señora de la Concepcion* taken by Drake was more earthily known as *Cacafuego*; she failed signally to live up to her sobriquet, of which the standard translation 'Spitfire' is out by one consonant.

As for the commodities handled in this lively traffic, their general nature stems from the general economic development of the Pacific Indies. Passenger trade was mainly, though of course far from entirely, inwards to Peru; it ranged from great parties bringing new Viceroys down to the trader with a handful of Negro slaves. Basically the Peruvian cabotage looked after provisioning and the exchange of primary products and obraje wares, all the way from the timber, cacao, and cotton of Guayaquil to the copper, hides, tallow, and fish (later the wheat and wine) of Chile. Callao itself was the entrepôt redistributing the merchandise brought on the long-distance truly intercolonial—or intercontinental—trade. Northwards it sent government silver for Seville, private silver for Seville or the Puerto Bello fairs or New Spain (and so much ultimately to China); sometimes, in the seventeenth century, mercury for the mines of New Spain; wine for central America and New Spain. Other exports were few and exotic: perhaps most important were drugs, especially Peruvian or Jesuits' bark, the source of cinchona

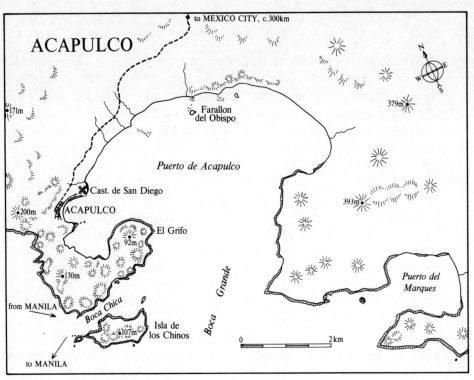

ACAPULCO

to MEXICO CITY, c.300km

•171m

Farallon
del Obispo

379m•

N
W E
S

Puerto de Acapulco

✠ Cast. de San Diego

393m•

•200m

⌂ ACAPULCO

El Grifo

•92m

*Puerto del
Marques*

•130m

from MANILA →

Boca Chica

Isla de
los Chinos

•107m

Boca   Grande

to MANILA →

0   2km

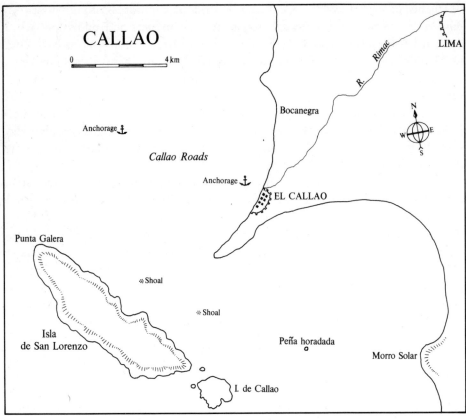

CALLAO

0   4km

LIMA

Bocanegra

R. *Rimac*

N
W E
S

Anchorage ⚓

Callao Roads

Anchorage ⚓

⛫ EL CALLAO

Punta Galera

❋ Shoal

❋ Shoal

Peña horadada

Morro Solar

Isla
de San Lorenzo

I. de Callao

or quinine, brought to Europe in 1640 by a grateful Vicereine, the Marquesa de Chinchon, whose fever it had cured. The merchants coming to Callao from the Isthmus fairs carried a wide range of goods to spread their risks;[42] Borah gives a full and fascinating list from which one may extract: textiles, European or Mexican, including cheap hats for Indians; dyestuffs; furniture, including even beds and writing desks; small metal wares, clocks, crockery, lacquered gourds and cups for chocolate drinking, luxury toilet utensils and cosmetics, jewellery; artisans' tools, leather goods, harness and saddlery; ointments (including salves for piles, 'a complement of the riding equipment'); ecclesiastical and devotional gear of all sorts; toys, guitars; stationery, books—a surviving list comprises mainly works of the Fathers, breviaries and so on, but also Virgil, Ovid, and Quintilian. And once the Galleon trade was opened, the wealthy of Peru increasingly used their abundance of silver to buy Asian luxuries.

This traffic, as Chaunu remarks, was not part of the world of Seville; its Asian component was indeed incongruous to the Sevillean scheme of things, even menacing to it. The conflicts and confluences of interests between Mexico, Lima, Manila, Macao, and both the public and the private sectors in Seville and Lisbon are curious and complex. It goes without saying that the Crown made every effort, counterproductive for the most part, to control and to tax intercolonial and Pacific trade: for one thing, Peruvian silver going to Acapulco meant a direct loss to the Treasury, since it avoided the 'averia both in this sea and in the Mar del Norte' that it would have paid going to Spain by the Isthmus. The bureaucracy was naturally enough obsessed by the possibilities of fraud, and yet many of its members of necessity owed much of their living, at least their good living, to fraud; at the least and best, dependency on fees meant that they had an interest in keeping things moving despite irregularities and hence in winking at infringements, while so complicated were the rules that with the utmost good faith a merchant could hardly help breaking them. Money was the best lubricant of 'passive administration', and this institutionalised rather than personal corruption was left as a legacy to the successor Republics. There was a burdensome mass of taxes, fees, licences, evaluations, backed by heavy bonds which meant that only bigger capitalists could cope. Initiative was paralysed, and 'As the [Crown's] necessities grew, the fiscal jungle grew more and more tangled' and proliferated more regulations which were mostly 'de observación momentánea'.[43]

Relative to Peru, New Spain was short of specie—the Crown's fiscal agencies seem to have been more efficient there, the Philippines had to be subsidised, and private fortunes were perhaps more readily returned to Old Spain; on the other hand Peru was industrially more backward and offered a good market for

◄*Figure 19.* ACAPULCO AND CALLAO. Acapulco about 1625, based on map in P. Gerhard, *Pirates on the West Coast of New Spain 1575–1742* (Glendale 1960); Callao from map in A. F. Frezier, *A Voyage to the South Sea* (London 1717).

Mexican production. It was the merchants of Mexico City who took the initiative in the intercolonial trade, and since they also monopolised the Manila trade, Mexico rivalled Seville as an economic metropolis of the Empire. The Philippine domination was at first entirely in order from the Castilian point of view, since it was New Spain which found the heavy situados which alone maintained those islands for the prestige of the Faith and the Crown. This picture, from the Sevillean viewpoint, was to change drastically when remittances to Spain declined *pari passu* with the increase of those to Manila, and when not only did cheap Mexican products cut into Seville's sales at Puerto Bello, but Peru's increasing demand for the luxuries of Acapulco began to drain off her silver as well.[44] But when the question of direct Peruvian-Asian trade arose, the interests of Mexico and Seville were one. Governor Ronquillo sent two ships from Manila for Peru in 1581 and 1582; the first was lost, the second reached Callao with a cargo of silks, porcelain, spices (mainly cinnamon), and iron, the last two items on government account. The ships were sent on the authority of a royal cédula, ostensibly to help supply a rearmament program, in fact as a cover for trade; but as soon as the news reached Spain, any further voyages were forbidden. In 1590 Viceroy Cañete tried again, on the grounds that Peru was short of iron and copper for the mines and that goods were not coming through from Seville; but although he and other high officials had invested heavily in the venture, the ship was condemned by the officials of Asia. Again in 1618 another Viceroy of Peru pleaded for opening a silk trade with China, for fiscal reasons, but was again turned down.[45]

The merchants of Lima were themselves, of course, quite willing to fight their own battles. In 1609–10 Peruleros came to Seville itself, with their own or their Lima principals' money, and bought direct, even from foreign suppliers, thus breaching the monopolistic hold of the Seville Consulado.[46] But the Limeños, like most men of the market, and certainly like Spain's rivals Dutch or English, had no abstract or *a priori* prejudice against monopoly, provided it were their own. There were, it is true, more rational arguments than are generally allowed for virtually sealing off Upper Peru's alternative outlet or supply line by La Plata: carrying the Potosi trade via Buenos Aires would have greatly lengthened the Atlantic leg of the total route, giving it a greater exposure to piratical attacks and demanding more shipping, and it would have meant diversion of naval resources from the Carrera—altogether a dangerous diffusion of energies. It is true again that the Portuguese and others made a very good thing out of illicit trade by this route, which became one of the major leaks in a leaky system; but this was due to no inherent advantage of the route itself, but to the insatiable demand of Potosi and the high added costs imposed by the Spanish protective system, which made smuggling profitable in almost any circumstances; as Jara puts it, this route 'created such problems of fiscal control (or better, of uncontrol) that it was thought most dangerous to the interests of the Crown.'[47] But the point is that any suggested relaxation of the ban was bitterly opposed by Lima: 'the trade of Buenos Aires was frozen, on the demand of the Peruvians, who thus closed a continental port which would have taken from them the monopoly of Chile, Charcas, and Upper Peru.'[48]

There was doubtless quite as much rationale, if not more, in the decision to prohibit direct Peruvian intervention in the Asian trade; after all, it had been empirically ascertained that New Spain's relation to the circulation of winds and currents in the North Pacific approximated that of Seville in the North Atlantic, and there was now a known route which, with all its limitations, was speedier and safer than trying to develop new courses right across the wind-belts and the equatorial calms. Moreover, direct Peruvian trade meant not only a direct drain of silver, but also a competitive buying at Manila, which might well force prices up and so add to the drain. Already the activities of Peruleros in New Spain seemed to threaten the system of supply to Tierra Firme, since their heavy silver backing gave Lima something of a monopsony position. The first official reaction was to prohibit the import or sale in Peru of all goods from the Philippines; this was a dead letter until in 1587 the Court, Seville, and the Cabildo of Mexico City together put pressure on the Viceroys to enforce the ban.[49] Typically, the prohibition had to be reissued thrice by 1600. There were vacillations of policy in response to local and temporary dearths and gluts; the main result of restriction was probably merely an increase in the overheads for bribery. In 1604 trade between New Spain and Peru was limited to three ships a year, each of 300 tons, to carry only regional products for exchange: no specie. Penalties for infringement were severe, but naturally evasion was still the order of the day, for instance by slight re-working of Chinese goods into a New Spain product and similar tricks of the trade. In 1609 the number of 'permission ships' was cut to two of 200 tons, in 1620 to one, which could carry specie to the amount of about 300,000 pesos; it was to ply between Callao and Acapulco only, with no intermediate calls, and to bring back produce of New Spain only: and there were seventy merchants interested in the ship of 1629, with an investment of over 1,000,000 pesos! In short, it proved impossible to stop Chinese goods reaching Peru without likewise stopping all shipping between the two Viceroyalties—or even with such a ban. In 1631 a total suspension for five years was promulgated, and this was repeated in 1634. The Procurator-General for Manila at the Council of the Indies, Juan Grau y Monfalcon, put up a lengthy and strong case for re-opening—the ban was 'so menacing to the Filipinas, that it alone may prove sufficient to ruin them.' In response to his protests, in 1640 an 'Informatory decree' was issued to Bishop Palafox of Puebla, directing him

> to inform me [Philip IV] very thoroughly of all that you shall
> ascertain and understand to be most expedient, in order that when
> I have considered all the reliable information in your report,
> I may take such measures as may be most fitting—

how small, how exceedingly slowly, ground the mills of Madrid![50] Four years later the Council once again debated the matter: Manila, Peru, and even Mexico were now for re-opening the trade, Seville was opposed. So important a point 'necessita de resolucion', but, typically, nothing was resolved. Occasionally, when New Spain was in urgent need, a mercury ship might be sent, licensed to take a limited amount of merchandise from Callao to Acapulco; and less licit Peruvian ships continued to tap the trade from minor ports, Guatulco or even the Puerto del Marques, under 10km from Acapulco, eventually from that very harbour: in 1685 Townley and Dampier tried, unsuccessfully, to cut the 'Lima ship' out from Acapulco itself.[51] Guatemalan and Nicaraguan ports seized the opportunity provided by the ban; indeed in the 1570s a disregarded appeal had been made to have Realejo appointed as the American terminal of the Galleon trade, supplanting Acapulco itself. After the official closure of trade between New Spain and Peru, the re-export of Chinese goods from Mexico by land remained legal, and the customs of Acapulco and Guatulco were evaded by this route, to the profit of Realejo and Acajutla. However, contraband had its own channels, so well established that the share of these ports was never more than marginal.[52] Both the illegal trade and its indefinite legal suspension lasted on into the eighteenth century—there was a reissue of the ban in 1706—to become yet another item on the agenda of Bourbon reform. The suspension was not formally rescinded—or rather itself suspended!—until 1779.

Paradoxically, the intercolonial trade had invited its official death-sentence by its success—that is, by its success in buying, however indirectly, into the intercontinental trade of the Manila Galleon.

The Philippines and the Galleon trade

Striking as it is, Wallerstein's dictum that 'in the sixteenth century, Iberia establishes *colonies* in the Americas, but *trading-posts* in Asia' over-simplifies the variety of political relations involved. It was one of the most notable Dutch rulers in the Indies who wrote of the Portuguese that

> The greater number regard India as their fatherland, thinking no
> longer of Portugal; they trade thither little or not at all, living
> and enriching themselves out of the treasures of India, as though
> they were natives and knew no other fatherland.[53]

Hence the stubborn and prolonged Lusian resistance to the assaults of the better-found and better-organised naval power of the Dutch; hence too, together with Albuquerque's conscious policy of integration by miscegenation, the much more marked cultural impression left by the 150 years of Portuguese rule in littoral Ceylon compared with that of the succeeding 150 years of Dutch rule. Malacca, Macao, Nagasaki may look like trading-posts pure and simple; yet perhaps only the last of these was truly one in the sense that the European factories of the seventeenth century in India, of the eighteenth at Canton, were such. From the start, the Iberian 'trading-posts' were bases not for wide political dominion but for extensive political and social influence (the latter largely mediated by religious missions) as well as trade. And if this is true of the scattered Portuguese holdings, it applies perhaps *a fortiori* to the relatively large but more concentrated

Spanish base in the Philippines, which lasted until 1898 and whose legacy of 'Hispano-Malayan Catholicism has survived the double collapse of the political and the linguistic presence of Spain.'[54]

This is perhaps the key. Philip II may not actually and cold-bloodedly have made the magnificent, if Quixotic, assertion that 'for a single hermitage, in which the Holy Name of God should be maintained in the Filipinas, he would expend the whole revenue of his Kingdoms'[55]—but it is significant that it could be ascribed to him, and it is certainly a highly symbolic statement. It is as certainly not consistent with a view of Iberia as merely planting trading-posts. It is of course true enough (and this is doubtless the core of Wallerstein's approach) that wide-ranging Conquistas, extensive colonies of settlement, were not possible in Asia as they were in the Americas. Entradas in Siam and Cambodia came to sticky ends, and serious contact with China and Japan soon dissipated such early dreams of glory as Sande's and Riquel's; the effectively organised and ruthless Dutch took the better part of a century to complete the subjugation of even the small island realms such as Mataram, Bantam, Makassar. By the same token, neither Spanish nor Portuguese ever displaced Asian shipping from a large share of the regional carrying trade; they ran the long-distance lines to other parts of the world, but these were fed by locally built, owned and managed craft.

But when Legazpi arrived on Cebu, the people of the archipelago had not developed for themselves political structures larger or more solid than loose associations of a few villages; 'for themselves', since in the south Islam was bringing new forms of political and social life, and here, in Sulu and Mindanao, it was not until within two or three decades of her own supersession in 1898 that Spain was able to claim anything more than the most nominal authority. North of Mindanao, however, the Spaniards found little difficulty in extending their control in the first place, and then in enlisting 'Indios' to maintain it by the represssion of their fellows: in both phases they had powerful support from the spiritual arm. There was it is true much resistance—Zaide lists over a score of risings between 1574 and 1762, and this is not exhaustive—but it was sporadic, local in inspiration and leadership; there was no unity.[56] Manila *intra muros* became a central Spanish strongpoint, uneasily watching over suburbs of Indios and the more sinister-seeming Parian, a solidly Chinese town of perhaps 30,000 people in 1627; and although the encomendero system was not so central to society as it was in the Americas, over half a million Indios lived in the nearly 200 encomiendas of 1621. But the real colonisers were the clergy, who covered the islands north of Surigao Strait with over a thousand 'towns': most of them poor places, no doubt, but forming a network for cultural impregnation and social control.[57] This is hardly the work of a trading-post.

Yet, if something more than a trading-post, the Philippines were something less than a full-fledged colony, and Manila has the air of being superimposed onto the islands, not growing from them. In contrast to Anthonio van Diemen's Portuguese, the Castilians of the Philippines did not even in thought detach themselves from Spain, still less perhaps from New Spain; and they enriched themselves not from local resources but by playing middleman between the treasures of America and the luxuries of Asia. A certain amount of gold was received from the Indios in trade or tribute, and from time to time there was a flurry of interest in reports of new finds; but nothing came of these. After the first few years, nothing was done to tap the potential of Mindanao in nutmeg and cinnamon, though the latter had formed part of one of the earliest cargoes shipped for New Spain: the local variety was inferior, but hardly enough so to warrant importing the spice from Ceylon, as was done. Intermittent attempts were made to export Indio-woven cottons to New Spain, but this industry could hardly stand up to Chinese and peninsular Indian competition even on its home ground. Tobacco seeds were brought from Cuba before 1600, and in 1641 Governor Corcuera presented the Viceroy of New Spain with two chests of Manila cigars; but the great days of their world fame, when the tobacco monopoly became the chief source of government revenue, had to wait until late in the eighteenth century. Some indigenous products—honey, wax, deer-skins, civet cats—went to Japan; China was as yet, and would long remain, sublimely independent of European wares. So by and large the exports of the Philippines were re-exports, to such an extent that when Grau y Monfalcon says that the islands 'abound in copper' while 'the quicksilver of the Filipinas' is of no less importance, the context makes it clear that he is speaking of imports from China. The lure of the super-profitable entrepôt trade stifled all other enterprise.[58]

'The manifest lists of the galleons are a veritable catalogue of the products of the Orient', and after over a page of enumeration of the rareties brought from China, Morga gives up: 'to recount all would mean never finishing, nor would even masses of paper suffice for the task.'[59] More prosaically, Guzmán-Rivas classifies the main lines exported to New Spain: food products—spices and later tea (both re-exports), palm wine; raw materials and drugs—amber, benzoin, borax (from inner China), Manila hemp, raw cotton and silk, iron, sandalwood, dyestuffs, tin, wax; manufactures—ceramics, many lines in silk and cotton textiles, jewellery, escritoires, screens, fancy boxes, and all sorts of curios and knick-knacks, chinoiserie in short. Obviously, with China and tropical Southeast Asia at hand to supply the luxuries of life, Japan the necessities such as iron, copper, lead, saltpetre, and Chinese artisans at Manila itself to provide domestic comforts, clothes, and furnishings, there was little call to import consumption goods from across the oceans. Some such there were, cacao and cochineal from New Spain, from Old 'peculiarly national goods' such as olive oil, wine, and books; but returns 'were of so little bulk that the galleon virtually sailed in ballast.' Basically the trade remained the exchange of silver for silk, much of which reached Europe itself.[60]

The effect of the Galleon trade in Asia, strictly commercial exchanges apart, was essentially to maintain the Spanish presence in the Philippines; Spanish action outside those islands (the Japanese and later the Marianas missions excepted) was military and ineffectual; the Portuguese seem to have had more intimate contact with local populations, over a wider field, and hence much more of a cultural impact. In the Philippines themselves, of course, things were different. Apart from direct religious indoctrination, romances such as those of Charlemagne and the Twelve Peers inspired Tagalog verse narratives, and there were many linguistic borrowings—over 150 plant names, hundreds of personal names.[61] Plants introduced via the Pacific included acacias, capsicums, groundnuts, papaya, indigo, manihot, tobacco; maize was probably already in Southeast Asia before any Spanish introduction. The agave or maguey was also brought in, but its use for *pulque*, the universal fermented drink of Mexico, did not catch on; rather the Indios who came to New Spain corrupted the natives of Colima and Acapulco by introducing them to *tuba* or palm 'wine': this was distilled, 'as strong as brandy, [so that] they crave it rather than the wine of España', a manifest menace to the vintners of Spain (and probably Peru!). This apart, there was little plant transferral from Asia; in contrast to the westbound sailings, the cold on the northern reaches of the eastwards run was probably enough to inhibit success with seedlings, which were space- and labour-demanding on the tight-packed ships to Acapulco; in any case, such traffic was not likely to appeal to the Manileño penchant for large profits and quick returns. There is a possible Japanese influence, dating from Vizcaino's times, on house-types in Michoacan, and more definite Malayan and Chinese motifs in ornamental glazed tiles (*azulejos*) and jars made for the mass market in New Spain. There were also some thousands of Chinese and Filipino immigrants, either as slaves or as Indio crewmen deserting the Galleon after the inhuman treatment and climatic rigours of the voyage. This seems to be almost the total cultural influence of the trans-Pacific trade in New Spain.[62] Indeed, if we wished to find a trading-post in connection with the Galleon route, we might find it on American rather than Asian shores: Acapulco was entirely a town of trade, and that concentrated on the *feria* when the Galleon was in. As in Puerto Bello, there were then a few weeks of frantic activity, a milling population of 12,000 or so, rich and poor, officials and seamen, merchants and muleteers, clergy and slaves; afterwards, as all who could afford to do so fled the stifling cauldron-like bay, the lowly permanent residents—Indians eastern and western, Negroes, Chinese, and all possible combinations—relapsed into months of monotony under the brazen sky of the *tierra caliente*.[63]

The Galleon trade: its geopolitical economy

'Manila remained all this time the meeting ground, halfway round the world, of the heirs of Columbus and Vasco da Gama: a triumph of maritime communication in defiance of probability.'[64] The meeting was never without some tension, and this is a *leitmotiv* of the first forty years of the seventeenth century. For the first fifty, until the news came that by the Treaty of Munster (1648) the Spanish Crown had at last admitted reality and recognised the independence of the northern Netherlands, there was a deeper burden: for throughout this period the Philippines were a beleaguered outpost, exposed to almost constant Dutch attacks. There was an offensive triumph at the beginning, Acuña's Moluccan expedition of 1605–6, and a defensive triumph at the end, 'La Naval de Manila' in 1646; but most of the actions between these dates, though generally successful, were in fact the *reactions* of a tough but hard-pressed static garrison. The Dutch pressure must be borne in mind as a persistent abrading factor, a tide constantly returning to beat upon the coast. The tone of the times can be caught from the Jesuit annual letter for 1618–19:

> The Hollanders came to these islands with their fleet of five galleons to plunder the Chinese ships, as they have done in former years. The fleet entered the Bay of Manila . . . [and] went back and forth on these seas just as if it were at home. But its appearance caused so little disturbance that everything remained as quiet as before, which illustrates the force of habit. . . .[65]

Paradoxically, the Dutch rush to the Indies, East and West, was expedited by Philip II himself. In a desperate attempt to cut off that trading with the enemy which was at once a running sore and a necessary nourishment of his own war effort, Philip in 1585 and again in 1595 closed Iberian ports to the shipping of England and the United Provinces, on the second occasion seizing some 400 Holland and Zeeland ships. It is highly likely that both countries, sooner rather than later, would have tried to tap the trade of the Indies at source—the English had already sought to find both a Northwest and a Northeast Passage to the Orient, the Dutch the latter only—and Philip's action by itself was neither a necessary nor a sufficient cause of the Dutch expansion. But it was a stimulus, a straight challenge, and with the confidence born of twenty or thirty years of privateering, good geographical intelligence, and a wealth of ships and shipping skills, the Netherlanders turned enthusiastically to direct long-distance trade. By mid-1596 the first fleet from the Texel had reached Bantam, and by the end of the century sixty-five Dutch ships had been sent out, all but eleven of them returning safely, and most of them profitably.[66]

In March 1603 one of their commanders, Jacob van Heemskerck, was not doing too well in legitimate trade: there was already too much competition amongst the Hollanders, and indeed just twelve months earlier, in March 1602, the seal had been affixed to the charter of the association designed to limit it, the famous *Vereenigde Oost-Indische Compagnie* or VOC. But that was on the other side of the world, and hearing of two carracks on their routine voyage from Macao to Malacca, van Heemskerck fell upon them and took the 1500-ton *Santa Catharina*. This was indeed a prize: Japanese copper, American silver, Chinese porcelain and above all silks, to the value of over 1,200,000 pesos, making this one of the richest single captures of the age. The news did not reach Macao, brought by a Japanese junk, until July; and the same evening two Dutch ships entered the port and took a carrack already laden for Japan.[67]

Macao now faced probable disaster: 'In a few years, the cunning and complex net which, from Lisbon to Macao and the Moluccas, held the Indian Ocean in the bonds of Portuguese trade, was torn to shreds . . . Macao was condemned to death, unless she could adapt herself; and she adapted.' The Macaonese were risk-takers in a sense the Manileños were not, versatile and persistent traders, as the career of Francisco Vieira de Figueiredo shows. By 1604 their ships had entered directly into the Manila trade, hitherto carried entirely in Chinese bottoms, taking over much of the high-value low-bulk *trafic de choix*. From 1618, the Dutch blockades were countered, with a good deal of success, by using numbers of lighter and handier galliots instead of the annual carracks; the Straits of Formosa were more difficult for the Dutch to block than those of Malacca, and so long as relations with the Japanese Court remained good (and nobles from the Shogun down had investments in Portuguese cargoes) the Dutch were held in check by diplomatic pressures. The Great Ship from Amacon was no more, but the traffic went on. The Portuguese came to be regarded by the Spaniards as masters of the Philippines;[68] but, just as with the intercolonial trade on the other side of the Pacific, the success of this trade—not between two Viceroyalties but between two Empires, albeit under one Crown—imperilled, or seemed to imperil, the whole system. It raised, even more acutely than before, the question of the 'drain'.

In the earlier years of the Union of the Crowns it was the Portuguese who feared trespass from Manila across the invisible boundary, arguing that all the treasure would go from New Spain to China, none to Old Spain, and even a Spaniard— although a bishop, and hence an enemy of Francisco Tello—could say that the Governor's shipment to China could utterly ruin Macao and with it the Japanese mission and all Luso-Castilian interests in the Orient, 'for all these affairs are moved but by one wheel, namely, Macan.'[69] It was on Lusian insistence that the Manila-Macao trade was banned in 1593, since at this time the Portuguese could freely send Japanese silver not only to China but to their Indian Ocean trading zones. But from 1605 the Malacca Straits were always liable to Dutch blockade, and in 1612 and 1613 there were premonitions of religious troubles in Japan, where the VOC had recently (1611) established a factory at Hirado. Access to the Manila trade thus became vital to Macao just as that trade was coming under attack; as we have seen, the Cabildo of Mexico City was early on the scene with complaints. Its real concerns were probably the cutting-in of Peruvian merchants and the competition of Chinese with Mexican goods, but it was of course more tactical to express great anxiety over the silver drain; it alleged that in the peak year of 1596 this amounted to no less than 12,000,000 pesos; actually a quarter of that amount was probably exceptional, though of course even this reduced figure was six times the legal limit—when Anson took the Galleon in 1743, she was carrying about 1,300,000 pesos, plus 35,582 ounces of silver— some of it disguised as cheeses![70] Sevillean hostility could be taken for granted, but Lisbon interests also saw in the Manila-Macao link a squandering into China of silver needed for the Indian Ocean trade, and condemned the Manileños for reckless competitive bidding and a general forcing up of prices. Nevertheless, the trade across the South China Sea was flourishing until the early 1620s, when, on any reckoning, New Spain's silver output began to drop. The position was clearly seen by Grau y Monfalcon in 1637: the fall in trade that then set in was due to monetary inflation succeeded by declining output of precious metals, decrease in the number of Indians considered both as consumers and as workforce, falling purchasing power offsetting the increase in the number of Spaniards, and the high imposts, increasing averia, and fear of sequestrations and forced loans.[71] The Dutch establishment of Fort Zeelandia in Formosa (1624), inside the Manila-Macao-Nagasaki triangle, of course did not help.

Even before this decline, drastic action to stop the drain had been requested by the Consulado of Seville—nothing less than the prohibition of Mexican trade to the Philippines, replacing it by direct trade between Spain itself and the archipelago, via the Cape of Good Hope. This was countered, ably and at length, by the Marques de Monteclaros, who pointed out that there were many other leaks, and at least 'the Chinese do us no other harm than to keep the silver', unlike 'the French and the rebels [who] are so skilful in getting this product away from us'; the Pacific route was more secure.[72] Administrative measures were tried: in 1635 Pedro de Quiroga was sent to Acapulco to enforce the legal limits, which he tried to do *inter alia* by the outrageous procedure of insisting on opening boxes and bales to see that their contents conformed to the consignor's sworn statement. The row was tremendous: there was a shipping strike at Manila, and for two or three years no laden Galleon reached Acapulco. Quiroga was snubbed and died in disgrace, and reform died with him.[73]

Proposed remedies were many, and conflicting. Grau y Monfalcon argued for lower imposts and fewer restrictions; he admitted that others stood for an opposite policy. In 1619 the Dominican Diego Auduarte put forward a drastic solution: forbid the Macaonese to trade with Japan, so that they would simply have to move to somewhere else in Portuguese India, where they would be more useful: there were only about 300 anyhow, an independent and irresponsible lot and 'evil examples'; Manila could take over the Japan trade and the conversion of China. The proposal was referred to Governor Fajardo, who thought that the Dutch or English would seize the place, destroying the Galleon trade; perhaps better to move the Macaonese to northern Luzon or Formosa, to keep open the Japan trade, but then again any action would be most difficult, and, on the whole, the time was not ripe for a definite decision. . . .[74]

On an opposite tack, there were suggestions for exchanging the Philippines for Brazil, or even for abandoning them altogether, as a fiscal and strategic liability. This of course was all but unthinkable, and the Manileños' spokesmen in Madrid, Rios Coronel and Grau y Monfalcon, loosed salvoes of counter-reasons, sacred and profane: first, the islands were as a firm column, a strong rock, whereby the Faith may be propagated and the heretics, Moors, and heathen broken; then they were necessary as a base to defend the Spiceries; they forced the Dutch to divide their forces and so they protected the whole of India, and indirectly the Spanish Main as well; victories in the Filipinas added to the honour and profit of the Crown, and cemented the fraternal union of Castile and Portugal; 'on the preservation of these islands depends that of the China trade'; and finally, if from Philippine expenditures were deducted those properly attributable to general imperial purposes (such as the defence of the Moluccas), then the Manila establishment was not so expensive after all.[75] Between the suppression of Macao and that of the Galleon trade, which it was understood on all hands would destroy the *raison d'être* of the Philippines, a wide variety of compromises was canvassed, their particular biases depending on whether their promoters thought the Macaonese, the Manileños, or the Mexicans were the villains of the piece. Chinese goods might be taken to Japan, whence so much silver 'is and may be obtained' to stop the drain from America; or the Philippines should be confined to paying for Mexican imports with their own local gold. And so on, and so on . . . Little wonder that Philip III, anything but a strenuous or intellectual monarch, minuted wearily 'All has been carefully considered, but the remedy is not easy.'[76]

In the 1620s Macao and Manila seem to have had a momentum of their own, since all the time the trade between them was officially without the law, and yet officialdom itself was often drawn in, by the mere necessities of the case. The semi-autonomy of the Senate of Macao may have accounted for something in this, as also of course the distance-time from Lisbon and Madrid; but the essence of the situation was that the fortunes of the two cities were bound together: if 'the ships from China do not come', there would be nothing for the Galleons. Both contributed to the cost of defending the communications between them.[77] Yet the tension remained, and became more acute with the depression in Mexican mining; it was exacerbated by mutual resentments stemming from the missionary rivalry in Japan, and doubtless by the reflex of events in the homeland, or rather the homelands. By 1624 Olivares had planned the 'Union of Arms'—in itself a sensible, even statesmanlike, proposal to pool Iberian resources in face of common danger, but in peninsular circumstances one bound to strain the loyalties of the non-Castilian realms, traditionally jealous of their ancient privileges; it was to lead by 1640 to secessionist revolt in Catalonia, revolution in Portugal. It had its reflection in the Orient: in 1630 Governor Niño de Tavora wrote to the King on the advantages of a 'union of posts and arms in the South Sea', but he had to admit that auditors and citizens bitterly opposed the experienced and meritorious, but Portuguese, Diego Lopez Lobo as admiral: 'I am not aware that it is a crime or a demerit to be a Portuguese.' (This was in face of a feared joint attack by Dutch and Japanese; nor did Tavora receive much help from the Viceroy in Mexico, who sent ninety men, little money, and gratuitous advice to reduce the military establishment—'he does not know what it means to have Dutch enemies about us . . .'.) Malacca and Macao should be joined with Manila; otherwise there was little hope for the Indies.[78]

As silver output continued to fall in the next decade, the 1630s, crisis deepened; with a smaller cake to share, the old links of interest began to snap. The complaints against the men of Macao, regarded as bigger profiteers than even the Sangleys, became more bitter, until in 1632 seventeen articles, leading up to a demand for the total prohibition of Portuguese trade at Manila, were adopted, unanimously, by the Manila town council. Two years later, on the insistence of Grau y Monfalcon, royal decrees were issued for the enforcement of the old law, though perhaps the expression was not so stringent as it might have been; and in 1636 the Governor reported that trade with Macao had in fact been banned. The natural result, of course, was that the Sangleys, who had always carried the bulkier portion of the trade, moved in on the rest; and not only that, but Spanish ships put into Macao, with or without the excuse of stress of weather, and drove a roaring trade. Even the Governor of Formosa tried to smuggle so blatantly from Macao harbour that he had to leave under fire from its defences, while in 1637 the Acapulco Galleon itself put in. After the expulsion from Japan in 1639–40 the Macao Senate tried to get their trade to Manila licensed, or even extended to the Americas:

> They pointed out that the rigid enforcement of the royal
> prohibition in 1633–34, had merely diverted the treasures of Potosi
> from the pockets of His Catholic Majesty's subjects at Macao into
> the coffers of the heathen Chinese at Canton and Amoy. 'Better to
> give the bread to the children than to the dogs' they protested, but
> by the time this remonstrance reached Europe, their liege lord was
> no longer King Philip of Hapsburg but King John of Braganza.[79]

Perhaps in the end the divorce was a relief to both parties.

The fall of Malacca to the Dutch in 1641 cut Macao off from Goa and the rest of the Estado da India; with remarkable resilience the Macaonese turned to Indochina, Makassar, and Timor, fitting themselves into the regional carrying trade and surviving as an almost indigenous element; as Anthonio van Diemen put it, as if 'they knew no other fatherland.' The Galleon, supported now by the American market, continued to carry silk to New Spain and indirectly to Peru; Mexican competition in silks was all but eliminated.[80] But the mastery of the Indonesian and China Seas was falling to the Dutch and the Mar del Sur itself was no longer *mare clausum*: it was still a Spanish lake, but one increasingly traversed by English and Dutch keels.

Chapter 9

THE FIRST IRRUPTION: FRANCIS DRAKE

... the ticklish and brittle state of the greatness of Spain. Their
greatness consisteth in their treasure, their treasure in their Indies,
and their Indies, if it be well weighed, are indeed but an accession
to such as are masters by sea.

what English shippes did heeretofore euer anker in the mighty
riuer of Plate? passe and repasse the vnpassable (in former opinion)
straight of Magellan, range along the coast of Chili, Peru, and all
the backside of Noua Hispania, further than any Christian euer
passed, travers the mighty bredth of the South sea, land upon the
Luzones in despite of the enemy, enter into alliance, amity, and
traffike with the princes of the Moluccaes, & the Isle of Java,
double the famous Cape of Bona Speranza ... & last of al returne
home most richly laden with the commodities of China?

Northern ways to the South Sea: Anian and the Three Brothers

Englishmen were the first outsiders to break into the Spanish Lake, although
apart from the Bristol venturers into and across the North Atlantic, who were
sailing at least as early as 1480,[1] they were slow in taking to long-distance voyaging
under their own colours; but this did not preclude some academic speculation
and lively projecting. The wealthy merchant Robert Thorne, Seville-based and
like Magellan's gunner Master Andrew a Bristol man, invested in Sebastian
Cabot's Spanish voyage for the South Sea (1526) and so was able to place with
it two Englishmen, Roger Barlow and Henry Latimer, in the unavowed pursuit
of knowledge as to whether the seas extended from the Spiceries 'without interposition of londe . . . to the newe founde landes that we discovered' across the
North Atlantic;[2] a pursuit unsuccessful since the voyage was diverted, by tales
of a silver Sierra, to La Plata and up the Parana. In the next year, 1527, there
was some diplomatic talk looking to a purchase of the Spanish claims to the
Moluccas by Henry VIII, and indeed his father had made it clear, as early as
1502, that he would not recognise claims based simply on discovery without
effective occupation.[3] As a matter of practical politics and logistics, however, for
the first half of the century English interests and activities had by and large a
northerly bias, with only one really important exception.[4] This was the early

'Considerations touching the War with Spain', *The Works of
Francis Bacon* (London 1824–34), V. 229–85 at 282–83; R. Hakluyt,
'Epistle Dedicatorie' to *The Principall Navigations, Voiages and
Discoveries of the English nation* (London 1589).

trespassing on Portuguese preserves in Guinea and Brazil, often using as a forward base the Canaries, a relatively free-trade area in the Spanish system, where English merchants had rights by the Treaty of Medina Campo (1489).[5] The resulting Anglo-Portuguese friction was less important, both in the long and short run, than the opportunity provided for John Hawkins's economically well-conceived, if politically unfortunate, pioneer enterprise in slaving from West Africa to the Caribbean: long term, the precursor of the great 'triangular trade' of the eighteenth century; short term, the occasion for the clash at San Juan de Ulua, perhaps not quite so sharp a turning-point in Anglo-Spanish relations as is generally reckoned, but of immense significance in the career of Francis Drake.[6] Without it there would doubtless still have been challenges to the Spanish monopoly, but the affair ensured that Drake would be a special agent in the process.

Early efforts by Thorne and Barlow to secure royal support for a northwards search for Cathay had no effect: the manuscript docketed *Geographia Barlow* lay in the archives for nearly 400 years.[7] However, the readjustment of the currency in 1551 and the consequent fall in exports, perhaps also the simultaneous isolation of Protestant England from both Habsburg and Valois, made the England of Edward VI's time more receptive to overseas projects: there was a need for alternative outlets for mercantile capital. In 1548 the veteran Sebastian Cabot, who had first sailed from Bristol about 1509 (if not with his father in 1497!) was attracted from his office of Pilot-Major to the Casa de Contratacion, to become an expert adviser to the English government; three or four years later we find him discussing with the Duke of Northumberland an attempt on Peru, perhaps by sending 4000 men in pinnaces up the Amazon! More to the point, Richard Eden and John Dee were beginning a program of geographical education. The first fruit of the new interest was the chartering (1552-3) of the Merchant Adventurers, for discovery and trade to the northeast, north and northwest, with Cabot as Governor for life: by 1558 the voyages to the White Sea promoted by this 'Muscovy Company' had opened up an important new market in Russia for the badly depressed cloth trade, and the company's agent Anthony Jenkinson had reached Bokhara. Not surprisingly in view of the hardships and hazards of the boreal seas, where Hugh Willoughby and all his men perished, the company tended to discount the distant vision of opening the Arctic ways to Cathay and the South Sea, in favour of the more solid prospects of profit from clothing the shivering Russians in good English wool.

The thinking of England's pioneer geographers was global, not flat-map: the use of 'Mercator's projection' (1569) as a navigational aid, with all that has implied for the image of the world, had to wait until Edward Wright applied it in his 'Azores' chart of 1599.[8] It was indubitable that the shortest routes from England to Cathay and the South Sea lay northabout. These were also the most free of political hazard or objection; indeed, in the view of that good Welshman John Dee, the Tudor Crown had an indefeasible title to those countries beyond

Iceland that had been colonised by King Arthur.[9] Even on Cabot's southern
voyage, Barlow's aim had been to find if there were unbroken sea between the
Moluccas and Newfoundland, 'without interposition of londe'; that indeed was
the nub. In the last resort only experience could decide—as Richard Willes put
it, 'It must be Peregrinationis historia, that is, true reportes of skilfull travailers,
as Ptolome writeth, that in such controversies of Geographie must put us out
of doubt.' There were, however, plenty of theorists prepared to discount the
obstacles of climate and ignorance: whatever the risks and hardships of an Arctic
route, the reward would be commensurate, for had not the King of Portugal
given the Emperor 350,000 crowns 'to leave the matter unattempted', and was
not that too much to pay for 'egges in moonshine'?[10]

The arguments, as exemplified in Sir Humphrey Gilbert's famous discourse
on the Northwest Passage, were wonderfully mixed appeals to authority, to
experience, and to unnatural physiography, and the proponents of northern
Passages were far from agreed on the layout of circumpolar lands and seas;[11]
but by mid-century it was generally agreed that a way through did exist. From
the Atlantic side there had been various probes. Verrazano, looking over a low
neck of land, had seen a great open water, which he thought must be the South
Sea; it was probably Chesapeake Bay or Pamlico Sound. A year or two later,
in 1524–5, Estevão Gomes (Magellan's deserter) carefully surveyed the whole
coast from the Bay of Fundy to Florida, finding no passage, and by 1535 Jacques
Cartier had eliminated the promise of the Gulf of St Lawrence: as on the Pacific
shores, any 'doubtful strait' must lie well to the north.[12] Danes and Portuguese
may well have been in the waters between Labrador and Greenland as far back
as the 1470s; here the Corte Reals had sailed and vanished in the first years of
the new century, and here about 1509 Sebastian Cabot had very likely penetrated
into the very portal of Hudson's Bay—in his own view, between the horns of
Asia and America. It is possible that the mysterious name 'Fretum Trium Fratrum'
refers either to the Corte Reals or the Cabots.[13]

This Strait of the Three Brothers was the eastern end of a waterway shown on
the very influential 1537 globe of Gemma Frisius, Cosmographer to the Emperor;
it was thought to lie in about 61–64°N, trending southwest and after about 200
leagues broadening out, to merge into the South Sea in a much lower latitude
than its Atlantic entry. This eastern mouth was thought of as reasonably well
fixed as to position, but difficult as to access; on the Pacific side was nothing
but a vagueness, in which the western entrance to the Passage, the Strait of
Anian, could be inserted at any point between Cipangu and Nueva España that
might suit the cosmographer's or projector's fancy. In a sense of course Anian
was really there, since a watergap does exist between Asia and America; but the
discovery of this genuine strait by Bering in 1728 did not end the career of the
Anian claim. It became associated with mythical voyages by the real Greek
pilot Juan de Fuca, the seedy and shadowy Lorenzo Ferrer Maldonado, and the
fictitious 'Admiral of Mexico and Peru' Bartholomew de Fonte—the last two

complete hoaxes; but belief in a waterway through America much to the south of Bering Strait was held, sometimes passionately, far into the eighteenth century, and the idea was a factor in the planning of the voyages of Byron, Cook (1776–8), La Pérouse, Vancouver, and Malaspina. In Spain the ghost of Anian was not finally laid to rest until 1802.[14]

More particularly to our point, whether or not Anian was a factor in the initial planning of Drake's voyage around the world, in the working-out of that voyage it led to the first non-Iberian European discovery in the South Sea, the only non-Spanish exploration of a Pacific mainland coast before the Russians reached the Sea of Okhotsk in 1639.[15]

The shift to the south and the rise of Drake

Two essential elements in this enterprise were converging by the mid-1570s. Francis Drake had established himself as an outstanding seaman and commander; and, although the most famous northwestwards voyages were yet to come, this approach was relatively losing ground. Expert opinion, which had begun by seeking northern ways into the South Sea, was now paradoxically swinging round to southern approaches to a Northern Passage. With Richard Grenville's project of 1573–4, the wheel had turned: where Barlow had told Henry VIII that to discover 'this waie of the northe onlie . . . resteth unto your graces charge', Grenville, leaving that route to the French, tells Elizabeth that 'the fourth [way] to the south is by God's providence left for England'.[16]

Gilbert's discourse seems to have been the first proposal for an English settlement in the Mar del Sur, 'about Sierra Nevada', that is in our California, Drake's Nova Albion. From the generally assumed lie of the Strait of the Three Brothers, and from experience of its ice-ridden eastern approaches, it seemed fair to reckon that a Pacific entrance at say about 44°N, or even down to the Tropic, would be easier to find and negotiate; and indeed Gilbert tells a circumstantial story of having himself been told by a gentleman of New Spain that sometime before 1560 Urdaneta in person had come from the Mar del Sur to Germany by the Northwest Passage.[17] A new factor enters with the first reports of Mendaña in the Solomons: these reached England not later than 1572,[18] and appear to have inspired, at least in part, the project of Grenville and his friends for 'the discovery, traffic and enjoying . . . of all or any lands . . . southwards beyond the equinoctial', not being already in the possession of any other Christian Prince in Europe. Such lands, beneath the Pole Antarctic and to be reached through the Straits of Magellan, imply the great Terra Australis of Mercator and Ortelius.

The antithesis between the two approaches is sharpened by a later version (c. 1575–6) of Grenville's project, made apparently with direct reference to Gilbert. Admitting the Northwest Passage exists, Grenville asks whether it is better to seek it by 'passing under the congealed Arctic circle, for so high the main of America reacheth', or by Magellan's way—a longer course, but over known seas with better weather, so that full sail could be carried night and day until the Strait of Anian was approached, and moreover passing by regions likely to be in all respects much richer than the boreal lands (this was before Frobisher had returned from the north with his fool's gold). The Magellanic tract might be searched to discover sites for fortifying the Straits 'if need were'; in effect, England might secure both the austral and the boreal approaches to the South Sea.[19] Terra Australis now seems not altogether ignored, but to have slipped out of focus. A grandiose plan, and so much would surely be too much for the canny Gloriana.

Yet the reception of the first project was initially favourable, though it might well be doubted (and it probably was) whether Richard Grenville was the man to respect the more distant bounds of any Christian Prince. According to John Oxenham's deposition to his Spanish captors, the plan included a settlement at La Plata (obviously a sensitive spot) and then passing the Straits to 'establish settlements wherever a good country for such could be found.'[20] A patent for the voyage was drawn up, but this provisional approval was withdrawn for fear of consequences: while in the early seventies Anglo-Spanish relations were at a nadir (with the seizure of the silver for Alba's troops, San Juan de Ulua, and the Ridolfi Plot), by 1574 a new understanding had been reached by the Convention of Bristol, and this 'was the reef upon which Grenville's project foundered'. An expedition into the Spanish Mar del Sur, with its standing temptation to treasure-raiding, would be a provocation which Elizabeth could hardly afford as yet.[21] But clearly South Sea venturing was in the air, and Grenville's plan remained in effect a blueprint for Drake's performance. Already indeed the aftermath of Spanish foul play at San Juan de Ulua had brought Englishmen, armed, across the Isthmus to the Mar del Sur: John Oxenham briefly on to its very waters, Francis Drake as yet only to a peak in Darien, a Pisgah-sight of the Ocean, a glimpse which led him to a longer voyage than Magellan's.

The hero of the Spanish Main, romantic theatre of Kingsley's schoolboy fiction and Froude's scarcely less impressionistic essays,[22] was born in the early 1540s, of a strongly Protestant Devonshire family, forced by the Catholic rising of 1549 to fly to more congenial Kent, which became four years later the very hearth of Wyatt's rebellion against Queen Mary's marriage with Philip of Spain.[23] The boy thus grew up in an atmosphere compounded of Protestant Hot Gospelling and the maritime activity of the Medway estuary. A family relationship with John Hawkins gave him a post with John Lovell, who in 1566 took four of Hawkins's ships on the almost routine run to Guinea for slaves (as often as not seized from Portuguese ships) and across to the Indies, where these and other commodities would be disposed of in flagrant breach of Spanish law. Often there was a hint of force, just sufficient to give the labour-hungry Spanish colonists an excuse to 'submit' to the exchange:

> the general landed with one hundred men and the people of the
> town came down under a captain; and with their agreement a

> shot was fired and an old house burned, and they did
> business together . . .[24]

Scruples were not nice on either side in such a trade, and at one of the tiny ports of Tierra Firme the Governor refused to pay for ninety Negroes already landed; twenty-five years later Drake was still recalling 'the wrongs received at Rio Hacha', the beginning of his personal war with King Philip and his officers.[25]

In October 1567 Drake sailed on Hawkins's 'third troublesome voyage', and was sent ahead in the 50-ton *Judith* to Rio de la Hacha. Here he was fired on and replied in kind, blockading the port until Hawkins arrived with superior force; after some violence, trade proceeded amicably. Now the troubles began: Hawkins was forced by storm damage to put into San Juan de Ulua, the port of Vera Cruz, to refit; his entrance was unopposed as the fleet was mistaken for the expected flota. When this did arrive a few days later, with the new Viceroy Don Martin Enriquez, Hawkins controlled the harbour mouth with a battery and was able to make terms before permitting its entry. Once in, however, Enriquez covertly prepared to attack, indubitably in gross and premeditated breach of faith.[26] After hard fighting only two of the five English ships got away—the *Minion* with Hawkins himself, and the *Judith*. Drake reached England in January 1569, a few days ahead of Hawkins, who had a nightmare voyage in the overcrowded and under-rationed *Minion*, even though half her crew had voluntarily taken their chances ashore in New Spain; and an ill chance it was. Hawkins wrote that the *Judith* 'forsooke us in our greate miserie', and he cannot be blamed for taking hard the apparent desertion by a young relative whom he had advanced; but then Drake may well have thought that his first duty was to bring his own tiny vessel safely home. It was not a brilliant start in command, though the estrangement from Hawkins does not seem to have remained serious for long.

For a time Drake returned to an obscurity from which he had only begun to emerge. In 1570, however, he made the first of three definitely known annual Caribbean voyages, probably largely financed by Hawkins, which brought him to the portal of the Pacific. Little is known of the first; on the second he went up the Rio Chagres as far as Cruces, and at the eastern end of the Isthmus marked down a well-hidden cove as a base for next year's voyage.[27] These forays were simply freebooting—if Drake had a commission at all, it would probably have been a Huguenot one, of doubtful avail against non-French Catholics.

The objective of the third voyage was far more than the usual snapping-up of coastal traders and raiding of undefended coastal towns; Drake had determined to seize the Peruvian treasure itself, by a surprise raid with only two small ships (70 and 20 tons) and seventy-three men. He had now a close acquaintance with the coast from the Chagres to Cape Tiburon, on the present Panama/Columbia border; but, strangely, he seems to have had only imperfect intelligence on the seasonal flow of traffic across the Isthmus. This was active only when the galeones were in, during the first four or five months of the year; for the remainder, the silver of Peru piled up in Panama City, but naturally was not portaged to the vulnerable northern shores until its onward shipping was becoming available. Since Drake left Plymouth on 24 May 1572, he was far too late to intercept treasure for that year's Seville fleet. In a more general view, however, the timing for a real blow at 'old Philip's treasury' was appropriate, since in January the Spanish Ambassador had been expelled for involvement in the Ridolfi plot against Elizabeth's crown and life. A damaging unofficial counterstroke was not likely to be frowned upon.

The magnificent adventure story of the Isthmus raid can be only outlined here. Although he found that his hidden Port Pheasant was no longer a secret to friend or foe, Drake assembled there his three pre-fabricated pinnaces, and at the end of July took them into Nombre de Dios at moonrise. Brilliantly successful at first, the surprise lost impetus, and when Drake himself fainted from an early wound, the seventy-odd assailants took to their pinnaces in some disorder.[28] This first attempt was a failure, though hardly a fiasco; and from the Cimarrons or Bush Negroes with whom contact was now made, it was clear that there would be no point in a second try until silver again began to move over the trail, in about five months' time. Apart from an outbreak of yellow fever, this interval was filled in agreeably enough by minor feints and forays, playing havoc with the cabotage carried on by the scores of small 'frigates' of the coast, and planning the next attack with the Cimarrons, who proved admirable allies, intelligent, born to the bush, physically tough, valiant and loyal.

The galeones arrived in January 1573, and Drake immediately set out with John Oxenham and sixteen others, accompanied by thirty Cimarrons, to ambush a requa near Casa de Cruces. On the way the guides took Drake to a look-out in a tall tree, whence he could see at once both the Caribbean and the South Sea, begging 'Almightie God of his goodnesse to give him life and leave to sayle once in an English Ship in that sea'; and Oxenham 'protested . . . that he would follow him by Gods Grace.' The prayer was granted, but it was Oxenham who led, to his own destruction.

The ambush was set, but one Robert Pike 'having drunken too much Aqua vitae without water . . . unadvisedly he rose up', and although 'the *Symeron* (of better discretion) puld him downe, and lay upon him', the alarm had been taken. The loot of the little village of Cruces was poor consolation for being 'defeated of our golden Recoe'; so far the voyage had been only modestly successful, and the company had dwindled to thirty-odd. They now fell in with a Huguenot party under the cartographer Guillaume Le Testu (Tetu), who brought news of the Massacre of St Bartholomew and proffered alliance: Drake was wary, but had little choice save acceptance, since the French had more than double his resources.[29] A new ambush was set near Nombre de Dios, this time successfully, though Le Testu was killed. Little of the massive haul of silver could be carried off, but gold to the value of 80–100,000 pesos was taken away: after the disappointments of Nombre de Dios and Cruces, 'our voyage was made.'

There was a last wild adventure, a raft voyage to regain the pinnaces, driven off by a storm; then an emotional leave-taking from the Cimarrons, whose leader Pedro was given the gilded scimitar, once owned by Henry II of France, which Le Testu had presented to Drake. On 9 August, 1575 a Sunday, Drake reached Plymouth 'about Sermon-time . . . very few or none remained with the Preacher. All hastning to see the evidence of Gods love and blessing towards our Gracious Queene and Countrey . . .' More to the point, Drake had exposed Spanish weakness, not least to the Spaniards themselves, and had pioneered a long series of attempts against the Isthmian node, the 'door of the seas, the key of the universe':[30] by Oxenham, Parker, Morgan and later buccaneers, Paterson, Pointis, Vernon.

Interlude: Oxenham on the Mar del Sur

Once again, like any Toynbeean hero, Drake withdrew, to wait for a return of greater renown. The negotiations for the Convention of Bristol were now in full swing (if that is the right phrase for any dealings between those incomparable deferrers Elizabeth and Philip), and any prominence for so successful a corsair would have been most inconvenient. Drake betook himself to the Irish wars, leaving to his companion on that peak in Darien the by now traditional free-booting on the Main. Oxenham's penetration right across the Isthmus was probably not the 'if of history', the 'Gallipoli campaign of the sixteenth century', that J. A. Williamson once called it—the lines of communication were too tenuous for Panama to have been held, had Oxenham taken it—but it has the interest of being the first European but non-Iberian enterprise on the waters of the Mar del Sur.[31]

Oxenham sailed from Plymouth in April 1576, with two small vessels and only fifty-seven men. After the usual marauding between Veragua and Acla, he came to the Cimarrons at their town of Ronconcholon—a considerable place, 217 houses, four or five times the size of Cruces. Meanwhile the President of the Panama Audiencia, Gabriel de Loarte, had sent out a small force from Nombre de Dios, which found Oxenham's hidden ships and took most of his guns and ammunition, with the goods which he carried to back up his cover story of innocent trading with the Cimarrons; but the English salvaged enough iron-work and cordage to build a new vessel. With the help of the Cimarrons, on whom he was now dependent, Oxenham took these materials across the Isthmus and built a 45-ton pinnace, and in February 1577 raided the Pearl Islands.

Here there was a good deal of wanton sacrilege: John Butler, the pilot and interpreter, opened a child's lesson-book, and 'when he came to the command-ment: *Thou shalt not steal*, he laughed loudly at it. . . .'[32] There was loud talk of returning with 2000 men 'to make himself master of all this realm', and altogether the party behaved recklessly. Oxenham captured a ship from Guayaquil—the first European prize ever taken in the Pacific—with 38,000 pesos in gold, a figure soon inflated to 100,000;[33] but by this time all Tierra Firme was aroused. Loarte had mobilised 500 men at Panama and sent 200 in search of the raiders;

he appealed to Peru for aid, expended money 'in anticipation of sanction' (to use a classic phrase of the British Raj), and in general displayed a most unbureau-cratic energy. Oxenham retired to Vallano, the Indian country, and might have got away (for the time being) but for carelessness: the pursuing Spaniards were baffled until they noticed a trail of food scraps—in one version, chicken feathers floating down a creek. Some of the English were killed or taken; the Spaniards reached and burnt Ronconcholon, which, as they calculated, led to trouble between the allies.

In Peru, Francisco de Toledo was not the man to ignore Loarte's appeal, and sent succours from Trujillo and Manta. Loarte tried to stop them, thinking he now had the situation well in hand and not wishing to share the credit; but an officer of Toledo's was not likely to desist at the behest of a legal official, however eminent. After tedious and confused 'campaigns' by handfuls of men in the jungly hills of Darien, all but a few of the English were rounded up: Oxenham's account of his own capture is one of the most vivid episodes in the whole story of the Spanish Main.[34] Thirteen were hanged at Panama, but Oxenham, Butler, and one 'Xerores' or 'Xervel' were taken to Lima for examination by the Inquisition: they were there when Drake came to Callao, and were at last hanged in 1580, a bitter payment for the sacrilege at the Pearl Islands. The handful who had escaped the Spanish net managed to seize a small vessel and sail away; their fate is unknown. As for the Cimarrons, many made terms, and were given letters of freedom and resettled with some degree of autonomy; others remained recalcitrant, and as late as 1580 were still waiting for the return of Oxenham's remnant showing the agreed signal, a black flag.[35]

Oxenham's raid was merely a disastrous episode, but not without some wider significance, even if its immediate result was only to impel the Spaniards to deal more effectively than before with the Cimarrons. The simplest English approach to the South Sea was indeed his: march across the Isthmus and build a ship. 'But that method was available only for a grab-and-run pirate raid, and was useless for serious empire-building.'[36] In their depositions at Lima, Oxenham spoke quite freely of Grenville's discarded project; Butler scouted the idea that a poor man like Drake could mount an expedition through the Straits. Oxenham thought that he could and would do so if he had the royal licence—but that this was impossible so long as Elizabeth was Queen. The net effect of the activities of Drake, Oxenham, and other corsairs of the 1570s may well have been to concentrate Spanish attention on the Caribbean side, so that when Drake did irrupt into the South Sea, with more force than Oxenham's pinnace, its shores were naked of defence. 'The colonists of [Chile and Peru], when they saw a sail approaching, knew no misgiving, and never dreamt that it could be other than a friend.'[37]

The problem of Drake's plan

The mass of literature surrounding the second circumnavigator seems proportion-ate to the loot he brought back; some of it seems bad Hollywood, though one contemporary account—Cooke, on the trial of Thomas Doughty—provides a tense and authentic court-room scene.[38] On the vexed question of Drake's aims and motives, the trend is to accept K. R. Andrews's closely argued position, but it would perhaps be premature to claim a consensus;[39] and there will probably always be obscurities about the Doughty affair, Drake's movements in Magellanic waters, his Californian landing, his 'Island of Thieves'.

Concerning the objectives, it would be as well to recall Williamson's remark that Drake combined 'all aims and all motives' of the 1570s—not perhaps in the planning, but in the event;[40] there was undoubtedly an element of *on s'engage, et puis on voit*. Precisely because the question of the plan gathers together so many strands—political, exploratory, economic, psychological—it transcends such matters as Cape Horn or the Plate of Brass, and indeed lies central to any discussion of the gathering stand against Habsburg dominance; even though the voyage itself, in its immediate political effects (not its long-term economic results) was no more than a foray, Corbett leads up to it under the significant heading 'Drake and the War Party'. Zelia Nuttall took this line of thought to an extreme, suggesting that 'the present occupation of the North American Continent by the Anglo-Saxon race is, after all, but a realisation of what may be called Drake's Dream'; but the evidences she cites are at times misinterpreted and in any case cannot bear the weight of the colonising designs she infers.[41] This enthusiastic vision received severe, though not short, shrift from H. R. Wagner, who saw the expedition as a trading venture to the Moluccas, and possibly China, diverted by Drake to plundering Peru. His massive study might have settled the issue for decades, had not Eva Taylor, only three or four years later, signally refuted his forecast that 'no other document of real value' was likely to be found—by turning up a draft plan for the voyage.[42]

The important points in the draft (some words in which are conjectural) are that Drake is to enter the South Sea by the Straits of Magellan and then sail north as far as 30° 'alonge the saeied coaste', where there should be countries not subject to any Christian Prince but offering great hope of profitable commodities; and having gone to 30° or as close as he thinks fit, he is to return the same way as he went out. Nothing on Anian, nothing on the Moluccas, a general resemblance to Grenville's first project. The immediate questions are: which is 'the said coast' and which 'the other coast' associated with it? Andrews argues that there are simply the west and east coasts of South America respectively. To Taylor, followed by Williamson, the latter merely suggests some earlier reconnaissance, but 'the said coast' is Terra Australis as shown on the standard Ortelius/Mercator maps (Plate XVI), trending from Tierra del Fuego towards the Spice Islands, the intended term of the voyage: 'Clearly its objective was not the American coast already under the obedience of Spain' as far south as Valdivia (39° 46′S), founded in 1552. So far Taylor; but for the Moluccan aspect—which is to the fore in his version—Wagner relies on statements by Francis Fletcher, chaplain to the expedition: a man with a good gift of phrase, often a good observer (he even

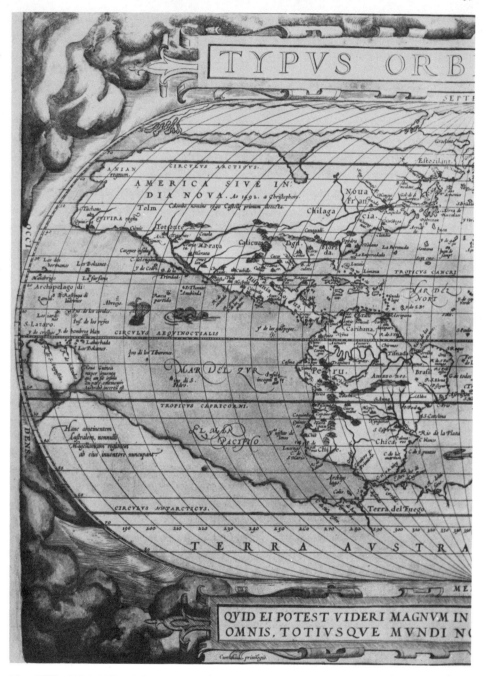

Plate XVI. DRAKE'S PACIFIC: ORTELIUS 1570. The standard view of the later sixteenth century. Note the run of New Guinea-Terra Australis-Tierra del Fuego, the passage from Anian to Greenland, and the Chilean bulge. From *Typis Orbis Terrarum* (Antwerp 1570). NLA.

gives an inventory of the 'furnishings' of a Fuegian hut), but pedantic and quite often muddle-headed: a minor Shakespearean character, comic but unpleasant, one moreover on bad terms with Drake. Andrews is quite warranted in dismissing such a witness on such a point.

Taylor bases herself rather on the seemingly more respectable evidence of John Winter, who as Drake's second should have known the real objective. His statement is self-exculpatory, to explain away what looks like desertion with his ship the *Elizabeth*; he gives no indication of a definite rendezvous, but says that after an accidental separation he tried to get his crew to sail for the Moluccas, but was overborne—and then, most revealingly, he 'despair[ed] utterly of the favourableness of the wind for to go to the Peru.' Edward Cliffe, one of his company, denies that the crew wished to give over the voyage but confirms that Winter 'alleged, he stood in dispaire, to haue winds to serue his turne for *Peru*'. According to John Cooke, Doughty pleaded with Drake 'I pray yow cary me with you to the Perwe', and Fletcher himself (or *The World Encompassed*, based on his notes) says that after the separation they sailed 'to coast alongst the parts of Peru . . . that we might fall . . . with the height of 30 deg., being the place appointed for the rest of oyr fleete to reassemble.'[43] Against all this stress on Peru, there is nothing in Winter's statement to indicate the Moluccas as an *original* objective.

Taylor's insistence that 'the said coast' was that of Terra Australis thus seems odd, quite apart from the fact that on current maps this supposed coast trended not north but initially south, then west swinging round to northwestwards. As for Anian, Taylor thinks that under John Dee's influence this was added as a possible objective, before the sailing. She makes much of a passage in one of Dee's manuscripts (mid-May 1577) which speaks of a great exploring expedition to be carried out 'presently' (i.e. immediately) by a British subject who has 'se[cret]ly' undertaken this exploit for God, Queen, and Country; she takes this to refer to Drake, since the objective of Frobisher, who was to sail in a week or two after Dee's writing, was perfectly well known to be the Northwest Passage. As Andrews points out, 'presently' could well mean Frobisher, but not Drake, since he was not to sail for six months; 'secretly' could suggest Drake but not Frobisher—'but the middle four letters of this word are putative. In effect there is room for doubt about Taylor's inference.'[44] Indeed, there is, for what if we read 'se[cure]ly', in its older sense of 'assuredly, of a certainty'? This would fit the Frobisher context, and it seems to have a good Elizabethan ring. The fact that Drake did make a move towards Anian and did go to the Moluccas is explicable by events: there was no other way for him to go. The Magellanic waters had proved highly hazardous by nature, and by the time that 'the voyage was made' nothing would seem more likely than an attempted Spanish interception at the Straits, only twelve degrees south of Valdivia, of whose existence Drake was now aware.

But if not Terra Australis nor the Moluccas nor Anian, what then? In Andrews's opinion, the voyage was really to explore the commercial opportunities (plunder-age not excluded) of South America beyond the Spanish limits: a trade recon-naissance in some force, but hardly a trading voyage, since there were no letters for foreign princes (surely essential for the Moluccas?) and scarcely any trade goods. One need not take too seriously the pious preamble about places not under the obedience of any Christian Prince; although Andrews says that the English might reasonably think the coast would be unoccupied by Spaniards south of 30°S, one must agree with Williamson that such ignorance would be remarkable, since Santiago in 33° 30′ had been founded for over thirty-five years, and Ortelius's map of 1564 shows several towns between 30° and 35°, including '[Val]paraiso'. However, the draft is careful to allow Drake the option of turning back before 30°; very possibly this clause was to facilitate a royal disavowal if need be. Nevertheless, even with this safeguard, the promoters must have known that to Philip of Spain an exploration from La Plata to Chile would appear a wanton provocation. Hence the cover stories: there was a rumour, doubtless leaked, that 'Drake the pirate' was going to Scotland to kidnap the little James VI; the official destination was Alexandria for currants,[45] a commodity in which Captain Drake had so far shown little interest. It is not very likely that many of the complement were fooled by this tale, though later on it suited some of them to say they were.

Wagner and Taylor regard the project as basically a peaceful venture: this is difficult to square with Drake as leader and (at this stage of his career) John Hawkins as a principal backer. Other supporters included Leicester, Walsingham, Hatton, the Navy's Master of the Ordnance Sir William Winter and his brother George; Drake himself subscribed £1000. The draft says that the Queen should be 'made pryve to the trewthe of the viage' and asked to contribute a royal ship; this she did not do, but very probably she did invest in the enterprise. It is scarcely possible to believe, however, that Drake held any formal commission from the Queen; though he assiduously spread around this impression, no reliable document was ever produced, even when Doughty—on trial for his life—directly asked for it, nor was one used to quash the 'appeal of murder' brought against Drake by Doughty's brother.[46] That the plan existed on paper before the Queen had been informed of its real object tells strongly against Drake's claim that Elizabeth had directly and spontaneously incited him to reprisals against Spain; an unlikely story, produced with splendid bravura at a crisis in the voyage.[47] Francis Drake was a great man; he was also a great con man or, if you prefer it so, a master of psychological warfare.

On the peaceable view, we have to explain a 'trading' voyage carrying only one identifiable merchant and a few presents, and with no mercantile element amongst its backers, all of whom 'were associated with maritime enterprise of a predatory kind, and all, with the exception of the Queen, advocate[s of] a vigorous anti-Spanish policy.'[48] It is significant that what in the last resort seems to have cost Doughty his head was the admission that he had revealed the true 'plott of the voyage' to Burghley who, if not the appeaser he is often made out to be, disapproved of plundering to the extent of refusing a proffered share of Drake's booty. As a reconnaissance for future operations, and perhaps for political benefits from contacts with Indians beyond the Spanish limits (a concept which certainly appealed to Drake),[49] the plan makes sense. But it is unlikely that its Court backers would have seen much sense in a reconnaissance which did not meet expenses; and who more likely to make it pay its way than the captor of the Nombre de Dios treasure train?

Port St Julian: a new Plutarchan parallel

The fleet which Drake took out of Plymouth late in 1577 consisted of the *Pelican* of over 100 tons; *Elizabeth* of 80, under John Winter; *Marigold* of 30, a storeship and a pinnace, not to mention the taken-down parts of four more pinnaces, hardly needed for peaceful trade.[50] The complement of at least 160 was also a heavier man/ton ratio than usual for trading voyages, though 'normal for a long-distance plunder cruise.'[51] Ten were gentleman-adventurers, not one of whom, despite Spanish fears, was to profit by this sea-cadetship to become a leader in naval affairs. The most notable of them was Thomas Doughty, a client of Hatton's with a rather ambiguous record in the past and a very ambiguous position now. Like Juan de Cartagena, he has been suspected by some scholars of being a spy (for Spain) or a secret agent (of Burghley's),[52] and he clearly regarded himself as an equal to his commander, or more; in a 'Society' sense he was Drake's superior, and though he seems to have had no definite posting on the staff, this higher social standing would have entitled him, by normal Elizabethan notions, to a major say in the direction of the undertaking. Such rule by committee was not Drake's way, and while Doughty was not Spain's man, and probably not Burghley's man in any sinister sense, he was surely Thomas Doughty's man; and that proved enough to chafe the latent ill-feeling between gentlemen and common mariners into a flame.

The Alexandrian story was soon exploded, for the fleet sailed down the Moroccan coast, robbing stray Iberian fishing smacks and coasters of their provisions.[53] At the end of January 1578, when off Santiago in the Cape Verdes, they took and retained a Portuguese ship laden with wines, cloth, and other goods for Brazil. This was significant in several aspects. First, it was naked piracy: there could be no question of reprisals, the islands had been Portuguese for over a century, and it was only two years since Elizabeth had signed a treaty to stop English incursions in these parts.[54] Second, while Drake released the rest of the company, he took good care to keep Nuño da Silva, a pilot highly experienced on the Brazilian coast. Finally, it was here that serious friction began, with charges and counter-charges between Doughty and Drake's brother Thomas over the pilfering of prize goods.

As the ships crawled slantwise and slowly through the Doldrums, friction grew into disaffection: there were petty squabbles, crude horseplay, arrogant or ironic speeches, ostentatious avoidances between gentlemen and mariners, and Drake's attempts at alleviation by shifting commands were unsuccessful. Early in April they saw land somewhere in the modern Rio Grande do Sul; the next

Figure 20. THE ENGLISH RAIDS, 1578–94

ten weeks were spent in reconnaissance almost to the Straits. After the equatorial heats and calms, they now had to contend with storm, fog, and cold, and tensions worsened: according to Cooke, Drake called Doughty 'a coniurer and witche, and, at eny time when he had any fowle wethar, he . . . wolde say that it came out of Tom Dowghtys· capcase, and wold avouch the same with greate othes.' No suitable wintering-place was found, and the little fleet turned north to enter, on 20 June, Magellan's Puerto San Julian. The ill omen of the place—they found his gibbet, 'with mens bones vnderneath'—was soon fulfilled. Hitherto contacts with the Patagonians had been friendly, if uncomprehending, on both sides; now a small shore party was attacked, and two killed by arrows. 'This bloudy Tragedie being ended another more greivious ensueth . . . more grevious because it was among ourselves begunn contrived & ended'.

The 'authorised' narrative (as Wagner says, 'the most untrustworthy of all') draws the Plutarchan parallel between Magellan and Drake, Cartagena and Doughty—but doctors Fletcher's notes to the extent of omitting Doughty's name; the 'famous voyage' version in Hakluyt mentions Doughty by name but is if anything even smoother. Cooke's account is a passionate brief in Doughty's defence and for Drake's conviction of judicial murder. (It is also one of the most vivid and 'immediate' things in Elizabethan prose, an artless masterpiece of reportage.) It is impossible now to unravel the truth from the tangle of charges, ranging from slander to high-level political betrayal; there seems to have been no question of real principle involved, such as a stand by Doughty against plundering. Through the confusion we can at least see that Doughty was at the head of a dangerously strong trend towards insubordination amongst the gentlemen-adventurers, and from Drake's point of view this put the whole voyage at hazard—and with it the whole career, if not the life, of Francis Drake.

Some of the large jury empanelled were clearly most ill at ease, and Drake forced a decision with a high hand: it was a kangaroo court, its proceedings full of challenges, sudden shifts of mood, catastrophic admissions. In the event, according to Cooke (who despite his obvious bias tells a much more likely tale than the smooth and sanctimonious official version), the jury, under pressure, answered for a verdict of guilty, Drake undertaking to answer for the sentence. He made an unconvincing show of reprieve, but decided (and from a realist point of view, almost certainly correctly) that after what had happened, it would be too dangerous to hold Doughty prisoner, to be a continuing centre of dis-affection. To him, his problem was the same as Magellan had faced in this very port, and his solution also had to be Magellan's: Stone dead hath no fellow. Only the mode differed, not the end. It is an ugly episode, lightened only by the Elizabethan genius for the great gesture: the die once cast, Drake and Doughty took Communion together, dined at the same table, and then took their leave in the high manner of the age, 'by drinking each to other, as if some journey oneley had beene in hand.'[55]

The troubles were not yet over. Drake had asserted his authority, but there were still murmurings sufficient to account for the scene a few weeks later when he discharged all his captains and masters, only to reinstate them after some remarkable justificatory speeches. Beginning conventionally 'My mastars, I ame a very badd orrator', he gave his version of the Queen's initiative in setting out the venture, and played on patriotism and greed, hopes and fears, as cunningly as that other poor orator Mark Antony. It was now that he spoke the famous words that in Williamson's opinion marked 'the beginning of a new tradition in English leadership,'[56] and ironically are recorded by his bitter enemy John Cooke: for the controversy and 'stomakynge between the gentlemen and saylars . . . I must have it lefte, for I must have the gentleman to hayle and draw with the mariner, and the maryner with the gentleman . . .' If at Port St Julian he has seemed almost paranoid, or else acting a magnificent but unscrupulous bravura role, from now on we shall see Francis Drake at his best, superbly in command of himself as well as of his company.

'the Southermost knowne land'

Three ships only, the *Pelican*, *Elizabeth*, and *Marigold*, left the port on 17 August 1578, Nuño da Silva's and the others having served their turn and been abandoned or broken up. Only three days brought them to Cape Virgins, where the *Pelican* was given the more famous and resounding name of the *Golden Hinde* (Plate XVII)—a compliment to Hatton, whose crest bore that heraldic beast, and doubtless a bid for a friend at Court should things go wrong. For the next phase of the voyage, Drake had a large and costly world map obtained from Lisbon, probably drawn by the great Portuguese cartographer Vaz Dourado, and it is also possible that he carried a Portuguese rutter of 1577 giving the coasts and courses from Brazil round to Chile, though beyond La Plata only sketchily;[57] his exploit was not such a daring of the unknown as Magellan's.

The passage was unhurried: islands were annexed, according to da Silva a great tree was taken as a souvenir—if so, it is perhaps a hint that he did not mean to return this way. It was however remarkably swift, only sixteen days, and this in mid-winter. By 6 September they had emerged into the South Sea, and for the next three days they sailed northwest, parallel to the Chilean coast as shown on Ortelius's standard map, but away from the immediate trend of that of Terra Australis.[58] But now their winter's luck ran out: tremendous contrary winds drove them for three weeks far to the south, down to 57°; the *Marigold* was lost 'in the uiolent force of the winds intollerable workinge of the wrathfull seas . . .'[59] Early in October the wind changed, and in a week the two remaining ships were among islands a degree or two north of Cabo Deseado: but almost at once a new storm forced them to sea, and by the morning of 8 October the *Elizabeth* had disappeared. Her captain John Winter lit fires just inside the Straits, but after two or three days he retreated further in and stocked up with penguin meat before returning to England, whether compelled by his crew or compelling them is now impossible to say.

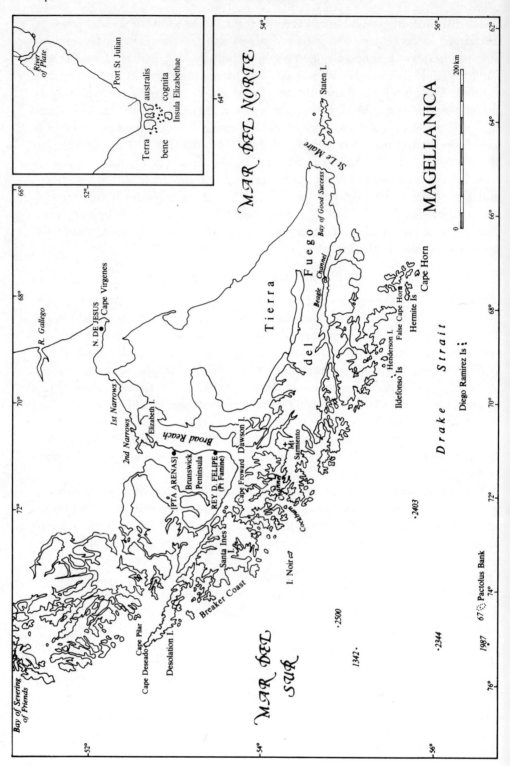

MAGELLANICA

MAR DEL NORTE

MAR DEL SUR

Tierra del Fuego

Drake Strait

0   200 km

Terra australis bene cognita
Insula Elizabethae
River of Plate
Port St Julian

R. Gallego
R. Gallego

N. DE JESUS
Cape Virgenes

1st Narrows
2nd Narrows
Elizabeth I.
Broad Reach

[PTA ARENAS]
Brunswick Peninsula
REY D. FELIPE
(Pt Famine)
Dawson I.
Cape Froward
Mt Sarmiento

Santa Ines I.
I. Noir
Cape Deseado
Cape Pilar
Desolation I.
Breaker Coast

Bay of Severing of Friends

Beagle Channel
St Le Maire
Bay of Good Success
Staten I.

Henderson I.
Ildefonso Is
False Cape Horn
Hermite Is
Cape Horn

Diego Ramirez Is

Pactolus Bank
67

1342.
•2500
•2344
1987
•2403

Meanwhile the now solitary *Golden Hinde* was again driven south, once more to 55–57°, but this time with more easting, closer to the 'Breaker Coast' and the wild fiord shores southeast from Isla Santa Ines. While his actual tracks and landfalls remain matters of dispute, Drake now indisputably made what may fairly be claimed as the most notable geographical discovery by any Englishman before James Cook: in Fletcher's fitting words, 'The vttermost cape or hedland . . . without [outside] which there is no maine or Iland to be seene to the Southwards, but that the Atlanticke Ocean and the South Sea, meete in a most large and free scope.'

Plate XVII. THE *GOLDEN HINDE.*   Reconstruction by Gregory Robinson. By permission of the National Maritime Museum, London.

The precise location of the uttermost cape is indeed most uncertain. Consciously or subconsciously, the student of such a problem will always be torn between a feeling of 'How splendid if it really were so!' and a desire to maintain a cool scepticism, unseduced by the romantic or ironic but in any case dramatic co-

◄*Figure 21.* MAGELLANICA. Inset: Francis Fletcher's map of southern South America. Fletcher's original is oriented with south at top. On main map, figures thus, '.2403', are depths in fathoms.

incidence; anyone who claims immunity must either deceive himself or be singularly insensitive. In British tradition, Drake's landfall has been associated with Cape Horn itself, the true southernmost land, and Corbett gave this belief his sober and weighty support. Although this view has been somewhat blown upon, as late as 1971 Richard Hough admits uncertainty in his text, but on his map opts clearly for Cape Horn; and its case has recently been revived, on new lines, by Robert Power.[60]

H. R. Wagner, arguing mainly from distances and bearings, made a plausible case for Henderson Island (55° 40'S; cf. Fletcher's 'necre in 56'), and is followed by S. E. Morison: these are weighty authorities. Felix Riesenberg, a sea captain with much experience in Magellanic waters, reconstructed a possible course from Nuño da Silva's log, allowing for usually neglected currents, and came up with the novel suggestion that this farthest south point of land is now under water: the Pactolus or Burnham Bank, where a sounding of 67 fathoms, black sand and small rocks, is surrounded by depths of 2000 fathoms and more: clearly a volcanic sea-mount, and such are notoriously likely to disappear. Moreover, several maps—French, Spanish and German as well as English, and as late as 1775—show in this general area the 'Elizabethides' or a port or land named for Drake. Again, while Fletcher's concept of an island is normally a crude rectangle, in this instance he does give some internal detail, a water body suggesting a (still rectangular!) crater lake. But the position seems much too isolated to square with Fletcher's suggestion of near-by inhabited islands, and this also weakens the likelihood of the assumption that has to be made, that this volcanic summit was well supplied with wood and 'herbes of great virtue': Horn Island has at least some vegetation, but obviously there can be no evidence at all of its existence on a hypothetical island. It is risky to rely too implicitly on the accuracy of da Silva's observations, made by astrolabe in far from ideal conditions and with some gaps; and indeed, like Riesenberg using nautical rather than academic arguments, Brett Hilder analyses the same data and concludes that the solution is the Diego Ramirez group, which seems as reasonable as Henderson Island and more reasonable than Cape Horn.

Power's argument for the latter is novel and ingenious. Its main thrust is that the four islands shown south of the Straits on the well-known sketch map of South America in Fletcher's notes are to be read on two different scales:

What we really have in this Fletcher map of South America
are two plans in two vastly different scales which have been
spliced together to dramatize what the uttermost Cape below
South America looked like to the Elizabethans.

This would be highly unorthodox but not impossible cartography. On one scale, the spread of the four islands would be comparable in size and shape to the Fuegian archipelago as a whole; on the other, to the southern Hermite Islands and Cape Horn. Apart from one or two side-points, the case really depends on whether one can reasonably make sophisticated inferences from maps admittedly drawn in a 'crude simplistic style'; so rudely drawn indeed that were it shorn of place-names, one might well fail to recognise West Africa on what Power calls a 'crude but identifiable Map'. Given the premise, things fall neatly into place; but to deduce measurements from such barbarous cartography as Fletcher's seems very hazardous. Nevertheless, there is the striking though rough coincidence of the layout of his islands with the Hermite group, and if one could have confidence in Fletcher's cartography the case would be quite strong. As it is, it seems fair to say that Power has put the Cape Horn claim on a more reasoned basis than has been done heretofore.[61]

However, as Hough says, the precise island, existing or not, does not matter much: the real point is that though Drake had not actually demonstrated the existence of what is now Drake Passage or Strait, he had sailed far enough to establish the virtual certainty that the two Oceans did indeed 'meete in a most large and free scope.' Fletcher's denial that the Strait of Magellan was a strait is pedantic perversity, and Terra Australis was broken down into islands for but a small sector of longitude; his riders owe more to bigotry than geography, but on the main point he did put the matter succinctly. Immediately, there was no attempt to use the route thus indicated, but this was probably not due, as has been suggested, to an English policy of secrecy. It is true that while the disposal of the treasure, with its political bearing, was still under advisement, publicity about the voyage was naturally muted; but in 1587 Richard Hakluyt himself

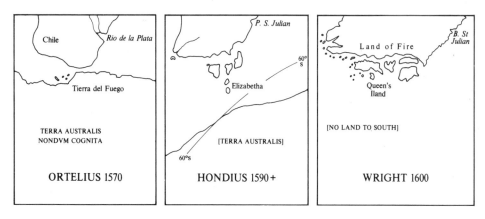

Figure 22. BEFORE AND AFTER DRAKE. The Ortelius is the standard sixteenth-century version before Drake (see Plate XVI); the Hondius from the famous broadside *Vera Totivs Expeditionis Navticæ* (*c.* 1593) showing the tracks of Drake and Cavendish; Wright's map was published in the 1600 edition of Hakluyts's *Principall Navigations*, with the note 'By the discouerie of Sʳ Francis Drake made in the yeare 1577 the streights of Magellane (as they are comonly called) seeme to be nothing els but broken lands and Ilands and the southwest coast of America called Chili was found, not to trend to the northwestwards as it hath beene described but to the eastwards of the north as it is heere set down: which is also confirmed by the voyages and discoueries of Pedro Sarmiēto and Mʳ Tho: Cavendish A° 1587.'

published, in Paris, a map showing open water south of the Elizabethides, and by 1593 Hondius, in his famous *Vera Totivs Expeditionis Navticae*, showing Drake's and Cavendish's tracks, pushed Terra Australis (in these longitudes) down below 60°—in fact, almost to Graham Land. Moreover, as early as April 1582 Philip II's ambassador in England, Bernardino de Mendoza, reported to the King that a person who claimed to have seen Drake's own chart had affirmed to him that 'there was the open sea beyond Tierra del Fuego.'[62] For some thirty years before the new passage was actually used its secret, like its seas, was open.

The delay in using this new Southwest Passage was not without good reason. Drake's immediate successors (Cavendish, Chidley, Richard Hawkins) must have been greatly impressed by his amazingly quick transit, barely a fortnight from Cape Virgins to Cape Desire; and no less by the frightful tempests met in latitudes south of the exit into the South Sea. The Straits had also an important advantage in the many anchorages where wooding and watering were easy, and fresh stocks of penguin meat might be had for the taking—a matter of particular significance to those on plunder bent, whose ships were of necessity heavily manned.[63] In contrast, the supremacy of Dutch shipping in the seventeenth century carrying trade was largely due to ship design which gave a maximum ratio of cargo space to crew; and the Dutch traders, Schouten and Le Maire, were to be the first to sail from ocean to ocean round the Horn—for the very Batavian technical reason that they desired to circumvent the [Dutch] East India Company's legal monopoly of trade by the Cape of Good Hope and the Straits of Magellan—nothing said of a by-pass!

The shores of silver

Cape Horn or Pactolus Bank or somewhere in between, the Elizabethides offered no inducements to linger, and on 30 October the *Golden Hinde* sailed 'right Northwest, to coast alongst the parts of Peru', as these were shown on the 'generall mappes', in search of the rendezvous in 30°; the great Chilean bulge on these maps (Plate XVI) was not due (as Fletcher asserted with much moral unction) to deliberate Spanish distortions, but to mistakes of compilation, as is shown by the 1577 rutter itself.[64] Realising that the maps were in error, Drake changed course and by 25 November was off Mocha Island (38° 25'S), about half-way between Valdivia and Concepcion and in that debatable land where warfare with the Araucanians was endemic. After an initial welcome by the Indians, a small watering party was attacked, two being captured and the rest, including Drake, wounded: a very close call, since had not 'one of the simplest of the company' cut the painter, all might have been lost. Naturally enough the English assumed, and it has been generally accepted, that they had been mistaken for hated Spaniards, and hence Drake refused to take revenge by bombardment. But not all Indians were freedom fighters, and this group had in fact been incited to attack by two local Spaniards; other Indians had in fact reported to Valdivia the passage of ships with black sails, but the local commander had refused to divert troops from the Araucanian front, since there was little truth in these Indians.[65]

Just north of Valparaiso Drake learnt from an Indian fisherman of that harbour and of a large ship lying there; he turned back, reaching it on 5 December. Valparaiso was as yet a wretched place, some nine households and a little church; but the ship was no less than Mendaña's capitana on the Solomons voyage. The eleven men aboard innocently invited the newcomers to drinks; the guests came aboard with a shout of 'Abaxo Perro, that is in English, Goe downe dogge.' The loot of the 'town' was not much—trifles of church silver (duly handed to Fletcher), wine, cedar boards for fuel—but the ship herself had a cargo of wine, at least 25,000 pesos in gold, and at this stage perhaps the most precious booty of all, an experienced pilot: Juan Griego, possibly that Juan de Fuca whose Strait is the last relic of Anian.[66] With this guide, Drake took a leisurely way north, twelve days, sailing with wind and current, to cover the roughly 330 km between Valparaiso and La Herradura, just south of Coquimbo. This was only some 15 km from La Serena, which had been warned: women and children were sent inland, and Drake's watering party was attacked by some scores of Spanish horsemen, plus Indians; he sheered off. Nearly a month was spent in careening and assembling a pinnace in Salada Bay, near Copiapo; perhaps Drake was still hoping for the *Elizabeth* to rejoin and give sufficient strength to attack Panama, though obviously this delay increased the risk of warnings reaching the north. That no alarm was in fact raised beyond La Serena was due to a bureaucratic ineptitude on which he could not reasonably have reckoned: the gamble came off because the local treasury, alleging strict orders, refused to advance the Santiago Cabildo 400 pesos for a fast boat, and nothing could be done until the Governor returned from the frontier wars. Then on 14 January 1579, seven weeks after the sack of Valparaiso, a message was sent: it reached Callao on 26 February, thirteen days after Drake.[67]

On 19 January Drake sailed north, still ahead of any warning; so complete was the surprise that at Tarapaca he snapped up thirteen bars of silver whose owner was asleep, and at Arica (5 February) over fifty bars, perhaps half a tonne of silver, were taken from two or three unguarded ships: there is a sportive note in the Hakluyt account of these doings, and that night Arica's score or so of households were in a manner serenaded by the *Golden Hinde*'s musicians. However, messengers were sent out from Arica, and near Arequipa a much more valuable cargo, 500 bars, was unloaded only two hours before the corsair's arrival. But a few leagues south of Callao a coaster was taken, and this had great news: two ships were taking on really large quantities of bullion at that port, while a third, San Juan de Anton's *Nuestra Señora de la Concepcion* (or *Cacafuego*) had just left for Panama and intermediate ports. Taking a couple of local pilots, Drake entered Callao harbour on the night of 13–14 February.

Rapid and doubtless forceful enquiries around the shipping showed that the silver was not yet loaded; meanwhile a customs boat sent to examine a ship just in from Panama hailed the *Golden Hinde*, who replied that she was Miguel

Angel's ship from Chile. But an official sent on board 'light[ed] upon one of the great peeces'—and no Spanish ship from Acapulco to Valdivia carried heavy guns. A flight of English arrows followed on the alarm so given, and the port fell into uproar as the English cut the cables of the ships and cut or damaged the masts of the two largest. This would be an obvious precaution against pursuit, and it is difficult to believe John Drake's story that the object was to gather the ships up and use them as an exchange for Oxenham; even if Drake knew that his old comrade was held in Lima (he did know it a little later), he took no action.[68] In any case, he had drawn a blank, but the rich *Cacafuego* was ahead, while despite his damage to the Callao shipping, he could not know what other military resources might be at hand, nor risk a second San Juan de Ulua.

Drake entered the port about 10 p.m.; the news reached Lima in time for the Viceroy, the great Toledo, to order candles to be set in all the waterfront windows, to simulate ranks of arquebusiers ready with lighted match.[69] The sense of outrage must have been intense, but little could be done about it. On Toledo's orders some 300 men piled into two ships and set out after the pirate, now standing out northwest from Callao. The Panama ship had been taken, but her cargo was of little interest, and seeing two large ships coming out in pursuit, Drake abandoned his prize, together with his conscripted pilots. Everything now went wrong for Toledo's gallant three hundred: the capitana was becalmed under the lee of Isla San Lorenzo, the ships were unballasted and very crank, and by sunset on the 14th the *Golden Hinde* was almost out of sight. Obviously they were not going to catch Drake, and to many it seemed just as well: their fire-power was only arquebuses, quite inadequate to meet the English guns; in their haste they had not taken on food; and 'the most imperative reason for returning seemed to be that many of the gentlemen were very seasick . . .'[70] They returned to face the anger of Toledo, who promptly gave orders to fit out two ships properly, with good pilots, 120 soldiers, his own son Don Luis in command, and the redoubtable Pedro Sarmiento de Gamboa on the staff. The ships were readied with despatch, and left Callao on 27 February.

Meanwhile Drake had made some minor but profitable captures, and at Paita learnt that the *Cacafuego* was only two days ahead: on 1 March she was sighted near the modern Esmeraldas in northern Ecuador. The *Golden Hinde* made all sail but put out drags astern, an old corsair's trick to disarm suspicion and yet to delay coming alongside until nightfall. The bewildered Anton had barely time to refuse to strike sail before he was shot up with bow and arquebus, lost his mizzen by a chain-shot, and was boarded; despite her name, the *Cacafuego* was virtually unarmed. A couple of days later, out of sight of land, she was searched: 360,000 pesos of registered treasure, perhaps as much more unregistered. The English vastly enjoyed the wry comment of one of their victims, that the *Golden Hinde* should be styled *Cacafuego* and her prize *Cacaplata*, 'Shitsilver', 'which pretie speech of the Pilots boy ministred matter of laughter to us, both then and long after.' The voyage was now indeed 'made', and Drake, naturally a generous man, could afford to be expansive: all prisoners were released, the crew with thirty or forty pesos each, the officers and gentlemen with gifts befitting their rank. As other witnesses testified, Drake robbed with a courtly air, dining and wining his involuntary guests well (on their own stores) and making elaborate presentations; but certainly losing nothing on the exchange:

> Highwayman's manners no less polite,
> Hoped that their coppers (returned) were right. . . .[71]

He also gave Anton a safe conduct addressed to Winter, which would of course suggest at least one other English ship on the coast, and openly discussed possible return routes. The known routes were by 'China' (the Moluccas and the Cape), 'Norway' (the Northeast Passage), and the Straits of Magellan, which could now be discounted as liable to interception, even had the western entrance been easy and safe. A fourth route was mentioned, but its location kept secret. Hints and enquiries from Drake's company suggested to some Spaniards that this undisclosed route might be by crossing Panama or Nicaragua and seizing shipping on the Atlantic side; Corbett thought it was the new way south of Tierra del Fuego, but this seems unlikely, and probably Sarmiento was right in thinking that it was by Cape Mendocino and Labrador, that is Anian. Drake's design was to create the utmost doubt about his intentions, and although Anton (who on his release went to Panama) correctly deduced that immediately Drake would make for Nicaragua to water and careen, the Spanish authorities were indeed totally bemused by these seemingly casual but, in retrospect, carefully planted stories.[72] Licentiate Valverde of Guatemala even built up an elaborate argument that Drake would winter in California and then return by the Straits of Magellan, gravely citing the fact that he had carried off from Guatulco the entire stock of Indian women's petticoats, obviously to use as trade goods along the coast, 'for he was not going to wear [them], nor would [they] be of utility in England. . . .'[73] Toledo's pursuing force was hamstrung by dispute between those who wished to follow up the coast to Panama, looking into every creek, and the bolder spirits who were for striking across to Nicaragua: this, the correct course if an interception was really desired, was forcibly and ably argued by Sarmiento, and his remarks when the more timid decision was taken had to be conveyed to Luis de Toledo 'algo glosado', somewhat toned down. The little fleet simply dithered around for over four months before returning to Callao on 12 June, by which date Drake was about to leave Nova Albion.

By whatever passage Drake was to return, at the moment he had no choice but to go north: all to the south of him was now alert and hostile, and he could not sail directly for the Moluccas without giving his ship a thorough overhaul. He might well reach New Spain ahead of any alarm, and there also he might get information on sailing courses and seasons for the Moluccas, while Anian remained a possibility, either as major objective or *pis aller*.

After stripping the *Cacafuego*, then, Drake stood out across the Gulf of Panama, and by mid-March reached the island of Caño (Costa Rica), where he took a bark which he used to lighten the *Golden Hinde* for caulking. The cargo, sarsparilla and local produce, was thrown aside; the real prize was one Colchero, an experienced pilot on the Manila run.[74] Despite strong pressure, including apparently physical maltreatment, Colchero turned down Drake's efforts to enlist him as a pilot, but his charts and sailing directions were invaluable, confirming that this was not the right time of year to make for the Moluccas: Drake must wait for some months, out of reach of Spanish power.

It seems likely that he intended his next call to be at Acapulco. A few days after leaving the island he fell in with a ship a week out of that port, and, still passing himself off as Miguel Angel, took her by surprise: she belonged to a gentleman of good family, Don Miguel de Zarate, and carried a typical Acapulco cargo, largely Chinese silks and porcelain. Drake took 'some trifles . . . for his wife', and the meeting passed off on a chivalrous note—but with touches of realism: Colchero was a prisoner on the ballast, and some of Zarate's men headed Drake off Acapulco by saying that there were ships and men already there. Instead, Drake settled for the tiny and decaying port of Guatulco. Here, in an almost farcical Easter interlude (13–16 April), Drake's people sacked a church being decorated for Easter, ostentatiously held 'Lutheran' services, and invited the handful of local officials to the *Golden Hinde*: these prudently took their dinners first, lest they should have to eat meat on Ash Wednesday. Drake loaded up with water for fifty days; and he set ashore Nuño da Silva.

Unless da Silva was a willing party to some subtle counter-intelligence scheme, this seems an inexplicable and uncharacteristically heartless action. Despite a marked reserve, da Silva had been seen by some of Drake's temporary guests in situations very compromising for a good Catholic, and even without this he would have much to explain to the secular authorities. He did in fact survive severe interrogation by the Inquisition, being sentenced to public abjuration at an *auto-de-fe* and to exile from the Indies; but by 1583 he was in Spain, apparently in royal favour.[75] But in a sense this abandonment of Nuño was symbolic: the Iberian and piratical phase of the voyage was over.

Nova Albion

Colchero's information and the state of the ship must have decided Drake's next move after Guatulco, with Anian as an entirely compatible secondary factor.[76] To leave New Spain for 'China' after mid-April would be to risk arriving at the height of the typhoon season, and he could not sail at once since the *Golden Hinde*, probably straining from the weight of bullion aboard, needed a full overhaul. A northern sweep would at one and the same time secure a place for thorough careening well beyond any risk of Spanish interference; fill in time until a less hazardous season for crossing the Ocean; and perhaps disclose a short and safe passage for home, should there really be a Strait of Anian near the Sierra Nevada of Ortelius and Gilbert's map. Not the least of Drake's gifts

was a flexibility of mind which enabled him to make good use of an enforced
waiting-time, as on the Isthmus in 1572–3, and again now.

Even apart from the risk of interception from an aroused Acapulco, a direct
course along the coast was impracticable; before reaching Guatulco, Drake had
'notice that we shoyld be troubled with often calmes and contrary windes, if we
continued neere the coast, and did not run of[f] to sea to fetch the wind.' From

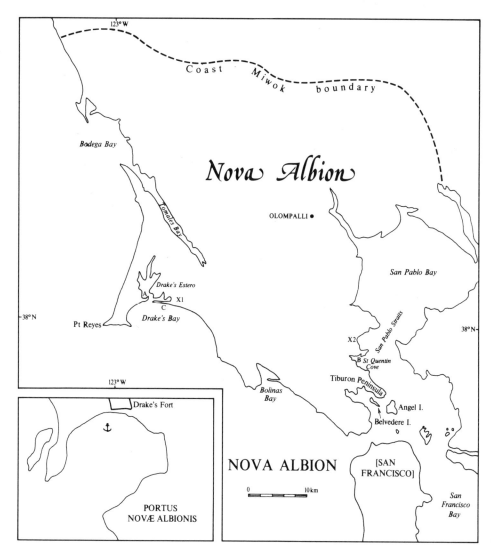

Figure 23. NOVA ALBION. Inset: outline of Portus Novæ Albionis. On main map: A,
anchorage in hypothetical Drake's Cove; B, in Bahia de las Calaveras; C, Cermeño's camp 1595;
X1, X2, sites where the Plate of Brass was said to be found in 1933 and 1936 respectively. Coast
Miwok boundary after R. F. Heizer, *Elizabethan California* (Ramona 1974), Fig. 6. Inset from
Hondius, *Vera Totivs Expeditionis Navticæ* (c. 1593), omitting detail; original is 64 x 44 mm.

Guatulco, then, he sailed west for some 500 leagues, then swung north in a great arc to meet the coast again: the northern mirror-image of Juan Fernandez' passage from Callao to Chile. They made a landfall on 5 June, above 42°N and perhaps as high as 48° or even Vancouver Island; the sources are confused and confusing.[77] Like Arellano, they met with a very surprising degree of cold for the latitude and season (but then they were straight from the *tierra caliente*), with snow lying even on low coastal plains. Mount Olympus (47° 43′N, *c.* 2240 metres) carries snow in June, but this scarcely suffices, nor does the tree-ring evidence for cooler and longer winters in this region and period.[78] It seems likely that dense mists, or the great dunes which blanket the coast in many places, were mistaken for snow. As evidence for a landfall well to the north, Eva Taylor stressed contemporary reference to 'that part of America . . . running on continually North-west, as if it went directly to join with Asia'; but so tangled is the argument that even that formidable lady was willing to defer to the authority of Wagner, who drew an opposite conclusion from the same text.[79] The weight of much discussion is for Cape Arago (Oregon) in 43° 20′N.

If there is some doubt as to the landfall, the case is even worse as to the precise site where Drake careened the *Golden Hinde*; the polemic is almost a minor industry in the Bay area, and an adequate review would fill a monograph. The linguistic, cultural, and archaeological evidence (which includes undoubted relics, such as Ming porcelain, of Cermeño's camp at Drake's Bay in 1595) establishes that the landing was in the territory of the Coast Miwok Indians (Fig. 23), so that basically the choice lies between Bodega, Drake's, and San Francisco Bays, though Wagner favoured Trinidad Bay, north of the Miwok area. This has scarcely anything to recommend it except his own authority, and he pretty conclusively demolishes Bodega Bay. As he says, it was until recently almost an article of local faith that Drake's Bay was precisely what its name asserts, but there is now a party for San Francisco Bay itself. The protagonists handle their cases with such skill and detail that the outsider finds himself in a sad state of alternating conviction. *Sub specie aeternitatis*, it does not matter much; but 'There is nothing so minute or inconsiderable, that I would not rather know it than not'.[80]

Everything has been pressed into service, literally from lettuces to coneys, and the texts have been analysed with a close exegesis usually reserved for Holy Writ: inferences have even been drawn from the imputed attitudes and gestures of engraved human figures on the Hondius map, which in the original are under 3 mm high and when enlarged not 10mm. But it is at least agreed on all hands (except, perversely, by Wagner) that the 'white bancks and cliffes, which lie towards the sea' and led Drake to call the country Nova Albion, are those inside Point Reyes, at Drake's Bay, which indeed bear a striking resemblance to the Seven Sisters near Beachy Head; but it does not follow that this was the actual careening place. A. S. Oko made out a strong navigational case that it was so, showing for example how easily a small ship might miss the Golden Gate; he is implicitly supported by Alan Villiers,[81] and the views of practical seamen are entitled to respect.

Any identification, however, must come to terms with the tiny (64 × 44 mm) but quite detailed inset of 'Portus Novae Albionis' on the 1593 Hondius map; as Power has shown, this may derive from Drake's own record (known to have been presented to the Queen), since in 1589 Hondius was in close association with Thomas Talbot, keeper of the records in the Tower. It is true that the main map shows Drake's course inaccurately—there is no call shown between Mocha and Callao, nor at Guatulco, and the track is laid down close to the Californian coast; only the latter error could perhaps be ascribed to 'security'. But the track may be conventionalised, while the inset is circumstantially detailed, and Aker shows that the other insets have a high degree of specificity. It is true that when he has to get rid of a crux, he rather weakens the argument by remarking that 'Hondius did not really understand what he had engraved';[82] but the insets do represent real places, and it seems extreme to set the Portus map aside altogether.

Accepting it as evidence, the crux is the island lying parallel to the 'Portus Peninsula', which cannot be reconciled with any *existing* claimant except within San Francisco Bay itself. To the Drake Navigators Guild, the solution is found in regarding the island as a temporary but recurrent sand spit formed in Drake's Estero, the inlet within the Bay.[83] This may be so, but obviously it can only be hypothesis that the Estero had this conformation in 1579, and while the geo-morphological argument is persuasive, it is not the absolute demonstration that the Guild rather dogmatically asserts. The Guild's arguments in other respects—notably the ecological—are much less convincing, and the problem is not to be solved on one criterion only. Above all, perhaps, much archaeological digging in and around Drake's Bay has produced nothing that can with probability be referred to Drake's visit, but plenty to Cermeño's; and yet the *Golden Hinde's* cargo must have been piled on the beach, and some eighty men ashore for over seven weeks where the Guild claims to have found the probable careening basin. (This argument is not available against San Francisco Bay sites, since these are built over.)

For Power, the island can be matched by Belvedere Island, which lies in the right relation to the Tiburon Peninsula: the problem now becomes one of accounting for the omission of Angel Island, off the tip of Tiburon, and of San Pablo Strait. Power gets over this by regarding the inset as a 'cartographic view' from Angel Island itself, rather than a map in the strict sense—a much more likely sixteenth century device than Fletcher's bifocal scale for Cape Horn. In my opinion Power deals successfully with the navigational problem, always regarded as a strong point for Drake's Bay, and is very convincing on the ecological side.

Either case can be made without appeal to the famous Plate of Brass (or lead, in one contemporary account) with an inserted sixpence, set up to record Drake's Act of Possession. Such a plate was found near the Tiburon Peninsula in 1936; it has been claimed that it was first found near Drake's Bay in 1933; much ink has been wasted on this side-issue. Some Californian scholars had almost invited a hoax, and there was initially an odd reluctance to submit the Plate to test; nor is it true, as has been claimed, that the metallurgical analysis when made was not challenged; challenges were made but brushed aside or ignored.[84] The orthography and style of the inscription have been generally suspect to experts in these matters, and Wagner has shown that lead and not brass was used for such plates, for good reasons.[85] Altogether, pending a metallurgical analysis with more refined techniques than were available in the 1930s, the Plate must be regarded with much suspicion; but even were it genuine, so portable an object, unless it had been found in a definite archaeological context, can say nothing as to the actual site of Drake's camp. As to that, the weight of evidence and argument, particularly as presented by Power, seems to me to point, though not strongly, to San Francisco Bay; but see p. 261.

A question of much more import than 'this bay or that bay?' is that of the significance to be granted to Drake's formal acceptance from the Miwok Indians of sovereignty over their country, 'the King and diuers others [having] made seuerall orations, or rather, indeed, if we had understood them, supplications, that hee would take the Prouince and kingdome into his hand.' To British students, this has seemed simple opportunism; as we have seen, the Draft Plan does not support any premeditated scheme of colonisation, and Zelia Nuttall mistook a wish that the country *might* 'have layen so fitly for her maiesty to enjoy . . . that the riches and treasures thereof . . . might with as great conueniency be transported' to England into a statement that they *were* to be so transported.[86] Any tentatives towards a follow-up of Drake's action were forgotten; even when Oregon was disputed between the United States and the United Kingdom in the 1840s, 'Drake's discovery appeared out of the haze again for a brief moment', but Britain had debarred herself from pressing any claim based upon it, because since the Nootka affair in 1790 (if not since Henry VII) she had insisted on occupation as well as discovery being necessary to secure title.[87] Recently, however, the claim that Drake was in effect the founder of British dominion in North America has been revived, in a more sophisticated style than Nuttall's hero-worshipping rhetoric.

Like Nuttall, proponents of this view attach a rather literal significance to the dotted lines between Nova Albio [sic], Nova Hispanie, and Nova France on maps such as the French version of 'La Herdike Enterprinse' (Plate XVIII). Setting aside all doubts as to the date of this document,[88] reputedly of the 1580s, and the undoubted fact that though allegedly 'veuee et corige par le dict siegneur drack' it shows his track wrongly, those who assert that it represents a conscious claim for English dominion from sea to sea should explain why the Atlantic frontage claimed between New France and New Spain is squeezed into the peninsula of Florida, where the Spaniards had founded St Augustine in 1565, and slaughtered a Huguenot colony: a region surely in the obedience of that

Christian Prince Philip II. More weight should be given, not only in this case, to J. A. Williamson's words:

> Some yield to the fascination of maps, wildly incorrect maps as
> they obviously are, and strive to extract from them secrets which
> for the most part they do not contain . . . a form of self-deception
> unrecognised by [its victim] and increasing its influence as his
> mind becomes more absorbed in the study. His minutely
> detailed scholarship becomes ever more admirable, while his
> judgment of the broad implications of evidence decays.[89]

Nevertheless, these lines of dots presumably did not spring out of thin air, they

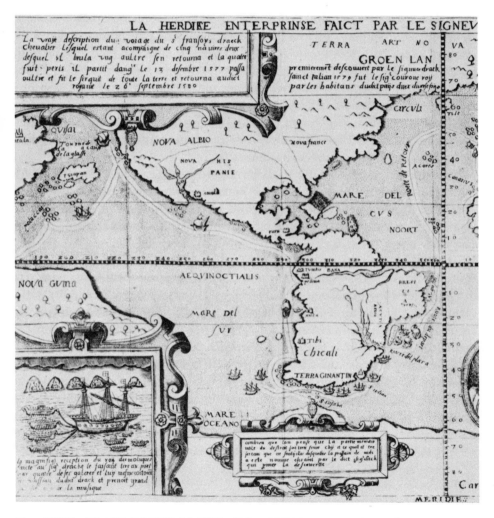

Plate XVIII.   DRAKE IN THE PACIFIC: 'LA HERDIKE ENTERPRINSE'.   For comment see text, pp. 259ff. Reproduced in Zelia Nuttall (ed.), *New Light on Drake* (London 1913). By courtesy of the Hakluyt Society. ANU.

must have had some rationale, even if a distorted one, and the question cannot be resolved by a mere denial of significance.

To begin with, Power points out that Drake's patron Hatton was also the patron of John Dee, who was undoubtedly a protagonist of a British Empire—indeed, it was he who coined this term which was to have so long a history. In 1577 Dee published an *Arte of Navigation* with a highly symbolic title page showing Elizabeth as patroness of a fleet of five ships prepared for overseas enterprise. In the same year Richard Willes issued his *History of Travayle* with an epistle to Anne, Countess of Bedford, whose husband was none other than Drake's godfather. Both these books were clearly propaganda for expansion, and their publication may well have some relation to Drake's enterprise, then on the stocks. It is also perhaps significant that immediately after Drake's return, according to William Camden, Elizabeth responded to Mendoza's protests by asserting, very forthrightly, the right not only to trade in the New World, but to 'transport colonies thither'.[90]

Probably more significant is a manuscript map in the Mellon Library, similar to *La Herdike Enterprinse* and possibly derived from a great wall map known to have existed in Whitehall Palace. This shows the Nova Albion/Nova Hispania boundary and a very suggestive distribution of banners of St George, which are placed on Meta Incognita (Baffin Land), Virginia, the Straits of Magellan, and Nova Albion. This recalls Grenville's project with its desire to secure an English foothold on both the northern and the southern approaches to the Mar del Sur: it will be noted that two of Drake's Acts of Possession fit in with Grenville's ideas. This certainly suggests a conscious rather than an absent-minded claim to Empire.[91]

Finally there is the remarkable poem *De Navigatione . . . Humfredi Gilberti . . . Carmen* (1582) by the young Hungarian scholar Stephen Parmenius, who was drowned off Newfoundland on Gilbert's 1583 voyage.[92] This is a most high-spirited call for English (and Protestant) colonisation, and Power very plausibly argues that the 'Speech of America' is an imagined plea by the Miwoks for the protection promised by Drake. The one brief mention of Drake himself in the poem is conventional, but notable for its early date, when publicity about the voyage was seemingly still not favoured; and a poem of 1582 is of course not evidence that Drake himself had any definite ideas of a continent-spanning dominion when he proclaimed Nova Albion. It might also be said that the 'America' of the poem is merely one of the standard rhetorical personifications so dear to Renaissance poets; but the phrasing seems too explicit for this:

> . . . You surely see that sad
> America, who proffered recently
> (With downcast crown) her rights and loyalty
> To independent England. . . .

In any case, Drake's Californian activities, even were they merely opportunistic, were intensely interesting to Gilbert, Hakluyt, and others of the 'forward school' with whom Parmenius was on intimate terms; and indeed in Hakluyt's 1600 reprint of the poem there is a marginal note 'Nova Albion' at the beginning of America's appeal.[93]

It is more difficult, however, to trace any continuity of this incipient imperial idea. It is all very well to cite the seventeenth century charters to English colonisers of America, running 'from sea to sea'; but there is the difficulty that these do not begin until *after* 1606.[94] It is probably too much to claim with Power that the maps and the poem amount to 'a continental claim, [a] concept [which] was later identified by historians as a manifest destiny'; but even the hard-headed Wagner admitted that 'If a navigable Northwest Passage had been found by John Davis in his voyages after 1585, perhaps there would be another story to tell' of Nova Albion.[95] At the least we have here a new and challenging view on an old question, a new field for enquiry which might well lead to the revision of some received ideas.

[Although it is now generally accepted that the Plate of Brass is most likely a hoax, a Brazen Plate, controversy is not yet dead. Robert Power has issued *A Study of Two Historic Maps* (Nut Tree 1978), in which he abandons his original idea that the Hondius 'Portus Novae Albionis' was a 'perspective rendering' in favour of its being a properly surveyed 'planimetric map'. Computerised comparisons of distances and bearings on this inset and on a chart of San Francisco Bay (1856) show a close fit, although at one point it is necessary to invoke two separate maps and an erroneous scale reduction of one of them when they were put together. There remains the very difficult crux that Angel Island is omitted on the 'Portus', and San Pablo Strait is crossed by a shoreline. One cannot see why 'these points are no longer material to the identification'.

Admitting the likelihood of some lingering subjectivity in one's personal choice, I now feel inclined to attach rather more weight to the Drake Navigators Guild geomorphological argument, admittedly not a conclusive demonstration, as indicating the probable solution.]

The return and the reckoning

Drake left his anchorage on 23 July, calling at the Farallon Islands next day. After that there was no landfall until 30 September, when they fell in with islands in 8–9°N; many canoes came off, but so thievish were the people that to be 'ridde of this vngracious company' it was necessary to make 'some of them feele some smart as well as terror'—according to John Drake, a score were killed. The identity of this 'Island of Theeues' has hardly such interest or importance as attaches to Drake's Magellanic or Californian visits, but it has attracted its share of attention. The choice lies between Yap, favoured by Wagner and Power, and Palau, and after an exhaustive analysis of every scrap of ethnographical data which can be extracted from the narratives, the anthropologist W. A. Lessa opted for Palau over Yap, in the last resort on the ground of location; but this seems his weakest ground since, as Robert Power points out, the distance from Palau to the next landfall a fortnight later on Mindanao is such as to give an unacceptably slow rate of sailing, under half the average on the whole California-Mindanao run. Lessa does, however, convincingly refute Andrew Sharp's view that both the first and second landfalls were on Mindanao (this depended on a misreading of 'within' for 'without' sight of land, which has crept into modern editions of *The World Encompassed*); and he has also probably established the position of the Mindanao landfall, about 75 km north of the Gulf of Davao.[96]

Passing down the coast of Mindanao, Drake had a brush with a Portuguese galleon, and rumour of his presence filtered through to Manila. He was making for Tidore when a chance encounter diverted him to Ternate, whose Sultan Baber was bitterly hostile to the Portuguese who had murdered his father. Hence the welcome to Drake was princely, and the English were much impressed by the colour and civility of the Court. The Sultan offered to 'sequester the commodities and traffique of his whole Iland from others . . . and reserue it to the intercourse of our Nation'; nevertheless, though he formally came out to the *Golden Hinde*, he did not venture aboard, and Drake in turn declined a personal visit ashore. Beneath all the courtesies there was mutual suspicion; and it is significant that there is no mention of any presentation of official credentials from the Queen—so much for that much-vaunted commission, and for Wagner's insistence on a Moluccan motive. As for the treaty, nothing was formalised, nothing written down. Although to English minds the visit marked a great break-through into the eastern trade, and was the proximate inspiration of Fenton's expedition of 1582–3 (the first English voyage destined for, though not reaching, the East Indies), the immediate results were six tons of cloves, a vague feeling of goodwill mixed with uneasiness, and some useful intelligence.[97] This included a first-hand but much slanted report on China by an exile from that country—amongst other items, the Chinese had 'brass ordnance of all sorts (much easier to be trauersed than ours were, and so perfectly made that they would hit a shilling) aboue 2000 yeares agoe': rating this at what it was worth, Drake cannily declined a pressing invitation to the Celestial Empire, but this was very likely the first face-to-face meeting of an Englishman and a Chinese.

The *Golden Hinde* spent only four or five days (5–9 November) in this Moluccan paradise, just about enough time to load the cloves. The passage onwards through the archipelago was not without incident: a month was spent on a small island near Celebes (Sulawesi), careening and refitting and enjoying the land-crabs, so big 'that one was sufficient to satisfie foure hungry men at a dinner, being a very good and restoratiue meate'. This idyllic interlude was followed by near-disaster, when on 8 or 9 January 1580 the ship struck a reef off Celebes: for some time they were in serious danger, and Fletcher preached a moralising sermon on judgments—probably too near the bone, for once they were free Drake put him in the stocks with a mocking inscription. The *Golden Hinde* was got off by jettisoning some stores and guns and (what must have hurt) three tons of cloves. Drake probably passed between Alor and Timor, and spent an agreeable fortnight (10–26 March) in Southern Java, most likely at Tjilatjap, victualling, cleaning the ship, and hobnobbing with half a dozen or more local rajas. They passed the Cape of Good Hope in June, called at Sierra Leone for water and provisions, and on 26 September 1580 the *Golden Hinde* entered Plymouth harbour:[98] a great voyage, some thirty-four months, with remarkably few lives lost, and the first circumnavigation carried out by the one commander.

Boldness at sea must be matched by caution at Court: this Drake well knew, and his first act was to communicate to the Queen, urgently and confidentially, the results of his campaign. News of his depredations had of course reached Spain and England, but Philip had instructed his new ambassador Mendoza to hold his hand until Drake should return. When he did, probably no English commoner had as yet been so popular a hero: amongst the more respectable there were some murmurings over Doughty, over Nuño da Silva, over the negress carried off from New Spain and abandoned, pregnant, in the Indies. But these were whispers in a storm. San Juan de Ulua was more than avenged.

There was a party on the Queen's Council for returning the booty, and also a compromise proposal to repay the promoters their capital plus 100 per cent, restoring the rest on condition that Spanish subversion in Ireland should cease. The recent abortive invasion of Ireland by Papal volunteers, massacred at Smerwick, and the fact that much of the plunder, being unregistered bullion, had no really licit ownership, greatly strengthened the Queen's hand in playing Mendoza, a game in which she seemed to take an aesthetic delight. It could be argued that refunding so much treasure would simply build up Philip's power for the subjugation of the Netherlands, if not England itself, and that a repudiation of Drake (dangerously unpopular as that would be) could only lead to further abject appeasement, putting the whole cause of the Reformed Churches at grave risk. Though Burghley and Sussex refused Drake's proffered douceurs, the big investors—Leicester, Hatton, Walsingham—soon prevailed over any further tendency to morbid probity; and indeed, a year before Drake's return steps were being taken to receive—and conceal—his treasure.[99] The stakes were simply too high for customary morality to hold.

Just how high they were can never be known. Even before the registration for the Crown began, Drake was allowed to abstract £10,000, but this was far from the total of preliminary deductions. The recorded bullion came to £307,000 and altogether the treasure must have exceeded £600,000, or say £18,000,000 in the early 1970s; perhaps it may have been twice as much. The return to the shareholders was stated on good evidence at a trifle of 4700 per cent, on an investment of the order of £5000. The Crown itself seems to have received around £300,000, more than a year's Exchequer receipts. The result of course was a boom in the privateering industry; but beyond that, in the much-quoted words of Keynes,

The booty brought back by Drake may fairly be considered the
fountain and origin of British foreign investment. Elizabeth paid
off out of the proceeds the whole of her foreign debt and invested
a part of the balance (about £42,000) in the Levant Company;
largely out of the profits of the Levant Company was formed the
East India Company, the profits of which during the seventeenth
and eighteenth centuries were the main foundation of England's
foreign connections. . . .[100]

This in the long term. Immediately, the monopoly of the Spanish Lake had been
broken, and clearly from the Spanish official point of view, this was no time for
the diversion of forces, needed for the defence of existing holdings, into the founding of new and yet further-flung colonies, mere tempting trifles to be snapped
up by the heretic sea-rovers: a factor in the long gap between Mendaña's first
and second voyages. Meanwhile, Anglo-Spanish tension was screwed up to a
new pitch; but so too was the English temper: as massive and as enduring as the
fiscal dividend was the gain to the nation's confidence and pride. The great
clash was to be fought out in Atlantic waters and the English Channel; but
before it took place the Pacific was to be the scene of Cavendish's reprise of
Drake's exploit, and before that of a heroic but tragic Spanish riposte,
Sarmiento's.

Chapter 10

RIPOSTE AND REPRISE

> ... I have given the name of the Strait of the Mother of God, to
> what was formerly known as the Strait of Magellan. . . because
> she is Patron and Advocate of these regions. . . . From it will
> result high honour and glory to the Kings of Spain . . . and to the
> Spanish nation, who will execute the work, there will be no less
> honour, profit, and increase.

> ... they died like dogges in their houses, and in their clothes,
> wherein we found them still at our comming, untill that in the
> ende the towne being wonderfully taynted with the smell and the
> savour of the dead people, the rest which remayned alive were
> driven . . . to forsake the towne. . . . In this place we watered and
> woodded well and quietly. Our Generall named this towne
> Port famine. . . .

The Spanish riposte: Sarmiento[1]

Francisco de Toledo lamented briefly that 'the sea is so wide, and [Drake] made
off with such speed, that we could not catch him'; but he was 'not a man to dally
in contemplations',[2] and within ten days of the hang-dog return of the futile
pursuers of the corsair he was planning to lock the door by which that low fellow
had entered. Those whom he had sent off on that fiasco seem to have been
equally, and reasonably, terrified of catching Drake and of returning to report
failure; and we can be sure that the always vehement Pedro Sarmiento de Gamboa
let his views on their conduct be known. He already had the Viceroy's ear,
having done him signal if not too scrupulous service in the taking of the unfortunate Tupac Amaru (above, Ch. 3) and in the denigration of Inca polity by the
compiling of the *Historia de los Incas*, an enquiry designed to contrast the benevo-
lence of Spanish rule under law with the capricious tyranny of the Incas;[3] and
it was natural that Toledo should choose him to lead the expedition to the Straits,
his first independent command.

Sarmiento was indeed one of the most remarkable men of his age; perhaps
the last in whom the ardent and indomitable spirit of the Conquistadores burned
with all its ancient power. Seaman and soldier, navigator and cosmographer,
scholar and explorer, poet of sorts and an official censor of poets,[4] he was also

---

Pedro Sarmiento de Gamboa, 12 February 1580 (in Markham,
Narratives, 121); Francis Pretty, January 1586 (Hakluyt, VIII.214);
both at the site of Ciudad del Rey Don Felipe, now Port Famine
or Puerto Hambre.

something of a sorcerer, specialising in love-magic, and hence more than once in serious trouble with the Inquisition and needing all Toledo's influence to get him out of it; quarrelsome, and obviously not one to suffer fools gladly or at all, still less knaves and poltroons, and far too ready to pass such judgments; but at all times and in all emergencies possessed of a clear and practical head, unlimited devotion to his duty and all but unlimited faith in his star, and above everything a most iron resolution—

> A Frame of Adamant, A Soul of Fire,
> No Dangers fright him, and no Labours tire.[5]

He was to have more than his share of both.

Toledo, though unwell, came down to Callao to inspect the available ships by lantern light, right down to the keel; for all that, and in part due to Toledo's drive for haste, the capitana began to leak as soon as they sailed, and had to put into Pisco for repairs. Sarmiento was given two ships, the *Nuestra Señora de Esperanza* as flag and the *San Francisco*, under Juan de Villalobos, as almiranta. Their complements were about 110 officers, sailors, and soldiers, plus a few Indian or mestizo servants; and each ship had two medium-sized artillery pieces and forty arquebuses. This slight armament gives a touch of unrealism to the instruction that should Sarmiento fall in with 'Francisco Draquez, the English Pirate . . . you are to endeavour to take, kill, or destroy him. . . .' It is not surprising that recruitment was Sarmiento's greatest difficulty.

His instructions were lengthy—ten pages in Markham's translation—but their essence was that he should carry out a detailed exploration of the Straits, including all entries into them, so that all pirates' holes should be stopped; he was to prepare charts and sailing directions and to note the most promising places for settlements and especially for fortifications, and to take formal possession wherever he landed. After entering the Atlantic, one ship was to be sent back to Peru with despatches (reports should also be sent overland from La Plata), while Sarmiento himself was to go on to Spain to report to the Council of the Indies and the King. This program was faithfully executed: Sarmiento's descriptions of the Straits themselves and their tangled western approaches were extremely detailed, many of his names surviving: the monument to this part of his work is the towering Mount Sarmiento, so named by Robert Fitzroy. And he made no fewer than thirteen Acts of Possession.

Sarmiento sailed from Callao on 11 October 1579, but was held up for some days repairing at Pisco. He took Juan Fernandez' recently discovered course, well to the west of his island, and saw land on 17 November on Golfo Trinidad (50°S). The next two months were spent in the detailed and arduous exploration, largely by boat, of the intricate channels between Isla Hanover and the mainland (Fig. 21), penetrating as far as the southern end of Cordillera Sarmiento in about 52° 10'. Christmas was spent at Puerto Bermejo in the south of Isla Madre de Dios, where Villalobos had been building a bergantin and (according to Sarmiento) deliberately using up provisions to have an excuse for returning home: Sarmiento put a stop to this. But discussion with his pilots convinced him that there was no point in continuing to search for a passage in the labyrinth of inner channels, where indeed the British naval hydrographers of the nineteenth century bestowed such names as Obstruction Sound, Disappointment Bay, Small Hope and Last Hope Inlets . . .

On 21 January 1580 they left Puerto Bermejo to sail south into the open ocean, and on the 30th the *Esperanza* entered the Strait itself; but meanwhile Villalobos, who in Sarmiento's opinion had been dragging his feet ever since Pisco, had parted company in a tempest and returned to Valparaiso. He may have been driven as far south as 56° or more, to find like Drake that the two Oceans joined 'sin impedimentos ni barreras'; but if he did so report, no notice was taken: the belief that the barrier was pierced by but a single channel was too useful for Spain to be lightly given up.[6]

Inside the Straits, Sarmiento waited for a few days for the *San Francisco* and then, overruling the strong pleas of his pilots for a return, went on his way, again carefully charting and recording the topography, occasionally contacting the Indians and collecting (naturally) very confused misinformation from them, kidnapping a few to be baptised and trained as interpreters, liberally taking possession, and renaming the Strait for the Mother of God: as Subercaseaux remarks, posterity paid not the slightest attention to this. He never lost sight of his major task of assessing the potentialities for settlement and defence. His evaluation is hardly glowing: between the Second and First Narrows they saw 'great downlands . . . very agreeable to the sight and with very beautiful greenery, like arable fields',[7] and although hereabouts it was still liable to cold squalls, it was warmer than the country to the west, with potential for livestock, grain, and a large population; according to one of the natives, there was cotton, a sure sign of mild climate. This is very tepid as the prospectus for a colony, and clearly Sarmiento's zeal for his patriotic assignment led him later on to take, in retrospect, too rosy a view of these inhospitable shores, whose exploitation with the vastly enhanced resources and techniques of the later nineteenth century was to prove partial and painful enough.

The hazards of the voyage were not over when they emerged into the Atlantic on 24 February. Blown far offshore, they had hardly the vaguest idea of their position until Sarmiento improvised an instrument to find the longitude by lunar distances, in itself a notable feat.[8] On 23 May they had a successful brush with a better-armed French corsair off Santiago in the Cape Verdes, and later in the day were looked on askance in the port: they had wild long-haired Indians with them, were powder-grimed from the fight, and could scarcely spare water to freshen themselves up. They managed to establish their *bona fides* as Spaniards most surprisingly from Peru, and at the Governor's request Sarmiento took on men and guns and drove the pirates away; but for all that, they were not welcome. King Sebastião's mad crusade into Morocco had ended in the annihilation of

Alcacer-Kebir, and in the interregnum following the death of his aged successor, the Cardinal-King Henrique, the political crisis in Portugal had reached explosion-point. On the very day that Sarmiento weighed from Santiago, the bastard Dom Antonio was popularly acclaimed King; but Philip II had as good or better a title and bigger battalions, and within a week the Duke of Alba was marching on Lisbon. When Sarmiento reached the Azores in mid-July, followed immediately by a Portuguese Indies squadron, the situation was so tense that his people stood to arms, with lighted match, all night, to be relieved next day by the arrival of the New Spain fleet of twenty-two sail, more than enough to overawe Dom Antonio's followers. Sarmiento went on with this fleet, and on 19 August reached Spain: under ten months and two weeks from Callao to San Lucar.

This voyage, as Clissold remarks, was Sarmiento's most successful exploit, though not his most ambitious. It was not, as is sometimes stated, the first west to east passage of the Straits: setting aside the very dubious instances in the 1520s mentioned by Landín Carrasco, there was Ladrillero in 1558 and from Drake's fleet Winter, possibly Carder.[9] But it was certainly the first direct voyage from Peru to Spain, and in Toledo's view the expected fortification of the Straits would provide a more economical trade route between the two, by cutting out the Isthmus portage, and would enable the endless wars in Chile to be more efficiently supported.[10] Moreover, Sarmiento's careful sailing directions were to meet with very appreciative recognition by Fitzroy and King, more than two centuries later.[11] But the immediate sequel was to see the utter wreckage of his hopes.

A mismanaged Odyssey

Sarmiento reported in person to King Philip in September 1580, a few days before Drake reached Plymouth. At the Cape Verdes and the Azores he had picked up wild rumours of English fleets for the Straits, English settlers in Brazil; and in the midst of his Portuguese venture, Philip had to turn his attention to this threat on the other side of the ocean. Morale, however, had been much enhanced by the acquisition of the neighbour kingdom with its naval strength, and for once at least little time was lost in deciding to mount a powerful expedition to settle and fortify the Straits, which would be much facilitated by the Brazilian bases.

As to the fortifications, the most expert opinion was sought: the Duke of Alba and the great admiral Santa Cruz approved, the former at first with reservations— it was a most important thing to be done *if* it could be done, and perhaps a stout boom across the narrows and some gunboats would be cheaper and as efficient. But Sarmiento's conviction prevailed: solid forts, backed by a colony to provision them, would be the real answer, and the Italian military engineer Juan Bautista Antonelli was called in to design them.[12] Following Toledo's hint, the fleet was to take out 600 soldiers for Chile, under Don Alonso de Sotomayor. In contrast to this careful military planning, the arrangements for a colony, so distant and in so little-known a region, were cursory: simply that Sarmiento was authorised to recruit, 'without expenses to His Majesty', a hundred or so settlers.[13]

Preparations were put in hand at Seville with much vigour; but they were vitiated by a fatal flaw in the command structure. Despite his relative lack of experience in command, Sarmiento had shown himself not only a very skilful navigator but a most resolute leader; he had succeeded in all his public under-takings and fully justified the trust of so notable a ruler of men as Toledo. He might therefore have reasonably expected overall command of the enterprise; but by the norms of Court life, so great an armada—twenty-three ships—should be headed by a man of high social standing. It is difficult to see Sarmiento working happily under any leader but one of the stature of Toledo or Alba or Santa Cruz; and even a milder man than he, one less utterly convinced of his own rightness and powers, might have resented being passed over. Almost any available choice of a commander over Sarmiento would probably have led to great difficulties; the actual choice of Diego Flores de Valdes was a disaster.

As prickly and quarrelsome as Sarmiento himself, he had the appropriate social rank and considerable experience in the more or less routine task of convoy-ing the Seville fleets across the Atlantic, but these seem the sum total of his qualifications. He had no initiative and was no leader, his very inept showing as the reluctant chief of staff to the reluctant commander Medina Sidonia in 1588 finally demonstrating his unfitness.[14] From the start he was averse to the Straits project, perhaps resenting being taken from his comfortable and profitable convoy command to face unknown hazards and hardships. We need not believe more than a fraction of Sarmiento's anguished allegations of malevolence, deliberate sabotage, corruption (though this was likely enough in a convoy commander), and even personal cowardice; discounting a great deal, it remains clear that his appointment to overall command of the fleet—but of the fleet only, Sarmiento being designated Governor and Captain-General of the projected colony—was a recipe for fiasco; not to mention the insertion of a third element in the command, Sotomayor and his Chilean force.

Sarmiento accepted the situation, after a protest of a stiffness to which His Majesty was probably unaccustomed, and set to work. At Seville, conditions were chaotic. To begin with, Diego Flores practically washed his hands of the detail work. Everything, except bureaucracy and peculation, was in short supply. Somehow or other Sarmiento and a few other devoted officials managed to collect ships and stores, men and munitions, including some 300 colonists (nearly a third of them children) caught up, by God knows what inducements, from the grinding life of the Andalusian peasantry: the nominal roll still exists, the names of the nameless, 'Juan perez su mujer maria y tres hijos. . . .'[15] By the time that all was more or less ready, the season was so far advanced that it would have been better to wait till the next year; they should have left in August at latest, and when that month was past they risked losing all, 'as one who goes to slaughter',[16] and Flores and Sarmiento were for once agreed in protesting when Medina Sidonia forced them to put to sea, being towed out over the San Lucar bar, on 25 September 1581.[17] The expected equinoctial storm did not fail them: within a week six ships and 800 men were lost, and the battered remainder made Cadiz with great difficulty.

They sailed again on 9 December, with orders to winter at Rio de Janeiro, to ward off expected French corsairs; this to the dismay of Sarmiento, who feared the ravages of the *broma* (ship-worm) and 'other inconveniences'. His fears were well founded: they reached Rio on 24 March 1582, and from then on Sarmiento's narrative, not lacking in complaints hitherto, becomes an unending round of recrimination. As he had no authority over the fleet, he was able only occasionally, and then by violent action, to check the ships' companies (from the highest officers down) from selling gear and stores and stocking up with profitable Brazil timber and dye-wood. Much powder was wasted in salutes and fireworks, and Sarmiento trembled for fear of shortages in the Straits: they fired off more arquebus shots than there were hairs on his head, and each shot 'struck me to the heart . . . Your Majesty ties my hands . . . alone and without authority, I can do no more, but my blood scalds me. . . .'[18] Clearly by this time Sarmiento is almost paranoid in his anguish; yet he did his best to look after the sick and to keep his people employed in constructing prefabricated houses for the Straits; even so, morale was naturally abysmal. Soon it was being said that not even to seduce a soul would the Devil himself dare to enter the Strait.[19] Only a madman like Pedro Sarmiento. . . .

When at last they left Rio, Flores insisted that Sarmiento should not sail with him in the flagship, but in the slow *Begoña*. The broma had done its work so well that a 500-ton ship foundered with much loss of life and stores. Many officers now wished to return, but it was agreed to refit at Santa Catarina, where there was news of Edward Fenton's English fleet in nearby waters: against his orders, Flores made no attempt to intercept them. There were more bitter disputes at Santa Catarina, where Flores sent three ships back to Rio de Janeiro for repairs. When the rest sailed again, on 13 January 1583, Alonso de Sotomayor, who seems to have tried to mediate, had had enough: he took his three ships (and according to Sarmiento many of the stores for the Straits) into La Plata and thence marched his 600 men across the Andes to Chile. The diminished fleet pressed on, and by February was at the Straits: twice Flores tried to enter, but each time the notorious tidal currents drove him out, and his honour, such as it was, was satisfied by the attempt. Disregarding pleas to wait in the shelter of Cabo Virgenes or the Rio Gallego, he set a course for Brazil, and Sarmiento, in far from speechless fury, had perforce to follow.[20]

The ships were scattered by a storm, and Sarmiento reached São Vicente (near modern Santos) to find that the three sent back from Santa Catarina had attacked Fenton's ships, which got away after sinking the *Begoña*. Early in May what was left of the armada reassembled at Rio de Janeiro, and here Diego Flores announced that he would have no more of the enterprise. His arguments did not lack substance: the Straits did not lend themselves either to fortification or settlement, and it was more important to make sure of the Brazilian bases, threatened by French and English privateers and Portuguese sedition.[21] By his own account, Sarmiento humbled himself—we may doubt by how much!— but in vain. Flores took himself off with six ships, and at Parahaiba was lucky enough to surprise five French corsairs loading Brazil wood: as four of them were careening, the victory was easy, and on his return to Spain—getting in first with his story—it served to divert attention from his general conduct.[22]

Sarmiento remained with five ships under Diego de Ribera; after some reinforcements and further desertions (including his engineer, J. B. Antonelli's brother), he was left with 548 men, women, and children. At least he was now his own master. It is a tribute to his astonishing drive and powers of command that the expedition did not collapse there and then. All but two years to the day from their final sailing from San Lucar, they wearily put to sea again (8 December 1583). On 1 February 1584 they were again off Cabo Virgenes, and the promised land was near.

The Cities of Jesus and the King

Three times they entered the Straits, penetrating almost to the Second Narrows, only to be thrown out again by the appalling tidal currents; finally Sarmiento decided to land in the shelter of Cabo Virgenes itself. The little colony began with a total population of under 350, of whom 177 were soldiers and 81 'pobladores', including 13 women and 10 children. For the formal founding of the City of the Name of Jesus, Sarmiento himself landed, according to Arciniega in full parade armour, and although on more workaday occasions he wore seamen's clothes, this would be in character. The colonists were in rags, 'and he who had a waistcoat had no jacket.'[23] To their leader, the 'plain clothed with odoriferous and consoling herbs' was indeed a promised land; what the wretched Andalusian peasants and artisans thought of these windswept and inexpressibly bleak steppelands cannot be imagined, the more so as the ships were at once blown off out of sight, and they were left with less than four days' rations, apart from some manioc flour and two sacks of biscuit. Soldiers and settlers alike, they were used to buckling to under hardship, and Sarmiento saw that they did so. He made inspiring speeches, and 'All answered that they were ready to obey and to follow to the end of the world as they had no other father'—and no other option; and for all but two of them this was to be in truth the very end of the world.

They scouted about for food, finding various edible roots and berries, fish and shellfish; vegetables, vines, and fruit trees were planted, including of all things quinces and ginger. Half a league from Cabo Virgenes a township was laid out, with town square (and gallows) and a sail-roofed church. Then, three days later, the ships came back and more stores were landed. It was agreed to beach one of the ships and use her timbers for building; unluckily, the beaching was mismanaged and many stores, including half the flour, wine, and cannon were lost—even so, they were more than amply gunned, with twenty-two pieces in charge of Andrés de Viedma. But this incident led to a quarrel with Diego de Ribera, up till now a staunch supporter, and he left hastily, without waiting for despatches: *more suo*, Sarmiento put the worst possible construction on this defection. He was left with one small ship, the *Santa Maria de Castro*, in bad shape and lacking much of her gear.

Nombre de Jesus, although formed into a municipality, was only an advanced base, and the main work lay ahead. As regards terrain, the best site for a fort blocking the Straits would have been at the Second Narrows, but Sarmiento ruled this out as he feared that the currents would make it almost inaccessible to shipping, which would face a constant risk of being forced out into the Atlantic, as had happened so often already and was to happen again to the *Maria* on her first voyage west. He decided that the main position should be at Cabo Santa Ana, some forty kilometres on the hither side of the southernmost point of the mainland. On the first voyage to Spain he had noted this as a suitable site: it lay on the frontier between the two main Indian groups, with generally open steppe country towards the Atlantic, forested mountains to the west; a convenient port with ample wood and water, harbouring many deer and parroquets, which hinted at a mild climate; and a projected fort at the First Narrows could be reached in one tide.

Andrés de Viedma was to be left in command at Nombre de Jesus; it needed a resolute man, for the tiny settlement had already been attacked by the Indians. The *Maria* was sent ahead to Cabo Santa Ana to begin cutting timber, and after waiting three days lest she should again be driven back, Sarmiento set off by land on 4 March 1584, with a hundred soldiers. The many detours on this indented coast meant a total distance of seventy or eighty leagues; to make it on the eight days' rations they carried would have meant covering over fifty kilometres a day; Sarmiento, always reconnoitring ahead, must have covered a greater distance still. It was a ghastly traverse: clothing was inadequate to the autumn cold, shoes gave out and had to be improvised from hide and goatskin. Foraging produced occasional eggs of 'vultures' (rheas?), deer, berries, nuts and roots, but above all shellfish. They had to sacrifice their two remaining dogs and the few goats they had brought as stock; some very pleasant nuts, like chestnuts (probably Antarctic beech) gave them violent colics. There was a fight with some very tall and very valiant Indians, who killed one man and wounded ten. A little wine could be doled out to the wounded, but they, and some sound men, wished nothing more but to die among the reeds and bushes, and there were murmurings; somehow Sarmiento drove and cajoled them on, until on the nineteenth day they reached the limits of endurance: 'they would wait where they were, either for the mercy of God, or for death.' Sarmiento, whose writings show a compassion for the rank and file rare in his age, tried to rally them for a last effort: let it not be said that the King 'had no longer such men as he was wont to have in olden days',[24] and

Cabo Santa Ana was in sight. Next daybreak he set out with a handful of followers, promising—with how much conviction?—to return when he met the *Maria*. Before he had gone two hundred paces he sighted her boat, and sent back the news: all came down to the beach, some crawling on hands and knees, and they learnt that the ship was harboured barely an arquebus shot away. An issue of bread and wine worked wonders.

On 25 March 1584 Sarmiento founded his second city, Rey Don Felipe; large wooden buildings were erected for the church and the royal magazine, sites allotted for town hall, clergy house, and a Franciscan monastery, magistrates were appointed, the township was palisaded and six guns mounted on a seaward bastion. There were the usual pathetically hopeful plantings. But rations were severely limited—twelve ounces of flour or biscuit and a half a gill of wine a day; basically they would have to live on the country. Shellfish, stewed with a bark like cinnamon, were a staple food, and there was a bizarre and macabre note: they contained so many pearls that it was tiresome to pick them out, 'and at first, when they had no thought of perishing, and had hopes of escaping, they kept them . . . but, afterwards, when they found themselves in such hopeless case, they took no care of them'.[25]

Not surprisingly, there was an incipient conspiracy to seize the *Maria* and escape; as soon as this was crushed, and fortunately after the people were under some sort of cover, it snowed for fifteen days. Sarmiento then decided to return to Nombre de Jesus, taking with him some guns for the First Narrows; he sailed on 25 May and reached the town that same night, to find that here also there had been a mutiny and an execution, short rations, and a fight with the Indians. Before he was able to land, a furious gale broke his sole remaining cable and drove the *Maria* out to sea. It raged for twenty days and return was impossible; after a nightmare voyage, in which they were reduced to gnawing leather, Sarmiento reached São Vicente on 27 June: the beginning of a new act in his tragedy.

At São Vicente, Sarmiento received little help; he went on to Rio de Janeiro, where the Governor Salvador Correa de Sá was more sympathetic, and indeed by and large the Portuguese seem to have been more helpful than his own countrymen. Diego de Ribera had not been unmindful of the colony, and with the stores he had left at Rio Sarmiento was able to despatch a small ship with flour and other supplies for the Straits; but Rio was then only a minor port, and it was necessary to go to Pernambuco for more adequate provisioning. Thence he headed south again, only to be wrecked at Bahia: ship and stores were a total loss, but for two or three barrels of wine and a gun, and Sarmiento, who had once declared that he would reach the Straits if he had to sail there on a plank, now got ashore, bruised and bleeding, on two boards roughly nailed together. . . . Here and at Espíritu Santo he was given every help, and collected more stores, with which on 13 January 1585, he left for Rio de Janeiro, whence his supply ship had sailed in December. He set off at once with his succours; once more a terrible seven weeks' storm drove him back to Rio, having jettisoned most of the stores and only holding the ship together with improvised cables. And there he found that the supply ship sent off in December had itself been driven back to that port.

He did not yet despair. His ship was patched up by pulling to pieces and burning an old wreck for its nails and iron gear; tar had to be got from Bahia, grease by catching two whales in the harbour. Now he had to face open mutiny: he quelled it by physical assault on the ringleaders and fair words to the rest. But the months dragged by, it seemed hopeless to continue these desperate improvisations in Brazil, and he decided to seek more effective aids in Spain. At the end of April 1586, Sarmiento sailed from Rio de Janeiro, ill but keeping on deck lest there be further insubordination. On 11 August he was in the Azores and there, in what were now *de facto* Spanish waters, he fell in with two well-armed English pinnaces. He had only twenty men; surrender was inevitable.[26]

Prisoners of starvation

At Nombre de Jesus, Andrés de Viedma decided that anything was better than the inexpressibly bleak and wind-swept Patagonian steppes, and took his 200 or so souls to Rey Don Felipe, which from Sarmiento's accounts should at least offer them better shelter and more varied resources. They reached the town in August 1584, in the depths of winter, and were soon disillusioned: the forests and the beaches could support the small bands of Indians, habituated to the climate and with generations of experience in hunting and gathering; but not a large body of civilised men bewildered in their new and savage environment. In despair, Viedma sent 200 of them to make their way back to Nombre de Jesus, virtually a sentence of death on these prisoners of starvation: they were instructed to keep a close watch for any ships that might pass. . . . The rest waited at Rey Don Felipe. They waited through winter and the next summer; in the autumn of 1585 Viedma and his sixty or so survivors built two boats and set out for Nombre de Jesus. One boat was soon wrecked, though all in it were saved; Viedma took twenty men back to Rey Don Felipe, telling the rest to live as best they could along the beach. When summer returned he collected the survivors: all told fifteen men and three women. Towards the end of 1586 this handful set off eastwards again, with the aimless aim of reaching Nombre de Jesus:[27] the way was dotted with the bodies of those sent off on the same track two years before.

Off Terceira, Sarmiento had managed to throw overboard his papers and charts, but his rank was betrayed by his pilot. So notable a captive was received in England with honour. The English ships belonged to Walter Raleigh, prisoner and gaoler were kindred spirits, and it is very likely that Raleigh's obsession with El Dorado owed much to their long and friendly conversations. Far distant from his Governorship, in more than a merely geographical sense, the Captain-General was received by Burghley, Howard of Effingham, and Elizabeth herself: he plumed himself on his conduct of an hour and half of Latin discourse with the heretic monarch, discourse so important and confidential that it could be reported only verbally to the King in person. He was soon released, in October 1586, without ransom, but charged with an ambiguous personal message from Raleigh to Philip, and almost certainly with peace feelers from Elizabeth herself.

He had a long conference with Parma, Philip's Governor in the Netherlands, and then set off, with Elizabeth's passport, across France: Viedma's remnant was probably nerving itself for the hopeless trek to Nombre de Jesus. And then, in a wayside tavern near Bordeaux, he was snapped up by a band of Huguenot partisans. This time his captivity was not to be as elegant as that in Raleigh's hands: eventually he was confined in a foul dungeon, where he lost teeth and hair, all the time negotiating for his ransom—a double haggle, with his captors and Philip's bureaucracy—and pleading for succours to be sent to his colony. At last Treasury agreed to advance the money—but only as a deduction from the considerable debt on the colony's account which was owed to Sarmiento by the Crown.

He was freed, broken in health and fortune, in October 1589; two years later the 'singular grandeza' of the King, and the liberal hand for which Sarmiento thanked him (perhaps not without irony), had not got round to settling his accounts. He had a fruitless interview with Philip, and then, like Quiros, entered on the dreary course of submitting memorial after memorial, moving but useless, crying out for the rescue of his colonists. The year after the Invincible Armada's shattered return was no time to put forward projects which could only weaken Spain in the main theatre of war; and in fact the non-decision had already been taken. In December 1586 Philip had asked three of his advisers what should be done: he had ordered two ships from Peru (we hear no more of these), should he send two from Spain? Only Santa Cruz approved; Medina Sidonia more realistically said that it was too late, the settlers by now would be back in Chile, or dead; soon this latter was to be true.[28]

The rest is anticlimax. Sarmiento was employed as a censor of poetry, deleting at a stroke 109 sheets of a long verse narrative whose author was unduly appreciative of the pirate Drake, and of Mendaña, hardly less of a sin. When at last recalled to active service, he must have felt it too reminiscent of Diego Flores (now in prison for his Armada failure), for it was as almirante to an Indies convoy. His appointment to the fleet about to sail in October 1592 is the last we know of Pedro Sarmiento de Gamboa; probably he died on the voyage, and all but one of his colonists had died before him.

January 1587: a ragged handful on a Patagonian beach saw four ships standing into the Straits; that night they lit fires, the ships' lanterns signalled back. In the morning a boat was seen pulling along the shore, and with Viedma's permission

—there was so much discipline left!—three soldiers ran to show a white flag where the boat must pass. It came to the beach, but the joy of the moment was shattered: the newcomers were not reliefs from Spain or Brazil, but Englishmen going to Peru. They offered passage, but the Spaniards drew back, fearful: these heretics would be quite capable of throwing their dupes into the sea. The English reassured them, saying that they themselves were the better Christians, and one of the three, Tomé Hernandez, stepped into the boat, which pushed off. Hernandez begged the leader to pick up his two comrades, and was asked how many Spaniards there were in all; he replied: twelve men, three women.

> The General then desired this witness to tell the other two soldiers
> to go to the rest of their people, and that for his part he would
> come to embark them all, and that they were to wait for him . . .
> [but] When Thomas Candi went on board, seeing it was good
> weather for navigating, he made sail without waiting for the rest
> of the people to whom he had sent . . .[29]

Still, after four centuries, the bald statement chills the blood.

So Cavendish sailed on, to peer curiously through the streets of Rey Don Felipe, with its gibbet and its dead 'in their houses, and in their clothes'; also, providently, to dig up four guns, and to give it the name it still holds: Port Famine, Puerto del Hambre (Plate XIX). This was not quite the end: three years later the *Delight* of Bristol was in the Straits: 'by Port famine we spake with a Spaniard, who told us he had lived in those parts 6. yeeres . . . in an house by himself a long time, and relieved himself with his caleever [firearm] until our comming thither.' They took him aboard, but on the return the *Delight* was wrecked near Cherbourg, and he was not among the six survivors.[30] Tomé Hernandez got away from Cavendish in Chile, and lived to make his Declaration in Lima in 1620: our only direct witness to those days of anguish and despair.

So ended Sarmiento's dream: the last great Spanish action in these regions, and either the most useless and tragic in the annals of the sea or the apex of Spanish heroism, according to choice;[31] but indeed one need not choose, for it was both. Nor, of course, was Spain the only country compelled 'by pressing and perhaps greater exigencies to leave to their fate many heroic settlers': at the very time of this agony in the Straits, far to the north the six-score English men and women of the lost Virginia colony were suffering and dying.[32] With the resources of the time, colonisation of so remote and harsh a region as the Straits was probably logistically impossible, even had the expedition moved smoothly and well-found to its destination. Even in detail, the site chosen was unfortunate: when in 1843 the Chileans asserted their claim to the Straits, their original settlement of Puerto Bulnes, actually at Puerto del Hambre, lasted only six years before being transferred to a much more favourable position at Punta Arenas,[33] but the existence of this modern city of over 67,000 is scarcely conceivable without fuel-powered shipping.

Plate XIX.   SARMIENTO IN THE STRAITS.   An idealised Ciudad Rey Don Felipe realistically labelled 'now Port Famine', the fires of Tierra del Fuego, and an assortment of giants, including Pigafetta's arrow-swallower (cf. Plate VII). The toponymy reflects Magellan (B. de S. Iulian, C. 1100 Virgines), Drake (3 Ins. Draco), Sarmiento (Philippopolis), Cavendish (P. Famin, C. Frowart), and the Dutchmen Cordes and van Noort in 1599–1600 (Oliuers B., Canal Maurity). From L. Hulsius's 'Collection of Voyages'; reproduced in J. Parker (ed.), *Merchants and Scholars* (Minneapolis 1965). By courtesy of University of Minnesota Press. ANU.

Yet legend would not let Sarmiento's colonists die so easily; together with the imaginary survivors of other luckless voyages, Simon de Alcazaba's and Camargo's, they were translated by popular imagination into the founders of the fantastic and magnificent 'enchanted city of the Caesars', hidden, somewhere in Patagonia, between two border ranges of diamond and of gold. As late as 1782, in the last great Indian rebellion, Gabriel Condorcanqui, styling himself Tupac Amaru II, 'raised multitudes, proclaiming himself "Inca, señor de los Césares y Amazonas".'[34] Irony could hardly go further than this evocation of ghostly splendour.

The English reprise: Fenton and Cavendish

In England, the years after Drake's return were alive with predatory projects: 'Gentlemen of fortune, and gentlemen of no fortune, were about this time equally encouraged to distress the enemy.'[35] Already before he was back, but after it was known from John Winter that he had passed into the South Sea, the younger and greater Richard Hakluyt had envisaged, with considerable panache, the seizure of the Straits and São Vicente: a reclaimed pirate could be sent out 'as of himselfe, and not with the countenance of thenglish state', and a colony peopled with Cimarrons and convicts, men and women—

>	And planting over them a few good English captens . . . there is
>	no doubt but that we shal make subjecte to England all the
>	golden mines of Peru and all the coste and tract of that firme of
>	America upon the Sea of Sur.[36]

Officially, however, so long as relations with Spain were still fluid, though fragile, attention was directed rather to following up Drake's success with the Sultan of Ternate; this seems indicated by 'A project off a corporatyon of sooche as shall ventere unto sooche domyniones & contries scytuat beyonde the equynoctyall lyne', apparently of November 1580.[37] Drake was specifically proposed as life-governor of the company, and there is added an interesting request for the establishing of 'an howse of Contratacon w^t sooche orderes as weare grawnted by the K. of Spayne.' There seems to have been objection by the Muscovy Company, since the Moluccas, being north of the Line, were in its sphere, and the project was lost in the more exciting possibilities raised by the presence of the refugee Dom Antonio in England. These included occupation of Terceira in the strategically immensely important Azores, and as an alternative to go to Portuguese India, expected to rally to the Pretender, and to establish the spice trade from Calicut.[38] Ours was not the first 'Global Century'.

Despite the many alarmist despatches of the Spanish ambassador Mendoza (soon to be expelled for his plotting), these schemes got bogged down in personal and political disputes, and when Drake took to the seas again it was for the great West Indies raid of 1585–6, in which he took Cartagena but was not strong enough to go on to Panama itself. The Dragon's mantle fell in the first place on to the inadequate shoulders of Edward Fenton, a soldier not a seaman, who replaced the original choice of Martin Frobisher as leader of the follow-up expedition; Frobisher's known toughness would at least have ensured that any piratical diversions would have been efficiently conducted. As it was, Fenton's voyage was as thoroughly mismanaged as any of which we have record, except Diego Flores's. Though Drake and the Muscovy Company had large shares in it, the enterprise was essentially Leicester's—the flagship of 400 tons and 40 guns was renamed the *Galleon Leicester*—and was well-found; it was wrecked by personal incompatibilities and the lust for the plunder of Peru. It never got anywhere near its objectives, official or other, and in fact its main interest is in the lurid diary, for very obvious reasons kept largely in cipher, of the chaplain Richard Madox.[39]

Fenton's instructions were for a voyage to the East Indies and Cathay by the Cape of Good Hope, the Straits being specifically barred either going or returning, 'except upon great occasion incident'. This loophole was enough for the more ardent spirits, who included Sir John Hawkins's nephew William and Drake's cousin John, together with Drake's pilots on the circumnavigation, Blacoller and Hood; also the shady Protestant Portingall Simão Fernandez, who was all for plunder though not for the Straits, hedging neatly when the decision had to be made. The details of the fiasco need not detain us long. The four ships sailed in May 1582, far too late, and after some misadventures in Sierra Leone reached Brazil, where as we have seen they crossed the tracks of Diego Flores and Sarmiento. Dissension had begun in the English Channel, and now came to a head. Fenton himself, in his post-mortem apologia to Burghley and Leicester, stresses his honest intent; but according to Madox (who was an upright man) and William Hawkins, he had ideas of making himself a Pirate King at St Helena, counterfeiting the Portuguese flag and taking the carracks of the Carreira; 'He saith the queen was his love. He would go through the South Sea to be like Francis Drake.'[40] When it came to the point, he drew back, fearful of Spanish forces in the Straits. Off southern Brazil a council of December 1582 decided to turn back to trade and revictual at São Vicente; John Drake deserted and took his bark into La Plata, naturally to fall into Spanish hands. The Cape of Good Hope option was theoretically kept open, though Fenton probably meant to sell off his merchandise and make for home. At São Vicente prospects were ruined by the fight with the *Begoña*, and despite the murmuring of the crews, still eager for loot, Fenton gave over the voyage.

The real significance of this miserable affair is in its evidence of the over-mastering lure of the South Sea; in William Hawkins's words, 'ther is no hope for money . . . but by passynge the Straytes.'[41] This, coupled with abysmal leadership, was enough to wreck a well-considered venture which might have taken English trade to south and east Asia two decades before the East India Company's eventual success. Yet Drake had shown that the two objectives of the Moluccas and Peru were not entirely incompatible, that a resolute leader might tap at once 'both the Inidia's of spice and Myne'.[42]

Anglo-Spanish relations worsened in 1584, and Elizabeth, though still averse to open war, felt less need to maintain even an ostensible regard for Philip's claims and susceptibilities. A powerful fleet was planned for the Moluccas, probably to go by way of the Straits—fifteen ships and barks, twenty pinnaces, 1600 men, a third of them soldiers—under Drake's command; scarcely a peaceful trading venture. But the deepening crisis in the Netherlands after William of Orange's murder by a Spanish agent (July 1584), the seizure of English shipping in Iberian ports in May 1585, followed by the commitment of English troops under Leicester to the Dutch 'People's War'—all these compelled the retention of so great an armament in waters nearer home, and hence Drake was diverted to the West Indies.[43] The more distant field of the South Sea was left to private enterprise, and the first entrants were the dazzling courtier George Clifford, Earl of Cumberland,[44] and Thomas Cavendish, a young gentleman of good family and fortune from East Anglia, not one of the West Country brood of corsairs. Cumberland, apparently in collaboration with Cavendish, sent out two ships for the Straits and Peru in 1586, but they got only as far as 44°S and apart from the wanton robbery and burning of Negro villages in Sierra Leone and some scrappy fighting in Brazil, his captains achieved little. Their most useful prize was the Portuguese Lopez Vaz, captured off the Plate and brought to England to become a prime informant for Hakluyt.

Cavendish, who had gained experience on Grenville's 1585 Virginia voyage, was his own master: he sailed himself and had better fortune.[45] With his newly built *Desire* of 120 or 140 tons and two smaller ships, he left Plymouth on 21 July 1586 and reached Port Desire, north of Port St Julian, in mid-December, sailing again on the 28th. Cavendish had timed himself well, avoiding the need to winter in Patagonia, a sure breeding-ground for dissension and often mutiny and the overthrow of the voyage.[46] On 6 January 1587 he entered the Straits and, as we have seen, picked up Tomé Hernandez and examined the grim relics of Rey Don Felipe. He named Cape Froward, the southernmost point of the mainland, and beyond it was held up for a month by 'most vile and filthie weather', though finding 'at every myle or two myles ende an Harborough on both sides of the land.' On 24 February he passed into the South Sea, a passage of fifty days against Magellan's thirty-eight and Drake's sixteen.

At Mocha they had a brush with Araucanians who took them for Spaniards, but at St Mary (Isla Sta Maria) the subjugated Indians were very friendly after they had been 'made merie with wine' and convinced that the newcomers were none of their old masters. By 30 March they were at Quintero Bay, where Tomé Hernandez, naturally enough disregarding his 'deepe and damnable othes' of loyalty, made his escape, and two days later brought down upon them 200 horse; a dozen Englishmen were killed in the fight, and others captured. On 23–25 April they took a large ship and two barks in Arica roads, but the place was too well defended to risk a landing. The Spaniards had learnt the lesson of 1579, if as yet inadequately; two days later, Cavendish took a bark (with a useful

Greek pilot), and under torture the prisoners confessed that they had been carrying 'letters of adviso' for Lima. A raid near Pisco produced nothing but some provisions, and the taking of a 300-ton ship yielded no better plunder; the best prize had a general cargo worth £20,000 'if it had bene in England or in any other place in Christendome where we might have solde it.' Paita was sacked and wantonly burnt, by no means the last time that this little town 'of more importance than its wretched appearance would indicate' was to pay such a penalty for having the only safe anchorage on this part of the coast.[47]

There had been sundry partings and rejoinings, but by 25 May all three ships, plus a prize, were assembled at Puna. The Indian lord of the island and his 'marvellous faire' Spanish wife had fled with 100,000 crowns, but his sumptuous house made a convenient headquarters and in a great storehouse there were ample supplies of pitch and fibre for cables; Pretty's description of the island, almost as large as Wight, is idyllic. Here they careened and secured a great deal of ships' tackling and iron gear, as well as the bells of the church, which they burned. There was some sharp fighting, in which nine men were killed and three taken, though they claimed to have slain nearly fifty Spaniards and Indians; after this they burned the town of 300 houses and four ships on the stocks, and 'made havocke of their fields, orchards and gardens'. An exciting fortnight; it is true that there was now open war with Spain, but it is also clear that Cavendish can hardly be described, like Drake, as 'un corsario sin crueldad'.[48]

Soon after reaching Puna on 5 June, they burned their smallest vessel, for want of men to man her, and set course for New Spain, making a landfall in Costa Rica on 1 July; news of the raid reached Panama and two ships were sent out, two weeks late, while the Viceroy of New Spain did not receive warning in time. Two ships from Sonsonate were taken and burnt; they were of most value for the information received from a French pilot, Michael Sancius (Miguel Sanchez) of the course and expected time of arrival of the Manila Galleons. Guatulco was thoroughly sacked, the customary church-burning being marked, according to local tradition, by the miraculous preservation of a much-venerated Holy Cross; which then fell a prey to souvenir hunters and, after a 2000-folio enquiry into the incident, was removed to the cathedral of Oaxaca.[49] Cavendish bypassed Acapulco and touched at a number of small ports and bays to the northward, careening at Mazatlan before reaching Cape St Lucas, where he meant to lie in wait for the Galleon, on 14 October.

Up till now the voyage had not been very profitable: at least a score of ships and small craft had been taken and destroyed, but none of them had any treasure or small-bulk goods of great value. Real success, however, was now at hand, for on 4 November the 600-ton *Santa Ana* was sighted. The English were greatly outnumbered, but the Galleon had no guns mounted: 'As no other ships but ours have ever been sighted on this voyage . . . [the Galleons] have always sailed with little or no artillery, and with as little fear of corsairs as if they were in the river of Seville.'[50] The *Santa Ana* beat off the first English attack with small arms, but could not cope with two handy ships carrying twenty-eight guns in all, and after a stiff fight of five or six hours she surrendered.

The voyage was now indubitably 'made': 122,000 pesos of gold, or about £70,000; pearls, rich silks, musk, altogether an investment of 1,000,000 pesos in Manila, worth twice that in New Spain.[51] There was more than could be carried off, and most had to be burnt with the ship, but ample remained. Prisoners also were interesting: most of them, including Sebastian Vizcaino, were set ashore in Baja California, but Cavendish carried off two Japanese and three Filipino lads, a Portuguese 'Old China Hand', and a pilot who knew the Ladrones and the Philippines. For these he now set sail, reaching Guam on 3 January 1588 and passing through the San Bernardino Straits on the 14th.

The smaller of the two remaining ships had disappeared when they left California, and Manila was too tough a nut to crack with one galleon. Cavendish spent a fortnight cruising at will among the southern Philippines; he attempted to seize a new Galleon being built on Panay, but the local Spaniards were on the alert and beat him off. He departed with a flourish: 'our Generall sent commendations to the Spanish captaine . . . and willed him to provide great store of gold: for he meant for to see him with his company at Manilla within fewe yeeres. . . .' Bishop Salazar of Manila had to admit the 'more than human courage' of 'this barbarian infidel'; his bitterest grief was not for the loss of the Santa Ana and the ruin so caused, but that a mere youth in a wretched little ship should sail gaily and boastfully through 'an army of [your Majesty's] captains . . . he went from our midst laughing, without anyone molesting or troubling him; neither has he felt that the Spaniards are in this land to any purpose.'[52]

On 8 February Cavendish was off Gilolo; for some reason he did not repeat Drake's call at the Moluccas; perhaps the sickness which broke out a few days later was already showing itself. Instead he refreshed himself in southeastern Java, where he cultivated very friendly relations with the local raja and also with two Portuguese, who enquired after their King Dom Antonio, reported by the Spaniards to be dead. Cavendish assured them that he was alive and honourably maintained in England, 'and that we were come under the King of Portugall into the South sea, and had warred upon the Spaniards there.' He also left three large guns, whether for the Portuguese or Javanese was not clear, and received enthusiastic offers that should Dom Antonio arrive, he would have at command the Moluccas, China (i.e. Macao), and the Philippines. This apparently successful piece of propaganda warfare did not prevent the two Portuguese informing the Malacca authorities about the visit.[53] Having thus laid foundations of a sort for future projects, Cavendish sailed for home on 14 May, by the Cape and St Helena: a week before entering Plymouth on 9 September they learnt from a Flemish ship of the defeat in August of the Armada, 'to the singular rejoycing and comfort of us all.' Truly a happy return.

The booty of the Santa Ana, much exaggerated by rumour, was substantial enough: probably about £125,000, perhaps two-fifths of the ordinary yearly revenue of the Crown. Cavendish banqueted the Queen at Greenwich, but his reprise of Drake's achievement did not extend to a knighthood. Apart from its financial success, the voyage was very profitable from an intelligence point of view: it is apparent that in the East Indies Cavendish had been at least as much concerned with political warfare and the gathering of information as with plunder or spices, for which he had little room. The master of the *Desire*, Thomas Fuller, brought back detailed sailing directions for the whole voyage, and Cavendish had secured a great map of China, from which were deduced Chinese armed forces of 7,923,785 horse and foot! The English name had been brought to the Philippines, where Cavendish had been at pains to ingratiate himself with the Indians of Capul, who promised 'to ayde him, whensoever hee shoulde come againe to overcome the Spaniards'; in Java also his contacts were very genial. He might therefore congratulate himself on a well conducted and very promising reconnaissance, and he undoubtedly looked forward to a more solid exploitation of it on a second voyage.[54] That voyage was to be a disaster, and in fact no Englishman coming by the South Sea was to repeat his success until the days of the buccaneers, a century later.

The first attempt to do so was made within a year of Cavendish's return, by John Chidley and Andrew Meyrick, who sailed from Plymouth in August 1589 'for The South Sea, and chiefly for the famous province of Arauco on the coast of Chili', reported by Cavendish to be full of gold mines. Of Chidley's three tall ships, only one—the *Delight*—is heard of again, wrecked in Normandy with, as we have seen, the last Spaniard from Rey Don Felipe.[55]

Already in 1589 Spanish reports were speaking of another linked venture by Cumberland and Cavendish, both for the South Sea and the latter for China as well. In the event, Cumberland went only to the Azores and Cavendish seems to have rapidly expended his gains from the *Santa Ana*, redeeming lands mortgaged for the first voyage, investing in some not very profitable semi-piratical ventures, and fitting out his second fleet.[56] This was on a large scale: he had the big *Galleon Leicester*, his own old *Desire* refitted, the *Roebuck* of 240 tons and 20 guns, *The Black Pinnace* which had brought Sir Philip Sydney's body home to a mourning England, and a small bark: at least 80 guns and some 350 men. His captains included John Davis, regarded by many then and since as England's greatest navigator of the day, under promise that 'when wee came back to the Callifornia, I should haue his Pinnace with my own Barck (which for that purpose went with me to my great charges) to search that Northwest discouery vpon the backe partes of America. . . .'[57] In Quinn's view, Cavendish's objective was not only the routine plunder of Peru, but also 'an English galleon trade with China [and perhaps Japan] that might emulate the fabulously rich Manila galleon itself.' To this end his two young Japanese and his Portuguese China expert would doubtless be most useful intermediaries.[58] With these high prospects he sailed from Plymouth on 26 August 1591.

Cavendish intended to begin by taking Santos in Brazil as a base, but they were becalmed in the Doldrums, and here, on a charge by the two Japanese that a Portuguese pilot was plotting desertions at Santos, Cavendish had 'the poore Portingall' hanged.[59] They suffered from scurvy and food shortages before reaching Brazil, but Santos was duly taken on 16 December (the people were all rounded up at Mass), though through negligence most of the local provisions on which Cavendish had relied were spirited away by the inhabitants. They did not sail again until 24 January 1592, sufficiently late in the season. The fleet was scattered by a storm off the Plate; although Cavendish had not fixed a rendezvous, the three large ships and *The Black Pinnace* were reunited in Port Desire on 16 March—already autumn. By this time morale was exceedingly low amongst what Cavendish called 'the moste abiect & mutanus Companye that ever was Caried out of Englande by anye man livinge'. It was not improved by the weather in the Straits, 'not durable for Christians', where in late April they had to shelter a few miles west of Cape Froward. Like Sarmiento's men, they were reduced to shellfish, cinnamon bark, and seaweed; on the *Galleon Leicester* forty men died in seven or eight days and seventy were ill, 'so that there was not 50 men that were able to stand vppon the hatches.' All the ships had lost or worn out many of their sails and cables; and it was not yet full winter.

In this extremity, Cavendish decided to put about and reach the East Indies by the Cape; after representations by the crews, and since neither Port Desire nor Port St Julian was really suitable as shelter for the larger ships, he agreed to return to Brazil to recuperate. As Richard Hawkins was to warn, 'all men are to take care, that they goe not one foote backe . . . for I haue not seene, that any who haue yeelded therevnto, but presently they haue returned home'—and he makes specific reference to Fenton and Cavendish.[60] Such a decision was all but inevitably fatal to the voyage, though perhaps often enough the only salvation for the voyagers, or some of them.

On the night of 20 May, not very far from Port Desire, Davis in the *Desire*, with *The Black Pinnace*, parted company. Once again, Cavendish had inexplicably failed to appoint a rendezvous; inexplicably again, although he thought that the two missing ships would make for Port Desire, he made no attempt to find them: all he did was to denounce 'that villaigne that hath bynn the death of mee and the decaie of the whole Accon, I meane Davys', and to sail on for Brazil. Meanwhile his scapegoat Davis, not meeting the General at Port Desire, refitted there and pressed on with the voyage, although it is true that his interest was probably exclusively with the Northwest Passage. He could not leave the port until 7 August, and may have been blown within sight of the Falklands; thrice he pushed through into the South Sea, in the dead of winter, losing *The Black Pinnace* there, until on 10 October he was finally driven back into the Straits. By the 30th he was back at the Penguin Island off Port Desire: they had made the second full passage from Cabo Deseado to Cape Virgins in seventeen days. They took on 20,000 penguins—dried, as they had not enough salt—and sailed for England on

22 December. They lost twenty-one men in Brazil, surprised by the Portuguese while watering, and as a final horror the poorly preserved penguins rotted and produced a most loathly worm: 'there was nothing that they did not devour, only yron excepted.'[61] Davis, more of a leader and less of a driver than Cavendish, kept them going, and on 11 June 1593 they reached Berehaven in Ireland—sixteen men, of whom only five were fit enough to work the ship.

Seven months earlier Cavendish had died. He had made his way up the Brazilian coast, fighting the Portuguese with more ill than good fortune. He considered—secretly, for fear of mutiny—stripping the *Roebuck* to refit and man the *Galleon Leicester*, pretending that he would make for St Helena to prey on the carracks of the Carreira, but really meaning to slip back to the Straits. But in the second of three fights with the Portuguese he lost twenty-five men out of eighty committed, and at this point the *Roebuck* deserted. On the flagship Cavendish managed to maintain his authority, partly by physical violence like Sarmiento's in like case, and even to induce his men—nominally at least—to make once more for the Straits. But the slaughter of all but two of thirty sick men ashore was too much for any remaining morale, and Cavendish bore up for St Helena. He missed it, and his men compelled him to go on northwards for Ascension. Cavendish was preparing himself to die; one can hardly say composing himself, for the bitter apologia he wrote, blaming everyone but himself, is the work of a man brought near to madness: 'amongst such hel houndes my spirit was Cleene spent wishinge my self vppon any desarte place in the worlde there to dye' and at Ascension he meant 'to haue there ended my vnfortunate lief.' But he missed that island also, and died at sea: a ruffianly spoiled child of fortune yielding up his life in an agony of spirit. Davis survived, to defend himself with dignity but point in *The Seamans Secrets*: after all, the 'runaway' was the last to return home.

The last English foray: Richard Hawkins

Sir William Monson, England's leading naval publicist of the early seventeenth century, was of opinion that the incursions of Drake and Cavendish, spectacular as they were, merely 'warned [the Spaniards], without annoying [i.e. injuring] them, to strengthen themselves in those parts . . . as appeared by the taking of Mr Hawkyns in the South Sea, 1594.'[62] Stung by the Callao affair, the Viceroy Toledo had grandiose plans for fortifying Guayaquil, Paita, Callao, and Arica; these were lost in the obstructed 'official channels' of the Council of the Indies, but after Drake the engineer Bernardino de Tejeda came to Peru and by mid-1587 had cast forty-four pieces for the new Viceregal navy; after Cavendish, he took in hand four forts at Callao, and gun-turrets were added to the Casas Reales on its waterfront.[63] Although the defences were still inadequate by 1590, Cavendish's successor Sir Richard Hawkins met with a much more efficient Spanish response.

Hawkins, son of the great Sir John, was twenty-five when he commanded a small galliot on Drake's West Indian expedition of 1584–5, and had a Queen's ship of 250 tons in the Armada fighting. His incomparable *Observations* show him as a thoughtful seaman and a delightful writer, though too easy-going as a commander.[64] Years later, after the peace with Spain, he stated his design as a trade reconnaissance in Cavendish's tracks; but it did not exclude plundering the Queen's enemies in Peru, and J. A. Williamson thinks that it may also have included a search for Terra Australis. It is rather doubtful that he had a proper commission, though he did have some official sanction. He sailed from Plymouth on 12 June 1593 with two ships, the *Dainty* of 300–400 tons and the *Fancy*, and a storeship.[65]

The trans-Atlantic voyage was uneventful: English seamen had not yet learnt to appreciate the Portuguese course, which made its westing well north of the Doldrums, and although Hawkins made no stops in the Canaries or Sierra Leone, it was the end of October before he made a landfall at Santos.[66] By this time he had only a couple of dozen sound men out of his original 164, owing to scurvy; but treatment with oranges and lemons, 'a certaine remedie for this infirmitie', produced a rapid recovery. This was all he could get at Santos, however; the Portuguese politely warned him off, and in his weakened condition he could only obey; in any case, he had neither the calculated daring of a Drake nor the bandit instincts of a Cavendish to lead him to defy the warning. He was able to complete recuperation at some islands north of Rio de Janeiro, where he burnt the storeship. Sailing again for the Straits on 10 December, he ran into a storm off the Plate, and the *Fancy* deserted: almost a standard combination. On 2 February he sighted an unknown land, and 'in perpetuall memory' of his Virgin Queen's chastity he named it 'HAVVKINS-*maiden-land.*' This, though his description is rather too favourable, must have been the Falklands.[67] He sighted Cape Virgins on 10 February 1594 and had a difficult passage of forty-six days; his account is chiefly notable for an entertaining essay on penguins—the word seemed Welsh, and brought to mind Prince Madoc and '*Motezanna* King (or rather Emperour) of *Mexico*.'

On 29 March he entered the South Sea and three weeks later was off Mocha Island, making very wary contacts with the Indians. Hawkins intended to keep well out to sea to escape observation and to make his first strike well north of Callao; but his company was avid for loot and forced him to raid Valparaiso. Here they took four ships with general cargoes, 'good Merchandize in *Lyma*, but to vs of small accompt'; but a fifth ship came in from Valdivia with 'some good quantitie of Gold'. Hawkins ransomed the ships, exchanging courtesies with the local notables; but Alonso de Sotomayor ('a noble Souldier, and liberall Gentleman') was waiting on the shore: in Lima he told Hawkins that he had set an ambush with 300 horse and foot. Hawkins was naturally on edge, regretting the impetuous greed of his crew, and especially nervous of the local wine, which despite all precautions by 'day and night, overthrew many of my people.' It was clearly not going to be, as heretofore, an easy walkover; and, as he had feared, messages were already on their way north. The *Dainty* put in at Coquimbo and looked into Arica, and now Hawkins had more trouble with the crew, who were fearful of being defrauded of their share of the prize and insisted that all treasure should be locked up, one of the three keys to be held by their delegate. Too many captains did so defraud their men, and it is typical of Hawkins's fair-mindedness that he recognised this and condoned (he could hardly help it) this first appearance of the shop-steward in English history.

Surprise was now lost: the Viceroy at Lima, the Marquis de Cañete, had already received news from Valparaiso and sent out six ships under his brother-in-law Don Beltran de Castro, while the whole coast northwards was alerted.[68] Three of the ships were well-gunned, but the crews, though enormously outnumbering Hawkins's seventy-five men, were a scratch lot, apart from 300 trained soldiers. Off Pisco, south of Callao, a sharp little engagement took place: the Spanish ships, though useless in bad weather, were much better adapted to the normally light winds of the coast than was the *Dainty*, and showed a disconcerting ability to get to windward. Luckily for Hawkins, lack of fighting experience caused the Spaniards to miss their opportunity, and when unusually heavy weather came on, their light spars and large expanses of light cotton sail could not take it: the capitana lost her mainmast and both the other large ships were also damaged in spars and sails. The *Dainty* was able to slip away between them, but it was a narrow escape.

Hawkins now set course for the Bay of Atacames in northern Ecuador, purposing to refit and then 'depart vpon our Voyage, with all possible speede': he reckoned without his crew. Don Beltran returned to Callao, where he was received with popular insult; but he was soon to put out again with two ships and a pinnace; his flagship, according to Hawkins, had thirty bronze guns, most of them heavy pieces. The crews were weeded out, but still outnumbered the English by at least ten or twelve to one; it seems that they now had some more efficient officers, the almirante, on Hawkins's own showing, being a really first-class fighting seaman.[69]

On Hawkins's way to Atacames two ships were chased but got away; he had thought that no ship afloat could have gained so much on the *Dainty*, but to his grieved astonishment the Spanish ships were able to outsail him with foresail and mizzen only. He was now anxious only to get away, but once more the insubordination of his crew ruined his chances. They insisted on taking a pinnace to chase a sail sighted from Atacames and failed to return, as ordered, on the next day, when Hawkins meant to sail for New Spain; he was detained in the bay four days longer than he had reckoned. He was actually weighing anchor, on 18 or 19 June, when Don Beltran's ships stood in. Despite their apparently overwhelming superiority, however, it took three days' hard fighting to overcome Hawkins's little company. At one point the Spaniards offered good terms, but Hawkins in a magnificent speech—doubtless embellished in tranquillity, but still magnificent—rallied his men: 'Came we into the South-sea to put out flagges of truce? And left we our pleasant *England*, with all her contentments, with intention or purpose to avayle our selues of white ragges?' They were also fired with wine. But at last the *Dainty*, riddled with great shot and with nineteen dead, was brought to surrender; Hawkins had received six wounds, two of them serious, and was 'out of hope to liue or recover'; considering that 'the honour or dishonour, the wel-fare or misery, was for them, which should be partakers of life', he consented that they should accept the twice-offered terms not only of quarter but of repatriation to England.[70] The English were treated with every kindness and courtesy, but it took a long time, and much effort by Don Beltran,

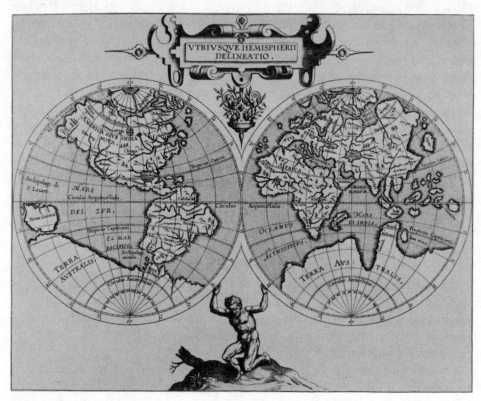

Plate XX. PTOLEMY TRANSFORMED: WYTFLIET 1597. An academic view: remnants of Marco Polo's geography (Beach, Maletur, Locach) are linked by Terra Australis to Tierra del Fuego; Japan has more or less fallen into its right place, Anian and Quivira are prominent; but although Noua Guinea is separated from Terra Australis (mere guesswork) the Spanish discoveries in the Pacific are ignored, and the Indonesian region is less realistic than on Ribeiro's maps of 1527–9 (cf. Fig. 4). But fundamentally Ptolemy has been not so much augmented as demolished: his enclosed Indian Ocean and his Sinus Magnus, the great gulf beyond Farther India (Plate I), have vanished for all time. From C. Wytfliet, *Descriptionis Ptolemaicæ Augmentum* (Louvain 1597), facsimile published by Theatrum Orbis Terrarum BV (Amsterdam 1964). By courtesy of Mr N. Israel, Amsterdam. ANU.

who considered his personal honour at stake, before the Spanish authorities were
brought to fulfil the terms. Hawkins himself did not reach England until 1602,
though most of his men had preceded him. Meanwhile the *Dainty* was exhibited
at Panama as a trophy of war: the first prize taken by the Spaniards in the South
Sea.

This was not quite the last fling: in 1596 Sir Robert Dudley, Leicester's son,
sent out three ships under Benjamin Wood 'for the straights of Magellan and
China', but Wood took them by the Cape route and the expedition dissipated
itself in aimless incursions in the Indian Ocean.[71] But indeed the war itself had
become an aimless stalemate: Drake and Sir John Hawkins had died on their
mismanaged West Indian voyage of 1595–6, and although Cadiz was sacked in
1596, in the next year both Essex's 'Islands Voyage' and the last great Spanish
invasion effort were fiascos; Burleigh and King Philip died in 1598, an era was
ending. But in 1600 the East India Company was chartered, and in the next two
years James Lancaster opened the path of the future for English enterprise by his
successful trading voyage to the East Indies by the Cape of Good Hope.[72]

The final English attack on Spanish America returned to the Isthmus where
Drake and Oxenham had begun: in 1601 William Parker, in a brilliant surprise,
took the newly fortified Porto Bello; but the treasure fleet had sailed only a
week before, and 'the treasure-house of the world' was empty.[73] The old Queen
died, and in 1604, under James I and VI, came peace; there was to be no further
English attempt on the South Sea until Sir John Narborough's in 1669. The little
ports between Valdivia and Acapulco were indeed often to be in terror of
corsarios luteranos, Callao itself blockaded; but the flags arrayed against them
were not English but Netherlandish. The Hollanders had taken over.

The century's work

When our story opens, Europeans were merely on the threshold of the Pacific:
in 1500 no European had seen any shore of the Ocean, and since Marco Polo
probably only a few missionaries had ever been even on its border seas. By 1600
the outlines of the East Indies and the China coast were tolerably clear, there
was active trade with Japan, and a regular shipping line across the Ocean between
Manila and Acapulco; the eastern shores from California to Tierra del Fuego
were known to Europeans, and from Acapulco to Valdivia were the scene of a
lively coastwise traffic. The northern coast of New Guinea was known, though
Australia was scarcely imagined, unless as a hypothetical Terra Australis; the
Portuguese may well have sighted much of the continent in the 1520s, but this
was not on record. In the Ocean itself, many islands had been sighted, some
visited, including the great Solomons group; and if they were cartographically
floating islands, at least the Ocean was delimited east and west, and it was known
that within it were many places of rest and refreshment (Fig. 24). The geographical revolution may be evaluated by comparing the fifteenth century world

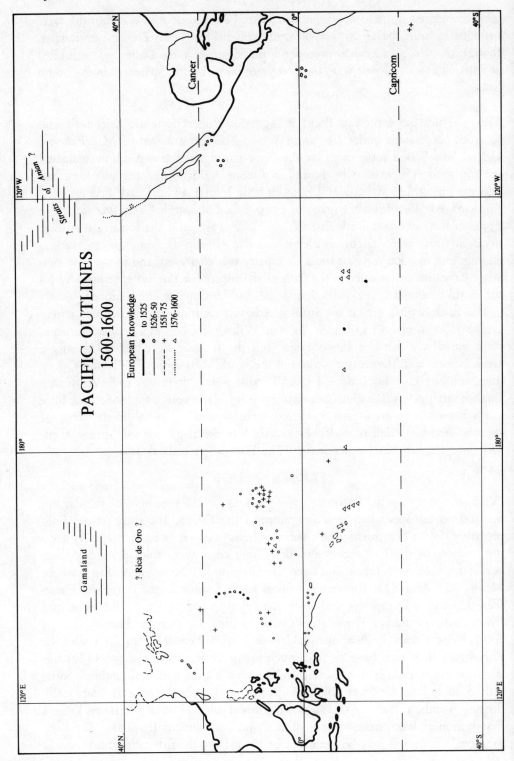

PACIFIC OUTLINES
1500-1600

European knowledge

	to 1525
○	1526-50
+	1551-75
△	1576-1600

Gamaland

? Rica de Oro ?

Straits of Anian ?

Cancer

Capricorn

map of Ptolemy in Plate I with its academic revision by Wytfliet in 1597 in
Plate XX. It was a great achievement, attained with wretched technical resources
and by scarcely imaginable suffering.

Despite Jesuit and other relations, the great empires of Asia were still, in
European minds, lands of mystery and fable, although in total there was an
immense amount of solid information available to merchants and scholars, and
this was already exerting a marked influence on European thought and art, as
Donald Lach's massy volumes attest.[74] Across the Ocean, two great unknown
empires had been discovered and subverted, whole nations all but extirpated,
and on their ruins had been erected a strange new imperium stretching from
New Spain to Chile and La Plata; their treasures had at once enormously stimulated and distorted European economies. And already some of the finer spirits of
Europe were drawing inferences unflattering to the assumptions and the self-
image of Western Christendom: Montaigne had written those devastating
essays 'Of Cannibals' and 'Of Coaches', in which by implication the court of
Charles IX appears scarce as civilised as that of some petty Brazilian chief. The
silks of China, the spices of Ternate and Tidore, the silver of Zacatecas and Potosi,
had been bought with blood and iron 'and the sweete liues of multitudes of
men.'[75]

◄ *Figure 24.* PACIFIC OUTLINES, 1500–1600. Placing of islands perforce somewhat approximate.

NOTES

Notes for Chapter 1

[1] It is generally stated, and almost certainly with truth, that Magellan himself gave the name; but there is no hard evidence. On the use of 'South Sea' or 'Pacific', note that C. de Brosses, *Histoire des Navigations aux Terres Australes* (Paris 1756), uses 'Mer du Sud' over twice as often as 'Pacifique', and in his supporting texts the ratio is seven to one. See O. H. K. Spate, '"South Sea" to "Pacific Ocean": a note on nomenclature', *Jnl Pac. Hist.* 12, 1977, 205–11.

[2] As cited in J. T. Medina, *El Descubrimiento del Océano Pacifico: I. Núñez de Balboa* (Santiago 1914), 92–3. Actually at this time, after the death of Isabella of Castile, Ferdinand of Aragon was Administrator of Castile for their mad daughter Juana.

[3] The reference is to the Korean world-map of 1402, reproduced in part as Plate CDXII (Vol. IV Part 3) in J. Needham, *Science and Civilisation in China* (Cambridge 1971), and discussed there and in Vol. III (1959), 554–5 [*Science in China*]. Some versions show England and Ireland (Ying-chi-li Kuo and I-erh-lang-ta); all give a recognisable delineation of the Mediterranean lands. Despite some oddities—Columbus really did not need to learn of the sphericity of the earth from hypothetical traditions, through Marco Polo, of Chinese globes!—there is much useful information in K. Chang, Chinese Great Explorers: Their Effect upon Chinese Geographic Knowledge prior to 1900 (Univ. of Michigan Ph.D. thesis 1955).

[4] See the discussion in F. Morales Padrón, *Historia del Descubrimiento y Conquista de América* (2nd ed., Madrid 1971), 11–14 [*Historia*].

[5] K. B. Cumberland, *Southwest Pacific* (Christchurch 1954), 5.

[6] C. W. Brooks, *Japanese Wrecks . . . in the North Pacific Ocean* (San Francisco 1876), 9–17, and a rather better treatment in H. E. Wildes, 'The Kuroshiwo's Toll', *Trans. Asiatic Soc. Japan* 2nd Ser. 17, 1938, 210–33. T. G. Nelson, 'Drift Voyages between eastern Asia and the Americas', *Canadian Geogr* 6, 1962, 54–9, adds little.

[7] For metallurgy, R. von Heine-Geldern, 'American Metallurgy and the Old World', in N. Barnard (ed.), *Early Chinese Art and its Possible Influence in the Pacific Basin* (New York 1972), III.787–822; he slides too easily from 'may have' to 'must have', and cites no Chinese documentary evidence for a traffic so active as to have made the Pacific, in his own phrase, 'a Chinese Mediterranean' (817). One can hardly follow him in the suggestion (811) that Argentinian stone tools were influenced by the Indo-Chinese Dong-son culture (1st millenium B.C.). The close contemporaneity of some developments in China and South America (790) would seem to weaken rather than strengthen his case, which is strongest on the very sophisticated technique of decorating gold work by granulation, common to both areas. Cf. in the same volume (823–41) P. Tolstoy, 'Diffusion: as Explanation and as Event', though this is perhaps more significant as a very elegant essay in methodology. For a balanced discussion see Needham, *Science in China*, IV.540–53.

[8] J. Golson, 'The Remarkable History of Indo-Pacific Man', *Search* (Sydney) 3, 1972, 13–21.

[9] 'por mares nunca dantes navegados'—Luis de Camões, *Os Lusiadas* (Lisbon 1572), I.1.

¹⁰ de Menezes, on his way to govern the Portuguese stations in the Moluccas, was blown to the northwest corner of the 'island of the Papuas' and waited there for the monsoon—A. Sharp, *The Discovery of the Pacific Islands* (Oxford 1960), 13; G. Souter, *New Guinea: The Last Unknown* (Sydney 1963), 18. For white penetration, Souter, 181–4, and 118–24 for the German officer Hermann Detzner, who allegedly spent the entire 1914–18 war in prolonged wanderings to avoid the Australian forces which had taken Kaiser Wilhelmsland. His survival was a remarkable achievement, but he later admitted that much of his story was fictitious, and he did not anticipate the Australian patrols of the 1930s—P. Biskup, 'Hermann Detzner: New Guinea's First Coast Watcher', *Jnl Papua & New Guinea Soc.* (Port Moresby) 2, 1968, 5–21.

¹¹ Barron Field, 'The Kangaroo' in *First Fruits of Australian Poetry* (Sydney 1819):

'. . . this fifth part of the Earth,
Which would seem an after-birth,
Not conceived in the Beginning'

¹² R. Jones, 'Emerging Picture of Pleistocene Australians', *Nature* 246, 1973, 278–81, and in general D. J. Mulvaney, *The Prehistory of Australia* (London 1969).

¹³ Cosmas is entertaining in small distilled doses, and is a witness of some merit for countries he had visited, from Egypt perhaps as far as Ceylon—see the translation by J. W. McCrindle, HS 2nd Ser. 98 (London 1897), and C. R. Beazley, *The Dawn of Modern Geography* (London 1897–1906), I.273–303 [*The Dawn*]. The old error dies hard; in May 1974, while writing this chapter, I came across it twice in statements by contemporaries of wide general culture.

¹⁴ A. Rainaud, *Le Continent Austral* (Paris 1893), 110 [*Austral*]. The views of the Fathers are canvassed in Beazley, *The Dawn*, I.272–83, 327–32.

¹⁵ G. H. T. Kimble, *Geography in the Middle Ages* (London 1938), 37 [*Geography*]; cf. E. G. R. Taylor, *Ideas on the Shape, Size and Movements of the Earth* (London 1943).

¹⁶ Beazley, *The Dawn*, III.501–2.

¹⁷ Rainaud, *Austral*, 124; cf. note 13 above.

¹⁸ The texts quoted are *Psalms* 93.1, *Job* 26.7, *Isaiah* 40.22, *Mark* 16.15.

¹⁹ E. H. Bunbury, *A History of Ancient Geography* (2nd ed., London 1883; reprint, New York 1959), I.125, II.228 [*History*]; Rainaud, *Austral*, 19–23 for classical and 128–65 for mediaeval times; numerous references in Beazley, *The Dawn*, but especially I.343–73.

²⁰ Kimble, *Geography*, 84–8; Rainaud, *Austral*, 145–6.

²¹ M. Letts, *Mandeville's Travels: Texts and Translations*, HS 2nd. Ser. 101 (London 1953), 129; cf. 204–17, 333–4, and E. G. R. Taylor's introduction on 'The Cosmographical Ideas of Mandeville's Day', li–lix. On the book's popularity, see A. D. Greenwood in *The Cambridge History of English Literature*, 1907–16, II.78–9, 82–3. There is a good discussion in A. Cortesão, *History of Portuguese Cartography* (Lisbon 1969–71), I.302–5 [*Cartography*]. The first volume of this masterly work is in effect a history of European cartography from the earliest times to Marco Polo, and is relevant to many topics in this chapter.

²² S. T. Coleridge, *The Rime of the Ancient Mariner*. There is an engaging assortment of monsters and other Perils of the Deep in J. L. Lowes, *The Road to Xanadu* (revised ed., Boston 1927), 116–20.

²³ Beazley, *The Dawn*, I.394, 465 and II.419, 533. The 'hand of Satan' tale may be the legend of a legend: Rainaud refers it to P. Denis, *Le Monde Enchanté* (Paris 1843), 121—but while Denis knows his way about the obscure literature of marvels, he gives no specific reference. (There is an undated modern reprint of his book put out by Burt Franklin, New York.) The mysterious Atlantic isle 'de la man de Saranaxio' is discussed in Rainaud, *Austral*, 165, and in more detail by A. Cortesão, *The Nautical Chart of 1424* (Coimbra 1954), 74–6. This is now more accessible in the third volume of his *Esparsos* (Coimbra 1974–5)—see 134–6 for the rejection of Armand d'Avezac's intriguing

conflation of Satan with St Athanasius! Of course, it was probably not such tales which kept the Arabs of the Maghreb from sailing to Guinea, but rather the lack of economic motive—they had the caravan routes across the Sahara; cf. E. G. R. Taylor, *The Haven-Finding Art* (London 1956), 130 [*Haven-Finding*].

[24] E. Prestage, *The Portuguese Pioneers* (London 1933), 54–6 [*Pioneers*]. But the Catalan Atlas of 1375 represents the African coast beyond Cape Bojador—V. M. Godinho, *L'Économie de l'Empire Portugais aux XVe et XVIe Siècles* (Paris 1969), 29, 52 [*Économie*].

[25] Kimble, *Geography*, 8–10, 48–9; Rainaud, *Austral*, 114.

[26] D. Lach, *Asia in the Making of Europe* (Chicago 1965), I.67–9 [*Asia*].

[27] The Alexandrian authenticity of the Ptolemaic maps is strongly impugned by L. Bagrow, 'The Origin of Ptolemy's Geographia', *Geografiska Annaler* (Stockholm) 27, 1945, 319–87; and cf. his *History of Cartography*, translated and enlarged by R. A. Skelton (London 1964), 34–6. But their likely Byzantine origin is not greatly to the point—what matters is what the fifteenth century accepted as being on Ptolemy's authority.

[28] Cf. below, Ch. 2; also B. Penrose, *Travel and Discovery in the Renaissance 1420–1620* (Cambridge (Mass.) 1952) [*Travel*] and L. Wroth, 'The Early Cartography of the Pacific', *Papers Biblio. Soc. of America*, 38 No. 2 (New York 1944), 87–268, at 91–103 ['Cartography'].

[29] Ptolemy's figure was 180,000 stadia against Eratosthenes' 252,000; there is no certainty as to the length of the stadium used by the latter, but on one value he may have been only about 1 per cent out—G. Sarton, *A History of Science* (Cambridge (Mass.) 1959), II.103–6; M. R. Cohen and I. E. Drabkin, *A Source Book in Greek Science* (New York 1948), 149–53.

[30] Bunbury, *History*, I.627; *The Geography of Strabo*, trans. H. L. Jones (Loeb ed., London 1917), 241.

[31] Kimble, *Geography*, 8–9, 86–7, 210; Cortesão, *Cartography*, I.191–8.

[32] Kimble, *Geography*, 208–12; J. H. Parry, *The Age of Reconnaissance* (Mentor ed., New York 1964), 25–9 [*Reconnaissance*]. In the fifteenth century, influential supporters of a seaway to Cathay and the Indies included Pope Pius II (Aeneas Sylvius) and of course Toscanelli, who at Columbus's request sent him a copy of his letter of 1474 addressed to Afonso V of Portugal, which in S. E. Morison's phrase became 'Exhibit A' for Columbus. The latter also studied d'Ailly's works with meticulous care, and whether his still-extant marginalia, picking out every hint which might bolster his case, were made before or after his first voyage seems scarcely to affect the issue— Morison, *Admiral of the Ocean Sea* (Boston 1942), 33–5, 64–9, 92–4, in my opinion a reasonably strong case for the earlier date. For a different view see C. Jane's introduction on 'The objectives of Columbus' in his *Select Documents illustrating the Four Voyages of Columbus*, HS 2nd Ser. 65 and 70 (London 1930), 1933—a beautifully written essay on 'History in the Subjunctive Mood', which in this context may be the right mood.

[33] Morison, *Admiral of the Ocean Sea*, 68; A. von Humboldt, *Cosmos* (London 1864), II.645; cf. R. A. Skelton, *The European Image and the Mapping of America* (Minneapolis 1964), 12–16.

[34] Prestage, *Pioneers*, 16, 32; J. A. Williamson (ed.), *The Cabot Voyages . . .*, HS 2nd Ser. 120 (Cambridge 1962), 5–7. Cortesão, *Cartography*, I.295–7 is full and decisive.

[35] J. H. Parry, *The European Reconnaissance* (New York 1968), 16.

[36] H. Yule, *Cathay and the Way Thither*, HS 2nd Ser. 37 (Vol. III) (London 1914), 151. See also E. Power, 'The Opening of the Land Routes to Cathay', in A. P. Newton (ed.), *Travel and Travellers in the Middle Ages* (London 1926), 124–58 [*Travellers*].

[37] J. H. Kramers, 'Geography and Commerce', in T. Arnold and A. Guilleaume (eds.), *The Legacy of Islam* (Oxford 1931), 79–107 at 83.

[38] Beazley, *The Dawn*, III.439; Prestage, *Pioneers*, 32—suggesting that a copy may have been used

by Prince Henry; Cortesão, *Cartography*, I.290; Bagrow, *History of Cartography*, 66 and Plate XXXVI; and especially G. H. T. Kimble, 'The Laurentian world map . . .', *Imago Mundi* 1, 1935, 29–33. The Sanuto and Laurentian maps are presented by Beazley, III.439 and 521; cf. also the sketches of world-maps from 1321 to 1457–9 in Cortesão, *Cartography*, II.159.

[39] Cortesão, *Cartography*, I.398–9, II.60–3; Wroth, 'Cartography', 103.

[40] For the romantic tale of the Bristolian Robert Machin's ill-fated honeymoon on Madeira, see F. Machado in A. Baião *et al.* (eds.), *História da Expansão Portuguesa no Mundo* (Lisbon 1937–40), I.280–4 [*Expansão*] and A. Cortesão, 'The Story of Robert Machin's Discovery . . . in the XIV Century', *Rev. da Univ. de Coimbra* 23, 1973, 393–409. More generally, Prestage, *Pioneers*, 35–54; Cortesão, *Cartography*, II.52–72; Godinho, *Économie*, 19–26.

[41] A. Cortesão, 'Nautical Science and the Renaissance', in *Esparsos*, II.86–111, at 94. The general story has been told, and well told, too often to need detailed reference here; but on the motivation see Prestage, *Pioneers*, 29–32, 164–7; Veiga Simões in Baião, *Expansão*, I.311–56 (especially 'Sua pretenza Crusada', 319–37); and the thoughtful recent treatment in C. R. Boxer, *The Portuguese Seaborne Empire* (Harmondsworth 1973), 15–38 [*Empire*].

[42] Casting about for some respectable source for this old story, remembered from undergraduate days (if not earlier), I tried the obvious places such as Kimble and the great Madrid *Enciclopedia Universal Ilustrada*, without success. A chance look at the first page of E. O. Winstedt's edition of Cosmas Indicopleusthes (Cambridge 1909) gave Glanvill's 1702 translation of Fontenelle's *Plurality of Worlds*. See R. Shackleton (ed.), *Entretiens sur la Pluralité des Mondes* (Oxford 1955), 14, 180–1. Such are the pleasures of serendipity.

[43] João de Barros, *Asia* (1552), Dec. I, Liv. 2, Cap. iv (Lisbon ed. 1945–6, I.93).

[44] K. F. Helleiner, 'The Population of Europe . . .', in *The Cambridge Economic History of Europe*, 1942–65, IV.1–95 at 7–9 [*Cambridge EHE*].

[45] H. A. L. Fisher, *A History of Europe* (London 1948), 390–1.

[46] E. Armstrong, 'The Papacy and Naples in the Fifteenth Century', in *The Cambridge Mediaeval History*, 1911–36, VIII.158–201 at 195.

[47] R. Doucet, 'France under Charles VIII and Louis XI', in *The New Cambridge Modern History*, 1957–70, I.292–315 at 309–10 [*New CMH*].

[48] E. E. Rich, 'Expansion as a Concern of All Europe', in *New CMH*, I.445–69 at 447.

[49] F. Braudel, 'European Expansion and Capitalism: 1450–1650', in J. L. Blau (ed.), *Chapters in Western Civilization* (2nd ed., New York 1954), I.245–84 at 250 ['Expansion'].

[50] Cf. the discussion in M. Gilmore, *The Age of Humanism* (New York 1952), 49–56 [*Humanism*].

[51] For a concise account of the Fuggers, see S. P. Clough and C. W. Cole, *Economic History of Europe* (3rd ed., Boston 1952), 154–7.

[52] Braudel, 'Expansion', 260.

[53] '. . . it was not new lands that the European adventurer discovered or rediscovered; it was rather the unending salt-water routes . . .'—Braudel, 'Expansion', 249. Cf. Chaunu, 52.

[54] R. B. Merriman, *The Rise of the Spanish Empire* (New York 1952; original ed. 1918), II.220–1. But cf. M. Mörner, 'Spanish Migration to the New World prior to 1800', in F. Chiappelli (ed.), *First Images of America* (Berkeley 1976), II.737–82 at 738.

[55] R. Lapa (ed.), *Quadros da Crónica de D. João I* (Lisbon 1943), v–vi; Boxer, *Empire*, 17, 28–33; and the brilliant background sketch in Godinho, *Économie*, 31–40. The internal stability of Portugal as a factor in her rise to world power seems to be generally overlooked; for an exception, see I. Wallerstein, *The Modern World System* (New York 1974), 50–1.

[56] H. V. Livermore, *A History of Portugal* (Cambridge 1947), 185.

[57] Bunbury, *History*, II.443; its date is between A.D. 50 and 100.

[58] R. A. Mortimer Wheeler *et al.*, 'Arikamedu: an Indo-Roman Trading Station on the East Coast of India', *Ancient India* (New Delhi) 2, 1946, 17–24. Lach's *Asia* provides a richly detailed survey of the whole theme; for the pre-Discovery phases see Chapters I and II, 5–88, and also G. B. Sansom, *The Western World and Japan* (Vintage ed., New York 1973), 17–18, 20.

[59] John de Piano Carpini and Ascelin of Lombardy (who got no farther than Tabriz) were sent by Pope Innocent IV in 1245, Andrew of Longjumeau and William of Rubruck (Rubruquis) by Louis IX of France in 1249 and 1253; see Beazley, *The Dawn*, III.175–91; Lach, *Asia*, I.30–4; and especially the first six chapters of I. de Rachewiltz, *Papal Envoys to the Great Khans* (London 1971). Rubruquis was a remarkably good observer, still very pleasantly readable. Later Franciscans succeeded in setting up an Archbishopric at Cambaluc (Peking), with a Bishop at Canton, but not, apparently, many converts. For Prester John and his translation to Ethiopia, see i.a. E. D. Ross, 'Prester John and the Empire of Ethiopia' in Newton, *Travellers*, 174–94; and Cortesão, *Cartography*, I.255–75—this 'greatest hoax in the history of geography' was of much but ambivalent significance in Portugal. There is a full and admirable recent treatment of the whole amazing story in R. Silverberg, *The Realm of Prester John* (New York 1972).

[60] Lach, *Asia*, I.49–50; there is an all-too-obvious parallel with oil prices in 1973. . . . It should be noted that the Venetian trade was not immediately and utterly supplanted by Lisbon; and indeed it revived remarkably later in the sixteenth century. For the vicissitudes of the spice trade, especially in pepper, see Lach, I.91–147; F. C. Lane's papers of 1933 and 1940 in his *Venice and History* (Baltimore 1966), 12–14, 25–34 (the birth of a great historical revision), and 373–82; Godinho, *Économie*, 713–31, 773–80 ('la Mer Rouge n'a jamais pu être complètement coupée de l'océan Indien . . . la route du Cap n'a jamais pu la remplacer totalement'); F. Braudel, *La Méditerranée . . . à l'epoque de Philippe II* (Paris 1949), 421–47—there was a 'revanche méditerranéenne' by the Red Sea route in 1550–70, and in 1585 Philip formally offered Venice what was in effect an agency for pepper brought to Lisbon. As his subtitle suggests, N. Steensgard goes further in revisionism in *The Asian Trade Revolution of the Seventeenth Century: The East India Companies and the Decline of the Caravan Trade* (Chicago 1974); see 96–101, 154–6, and especially 163–9—in the later sixteenth century, 'Only in a few years was as much as half [of pepper and spice imports] brought to Europe by the route around Africa.' Yet one may still meet the old errors that the fall of Constantinople in 1453 saw a complete blockage, as completely broken by Vasco da Gama.

[61] J. U. Nef, 'Mining and Metallurgy in Medieval Civilisation', in *Cambridge EHE*, II.430–93 at 457 and 470.

[62] I have relied heavily in this section on R. M. Nance, 'The Ship of the Renaissance', *MM* 41, 1955, 180–92 and 281–98, and on the admirable discussion in Parry, *Reconnaissance*, 67–84; more detail, perforce omitted here, may be found in S. E. Morison, *The European Discovery of America: The Northern Voyages A.D. 500–1600* (New York 1971), 112–56. See also the section on 'Types de Navires et Constructions Navales' in M. Mollat and P. Adam (eds.), *Les Aspects Internationaux de la Découverte Océanique aux XVe et XVIe siècles* (Paris 1966), 137–222, especially F. Mauro on the organisation of shipbuilding, at 184–9 [*Aspects*].

[63] See *MM*, *passim*.

[64] For Chinese developments, comparisons, and possible influences, see Needham, *Science in China*, IV Section 29, especially 492, 509–14, 638–55, 695–9. Cf. J. Poujade, *La Route des Indes et ses Navires* (Paris 1946), 258–9, 268.

[65] For the development of ordnance in general see A. R. Hall, 'Military Technology', in C. Singer *et al.* (eds.), *A History of Technology* (Oxford 1954–8), III.347–76, and for naval applications F. C. P. Naish, *ibid.*, 478, 481; Parry, *Reconnaissance*, 133–40; C. Cipolla, *Guns and Sails in the Early Phase*

of European Expansion 1400–1700 (London 1965), especially 81–3 on the 'bigger and better' arms race before 1550.

[66] M. Lewis, *The Spanish Armada* (Pan ed., London 1960), 75–8; cf. G. Mattingly, *The Defeat of the Armada* (London 1959), 345–6. Note, however, the difference between English and Spanish reckonings, and the 1590 change in the latter—above, pp. xxii–xxiv.

[67] Q. da Fonseca, 'A arquitectura naval no tempo dos Descobrimentos', in Baião, *Expansão*, II.39–46 (100 tonéis = 125 metric tons); R. M. Nance, 'Caravels', *MM* 3, 1913, 265–71; for the Spanish caravel, Morales Padrón, *Historia*, 33–5. For fluyts, R. Davis, *The Rise of the English Shipping Industry* (Newton Abbott 1962), 48–50.

[68] R. L. Scheina, 'Mass Labour: the Key to Spanish Maritime Construction', *MM* 58, 1972, 195–204, and in general the papers on 'Brigantines' in the same journal by E. A. Dingley (6, 1920, 292–4), R. M. Nance (7, 1921, 22–4), and A. Balsen (7, 1921, 79–82). Perhaps the best description is in S. E. Morison, *The European Discovery of America: The Southern Voyages A.D. 1492–1616* (New York 1974), 187, 549–50 [*Southern Voyages*].

[69] Chaunu, 667–8—those built at Maracaibo were up to 180 *toneladas* by 1637. For some specific points on Spanish Pacific shipbuilding, see H. A. Morton, *The Winds Command: Sailors and Sailing Ships in the Pacific* (Vancouver 1975), 127–9; he is also good (221–35) on the typology of masting and rigging in general [*Winds Command*].

[70] P. Chaunu, *Conquête et Exploitation des Nouveaux Mondes* (Paris 1969), 279–80.

[71] Taylor, *Haven-Finding*, 174. Drake's method was simple—kidnap a local pilot (ibid., 208).

[72] Cortesão, *Cartography*, II.96, 103, 227, and cf. E. Axelson, 'Prince Henry the Navigator and the Discovery of the Sea Route to India', *Geogl Jnl* 127, 1961, 145–58 at 153. The limitations of dead reckoning, and the implication of an earlier introduction of instrumental navigation than is allowed by some writers, are discussed in C. V. Sölver and G. J. Marcus, 'Dead Reckoning and the Ocean Voyages of the Past', *MM* 44, 1958, 18–34.

[73] Taylor, *Haven-Finding*, 162–3. For details of the development of instrumental navigation, see Parry, *Reconnaissance*, 103–15; J. B. Hewson, *A History of the Practice of Navigation* (revised ed., Glasgow 1963); C. H. Cotter, *A History of Nautical Astronomy* (London 1968) [*Astronomy*]; but especially D. W. Waters, *The Art of Navigation in Elizabethan and Early Stuart Times* (London 1958)—a superb work crammed with fascinating detail [*Navigation*].

[74] The lunar eclipse method had been suggested by Hipparchus, c. 160 B.C. (Bunbury, *History*, I.633), but as Sir Isaac Newton reputedly remarked that working out future lunar positions was 'the only problem that ever made my head ache', it is not surprising that few seamen tried their hands!—Cotter, *Astronomy*, 14, 195–205, and J. G. Crowther, *Founders of British Science* (London 1960), 264; cf. Morison, *Southern Voyages*, 295–6. Much progress in the study of magnetic variation was made by Pedro Nuñes, and in the field by D. João de Castro—Taylor, *Haven-Finding*, 175–84, and L. de Albuquerque in Cortesão, *Cartography*, II.420–3. Since Taylor wrote, Cortesão and Albuquerque have published D. João's 'magnificent rutters' of his Indian voyage in *Obras Completas de D. João de Castro*, I (Coimbra 1968). An anonymous Portuguese chart of c. 1585 even shows rough isogonic lines—A. Cortesão and A. Teixeira de Mota, *Portugaliæ Monumenta Cartographica* (Lisbon 1960), III.71–2 and Plate 363.

[75] Taylor, *Haven-Finding*, 160, 167, 201–2; the log-and-line appears to be the first English contribution to the art.

[76] C. Jack-Hinton, *The Search for the Islands of Solomon 1567–1838* (Oxford 1969), 182–3, 218–20, 227–31, and Maps XXXIII, XXXIV.

[77] For a clear account of the use of wind-roses and the rhumbs drawn from them, see Taylor, *Haven-Finding*, 109–13.

[78] Cortesão, *Cartography*, II.93–7; Taylor, *Haven-Finding*, 174–81; Parry, *Reconnaissance*, 111–30; and for the relationship of Wright and Mercator, Waters, *Navigation*, numerous references but especially 121–2, 228–9.

[79] Ma Huan, *Ying-yai Sheng-lan* [*The Overall Survey of the Ocean's Shores*], trans. J. V. G. Mills, HS Extra Ser. 42 (Cambridge 1970); cf. below, Ch. 6.

[80] The 'ideological' factors are interestingly discussed in Gilmore, *Humanism*, 32–7, and Braudel, 'Expansion', 246–54.

[81] C. Marlowe, *The First Part of Tamburlaine the Great*, V.i.

[82] Rich, in *New CMH*, 446.

[83] Parry, *Reconnaissance*, 67; see his Chapters II and IV on organisation and manning. The changing relative shares of local enterprise and outside finance are discussed in J. Heers, 'Le rôle des capitaux internationales dans les voyages de découvertes aux XVe et XVIe siècles' in Mollat and Adam, *Aspects*, 273–93. For an analysis of the investments in several important Spanish voyages, see F. de Solano, 'Navios y Mercaderes en la ruta occidental de especies (1519–1563)', in *A Viagem de Fernão de Magalhães* (Lisbon 1975), 579–610 (see full reference in Ch. 2, note 24).

[84] C. Day Lewis, *Transitional Poem* (London 1929), 10.

[85] For the (not so very) 'minor horrors of the sea', see the elaborately facetious letter of 1573 by Eugenio de Salazar in Parry, *The European Reconnaissance*, 348–64. Morton, *Winds Command*, Chs. 17–24 *passim*, gives many picturesque details of life on board in sailing days.

Notes for Chapter 2

[1] C. E. Nowell, 'The Columbus Question', *Amer. Hist. Rev.* 44, 1938–9, 802–22, canvasses in a moderate spirit some of the theories and heresies surrounding the problem of Columbus's intent; cf. C. Jane's introduction to *Select Documents illustrating the Four Voyages of Columbus*, HS 2nd Ser. 65, 70 (London 1930), stressing the mystical element in his concepts and tending to discount the simple search-for-the-Indies thesis. There is a balanced review in G. F. Hudson, *Europe and China* (London 1961; original ed. 1931), 204–28. The views of the Vignaud school seem in the discard since the appearance of S. E. Morison's *Admiral of the Ocean Sea* (Boston 1942) [*Admiral*]; for a more recent discussion, G. R. Crone, *The Discovery of America* (London 1969) [*Discovery*].

[2] A. P. Newton, 'Christopher Columbus and his First Voyage', in A. P. Newton (ed.), *The Great Age of Discovery* (London 1932), 73–103, at 85–9; see also his 'Asia or Mundus Novus' in the same volume, 104–28 [*Great Age*].

[3] D. Peres, *História dos Descobrimentos Portugueses* (Oporto 1943), 254–6, 263; E. A. Prestage, *The Portuguese Pioneers* (London 1933), 230–1; royal support for Dulmo (actually a Fleming, van Olmen) may have been meant 'as a warning to Ferdinand and Isabella, to prevent them from coming to terms' with Columbus. Cf. V. M. Godinho, *L'Économie de l'Empire Portugais aux XVe et XVIe siècles* (Paris 1969), 44–6.

[4] J. de Barros, *Asia* (Lisbon 1552–63), Dec. I, Liv. 2, Cap. xi (Lisbon ed. 1945–6, I.118–22).

[5] See C. R. Boxer, *The Portuguese Seaborne Empire 1415–1825* (Harmondsworth 1969), 20–4; J. H. Parry, *The Spanish Seaborne Empire* (Harmondsworth 1973), 22, 123–9.

[6] H. Vander Linden, 'Alexander VI and the Demarcation . . . of the Domains of Spain and Portugal, 1493–94', *Amer. Hist. Rev.* 22, 1916–17, 1–20, at note 40 ['Alexander VI']. See also C. E. Nowell, 'The Treaty of Tordesillas . . .' in A. Ogden and E. Sluiter (eds.), *Greater America* (Berkeley 1945), 1–8; R. B. Merriman, *The Rise of the Spanish Empire* (New York 1962; original ed. 1918),

II. 199–205 [*Spanish Empire*]; Crone, *Discovery*, 96–103; L. Weckmann-Muñoz, 'The Alexandrine Bulls of 1493', in F. Chiappelli (ed.), *First Images of America: The Impact of the New World on the Old* (Berkeley 1976), 201–20 [*First Images*]. There is an extremely detailed and objective study, with Latin and Spanish texts of the Bulls, in M. Gimenez Fernández, *Nuevas Consideraciones sobre la História, Sentido y Valor de las Bulas Alejandrinas referentes a las Indias* (Seville 1944)—see especially 44–51, 113 [*Bulas*]. English translations of the Bulls and other relevant documents, such as the Treaties of Tordesillas and Zaragoza and the proceedings of the Badajoz junta, will be found in Vol. I of Blair & Robertson. I regret not to have seen the obviously important *El Tratado de Tordesillas y su Proyeción*, Primer Coloquio Luso-Español de Historia de Ultramar (Valladolid 1973–4).

⁷ G. Mattingly, 'No Peace Beyond What Line?' *Trans. Roy. Hist. Soc.*, 5th series 13, 1963, 145–62, at 152, 161. ['No Peace']. Some of the confusion arose from the seaman's colloquial usage of 'the Line' as shorthand for the Equinoctial Line, 0°.

⁸ Blair & Robertson, I.112.

⁹ Vander Linden, 'Alexander VI', at note 45.

¹⁰ Either by accident or design, Columbus had reported his discoveries as 34 or 32°N, instead of 20–24—Crone, *Discovery*, 84. See also F. Morales Padrón, *Historia del Descubrimiento y Conquista de América* (2nd ed., Madrid 1971), 98–9 (with map) [*Historia*].

¹¹ Gimenez Fernandez, *Bulas*, 136, 148; Morales Padrón, *Historia*, 109–11, cf. Mattingly, 'No Peace', 151–3.

¹² The saying goes back to 1518—E. G. Bourne, 'Historical Introduction' to Blair & Robertson, at I.25; cf. Maximilian of Transylvania in C. E. Nowell, *Magellan's Voyage Around the World* (Evanston 1962), 277 [*Voyage*]. For the beginnings of the idea of a global demarcation (as against one in the Atlantic hemisphere only), see R. E. Abadía, 'La idea del antimeridiano', in A. Teixeira da Mota (ed.), *A Viagem de Fernão de Magalhães e a Questão das Molucas*, Actas do II Colóquio Luso-Espanhol de História Ultramarina (Lisbon 1975), 1–26 ['antimeridiano']; L. de Albuquerque and R. Graça Feijó, 'Os pontos de vista de D. João II na Junta de Badajoz', ibid. 527–45 at 532 ['Badajoz']. But 'such an antimeridional boundary is a mere supposition or logical inference, which lacks the slightest textual mention in the famous treaty of 1494'—J. P. de Tudela y Bueso, 'La especería de Castilla . . .', ibid. 627–87 at 632 ['La especería']. References to this most important work, which subsumes a vast amount of Magellanic scholarship, are by author and title of paper 'in Actas II'.

¹³ O. H. K. Spate, 'Terra Australis—Cognita?', *Hist. Studies* (Melbourne) 1957, 1–19, at 13–14. Ludovico de Varthema *may* have reached the Moluccas, but if he did so it was not until 1505, so the area was still 'utterly unknown' to any Europeans at the end of the fifteenth century—B. Penrose, *Travel and Discovery in the Renaissance 1420–1620* (Cambridge (Mass.) 1952), 28–32.

¹⁴ C. O. Sauer accepts early Spanish statements, based on accounts made through the Indian chiefs (who would have had good reason not to exaggerate) that the adult aboriginal population of Española in 1496 was over 1,000,000; a density of 13 or 15 per km², excluding children. This would be ecologically feasible, but 'In less than twenty years from the founding of Isabela the impending extinction of the natives was apparent and in another ten it had occurred'—*The Early Spanish Main* (Berkeley 1968), 65–9, 200–4.

¹⁵ Morales Padrón, *Historia*, 149.

¹⁶ Details in already cited works by Crone, Morison, Parry, and Penrose; also the relevant chapters of J. B. Brebner, *The Explorers of North America 1492–1806* (Meridian ed., Cleveland 1964); F. A. Kirkpatrick, *The Spanish Conquistadores* (3rd ed., London 1967); J. H. Parry, *The Age of Reconnaissance* (Mentor ed., New York 1964) [*Reconnaissance*]; and especially S. E. Morison, *The European*

Discovery of America: The Southern Voyages A.D. 1492–1616 (New York 1974), Chs. IX–XI [*Southern Voyages*]. For the remote possibility that Englishmen of John Cabot's 1498 voyage may have preceded the Spaniards on the Darien coast, see J. A. Williamson (ed.), *The Cabot Voyages and Bristol Discovery under Henry VII*, HS 2nd Ser. 120 (Cambridge 1962), 107–12 [*Cabot Voyages*].

[17] Crone, *Discovery*, 126–7, and see his whole Ch. IX, a moving story; cf. Morison, *Admiral*, 580–2, 594–621.

[18] The Spanish form of Columbus.

[19] Santa Maria was abandoned in 1523–4, and 'Since that day no white settlement has ever been able to maintain itself permanently in the Darien section of the isthmus'—G. Mack, *The Land Divided: A History of . . . Isthmian Canal Projects* (New York 1944), 31.

[20] The tragical history of these beginnings is vividly and thoughtfully told in J. Mirsky, *The Westwards Crossings: Balboa, Mackenzie, Lewis and Clark* (2nd ed., Chicago 1970) [*Crossings*]; the significance of the 'cycle of gold and depopulation' is brought out in Chaunu, 898–903. There is a full and sympathetic study of Balboa and a mass of documentation in the first two volumes of J. T. Medina, *El Descubrimiento del Océano Pacífico* (Santiago de Chile 1913–14) [*Descubrimiento*]. More accessible is the biography by K. Romoli, *Balboa of Darién* (New York 1953) [*Balboa*].

[21] The detail of this solemn act is given in Medina, *Descubrimiento*. I.92–4; for the precise date Romoli, *Balboa*, 160–1. A day or two earlier one of Balboa's men, Alonso Martin, in command of a patrol to find the best way to the sea, had actually pushed off in a canoe, claiming to be the first Spaniard on the new sea. There is no foundation for Sir Clement Markham's story (*Geogr Jnl* 41, 1913, 519) that the sea was called 'Pacific' because the young chief Panciaco told Balboa that 'the great ocean was always smooth'; as a matter of fact some of the first Spaniards to sail in these waters found them 'turbulent' and 'raging' (H. J. Wood, in Newton, *Great Age*, 161), and Balboa's first attempt to reach the Pearl Islands by canoe failed miserably—he had been warned that the season was always stormy—Romoli, 165–8. As for the name, on 3 December 1514 there was a formal proclamation in Santa Maria of the 'Tierra Nueva a la parte del Mar del Sur'—Medina, *Descubrimiento*, I.87 and III (*Fernando de Magellanes*, 1920) cclxviii.

[22] In his paper 'The Discovery of the Pacific: A Suggested Change of Approach', *Pac. Hist. Rev.* 16, 1947, 1–10 ['Pacific'], C. E. Nowell claims that Antonio de Abreu and Francisco Serrão were 'by all accepted standards' the first European discoverers of the Pacific, having reached the Moluccas and the Banda Sea towards the end of 1511. The two encyclopaedia references given as 'accepted standards' are not convincing, and in contrast e.g. the official Australian chart *Australia and Adjacent Waters: Limits of the Oceans and Seas*, RAN Hydrographic Office (Sydney 1972), links the Banda Sea with the Indian not the Pacific Ocean. This has international standing, though the boundaries shown have of course no political significance. In fact, Nowell explodes his own claim by saying that Balboa was probably not even the thousandth European to 'behold the Pacific', being anticipated by Polo and many missionaries (not hundreds, but scores?). But there is a vast difference between thalassic waters and the great Ocean, and commonsense as well as tradition accord in awarding the honour to Balboa. Nevertheless, Nowell's paper is important and valid in stressing the significance of the Portuguese approach via the Indian Ocean.

[23] Cited in Mirsky, *Crossings*, 81, but here quoted from Richard Eden's translation of the Decades, in *A Selection of Curious, Rare, and Early Voyages . . .* (London 1812), 541.

[24] My treatment of Magellan is in the main based on the standard Portuguese biography by the Visconde de Lagôa, *Fernão de Magalhãis (A sua Vida e a sua Viagem)* (Lisbon 1938) [*Vida e Viagem*]; J. Denucé, *Magellan: La Question des Moluques et la Première Circumnavigation du Globe* (Brussels 1911) [*Moluques*]; and A. Teixeira da Mota (ed.), *A Viagem de Fernão de Magalhães e a Questão das Molucas, . . .*, cited in note 12. The third volume of Medina, *Descubrimiento*, is also devoted to

Magellan, and there is an immense documentation in P. Pastells SJ, *El Descubrimiento del Estrecho de Magellanes* (Madrid 1920) [*Estrecho*]. For the basic narrative of Pigafetta the translation in Nowell, *Voyage* (which also has Maxmilian of Transylvania and Gaspar Côrrea), and the splendid facsimile French text in R. A. Skelton, *Magellan's Voyage* (New Haven 1969), have been used. The first printed version of Pigafetta, *c.* 1525, is given in facsimile and translation in P. S. Paige, *The Voyage of Magellan* (Englewood Cliffs 1969).

There are recent biographies in English by C. McK. Parr, *So Noble a Captain* (London 1953) and E. Roditi, *Magellan of the Pacific* (London 1972). Both are based on solid research, but Parr seems to extrapolate from the sources too readily: thus he is able 'to sketch with confidence' a 'probable' voyage of Magellan to the Philippines in 1512 (96–8); later (250) 'since he reached the Philippines for the second time *from the opposite direction* [Parr's italics] *it is evident* [my italics] that he was the first man ever to complete the circumnavigation of the globe.' This does not seem accepted by any other authority known to me; cf. M. Torodach, 'Magellan Historiography', *HAHR* 51, 1971, 313–35. Morison (*Southern Voyages*, 217) makes a somewhat similar claim, stating as a fact that Magellan was with de Abreu in 1511 (not generally accepted) and that the longitudes he reached in 1511 and 1521 overlap; elsewhere (421, 435) he inclines to award the honour to Magellan's slave Enrique, a point made in a more guarded way by Stefan Zweig: much as one might like to believe this, the evidence is highly inferential.

Finally, S. Zweig, *Magellan: Pioneer of the Pacific* (London 1938) [*Magellan*] has some romanticism and a good deal of psychological interpretation (of a licit type) but is a work of beauty and power.
25 It is interesting to note that the Egyptian riposte was strongly supported by Venice—D. Lach, *Asia in the Making of Europe* (Chicago 1965), I.106, 112 [*Asia*]; H. V. Livermore, *A History of Portugal* (Cambridge 1947), 233.
26 E.g. F. H. H. Guillemard, *The Life of Ferdinand Magellan* (London 1890), 81–2 [*Life*]; Merriman, *Spanish Empire*, II.420; Medina, *Descubrimiento*, III.xxxv.
27 Visconde de Lagôa, 'Fernão de Magalhães ...', in A. Baião *et al.* (eds.), *História da Expansão Portuguesa no Mundo*' (Lisbon 1937–40), II.305–28 at 313 [*Expansão*].
28 *Asia*, Dec. III, Liv. 5, Caps. vi, vii (Lisbon ed. 1945–6, III.272, 282).
29 Lagôa, in Baião, *Expansão*, II.307. Italian navigators, without their own bases to work from, were in effect professionals out for hire. Some of these mercenaries of the sea were rather disreputable adventurers, such as Solis; but this cannot be said, for example, of Vespucci, Verrazano, the Cabots, Hudson. At the Junta of Badajoz both Portuguese and Castilians refused, nominally at least, to accept as participants their respective defectors, who were plenty—Blair & Robertson, I.176, 216; Albuquerque and Feijo, 'Badajoz', in Actas II at 540.
30 Zweig, *Magellan*, 82–84, takes a sterner view, pointing out that Magellan not only left but 'deliberately harmed his country', but excuses this as the prerogative of creative genius. Lagôa rather grandly compares Magellan to Alcibiades and Coriolanus, and remarks that Brutus is praised for cutting short 'the greatest flight of human glory'; more to the point than this out-dated romantic classicism is his further observation that there was no translation of Pigafetta into Portuguese (until his own of 1938)—*Vida e Viagem*, I.xiii, xvi. For a very full and fair discussion, see A. A. Banha da Andrade, 'Sentimentos de honra e direitos de justiça, na viagem de Fernão de Magalhaes', in Actas II, 451–65.
31 Albuquerque and Feijó, 'Badajoz', in Actas II, at 534–5; Portuguese claims were based rather on their ten years of trading presence in the Moluccas. According to Enciso in his *Suma de Geographia* (1519) the antimeridian of the Tordesillas line was in the Ganges delta; Magellan, in a memorial to the King (also 1519) put it at Malacca, whose position on his reckoning lay in the middle of Borneo; the Moluccas were thus safely in the Spanish hemisphere—R. A. Laguarda Trias, 'Las longitudes

geograficas de la membranza de Magallanes', in Actas II, 135–78. Enciso took a value of 16⅔ leagues to the degree instead of the 17½ of the Portuguese, thus shrinking the Portuguese hemisphere when degrees were turned into leagues; he appears to have falsified diagrams taken from Portuguese sources—E. G. R. Taylor (ed.), [Roger Barlow's] *A Brief Summe of Geographie*, HS 2nd Ser. 69 (London 1932), xiv–xvii.

[32] Lach, *Asia*, I.113–15; Parry, *Reconnaissance*, 173. For the entertaining history of the elephant Hanno, see Lach, *Asia*, II.135–9 (physically the third volume, 1970).

[33] Denucé, *Moluques*, 72–7; Lagôa, *Vida e Viagem*, I.35–7; Nowell, *Voyage*, 24–5; Skelton, *Magellan's Voyage*, I.155.

[34] Nowell, 'Pacific', 8.

[35] Morison, *Southern Voyages*, 321, 351–2.

[36] Parry, *Reconnaissance*, 173; cf. Morison, *Southern Voyages*, 288–97. The name 'America' was not generally accepted by Spaniards until the eighteenth century; they kept to their own term 'Indias'— Morales Padrón, *Historia*, 154–5. There is a brilliant philological analysis of the naming of America in H. Jantz, 'Images of America in the German Renaissance', in Chiappelli, *First Images*, I.91–106 at 97–100: '. . . America was just right, Columbia might have done, but Vespuccia or Christophoria would have been sad absurdities.' One reason why 'America' won out is given by D. B. Quinn, 'New Geographical Horizons: Literature', ibid. 635–58 at 638–47: Vespucci's literary output was larger, better, and more accessible than Columbus's. We need not go into the vexed question of the authenticity of Vespucci's 1497 voyage, denied by Morison and many others; for an amusing review of the matter, see *Southern Voyages*, 306–12.

[37] See L. Wroth, 'The Early Cartography of the Pacific', *Papers Biblio. Soc. of America* 38 No. 2 (New York 1944), 85–268 at 119–40 ['Cartography'].

[38] See i.a. A. P. Newton in *Great Age*, 122–27. R. Levillier in *America la Bien Llamada* (Buenos Aires 1948), takes him down to Golfo San Jorge in 46°S (not seen, but see Levillier's map in Morales Padrón, *Historia*, 141).

[39] For the significance of these voyages see D. Ramos Perez, 'Magallanes en Valladolid: la capitulación', in Actas II, 179–241, at 189–95 ['capitulación']. A. von Humboldt, *Examen Critique de l'Histoire de la Géographie du Nouveau Continent* (Paris 1836), I.348–53, is still of interest.

[40] For the complexities in the interpretation of 'these meagre indications', see J. da Gama Pimental Barata, 'A armada de Fernão de Magalhães', in Actas II, 109–34. At least 50 per cent must be added for modern reckonings. As usual, Morison is excellent on the detail of ships, crews, and equipment —*Southern Voyages*, 342–7, 352–5.

[41] He added that their sides were soft as butter. As Morison remarks (*Southern Voyages*, 357) this was doubtless sour grapes; after her return the battered *Victoria* was repaired and crossed the Atlantic each way before being wrecked in the Caribbean.

[42] Other investors were less lucky: Aranda lost his whole investment, and the Fuggers put in 10,000 ducats and lost the lot, being tartly told by the courts twenty years later that 'the said Antonio Fucar y Ca. shall for ever hold their peace'—Lagôa, *Vida e Viagem*, I.233–6; Guillemard, *Life*, 125–6.

[43] 'Maestre Andrés, lombardero condestable de la dicha nao natural de Bristol que es en elreino de Inglaterra, marido de Ana de Estrada viuda, de Sevilla'—Pastells, *Estrecho*, I.213, 235. The careful computation of L. Diaz-Trechuelo, 'La organización del viaje Magallanico', in Actas II, 265–314, gives a total of 136 Spaniards and 79 assorted Europeans, plus 16 higher officers and 6 Africans or Asians.

[44] On this tangled question of Faleiro and Juan de Cartagena, Lagôa gives a full and balanced discussion—*Vida e Viagem*, I.158, 223–31; but for differing emphases, see Denucé, *Moluques*, 220–1,

and Nowell, *Voyage*, 65–7; cf. Tudela y Bueso, 'La especería', in Actas II at 548 note 48. On Faleiro's isogonal method, see A. Teixeira da Mota, 'A contribução dos irmãos Rui e Francisco Faleiro . . .', in Actas II, 315–41 at 321, 337–9; he attaches much more general importance to the lesser-known Francisco.

⁴⁵ *Vida e Viagem*, I.229. For a similar case of Fonsecan sharp practice in relation to Solis, see Tudela y Bueso, 'La especería, in Actas II at 638.

⁴⁶ Nowell, *Voyage*, 54–5; Perez, 'capitulación', in Actas II, 220–7 (which might tend to support Nunn's view of Magellan's ideas).

⁴⁷ 'The authorities' are divertingly divergent on the precise date of these events. Denucé puts them on Easter Sunday and Monday, 1–2 April; Merriman on Easter Sunday and Monday, 8–9 April; Nowell on Palm Sunday and the next day, with the trial verdict on 7 April. By the Julian calendar, in use until 1582, the dates would be 1–2 April; by the Gregorian, ten days later. Pigafetta and Maximilian, who slur over the whole affair, give no dates at all. It is not of vast moment.

⁴⁸ J. A. Williamson (ed.), *The Observations of Sir Richard Hawkins* (London 1933), 87, 89 (quotations transposed). Williamson draws attention to the appositeness of this observation in his 'The First Circumnavigation', in Newton, *Great Age*, 181–98 at 187–8.

⁴⁹ K. R. Andrews, *Drake's Voyages* (London 1967), 63–8. According to Drake's chaplain Francis Fletcher, who was more than a little of a Malvolio (below, Ch. 9), the cooper made tankards of the timber 'for such of the company who would drink of them, whereof for my own part, I had no great liking'—J. Hampden (ed.), *Francis Drake Privateer* (London 1972), 150.

⁵⁰ Zweig, *Magellan*, 203–4.

⁵¹ G. E. Nunn's views are set out in *The Columbus and Magellan Concepts of South American Geography* (Glenside 1932), and 'Magellan's Route in the Pacific', *Geogr. Rev.* 24, 1934, 625–33; Nowell's in *Voyage*, 28–9—see the Behaim-style map at 29, from which my quotation about the Strait is drawn. It seems unlikely that Magellan was so much behind the times, and as regards Behaim and the Pacific track the Nunn-Nowell thesis has received little acceptance, and perhaps less careful consideration than it warrants; Morales Padrón, however, accepts both Nunn's track and Behaim's influence—*Historia*, 193, 200. Lagôa (*Vida e Viagem*, I.48–53) argues, to my mind convincingly, against Behaim's significance, in general and in this case; cf. also Wroth, 'Cartography', 143–5, and E. A. Heawood, 'The World Map before and after Magellan', *Geogr. Jnl* 57, 1921, 431–46 ['World Map']. On Behaim's doubtful standing as a cosmographer, see G. R. Crone, 'Martin Behaim . . .', and H. Winter, 'New Light on the Behaim Problem', in Actas do Congreso Internacional de História dos Descobrimentos (Lisbon 1961), II.117–33 and 399–411; both devalue him. On Schöner, G. Schilder, *Australia Unveiled: the share of the Dutch navigators in the discovery of Australia* (Canberra 1976), 10.

⁵² Gomes may have called at Puerto San Julian to look for Juan de Cartagena; in the normal manner of deserters, on his return to Spain he spread the most prejudicial stories about Magellan. He may also have sighted the Falklands long before Richard Hawkins or Sebald de Weerdt (1594, 1598): various Argentinian references are summarised in E. J. Goodman, *The Explorers of South America* (New York 1972), 160–4. The loyal Alvaro de Mesquita, arrested first by the mutineers at San Julian and then by Gomes, was imprisoned until after the return of the *Victoria*.

⁵³ Translations from the French text in Skelton, *Magellan's Voyage*. Cabo Deseado is the only place where Pigafetta tells us that Magellan *himself* bestowed a name.

⁵⁴ Tudela y Bueso argues plausibly that Albo's rutter is really del Cano's—Actas II at 656. For criticism of Nunn see D. D. Brand, 'Geographical Exploration by the Spaniards', in Friis, *Pacific Basin*, 109–44 at 115, and especially Appendix I in H. Wallis, The Exploration of the South Sea, 1519 to 1644 (Oxford D.Phil thesis 1953–4); she points out that Nunn overlooks the evidence of

Magellan's own memorial. H. E. Maude also criticises Nunn, and in a closely reasoned analysis identifies San Pablo as Pukapuka and Tiburones very firmly as Flint—*Of Islands and Men* (Melbourne 1968), 38–48.

55 Details of events from the sighting of Samar onwards are from Pigafetta's moving and vivid narrative; Morison, *Southern Voyages*, 417–32, is detailed and perhaps a little too colourful.

56 He is variously alleged to have been poisoned by the Rajah of Tidore, in revenge for his successful leadership of Ternatean forces, or by a Malay woman at Portuguese behest, or to have died on a Portuguese ship en route to Goa.

57 I. A. Wright, Early Spanish Voyages to the Far East, 1527–1565 (Univ. of California P.D. thesis 1940), 99.

58 There is a good biography by M. Mitchell, *Elcano: The First Circumnavigator* (London 1968).

59 A. Sharp gives good reasons for equating these islands with the Maug group and Agrigan (Asuncion) in the Marianas and Sonsorol in the Carolines; this last would have been the first European sighting in the group—*The Discovery of the Pacific Islands* (Oxford 1960), 8–11.

60 The almost intolerable complexities of both the Portuguese and the Castilian stances at Badajoz are analysed by Tudela y Bueso, 'La especería', in Actas II at 664–73. See also Albuquerque and Feijó, 'Badajoz', ibid.; Blair & Robertson, I.195–221; Denucé, *Moluques*, 393, 399–401; C. W. Nowell, 'The Loiasa Expedition and the Ownership of the Moluccas', *Pac. Hist. Rev.* 5, 1936, 325–36. It passes understanding that Morison, apparently quite seriously, can call the negotiations 'a sincere attempt' at a settlement—*Southern Voyages*, 476.

61 Cf. Heawood, 'World Map' at 437, 440; reckoning from Santo Antão, the most westerly of the Cape Verdes and hence the most favourable to Spanish claims. Cf. note 31 above. Other reckonings put the antimeridian between 131°18' and 133°21'E—Abadía, 'antimeridiano', in Actas II at 22–5.

62 Denucé, *Moluques*, 401. As late as 1575 Lopez de Velasco's MS. maps still show the demarcation line through the tip of Malaya—Wroth, 'Cartography', 159.

63 In 1519 Davila and Niño were sent from Spain 'to take over Balboa's ships, or build new ones, and explore the South Seas for a thousand leagues, in the hope of finding the Spice Islands. They did not get very far. Some years were to elapse before the little bush harbors of the Pacific could build ships reliable enough for long ocean passages.'—J. H. Parry, *The European Reconnaissance* (New York 1968), 236. Cf. Tudela y Bueso, 'La especería', in Actas II, 649 note 50.

64 Parry, *The European Reconnaissance*, 238.

Notes for Chapter 3

1 Bernal Diaz del Castillo, *The Conquest of New Spain*, trans. J. M. Cohen (Harmondsworth 1963), 214.

2 The Third Letter of Cortes, trans. F. A. McNutt, in P. de Fuentes, *The Conquistadores* (New York 1963), 49–133, at 123.

3 F. Morales Padrón, *Historia del Descubrimiento y Conquista de América* (2nd ed., Madrid 1971), 229 [*Historia*]. He says what can be said for Pedrarias—387, 395.

4 For this tangle of geography and intrigue, see J. Mirsky, *The Westwards Crossings* (Chicago 1970), 70–81; K. Romoli, *Balboa of Darién* (New York 1953), Chs. XX–XXI; C. O. Sauer, *The Early Spanish Main* (Berkeley 1966), Chs. XIII–XV [*Spanish Main*].

5 Sauer, *Spanish Main*, 220–9.

[6] On the locational factors involved in the decline of Darien and the rise of Panama, see Sauer, *Spanish Main*, 278–81, and Chaunu, 898–9, 906–8, 915–16, 941–5. By this time the old division of jurisdiction between Veragua and Darien had been overtaken by events and Pedrarias had a free hand, the claims of Columbus's heirs being bought off, twenty years later, by the grant of a somewhat titular Dukedom of Veragua, amongst whose holders was the son of the Duke of Berwick, bastard of our James II and VII—P. Pastells SJ, *El Descubrimiento del Estrecho* (Madrid 1920), table of Columbus's descendants; cf. Sauer, 264–5. For Old Panama city itself, cf. C. H. Haring, *Trade and Navigation between Spain and the Indies* (Cambridge (Mass.)), 185–8 [*Trade and Navigation*].

[7] W. Dampier, *A New Voyage Round the World* (1697; Dover ed., New York 1968), 124–6.

[8] For an elaboration of this argument, see O. H. K. Spate, 'How Determined is Possibilism?', *Geogr. Studies* (Leicester) 4, 1957, 3–12.

[9] G. Mack, *The Land Divided* (New York 1944), 31–3. For the Desaguadero, M. J. MacLeod, *Spanish Central America: A Socioeconomic History, 1520–1720* (Berkeley 1973), 155 [*Central America*].

[10] For these marches between Panama and Guatemala, see Morales Padrón, *Historia*, 389–98 and map at 399. MacLeod, *Central America*, 38–45, gives a good analysis of the Conquista in this fragmented region, a much messier process than the conquest of Mexico.

[11] See the elaborate calculations in W. Borah and S. F. Cooke, *The Aboriginal Population of Central Mexico on the Eve of the Spanish Conquest* (Berkeley 1963), especially Ch. VI, and their article 'La Despoblación del México Central en el siglo XVI', *Hist. Mexicana* 12, 1962–3, 1–12. The matter is discussed in more detail in Ch. 7 below.

[12] This is the Spanish and generally received story. For the Indian version that Montezuma was in fact killed by the Spaniards themselves, see Hernán Cortés, *Letters from Mexico*, trans. A. R. Pagden (London 1972), note 89 at 477 [Cortés, *Letters*].

[13] Apart from the old standard and very detailed narratives of W. H. Prescott, *History of the Conquest of Mexico* (New York 1843, numerous eds.) and H. H. Bancroft, *History of Mexico* (San Francisco 1883–6), accounts by participants are readily available in Bernal Diaz, *The Conquest of New Spain*, and de Fuentes, *The Conquistadores* (contains six reports as well as Cortes's Third Letter). Most of F. L. de Gomara's *Istoria de la Conquista de Mexico* (Zaragoza 1552) is translated by L. B. Simpson in *Cortés: The Life of the Conqueror by His Secretary* (Berkeley 1965) [Gomara, *Cortés*]. All of these have been used, for background if not for direct reference.

[14] Gomara, *Cortés*, 277–8. It is pleasant to record that the Tlaxcalans long retained the privileges, in some respects amounting to autonomy, awarded them for their indispensable support; some rights persisted to the end of Spanish rule—S. de Madariaga, *The Rise of the Spanish American Empire* (London 1947), 25 [*The Rise*].

[15] See G. C. Vaillant, *The Aztecs of Mexico* (Harmondsworth 1950), 199–200, 205–15, 229–54, for a sympathetic account of 'the death-throes of the Aztec nation', including remarks on the nature of Aztec warfare, the portents, and Montezuma's position; and the very thoughtful analysis in Chaunu, 150–5—though it is a little odd to find asserted a general European superiority, including the moral and spiritual (151), and on the next page a realistic comment on the 'incomparable bestiality' of Pizarro's men in their 'sinister enterprise'. But the Conquista, and Spanish rule in the Indies, are riddled with such human contradictions. For the portents again, see the very interesting study by N. Wachtel, *La Vision des Vaincus: Les Indiens du Pérou devant la Conquête espagnole* (Paris 1971), 36–8 [*Vaincus*].

[16] Cortés, *Letters*, 266–8, 270, 275–7, 318.

[17] Cortés, *Letters*, 326–8.

[18] D. D. Brand, 'The Development of Pacific Coast Ports during the Spanish Colonial Period in Mexico', in *Estudios Antropológicos . . . en homenaje al doctor Manual Gamio* (Mexico 1956), 577–91,

at 579 ['Coast Ports']; this is a main source for my Figure 6.

[19] C. R. Markham (ed.), *Early Spanish Voyages to the Straits of Magellan*, HS 2nd Ser. 28 (London 1911), 102–8.

[20] The first four chapters of W. Borah, *Early Trade and Navigation between Mexico and Peru* (Berkeley 1954) [*Early Trade*], are crammed with fascinating material on the shipping and commerce of the coast; a main source for this section. Cf. the analysis of ports and trade in Chaunu, 788–98, 826–32, 858–89. See also M. L. Moorhead, 'Hernán Cortés and the Tehuantepec Passage', *HAHR* 29, 1949, 370–9, and for Guatulco, Hakluyt, VIII.231–2.

[21] Brand, 'Coast Ports', lists fifty-three; to the obscurity of chronology must be added that of toponymy—he gives sixteen variants for Manzanillo, and for Sentispac he just gives up—'a wonderful variety of spellings'. There are maps of Acapulco and Guatulco in P. Gerhard, *Pirates on the West Coast of New Spain 1575–1742* (Glendale 1960) [*Pirates*], and further details in his *A Guide to the Historical Geography of New Spain* (Berkeley 1972), 39–42, 123–6, 264–7, 393–7.

[22] For early and later Acapulco, T. Oteiza Iriarte, *Acapulco: La Ciudad de las Naos de Oriente y de las Sirenas Modernas* ([n.p.] 1963)—somewhat popular and rhetorical, but not so much as the title suggests.

[23] Borah, *Early Trade*, 5, 65–8; cf. Haring, *Trade and Navigation*, 267, and a mass of detail in P. S. Taylor, 'Spanish Seamen in the New World during the Colonial Period', *HAHR* 5, 631–61. For Realejo itself, D. R. Radell and J. J. Parsons, 'Realejo: A Forgotten Colonial Port . . .', ibid. 31, 1971, 295–312 (with map), and for slaving. MacLeod, *Central America*, 51–6.

[24] Bancroft, *History of Mexico*, II.31–2; Prescott, *Conquest of Mexico*, Book VII Ch. II.

[25] J. Juan and A. de Ulloa, *Noticias Secretas de América* (London 1826), 114–28 (for the authenticity of this work, see below, Ch. 7 note 35). There is a handsome tribute to the Manila yards in D. R. Perez, *Historia de la Colonización Española en América* (Madrid 1947), 244 [*Colonización*].

[26] See the vivid description of worm damage from Oviedo's *Historia general y natural de las Indias* (1535–7) cited in Chaunu, 940; for the lead on Pedrarias's ships, Haring, *Trade and Navigation*, 277, and in general D. W. Waters, *The Art of Navigation in England in Elizabethan and Early Stuart Times* (London 1958), 92.

[27] Gomara, *Cortés*, 391 and Simpson's note; cf. F. Chevalier, *Land and Society in Colonial Mexico* (Berkeley 1963), 127–30 [*Land and Society*].

[28] They were used i.a. by Cavendish, Swan, Grogniet's deserters in 1686, Dampier, and Shelvocke —see Gerhard, *Pirates, passim*; R. Bonnycastle, *Spanish America* (London 1819), 153; and especially Woodes Rogers, *A Cruising Voyage Round the World* (1712; reprinted Amsterdam, 1969), 275–8.

[29] The standard modern treatments in English are by H. R. Wagner, *Spanish Voyages to the Northwest Coast of America in the Sixteenth Century* (Amsterdam 1966; original ed. 1929) [*Voyages to NW*] and *Cartography of the Northwest Coast of America to the Year 1800* (Berkeley 1937); see also M. G. Holmes, *From New Spain by Sea to the Californias 1519–1668* (Glendale 1963); briefer accounts in C. E. Chapman, *A History of California: The Spanish Period* (New York 1921), 43–54 [*California*]; S. E. Morison, *The European Discovery of America: The Southern Voyages A.D. 1492–1616* (New York 1974), 617–33; Gomara, *Cortés*, 396–402—vivid if confused. A. del Portillo y Diez de Sollano, *Descubrimientos y Exploraciones en las Costas de California* (Madrid 1947), gives little detail for the sixteenth century and astonishingly does not cite Wagner; he writes down Cabrillo in favour of Vizcaino, which may be just tenable, but writes up Pedro Porter y Casanate, which surprises.

For the 'insularity' of California, see R. V. Tooley, *California as an Island* (London 1964), and J. L. Leighley, *California as an Island* (San Francisco 1972), both richly mapped. On the name 'California', Chapman, *California*, 55–9 (with many references) and Portillo, 109–37; the latter thinks that the name was given in derision, which understandably causes some local heat. There are still some discrepancies and dubieties—e.g. the fate of Ulloa—but these are not material.

[30] See Wagner, *Voyages to NW*, 72–93 (with translation of the major contemporary account). I have not seen H. E. Bolton, *Spanish Exploration in the Southwest, 1542–1706* (New York 1916).

[31] C. Pisano y Saucedo, 'El Puerto de Navidad y la Expedición de Legaspi', *Hist. Mexicana* 14, 1964–5, 227–49—with a photograph of the tiny modern village.

[32] R. F. Heizer, *California's Oldest Historical Relic?* (Berkeley 1972).

[33] Borah, *Early Trade*, 8–21; Chevalier, *Land and Society*, 27–9; cf. P. Chaunu, *Conquête et Exploitation des Nouveaux Mondes* (Paris 1969), 158–64 [*Conquête*].

[34] J. Hemming, *The Conquest of the Incas* (Abacus ed., London 1972), 25 [*Incas*]; V. W. von Hagen, *The Desert Kingdoms of Peru* (Mentor ed., New York 1968), 131–6 [*Kingdoms*]. Hemming's richly detailed account is strongly sympathetic to the Indians; W. H. Prescott, *History of the Conquest of Peru* (New York 1847; numerous eds.), remains a standard narrative óf the in-fighting. For the 'feel' of time and place, as distinct from strict fact, there is nothing to match the 1500 or so pages of Garcilaso de la Vega, El Inca, *Royal Commentaries of the Incas and General History of Peru* (1609, 1616), trans. H. V. Livermore (Austin 1966) [*Commentaries*]—a wonderful book.

[35] Borah, *Early Trade*, 3; F. A. Kirkpatrick, *The Spanish Conquistadores* (London 1934), 146–7 [*Conquistadores*]—perhaps the most handy *short* account; for meticulous detail, see R. C. Murphy, 'The Earliest Spanish Advances Southwards from Panama . . .', *HAHR* 21, 1941, 2–28, with an excellent map. It is probable that before Pizarro arrived in Inca territory it had already been reached by a European, overland from Brazil—C. E. Nowell, 'Aleixo Garcia and the White King', ibid. 26, 1946, 450–66.

[36] T. Heyerdahl, *American Indians in the Pacific* (London 1952), 517–19; von Hagen provides cogent arguments to demolish Heyerdahl's structure of inference—*Kingdoms*, 135–7, 176. The raft's cargo is described in Hemming, *Incas*, 25.

[37] Kirkpatrick, *Conquistadores*, 149; J. Lockhart, *Spanish Peru 1532–1560* (Madison 1968), 234 [*Peru*].

[38] For a clear and brief but authoritative account of the Inca polity, A. Métraux, *The Incas* (London 1965). Métraux provides a balanced but incisive criticism of the anachronistic view of the Empire as a socialist welfare state; see especially 'The Organisation of the Empire', 87–115, and cf. J. A. Mason, *The Ancient Civilizations of Peru* (Harmondsworth 1957), 176–9. See also Part I, 'Le Traumatisme de la Conquête' of Wachtel, *Vaincus*.

[39] Métraux, *The Incas*, 111–14.

[40] Examples in Hemming, *Incas*, 139–40, 156. Pizarro may also have been favoured by an unusually wet 'El Niño' year (see below, Ch. 5) with a consequent unusual flourishing of pasture—personal information from Prof. C. N. Caviedes, University of Regina.

[41] Chaunu, 150–5. He credits the Incas with 'perhaps a better sense of economic statistics' than any other régime of their time, Europe included, thanks to the quipus, which are rather bizarrely described as the 'electronic calculators of a civilisation which practised trepanning with obsidian scalpels'; but he points out (*Conquête*, 163) that the key to their cipher is lost. What would historians make of our civilisation if the surviving documents were computer printouts?

[42] Morales Padrón, *Historia*, 418–22, 434–6, gives Atahualpa's threats and defends Pizarro from the blackest charges; his brothers were worse than he. He also points out (267), on the testimony of Pizarro's brother Pedro, that while waiting for Atahualpa's masses 'many Spaniards . . . urinated from sheer fright', and thinks that the tension of terror must account for much of the slaughter.

[43] Wachtel, *Vaincus*, 60–1.

[44] Acceptance, from geography books, of the great temperature anomaly caused by the Humboldt Current had hardly prepared me for wood fires, not exactly necessary but very gratifying, at

lunchtime in October—only 12° from the Equator and not much above sea-level.

[45] Métraux, *The Incas*, 173–5. Apart from the very full and vivid treatment in Hemming, *Incas* (see 459–73 for the tangled history of Manco's kin), a few pages (166–76) in Chaunu, *Conquête*, give a penetrating analysis of the Inca resistance, the civil wars, and the Chilean venture. For a legalistic defence of the Viceroy's action, see R. Levillier, *Don Francisco de Toledo: Supremo Organizador del Perú* (Madrid 1935), I.279–356: his line is that Tupac Amaru was responsible for the slaying of envoys (this is highly doubtful) but that even so all would have been well had he tamely surrendered; as it was, he was justly executed as taken in flagrant armed resistance to the Crown—to which, on Levillier's own showing (347, 355) he had never pledged obedience. Toledo's mistake was only the 'excessive theatricality' of the actual execution, which gave both occasion and opportunity for the expression of nativist resentment.

[46] S. Zavala, *El Mundo Americano en la Epoca Colonial* (Mexico 1967), I.15; J. Basadre, *Chile Perú y Bolivia Independientes* (Barcelona 1948), 477. Naval operations from Garcilaso, *Commentaries*, II.980–1129 *passim*, especially 1043–9, 1057, 1093.

[47] Lockhart, *Peru*, 16, 54; the succeeding figures are from this admirable study at 136–7, 150, 152.

[48] R. P. Barrenechea, 'Lima: el río, el puente y la alameda', *Estudos Americanos* 22, 1961, 1–37 at 15, and 'El Callao en la historia peruana', *Rev. Histórica* (Lima) 22, 1958–9, 255–65 at 257; J. Bromley, 'El Callao. Puerto de Lima', ibid. 26, 1962–3, 7–76 at 8.

[49] Chaunu, 1100; who adds 'La sanction . . . est bénigne'.

[50] L. Galdames, *A History of Chile*, trans. I. J. Cox (Chapel Hill 1941), 26–39, and for the later *conquista* 37–60. There is a useful map in F. A. Encina, *Resumen de la Historia de Chile* (4th ed., Santiago 1961), I.47.

[51] Lockhart, *Peru*, 43, 143–5; Chaunu, 135–42.

[52] Morales Padrón, *Historia*, 486.

[53] Chaunu, 141–2. Once he breaks away from his statistics, Chaunu is always brilliant and stimulating, but sometimes carried away by epigram or lyricism, and on this matter Wachtel, *Vaincus*, 289–95, is perhaps more to the point. For Osorno, G. Guarda, *La ciudad chilena del siglo XVIII* (Buenos Aires 1968), 52–4.

[54] Madariaga, *The Rise*, 39, where it is made the occasion for an unflattering comparison with uncultured Anglo-America. However, those who begin comparisons should finish them: if we take date of settlement, not just Anno Domini, the picture is very different. On Madariaga's own figures, the lag between settlement and printing ranges from 20 years (New Spain) to 271 (Chile) in Spanish America, 5 (Pennsylvania) to 122 (Virginia) in Anglo-America. Actually the first press in Chile was probably in 1776, not 1812, but this still leaves a lag of 235 years—C. H. Haring, *The Spanish Empire in America* (New York 1963, original ed. 1947), 230 [*Spanish Empire*].

[55] F. C. Lane, 'Force and Enterprise in Oceanic Commerce', in *Venice and History* (Baltimore 1966), 399–411, at 401.

[56] Chaunu, 130–4, 138, 144–55, and *Conquête,* 135–9; cf. A. Jara's Introduction ('Ocupación, pobliamento y frontera') to *Tierras Nuevas* (Mexico 1969), 1–10, at 3–6.

[57] J. H. Parry, *The Spanish Seaborne Empire* (Harmondsworth 1973), 82 [*Seaborne Empire*]; Haring, *Spanish Empire*, 19, 25, 33–7. A fuller account of the organisation and armament of the entrada is given in Morales Padrón's splendid section 'Las huestes indianas', *Historia*, 216–25; and cf. M. Góngora, *Studies in the Colonial History of Spanish America* (Cambridge 1975), 7–8 [*Studies*].

[58] Morales Padrón, *Historia*, 476–82 ('Los amazonautos'); *The Expedition of Pedro de Ursua and Lope de Aguirre . . .*, HS 1st Ser. 28 (London 1861).

[59] Haring, *Spanish Empire*, 40, and cf. his whole Ch. III; Parry, *Seaborne Empire*, 82–6 and Ch. 9; and L. B. Simpson, *The Encomienda in New Spain* (2nd ed., Berkeley 1950), especially xi–xii, 132–8,

154–8. The literature of the *encomienda* is large and technical, but the principles will be found in almost any substantial general work on colonial Spanish America.

I am conscious that my whole discussion of the Conquista, as of much else, is of necessity too brief to avoid over-simplification. For a modern Spanish 'revisionist' view, which is long on jurisprudence and administration but seems short on the facts of life, see Perez, *Colonización*.

[60] C. Churchill, *Gotham* (London 1764), I.11–12; the opening pages of this poem are a fine sardonic comment on the theme of this section.

[61] L. Hanke, *The Spanish Struggle for Justice in the Conquest of America* (Philadelphia 1949), 32–6 [*Justice*].

[62] M. Gonzáles Prada, cited in J. H. Rowe, 'The Incas under Spanish Colonial Institutions', *HAHR* 37, 1957, 155–91, at 191—a dispassionate but devastating analysis of the working of the system. For a superb example, see Solorzano Pereira's conscientious and meticulous analysis (1630) on the employment of *mitayos*, the forced labourers of Huancavelica: experience 'made him rein in [*frenar*] his impulses of humanitarian dialectic'—G. Lohmann Villena, *Las Minas de Huancavelica* (Seville 1949), 270–83. See also Góngora, *Studies*, 145–7.

[63] 'Succeeding Times did equal Folly call/Believing nothing, or believing all'—J. Dryden, *Absalom and Achitophel* (London 1681), lines 118–19.

[64] R. Menéndez Pidal, *El Padre Las Casas. Su doble personalidad* (Madrid 1963), cited in L. Hanke, 'More Heat and Some Light . . .', *HAHR* 44, 1964, 293–340; admittedly Pidal was 90 when he wrote this. One may also find rather odd Kirkpatrick's reason (*Conquistadores*, x) for not citing Las Casas (whom it was not really necessary to cite)—simply that his testimony 'is suspect to some Spaniards'! On this principle, very few actors in history could ever be cited: Trotsky on the Russian Revolution, for example or Clarendon on the English 'would be suspect to some . . .'. The legend certainly needs some toning down, but not so much as it is given in, for example, B. W. Diffie, *Latin American Civilization: Colonial Period* (Harrisburg 1945), *passim*, where it becomes positively gilded [*Colonial Period*]. There is an admirable selection of source extracts, from Las Casas to Menéndez Pidal, in C. Gibson (ed.), *The Black Legend* (New York 1971).

[65] For example, Pedro de Alvarado on himself and Garcia del Pilar on Nuño de Guzman in de Fuentes, *The Conquistadores*, 187, 199–208.

[66] It is impossible here to go into the detail of this fascinating episode in the history of ideas; see i.a. Hanke, *Justice, passim*; Parry, *Seaborne Empire*, 126–39; Morales Padrón, *Historia*, 212–16; and especially J. H. Parry, 'A Secular Sense of Responsibility', and E. Grisel, 'The Beginnings of International Law . . . Vitoria's *De Indiis prior*', 287–304 and 305–26 in F. Chiappelli (ed.), *First Images of America* (Berkeley 1976) [*First Images*]. It is ironic that Las Casas and his chief intellectual opponent Sepulveda debated the issue face to face, but that the latter was not permitted to publish his reply *Democritus Alter*. Many facets of this human problem are brought out in the controversy, amusing were not its theme so deeply tragic, between Hanke and Benjamin Keen in *HAHR* 49, 1969, 703–19, and 51, 1971, 112–28 and 336–55.

[67] Chaunu, *Conquête*, 136; cf. A. W. Crosby, 'Conquistador y Pestilencia: The First New World Pandemic and the Fall of the Great Indian Kingdoms', *HAHR* 47, 1967, 321–37.

[68] J. H. Parry, *The Age of Reconnaissance* (Mentor ed., New York 1964), 192–3.

[69] Lockhart, *Peru*, 61–2, 68–9; Góngora, *Studies*, 27–9.

[70] Haring, *Spanish Empire*, 101–5. Once again, the outlines will be found in any substantial history of Latin America. For the earliest phases of territorial organisation, see C. W. Hackett, 'The Delimitation of Political Jurisdiction in Spanish North America to 1535', *HAHR* 1, 1918, 40–69, and for the development and working of the machinery, B. Moses, *The Establishment of Spanish Rule in America* (New York 1965, original ed. 1898).

⁷¹ B. Moses, *Spain's Declining Power in South America 1730–1806* (Berkeley 1919), 46–9.

⁷² Moses, *Spain's Declining Power*, xviii–xix.

⁷³ D. M. Dozer, *Latin America: An Interpretative History* (New York 1962), 102 [*Latin America*].

⁷⁴ These changes can be followed in outline in *The New Cambridge Modern History: XIV. Atlas* (1970), plates at 229, 230, 235, 236.

⁷⁵ A. S. Aiton, 'Conquest and Settlement . . .', and R. D. Hussey, 'Colonial Economic Life', in A. C. Wilgus (ed.), *Colonial Hispanic America* (Washington 1936), 148–65 and 305–32.

⁷⁶ For town planning, Z. Nuttall, 'Royal Ordinances concerning the Laying Out of New Towns', *HAHR* 4, 1921, 743–53—including such sensible provisions as broad streets in cold climates but narrow ones in hot, with the rider that for 'defense, where horses are to be had, they are better wide.' Cf. D. Stanislawski, 'Early Spanish Town Planning in the New World', *Geogr. Rev.* 37, 1947, 94–105, and Dozer, *Latin America*, 148–51.

⁷⁷ Haring, *Spanish Empire*, 189–90.

⁷⁸ See the astonishing figures for book imports, and Bolivar's early reading, in Haring, *Spanish Empire*, 225–8. There is a full treatment in I. A. Leonard's delightful and instructive *Books of the Brave* (2nd ed., New York 1964), where we find (301–12) that within three years of his first appearance in print Don Quixote was the central figure of a hilarious skit presented in the Peruvian Sierra at the remote mining camp at Pausa, which had twelve Spanish families. Madariaga (*The Rise, passim*) perhaps takes a euphoric view of the *general* level of culture, but many of his details are striking; cf. Diffie, *Colonial Period*, 502–7, 545–6. Sor Juana Ines de la Cruz, the first notable Mexican poet (1648–95), had a library of 4000 volumes—A. Flores (ed.), *An Anthology of Spanish Poetry* (Garden City (New York) 1961), 145.

⁷⁹ D. Ramos, *Mineria y Comercio Interprovincial en Hispanoamerica* (Valladolid, n.d.), 117–18 [*Mineria*].

⁸⁰ Borah, *Early Trade*, 126–7, and below, Ch. 8.

⁸¹ Perez, *Colonización*, 207–8.

⁸² Haring, *Spanish Empire*, 297–300. For the Casa's geographical work, its successes and limitations, see the excellent essay by Ursula Lamb, 'Cosmographers of Seville: Nautical Science and Social Experience', in Chiappelli, *First Images*, II.675–86.

⁸³ Ramos, *Mineria*, 115.

⁸⁴ A. von Humboldt, *Cosmos* (Bohn ed., London 1864), II.649.

Notes for Chapter 4

¹ Setting aside the doubtful tales of Fernão Mendes Pinto, the deepest inland penetrations before 1555 were probably Tomé Pires's embassy to Peking (1517) and Galeote Pereira's journey, as a captive, from Foochow to Kueilin in Kuangsi (1549–50)—C. R. Boxer (ed.), *South China in the Sixteenth Century*, HS 2nd Ser. 106 (London 1953), li–liv.

² For the importance of Malacca, see M. A. P. Meilink-Roelofsz, *Asian Trade and European Influence in the Indonesian Archipelago between 1500 and about 1630* (The Hague 1962), *passim*—a richly detailed and documented study [*Asian Trade*]; and P. Wheatley, *The Golden Khersonese* (Kuala Lumpur 1961), 306–25, particularly good on site-values; and especially L. F. F. R. Thomaz, 'Maluco e Malaca', in A. Teixeira de Mota (ed.), *A Viagem de Fernão de Magalhães e a Questão das Molucas*, Actas do II Coloquio Luso-Espanhol da História Ultramarina (Lisbon 1975), 29–48. References to papers in this volume are given as 'in Actas, II'.

[3] D. Lach, *Asia in the Making of Europe* (Chicago 1965), I.732 [*Asia*]; for Cheng Ho, see below, Ch. 6.

[4] Meilink-Roelofsz, *Asian Trade*, 87–8; for the 'Gores', A. Kobatu and M. Matsuda, *Ryukyuan Relations with Korea and South Sea Countries* (Kyoto 1969), 126–9, and A. Cortesão's note in *The Suma Oriental of Tomé Pires*, HS 2nd Ser. 89–90 (London 1944), I.128 [*Suma*]. Boxer thought that the Gores were Japanese, Denucé that they were Koreans. No doubt the seafaring men of the region, especially the quasi-piratical (no small contingent), were as cosmopolitan as the Caribbean buccaneers.

[5] Pires, *Suma*, II.269–70; Meilink-Roelofsz, *Asian Trade*, 76.

[6] Pires, *Suma*, II.287; Meilink-Roelofsz, *Asian Trade*, 132–5; Lach, *Asia*, I.128–30.

[7] Pires, *Suma*, I.219–20.

[8] Lach, *Asia*, I.608; see his whole section, 592–623, on the 'Spiceries'; and Thomaz, 'Maluco e Malaca'; in Actas II at 30–4.

[9] R. B. Merriman, *The Rise of the Spanish Empire* (New York 1962, original ed. 1918), III.445–7 [*Spanish Empire*].

[10] For the Casa at Corunna, F. de Solano, 'Navios y mercaderes en la ruta occidental de las especies (1519–1563)', in Actas II, 579–610 at 583–9.

[11] I. A. Wright, Early American Voyages to the Far East, 1527 (Univ. of California Ph.D. thesis 1940), 199 [*American Voyages*]; Meilink-Roelofsz, *Asian Trade*, 158. For the voyage itself: Urdaneta's account in C. R. Markham (ed. and trans.), *Early Spanish Voyages to the Straits of Magellan*, HS 2nd Ser. 28 (London 1911), 41–89 [*Early Voyages*]; C. E. Nowell, 'The Loiasa Expedition and the Ownership of the Moluccas', *Pac. Hist. Rev.* 5, 1936, 325–36 ['Loiasa']; and H. M. Wallis, The Exploration of the South Sea, 1519 to 1644 (Oxford D.Phil thesis 1953–4), 92–117 [*Exploration*]. The first two are markedly pro-Spanish, and Markham not always accurate in detail; Helen Wallis's thesis, unfortunately unpublished, is probably the best analysis of early European voyaging in the Pacific, especially in relation to winds and currents. S. E. Morison, *The European Discovery of America: The Southern Voyages A.D. 1492–1616* (New York 1974), 477–92, gives details of the ships [*Southern Voyages*].

[12] R. A. Langdon, *The Lost Caravel* (Sydney 1974), 12–23, 43–6 [*Caravel*].

[13] Markham, *Early Voyages*, 31, 33, 34.

[14] This little Moluccan war can be unravelled, with patience and from opposite points of view, in Urdaneta's account (Markham, *Early Voyages*, 55–76) and J. de Barros, *Asia*, Dec. IV Liv. 1 Caps xiv–xvii and Liv. 2 Cap. xviii (Lisbon ed. 1945–6, IV.50–65 and 116–19). For the economic background of this literally cut-throat competition, Meilink-Roelofsz, *Asian Trade*, 154–9, and the excellent analysis in V. M. Godinho, *L'Économie de l'Empire Portugais aux XVᵉ et XVIIᵉ siècles* (Paris 1969), 787–94, 812–20 [*Économie*]. There is a clear and concise narrative in N. P. Cushner SJ, *Spain in the Philippines* (Quezon City 1971), 21–9 [*Spain*].

[15] On Portuguese evidence, Meneses was a sadist: see Castanheda's appalling account of his atrocities in Barros, *Asia*, IV.3.xx (Lisbon ed. 1945–6: IV.120–3). It is fair to add that the next Governor sent him to India in disgrace, and he died an exile in Brazil (ibid. IV.6.xx (IV.352–3)).

[16] Wright, *American Voyages*, 155–6, and her paper 'Early Spanish Voyages from America to the Far East, 1527–1565', in A. Ogden and E. Sluiter (eds.), *Greater America* (Berkeley 1945), 59–78, at 63. ['Spanish Voyages']. Wright has also a detailed account in 'The First American Voyage across the Pacific, 1527–28', *Geogr Rev.* 29, 1939, 472–87 ['First Voyage']; see also Wallis, Exploration, 117–33. The narrative of Vicente de Napoles is in Markham, *Early Voyages*, 109–34. Sebastian Cabot's expedition to La Plata in 1526–30 was originally intended for the Moluccas, 'Tarshish and

Ophir', and Cortes expected Saavedra to link up with him—Morison, *Southern Voyages*, 537–8, 559.

[17] Identified as Utirik, Taka, Rongelap, and Ailinganae; the latter pair were named Los Reyes for the Three Kings of the Epiphany, being found on that day (6 January); the people declined or soon broke off contact. It is just possible that the lost ships reached Japanese waters—A. Sharp, *The Discovery of the Pacific Islands* (Oxford 1960), 17–18, 22–3 [*Discovery*]. Wright's identification of Los Reyes with the Palaus ('First Voyage', 477) is improbable.

[18] For contemporary views on the atmospheric circulation, see Wallis, Exploration, 14–26.

[19] Ibid., 122, 126, 163–7.

[20] Ibid., 168; cf. 169–75 for an analysis of the two return attempts, and Sharp, *Discovery*, 19–23 for the islands seen. The route of the second voyage in Wright's map ('First Voyage') seems erroneous.

[21] Markham, *Early Voyages*, 131.

[22] Merriman, *Spanish Empire*, III.452–3; Wright, American Voyages, 197–8; J. P. de Tudela y Bueso, 'La especeria de Castilla . . .', in Actas II, 627–87 at 676, 683–7. For the possible bearing of the new line on the question of Portuguese priority in Australia, see O. H. K. Spate, 'Terra Australis —Cognita?', *Hist. Studies* (Melbourne) 8, 1957, 1–19 at 14 ['Terra Australis'].

[23] Nowell, 'Loiasa' at 335.

[24] Godinho, who stresses the difficulty of the Goa-Moluccas voyage and the feebleness of Malacca as an intermediate base, yet implicitly concedes that the Spanish logistic position was worse; he gives an appalling picture of Portuguese internal feuds and corruption—*Économie*, 792–4.

[25] W. L. Schurz, *The Manila Galleon* (Dutton ed. New York 1959, original ed. 1939), 19–20 [*Galleon*].

[26] Markham, *Early Voyages*, 135–56, 161–8; C. F. Duro, *La Armada Española desde la Union de los Reinos de Castilla y de León* (Madrid 1895–1903), I.292 [*Armada*]; B. Subercaseaux, *Tierra de Océano* (5th ed., Santiago 1965), 88–92; Morison, *Southern Voyages*, 596–600. For the possible first discovery of Juan Fernandez, D. D. Brand, 'Geographical Exploration by the Spaniards', in H. Friis (ed.), *The Pacific Basin: A History of Its Geographical Discovery* (New York 1967), 109–44 at 126 [*Pacific Basin*].

[27] A. Denucé, *Magellan: La Question des Moluques . . .* (Brussels 1911), 397–8. The idea seems to have stemmed from Ojea's failure in 1557–8 to find the western entrance to the Straits; see below, Ch. 5.

[28] Richard Hakluyt's translation in A. Galvano [Galvão], *The Discoveries of the World*, HS 1st Ser. 30 (London 1852), 202–5. The view that the mutineers demanded a course for the Moluccas stems from do Couto—Wright, American Voyages, 194–215 at 211; Wallis, Exploration, 133–8. The more detailed account of what is probably the first draft of Galvão's lost *Historia das Molucas* says nothing of Grijalva's murder (simply 'The chief captain having died . . .'), but then it is the muti-neers' story; see H. T. T. M. Jacobs SJ (ed.) *A Treatise on the Moluccas* (Rome 1971; written *c*. 1544), 312. Galvão, a vast contrast to Meneses, restored decent order among his compatriots, conciliating the local people and spreading the Gospel into nearby groups; it is especially pleasing that so stout a Protestant as Hakluyt, in the Epistle Dedicatorie to *The Discoveries*, puts 'pietie towards God, equitie towards men' first in his list of Galvão's virtues; but like Camões himself, he was one of those who were 'bulwarks to the King and Faith, But died in hospitals, in wretched beds'—*Os Lusiadas*, X.23.

[29] For island identifications, see Sharp, *Discovery*, 24–6, and H. E. Maude, *Of Islands and Men* (Melbourne 1968), 48–50 [*Islands*]—the first, 'o Acea', has been identified with Christmas I. in the Line group, but may have been in the northern Gilberts, as the second, 'los Pescadores', certainly was.

[30] For the Villalobos expedition in general, see Wallis, Exploration, 138–52; Wright, 'Spanish Voyages', 218–38, and American Voyages, 69–72; C. Perez-Bustamenta, 'La expedición de Ruy Lopez de Villalobos . . .', in Actas II, 611–26; and H. R. Wagner, *Spanish Voyages to the Northwest Coast of America in the Sixteenth Century* (Amsterdam 1966, original ed. 1929), 98–101 [*Voyages to NW*]. Details of the bargaining with Mendoza in Blair & Robertson, II.48–56, and A. Gschaedler, Mexico and the Philippines: The Voyages of Villalobos and Legaspi (Columbia Ph.D. thesis 1954), 30–4 [Mexico].

[31] Sharp, *Discovery*, 13–16, 26–32. In 1525 Gomes de Sequeira had been windblown for some 300 leagues east of Celebes (Sulawesi), reaching an island identified by Sharp as Yap, by Cortesão as Palau, and Gago Coutinho as Cape York in Queensland—Spate, 'Terra Australis', at 15–16. Other ships might have come from the west as far as the Palaus, which have been perhaps most widely accepted as the Ilhas de Sequeira; but W. A. Lessa makes out a convincing case, based in part on the nakedness of the Palauese, for Ulithi, 6° further east—The Portuguese Discovery of the Isles of Sequeira, unpublished (1974), citing much ethnographic as well as documentary evidence. K. G. McIntyre, *The Secret Discovery of Australia* (Medindie (S.A.) 1977), 296–310, follows Gago Coutinho in bringing Sequeira to Australia, but to Arnhem Land or the islands off it; he admits the obscurities in the evidence.

[32] Fray Geronimo de Santiesteban in Blair & Robertson, II.65, 67–8.

[33] D. D. Brand, in Friis, *Pacific Basin*, at 123.

[34] Merriman, *Spanish Empire*, III.454–5; Sarangani was named 'Antonio' for the Viceroy Mendoza.

[35] Wallis, 'Exploration', 186; see also Wright's acute remarks on the false goal of the Moluccas, as against the Philippines, in 'Spanish Voyages', 74–5.

[36] M. Cuevas SJ, *Monje y Marino: La Vida y los Tiempos de Fray Andrés de Urdaneta* (Mexico 1943), 184 [*Monje y Marino*].

[37] H. R. Wagner, *Cartography of the Northwest Coast of America to the Year 1800* (Berkeley 1937), 66–7 [*Cartography of NW*]; L. Wroth, 'The Early Cartography of the Pacific', *Papers Biblio, Soc. of America* 38 No. 2 (New York 1944), 85–268 at 161–2 ['Cartography'].

[38] Wallis, 'Exploration', 144–5, 163.

[39] As may be seen from the sixth (and penultimate) summons for Legaspi to depart made by the Portuguese commander Gonçalo Pereira—Blair & Robertson, II.303. The whole correspondence (244–329) is high-flown, meticulously notarised, insincere on either part (though the Portuguese had the law, as Urdaneta at least well knew), and extremely diverting.

[40] Cushner, *Spain*, 39–40; Blair & Robertson, II.78—most of this volume is devoted to documents on the voyage and the founding of Spanish rule, of which Cushner (30–73) gives a good general account. G. F. Zaide, *Philippine Political and Cultural History* (revised ed., Manila 1957), is more detailed but less well organised. For the preparations and problems surrounding the voyage: Gschaedler, Mexico, *passim*; Wagner, *Voyages to NW*, 94–120; Wallis, Exploration, 152–67; Wright, American Voyages, 240–4, and 'Spanish Voyages', 73–7.

[41] Blair & Robertson, II.80–1; Wagner, *Voyages to NW*, 104, and 105–6 for Urdaneta's memorandum.

[42] Confusingly for a later age, the overall commander of a Spanish fleet was the General and his flagship was styled the *capitana*; the second in command was the *almirante* and his ship the *almiranta*. On the Carrion-Urdaneta question, see M. Mitchell, *Friar Andrés de Urdaneta, O.S.A.* (London 1964), 140–6—a better biography than Cuevas's rather *arriéré* work.

[43] Blair & Robertson, II.84; Wallis, Exploration, 193–4.

[44] Wagner, *Voyages to NW*, 107; instructions summarised in Blair & Robertson, II.89–100.

[45] The other ships were the *San Pedro*, 500 tons, *capitana*; *San Pablo*, 300 or 400, *almiranta*; *San Juan*,

80. There was also a smaller craft, either a fregata towed by the *San Pedro* or a bergantin carried on her deck. The patache *San Lucas* was 40 tons.

⁴⁶ Blair & Robertson, II.108; for the islands, Sharp, *Discovery*, 36–9.

⁴⁷ Cushner, *Spain*, 53–5; Blair & Robertson, II.120–1; for photograph of 'El Niño', Plate 1 in K. Lightfoot, *The Philippines* (London 1973).

⁴⁸ The title of J. L. Phelan's study, subtitled *Spanish Aims and Filipino Responses, 1565–1700* (Madison 1959).

⁴⁹ See the extremely interesting lists in Blair & Robertson, II.182–95.

⁵⁰ Cushner, *Spain*, 65–70, for the move to Manila; for its advantages, Lightfoot, *Philippines*, 73.

⁵¹ P. Chaunu, *Les Philippines et le Pacifique des Ibériques* (Paris 1960), 20–1.

⁵² Blair & Robertson, II.214.

⁵³ Wallis, Exploration, 191. Sources for this section in general those in note 30 above, with Sharp, *Discovery*, 33–6 for Arellano. Cf. also E. W. Dahlgren, *Were the Hawaiian Islands Visited by the Spaniards before their Discovery by Captain Cook in 1778?* (plus an even longer subtitle!) (Stockholm 1916, 34–9) [*Hawaii?*].

⁵⁴ Wallis, Exploration, 192; though the latitudes given by de la Torre and Urdaneta differ by 4°. Parece Vela = 'looks like a sail'; Abreojos = 'keep your eyes open'—in its Portuguese form 'Abrolhos' it became almost a generic term for a low dangerous reef, as in the Dutch + Portuguese name Houtmans Abrolhos off Western Australia. Cf. Miro como vas = 'watch how you're going'.

⁵⁵ The question of desertion is resolved in Arellano's favour, but against Lope Martin, in A. Sharp, *Adventurous Armada* (Christchurch 1961), 23–7, 110–12; he also gives a vivid account of the San Geronimo affair, 113–45; this is a 'juvenile' book, but thoroughly based on the original documents. Cuevas, *Monje y Marino*, 235–7, also acquits Arellano.

⁵⁶ P. Chaunu, 'Le galion de Manille', *Annales Économies Sociétés Civilisations* 6, 1961, 447–62 at 452.

⁵⁷ Blair & Robertson, II.101–2; Wallis, Exploration, 201; Cuevas, *Monje y Marino*, 271–8 (criticism of Wagner); H. R. Wagner, 'A Discussion of Urdaneta and the Return Route from the Philippine Islands', *Pac. Hist. Rev.* 13, 1944, 313–16.

⁵⁸ A. F. González González, 'La dispersión de la escuadra magallánica. El problema del regresso a las costas americanas', in Actas II, 435–9 at 448.

⁵⁹ Schurz, *Galleon*, 216–83 *passim*, but especially 216–17, 251, 279–81; Wallis, Exploration, 207–8; Dahlgren, *Hawaii?*, 41–58, gives an annotated list of sailings to 1609.

⁶⁰ S. Zavala, *El Mundo Americano en la Epocha Colonial* (Mexico 1967), II.173; Cuevas, *Monje y Marino*, 203, and text at 377–81; text and translation also in Blair & Robertson, II.220–31.

⁶¹ E. Chassigneux, 'Rica de Oro et Rica de Plata', *T'oung Pao* 30, 1933, 37–84, at 38 ['Oro et Plata']. *The Times Survey Atlas* of 1922 still has 'Roca de Plata or Crespo', along with the 'Anson Archipelago' in the empty waters between Marcus Island and Hawaii, and separates Lot's Wife and Coluna Island (Plate 103); the longest-lived of these mythical islands, Ganges, survived in some maps until 1952. Some of these 'islands' may be due to breakers on a submarine sea-mount or volcano, but other anachronistic survivals seem to stem from the real existence of an isolated stack, Arellano's 'una Coluna', which was sighted and named 'Lot's Wife' by John Meares (of Nootka ill-fame) in 1788, and is really Sofu Gan north of the Bonins. Meares placed it 16° too far east, near enough to the reputed but vague position of Rica de Oro for a conflation which misled cartographers—Chassigneux, 160. This is probably the fullest discussion, but see also Dahlgren, *Hawaii?*, 66–9; Schurz, *Galleon*, 230–8; Wagner, *Voyages to NW*, 125–43; Wroth, 'Cartography', 207–15.

⁶² J. C. Findlay, *A Directory for the Navigation of the North Pacific Ocean* (2nd ed., London 1870), 875–6.

⁶³ Chassigneux, 'Oro et Plata', 64–71; Dahlgren, *Hawaii?*, 67–8.

⁶⁴ Schurz, *Galleon*, 236–7.

⁶⁵ Wagner, *Cartography of NW*, 125–41; and for the Anian element, 177–8.

⁶⁶ Schurz, *Galleon*, 232–5; Blair & Robertson, XIV.275–7. Vizcaino spent six weeks on this search (Dahlgren, *Hawaii?*, gives dates—25 September to 7 November), not Schurz's three months or E. C. Chapman's three weeks.

⁶⁷ Blair & Robertson, XVIII.326; Duro, *Armada*, III.378–80; and cf. below, Ch. 5. Rios Coronel thought Rica de Plata was 100 leagues in circumference.

⁶⁸ Dahlgren, *Hawaii?*, 49–51.

⁶⁹ J. K. Heeres, in *Abel Janszoon Tasman's Journal* (Amsterdam 1898, reprinted Los Angeles 1965), 15–37; Chassigneux, 'Oro et Plata', 46–8; Dahlgren, *Hawaii?*, 74–7; Wagner, *Cartography of NW*, 138; J. O. M. Broek, 'Geographical Exploration by the Dutch', in Friis, *Pacific Basin*, 151–69 at 166–7; J. J. Stephan, *The Kuril Islands* (Oxford 1974), 32–6. Much of the extreme confusion of cartography in these parts is sorted out in Wroth, 'Cartography', 201–6, and J. A. Harrison, *Japan's Northern Frontier* (Gainesville (Florida) 1953), 145–55.

⁷⁰ G. F. G. Careri, *A Voyage to the Philippines* (Manila 1963), 150; this is Awnsham Churchill's 1704 translation from first edition (Naples 1699–1700). The pilots supposed these islands to be those 'of Salomon'—the old Ophirian conjecture which played so large a part in Pacific imaginings —but Careri opines that they were imaginary, which does not stop him from a wildly garbled linkage with Mendoza's [*sic*: Mendaña's] 1596 voyage. Wagner (*Cartography of NW*, 139) doubts Careri's authenticity, but this scarcely detracts from the narrative: whoever wrote it had experienced it, and one feels 'Yes, that is what the passage *must* have been like'.

⁷¹ Quoted Schurz, *Galleon*, 237–8.

⁷² Sharp, *Discovery*, 66–8, sets out the elements of the cartographical problem; the currently accepted negative view is based on Dahlgren, *Hawaii?*, and J. F. G. Stokes, 'Hawaii's Discovery by Spaniards: Theories Traced and Refuted', *Papers Hawaiian Hist. Soc.* 20, 1939, 38–113. R. Yzendoorn, 'A Study in Hawaiian Cartography prior to Cook's Rediscovery', *21st Annual Report Hawaiian Hist. Soc.*, 1913, 23–32, raises the telling point that several Mercator-Ortelius maps of the sixteenth century show a group of islands named 'Los Bolcanes' in the appropriate latitudes, and claims that, apart from Hawaii, the only other volcanoes of the North Pacific are in the Aleutians; but Stokes identifies these with the Bonin or Volcano Islands discovered by Bernardo de la Torre in 1543. For counter-arguments to Dahlgren and Stokes, plausible but not entirely convincing, see B. Anderson, *The Life and Voyages of Captain George Vancouver* (Toronto 1960), 128–34.

⁷³ Quoted Chassigneux, 'Oro et Plata', 37.

⁷⁴ Work on these is being undertaken by a Hawaiian student, Mr Paki Neves, in the Department of Pacific and SE Asian History, Australian National University. Neves stresses persistent traditions about 'Lono' and 'Paao', respectively Captain and Priest 'of the ship', and the banner- or sail-like Lono image. Together with the importance of Kealakekua Bay in the procession of the image, these traditions might account, at least in part, for the reception of Captain Cook as a God.

⁷⁵ Cf. Maude, *Islands*, 60, and T. A. Rickard, 'Drift Iron: A Fortuitous Factor in Primitive Culture', *Geogr. Rev.* 24, 1934, 525–43. On junks, W. E. Braden, 'On the Probability of pre-1778 Japanese Drifts to Hawaii', *Hawaiian Jnl of History* 10, 1976, 75–89.

⁷⁶ See Langdon, *Caravel*, 272–80, for a general restatement of the case for Spanish contact.

⁷⁷ Broek, in Friis, *Pacific Basin* at 167.

Notes for Chapter 5

[1] H. R. Wagner, *Spanish Voyages to the Northwest Coast of America in the Sixteenth Century* (Amsterdam 1966, original ed. 1929), 128–33, 152–3 [*Voyages to NW*]. Chapters IX–XII form a major source for this section and include Ascension's narrative (180–272). C. E. Chapman, *A History of California: The Spanish Period* (New York 1921), 112–42, gives more weight to the impact of Drake and Cavendish on Spanish thinking than does Wagner [*California*].

[2] Wagner, *Voyages to NW*, 155 and 362 note 44, and his *Sir Francis Drake's Voyage Around the World* (Amsterdam 1969, original ed. 1926), note 23 on 490–2—102 lines in minion or 7-point type! I no longer feel the need to apologise for the length of my own notes.

[3] Wagner, *Voyages to NW*, 163 and 373 note 78; the port of arrival is usually given as Navidad.

[4] Wagner, *Voyages to NW*, 280; the letter is in Hakluyt, VIII.133–5. Vizcaino's eye for the main chance was shared by many Spanish pioneers, but few were quite so earthy about it. Cf. A. del Portillo y Diez Sollano, *Descubrimientos y Exploraciones en las Costas de California* (Madrid 1947), 174–204 [*Descubrimientos*], and M. del Carmen Velasquez, 'La navegacion transpacifica', *Hist. Mexicana* 17, 1968–9, 159–75, which despite its title is mostly on Vizcaino in California. For Vizcaino and pearling, H. R. Wagner, 'Pearl Fishing Enterprises in the Gulf of California', *HAHR* 10, 1930, 188–220.

[5] Wagner, *Voyages to NW*, 363 note 49.

[6] Ibid., 174–6 and 376 note 27.

[7] Fray Antonio's bad calculations grossly inflated his 'island', making what is really the peninsula of Baja California correspond roughly to the entire modern state of California—J. B. Leighly, *California as an Island* (San Francisco 1972), 30–3, 39 [*California*].

[8] Wagner, *Voyages to NW*, 180–1, 165–8, and comment at 388–91; for scurvy and Monterey, 245–7, and the pelican in her piety at 187 and 212. There is another Ascension account in H. Aschmann, 'A Late Recounting of the Vizcaino Expedition', *Jnl Calif. Anthropology* 1, 1974, 174–85.

[9] Leighly, *California*, 23.

[10] Chapman, *California*, 137–8; Wagner, *Voyages to NW*, 180–1, 407 note 187.

[11] Chapman, *California*, 138–42.

[12] The most prominent figure was probably the Aragonese entrepreneur Pedro de Porter y Casanate, for whom, and for minor (mainly mission) explorations before Fr Eusebio Kino SJ finally established the peninsularity of Baja California (*c.* 1700), see Chapman, *California*, 156–79. To Chapman, Porter is a rather dubious character; to Portillo, a selfless hero comparable to Cortes—*Descubrimientos*, 245–90 at 273–4.

[13] J. R. Brebner, *The Explorers of North America* (Meridian ed., Cleveland 1964), 339. Exports were practically confined to hides and tallow; for a vivid acount of Mexican California, see R. H. Dana's classic *Two Years before the Mast* (Boston 1840).

[14] G. F. G. Careri, *A Voyage to the Philippines*, Manila 1963, 160–1; cf. note 70 to Ch. 4 above.

[15] H. R. Wallis, The Exploration of the South Sea, 1519 to 1644 (Oxford D.Phil. thesis 1953–4), 207 [*Exploration*]; A. de Morga, *Sucesos de las Islas Filipinas* (Mexico 1609), trans. and ed. J. S. Cummins, HS 2nd Ser. 140 (Cambridge 1971), 319 [*Sucesos*]. Cf. R. Walter and B. Robins, *A Voyage round the World . . . by George Anson* (1748), ed. G. Williams (London 1974), 226.

[16] Compare the views of W. L. Schurz, *The Manila Galleon* (Dutton ed., New York 1959), 232–44; Chapman, *California*, 138–42—rather a median stance; Wagner, *Voyages to NW*, 275–83—the last seems to me the best-argued case.

[17] W. Borah, *Early Colonial Trade and Navigation between Mexico and Peru* (Berkeley 1954), 29–31,

and 31–6 for the discovery of the route and the ports. For El Niño, R. C. Murphy, *Bird Islands of Peru* (New York 1925), 165–8; C. N. Caviedes, 'El Niño 1972: Its Climatic, Human, and Economic Implications', *Geogr. Rev.* 65, 1975, 493–509, which gives many references; I have also received personal information from Professor Caviedes. There is an immense amount of data, which I confess I have not attempted to digest, in *El Mar Gran Personaje*, being Tomo I, Vols. 1 and 2, of the *Historia Maritima del Peru* (Lima 1975).

[18] For vivid accounts, B. Subercaseaux, *Tierra de Océano: La epopeya marítima de un pueblo terrestre* (5th ed., Santiago 1965), 115–34; S. E. Morison, *The European Discovery of America: The Southern Voyages A.D. 1492–1616* (New York 1974), 603–12. As an indication of the imperfect knowledge of these parts as late as 1946, Subercaseaux tells of an amusing find on the Taitao peninsula, supposedly uninhabited: not Man Friday's footprint, but 'un excremento humano fresco. . . .'

[19] D. D. Brand, 'Geographical Exploration by the Spaniards', in H. Friis (ed.), *The Pacific Basin: A History of Its Geographical Exploration* (New York 1967), 109–44, at 127 [*Pacific Basin*]. H. Kraus is in error in referring to Ladrillero's voyage as 'unsuccessful' (*Sir Francis Drake: A Pictorial Biography* (Amsterdam 1970), 118, 184–5); its purpose was not to go to Spain, but to reconnoitre the route, and in this it was successful. Kraus does however present Hernan Gallego's little-known but interesting *Declaracion del estrecho de Magallanes*.

[20] J. T. Medina, *El piloto Juan Fernández* (Santiago 1918), 39—a definitive work [*Fernández*]. R. L. Woodward, *Robinson Crusoe's Island* (Chapel Hill 1969), is a lively but scholarly history [*Robinson*].

[21] Sir Clements Markham's statement of 1904 that 'very little is known of Juan Fernandez' (*The Voyages of Pedro Fernandez de Quiros*, HS 2nd Ser. 14–15 (London 1904), II.526 [*Quiros*]) was true enough when made; but since it has been reprinted in an excellent work over sixty years later (C. Jack-Hinton, *The Search for the Islands of Solomon 1567–1838* (Oxford 1969), 26 [*The Search*]), it is as well to eliminate Markham's candidate. This man was building ships in Nicaragua in 1531; the Juan Fernandez who found the island said in 1590 that he was 60 (Medina, *Fernández*, 12–22, 66–7); and making all allowance for precocity, this exceeds! Markham's many translations for the Hakluyt Society do provide an easily accessible corpus of material, and his style, a little archaic but without undue archaism, 'has given us a story of singular charm and sustained dramatic quality . . . [with] some passages which would be difficult to improve upon' (Celsus Kelly); but wherever there is anything directional or numerical, he is excessively careless. Nor is he always objective, as any reader of his works on Peruvian history will see at once. Cf. H. Bernstein and B. W. Diffie, 'Sir Clements R. Markham as a Translator', *HAHR* 17, 1937, 546–7; C. Kelly OFM, 'The Narrative of Pedro Fernandez de Quiros', *Hist. Studies* (Melbourne) 9, 1959–60, 181–93 at 190 ['Narrative']; and the remarks of Robert Graves in the preface to his novel *The Isles of Unwisdom* (London 1950).

[22] Medina, *Fernández*, 118–70 *passim*; A. Dalrymple, *An Historical Collection of . . . Discoveries in the South Pacific Ocean* (London 1770), I.xxiv, xxix, 53–4; J. Burney, *A Chronological History of the Discoveries in the South Sea or Pacific Ocean . . .* (London 1803–17), I.300–2. The memorial of Dr Juan Luis Arias has been often reprinted and translated, e.g. in R. H. Major, *Early Voyages to Terra Australis*, HS 1st Ser. 25 (London 1859), 1–30, and Markham, *Quiros*, II.317–36. For alleged evidence of Spaniards in New Zealand, E. Stokes, 'European Discovery of New Zealand Before 1642: A Review of the Evidence', *NZ Jnl of History* 4, 1970, 1–9. For a possible earlier sighting of Juan Fernandez Islands, above, Ch. 4.

[23] Woodward, *Robinson*, 12–14, 20–63 *passim*.

[24] Ibid., 17–18.

[25] J. Juan and A. de Ulloa, *Relación Histórica del Viaje al América Meridional* (Madrid 1748), III.284–7,

and their *Noticias Secretas de América* (London 1826), I.71–7.

²⁶ Woodward, *Robinson*, 79–88; H. Wallis (ed.), *Carteret's Voyage round the World*, HS 2nd Ser. 123–4 (Cambridge 1965), I.128–40. Carteret had to go on the more difficult and less useful Mas Afuera.

²⁷ Jack-Hinton, *The Search*, 13—a meticulous and definitive work. For the background, see his first chapter ('The Ophirian Conjecture') and C. Kelly OFM, 'Geographical Knowledge and Speculation in regard to Spanish Pacific Voyages', *Hist. Studies* (Melbourne), 9 1959–60, 12–18 ['Geogl Knowledge']. Six narratives of Mendaña's first voyage, including those of Gallego, Sarmiento, Catoira, and Mendaña himself, are translated by Lord Amherst of Hackney in *The Discovery of the Solomon Islands*, HS 2nd Ser. 6–7 (London 1901) [*Solomons*]; the actual voyage is analysed in Wallis, Exploration, 212–54. All three Mendaña-Quiros voyages are vividly narrated in G. A. Wood, *The Discovery of Australia* (Melbourne 1969, original ed. 1922), 85–130 [*Australia*], and there is a very balanced account in J. C. Beaglehole, *The Exploration of the Pacific* (3rd ed., London 1966), 39–107 [*Pacific*].

²⁸ Jack-Hinton, *The Search*, 24–6; A. Galvano [Galvão], *The Discoveries of the World* (trans. R. Hakluyt), HS 1st Ser. 30 (London 1862), 213–14. The Tupac Yupanqui story has a strong bearing on Thor Heyerdahl's theories—see his *Sea Routes to Polynesia* (London 1968), especially 80–1. But much of his argument is fallacious, and he relies far too heavily on the examination under duress (even threat of death) of the centenarian Indian Chepo (for which see Amherst, *Solomons*, II.465–8).

²⁹ Kelly, 'Geogl Knowledge', 15 correcting Amherst, *Solomons*, I.lviii; Jack-Hinton, *The Search*, 31, and for official adoption of the name in 1580, 80–3.

³⁰ Amherst, *Solomons*, I.83, 103 (Mendaña), I.10 (Gallego); Wallis, Exploration, 220.

³¹ Jack-Hinton, *The Search*, 65–7; Wallis, Exploration, 218–19, 221–2.

³² Amherst, *Solomons*, I.100–5 (Mendaña), II.272 (Catoira); for identification of Ysla de Jesus, H. E. Maude, *Of Islands and Men* (Melbourne 1968), 53–9 [*Islands*] and A. Sharp, *The Discovery of the Pacific Islands* (Oxford 1960), 44 [*Discovery*].

³³ The navigation is analysed in detail by Jack-Hinton, *The Search*, 35–41, and Wallis, Exploration, 214–24. Jack-Hinton favours Roncador; Wallis and Sharp, Ontong Java.

³⁴ Mendaña's own narrative in Amherst, *Solomons*, I.108–12; the star was Venus, often visible in full daylight in these latitudes.

³⁵ Catoira, in Amherst, *Solomons*, II.215–462, gives much the most vivid and detailed account of affairs ashore; an honest man, giving full credit to Melanesian courage.

³⁶ Jack-Hinton, *The Search*, 64–7; Beaglehole, *Pacific*, 52–5; Amherst, *Solomons*, I.183–7 (Mendaña), II.417–21, 427–47 (Catoira).

³⁷ Amherst, *Solomons*, I.70–4 (Gallego).

³⁸ Ibid., I.77–8 (Gallego), I.186–90 (Mendaña), II.448–63 (Catoira). For Sarmiento's side, A. Landín Carrasco, *Vida y Viajes de Pedro Sarmiento de Gamboa* (Madrid 1945), 24–53.

³⁹ Amherst, *Solomons*, I.77–9 (Gallego), II.451–7 (Catoira).

⁴⁰ Jack-Hinton, *The Search*, 63–79.

⁴¹ 'A discourse of . . . the South sea written by Lopez Vaz . . .' in Hakluyt, VIII.153–206 at 204–6; hardly so 'cautious on the subject of gold' as Jack-Hinton suggests (*The Search*, 110).

⁴² The point is made by Mendaña himself in a complaint of harassment and obstruction by Toledo, under colour of the need to go against the corsairs. All would be well, at no cost to the Treasury, if His Majesty would give Mendaña a licence to sell 2000 quintals of mercury in Potosi or New Spain, so that he could prepare a new voyage—desirable, *inter alia*, since many young women expect to get husbands from such a voyage, and please God that waiting will not lead them to an

evil life!—letter to Council of the Indies, Lima, 24 March 1580, transcript by Zaragoza, MSS C 402, Mitchell Library, Sydney.

[43] The opening phrase is from the great eighteenth century Portuguese compilation of shipwrecks, the *História trágico-maritima*. The Quiros/Belmonte relation was published by J. Zaragoza in *Historia del Descubrimiento de las Regiones Australes hecho por el General Pedro Fernandez de Quirós* (Madrid 1876–82), and translated by C. R. Markham for the Hakluyt Society (above, note 21). I have relied mainly on Jack-Hinton and Wallis for dates and positions and courses, and have been content to quote Markham on the 'human interest' side, where he is better; but not without collating with Zaragoza (see next note). The authorship of the Quiros/Belmonte relation is ably discussed by Celsus Kelly in 'Narrative'—with notes on Markham's errors and on the big controversy (in a small pond) stirred up by Cardinal Moran, Archbishop of Sydney, who convinced himself but not many others that Quiros had discovered Australia, or at least Queensland; Kelly cites over forty items in this now happily dead polemic. The build-up was purely sectarian—the Mass in Australia had to antedate Holy Communion—and is now repudiated *in toto* by more conscientious Catholic historians such as Dr Eris O'Brien, formerly Archbishop of Canberra and Goulburn.

In a more refined form, the Mendaña-Quiros saga is part of the Australian mythos: see J. McAuley's poem *Captain Quiros* (Sydney 1964), and Rex Ingamells's ill-starred attempt at epic grandeur, *The Great South Land* (Melbourne 1951), as well as lyrics by poets such as Douglas Stewart and Ken Barrett. An English poet has retold it in an excellent novel: Robert Graves, *The Isles of Unwisdom*.

[44] This is Markham's constantly quoted version (Quiros. I.17); but Zaragoza (I.37) has 'es era toda tal, que puedo con razon decir, que en la vida tuve tanta pena como que tan bella criatura en parte de tal perdicion se quedase.' Markham seems to have slipped in the 'never', and my reading would be 'he was in all ways such that I can rightfully say that all my life I had so much pain that so fair a creature . . .'

[45] Both names are still in use, though Ndeni is now more common, and the group is still known as the Santa Cruz Islands. Although lying some 400 km east of the nearest point in the Solomons proper, they are administratively part of that group, so that in a purely technical sense Mendaña could be said to have rediscovered the Solomons.

[46] J. Allen and R. C. Green, 'Mendana 1595 and the Fate of the Lost *Almiranta*: An Archaeological Investigation', *Jnl Pac. Hist.* (Canberra) 7, 1972, 73–91; some of the finds were made by Melanesian schoolgirls.

[47] For navigational detail, Wallis, Exploration, 270–80, and Jack-Hinton, *The Search*, 129–32.

[48] This may seem a harsh judgment on a lady who died near 400 years ago; but be it noted that it is drawn from the Quiros/Belmonte relation, that Quiros appears almost pathologically loyal to his duty in her, and the criticism in this document is very restrained—and the more devastating for that.

[49] Morga, *Sucesos*, 104–5. The material is prolific: according to Celsus Kelly, more than 600 documents on the three voyages 1567–1606 have been found since 1930, and Quiros himself wrote some seventy memorials, of which about fifty are known to be extant—*La Austrialia del Espiritu Santo*, HS 2nd Ser. 126–7 (Cambridge 1966), I.ix, 4 [*Austrialia*]. Kelly gives, amongst other important documents, the *relacion* by Fray Martin de Munilla OFM (I.237–70) and the *sumario* of the accountant Juan de Iturbe (II.273–93). He also analyses, with much learning, 'Some early maps relating to the Queirós-Torres discoveries of 1606', in Actas of the Congreso Internacional de História dos Descubrimentos (Lisbon 1971), II.203–54.

The controversial account by Prado, translated by G. F. Barwick, is in H. N. Stevens (ed.),

New Light on the Discovery of Australia, HS 2nd Ser. 64 (London 1930) [*New Light*]—the new light did not dispel obscurities, and some heat was produced. The accounts of the Portuguese pilot Gonzalez de Leza and of Fray Juan de Torquemada are in Markham, *Quiros*, II.321–406, 407–54. There are analyses in Jack-Hinton, *The Search*, 133–83, and Wallis, Exploration, 286–335. Finally, for Torres and his Strait, it seems fair to say that B. Hilder, The Voyage of Torres along the Southern Coast of New Guinea in 1606 (Macquarie Univ. M.A. thesis 1976), may probably be taken as definitive [Torres].

[50] Jack-Hinton, *The Search*, 134, 167; Kelly, *Austrialia*, I.2, 114–15.

[51] There was at this stage no inordinate delay—Kelly (*Austrialia*, I.21) points out that though it was about eight and a half years between Quiros's return to and his second sailing from Callao, half this time was spent in travel and eighteen months in Rome.

[52] Stevens, *New Light*, 27–33; Kelly, *Austrialia*, I.35–7. Prado's account probably embodies three recensions; it is noteworthy that it has a scurrilous reference to Ochoa as a galley-slave, and yet Ochoa attests the truth of the document (*New Light*, 97, 203)! This is fishy, and it is difficult to believe Prado on personal matters. Stevens says (at 36) that 'after complaining of the conduct of Quiros he [Prado] was still loyal to him', because the heading of his *relacion* says that the discovery was begun by Quiros (which he could hardly deny) and completed for him by Prado with the help of Torres. This is thin evidence of loyalty; and the balance of evidence suggests that 'Torres with the help of Prado' is nearer the truth (cf. note 67 below). What Stevens modestly passes off as 'complaining' includes such amiable remarks as that Quiros was a liar and a fraud, 'fit to be of the Rua Nova in Lisbon, in whose mouth is nothing but lies, bragging, and disloyalty' (*New Light*, 241). One can only wonder at Stevens's odd notion of loyalty.

[53] Kelly, *Austrialia*, I.25–6, and II.357 (Iturbe, urging Quiros's unfitness for command).

[54] Jack-Hinton, *The Search*, 138–40; Wallis, Exploration, 286; Kelly, *Austrialia*, I.39 and II.276 (Iturbe).

[55] Marutea, Actaeon Group, Vaiaatea, Hao, Tauere or Amano, Rakaraka or Raroia, Raroia or Takume—Kelly, *Austrialia*, I.42, 55–8; Jack-Hinton, *The Search*, 141; Sharp, *Discovery*, 57–60; Maude, *Islands*, 66–70; and their following pages for San Bernardo and Gente Hermosa.

[56] Kelly, *Austrialia*, table at I.29 and Munilla's account, I.169–74; Markham, *Quiros*, I.209–17.

[57] Wallis, Exploration, 292–303; the various dead reckonings are discussed here and also by Jack-Hinton, *The Search*, 142–8. In the next paragraph I follow Hilder, Torres, 27.

[58] Jack-Hinton, *The Search*, 148–53, gives good reason for not making the facile identification Manicoco = Vanikolo = Vanikoro.

[59] It is generally held to be 'La Austrialia' in honour of the Habsburg House of Austria, to which the Spanish royal family belonged; but Quiros may in fact have named it 'La Australia', adding the complimentary 'i' later—Jack-Hinton, *The Search*, 154 note; Wood, *Australia*, 129–30; cf. C. Sanz, *Australia: su Descubrimiento y Denominacion* (Madrid 1963).

[60] See the divergent accounts of Quiros and Leza, in Markham, *Quiros*, I.241–4 and II.360–76; Munilla is vague—Kelly, *Austrialia*, I.210–11, and for Kelly's judicious comments I.86–8. It may be added that given the limitations of the arquebus, especially in a damp climate, its terror could wear off quite quickly—D. Shineberg, 'Guns and Men in Melanesia', *Jnl Pac. Hist.* 6, 1971, 61–82, though she perhaps makes too little allowance for the shock effect; cf. E. Bradford, *Drake* (London 1965), 73–4.

[61] Kelly, *Austrialia*, I.223 (Munilla) and II.286 (Iturbe); Prado in Stevens, *New Light*, 123, adding that Quiros intended to build a church of marble 'to rival that of St Peter at Rome'—perhaps mere camp gossip, but a touch characteristic of either man.

[62] Stevens, *New Light*, 125.

[63] No comment is made on this snap decision by Leza, Munilla, Torquemada, or Torres; Prado *more suo* says that Quiros left because he was 'so timid and fearful' of the poisonous fish, although he had not partaken (Stevens, *New Light*, 129); but Quiros and Leza make it clear that the decision was made before the poisoning, and Leza says that Quiros did eat and was ill as a result—Markham, *Quiros*, I.263, II.389–90. It is clear that Stevens's 'much-maligned man' was a much-maligner.

[64] The matter could be discussed endlessly and fruitlessly; see Jack-Hinton, *The Search*, 154–5; Kelly, *Austrialia*, I.88–96 (perhaps the fairest analysis); Beaglehole, *Pacific*, 96–9, and *The Journals of Captain James Cook: I. The Voyage of the* Endeavour, Hakluyt Society (Cambridge 1968), xlix [*Endeavour*]; Wood, *Australia*, 120–6.

[65] Markham, *Quiros*, I.281–6, and 291–2 for Quiros's will; Jack-Hinton, *The Search*, 156–7; Wallis, Exploration, 314.

[66] Torres to the King, Manila, 12 July 1607, in Markham, *Quiros*, II.455–66. His laconism compares very favourably with Prado's rhetoric.

[67] The Papuan coast is depicted on beautiful and detailed perspective maps drawn and signed by Prado as 'capitan' but referring to Torres as 'capitan y cabo', i.e. 'captain and commander'. Stevens's attempts to explain away this awkward fact and place Prado in command are roughly handled by W. Dixson, 'Notes and Comments on "New Light on the Discovery of Australia"', *Jnl Roy. Hist. Soc. Australia* 17, 1931, 289–330 at 302–6. A probable solution is put forward by Hilder (Torres, 7–10): the Viceroy's orders may well have nominated Prado to take over command in succession to Quiros; but Prado had transferred from the capitana to the almiranta, and after the separation it could not be known that Quiros was dead or incapacitated, whatever may have been thought or wished. On the almiranta, Torres was undoubtedly in command. Although Prado says that 'I' took possession at various points, and Torres that 'we' did, this would be at best a courteous deference to Prado's higher social standing on such formal occasions. See also B. Hilder, 'Torres or Prado?', *MM* 60, 1974, 133–42.

K. McIntyre thinks that both Quiros and Torres were aware of a passage south of New Guinea, but his arguments, though ingenious and worthy of serious consideration, are not altogether convincing—*The Secret Discovery of Australia* (London 1977), 320–3. It is fair to add that, while I have some reservations as to the mode of the discovery, I think that his main thesis—that the Portuguese, and specifically Cristovão de Mendonça, charted a good deal of the Australian coast in 1522–3—will be very difficult to refute.

[68] Kelly, *Austrialia*, II.353–4.

[69] The argument is as confused and tricky as the navigation. Select references: F. J. Bayldon, 'Voyage of Luis Vaez de Torres . . .', *Jnl Roy. Hist. Soc. Australia* 11, 1925, 158–95 (Torres hugged Papuan coast, or sailed north of Mulgrave I., out of sight of Cape York); Bayldon, 'Voyage of Torres', ibid. 16, 1930, 133–46 (latter option—this after *New Light*); Stevens, *New Light*, 45–70 (Endeavour Strait, in sight of Cape York); E. A. Parkyn, 'The Voyage of Luis Vaez de Torres', *Geogr. Jnl* 76, 1930, 133–46 (Bayldon's second option); A. R. H[inks], 'The Discovery of Torres Strait', ibid. 98, 1941, 91–102 (close to Papuan coast); A. Sharp, *The Discovery of Australia* (Oxford 1963), 23–30 (nothing proven). Wood, *Australia*, 133–4, is vague: Torres 'definitely saw the Southern Continent' yet 'writes as one who neither expected a continent, nor saw one.' The track shown by C. Prieto in *El Océano Pacífico: navegantes españoles del siglo XVI* (Madrid 1972), coasting most of the Gulf of Carpentaria, is quite imaginary.

[70] D. D. Brand, in Friis, *Pacific Basin*, 138; he confuses the Arias memorial with Torres's letter, which Dalrymple did not find until the 1790s—see H. T. Fry, *Alexander Dalrymple and the Expansion of British Trade* (London 1970), 112–13. For Dalrymple's map and Cook, Beaglehole, *Endeavour*, clxii–clxiv.

[71] Wallis, Exploration, 332-5, Jack-Hinton, *The Search*, 175-83, 222, 239-42 and his redrawings of the Duchess of Berry, Sanches, Van Langren, du Val, and Vaugondy maps. Eredia's maps (which show those hoary survivors Polo's Beach and Maletur) are in A. Cortesão and A. Teixeira da Mota, *Portugaliæ Monumenta Cartographica* (Lisbon 1960), IV.414 and 419. Hilder makes the intriguing suggestion that Prado's missing Mappa V may have been sent to Eredia, as the cartographer chiefly concerned with these regions—Torres, 172. J. O'Hagan, in The Use of Torres' Charts by Seventeenth Century Cartographers, unpublished typescript (1959) in the Mitchell Library, Sydney, draws attention to the remarkably correct outline of southern New Guinea in Sanson's maps of 1651 and 1659 and suggests that Ochoa may have sold a chart which became the source of the Van Langren globe.

[72] J. Forsyth analyses the process by which the change came about and makes strong case for a more general and persistent knowledge of Torres's results, even though some of his citations (e.g. from Burton's *Anatomy of Melancholy*) will hardly bear the weight he would put on them—Cook's Debt to Torres, unpublished typescript (*c.* 1960?) in the Mitchell Library.

[73] Beaglehole, *Endeavour*, 410-11.

[74] Beaglehole, *Pacific*, 105. The lingering misery of Quiros's last years is best followed in Kelly, *Austrialia*, I.105-16 (comment) and II.352-67 (documents). See also Jack-Hinton, *The Search*, 158-67.

[75] Also with da Gama, Magellan, Pizarro, and Cortes. Markham, *Quiros*, II.486, 503; Kelly, *Austrialia*, II.309, 362.

[76] Kelly, *Austrialia*, I.108-9. Twice *contredespachos* were prepared, in December 1609 and June 1610. The first really was a gross trick, the second merely told the Viceroy to limit Quiros to two or three ships and to stress missionary work, not conquest. Neither was used, since in each case Quiros, on sighting the open and favourable despatch, promptly raised the ante.

[77] Kelly, *Austrialia*, I.115-33. There was an extraordinary last fling in 1663-9, which ended in armed Franciscans arresting the Governor of the Philippines, while the promoter, a Peruvian astronomer, disappeared into Cochin-China. The mission to the Marianas of Fr Luis de San Vitores SJ (1667-72) was regarded as a first step towards further activity in the Austral regions, but local resistance and disorders killed any such project—Jack-Hinton, *The Search*, 171-5.

[78] Kelly, *Austrialia*, I.5.

Notes for Chapter 6

[1] The title of a book by F. B. Eldridge, Melbourne 1948: unacademic and unpretentious but stimulating; my reading of it a quarter of a century ago may have implanted the first seed of this work.

[2] C. R. Boxer, *The Great Ship from Amacon* (Lisbon 1959), 9 [*Great Ship*]; Tien-tse Chang, *Sino-Portuguese Trade from 1514 to 1644* (Leyden 1934), 7-9 [*Sino-Port. Trade*]; J. T. Pratt, *The Expansion of Europe into the Far East* (London 1947), 42-5.

[3] For the geopolitical background, see C. A. Fisher, *South-east Asia* (London 1964), 9-10, 83-95, 102-30.

[4] J. Needham, *Science and Civilisation in China* (Cambridge 1954), IV (1971) 452 note b, 467-84, especially at 481 [*Science in China*]. J. V. G. Mills in Ma Huan, *Ying-yai Sheng-lan: The Overall Survey of the Ocean's Shores*, HS Extra Ser. 42 (Cambridge 1970), 27-31, is more cautious on linear dimensions but agrees with the 3100 tons [*Overall Survey*].

⁵ Needham, *Science in China*, I.143, IV.486–503 and map at 560. The voyages are also discussed in some detail in K. Chang's thesis, Chinese Great Explorers, cited above, Ch. 1 note 3. The traditional motive of a search for the Emperor's dethroned predecessor (and nephew) is clearly inadequate for voyages of this range and duration.

⁶ Chang, *Sino-Port. Trade*, 33–5; C. R. Boxer, *South China in the Sixteenth Century*, HS 2nd Ser. 106 (London 1953), xix [*S. China*]. Earlier, however, the nascent Malaccan state had Ming support against Java and Siam, obviously for strategic and commercial reasons, in contrast to e.g. Brunei—see Wang Gungwu, 'Early Ming Relations with Southeast Asia', in J. K. Fairbanks (ed.), *The Chinese World Order* (Cambridge (Mass.) 1968), 34–62 at 56–9. The tribute system was of course far more complex and ideologically significant than can be explicated here; see Fairbanks's volume in general, and especially M. Mancall, 'The Ch'ing Tribute System', 63–89.

⁷ And indeed over the Ryukyus as late as the 1870s—see (of all places) W. de G. Birch (ed.), in the third volume of *The Commentaries of the Great Afonso Dalboquerque*, HS 1st Ser. 62 (London 1880), xiv–xx.

⁸ '. . . no serious attempt was made by either of the two great Far Eastern powers to dislodge the Spanish from Manila. Nothing shows more clearly than this the contrast between the aggressive navalism [of the maritime West] and the self-secluding policies inspired by the land-revenue ideology of Chinese civilization'.—G. F. Hudson, *Europe and China* (London 1961, original ed. 1931), 253.

⁹ Needham, *Science in China*, IV.314–30; Mills, *Overall Survey*, 3.

¹⁰ I have followed the convincing discussion (including the *raison d'être* of eunuchdom) in C. P. FitzGerald, *The Southern Expansion of the Chinese People* (Canberra 1972), Chs. 5 and 6 [*Expansion*]; some details from Needham, *Science in China*, IV.480–4, 526–30.

¹¹ Needham, *Science in China*, I.100, IV.527.

¹² And the 'Buyers . . . have a profitt adequate to the Risque they Run'—the South Sea Company factors at Kingston, Jamaica, 6 January 1736 (OS), cited in A. S. Aiton, 'The Asiento Treaty as reflected in the Papers of Lord Shelburne', *HAHR* 8, 1928, 167–77 at 167.

¹³ P. Wheatley, *The Golden Khersonese* (Kuala Lumpur 1966), 307–20; A. Cortesão (trans. and ed.), *The Suma Oriental of Tomé Pires*, HS 2nd Ser. 89–90 (London 1944), II.285 [Pires, *Suma*]. There is a very full account of Malacca's commerce in M. A. P. Meilink-Roelofsz, *Asian Trade and European Influence in the Indonesian Archipelago . . .* (The Hague 1962), especially Chs. II–IV [*Asian Trade*].

¹⁴ For these two paragraphs, Shunzo Sakamaki, 'Ryukyu and Southeast Asia', *Jnl Asian Studies* 23, 1963–4, 391–404, and R. K. Sakai, 'The Satsuma-Ryukyu Trade and the Tokugawa Seclusion Policy', ibid. 405–16 (with S. Crawcour's introduction to these papers); also Atsushi Kobata and Mitsugu Matsuda (eds.), *Ryukyuan Relations with Korea and South Sea Countries* (Kyoto 1969), v, 4–7, 13–14, 125, 177.

¹⁵ G. Sansom, *The Western World and Japan* (London 1950), 114 [*Western World*]; page references in the Vintage ed., New York 1973, run 10–20 pages earlier than those of this first edition. In general references to Japanese internal affairs in this chapter are drawn from Sansom's *A History of Japan 1334–1615* (London 1961) [*Japan 1334–1615*] and J. Murdoch, *A History of Japan*, II 1542–1651 (London, 3rd imp. 1949) [*Japan 1542–1651*].

¹⁶ D. Pacheco SJ, 'The Europeans in Japan, 1543–1640', in M. Cooper SJ (ed.), *The Southern Barbarians* (Tokyo 1971), 37 [*Barbarians*]: H. P. Varley, 'The Age of the Military Houses', in A. E. Tiedemann (ed.), *An Introduction to Japanese Civilization* (New York 1974), 61–96 at 89–90 [*Introduction*].

¹⁷ Sir Edward Michelbourne (1605), cited Boxer, *Great Ship*, 60. See i.a. D. Lach, *Asia in the Making of Europe* (Chicago 1965), I.663–70, and also 688–706 for the great impression made by

the four Japanese youths sent to Europe by the Jesuits in 1584-6. Lach also gives (687-8) some of the 'amusing and illuminating distichs' of Luis Frois SJ, contrasting Japanese and European ways.

[18] J. W. Hall, *Japan from Prehistory to Modern Times* (New York 1972), 130 [*Japan*]. There is of course much more detail in Murdoch and Sansom.

[19] Hall, *Japan*, 123-6; Sansom, *Japan 1334-1615*, 270-2, 304-5; Yosoburo Takekoshi, *The Economic Aspects of the History of the Civilization of Japan* (London 1930), I.356-68—a book crammed with picturesque and sometimes significant detail, but on the whole muddled and rather disappointing [*Economic Aspects*].

[20] Sansom, *Japan 1334-1615*, 265-70; FitzGerald, *Expansion*, 107-9; C. R. Boxer, *The Christian Century in Japan* (Berkeley 1951), 6-8 [*Christian Century*]. Takekoshi, *Economic Aspects*, has a chapter of lively detail entitled 'Japanese Pirate Fleet Spread All Over the Orient' (I.336-48). See also J. Gernet, *Le Monde Chinois* (Paris 1972), 365-9 (with map) and A. J. Marder, 'From Jimmu Tennō to Perry: Sea Power in Early Japanese History', *Amer. Hist. Rev.* 51, 1945-6, 1-34 at 19-20 ['Sea Power'].

[21] Chang, *Sino-Port. Trade*, 35-8; C. R. Boxer, *Fidalgos in the Far East* (The Hague 1948), 2 [*Fidalgos*]; Boxer, *S. China*, xix-xx; and cf. Cortesão's note in Pires, *Suma*, I.120. In general I have relied on Chang's unpretentious but valuable little book and Boxer's three—*Christian Century*, *Fidalgos*, and *Great Ship*—especially for the Macao-Japan trade.

[22] Chang, *Sino-Port. Trade*, 62-74; Boxer, *S. China*, xxi-xxv, 313-26.

[23] M. Fitzpatrick, Fighting Pirates in Northern Chekiang 1553-56 (unpublished, Dept of Far Eastern History, Australian National Univ.)—an excellent detailed account of defence measures.

[24] Meilink-Roelofsz, *Asian Trade*, 127-8.

[25] For the nomenclature, Boxer, *Fidalgos*, 3-4; the usual Spanish form was 'Macan'.

[26] Boxer, *S. China*, xxxv; Chang, *Sino-Port. Trade*, 87, 95-6. Chang refers to the alarmist memorials of scholars, for which, today, read 'wall newspapers'.

[27] See Boxer, *Christian Century*, 2-31, for a discussion of dates and priorities, including the confusions introduced by Fernão Mendes Pinto, who may or may not have been a worthy successor of Sir John Mandeville but was certainly in Japan soon after 1543.

[28] The Japanese were of course acquainted with gunpowder through their relations with China, but despite its limitations the arquebus was more tactically useful than anything they had yet seen. Opinions differ as to the impact of firearms on the wars of unification, but cannon (first used in 1558) led to changes in fortification, and only the most powerful warlords could afford ample armaments, so that (as in Europe a few decades earlier) guns promoted centralising trends. See Hall, *Japan*, 138, 145; Varley in Tiedemann, *Introduction* 90; Sansom, *Japan 1334-1615*, 263-4, 287-8; Boxer, *Fidalgos*, 96-7; but especially D. M. Brown, 'The Impact of Firearms on Japanese Warfare, 1543-98', *Jnl Asian Studies (Far Eastern Qly)* 7, 1947-8, 236-53 ['Firearms'].

[29] Boxer, *Great Ship*, 1-8, and *Christian Century*, 95-7, 119; Meilink-Roelofsz, *Asian Trade*, 132, 183.

[30] Despite the most ruthless persecution, crypto-Christian communities of some thousands survived near Nagasaki and on some islands, to come to light again in 1865—Boxer, *Christian Century*, 396; D. Pacheco in Cooper, *Barbarians*, 96; R. H. Drummond, *A History of Christianity in Japan* (Grand Rapids (Mich.) 1971), 112-17 [*Christianity*].

[31] Drummond, *Christianity*, 75, 91-2.

[32] According to Murdoch (*Japan 1542-1651*, 95-6), of an estimated 125,000 Christians in 1580, over 100,000 were in three fiefs, including those of 'Protasius' of Arima and 'Michael' of Amakusa. Cf. Takekoshi, *Economic Aspects*, I.442, 443-7, and Drummond, *Christianity*, 55-8.

[33] Boxer, *Christian Century*, 103-4; for motives in general, Sansom, *Japan 1334-1615*, 212-33.

Cf. L. Knauth, *Confrontación Transpacífica: El Japon y el Nuevo Mundo Hispanica* (Mexico 1972), 105—a book with much detail on the cross-currents of intrigue, pagan and Christian [*Confrontación*].

[34] Hall, *Japan*, 135.

[35] Boxer, *Christian Century*, 92, and *Great Ship*, 7–11.

[36] *Christian Century*, 97–103, 150–1; D. Pacheco in Cooper, *Barbarians*, 50–1—q.v. for beautiful colour plates of Portuguese shipping at Nagasaki.

[37] T. A. Agoncillo, *A Short History of the Philippines* (New York 1969), 45 [*Short History*]; the increase in the 1890s was due to troops brought in to suppress insurrection. For the missionary effort, J. L. Phelan, *The Hispanization of the Philippines* (Madison 1959), *passim*; N. P. Cushner SJ, *Spain in the Philippines* (Quezon City 1971), 74–101.

[38] Blair & Robertson, IV.166–70; Agoncillo, *Short History*, 47.

[39] P. Chaunu, *Les Philippines et le Pacifique des Ibériques* (Paris 1960), 43–6 [*Philippines*]; as Chaunu points out, the costs of the defences and the running of Acapulco were also basically on Filipino account.

[40] Chaunu, *Philippines*, 19.

[41] The direct quotations in this paragraph, in order of occurrence, are from Blair & Robertson, VI.63, VIII.278, 271, 272, 252–6 (list of consignors), XI.87, X.156. There is a wonderful immediacy in these on-the-spot reports. Cf. the comments of P. Chaunu in 'Le galion de Manille', *Annales Économies Sociétés Civilisations* 6, 1951, 447–62 at 457—a brilliant resumé of the 'Grandeur et decadence d'une route de la soie' ['galion'].

[42] Blair & Robertson, III.244, 247.

[43] The details of Limahon's raid, including the moonlight sighting of the pirate fleet and Salcedo's dash to Manila, are exciting. Sande's account and his reactions are in Blair & Robertson, IV.24–58, his schemes to conquer China and the royal brush-off in IV.58–62 and 94; the sensible comments of Fr José de Acosta SJ may be found in S. Zavala, *El Mundo Americano en la Epoca Colonial* (Mexico 1967), II.177 at note 34. The vivid account of Fr Gonzalez de Mendoza in his *Historia . . . del gran Reyno de la China* (Madrid 1580) is in Blair & Robertson, VI.91–124; to him we owe the story of the 'Indians' who spurned baptism since they did not wish to go to heaven in the company of Castilian soldiers—like the Indian Prince who thought that if Heaven were any good at all, the British would have annexed it long ago. Rada's narrative of his mission is in Boxer, *S. China*, 243–59; and see the introduction, xliii–l, for a 1581 mission from Spain to China, which got no further than Mexico. G. F. Hudson's comments in *Europe and China*, 248–51, that the ships Manila asked for were sent to their doom in the Armada, seem to ignore logistics. Finally for the warlike and vinous plans of the incomparable Picrochole, F. Rabelais, *Premier livre des faictes et dicts heroïques du noble Pantagruel* (Paris 1533, numerous eds.), Ch. XXXIII.

[44] The shocked expression of Bishop Salazar, Blair & Robertson, VII.68.

[45] Blair & Robertson, V.197, IX.39; for the Japanese raids of 1580–1, V.192–5. It is amusing to find the term 'heathen Chinese Indians'.

[46] Boxer, *Great Ship*, 18.

[47] For details, E. W. Dahlgren, *Were the Hawaiian Islands Visited by the Spaniards . . .?* (Stockholm 1916), 4–58.

[48] Blair & Robertson, IV.145.

[49] Chaunu, 'galion', at 458. An excellent sentence; but the reference he gives (Blair & Robertson, III.54–67; cf. III.184) does not bear out his further assertion that Legazpi proposed 'to abandon the hopes of pepper and put silk in the first place'; in fact, almost the contrary. The silk growers and weavers of New Spain were not pleased with this new opening.

[50] Chaunu, 'galion', at 458; W. L. Schurz, *The Manila Galleon* (Dutton ed., New York 1959),

27–39. Unreferenced statements on the Galleon trade are drawn from this comprehensive and well-written work [*Galleon*]. The regulations were extremely minute, descending to the position of fireplaces on the ships; though, admitting that *de minimis non curat lex* was a maxim of no applicability in Spanish bureaucracy, this at least was not trivial, in view of the fire risk—Blair & Robertson, XXV.23–47.

[51] Schurz, *Galleon*, 154–90.

[52] The mission from Manila which secured Macao's adhesion left when the Chinese became 'increasingly suspicious about the Spaniards' real intentions'. They sailed (1582) on a Portuguese ship which was wrecked on Formosa, most of the company reaching Macao after building a small boat; this seems to be the first European landing on an island which the Portuguese had coasted for forty years and had named for its beauty as seen from the sea—Boxer, *Fidalgos*, 43–4.

[53] Blair & Robertson, VI.243, and VIII.174–96 for the Manila Cabildo's views on the advantages of trading with Macao, and the large profits made by the Portuguese on this easy run.

[54] Blair & Robertson, VII.199–204, 269–71, 281–9.

[55] Blair & Robertson, VI.157–240—a wonderful synopsis of fears and hopes, splendid velleities and sordid realities. Other engaging points are that Chinese women 'lack only Christianity to be much beyond us in all matters of morality' (shades of *The Golden Lotus*!) and will make wonderful wives, mothers for a mixed race 'united and fraternal, and Christian'; that the Chinese will readily abandon their writing, so difficult that it is a 'diabolic invention' to retard men's minds; and that this conquest, conducted with impeccable civility and moderation, will forestall the French and English and other northern heretics who could make an entry by the strait (Anian) opposite Labrador.

[56] Blair & Robertson, IX.161–80, 197–203; A. de Morga, *Sucesos de las Islas Filipinas* (Mexico 1609), HS 2nd Ser. 140 (Cambridge 1971), 80–8, 119–36, 150–4 [*Sucesos*].

[57] Boxer, *Fidalgos*, 46–7, and *Great Ship*, 61–82; for the Spanish version, Morga, *Sucesos*, 136–49, including an interesting letter 'from the port of El Pinal, frozen with the cold' by Hernando de los Rios Coronel, who argues the advantages of direct trade to Canton and alleges, at this late date, that the Portuguese at Malacca had trespassed across the demarcation. *Per contra*, a Filipino Bishop argued eloquently that intervention in China would mean the destruction of Macao, and hence the ruin of the Japanese mission and of all Iberian interest in the East, since 'all these affairs are moved by but one wheel, namely, Macan'—Blair & Robertson, X.190–7.

[58] There was in fact no Shogun from 1573 to 1603, when Ieyasu assumed the title; Hideyoshi acted as Regent for the Emperor.

[59] Murdoch, *Japan 1542–1651*, 135–6.

[60] Takekoshi, *Economic Aspects*, I.371; Hall, *Japan*, 146; Sansom, *Japan 1334–1615*, 300–5.

[61] Boxer, *Christian Century*, 95–6. It is scarcely possible, even were it necessary, to give precise references for judgments compounded from scattered notices in many authorities; my sources will be clear from other notes.

[62] Mⁱˢ de la Mazelière, *Le Japon* (Paris 1907), III.32. Another triad has it that Nobunaga kneaded the dough, Hideyoshi baked the cake, Ieyasu ate it.

[63] Sansom, *Japan 1334–1615*, 303, 320.

[64] Andrew Marvell, *An Horatian Ode upon Cromwel's Return from Ireland*.

[65] In many respects the running of the country remained in the hands of local daimyo, but these were supervised by a bureaucracy drawn exclusively from the warrior class—cf. C. Totman, 'Tokugawa Japan', in Tiedemann, *Introduction*, 98–104.

[66] For all this see Boxer, *Christian Century*, 140–53, and *Great Ship*, 48–57; Sansom, *Japan 1334–1615*, 346–8; Pacheco in Cooper, *Barbarians*, 58–63.

[67] In 1586 the Great Ship went to Hirado, as Nagasaki was thought unsafe on account of the internal warfare in Kyushu which preceded the island's subjugation; it was still at Hirado when Hideyoshi was at Hakata in July 1572, and he asked for it to be brought round for his inspection. The commander declared this impossible for navigational reasons, but tactfully came to apologise in person, and the incident was apparently smoothed over; but it may have had some effect.

[68] Boxer, *Christian Century*, 152–3.

[69] The Portuguese account by Fr Luis Frois SJ is given in J. A. A. Pinto, Yoshitomo Okamoto and H. Bernard SJ (eds.), *Le Première Ambassade du Japon en Europe 1582–1592* (Tokyo 1942), Part I.

[70] Boxer, *Christian Century*, 153.

[71] Ibid., 150.

[72] G. Stramiglioni, 'Hideyoshi's Expansionist Policy on the Asiatic Mainland', *Trans. Asiatic Soc. Japan* 3rd Ser. 3, 1954, 74–116; Hall, *Japan*, 155–6; Sansom, *Japan 1334–1615*, 361–2. Hideyoshi is said to have told Nobunaga that if granted Kyushu for one year, he would take Korea and China 'as easily as a man rolls up a piece of matting and carries it under one arm'—Murdoch, *Japan 1542–1651*, 305.

[73] Murdoch, *Japan 1542–1651*, 311.

[74] Ibid., 348; cf. Robert Graves, 'Diplomatic Relations', in *Poems (1914–1926)* (London 1927), 129–32.

[75] Takekoshi, *Economic Aspects*, I.472. Sansom, *Japan 1334–1615*, gives a clear account of the land campaigns, and there is much detail (often picturesque) in Murdoch, *Japan 1542–1651*, 302–59 (with map); see also Brown, 'Firearms', at 240–1. The Spanish Armada carried some 31,000 men in all, the combined Christian fleets of southern Europe at Lepanto 75–80,000. For the naval side, see Marder, 'Sea Power', 21–31.

[76] Murdoch (*Japan 1542–1651*, 334–8) seems responsible for the view that the tortoise-boats were capital ships, heavily-armoured rams. He is followed by G. A. Ballard, *The Influence of the Sea on the Political History of Japan* (London 1921), 42–72 [*Influence of Sea*]. As might be expected of a Vice-Admiral, Ballard is good on the strategic aspects, and on a close reading it is clear that he gives more weight to fire-power than is implied in A. L. Sadler, 'The Naval Campaign in the Korean War of Hideyoshi (1592–1598)', *Trans. Asiatic Soc. Japan* 2nd Ser. 14, 1937, 177–208. Sadler corrects Murdoch on ships and armament and gives good accounts of the ten engagements, but his abominably drawn map is useful only after decipherment. He doubts the armour-plating (at 180), but this seems needless in view of the discussion of Yi-sun's tortoise-boats and their Chinese antecedents in Needham, *Science in China*, IV.682–8. Cf. also Brown, 'Firearms', 243, 250–3.

[77] Takekoshi, *Economic Aspects*, I.477–9.

[78] Ballard, *Influence of Sea*, 71.

[79] Boxer, *Christian Century*, 154–60; for what follows, apart from the specific references to Blair & Robertson, Sansom, *Japan 1334–1615*, 371–8.

[80] Blair & Robertson, VIII.256–69, and 285–97 for Dasmariñas's emergency measures, which went so far as to urge that if anyone should be captured, 'from myself and my son first, down to the least', there should be no thought of ransom. According to Murdoch (*Japan 1542–1651*, 282–3) Valignano refused to support Harada and wrote to the Jesuits of Manila about him, so that Dasmariñas may have had some warning. See also Knauth, *Confrontación*, 128–34.

[81] Boxer, *Christian Century*, 121; Murdoch, *Japan 1542–1651*, 282–5; Takekoshi, *Economic Aspects*, I.451–4; Blair & Robertson, IX.45.

[82] Boxer, *Christian Century*, 162; for the diplomatic exchanges, Blair & Robertson, IX.23–57, 122–35.

⁸³ In the first draft Dasmariñas gently reminded Hideyoshi that 'The Sun has no life or power than what God gave it, and this does not go to the extent of taking or giving away kingdoms . . .'—Blair & Robertson, IX.128.
⁸⁴ Blair & Robertson, IX.263.
⁸⁵ For the *San Felipe* affair, Murdoch, *Japan 1542–1651*, 267–99; Boxer, *Christian Century*, 164–6; Sansom, *Japan 1334–1615*, 374; and especially M. Cooper SJ, *Rodrigues the Interpreter* (New York 1974), 132–5, 150–60. Murdoch and Boxer accept the story of the pilot's boast; Sansom flouts it; Cooper, in a careful review (including Spanish counter-charges that the Portuguese Jesuits were responsible) suspends a definitive judgment but inclines towards acceptance. Morga, writing before 1609 and in close touch with the affair, also gives the story—*Sucesos*, 108.
⁸⁶ Morga, *Sucesos*, 111.

Notes for Chapter 7

¹ *Arbitristas*, as we should now say economic publicists, 'those contrivers of schemes, or *arbitrios*, who searched for a "universal means" to improve the situation'—J. Lynch, *Spain under the Habsburgs* (Oxford 1964–9), II.83 [*Habsburgs*].
² For instance, Philip's marital visits to Mary Tudor brought enough treasure into England to permit the revaluation of her badly debased currency—F. Braudel, *La Méditerranée et le Monde méditerranéen à l'époque de Philippe II* (Paris 1949), 377 [*Méditerranée*].
³ Cf. D. Ramos, *Minería y Comercio Interprovincial en Hispanoamerica (siglos XVI, XVII, y XVIII)* (Valladolid n.d.), 21, 50 [*Minería*].
⁴ P. W. Powell, *Soldiers, Indians and Silver* (Berkeley 1952), 204, and *passim* for a vivid description of the northern frontier; for the Tlaxcalans, E. Florescano, 'Colonización . . . en el norte de Nueva España, 1521–1750', in A. Jara et al., *Tierras Nuevas* (Mexico 1969), 43–76, at 55–61. See also M. L. Moorhead, 'The Soldado de Cuera', *Jnl of the West* 8, 1969, 38–57. N. Wachtel, *La Vision des Vaincus* (Paris 1971), 289–95, is good on the Araucanians [*Vaincus*]; for the retreat, L. Galdames, *A History of Chile* (Chapel Hill 1941), 88–9 [*Chile*]. There are many admirable general remarks and details in Chaunu, especially at 33, 145–9, 1111.
⁵ *Habsburgs*, II.213; see 200–12 for Mexican and 212–14 for Peruvian populations (including whites) and economic activity. Cf. also Chaunu, 1111, and Byron: 'A tyrant—but our tyrants then/Were still at least our countrymen.'
⁶ See *The Rise of the Spanish American Empire* (London 1947), 326–7 [*Rise*]. Madariaga wrote before modern analyses and purports to follow Angel Rosenblat. But he starts with Rosenblat's 3,500,000 for Mexico in 1570, and is thus able to show an increase to 3,700,000 in 1825, so that 'this all-important test . . . is decidedly favourable to the Spanish rule.' Since Rosenblat gives the 1492 population as 4,500,000, there is really a fall of 800,000 rather than a rise of 200,000. More modern Spanish apologists admit the decline, and refer it *inter alia* to some undefined shock at meeting a superior race. An extreme position is taken by B. W. Diffie, *Latin American Civilisation: Colonial Period* (Harrisburg 1945), 179–81—'the population of Montezuma's empire would not have reached one million people' [*Civilisation*].
    Rosenblat is the most serious proponent of a low starting figure; his calculations were first put forward in 1935 and in book form in *La Población Indígena de América desde 1492 hasta la Actualidad* (Buenos Aires 1945), reprinted, with documentation up-dated, in *La Población Indígena y el Mestizaje en América 1492–1950* (Buenos Aires 1950), and repeated unchanged in his critique of the 'Berkeley School', *La Población de América: viejos y nuevos calculos* (Mexico 1967). It should be said that he is

not unduly rhetorical nor chauvinist. Cf. W. Borah, *La Demografía Histórica de la América* (Bogota 1972), and P. Chaunu, *Conquête et Exploitation des Nouveaux Mondes* (Paris 1969), 378–83 [*Conquête*].

[7] W. Borah and S. F. Cook, *The Population of Central Mexico in 1548, The Indian Population of Central Mexico 1531–1610, The Aboriginal Population of Central Mexico on the Eve of the Spanish Conquest* (Berkeley 1960, 1960, 1963); see especially 2–7, 24–34, 41–4 of the last of these for the pictographic tribute lists, illustrated on Plate VIII of C. Gibson, *The Aztecs under Spanish Rule* (Stanford 1964) [*Aztecs*]. See also the Borah-Cook paper 'La Despoblación del México Central en el siglo XVI', *Hist. Mexicana* 12, 1962–3, 1–12. Even if we take the lower estimates of S. F. Cook and L. B. Simpson, *The Population of Central Mexico in the Sixteenth Century* (Berkeley 1948)— 11,000,000 in 1519, 2,014,000 in 1607—this is still genocide on a giant scale. Depopulation and gradual recovery after about 1630–50 can be followed in detail for many localities in P. Gerhard, *A Guide to the Historical Geography of New Spain* (Cambridge 1972). There is an acute analysis of the decline in a world-setting in M. J. MacLeod's introduction, 'The War of the Worlds', to his *Spanish Central America: A Socioeconomic History, 1520–1720*, 1–20 [*Central America*].

[8] W. Borah, 'America as Model: The Demographic Impact of European Expansion upon the Non-European World', *Actas y Memorias del XXXV Congreso Internacional de Americanistas* Vol. III (Mexico 1964), 379–87 at 387 (also as Berkeley Reprint No. 292).

[9] The Mayan Chilam Balam de Chumayel, cited Wachtel, *Vaincus*, 59; yet (at 48, note 1) the whites are also sons of the Sun.

[10] Including e.g. Lynch, *Habsburgs*, II.213, or E. Romero, *Historia Económica del Perú* (Buenos Aires 1949), 97, [*Perú*]; but L. A. Sanchez, *Historia General de América* (Santiago 1970), I.135 cites 8,000,000 [*América*].

[11] Chaunu, 1110; Wachtel, *Vaincus*, 138–52, 307, 333 (graph). Another estimate by D. N. Cook (1970) is 6,000,000 in 1531 (Lynch, *Habsburgs*, II.213), but more recently he gives 2,738,000 in 1530, 'certainly a revival of the conservative view' (not seen, but cited from review in *HAHR* 56, 1976, 297–9).

[12] Lynch, *Habsburgs*, II.201, 213. There is an important review of the question in M. Mörner, 'Spanish Migration to the New World prior to 1810', in F. Chiappelli (ed.), *First Images of America* (Berkeley 1976), II.737–82.

[13] J. Vicens Vives, *An Economic History of Spain* (Princeton 1969), 318 [*Spain*]. For New Spain, F. Chevalier, *Land and Society in Colonial Mexico* (Berkeley 1963), sections on 'The Land Grabbers' and 'Settlers' Encroachments', 135–46 and 207–20 [*Land and Society*]. See also MacLeod, *Central America*, 125–6.

[14] Cf. the 'assignment' of convicts at Botany Bay.

[15] This discussion is based mainly on W. Borah, *New Spain's Century of Depression* (Berkeley 1951), 32–42 [*Depression*]; C. H. Haring, *The Spanish Empire in America* (New York 1963, original ed. 1947), 42–63, 240–2 [*Spanish Empire*]; Lynch, *Habsburgs*, II.209–11; J. H. Parry, *The Spanish Seaborne Empire* (Harmondsworth 1973), 210–13 [*Seaborne Empire*]; L. B. Simpson, 'Mexico's Forgotten Century', *Pac. Hist. Rev.* 22, 1953, 113–21. There are interesting peripheral comments in Vicens Vives, *Spain*, 317–21, and Sanchez, *América*, I.333–43, and some very pertinent ones, on pre- as well as post-Conquest aspects, in S. J. and B. H. Stein, *The Colonial Heritage of Latin America* (New York 1970), 28–53—a miracle of concision and stimulation.

[16] Vicens Vives, *Spain*, 317. For the remarkable exceptions of Costa Rica and Antioquia, P. E. James, *Latin America* (New York [1942]), 100–5, 706–17; see the relevant chapters of this book for the geographical background of areas mentioned here.

[17] G. B. Masefield, 'Crops and Livestock', in *The Cambridge Economic History of Europe* IV, 1967, 275–301 at 275 [*Cambridge EHE*].

[18] D. Perez, *Historia de Colonización Española en América* (Madrid 1947), 158–9 [*Colonización*]; Haring, *Spanish Empire*, 235–8.

[19] W. Borah, *Early Colonial Trade and Navigation between Mexico and Peru* (Berkeley 1954), 10–18, 37–62, 84–6 [*Early Trade*].

[20] Chaunu, 741–4; Haring, *Spanish Empire*, 237–8; Madariaga, *Rise*, 58; but especially W. Borah, *Silk-Raising in Colonial Mexico* (Berkeley 1943), *passim*.

[21] Perez, *Colonización*, 197–9; cf. Chaunu, 787–8; Lynch, *Habsburgs*, II.207–9; Vincens Vives, *Spain*, 353. On the relation between mines and farming, cf. Humboldt's remarks cited in C. Prieto, *Mining in the New World* (New York 1973), 65–7 [*Mining*], and Chevalier, *Land and Society*, 102–7 and 154–5, the latter the specific case of a Governor of New Galicia who had 'huge droves, orchards, a winery, a water system, and four silver smelters with their charcoal heaps'.

[22] Chaunu, 772–3, 848–58, 885–92; Ramos, *Minería*, 225; MacLeod, *Central America*, 68–95, 274–5; for Guayaquil competition 146, 152; for indigo 176–86.

[23] Borah, *Early Trade*, 34–5, 65–6; Chaunu, 1071–4, 1083–90; Lynch, *Habsburgs*, II.198–9; Ramos, *Minería*, 215. MacLeod, *Central America*, 160–3, for attempts to have the transit trade of Panama diverted to Nicaraguan or Honduran ports, especially Realejo. The shipbuilding resources of Guayaquil are detailed in G. Lohmann Villena, 'La Marina Mercante', in *Historia Marítima del Perú* (Lima 1974–5), IV.213–369 at 215.

[24] S. Zavala, *El Mundo Americano en la Epoca Colonial* (Mexico 1957), I.15 [*Mundo Americano*]; Ramos, *Minería*, 214.

[25] J. Lockhart, *Spanish Peru 1532–1560* (Madison 1968), 186, 198; see 125 for truck-farming, which was looked down upon by Spaniards and was largely in Portuguese hands [*Peru*].

[26] Dates and other details in Romero, *Perú*, 98, 117–27; he has the delightful story that two or three survivors of the first olive seedlings, brought with loving care from Seville and guarded by Negroes and dogs, were stolen and turned up in Chile. Other points in Chaunu, 1094–7; Lynch, *Habsburgs*, II.215–28; Perez, *Colonización*, 163; Ramos, *Minería*, 216–20.

[27] For Jesuit activities in New Spain, Diffie, *Civilisation*, 385–6; Chevalier, *Land and Society*, 239–50; in Chile, Galdames, *Chile*, 103, 121–2.

[28] Thomas Gage, *The English-American* (1648; ed. A. P. Newton, London 1928), 45—this refers to New Spain, but could apply *a fortiori* to Peru. Gage, an English Dominican deserting to the Puritans, was a scoundrel who betrayed old comrades to their deaths, but he was a brisk reporter, invaluable as giving a non-Spanish view of life in New Spain and Guatemala.

[29] Haring, *Spanish Empire*, 236–7; Ramos, *Minería*, 236–7; Vicens Vives, *Spain*, 394.

[30] James, *Latin America*, 229. Chaunu, 139–42, 1171–5, has some acute remarks on Chile as the remotest frontier, but with a strangely moralising air, almost like Toynbee damning the Eskimos for living as they had to live.

[31] Galdames, *Chile*, 57–8, 72–4.

[32] Perez, *Colonización*, 199–200; Lockhart, *Peru*, 122; A. de Ovalle SJ, *Histórica Relación del Reino de Chile* (Rome 1646), cited from the 'Antología' ed. by R. Silva Castro (Santiago 1961), 37–41. Concision is not usually the strongest point of Spanish sixteenth and seventeenth century writers, and in bulk (503 pages in the complete Santiago 1967 ed.) the *Relación* might be tedious; but in excerpt the good Father (b. Santiago 1601, d. Lima 1651 on his way home from Europe) is irresistible in his ingenuous pleasure in almost everything and his style at once breathless and fresh. As for what sort of fish a *róbalo* might be, don't ask me: dictionaries give it as bass, sea-bass, bream, haddock, sea-pike, snook, and labrax. A queer fish anyhow.

[33] Lockhart, *Peru*, 103; see his listing of artisans at 243 (Table 5) and notes on skilled artisans, 126–7.

[34] Braudel, *Méditerranée*, 400; Haring, *Spanish Empire*, 60–1, 66, 242–4; Perez, *Colonización*, 190–1; Romero, *Perú*, 131–2. For the obrajes themselves and their products, see R. D. Hussey, 'Colonial Economic Life', in A. C. Wilgus (ed.), *Colonial Hispanic America* (Washington 1936), 305–32 at 322–3 ['Economic Life']; Chaunu, *Conquête*, 306; Diffie, *Civilisation*, 386–92; Ramos, *Minería*, 215–24; Perez, 193–9; Romero, 130–47.

[35] P. Guzmán-Rivas, Reciprocal Geographical Influences of the Trans-Pacific Galleon Trade (Texas Univ. Ph.D thesis 1960), 37–50; it was not a systematic slave trade. However, under the forms of law many Indians were virtually immured for life in obrajes—Gibson, Aztecs, 243–7. For corregidores and caciques, Haring, *Spanish Empire*, 57, 67, 132–3; Lockhart, *Peru*, 209. Their corrupt tyranny is still a main theme in J. Juan and A. de Ulloa, *Noticias Secretas de América*, written in the mid-eighteenth century but not published until 1826, in London. Although published as part of a propaganda campaign for American independence, the authenticity of the *Noticias* is accepted even by Madariaga (*Rise*, 391). Cf. Diffie, *Civilisation*, 389, 468—the more significant since he sees most things *couleur de rose*—and R. Donoso, 'Autencidad de las Noticias Secretas de América', *Rev. Chilena de Historia y Geografía* 138, 1970, 17–39.

[36] W. R. Ambrose, '3,000 Years of Trade in New Guinea Obsidian', *Nature* 237, No. 5349, 1972, 31–3—obsidian from New Britain was transported to the Santa Cruz about 1000 B.C. The total distance is 2000 km with one stage of 450 km over open seas, and the amounts suggest exchange, not a sporadic loss (personal communication).

[37] These included a tunnel between 5 and 6 km long and over 3 by 4 metres in section—H. H. Bancroft, *History of Mexico* (San Francisco 1883–6), III.7–11, 85–91 [*Mexico*]. But it narrowed at one point to about one metre each way—Gibson, *Aztecs*, 236–43.

[38] Hussey, 'Economic Life', 319; Gage, *The English-American*, 125–36—one of his most vivid passages; Prieto, *Mining* 68–9; Borah, *Early Trade*, 25–8; Chaunu, 713–19, for the Camino de Castilla between Mexico and Vera Cruz.

[39] A. P. Whitaker, *The Huancavelica Mercury Mine* (Cambridge (Mass.) 1941), 105 note 21 [*Huancavelica*].

[40] The classic source is E. J. Hamilton, *American Treasure and the Price Revolution in Spain, 1501–1650* (Cambridge (Mass.) 1934), especially 32–46 [*Treasure*]. Good summaries in Chaunu, *Conquête*, 302–15; Lynch, *Habsburgs*, II.204–9, 212–14; J. H. Elliott, *Imperial Spain 1469–1716* (London 1963), 174–88; comments in Vicens Vives, *Spain*, 322–4, 377–9. Recently, however, Alvaro Jara, *Tres Ensayos sobre Economía Minería Hispanoamericana* (Santiago 1966), has used Peruvian as well as Sevillean archives to revise Hamilton's figures upwards; he also puts the dominance of silver over gold later, not until the 1560s—26, 52 (table), 96–100, 103–6 [*Tres Ensayos*]. Cf. also P. Chaunu, *L'Amérique et les Amériques* (Paris 1964), 95 ff.

[41] D. A. Brading and H. E. Cross, 'Colonial Silver Mining: Mexico and Peru', *HAHR* 52, 1972, 545–79 at 568–71 and 579—an important paper.

[42] Vicens Vives, *Spain*, 323.

[43] Braudel in 1949 (*Méditerranée*, 400–1) seems to support the tripling of silver; but in 1967 he and F. Spooner indicate the 50 per cent increase—'Prices in Europe from 1450 to 1750' in *Cambridge EHE*, IV.378–486 at 445–50 ['Prices']. Cf. also Braudel, 'European Expansion and Capitalism, 1450–1650' in J. L. Blau (ed.), *Chapters in Western Civilisation* (New York 1961), I.245–84 at 260–3 ['Expansion'].

[44] Bancroft, *Mexico*, II.31–2; Prieto, *Mining*, 21 and the long quotation from Humboldt at 34–6. For the silver cannon, F. L. de Gomara, *Historia de la Conquista de Mexico* (1552; ed. J. Ramirez Cabanos, Mexico 1943), II.114–15 [*Conquista*]. The standard general survey of colonial mining seems to be M. Bargalló, *La minería y la metalurgía en la América Española durante la época colonial*

(Mexico 1955) [*La minería*], and its references to non-precious metals (mercury excluded) are cursory—77, 213–15, 295–6, 302–3.

[45] Chaunu, *Conquête*, 303; for mining expansion, Chevalier, *Land and Society*, 38–42.

[46] Whitaker, *Huancavelica*, 3. Valuable as this book is it is surpassed by G. Lohmann Villena, *Las Minas de Huancavelica en los siglos XVI y XVII* (Seville 1949) [*Las Minas*], which gives a vast amount of detail on the extraordinarily complex legal and technical tangles of the mines. Unreferenced statements to Huancavelica come from these works.

[47] Chaunu, 1112; Ramos, *Minería*, 240; Jara, *Tres Ensayos*, 70–3.

[48] Still used, though not for smelting, at the tin and bismuth mines which have revived Potosi— James, *Latin America*, 201. Collection was easier than might be thought, as a flock very decently deposits all its dung at a fixed spot—E. C. Rolls, *They All Ran Wild* (Sydney 1969), 257–8.

[49] There is no doubt that the process was known simply as a process well before 1554—see F. Spooner, *The International Economy and Monetary Movements in France, 1493–1725* (Cambridge (Mass.) 1972), 17–18 [*Movements*]—and Chaunu calls Medina 'only a diffuser' (*Conquête*, 305); but this seems to underrate him. The matter is discussed with much learning in M. Bargalló, *La Amalgamación de los Minerales de Plata en Hispanoamerica Colonial* (Mexico 1969), 50–91 [*Amalgamación*]; see also A. Probert, 'Bartolomé de Medina: The Patio Process and the Sixteenth Century Silver Crisis', *Jnl of the West* (Los Angeles) 8, 1969, 90–124. Perhaps Brading and Cross sum up fairly that 'it was the Spaniard who carried out the experiments which made it an industrial reality' —'Colonial Silver', 552.

[50] Chaunu, 1118, and 1112–22 for general discussion; also Borah, *Early Trade*, 88–93, and Brading and Cross, 'Colonial Silver', *passim*. For effects in Europe, Zavala, *Mundo Americano*, I.43, 216.

[51] Prieto, *Mining*, 79. Although Garcés was certainly very active, the paucity of references to him in Lohmann Villena, *Las Minas*, suggests that he was less important than Prieto implies. See also Lohmann Villena, 'Enrique Garcés . . .' *Anuario de Estudos Americanos* (Seville) 5, 1948, 439–82; Bargalló, *La minería*, 77–9, 134–7, and *Amalgamación*, 162, 166–74.

[52] Brading and Cross, 'Colonial Silver', 561, 573–6. Peru paid only the diezmo from 1548 till 1554, then the quinto until 1735—Bargalló, *La minería*, 82.

[53] M. F. Lang, 'New Spain's Mining Depression and the Supply of Quicksilver from Peru 1600– 1700', *HAHR* 48, 1968, 632–41 at 637–9. For a small shipment (200 quintals) from China in 1612, see Blair & Robertson, XVII.237; but most Chinese mercury went to Japan—VI.68. More could have been got from China for New Spain but for the perverse fear of adding to the silver drain to that country—P. J. Bakewell, *Silver Mining and Society in Colonial Mexico: Zacatecas 1546–1700* (Cambridge 1971), 152–4 [*Silver Mining*].

[54] Lohmann Villena, *Las Minas*, 173 (my italics); 'modorra' is heavy sleepiness, but the context calls for more than this; in veterinary usage, the dictionaries give it as meaning (1) the staggers (2) 'sturdy'! Cf. Chaunu, 1120–2; Whitaker, *Huancavelica*, 19–21. Perez in *Colonización* manages to mention hospitals but not mercury sickness.

[55] The main references in *Las Minas* are 169–77 (mercury poisoning, open-cut proposal), 189, 238, 258–88, 411–12; cf. Bakewell, *Silver Mining*, 158–64. The later history of the mine until its final ruin in the mid-nineteenth century is fascinating; see Whitaker's *Huancavelica*, from which one may pick out three points: ores found elsewhere were always assayed by Huancavelican experts, and 'invariably declared worthless' (50); after 1794 over two-thirds of output was by Indian *pallaqueadores*, i.e. virtually fossickers, and 'Thus the race in whose interest the court had formerly considered abandoning the mine was now its principal support' (74–5); and—a nice reprise of the first point—the final report on the worthlessness of Huancavelica was prepared for the (Californian) New Almaden Quicksilver Company (129, note 190).

[56] James, *Latin America*, 200–1.

[57] Chaunu, 1124–8. There is a careful and objective but finally condemnatory discussion in A. Crespo Rodas, 'La "Mita" de Potosí', *Rev. Histórica* (Lima) 22, 1955–6, 169–82. The comment on greed was made in 1715 about Huancavelica, but is even more applicable to Potosi—Lohmann Villena, *Las Minas*, 209.

[58] L. Hanke, *Potosí: Boom Town Supreme* (The Hague 1956), 1 [*Potosí*]; Chaunu, *Conquête*, 309–11; Lynch, *Habsburgs*, II.218–19. European comparisons from K. F. Helleiner, 'The Population of Europe . . .' *Cambridge EHE*, IV.1–95 at 81–3. There is a good account of Potosi in J. A. Crow, *The Epic of Latin America* (New York 1946), 267–73, and an excellent one in G. B. Cobb, 'Potosí, a South American Mining Frontier', in A. Ogden and E. Sluiter (eds.), *Greater America* (Berkeley 1945), 39–57.

[59] Brading and Cross, 'Colonial Silver', 553–4, 566–7; Hanke, *Potosí*, 15, 21—total water storage is said to have been 6,000,000 metric tons before the disastrous dam-break of 1626 destroyed 126 out of 132 mills and killed some 4000 people—Arzáns de Orsúa (see note 63 below), II.1–15, and W. E. Rudolph, 'The Lakes of Potosi', *Geogr. Rev.* 16, 1926, 529–54.

[60] G. B. Cobb, 'Supply and Transportation for the Potosí Mines, 1545–1640', *HAHR* 29, 1949, 25–45.

[61] R. N. Salaman, *The History and Social Influence of the Potato* (Cambridge 1949), 40–1, 101–3. With all respect, one cannot follow Salaman in his apparent inference (205–6) that the Spanish success in dominating the Indians, by the aid of the potato, may in some sense have inspired the English in dominating the Irish by the same means. It seems unlikely that knowledge of the specific —the use of *chuño*—could have been diffused to the English at the relevant time; Salaman's own rationale for the remarkable breach of conservative food habits in the adoption of the potato is very plausible; and he ascribes to Jacobean Englishmen a rather unlikely capacity for forward thinking. The whole notion is an offence against Occam's Razor; but it is a splendid book.

[62] Ramos, *Minería*, 241–2. A quintal was 40–5 kg.

[63] The romantic list is given in Prieto, *Mining* 71–3 (see also 31–4 for Potosi in general and 70–1 for the La Plata route), and Hanke, *Potosí*, 28–9, from Bartolomé Arzáns de Orsúa y Vela, *História de la Villa Imperial de Potosi* (Providence (Rhode Island) 1965), I.7–9, edited by L. Hanke and G. Mendoza in three splendid folios (clxxxv+1464 pages)—alas, that life is too short to do more than dip into them. Its remarkable flavour can be judged by the twenty pages of its chapter headings translated by Hanke in *B. A. de O. y V's History of Potosí* (Providence 1965), or better still in the extracts in R. C. Padden (ed.) *Tales of Potosí* (Providence 1975)—a riot of rape, elopement, abduction, duels, street fights, religious and imperial fiestas, gallantry and gallantries, drawn from a million-word tabloid which also contains a great deal of sober information. Often the bizarre and the mundane are juxtaposed: Book IV Ch. 13 is headed 'Of the Punishment which God executed in this Town on some sodomitic Indians, and of how in this same year there were found in the mines of its wealthy mountain admirable secret works of Nature'—but also contains (I.131–2) an account of the discovery of mercury at Huancavelica.

[64] For *Peruleiros* and *Peruleros* (sometimes confused) see Lynch, *Habsburgs*, II.59, 112, 187–8, 196.

[65] Hanke, *Potosí*, 2–3; C. R. Boxer, *Salvador de Sá and the Struggle for Brazil and Angola* (London 1952), 102–8. At least Potosi had *built* churches, unlike Mark Twain's Virginia City which had 'a whisky-mill every sixteen steps, half a dozen jails, and some talk of building a church'—hear H. Holbrook, *Mark Twain To-Night*, Columbia OL 5440, Side 1.

[66] *Conquista*, II.293–4; cf. Chaunu, 33, and Lynch, *Habsburgs*, II.200–1.

[67] Brading and Cross, 'Colonial Silver', 557–60, 564, 576–9; Chaunu, 786. In Chile Indians received one-sixth of placer gold produced (1559), but this was a collective payment—I. Wallerstein,

The Modern World-System (New York 1974), 94 [*World-System*].

[68] Chaunu, 756–9.

[69] James, *Latin America*, 615–22, 643–5; for desertion of Acapulco, W. L. Schurz, *The Manila Galleon* (Dutton ed., New York 1949), 74–6. For the geopolitics, Chaunu, 789–90, 1062; Ramos, *Minería*, 157–9, 212.

[70] Borah, *Early Trade*, 117–18.

[71] *Royal Commentaries of the Incas*, trans. H. V. Livermore (Austin 1966), II.645; cf. 636–7 for an extraordinary panegyric on Pizarro and his partners, who have enriched the world. Incidentally, Gomara himself may in a sense have anticipated by ten years Jean Bodin's famous enunciation of the quantity theory of money (1568), but the former's work was unpublished until 1912. Another Spaniard, Martin de Azpilcueta Navarro, actually published in 1556 a work ascribing the inflation to the influx of precious metal, but Bodin was the first to develop the idea systematically and to gain wide recognition for it. See Hamilton, *Treasure*, 292–3; Braudel, *Méditerranée*, 398–9; Lynch, *Habsburgs*, I.123–4; Spooner, *Movements*, 88–90, and 'The Economy of Europe 1559–1609' in *The New Cambridge Modern History*, III (1968) 14–43 at 18–19 ['Economy'].

[72] The 'long' sixteenth century is taken as from the mid-fifteenth to the Thirty Years' War; see i.a. Wallerstein, *World-System*, 67–9. See Chaunu, VIII.2.1 (1959), 10, for a rather verbose definition of 'conjuncture', and cf. Braudel and Spooner, 'Prices', 438. The opening of this essay is delightful as a comment on the history of price history, and admirable on its value and values. A rather clearer discussion of 'conjuncture' than Chaunu's may be found in F. Mauro, *L'Expansion Européenne (1600–1870)* (Paris 1967), 301–16.

[73] Hamilton's thesis is set out in *Treasure*, 283–306 ('Why Prices Rose'); several critiques of it are summarised in Wallerstein, *World-System*, 70–84. The following account is based on the relevant passages in the already cited works of Braudel, Chaunu, Elliott, Lynch, Parry, Spooner, Wallerstein and Vicens Vives. These overlap and interlock, so that several citations might be made on any one point. References below are therefore selective.

[74] Spooner, 'Economy', 22.

[75] Braudel, *Méditerranée*, 374–6—with details of some smuggling intercepts.

[76] Hamilton, *Treasure*, 33.

[77] A French estimate of 1691 reckoned that 25 per cent of 'Spanish' exports to the Indies were of French origin, 21 Genoese, 19 Dutch, 11 Flemish, 11 English, 7.6 Hamburgers, 3.8 Spanish—Vicens Vives, *Spain*, 433; cf. Lynch, *Habsburgs*, II.192.

[78] Parry, *Seaborne Empire*, 242–4; Spooner, 'Economy', 26–7.

[79] For the value of the Netherlands to Spain, and the cost of 'the provisioning of Flanders', see Lynch, *Habsburgs*, I.144–6, 272–3, 294–5, 346–7; for the asiento system, 131–4. See also Braudel, *Méditerranée*, 375–98, and Spooner, *Movements*, 26–7.

[80] J. E. Neale, *Queen Elizabeth* (London 1934), 181–3; J. A. Froude, *The Reign of Elizabeth* (Everyman ed.), II.471–7.

[81] H. Holborn, *A History of Modern Germany: The Reformation* (New York 1959), 75.

[82] C. H. Wilson, 'Trade, Society and the State', in *Cambridge EHE*, IV.487–575 at 494.

[83] Hamilton, *Treasure*, 90–1, 289. He is curiously precise: army disbursements on the Portuguese frontier in 1641–2 were 99.96 per cent in vellón. After an unsuccessful attempt to introduce vellón into New Spain in 1642, the Indians' fractional currency needs were met, until the eighteenth century, by the traditional medium of cocoa beans—Chevalier, *Land and Society*, 72, and E. J. Hamilton, *War and Prices in Spain 1651–1800* (Cambridge (Mass.) 1947), 72; see this work for the vicissitudes of vellón and the 1680 deflation. For the copper cargo, Parry, *Seaborne Empire*, 245.

[84] All this from J. McMaster's fascinating article 'Aventuras Asiáticas del Peso Mexicano', *Hist.*

Mexicana 8, 1958–9, 372–99; see Spooner, *Movements*, 27–9, for the world-meshing 'network of silver', and O. Pantaleão, *A Penetração Comercial de Inglaterra na America Espanhola de 1713 a 1783* (São Paulo 1946), 273.

[85] Lynch, *Habsburgs*, II.177; for the general theme of this section, 180–200.

[86] Lynch, *Habsburgs*, II.222–4.

[87] Chaunu, 758–9.

[88] Admiral de Bañuelos y Carilla (1638) in Blair & Robertson, XXIX.71.

[89] P. Chaunu, *Les Philippines et le Pacifique des Ibériques* (Paris 1960), 38–46, 268–9; cf. J. Grau y Monfalcon, 'Informatory Memorial' to Philip IV, in Blair & Robertson, XXVII.55–212 at 167–8.

[90] Lynch, *Habsburgs*, II.225.

[91] Ibid., II.193.

[92] MacLeod, *Central America*, 385–9. Very much has been written on the contraband penetration, sometimes amounting to domination, of Latin American markets in the eighteenth century, such as Olga Pantaleão's excellent study cited in note 84 above. This theme will be discussed in later chapters of this work.

[93] Ramos, *Minería*, 115–18.

[94] Chaunu, *Conquête*, 277–8; cf. 279–81 on 'le frein de poids moteur'.

[95] This epigram is often quoted; I have taken it from Vicens Vives, *Spain*, 464.

Notes for Chapter 8

[1] J. Vicens Vives, *An Economic History of Spain* (Princeton 1969), 398–9 [*Spain*], refers to Genoese and Portuguese, French and Netherlandish interests, and also 'another network, more obscure but no less powerful, between these same merchants and the great Andalusian latifundist magnates' such as the Count-Duke Olivares and that Aunt Sally of English popular navalism, Medina Sidonia, whose appointment to command the Armada, though a mistake, was by no means the mere nonsense that is so often stated or implied—for a welcome change, see W. Graham, *The Spanish Armadas* (London 1972), 78–80. For the Genoese, see I. Wallerstein, *The Modern World-System* (New York 1974), 49–50, 168–9, 173, 215 [*World-System*]; F. Braudel, *La Méditerranée et le Monde méditerranéen a l'époque de Philippe II* (Paris 1949), 395 [*Méditerranée*].

[2] In his chapter 'Le "monopole" de la Péninsule du Sud', Pierre Chaunu makes the point that 'The political and economic collapse of Spain in the 17th century did not carry with it, as would have been logical on the absurd hypothesis of a princely caprice, the disappearance of the "Carrera de Indias" but its internal colonisation by the colonies of foreign factors living at Cadiz'—*Conquête et Exploitation des Nouveaux Mondes* (Paris 1969), 245–76 at 268 [*Conquête*].

[3] For the Casa at Corunna, see F. de Solano, 'Navios y mercaderes en la ruta occidental de las especies (1519–1563)' in *A Viagem de Fernão de Magalhães e a Questão das Molucas* (Actas do II Colóquio Luso-Espanhol de História Ultramarina (Lisbon 1975), 579–610 at 583–7, and J. Pérez de Tudela y Bueso, 'La especeria de Castilla . . .', ibid., 627–87 at 658–9, 681 ['La especeria']. Chaunu, 177–201 has a lengthy analysis of the reasons for settling the monopoly at Seville; he formally repudiates the (conventionally immoral) stance of geographical determinism, but his narrowing of choices is difficult to distinguish from that position. See also J. H. Parry, *The Spanish Seaborne Empire* (Harmondsworth 1973), 31–6, 110–14 [*Seaborne Empire*]; C. H. Haring, *Trade and Navigation between Spain and the Indies in the Time of the Hapsburgs* (Cambridge (Mass.) 1918), Chs. I–II *passim* [*Trade*]; Haring, *The Spanish Empire in America* (New York 1963, original ed. 1947), 194–304

[*Spanish Empire*]; J. Lynch, *Spain under the Habsburgs* (Oxford 1964–9), I, 117–19, 151–5 [*Habsburgs*]. There are some perceptive remarks on the system, and especially its durability, in S. J. and B. N. Stein, *The Colonial Heritage of Latin America* (New York 1970), 46–53. [*Heritage*].

[4] Vicens Vives, *Spain*, 437–8; J. H. Elliott, *Imperial Spain 1469–1716* (London 1963), 173 [*Spain 1469–1716*]. The main liability of Cadiz was its vulnerability to attack, as in Essex's raid of 1596, when the President of the Casa de Contratacion himself was taken—A. L. Rowse, *The Expansion of Elizabethan England* (Cardinal ed., London 1973), 323–6.

[5] Vicens Vives, *Spain*, 370–1; for the persistent structural crisis of the American market, Chaunu, *Conquête*, 339.

[6] Stein, *Heritage*, 46. There is a clear account, including an interesting quasi-defence of the system, in E. W. Dahlgren, *Les Relations Commerciales et Maritimes entre La France et les Côtes de l'Océan Pacifique* (Paris 1909), 1–50 but especially 4–5.

[7] The causes are of course complex, but include the expulsions of Jews and *conversos*, who had many of the more progressive entrepreneurs and artisans, and the grossly inequitable official favour to the Mesta, the guild or corporation of sheep-rearers. Later, highly retrogressive taxation, especially the *alcabala* or sales tax, and the great inflation, which in so far as it stemmed from Indies treasure naturally struck Spain first and hardest, put Spanish industry at a great disadvantage compared with other countries—see i.a. Elliott, *Spain 1469–1715*, 179–81, 187–90; Lynch, *Habsburgs*, I.15–18, 119–21; Vicens Vives, *Spain*, 241–57, 401.

[8] '. . . the routine procedures and lack of imagination of the Spanish administration which, having prepared a system for transmitting merchandise to America and for receiving silver, allowed foreign interests to infiltrate and take advantage of it . . .', while 'the escort ships carried merchandise even in the mouths of their cannons'—Vicens Vives, *Spain*, 399. This last may seem a picturesque exaggeration, but even the forger of the convoy system, Menendez de Avila, though 'a stern disciplinarian, made a fortune by smuggling', and a flagship was reported so heavily laden that her lower gun-ports were below the water-line—Parry, *Seaborne Empire*, 122. The motto of the bureaucracy seems to have been *Quis custodiet ipsos custodes?*—unless it was a perversion of the Crown's great boast, *Plus Ultra*.

[9] Vicens Vives, *Spain*, 382–4; Braudel, *Méditerranée*, 375–97; see above, Ch. 7.

[10] The splendidly ingenious maps and diagrams in Tome VII ('Construction Graphique') of the Chaunu's *Séville* are probably more enlightening to the general historian than the details and tabulations of the actual trade movements in Tomes II–VI. More succinct accounts of the organisation of flotas and galeones may be found in Haring, *Trade*, 201–30, and *Spanish Empire*, 304–5; Parry, *Seaborne Empire*, 104–8, 120–2, 286–7, and Parry, 'Colonial Development . . . I. America' in *The New Cambridge Modern History* III, 1968, 507–32 at 516–20.

[11] Baptista Antonio [Juan Bautista Antonelli], 'A relation of the ports, harbors, forts and cities in the west India . . . Anno 1587' in Hakluyt, VII.109–27 ['relation'].

[12] D. Francis, *The First Peninsular War 1702–1713* (London 1975), 53–4; cf. Parry, *Seaborne Empire*, 260; Lynch, *Habsburgs*, II.74–5, 174–7, 191; M. Lewis, *The Spanish Armada* (Pan ed., London 1961), 88; P. Geyl, *The Netherlands in the Seventeenth Century 1609–1648* (London 1961), 88 [*Netherlands*].

[13] 'Tierra Firme' was the northern mainland of South America, roughly the modern Colombia (with Panama) and Venezuela, which until they were joined in the Viceroyalty of New Granada in the eighteenth century were attached respectively to Peru and New Spain. Tierra Firme was the original 'Spanish Main'; the use of this term for the adjacent seas is secondary. See *The New Cambridge Modern History*, XIV (Atlas), 1970, 229–30, and *The Oxford English Dictionary*, s.v. Spanish.

[14] D. R. Perez, *Historia de la Colonización Española en America* (Madrid 1947), 235 [*Colonización*].

[15] G. Mack, *The Land Divided: A History of the Panama Canal and other Isthmian Canal Projects* (New York 1944), 239–41, 151–8 [*Land Divided*]; for a modern first-hand account of the terrain, D. Howarth, *The Golden Isthmus* (London 1967), 11–14, 31–6.

[16] R. D. Hussey, 'Colonial Economic Life', in A. C. Wilgus (ed.), *Colonial Hispanic America* (Washington 1936), 305–32 at 324–5 ['Economic Life'].

[17] See above, Ch. 3, and references there. Locational and other factors are analysed with great skill and detail in Chaunu, 821–32, 869–89; while Mack, *Land Divided*, is unmatched for the meticulous treatment of all possible and impossible canal projects, not to mention the Eads Ship[-carrying] Railway.

[18] M. J. MacLeod, *Spanish Central America: A Socioeconomic History 1520–1720* (Berkeley 1973), 159–65 [*Central America*].

[19] P. Nichols, *Sir Francis Drake Revived*, in J. Hampden (ed.), *Francis Drake Privateer* (London 1972), 53–104 at 83; Chaunu, 916–21.

[20] A. Galvano [Galvão], *The Discoveries of the World*, trans. R. Hakluyt, HS 1st Ser. 30 (London 1862), 180. The Gomara list I know only from Mack, *Land Divided*, 42–3, and Haring, *Trade*, 192— where however there seems a misprint in the Spanish, as well as a careless description of Galvão and his book.

[21] For these early projects, see Mack, *Land Divided*, 40–6, and slighter mentions in Perez, *Colonizacion*, 264, and in H. M. Stephens and H. E. Bolton (eds.), *The Pacific Ocean in History* (New York 1917), at 118–21 (R. J. Taussig) and 45–6 (R. Altamira).

[22] Mack, *Land Divided*, 44–54; J. de Acosta SJ, *The Natural & Moral History of the Indies*, trans. C. R. Markham, HS 1st Ser. 60 (London 1880), 135–6; for a nicely muddled version of the tradition, J. B. Bishop, *The Panama Gateway* (New York 1913), 29–30 [*Gateway*].

[23] Mack, *Land Divided*, 53, 55; for another first-hand testimonial, Haring, *Trade*, 183—a priest living in Tierra Firme called it in 1640 'malissimo camino', the worst he had ever seen.

[24] Chaunu, 898, 901–8; and cf. 684, 825. The whole chapter 'Panama, Isthme de Seville' (898–958) is a magnificent piece of historical geography. However, in 1526 Panama had been formally designated as the terminal for the (putative) spice trade; but this was 'certainly beyond the economic possibilities of the isthmian area', pending the actual anchoring of a ship from Asia at Panama, which in turn would demand far more experience than was yet available—Tudela y Bueso, 'La especeria', in Actas II at 679.

[25] Although briefly responsible for everything from Nicaragua to the Straits of Magellan! This first Audiencia was established in 1542, and after some vicissitudes Panama became in 1567 a Presidency, with its own Audiencia, under Peru—Haring, *Spanish Empire*, 83–4.

[26] Chaunu, 905–8.

[27] Chaunu, 1013–33; Antonelli, 'relation', 110–15.

[28] Antonelli, 'relation', 116; Chaunu, 925–9; Parry, *Seaborne Empire*, 116.

[29] Thomas Gage, *The English-American* (1648), ed. A. P. Newton (London 1928), 367–9; Gage's admirations and complaints are echoed, in more exalted language, by J. Juan and A. de Ulloa, *Relación Histórica del Viage a la América Meridional* (Madrid 1748), I.139–40. The estimate of US$200 is from J. A. Crow, *The Epic of Latin America* (New York 1946), 180–1—a lively description of the fair. A. C. Loosley, 'The Puerto Bello Fairs', *HAHR* 13, 1933, 314–35, gives a long list of the wares exchanged.

[30] Antonelli, 'relation', 122; Gage, *English-American*, 364. Wood may have been favoured because of earthquake risk and for lack of good local stone.

[31] It is amusing, but also instructive, to compare the old translations quoted in S. de Madariaga, *The Rise of the Spanish American Empire* (London 1947), 114–15 [*Rise*] with A. O. Exquemelin, *The*

Buccaneers of America, trans. A. Broom (Harmondsworth 1969), 197–8. This is claimed in the Introduction (at 18) to be 'the first translation accurately based on the Dutch ever to appear in English', and is quite sober compared with the exuberance of earlier versions. On the other hand, J. B. Bishop's objection (*Gateway*, 21) that rich paintings in Panama are likely to have existed only in Exquemelin's imagination, since they would have had to come from Spain over 4000 miles of sea and the horrid mule-track, is quite absurd; there was no earthly reason why they should not have been so brought, many heavenly ones why they should; not to mention the artists of Mexico and Lima.

[32] Haring, *Trade*, 188.

[33] Chaunu, 910; Haring, *Trade*, 186–7; Gage, *English-American*, 365.

[34] Chaunu, 950–3; Haring, *Trade*, 187.

[35] W. Borah, *Early Colonial Trade and Navigation between Mexico and Peru* (Berkeley 1954), 11–13, 67, 71–2—a basic source for this section [*Early Trade*]; D. Ramos, *Minería y Comercio Interprovincial en Hispanoamerica* (Univ. of Valladolid n.d.), 212–13, misses Borah's point on Griajlva, but cf. 151–9 for some interesting general views. See also Chaunu, 757.

[36] J. Lockhart, *Spanish Peru 1532–1560* (Madison 1968), 117 [*Peru*]; H. Morton, *The Wind Commands: Sailors and Sailing Ships in the Pacific* (Vancouver 1975), 191–2, gives some extreme examples of the difficulty of working out of the Bay.

[37] Borah, *Early Trade*, 29–34, 63; Lockhart, *Peru*, 116–17, and 121–2 for an unlucky voyage in 1550–1. Some sailing details are given in G. Lohmann Villena, *Historia Marítima del Perú*, Tomo IV (*Siglos XVII y XVIII*) (Lima 1975)—see Cap. II, 'La Marina Mercante', 213–369 at 226–7 [*Hist. Marítima*].

[38] J. Frezier, *A Voyage to the South Sea* (London 1717), 193–4; cf. D. Whittlesey, *The Earth and the State* (New York 1939), 437, 463–4, for the locational values of Valparaiso and Callao. J. A. del Busto Duthurburu, in *Hist. Marítima*, Tomo III (*Siglo XVI: historia interna*) Parte 1 adds little on Callao (381–405) but gives much detail in Cap. VIII, 'Los Primeros Portos', 327–79.

[39] A. Jara, 'La flota del Mar del Sur . . .', in *Tres Ensayos sobre Economia Minera Hispanoamericana* (Santiago 1966), 55–97, at 74–7 [*Tres Ensayos*]. This essay also appears in *Les Grandes Voies Maritimes dans le Monde XVᵉ–XIXᵉ siècles* (Paris 1965), 247–75; this book is as difficult to track down, even in Berkeley, as any seventeenth century work; it is not, as most references suggest, solely by or edited by Jara but by M. Mollat. It is published by SEVPEN for the Ecole Pratique des Hautes Etudes.

[40] For this paragraph and the next, Borah, *Early Trade*, 63–9; Chaunu, 1104–10; Lockhart, *Peru*, 114–34; Lohmann Villena in *Hist. Marítima*, IV.215–18, 227–30.

[41] Haring, *Trade*, 261.

[42] Borah, *Early Trade*, 85–7. It is however perhaps too much to say, as Borah does, that the merchants 'were really engaged in long-distance peddling'; after all, if at one end they were supplied by a fair, they seem to have had fixed bases in Lima and definite factors and agencies elsewhere. There is an analogy with the classic peddling trade as described in N. Steensgaard, *The Asian Trade Revolution of the Seventeenth Century* (Chicago 1974), 22–59; but it seems to me rather a slight one.

[43] Ramos, *Minería*, 247–8; cf. 226 for 'vías extralegales' and 234–5 for illicit devices, such as Peruvian wine entering Guatemala 'under pretext of being vinegar'. Borah, *Early Trade*, 96–115, describes the web of tax and regulation.

[44] Borah, *Early Trade*, 80–4, 117–18; Chaunu, 752–9.

[45] Borah, *Early Trade*, 117–18; Lohmann Villena, in *Hist. Marítima*, IV.318; Ramos, *Minería*, 227–30; Blair & Robertson, IV.313–14, V.11, 30–1.

[46] Lynch, *Habsburgs*, II.187, 196.

[47] Jara, *Tres Ensayos*, 69; see 82–7 for the opening of a Chile-La Plata route.

[48] Perez, *Colonización*, 212; Haring, *Spanish Empire*, 308–9; Lynch, *Habsburgs*, II.178–9; Ramos, *Mineria*, 195–200; Romero, *Perú*, 177–8. The use of the Plate estuary to breach the monopoly reached its height in the eighteenth century: there are full studies by S. Villalobos R., *Comercio y Contrabando en el Rio de la Plata y Chile 1700–1811* (Buenos Aires 1965), and Olga Pantaleão, *A Penetração Comercial de Inglaterra na America Espanhola del 1713 a 1783* (São Paulo 1946). S. E. Morison's analogy of Montreal and Quebec confined to New York for an outlet is entertaining but ignores the differences in true locational factors—especially in regard to winds, an astonishing lapse for the Admiral—and is quite beside the point—*The European Discovery of America: The Southern Voyages 1492–1616* (New York 1974), 581.

[49] The detailed story of the end of the New Spain-Peru trade is in Borah, *Early Trade*, 116–27. The decrees are in Blair & Robertson, XVII.27–52. Many points stem from the long memorial on 'Reforms needed in the Philippines' (1620) by Hernando de los Rios Coronel, Procurator-General for Manila at Madrid, ibid. XVIII.290–342. Ramos, *Minería*, 230–5, brings out the threat of monopsony; there are other details in Lohmann Villena, *Hist. Marítima*, IV.314–18, and it becomes extremely difficult even for Ramos to discern that Common Market in which 'La defensa del consumidor es la unica ley' (*Minería*, 117–18, 229).

[50] Grau y Monfalcon's 'Informatory memorial' of 1637, Blair & Robertson, XXVII.55–214 at 165 [Grau, 'Memorial'], and the 'Informatory decree', XXX.97–101 at 101. Grau's 'Justification of the maintenance of the Philipinas Islands and their commerce', XXX.25–81, is addressed to Bishop Palafox and adds a few points.

[51] The debate of 1644 is reported in a printed *Relacion* bound with Prado's MS. narrative of his voyage through Torres Straits, in the Mitchell Library, Sydney, item 3–9A, Safe 1/73. For the decrees of 1706 and 1779, see W. L. Schurz, *The Manila Galleon* (Dutton ed., New York 1959), 366–70, 381–2 [*Galleon*]; but Puerto del Marques is southeast not north of Acapulco—see W. Dampier, *A New Voyage Round the World* (1697) (Dover ed., New York 1968), 170–2 and map at 26. Between 1711 and 1715 at least seven ships from Peru, with cacao, aguardiente, and wine, were embargoed in Acapulco harbour—N. P. Cushner SJ, *Spain in the Philippines* (Quezon City 1971), 136–7 [*Spain*]. For occasional licensed trading, see G. Lohmann Villena, *Las Minas de Huancavelica* (Seville 1949), 431.

[52] MacLeod, *Central America*, 165–70, including the amazing story of the Galleon which overshot Acapulco and put in at the Gulf of Fonseca.

[53] Wallerstein, *World-System*, 335; Anthonio van Diemen (1640), cited from Geyl, *Netherlands*, 186. In stating that 'Spain eventually gave up the Manila Galleon', impliedly c. 1640, Wallerstein must have misread his source. P. Chaunu, 'Le galion de Manille', *Annales Economies Sociétés Civilisations* 6, 1951, 447–62 ['galion'].

[54] Chaunu, *Philippines*, 22.

[55] Epigraph to Fr Francisco Colin SJ, *Labor evangelica . . .* (Madrid 1663), itself the epigraph to Chaunu, *Philippines*.

[56] T. A. Agoncillo, *A Short History of the Philippines* (New York 1969), 21–2, 45–6; K. Lightfoot, *The Philippines* (London 1974), 49–50; G. F. Zaide, *The Philippines since Pre-Spanish Times* (Manila 1949), 410–27, 438–9 [*Philippines*].

[57] Zaide, *Philippines*, 203, 229.

[58] A. De Morga, *Sucesos de las Islas Filipinas* (1609), trans. and ed. J. S. Cummins, HS 2nd Ser. 140 (Cambridge 1971), 261, 308, 310 [*Sucesos*]; Grau, 'memorial', 79–80, 198–201; Schurz, *Galleon*, 44–9. For spice-smuggling from the Moluccas by Portuguese and Sangleys, Blair & Robertson, XI.207; the information on tobacco I owe to Cushner, *Spain*, 202–3, and a control tag of La Flor de

Isabela, Inc., Manila. The mechanism of the trade at Manila is described above, Ch. 6.

[59] Schurz, *Galleon*, 31–3; Morga, *Sucesos*, 305–6, 308–9.

[60] P. Guzmán-Rivas, Reciprocal Geographical Influences of the Trans-Pacific Galleon Trade (Univ. of Texas Ph.D thesis 1960), 59 [*Influences*]; Schurz, *Galleon*, 275; Chaunu, 'galion', 458; Blair & Robertson, XXIV.286–8, for nature and importance of Japan trade.

[61] Guzmán-Rivas, *Influences*, 244–58.

[62] Ibid., 37–53, 99–107, 119–44, 196–208. The complaint about *tuba* is in a report on ship-building (1619) in Blair & Robertson, XVIII.169–85; in 1671 the inhabitants of Colima petitioned for licence to make tuba, described as very innocuous!—*Influences*, 104. For the inhuman treatment of Indio sailors, the details of which 'would fill many pages', Rios Coronel in Blair & Robertson, XVIII.299–300.

[63] Schurz, *Galleon*, 371–84, quotes vivid vignettes of Acapulco from a variety of travellers; see also M. Carrera Stampa, 'Las Ferias Novohispanas', *Hist. Mexicana* 2, 1952–3, at 329–34.

[64] J. H. Parry, 'Transport and Trade Routes', in *The Cambridge Economic History of Europe* III (1967) 155–222 at 210 ['Transport'].

[65] Blair & Robertson, XVIII.228.

[66] For the beginnings of Dutch expansion, B. H. M. Vlekke, *Nusantara: A History of Indonesia* (rev. ed., The Hague 1959), 101–9; G. Masselman, *The Cradle of Colonialism* (New Haven 1963), 62–105 [*Colonialism*]; C. R. Boxer, *The Dutch Seaborne Empire 1600–1800* (Harmondsworth 1973), 21–6. There were also plenty of Dutch proclamations against trading with the enemy, especially under Leicester—as ineffectual as the Spanish; see D. W. Davies, *A Primer of Dutch Seventeenth Century Trade* (The Hague 1961), 25–8.

[67] Masselman, *Colonialism*, 130–1, 141–50; C. R. Boxer, *Fidalgos in the Far East 1550–1770* (The Hague 1948), 50–1 [*Fidalgos*].

[68] Chaunu, 'galion', 458 and *Philippines*, 53, 152; Boxer, *Fidalgos*, 68–9; A. R. Disney, Twilight of the Pepper Trade, unpublished typescript, Ch. 2 (cited by courtesy of the author). Chaunu's figures for the actual entry of Macaonese ships at Manila (*Philippines*, Série 13) do not at first sight seem to bear out his reference to an 'entrée massive', but the Portuguese ships would be larger than the Chinese craft. Even after the catastrophe of the expulsion from Japan, followed by the loss (at least officially) of the Manila market after 1640, the Macaonese remained active entrepreneurs; e.g. their Bocarro gun-foundry was the best in the East, and English gun-runners took its products through the Dutch blockade to Goa—Boxer, *Fidalgos*, 110, 113. For the Makassar-based merchant adventurer Figueiredo, see C. R. Boxer, *Francisco Vieira de Figueiredo . . . 1624–1667* (The Hague 1967).

[69] Blair & Robertson, VII.199–204 (letter from Portugal, 1590); X.190–7 (Bishop of Nueva Segovia to King, 17 May 1599).

[70] Borah, *Early Trade*, 123; the figure of 12,000,000 pesos is given by Haring (*Trade*, 189) and accepted by Parry ('Transport', 210); but see Schurz, *Galleon*, 188–90; Chaunu, *Philippines*, 268–9; Grau, 'memorial', 167–8, 171–6, which cumulatively make such an amount highly improbable. For Anson's capture, R. Walters and B. Robins, *A Voyage round the World . . .* (1748), ed. G. Williams (London 1974), 344, 393—by Anson's time, Mexican silver output had recovered from the seventeenth century trough.

[71] Chaunu, 'galion', 459–61; Grau, 'memorial', 152–7; Boxer, *Fidalgos*, 133–4.

[72] Blair & Robertson, XVIII.212–32 at 200—Montesclaros at this time (1612) was Viceroy of Peru, and had been of New Spain—a man of experience in fending off unwelcome suggestions.

[73] Schurz, *Galleon*, 187–8, 379–80; cf. Grau's protests, and excuses, in 'memorial', 167–8.

[74] Blair & Robertson, XVIII.194–203, XX.131–2.

[75] Hernando de los Rios Coronel, 'Memorial y Relacion' for the King (Madrid 1621), Blair & Robertson, XIX.187–298 at 235–55; Grau y Monfalcon, 'Justificacion' (1640), ibid. XXX.25–81 at 28–47.

[76] Blair & Robertson, XIV.217, 231; XVIII.57–64.

[77] Chaunu, 'galion', 460; Boxer, *Fidalgos*, 132–57; Blair & Robertson, XX.129 (1621), XXII.97–101 (1626). The complex links and rivalries are emphasised in Chaunu's article 'Manille et Macao face à la conjoncture des XVIe et XVIIe siècles', in *Annales Economies Sociétés Civilisations*, 1962 (not seen, but quoted in F. Mauro, *L'Expansion Européenne (1600–1870)* (Paris 1967), 303, 306).

[78] Blair & Robertson, XXIII.112, 114 (1630), XXIV.218–20 (1632).

[79] Blair & Robertson, XXVI.269–90; quotation from Boxer, *Fidalgos*, 136–8.

[80] C. R. Boxer, *The Great Ship from Amacon* (Lisbon 1959), 18; Chaunu, 'galion', 452.

Notes for Chapter 9

[1] D. B. Quinn, 'The Argument for the English Discovery of America between 1480 and 1494', *Geogr. Jnl* 127, 1961, 277–85, also in his *England and the Discovery of America 1481–1620* (London 1973), 5–23 [*Discovery*]; J. A. Williamson, *The Cabot Voyages and Bristol Discovery under Henry VII*, HS 2nd Ser. 120 (Cambridge 1962), 19–32, 187–9 [*Cabot Voyages*]. The priority of Prince Madoc (A.D. 1170) is disputed, and anyhow he was Welsh.

[2] Thorne in R. Barlow, *A Brief Summe of Geography*, ed. E. G. R. Taylor, HS 2nd Ser. 69 (London 1932) at xxviii [*Brief Summe*]; also in Hakluyt, VIII.44–5; for Cabot's voyage, S. E. Morison, *The European Discovery of America: The Southern Voyages A.D. 1492–1616* (New York 1974), 537–61 [*Southern Voyages*].

[3] Henry VII's thinking and its evolution were subtle; see Williamson, *Cabot Voyages*, 50–3, 125–7, 132–3. The close relations of Bristol and the Azores are noteworthy.

[4] To avoid overlapping and repeating citations, it may be stated that unreferenced factual statements in this section are from: E. G. R. Taylor, *Tudor Geography 1485–1583* (London 1930), Chs. III and V–VII [*Geography*]; Taylor, 'Early English Empire Building Projects in the Pacific Ocean, 1565–1585', *HAHR* 14, 1934, 295–306 ['Early Empire']; J. A. Williamson, *The Ocean in English History* (Oxford 1941), Chs. I–III [*Ocean*]; Williamson, *The Age of Drake* (2nd ed., London 1946), Chs. I–III [*Age of Drake*]. There is a stimulating political and cultural commentary in A. L. Rowse, *The Expansion of Elizabethan England* (Cardinal ed., London 1973) [*Expansion*]. Rowse inclines somewhat to a more sophisticated rendering of the 'Dogs of Devon' tradition stemming from Charles Kingsley's *Westward Ho!* (1855) and J. A. Froude's *English Seamen in the Sixteenth Century* (1895), in which the chapter on Drake is totally chauvinist and largely erroneous. There is also much background material in the immense compilation (cccclxxvii + 5720 pages!) by E. M. Tenison, *Elizabethan England ... 'In Relation to all Foreign Princes'* (Leamington Spa 1933–61) [*Elizabethan England*]; but strangely enough, unless it be due to a subconscious desire to avoid questions of piracy, there is scarcely any reference to Drake's circumnavigation in this fascinating, highly idiosyncratic, and very courageous work.

[5] See for example John Hawkins's all too close relations with Pedro de Ponte, a shady magnate of Teneriffe, in A. Rumeu de Armas, *Los Viajes de John Hawkins a América, 1562–1595* (Seville 1957), 87–106, 202, 218; and 36–48 on the general position [*Hawkins*].

[6] Contrast e.g. Rowse, *Expansion*, 192, and Williamson, *Age of Drake*, 93, with the playing-down of the political effects in K. R. Andrews, *Drake's Voyages: A Re-assessment of their Place in Elizabethan*

Maritime Expansion (London 1967), 28–30 [*Voyages*]. But for the important purely naval aspect, see D. W. Waters, 'The Elizabethan Navy and the Armada Campaign', *MM* 35, 1949, 90–138 at 95.

[7] This is Barlow's *Brief Summe*, mainly a translation of Juan de Encisco's *Suma de Geographia* (Seville 1519), but adding Barlow's first-hand reports from the Parana region and ending with an appeal for northern discovery. For Northumberland's wild idea, Taylor in *Brief Summe*, liv.

[8] D. W. Waters, *The Art of Navigation in England in Elizabethan and Early Stuart Times* (London 1958), 157, 220–5, 229 [*Navigation*].

[9] E. G. R. Taylor, 'The Northern Passages', in A. P. Newton (ed.), *The Great Age of Discovery* (London 1932), 199–224 at 202–7. For the possible origin of the legendary Friseland and Estotiland and the disputed Zeni voyages, see her article 'A Fourteenth Century Riddle—and its Solution', *Geogr. Rev.* 54, 1964, 573–6; which is perhaps a little more convincing, if not quite so entertaining, as the account of a fourteenth century Italo-Scottish expedition to Massachusetts in R. H. Ramsay, *No Longer on the Map* (New York 1972), 53–76. C. Miller, *The Silver Map of the World* (London 1900), 49–67, is amusing and damnatory.

[10] R. Willes, 'Certaine other reasons . . . to prove a passage by the Northwest', in Hakluyt V.120–32 at 130; H. Gilbert, 'A discourse . . . to prove a passage by the Northwest to Cathaia', ibid. 92–120 at 117 ['A discourse']; the latter also in D. B. Quinn (ed.), *The Voyages and Colonising Enterprises of Sir Humphrey Gilbert*, HS 2nd Ser. 83–4 (London 1940), I.129–65 [*Gilbert*].

[11] The various combinations can be most readily grasped from the maps in Williamson, *Age of Drake*, at 21, and Taylor, *Geography*, at 80. See also the 1566 'General Map, made onely for the particular declaration of this discovery', in Quinn, *Gilbert*, at I.164.

[12] J. B. Brebner, *The Explorers of North America 1492–1806* (Meridian ed., Cleveland 1964), 25, 95–102.

[13] E. Prestage, *The Portuguese Pioneers* (London 1933), 187, 270–7, for the Azorean Corte Reals; for the name 'Trium fratrum', Taylor, *Geography*, 82. Of the three Cabot brothers, Ludovico and Sancio were 'unknown men', completely overshadowed by Sebastian (Williamson, *Cabot Voyages*, 114), while of the three brothers Corte Real only two sailed and perished in these waters.

[14] H. R. Wagner, *Spanish Voyages to the Northwest Coast of America in the Sixteenth Century* (Amsterdam 1960, original ed. 1929), 53, 111, 138, 162; Wagner, 'Apocryphal Voyages to the Northwest Coast of America', reprint from *Proc. of Amer. Antiquarian Soc.* (Worcester (Mass.) 1931); J. C. Beaglehole, *The Journals of Captain James Cook: III . . . 1776–1780*, HS Extra Ser. 36 (Cambridge 1967), xxxvii–xlviii. P. Novo y Colson, *Sobre los Viajes Apócrifos de Juan de Fuca y de Lorenzo Ferrer Maldonado* (Madrid 1881), gives damning documentation on the latter, and there are some interesting points in H. H. Bancroft, *Retrospection Political and Personal* (3rd ed., New York 1915), 528–34; but R. R. Owen, 'The Myth of Anian', *Jnl Hist. of Ideas* 36, 1975, 135–8 adds little or nothing. I regret not seeing G. E. Nunn, *Origin of the Strait of Anian Concept* (Philadelphia 1929). The name 'Ania(n)' was used by Marco Polo for a region in northeast Asia, and 'came into the literature' as the name of a strait with Gastaldi in 1562; oddly enough it seems to derive from 'Aniwa', the Japanese name for the real strait between Sakhalin and the mainland—Ramsay, *No Longer on the Map*, 150–1.

[15] D. M. Lebedev and V. I. Grekov, 'Geographical Exploration by the Russians', in H. R. Friis (ed.), *The Pacific Basin: A History of Its Geographical Exploration* (New York 1967), 170–200 at 170.

[16] Barlow, *Brief Summe*, 180–2; Grenville, quoted in A. L. Rowse, *Sir Richard Grenville of the 'Revenge'* (London 1940), 80 [*Grenville*].

[17] Gilbert, 'A discourse', at 102, 110–11 in Hakluyt VIII. The name Sierra Nevada comes from confused reports of Coronado's great inland exploration (1540–2) and was placed rather north of

the modern Sierra Nevada of California, as in Gilbert's map of *c.* 1563. The date of the talk about Urdaneta is given as 1568 ('A discourse' was drafted in 1566 but not printed until 1576), and obviously the story was much misrepresented or misunderstood; see Quinn in *Gilbert*, 30–1. Returning the compliment, the Spaniards of Mexico called the Passage 'the Englishman's Strait'.

[18] The reference in Henry Hawks's account of New Spain (Hakluyt, VI.279–96 at 291) is too brief and off-putting to have provided much of a lure, but it gives a definite date for English knowledge.

[19] Rowse, *Grenville*, 88–105.

[20] Zelia Nuttall (ed.), *New Light on Drake*, HS 2nd Ser. 34 (London 1914), 9–10 [*New Light*]: '. . . y despues pasarian al estrecho y poblarian donde hallasen buena terra para poblar. . . .' Oxenham claims, convincingly, to have seen the project or a draft of it, and from the deposition of his fellow-captive John Butler it seems that he need not have made such an admission unless there was reason behind it. At this time the original Spanish settlement at Buenos Aires (1536) had faded away, but Asuncion remained as a centre of dominion in the Parana-La Plata region, and Buenos Aires was refounded, permanently, in 1580.

[21] Rowse, *Grenville*, 90.

[22] I have read and re-read *The History of England* for years, always with pleasure and sometimes with profit; but it must be remembered that the treatment of Drake in *English Seamen* and 'England's Forgotten Worthies' is Froude at his unworthy worst. One may doubt the virgin purity of Queen Elizabeth's political attitude (Rowse, *Grenville*, 108), but this pales before Froude's 'simple majesty' as a term descriptive of the tangled and murky Doughty trial—*Short Studies on Great Subjects* (Fontana ed., London 1963), 175. For admirably pungent comment, see *The Letters of Sir Walter Raleigh 1879–1922* (London 1926), I.263.

[23] The standard biography is probably still Julian Corbett's massive (924 pages) *Drake and the Tudor Navy* (London 1898), good stuff though outdated [*Drake*]; G. M. Thomson, *Sir Francis Drake* (London 1972), is a reasonably good modern life [*Francis Drake*]. K. R. Andrews, *Drake's Voyages* is important, while J. Hampden (ed.), *Francis Drake Privateer* (London 1972), is a most useful volume, reprinting Hawkins's *Third Troublesome Voyage, Sir Francis Drake Revived* (1626, but vetted by Drake himself), and *The World Encompassed* (1628), as well as the accounts of Cooke and Winter, with intelligent comment [*Privateer*]. These have modern spelling; the original is retained in N. M. Penzer (ed.), *The World Encompassed and Analogous Contemporary Documents* (London 1926), which has also the important notes of Francis Fletcher and accounts by Cooke, Cliffe, Nuño da Silva, Zarate, and San Juan de Anton—a very useful collection, though the 'Appreciation' by R. C. Temple is sad stuff [*World Encompassed*]. There is a rich iconography in H. P. Kraus, *Sir Francis Drake: A Pictorial Biography* (Amsterdam 1970). For the Spanish side, Nuttall's *New Light*, despite some editorial naïveties, is indispensable for the circumnavigation, and I. A. Wright, *Spanish Documents Concerning English Voyages to the Spanish Main 1569–80*, HS 2nd Ser. 71 (London 1932), for Nombre de Dios in 1572–3 and for Oxenham [*Documents*].

[24] Deposition of Robert Barrett, master of Hawkins's *Jesus of Lubeck*, taken at San Juan de Ulua, in Wright, *Documents*, 153–60; documents 22–9 in this volume give the Spanish version. As Wright points out in her Introduction (at 21), Hawkins at San Juan for the first time faced not colonists and minor officials 'whose material interests and secret intentions were in harmony with his own', but a Viceroy and a Captain-General. For details of Rio de la Hacha, J. A. Williamson, *Hawkins of Plymouth* (2nd ed., London 1969), 96–9 [*Hawkins*].

[25] Hampden, *Privateer*, 27, 53.

[26] In the abstract, certainly dastardly; but for all the moral fury, one may wonder if a Spanish fleet driven into an Irish port would have fared much better; perhaps worse, judging by events in the Armada year, for which see C. Falls, *Elizabeth's Irish Wars* (London 1950), 163–7. Far worse by

any civilised standard is the treatment of prisoners by the Inquisition, though here again the English record in Ireland was ugly, e.g. the Rathlin massacre, where Drake was present but unlikely to have been involved (Falls, 116). For details of the fight at San Juan, Williamson, *Hawkins*, 135–47, and R. Unwin, *The Defeat of John Hawkins* (London 1960), 135–47; for a Spanish version, Rumeu de Armas, *Hawkins*, 265–304.

[27] See Thomson, *Francis Drake*, 341–2, for the claimants to Port Pheasant (so named 'by reason of the great store of those goodly Fowles'); one is tempted to opt for the Puerto Escoces of the Scots colony in Darien (1698–1700), but—like so many of Drake's localities—its site must be left an open question.

[28] For Spanish accounts, Wright, *Documents*, 48–73. All direct quotations in this section are from her reprint (245–326) of the very vivid *Sir Francis Drake Revived*.

[29] But 'the French Captaine cast abroad his hands, and prayed our Captaine to helpe him to some water, for that he had nothing but Wine and Cider aboard him, which had brought his men into great sicknesse.'

[30] The phrase is William Paterson's, cited in J. Preble, *The Lion in the North* (Harmondsworth 1973), 281.

[31] Williamson, *Age of Drake*, 133–44 at 134–5. There is a brief account by Lopez Vaz in Hakluyt, VIII.155–9, but no English primary sources except a few passing references (see Quinn, *Gilbert*, 32, 169); the depositions of Oxenham, Butler, and 'Xerores' (Sherwell—see Rowse, *Grenville*, 109) are in Nuttall, *New Light*, 1–12, and Spanish accounts in Wright, *Documents*, *passim*. The moral story of Oxenham's love for a Spanish lady, romanticised by Kingsley in *Westward Ho!*, is mere gossip—see J. A. Williamson (ed.), *The Observations of Sir Richard Hawkins* (1622), London 1933, 162–4 [*Hawkins, Observations*].

[32] Wright, *Documents*, 118. The Spanish evidence of outrages is too sober and circumstantial to be discounted, and says little for the commonsense of the party.

[33] Ibid., 112, 114, 128, 134.

[34] Ibid., 232–4.

[35] Ibid., 234–41; cf. Lopez Vaz in Hakluyt, VIII.159.

[36] Williamson in Hawkins, *Observations*, xxv; but cf. his *Age of Drake*, 134–5.

[37] J. A. Froude, *The Reign of Elizabeth* (Everyman ed.), IV.327–8—a most beautiful passage.

[38] Apart perhaps from Penzer's, the most comprehensive assembly of texts, and certainly the most detailed analysis, are in H. R. Wagner, *Sir Francis Drake's Voyage around the World* (Amsterdam 1969; original ed. 1926) [*Voyage*]. Like all Wagner's work, this volume of 543 pages is somewhat heavy and pontifical, but immensely thorough and immensely useful. A refreshingly cool and realistic view of Drake's motives and actions is taken by L. Gibbs, *The Silver Circle* (London 1963). All direct quotations on the circumnavigation, unless otherwise indicated, are from accounts in Penzer's *World Encompassed*.

[39] The *locus classicus* for this debate is now K. R. Andrews, 'The Aims of Drake's Expedition of 1577–80', *Amer. Hist. Rev.* 73, 1968, 724–41, to which my debt is obvious ['Aims']; see also Chs. 3–4 in his *Voyages*, and Hampden, *Privateer*, 107–21 (with transcript of the Draft Plan).

[40] *Age of Drake*, 145; cf. Morison, *Southern Voyages*, 636: 'an opportunist . . . what he would do when he got [to the Pacific] would depend on wind, weather, luck and circumstances.'

[41] Nuttall, *New Light*, lvi; there is a give-away reference (xiv) to Drake as a hero of her girlhood.

[42] Wagner, *Voyage*, iii. Taylor's new data and her views thereon are in *Geography*, 115–19; 'John Dee, Drake and the Straits of Anian', *MM* 15, 1929, 125–30; 'More Light on Drake', *MM* 16, 1930, 134–51 ['More Light']; 'The Missing Draft Project of Drake's Voyage of 1577–80', *Geogr. Jnl* 75, 1930, 46–7; 'Early Empire' at 300–6.

[43] The direct quotations are: Winter, in Taylor, 'More Light', 151; Cliffe and Cooke, in Penzer, *World Encompassed*, 198, 150. Nuño da Silva also speaks of a rendezvous between 30 and 31°S, and is not necessarily to be dismissed as a Portuguese anxious to placate his interrogators in New Spain. Incidentally, Winter read Magellan's voyage to his crew, 'who seemed to like well of [it]'—doubtless in a well-censored version.

I owe much to Eva Taylor's encouragement in my earlier career, but remain astonished that so acute and hard-headed a lady should take Winter's statement at face value.

[44] Taylor, *Geography*, 115–19; Andrews, 'Aims' at 738, and 732–3 for a cogent argument against the Moluccas and Dee's influence, at least to the extent asserted by Taylor.

[45] Wagner, *Voyage*, 465.

[46] See Hampden, *Privateer*, 229, 231. Zarate said that he was shown a commission, but there is no evidence that he could read English; Nuño da Silva's story (Nuttall, *New Light*, 378) of Drake producing papers at Port St Julian is neither clear nor decisive. What is, or should be, almost certainly decisive is the point brought out by W. Senior in his unduly neglected paper 'Drake at the Suit of John Doughty', *MM* 7, 1921, 191–7: production of a commission would have quashed John Doughty's suit at the beginning; no commission was produced, Doughty was non-suited on a technicality, and gaoled (for other aspects of this nasty affair, Corbett, *Drake*, I.340–3). As Queen Elizabeth was directly responsible, she can I suppose be held to have legitimised Drake after the fact; but this is a long way from the invariable chivalrous fairness which devotees like Froude, Tenison, and Geoffrey Callender stick to despite the evidence. See the amusing polemic between Gregory Robinson and Callender in *MM* 7, 1921, for the very tortuous knots into which the more devout believers in Drake as a knight *sans reproche* must tie themselves.

[47] It is true that the story comes from the bitterly hostile Cooke (Hampden, *Privateer*, 237); but his indignant bias is so open and sincere that he carries his own corrective. As Corbett says, 'In his heat . . . there is a certain honesty which betrays him into constant admissions' which he did not recognise as favouring his adversary (*Drake*, I.233, 424–6). Cooke could hardly have invented, or needed to invent, this point.

[48] Andrews, 'Aims', 749.

[49] As shown by his opportunistic exploitation of his welcome by the Californian Indians, and his desire (Penzer, *World Encompassed*, 38) to have been a patron to defend those of Chile.

[50] F. C. P. Naish, 'The Mystery of the Tonnage and Dimensions of the *Pelican-Golden Hind*', *MM* 34, 1948, 42–5, sums up: 'the 150-ton ship, the 120-ton ship, and the 100-ton ship were different ways of reckoning . . . one and the same ship'. There are several other papers in *MM* on the same subject, especially in 1950–1. Some writers say that there were two pinnaces, *Benedict* and *Christopher*, but these seem to be two names for the same craft. They sailed on 15 November but were driven back by tempest, finally leaving on 13 December.

[51] Andrews, *Voyages*, 59–60; cf. Williamson in Hawkins, *Observations*, liii.

[52] Tenison, *Elizabethan England*, IV.61–2 for Doughty as suborned by Spain; she gives no hint of evidence, and was answered far in advance by Corbett: the complete ignorance of Drake's intent shown by the Spanish ambassador, Mendoza, refutes this suggestion. On the other hand, his own suggestion that Doughty was Burghley's agent is also mere inference, though rather more responsibly put than Tenison's—*Drake*, I.266, 342–3.

[53] Drake's brother John, in Nuttall, *New Light*, 25.

[54] Williamson, *Ocean*, 38–9.

[55] It is pleasant to record that Fletcher and Cooke are substantially at one on the closing scene. My use of Cromwell's 'Stone dead hath no fellow' is independent of Gibbs, *The Silver Circle*, 47.

[56] *Age of Drake*, 181.

[57] There is a contemporary English translation in the British Library; see E. G. R. Taylor, 'The Dawn of Modern Navigation', *Jnl Inst. of Navigation* I, 1948, 283–9. Cf. Wagner, *Voyages*, 34–41, and R. Boulind, 'Drake's Navigational Skills', *MM* 54, 1968, 349–71.

[58] Andrews (*Voyages*, 69) takes this as clear evidence that Drake had no intention of looking for Terra Australis; however, Wagner (*Voyage*, 80) makes the point that Ortelius shows the Terra Australis coast here as running first southwest then northwest, so that 'every effort would be made to avoid running in either a south or southeast direction' for fear of embayment. An overlooked statement by Fletcher (in Penzer, *World Encompassed*, 30) might be taken as giving some support to the Terra Australis case—Drake was enforced by the increasing cold 'not to saile any farther towards the pole Antartick'. But it is rather too vague.

[59] Fletcher, in Penzer, *World Encompassed*, 133; *more suo*, he draws a pietistic lesson. It is of course not certain that the *Marigold* was so dramatically and immediately cast away as Fletcher implies (one fears for the sake of the moral!); Cavendish in 1587 saw in the Straits a wreck 'which we judged to be a Barke called the John Thomas' (Hakluyt, VIII.213), and John Thomas was captain of the *Marigold*. Wagner (*Voyage*, 81) suggests that the wreck might have been one of Sarmiento's but this is unlikely as it was pointed out to Cavendish by the survivor of that expedition whom he picked up. There is also the strange story of the pinnace lost shortly after the *Elizabeth* separated, which made its way as far as the Plate before being wrecked; the sole survivor, Peter Carder, reached England some years later, with many marvellous tales—see Hampden, *Privateer*, 156, 209–10, and Carder's narrative in S. Purchas, *Hakluytus Posthumus or Purchas his Pilgrimes* (1625) (Glasgow 1905–6), XVI.136–51.

[60] For the following discussion, see Corbett, *Drake*, I.266–75; Wagner, *Voyage*, 80–6; R. Hough, *The Blind Horn's Hate* (London 1971), 100–5; F. Riesenberg, *Cape Horn* (London 1941), 81–114; R. H. Power, 'The Discovery of Cape Horn by Francis Drake in the Year 1578', typescript lecture to the Society for the History of Discoveries, Hotel Sir Francis Drake, San Francisco 1975 (cited by permission) ['Cape Horn']; B. Hilder, 'Drake's Passage', *Navigation* (Jnl of Australian Inst. of Navigation, Sydney) 5, 1976, 507–12. All these have maps, though Corbett's inexplicably takes Drake through Cockburn Channel, in conflict with his text at I.266. The nature of Pactolus Bank is confirmed by Plate 165 of the authoritative *Fiziko-Geograficheskiy Atlas Mira* (Akademia Nauk CCCP, Moscow 1964).

[61] Fletcher's authorship of these maps has been doubted (Wagner, *Voyage*, 291–2), but this is irrelevant. Whether or not his southernmost island is accepted as Cape Horn, Power does at least sort out the confusion (which even Wagner left obscure) of Drake's Elizabethan names: 1. *Elizabeth I.*, the modern Isabel, in the Straits, where he took possession; 2. *Elizabethides*, a collective name for the archipelago south of the Straits; 3. *Elizabetha I.*, the southernmost. This makes sense of the tangle.

[62] E. G. R. Taylor (ed.), *The Troublesome Voyage of Captain Edward Fenton 1582–1583*, HS 2nd Ser. 113 (Cambridge 1959), lvi, 120–31 [*Fenton*]. For the maps, Wagner, *Voyage*, 406–37; Corbett, *Drake*, I.27–74; Taylor, 'Early Empire', 303; Power, 'Cape Horn'. Hondius hedged a little in his legend.

[63] Andrews, *Voyages*, 71–2, 83–4; Williamson, *Age of Drake*, 186. Hakluyt, always in modern parlance a 'North Atlantic man', seems to have thought of the new discovery more as an approach to the Northwest Passage than as with a specific Pacific context—Andrews, *Voyages*, 84, and H. Wallis, 'The Pacific', in D. B. Quinn (ed.), *The Hakluyt Handbook*, HS 2nd Ser. 144–5 (London 1974), I.223–33 at 232–3.

[64] See H. Wallis, 'English Enterprise in the Region of the Strait of Magellan', in J. Parker (ed.), *Merchants and Scholars: Essays in the History of Exploration and Trade* (Minneapolis 1965), 193–220

at 204–6. After Mocha, the account in *The World Encompassed* is no longer from Fletcher but uses 'The famous voyage of Sir Francis Drake …' in Hakluyt, VIII.48–74—see Wagner, *Voyage*, 286–93, and Hampden, *Privateer*, 120–1.

65 '… con poco verdad se traten estos Indios …'—quoted in Aida Chaparro Galdames, 'El corsario Francisco Drake en Chile', *Rev. Chilena de Historia y Geografía* 50, 1924, 109–31, and 51, 1925–6, 288–320 at 288–91 ['El corsario']. This paper adds several details to the English accounts. Drake's weathered canvas sails would have appeared 'black' in contrast to the white cotton used by local shipping; see H. A. Morton, *The Winds Command: Sailors and Sailing Ships in the Pacific* (Vancouver 1975), 128.

66 Wagner, *Voyage*, 477–8.

67 G. Chaparro, 'El corsario' at 51, 301–3; cf. Juan Griego and others in Nuttall, *New Light*, 69. For options at this stage of the voyage, Andrews, *Voyages*, 72–4. Wagner gives the most detailed itinerary, with maps, in *Voyage*, Chs. V–VIII.

68 Nuttall, *New Light*, 47; cf. Wagner, *Voyage*, 481. The number of ships damaged is stated at nine to thirty, but usually thirteen or seventeen.

69 J. A. del Busto Duthurburu, *Siglo XVI—Historia Externa*, being Tomo III Vol. 2 of the *Historia Marítima del Perú* (Lima 1975), 524–5; but according to E. Morales, *Aventuras y Desaventuras de un Navegante: Sarmiento de Gamboa* (Buenos Aires 1946), 139–40, this device was due to quick thinking by the wife and sister-in-law of a Callao port official; given the timing, this seems plausible.

70 Sarmiento's Narrative in Nuttall, *New Light*, 57–88—the basic source for the 'pursuit'.

71 '… que no perdio nada en las ferias'—Nuttall, *New Light*, 205; Austin Dobson, *The Ballad of 'Beau Brocade'*.

72 Nuttall, *New Light*, 172, 178. For the confusion, see in that volume 73–87 (Sarmiento), 216–25, 242–5, 252–5 (Viceroy Enriquez), 23–37 (Velasco); and from a different angle—that of one of Hawkins's men, captive in New Spain—the story of Miles Philip, Hakluyt, VI.325–8.

73 Nuttall, *New Light*, 101–7—a delightfully logical structure of absurdities.

74 It is usually stated that there were two pilots, but one, Martin de Aguirre, may have been only a mariner or successfully pretended to be so, in which Colchero failed.

75 See Nuttall, *New Light*, 295–399 *passim*, for much graphic detail, e.g. the Inquisition's meticulous tracking down of da Silva's personal effects, including a pair of women's boots, two pounds of soap, and half a pound of cinnamon and cloves, 'good for the womb'. Perhaps the real reason for dumping him is that had Drake brought him to England, he could have been an awkward witness in a prize court.

76 For Drake's course from Guatulco to Nova Albion, the best fairly recent discussions (though reaching opposite conclusions) are in Wagner, *Voyage*, 130–69, and R. P. Bishop, 'Drake's Course in the North Pacific', *Brit. Columbia Histl Qly* 3, 1939, 151–81 ['North Pacific'].

77 Bishop, 'North Pacific', 160–1, gives various English sixteenth century references.

78 Personal information from Asst Prof. R. Byrne, Dept of Geography, Berkeley.

79 E. G. R. Taylor, 'Francis Drake and the Pacific: Two Fragments', *Pac. Histl Rev.* 1, 1932, 360–9; Wagner, *Voyage*, 141; cf. Penzer, *World Encompassed*, 49, 51–2. I would like to support Taylor on this item—but Wagner has other points in favour of a lower latitude, as does Aker, *Report of Findings*, 245–60 (full title in next note).

80 J. Boswell, *The Life of Samuel Johnson, LL.D.* (Everyman ed.), I.553. In this laudable spirit, I have sighted just sixty (60) items on this sole point, many worthless. Besides Wagner, *Voyage*, 154–69 (below the master's best), and Morison, *Southern Voyages*, 669–80, 686–9, there are the earlier works of G. Davidson between 1887 and 1908 and J. W. Robertson in 1926–7, favouring Drake's and San Francisco Bays respectively. These give the basic arguments, but they have been supple-

mented by a recent explosion of pamphlet and periodical literature, from which may be mentioned:
California Hist. Soc. Special Publn No. 25, *The Plate of Brass*, 1953 (reprints Nos 13, 1937, the
initial report, and 14, 1938, the metallurgical analysis) [*Plate of Brass*]; R. F. Heizer, *Francis Drake
and the California Indians, 1579* (Berkeley 1947); W. A. Starr, 'Drake Landed in San Francisco Bay',
Calif. Hist. Soc. Qly 41, 1962, 1–29; A. S. Oko, 'Francis Drake and Nova Albion', ibid. 43, 1964,
145–58; R. H. Power, 'A Case for San Francisco Bay', ibid. 53, 1973, 100–28; R. H. Power,
Francis Drake and San Francisco Bay: A Beginning of the British Empire (Univ. of California, Davis
1974) [*Francis Drake*]. The numerous researches of the Drake Navigators Guild are summed up in
the 460 multilith pages of R. Aker, *Report of Findings Relating to Sir Francis Drake's Encampment . . .*
(Point Reyes 1970) [*Report of Findings*], criticised in an *Analysis* by Heizer and others, 1971. A
special number of the *Calif. Hist. Soc. Qly* 53, Fall 1974, is devoted to a debate between the Guild and
Power (A. V. Neasham intervening, to little effect, for Bolinas Bay). This has many maps and
illustrations, and a bibliography (incomplete) of 103 items. Finally, the best and most detached
summing-up is in R. F. Heizer, *Elizabethan California* (Bellena Press, Ramona (Calif.) 1974). 'Here is
God's plenty'—or the Devil's!

81 A. Villers, 'Queen Elizabeth's Favourite Sea Dog, Sir Francis Drake', *Natl Geographic Mag.* 147,
1975, 216–53. As well as these two sea-captains, the Drake Navigators Guild is supported by two
Admirals, Nimitz and Morison.

82 Aker, *Report on Findings*, 211–13.

83 Ibid., 70–93.

84 A. L. Chickering, 'Some Notes with Regard to Drake's Plate of Brass', *Calif. Hist. Soc. Qly* 16,
1937, 275–81 at 276; *Plate of Brass*, iii–iv, 1; E. R. Caley and R. B. Haselden, critique of the metallurgical analysis by C. G. Fink and E. P. Polushkin, *Amer. Hist. Rev.* 44, 1938–9, 879–80—an item
not included in the bibliography in the Fall 1974 *Quarterly*. The Plate was cleaned before being
submitted to analysis. An Elizabethan sixpence has been discovered in a properly excavated site at
Olompali, perhaps the chief village of the Coast Miwok—personal information from R. H. Power,
and visit to the site.

The suspicion indicated in the text may now be taken as confirmed by the up-to-date metallurgical analysis in *The Plate of Brass Reexamined 1977* (Bancroft Library, Berkeley).

85 H. R. Wagner, 'Creation of Rights of Sovereignty through Symbolic Acts', *Pac. Hist. Rev.* 7,
1938, 297–326—not a single reference to the use of brass 'down to the end of the 17th century, nor
indeed, until much later' (308). However, Fenton in 1582 is stated to have used a copper plate in
Sierra Leone—Taylor, *Fenton*, 104. M. Servin, Acts of Possession in the Age of Discovery (Univ.
of Southern California Ph.D. thesis 1959), makes only passing references to this point, but except
for Drake's Plate itself, all plates he mentions (ranging from Baffin Land in 1613 to Jarvis I. in
1935) were of lead.

86 Cf. Nuttall, *New Light*, xxxviii, with Penzer, *World Encompassed*, 59–60.

87 Wagner, *Voyage*, 153.

88 Ibid., 427–36; he argues strongly for a seventeenth century date.

89 Williamson, *Cabot Voyages*, 67.

90 *The History . . . of Elizabeth* (1630 ed.), quoted in Power, *Francis Drake*, 22–3; personal information from Mr Power. Cf. Taylor, *Geography*, 113–17.

91 Power, *Francis Drake*, 14–17; Morison, *Southern Voyages*, 668, 689.

92 Power, *Francis Drake*, 16–20; D. B. Quinn and N. M. Cheshire, *The New Found Land of Stephen
Parmenius* (Toronto 1972) (text and translation of the *Carmen*).

93 In 1584 Hakluyt referred to Parmenius as 'lately my bedfelowe in Oxforde'—D. B. Quinn (ed.),
The Hakluyt Handbook, HS 2nd Ser. 144–5 (London 1974), I.273–4.

[94] Bishop, 'North Pacific', 174–5; C. O. Paullin and J. K. Wright, *Atlas of the Historical Geography of the United States* (Washington 1932), 25–7 and Plate 42.

[95] Power, *Francis Drake*, 20; Wagner, *Voyage*, 152–3. There is a final mystery, which may have some bearing on the 'colony' question, in that while there were eighty or so men in Nova Albion, there seem to have been only sixty when Drake left Ternate, and there is no evidence of losses en route or of a factory being left there. Aker, *Report of Findings*, 330–42, discusses the matter in (admittedly speculative) detail; but cf. Wagner, 148–9.

[96] A. Sharp, *The Discovery of the Pacific Islands* (Oxford 1960), 49–50; W. A. Lessa, *Drake's Island of Thieves: Ethnological Sleuthing* (Honolulu 1975), 180–7, 236–55 at 240; Power's criticism is in an unpublished review, cited by permission; Aker favours Palau but on a different approach from Lessa's—personal information. Palau is probably right.

[97] Wagner, *Voyage*, 172–82; Corbett, *Drake*, I.315–18. Cf. Blair & Robertson, IV.313–14, VI.59.

[98] Andrews, *Voyages*, 79–80; Corbett, *Drake*, I.320–4; Wagner, *Voyage*, 185–92. There is some doubt about the precise date, due perhaps to 'security' considerations—Corbett, I.329.

[99] W. R. Scott, *The Constitution and Finance of English, Scottish, and Irish Joint Stock Companies to 1720* (New York 1951; original ed. 1912), I.78; see 75–88 for the best analysis of the amount and disposal of the loot (it is a pleasure to use once more a book which contributed to my doctoral thesis forty years ago!). Scott's figures are summarised in Gibbs, *The Silver Circle*, 114–18; Wagner, *Voyage*, 194–206, gives much political background.

[100] J. M. Keynes, *A Treatise on Money* (1930), in *The Collected Writings* (London 1970–3), VI.139–40.

Notes for Chapter 10

[1] The basic source in English is C. R. Markham, ed. and trans., *Narratives of the Voyages of P. S. de G . . .*, HS 1st Ser. 91 (London 1895), which contains Sarmiento's own accounts [*Narratives*]. There is an immense documentation—too immense for our purposes—in Vol. II of P. Pastells SJ, *El Descubrimiento del Estrecho de Magellanes* (Madrid 1920). Modern biographies: A. Landín Carrasco, *Vida y. Viajes de P. S. de G.* (Madrid 1945), perhaps the best technically [*Vida y Viajes*]; Rosa Arciniega, *P. S. de G.: (El Ulisses de América)* (Buenos Aires 1956), somewhat romanticised in expression but sound in substance [*Ulisses*]; E. Morales, *Aventuras y Desaventuras de un Navegante: P. S. de G.* (Buenos Aires 1946) [*Aventuras*], a reissue of *S. de G.: Un Navegante Español del Siglo XVI* (Barcelona 1932) [*Navegante*], and perhaps especially useful for Sarmiento's earlier career, as is A. Rosenblat's introduction to the *Historia de los Incas* (Buenos Aires 1942) [*Historia*]. In English again there is a good analysis in S. E. Morison, *The European Discovery of America: The Southern Voyages 1492–1616* (New York 1974), 690–708 [*Southern Voyages*]; a very readable account in R. Hough, *The Blind Horn's Hate* (London 1971), 108–51; and a complete, sound, and again very readable biography by S. Clissold, *Conquistador: The Life of Don P. S. de G.* (London 1954) [*Conquistador*].

The three Spanish biographies, and Clissold, traverse the same ground, and so far as this chapter is concerned are based essentially on Sarmiento's own accounts; it does not seem necessary to document statements of fact common to all of them. Unreferenced direct quotations in this and the next three sections are from Markham, *Narratives*. Markham and Morison also have good maps of Sarmiento's explorations in the very intricate western approaches to the Straits.

[2] J. A. del Busto Duthurburu, 'La Fortificación del Estrecho', in *História Marítima del Perú* (Lima 1975), T.III Vol. 2, 541–91, at 547–8 [*Hist. Marítima*].

3 Morales, *Aventuras*, 103–15; Rosenblat, *Historia*, 33–38; it is generally agreed that the 'validation' by Inca notables was so cursory as to be almost a farce. But see J. Hemming, *The Conquest of the Incas* (Abacus ed., London 1972), 413–16 and 609, and R. Levillier, *Don Francisco de Toledo* (Madrid 1935), I.279–356. One does not need to accept Markham's uncritical and indeed rabid Black Legend-mongering to find the apologia rather less than convincing.

4 For these activities, see Clissold, *Conquistador*, 198–9, and G. Callender, 'Fresh Light on Drake', *MM* 9, 1923, 16–28. His sonnets to Enrique Garcés, which I have read somewhere, are poor stuff.

5 S. Johnson, *The Vanity of Human Wishes* (London 1749).

6 Arciniega, *Ulisses*, 128; Clissold, *Conquistador*, 126; cf. B. Subercaseaux, *Tierra de Océano* (5th ed., Santiago 1946), 144–5. It is likely that Sarmiento was unfair to Villalobos, as he tended to be to any man (and they were numerous) who could not measure up to his rigid ideal of duty.

7 Landín Carrasco, *Vida y Viajes*, 94–5, q.v. for Argensola's inflation of Sarmiento's 'gente grande' into giants and 'shapes like houses' into the tall buildings of a city. Cf. Markham, *Narratives*, 125–7, 136–7, 147–8.

8 Claimed by Markham (*Narratives*, 164) to be the first such observation by a method suggested in 1522; it had in fact been attempted by Vespucci in 1499—E. G. R. Taylor, *The Troublesome Voyage of Captain Edward Fenton 1582–1583*, HS 2nd Ser. 103 (Cambridge 1959), 311 [*Fenton*].

9 Clissold, *Conquistador*, 136–7; Landín Carrasco, *Vida y Viajes*, 107–11.

10 Busto Duthurburu, *Hist. Marítima*, 570.

11 R. Fitzroy, *Narrative of the Surveying Voyage of . . . Adventure and Beagle* (London 1839), I.26–7, 29, 262— 'our favourite old navigator'.

12 Morales, *Aventuras*, 125, 130; Landín Carrasco, *Vida y Viajes*, 115; Arciniega, *Ulisses*, 151–4; Clissold, *Conquistador*, 137. Alba's opposition was not solitary, nor did Diego Flores lack maritime experience (Hough, *The Blind Horn's Hate*, 121–2); the admiral Cristobal de Eraso thought that a good squadron in Chilean waters would be more effective than forts in the Straits—C. Fernández Duro, *La Armada Española desde la Unión de las Coronas de Castilla y León* (Madrid 1895–1903), II.358 [*Armada*]. J. B. Antonelli was to have sailed with Sarmiento, but in the event his brother did so—fortunately for Spain, in view of J.B.'s services in strengthening Cartagena and other places after Drake's 1585 Caribbean raid.

13 Markham, *Narratives*, 222–4, 230. Perhaps the only similarly light-hearted 'forward planning' of a colony was the slinging round the world of 750 convicts in 1787, on little more than Sir Joseph Banks's say-so (after a week's visit in 1770) that Botany Bay was a good place.

14 See M. Lewis, *The Spanish Armada* (Pan ed., London 1966), 47–8, 187, 189.

15 Pastells, *Descubrimiento*, II.135.

16 Arciniega, *Ulisses*, 161.

17 The reasons are nowhere stated, but Medina Sidonia, as Captain General of Andalusia, was responsible for the good government of the region, and no local authority could view with equanimity the prospect of some 3000 soldiers, sailors, and semi-conscripted colonists hanging about Seville for months.

18 Landín Carrasco, *Vida y Viajes*, 130–2.

19 Arciniega, *Ulisses*, 188.

20 Busto Duthurburu suggests that Flores would not land for fear that once ashore, with Sarmiento as Captain-General of the colony, he might be arrested—*Hist. Marítima*, 576. This is speculation, but certainly nothing would have given Sarmiento greater pleasure.

21 Clissold, *Conquistador*, 156–8; Morales, *Aventuras*, 141–2.

22 Clissold, *Conquistador*, 158; as Duro says (*Armada*, II.366–8) the affair was a 'lightning-rod' for Flores, who was condemned even by Ribera, 'his fellow-provincial and kinsman'. There are hints

towards a defence of Flores in a review of Rosenblat in *Rev. Chilena de Historia y Geographia*, 118, 1951, 343–6.

[23] Arciniega, *Ulisses*, 189–90; Landín Carrasco, *Vida y Viajes*, 155–6.

[24] Arciniega, *Ulisses*, 203.

[25] Markham, *Narratives*, 374–5.

[26] Sarmiento says that there were three English ships with 34 guns and 170 musketeers, plus two armed launches (Markham, *Narratives*, 340); the English account (Hakluyt, IV.278–81) only two pinnaces, although even after sending away prizes they outnumbered Sarmiento by three to one, and much more at the time of the fight. Sir Richard Grenville was in the Azores with three ships at about this time, and they may have been visible in the offing; but there is no warrant for Markham's statement that Grenville must have been the captor—fitting as it would be that Sarmiento should be taken by a man as tough as himself. For Sarmiento's captivities, Duro, *Armada*, 423–43.

[27] Morales (*Navegante*, 259) says that they set out to walk to La Plata, and adds truly that 'The venture was Dantesque, the design very sixteenth century'. But this rests only on the statement in Hakluyt (VIII.214) that 'they were determined to have travailed towards the river Plate', which in turn Cavendish must have understood, or misunderstood, from Tomé Hernandez, while the latter says definitely (Markham, *Narratives*, 363) 'these survivors agreed to go to the first settlement', which was Nombre de Jesus.

[28] Landín Carrasco, *Vida y Viajes*, 197, 202–7; cf. 171 for an example of the reasoning which earned for Philip the somewhat ironic title of the Prudent King.

[29] Tomé Hernandez, 'Declaration', in Markham, *Narratives*, 352–75, at 364–5. The fourth ship was a pinnace built in Brazil. Morison's account of this incident (*Southern Voyages*, 714) is marred by a number of minor errors.

[30] Hakluyt, VIII.282–5.

[31] Subercaseaux, *Tierra de Océano*, 144; Morales, *Aventuras*, 163.

[32] Landín Carrasco, *Vida y Viajes*, 183; for the 'Lost Colony', D. B. Quinn, *England and the Discovery of America 1481–1620* (London 1973), 432–42 [*Discovery*], and the moving passage in Hakluyt, VI.221–2.

[33] A. Braun Menéndez, *Pequena Historia Magallánica* (5th ed., Buenos Aires 1969), 41–50. Population of Punta Arenas is 1966 estimate.

[34] Morales, *Aventuras*, 163, and *Navegante*, 259–75. The name comes from Francisco Cesar, an officer on Sebastian Cabot's 1526 voyage to La Plata, not from the Romans—until our own day, there were limits even to myth! Cf. E. J. Goodman, *The Explorers of South America* (New York 1972), 170–8 (it is odd that this otherwise comprehensive book manages to make only three slight passing mentions of Sarmiento) and R. H. Shields, 'The Enchanted City of the Caesars . . .' in A. Ogden and E. Sluiter (eds.), *Greater America* (Berkeley 1945), 319–40.

[35] [D. Henry], *An Historical Account of all the Voyages round the World performed by English Navigators* (London 1774), I.160.

[36] 'A Discourse of the Commodity of the Taking of the Straight of Magellanus', in E. G. R. Taylor (ed.), *The Original Writings . . . of the Two Richard Hakluyts*, HS 2nd Ser. 76–7 (London 1935), I.139–46, at 142. The ascription to Hakluyt was queried by J. A. Williamson (in E. Lyam (ed.), *Richard Hakluyt and his Successors*, HS 2nd Ser. 93 (London 1946), 27–8), on the grounds that Hakluyt 'never again showed much concern with the South Sea' but in general concentrated on the Northern Passages. But surely a man who published so much may be allowed a little divagation, and in this case Hakluyt's reference (at 140) to the feared death of Ivan the Terrible (with consequently a possible lapse of good relations with Russia), not to mention the réclame of Drake's

success, provides good reason for this flurry of interest in the Straits.

[37] H. R. Wagner, *Sir Francis Drake's Voyage around the World* (1936; reprinted Amsterdam 1969), 214; see his whole chapter on 'The Fenton Expedition'. The project was considered by Zelia Nuttall as one for a colony in Nova Albion—*New Light on Drake*, HS 2nd Ser. 34 (London 1914), xxxviii. For a discussion of the geopolitical atmosphere, see K. R. Andrews, *Drake's Voyages* (London 1967), 84–9.

[38] Taylor, *Fenton*, xxviii–xxxii and 5–8.

[39] *An Elizabethan in 1582: The Diary of Richard Madox, Fellow of All Souls*, ed. E. S. Donno, HS 2nd Ser: 147 (London 1976). It is understandable that Fenton does not figure in the work of a more distinguished Fellow of All Souls—A. L. Rowse, *The Expansion of Elizabethan England* (Cardinal ed., London 1973) [*Expansion*].

[40] Taylor, *Fenton*, xliv, 183, 278, 266–72. For the shifty career of Simão Fernandez, Quinn, *Discovery*, 246–63.

[41] Taylor, *Fenton*, 342, and following pages for the proceedings of the council.

[42] J. Donne, 'The Sunne Rising', in *Songs and Sonets* (1590–1601).

[43] See i.a. K. R. Andrews, *Drake's Voyages* (London 1967), 93–5.

[44] For Cumberland, see Rowse, *Expansion*, 310–14, and for the expedition he sent out Hakluyt, VIII.132–53, where the debates between the two captains (140–1, 151) give an excellent example of the divisions which paralysed so many ventures. The portraits of Frobisher and Cumberland in Rowse and of Cavendish in Quinn (see next note) repay study.

[45] For Cavendish, see D. B. Quinn (ed.), *The Last Voyage of Thomas Cavendish* (Chicago 1975) [*Last Voyage*]; Pretty's account of the circumnavigation is in Hakluyt, VIII.206–82, source of all direct quotations unless otherwise stated.

[46] See the very feeling remarks (already cited, Ch. 2) in J. A. Williamson (ed.), *The Observations of Sir Richard Hawkins* (1622) (London 1933), 87–9, 91–5 [*Hawkins, Observations*]. It was at Port Desire that Cavendish 'took the measure of one of [the Indians'] feete, and it was 18. inches long'— probably the length of a skin shoe, and one source of the long-lived legend of Patagonian giants; see H. Wallis, 'English Enterprise in the Region of the Strait of Magellan', in J. Parker (ed.), *Merchants and Scholars* (Minneapolis 1965), 193–220 at 200, and her essay 'The Patagonian Giants' in R. E. Gallagher (ed.), *Byron's Journal of his Circumnavigation 1764–1766*, HS 2nd Ser. 122 (Cambridge 1964), 185–96.

[47] P. C. Scarlett, *South America and the Pacific* (London 1838), II.137–8; cf. W. Dampier, *A New Voyage round the World* (Dover ed., New York 1968), 104–5.

[48] Morales, *Navegante*, 133.

[49] For this and other local incidents, see P. Gerhard, *Pirates on the West Coast of New Spain 1575–1742* (Glendale, Calif. 1960), 83–94.

[50] Santiago de Vera to the King, Manila, 26 June 1588, in Blair & Robertson, VII.53.

[51] W. L. Schurz, *The Manila Galleon* (Dutton ed., New York 1959), 308.

[52] Salazar to the King, Manila, 27 June 1588, in Blair & Robertson, VII.66–8. For details of Cavendish in the East Indies, see Quinn, *Last Voyage*, 14–15.

[53] Viceroy of (Portuguese) India to the King, 3 April 1589, in Blair & Robertson, VII.81–2.

[54] For Cavendish's return and the general results of his voyage, see Quinn, *Last Voyage*, 16–17.

[55] Hakluyt, VIII.282–9; see especially the vivid complaints of the *Delight*'s crew in the Straits.

[56] Quinn, *Last Voyage*, 18–19; G. Dyke, 'The Finances of A Sixteenth Century Navigator . . .', *MM* 64, 1958, 108–15. Quinn's volume has a facsimile of Cavendish's own account, with facing transcript (source of all direct quotations unless otherwise stated) and reproductions of two maps belonging to Cavendish. See also John Jane's account in Hakluyt, VIII.289–312.

[57] Dedication to Lord Howard of Effingham of *The Seamans Secrets* (1594) in *The Voyages and Works of John Davis*, ed. A. H. Markham, HS 1st Ser. 59 (London 1880), 232–3.

[58] He also had with him Thomas Lodge, one of the 'University Wits', who claimed to have written his romance *Margarite of America* in the Straits.

[59] 'The admirable adventures and strange fortunes of Master Antonie Knivet', a harrowing tale of hardships in the Straits and in Brazilian captivity, in S. Purchas, *Hakluytus Posthumus, or Purchas His Pilgrimes* (1622) (Glasgow 1905–6), XVI.177–289 at 178–9 [*Pilgrimes*]. Cavendish hanged two other Iberian pilots, and according to Knivet and Jane abandoned some of his sick.

[60] Hawkins, *Observations*, 87.

[61] See the terrible but heroic story in Hakluyt, VII.298–312.

[62] 'Naval Abuses', in *The Naval Tracts of Sir William Monson*, ed. M. Oppenheim, II.237–44, at 239 (Navy Records Society, Vol. 23), London 1902.

[63] G. Lohmann Villena, *Las Minas de Huancavelica* (Seville 1949), 218–19, and *Las Defensas Militares de Lima y Callao* (Lima 1964), 27–9.

[64] All direct quotations or statements in this section, unless otherwise stated, are from Hawkins's *Observations* or J. A. Williamson's valuable introduction in the Argonaut edition (London 1933).

[65] The *Dainty*, to Hawkins's chagrin, had been christened by his mother *Repentance*, as 'the safest Ship we could sayle in, to purchase the haven of Heaven', and to his delight renamed by the less puritanical Queen herself. As Hawkins wryly remarks, 'his mother was no Prophetesse'.

[66] As Williamson points out, not the (modern) Santos of Fenton and Cavendish, but Victoria, north of Rio de Janeiro.

[67] Doubts have been expressed, but in my opinion Williamson refutes them convincingly— *Observations*, lvii–lxi.

[68] For the Spanish response, see Busto Duthurburu, in *Hist. Marítima*, 608–12.

[69] See Hawkins's letter to his father Sir John, in *Observations*, 178–83.

[70] Our old acquaintance Tomé Hernandez was in the fight, and Hawkins notes with grim satisfaction that 'the judgement of God left not his ingratitude vnpunished . . . [for] I saw him begge with Crutches, and in that miserable estate, as he had beene better dead, then aliue!' The judgment of God kept him alive until 1620 at least . . .

[71] W. Foster, *England's Quest of Eastern Trade* (London 1933), 138–42.

[72] See Rowse, *Expansion*, 321–39, for a good account of the closing phases of the war.

[73] Purchas, *Pilgrimes*, XVI.292–97.

[74] *Asia in the Making of Europe*, Vol. I, Books 1 and 2 (Chicago 1965).

[75] Hawkins, *Observations*, 17.

Index

Merely 'marker' and *en passant* mentions omitted. References to authors, and to the notes, given only when there is comment or additional information. Abbreviations: *pm, passim*; GP, Governor of Philippines; VP, VNS, Viceroy of Peru/New Spain.

This book was designed by Adrian Young MSIAD
It was set in 12 pt 'Monotype' Bembo, one point leaded
and printed at Griffin Press Limited, South Australia

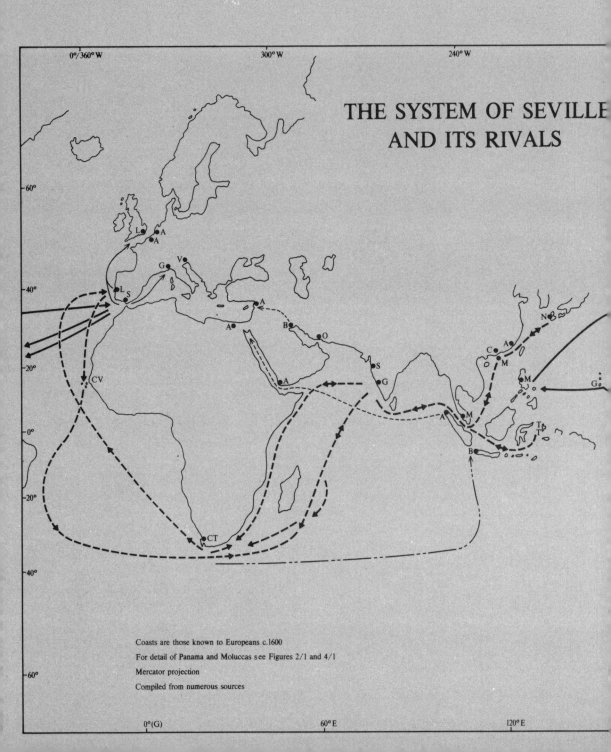

THE SYSTEM OF SEVILLE
AND ITS RIVALS

Coasts are those known to Europeans c.1600

For detail of Panama and Moluccas see Figures 2/1 and 4/1

Mercator projection

Compiled from numerous sources